THE NEW OXFORD HISTORY OF ENGLAND

General Editor · J. M. ROBERTS

A Polite and Commercial People

ENGLAND
1727–1783

PAUL LANGFORD

GUILD PUBLISHING

LONDON · NEW YORK · SYDNEY · TORONTO

This edition published
1989 by Guild Publishing
by arrangement with
OXFORD UNIVERSITY PRESS

©Paul Langford 1989

Filmset by Butler & Tanner Ltd, Frome and London
Printed in Great Britain by
Bookcraft Ltd, Bath, Avon

CN 2557

FOR
MARGARET

General Editor's Preface

The first volume of Sir George Clark's *Oxford History of England* was published in 1934. Undertaking the General Editorship of a *New Oxford History of England* forty-five years later it was hard not to feel overshadowed by its powerful influence and well-deserved status. Some of Clark's volumes (his own among them) were brilliant individual achievements, hard to rival and impossible to match. Of course, he and his readers shared a broad sense of the purpose and direction of such books. His successor can no longer be sure of doing that. The building-blocks of the story, its reasonable and meaningful demarcations and divisions, the continuities and discontinuities, the priorities of different varieties of history, the place of narrative—all these things are now much harder to agree upon. We now know much more about many things, and think about what we know in different ways. It is not surprising that historians now sometimes seem unsure about the audience to which their scholarship and writing are addressed.

In the end, authors should be left to write their own books. None the less, the *New Oxford History of England* is intended to be more than a collection of discrete or idiosyncratic histories in chronological order. Its aim is to give an account of the development of our country in time. Changing geographical limits suggest it is hard to speak of that solely as a history of England. Yet the core of the institutional story which runs from Anglo-Saxon times to our own is the story of the State structure built round the English monarchy, the only continuous articulation of the history of those peoples we today call British. Certainly the emphasis of individual volumes will vary. Each author has been asked to bring forward what he or she sees as the most important topics explaining the history under study, taking account of the present state of historical knowledge, drawing attention to areas of dispute and to matters on which final judgement is at present difficult (or, perhaps, impossible) and not merely recapitulating what has recently been the fashionable centre of professional debate. But each volume, allowing for its special approach and proportions, must also provide a comprehensive account, in which politics is always likely to be prominent. Volumes have to be demarcated chronologically but continuities must not be obscured; vestigially or not, copyhold survived into the 1920s and the Anglo-Saxon shires until the 1970s. Any one volume should be an entry-point to the understanding of processes only slowly unfolding, sometimes across centuries. My hope is that in the end we shall have, as the outcome, a set of standard and authoritative histories, embodying the scholarship of a generation, and not mere compendia in which the determinants are lost to sight among the detail.

Preface

I T is fifty years since the publication of Basil Williams's *The Whig Supremacy*, an early volume in the original Oxford History of England and one which dealt in part with the period covered by this volume of the New Oxford History of England. When the first series was in preparation it was perhaps easier than it is now to predict and fulfil the expectations of its readers. The demands of narrative and the hegemony of political history imposed a pattern which was widely accepted. Social, economic, religious, and cultural history were treated as separate and subsidiary matters. If the Oxford History of England lacked the familiar perspective and confident assumptions of its august predecessor the Cambridge Modern History, it rested on a considerable consensus about what was important and what was not. That consensus was weakening even before the completion of the first Oxford series, and it is certainly not available to its successor. History has expanded beyond what could have been conceived by Basil Williams's readers in 1939. It comprehends subjects which are found nowhere in his pages, draws on concepts which had not been heard of when he wrote, and sometimes appeals to values foreign to his experience. In terms of scholarly research it has become ever more specialized. As a discipline it has been enhanced or subverted, depending on standpoint, by a wealth of new techniques, many drawn from other disciplines. The consequences for history as an academic subject are endlessly debated. Whether there even remains a coherent and rational discipline worthy of the name is itself something which can be disputed. What is not in doubt is that it has become difficult to meet the diverse requirements of readers and students, and difficult, as well, to bring order and system to a vastly more complicated, considerably more professional, and arguably more faddish subject. There is no longer general agreement on what constitutes the proper province of the historian, let alone a ready formula for balancing the requirements of narrative and analysis. The composition of a historical 'survey' represents a problem to which there is plainly no correct, or even widely recommended solution.

My own solution is something of a compromise. There are four chapters of narrative (2, 5, 8, 11) to meet an indispensable requirement, that of describing matters of State as they evolved in respect both of relations with foreign powers and internal affairs. But politics is not confined to these chapters. There is a chapter (14) on the structure and development of the State as an institution, and questions of political theory and practice make frequent appearances elsewhere. For the rest I have opted for themes rather than neatly differentiated topics or broad categories such as 'social', 'economic', and 'cultural'. All the themes are selected with references to a major preoccupation of the time, and each chapter has a contemporary expression for its title. They are arranged in broadly chronological order, but I have felt free to follow the themes wherever they lead, sometimes pursuing them from the beginning of the period to the end, sometimes retracing my steps to pick up an important influence or analogy.

In addition to the brief indication of topics listed in the table of contents, each chapter is preceded by a short statement summarizing its argument and subject. Throughout my intention has been to integrate what are often treated as distinct areas of interest, partly in search of illuminating connections and parallels, partly to recapture something of the contemporary experience of the period. Two chapters centre on the nature of propertied society: 3 deals with some central middle-class concerns of the age, while 12 considers in more detail their social and cultural consequences in the later part of the period. Three chapters have to do with economic change: 4 examines the uncertain commercial trends of the second quarter of the century and assesses their implications for public morality and social policy; 9 and 13 analyse the growth and expansion which occurred especially after 1750, 9 with the emphasis on the campaign for 'improvement', 13 in relation to the impact of war and industrialization. Two profound cultural and ideological changes have a chapter to themselves: 6 explains the challenge which the evangelical revival presented to contemporary institutions and beliefs; 10 describes the sentimental revolution of the 1760s and the impulse which it gave to so-called reform. Chapter 7 assesses the image which the English presented to themselves and to foreigners.

I have sought as far as possible to take account of current scholarship, but this book is in no sense a résumé of recent research on eighteenth-century England. My main object has been to emphasize the changes which occurred in an age not invariably associated with change. To a great extent they have to do with the enrichment and influence of a broad middle class whose concerns became ever more central to Georgian society and whose priorities determined so much both of debate and action. The result is a bias perhaps, but one which seems to me to reflect the most significant developments of the mid-eighteenth century. I have also sought to convey something of the colour of a colourful era, not least by generous quotation from contemporary sources, many of them literary. The eighteenth-century Englishman's own perception of the changes which he lived through not only assists historical understanding of the changes themselves; it also does much to promote imaginative insight into the character of his age. In addition I have devoted some detail to the treatment of persons and things not of recognized importance in their own right, where it seems that they exemplify interesting developments. It is not my contention, for example, that Alexander Fordyce or John the Painter are important in the same historical sense as George Grenville or John Howard, only that their careers reveal some characteristic attitudes and anxieties. Examples of this kind can be more illuminating than any amount of authoritative assertion and generalization.

Dates before the introduction of the Gregorian calendar in 1752 are given in the old style, but the year is treated as beginning on 1 January throughout. Quotations are reproduced with the original spelling and punctuation unmodernized. The source of all quotations is identified in the footnotes. In a work of this kind it is not possible to acknowledge all secondary authorities. In the bibliography, too, it has been necessary to keep detailed references to a minimum. For these omissions I plead the nature of the enterprise. Other deficiencies are entirely my own. What merits it has are shared with others. The writing of this book has been made possible by the tolerance of my wife, to whom it is dedicated, and the more erratic but no less beneficial forbearance of my small son. It also owes much to the supervision of an unfailingly attentive and congenial general editor, on whose judgement and scholarship I have liberally drawn.   P. L.

Contents

Illustrations

BM numbers indicate Prints and Drawings: Personal and Political Satires in the British Museum. Plate 13 is reproduced by kind permission of Lord and Lady Monson being part of their collection of documents deposited at the Lincolnshire Archives Office reference MON 21/12/8.

Figures and Tables

CHAPTER I

Introduction

THE expression 'a polite and commercial people' was used by the distinguished academic, MP, and judge, William Blackstone, in his magisterial *Commentaries on the Laws of England*, published between 1765 and 1769.[1] Blackstone is a fitting source for the title of this volume. His lifetime, 1723 to 1780, coincides with the period which it describes, and his varied career touched many of the themes with which it is concerned. But similar terms were commonplace in the 1760s and 1770s, and suggest something of a consensus about the central characteristics of mid-eighteenth-century England. They also correspond well with the images of eighteenth-century life which were transmitted to posterity. Politeness conjures up some familiar features of Georgian society, its civilized if secular outlook, its faith in a measured code of manners, its attachment to elegance and stateliness, its oligarchical politics and aristocratic fashions. Politeness is stamped on the country houses and portraits which for many provide the most vivid introduction to the culture of the eighteenth century. It is to be found in the pages of the standard texts through which modern readers customarily encounter eighteenth-century literature, the *Spectator*'s journalism, Pope's poetry, Horace Walpole's letters, Gibbon's history, Burke's rhetoric, Boswell's *Life of Johnson*, Johnson's own *Lives of the Poets*. Commerce is not less redolent of an era in which the empire, built on trade and extended by arms, expanded beyond the empires of ancient as well as modern times. Moreover, it will forever be associated with the enterprise of an age of extraordinary economic growth, accompanied by the first clear signs of industrialization.

Associations of this kind conceal facile generalizations, over-simple conclusions, and dangerous misunderstandings. But the

---

[1] iii. 326.

terms themselves, rooted in the usage of the day, are none the less important. Understanding mid-eighteenth-century England involves deciphering the code in which it thought and wrote, rescuing its meaning from the contamination of modern usage, and testing its relevance against the hard historical evidence. Blackstone's phrase was not only meant to be descriptive: though it revealed what he believed the English to be, it also implied his own approval that they were so. Not least it associated his own age with the spirit of progress. His book was designed to explain the arcane mysteries of English law to an audience which had the intelligence and interest to grasp its principles, but was too busy serving the diverse requirements of a complex, developing society to put itself through the costly experience of a traditional legal education. Practically every learned and scientific specialism had its Blackstone in the middle of the eighteenth century, appealing to much the same readership. It was a readership which, these writers believed, would not have been available in an earlier, less enlightened age. In short, a polite and commercial people was peculiarly the accomplishment of Blackstone's own time, at least of his own century. What exactly did he mean by it?

Commerce did not merely signify trade. Rather it suggested a definitive stage in the progress of mankind, as evidenced in the leadership of western Europe, and the manifold social and cultural consequences thereof. The eighteenth century had many anthropologists, economists, and sociologists, though it did not call them by these names. Most of them agreed that they lived in a commercial age, an era in which the processes of production and exchange had dramatically increased the wealth, improved the living standards, and transformed the mores of western societies. They contrasted the results with the feudal conditions still to be found in much of Europe and with still more primitive societies discovered overseas. France, Holland, and Britain were the obvious leaders in this progress, but Britain, in particular, seemed to be in the very forefront, with its formidable intellectual inheritance, its admirable political institutions, its spectacular financial sophistication, its vast overseas empire, and its burgeoning industrial production.

Commerce not only expressed the peculiar modernity of the Hanoverian age, it also indicated the problems which preoccupied contemporaries and the uncertainties which clouded their confidence. Commerce in an international setting was an acutely competitive affair, in which the full power of the States competing was exerted to strengthen the national economy. The struggle for raw materials and tropical commodities, as well as for markets and the carrying trade which served them, was central to international relations. Mercantilism was not a contemporary term, and can be rather misleading. But its emphasis on competition is proper. Every war during this period was in essence a commercial war, and to a marked extent a colonial war, whether the enemy was a rival power or one's own insubordinate colonists. Every peace was the continuation of war by economic means. Views might differ on the commercial merits of one war or another, or one peace treaty or another, and different interests might be adversely or advantageously affected, but the essential object was the same. Since war and the conduct of foreign relations were the principal business of kings and their ministers much of the political and parliamentary history of the period was radically affected. The domestic consequences of commercial rivalry were hardly less far-reaching. Contemporary wisdom suggested the need for relatively free competition, but all kinds of covert interests, communal traditions, and collective sensibilities could be resistant to the requirements of an entrepreneurial order. Since Parliament was entrusted with oversight of the laws governing competition and government had a vital interest in the borrowing and taxation which bore on trade and industry, this too was a matter of supreme political importance.

Commerce was not just about exchange but more fundamentally about consumption. Adam Smith's celebrated *Wealth of Nations*, published in 1776, championed the interest of consumers against monopolistic producers, and identified their demands as the critical spur to the creation of wealth. Not inappropriately for a work by a Scot in an age of Scottish 'enlightenment' it was probably the most influential book produced in England between 1727 and 1783. Yet it was only the most distinguished contribution to a continuing debate about the means by which consumption could be maintained. Moreover the moral and social consequences provoked even more speculation and argument. A history of luxury and attitudes to luxury would come very close to being a history of the eighteenth century. There is a sense in which politics in this period is about the distribution and representation of this luxury, religion about the attempt to control it, public polemic about generating and regulating it, and social policy about confining it to those who did not produce it.

Luxury was the subject of endless controversy, not least when the object was to predict the future, one of the favourite objects of controversialists. Optimists saw no obvious limit to the enrichment of so vigorous a society, and endorsed the numerous improvements and changes which it brought to rural and urban life. They fearlessly replanned the education, supervision, and welfare of the lower class to fit it for such a society, assumed that British power would maintain the international competitiveness of this remorseless successful State, and made due allowance for the provision of godly discipline and pious benevolence in a commercial age. Pessimists worried about the economic nemesis which must befall a people unaware of the natural limits of expansion, doubted the demographic and commercial vigour of their own State, and deplored the transformations which economic change brought to traditional values, faiths, and customs. They denounced the corruption and hypocrisy which marred a once venerated political system, urged a reversion to fundamental religious values, and grimly looked forward to the collapse of what seemed in every sense a meretricious society. It was possible to entertain some of the confidence with some of the doubt, and few people took an extreme view on all of these questions. Complacency and despair were usually to be found in equal measure and often followed each other among the same people in rapid succession. But between them they embrace the most pervasive concerns of the age.

In a sense politeness was a logical consequence of commerce. A feudal society and an agrarian economy were associated with an elaborate code of honour designed to govern relations among the privileged few. Their inferiors could safely be left to languish in brutish ignorance under brutal laws. But a society in which the most vigorous and growing element was a commercial middle class, involved both in production and consumption, required a more sophisticated means of regulating manners. Politeness conveyed upper-class gentility, enlightenment, and sociability to a much wider élite whose only qualification was money, but who were glad to spend it on acquiring the status of gentleman. In theory politeness comprehended, even began with, morals, but in practice it was as much a question of material acquisitions and urbane

manners. It both permitted and controlled a relatively open competition for power, influence, jobs, wives, and markets. Though it
involved much emulation and admiration of aristocrats, it did not
imply an essentially aristocratic society. Britain in the eighteenth
century was a plutocracy if it was anything, and even as a plutocracy
one in which power was widely diffused, constantly contested, and
ever adjusting to new incursions of wealth, often modest wealth.

Politeness and politics had the same stem and were certainly
complementary terms in the eighteenth century. But there was a
significant distinction. Politeness was primarily about the social
control of the individual at a time of intense enthusiasm for
individual rights and responsibilities. Politics, at every level,
involved individuals in consciously making decisions which
affected large numbers of people. Assessing the consequences needs
a certain historical sensitivity to the personalities of those involved.
It is possible to be reasonably confident that the sentimental vogue
would have occurred in the 1760s and 1770s without the stimulus
supplied by the writings of Rousseau. It is even feasible to suppose
that infant mortality and prison conditions would have been
exposed to critical investigation without the leadership provided
by Hanway and Howard. But it is less easy to be sure that Canada
was destined to join the British empire without the generalship of
Wolfe, or the Stuarts condemned to stay at Rome without the
statesmanship of Walpole.

Yet the underlying tendencies of public life were closely related
to the themes displayed elsewhere. The traditions inherited from
the seventeenth century revealed the vigour on which the British
prided themselves, but not the discipline and order which they
sought to acquire. Popular libertarianism, religious conflict, party
strife, dynastic instability, all remained features of the decades
which followed the Revolution of 1688. The competition and
change so characteristic of the mid-eighteenth century might have
been expected to make these contentions worse. They also put a
still greater premium on regulating the consequent tensions, securing the highest possible degree of consensus, and generally averting
the chronic divisions which had threatened the stability of post-
Revolution in England. To this extent the politics of the period,
though not always very urbane, were the politics of politeness, the
pursuit of harmony within a propertied society. Nor was this a
matter of the operation of unseen forces. Rhetoric aside, all the

most successful politicians of the age, Walpole, Pelham, Newcastle, North, the two Pitts, were its practitioners, even when, as in the case of Walpole and the elder Pitt, they had made their name by confrontation. It is no coincidence that the very term 'patriotism', the battle cry of opposition and the reminder of a fundamental political division in the first half of the century, was first reduced to cant and then rendered anodyne as the expression of national unity in the second half.

The 'people' to whom Blackstone addressed his lectures, his books, and his parliamentary speeches, were certainly polite and commercial. But most people were neither, as he very well knew. Polite living and commercial consumption with any real degree of choice were for the propertied members of society. This was by no means a small class and it was a feature of the age that it was a diverse and a growing one. Even so it did not include more than a minority of the subjects of George II and George III. The great majority of the population were propertied only in the pedantic sense employed by political philosophers, that is that they had a property in their own lives and labour. They lacked the kind of property which made it practicable to acquire politeness and engage in conspicuous consumption, though there were always censors at hand to criticize the humble artisan or peasant for seeking to do both. To propertied people they were a continuing irritation, an implied rebuke and source of guilt, a cause for concern, a potential threat, and a stimulus to philanthropy. In short, they were the perpetual challenge of the age. The story of politeness and commerce as it developed in the mid-eighteenth century is not least an account of the way in which the polite and commercial class dealt with its inferiors.

It is also the story of a transformation, or rather a series of transformations. Politeness and commerce were already hackneyed terms in the 1730s, and Blackstone's expression would still have seemed appropriate in the 1780s. But this is not to say that they went with a static society. In fact it was the utility of both that they allowed for the dynamism of the age. The commercial spirit of the 1770s was as marked as that of the 1720s. But Walpole's generation would have been startled to find it threading the landscape with waterways, raising cities and suburbs where there had been only villages, revolutionizing farms and manufactures, dictating war against the American colonies, and promoting parliamentary legislation on an unprecedented scale. Politeness, too, was as necessary in the 1770s as the 1720s. But Lord Burlington's generation would have been astonished by the Gothic Revival, middle-class tourism, macaroni extravagance, evangelical puritanism, and the sentimental excesses of the cult of feeling. There was much that was even more revolutionary in the responses which both politeness and commerce provoked: Methodist 'enthusiasm', systematic collective philanthropy, subversive political radicalism, and, not least, critical interest in the status of women, children, foreigners, slaves, distant peoples, animals, and every other living creature not blessed with the inestimable divine gift of birth as a free-born, propertied Englishman. But Englishmen themselves were hardly the same people, and there was much less certainty by the 1780s about who precisely they were. The British empire in 1783 was not at all what it had been in 1727, nor were relations between the constituent peoples of the British Isles the same. Change, as many contemporaries insisted, was the endemic condition of the age. What lay beyond politeness and commerce themselves was something which perplexed and fascinated enquiring minds. For the rest, no doubt, it was sufficient to wrestle with the practical consequences of the transformation which they had already wrought.

CHAPTER 2

Robin's Reign, 1727–1742

THOUGH the accession of George II aroused wide-spread expectations of change, both at home and abroad, the new King eventually endorsed the men and measures of his predecessor. The reign began in remarkably tranquil circumstances, with no suggestion of a reviving Jacobite threat. It confirmed the growing stature of Sir Robert Walpole, and simultaneously served to identify him with the ills of contemporary society. A galaxy of literary talents exposed the faults of his 'system' and created an enduring image of corruption as the prime characteristic of the 'Robinocracy'. Yet Walpole's supremacy showed increasing signs of strain in the mid-1730s. His excise scheme proved a major miscalculation, and caused a crisis at court, as well as exposing him to severe criticism inside and outside Parliament. It enabled his opponents to appeal to 'Country' sentiment rather than to narrow party prejudices. Divisions within the royal family provided a focus for aristocratic opposition. Episcopal unrest at the deistic tendencies visible in court life endangered the alliance of Whig politicians and Whig Churchmen. An outbreak of anticlericalism in the House of Commons made it easier for Dissenters to challenge the privileges of the Church, and the consequent religious tensions added an element of instability to ministerial politics. Above all there was growing

evidence of popular alienation from the regime, cul-
minating in the pressures which forced Walpole to
declare war on Spain in 1739. Military failure and
the extension of the war to Europe provided the crucial
stimulus required to weaken Walpole's hold on power.
It needed only the general election of 1741 to bring to
an end an administration which had broken new
ground in British political history and firmly estab-
lished its head as a uniquely successful, if also uniquely
execrated Prime Minister.

THE ACCESSION OF GEORGE II

IN the monarchies of the eighteenth century no occasion raised more hopes and offered more disappointments than the accession of a new monarch. Especially was this the case in a limited monarchy, where the pattern of politics as well as the fate of individual politicians might be affected. In this and indeed in most respects the accession of George II in June 1727 turned out to be a curious anticlimax, more important for what it failed to change than for what it changed. There was no indication that the new King intended to challenge the laws and conventions which contemporaries inaccurately but reverently described as the Revolution Settlement. The champions of the new court stressed its mildness and benevolence, as well as its respect for traditional rights and liberties. The scientist and Freemason J. T. Desaguliers, mindful of Newton's death a few months earlier, celebrated the accession with Newtonian metaphors. His verse expressed both the contemporary faith in the unique virtue of England's balanced constitution, and the enthusiasm of the 1720s for mechanistic descriptions of the natural world. In his relations with his subjects, George was compared to the sun, though not indeed in the sense of a Sun King such as Louis XIV. 'His Pow'r, coerc'd by Laws, still leaves them free, Directs but not Destroys their Liberty'. The rules of gravity as well as of light operated to his advantage. 'Attraction now in all the Realm is seen, To bless the Reign of George and Caroline.'[1]

Less fancifully, and at the level which brought the monarchy into the minds of ordinary Englishmen, it was made clear that the customary rites would be strictly observed. Despite the factious politics of the City of London, party animosities were not permitted to mar the succession. The coronation, accounted by contemporaries a spectacular success, was held during a tumultuous parliamentary election in the City, but with no adverse effects. Loyalty was gratified by the report that the Corporation expended the large sum of £4,889 on the traditional royal banquet in the Guildhall.[2] The Queen was prominent in these festivities and did much to create a comforting atmosphere of normality. She was the

---

[1] *The Newtonian System of the World, the Best Model of Government: An Allegorical Poem* (Westminster, 1728), pp. 24, 34.

[2] W. Maitland, *The History and Survey of London* (2 vols., London, 1756), i. 541–3.

first consort to appear at the coronation by right of her husband's inheritance since 1625, as her husband was the first Prince of Wales to succeed his father since Charles I in 1625. Though the Jacobite threat could not be ignored there was a marked sense of dynastic continuity about the events of 1727. In time, admittedly, the public image of the new regime was to be sullied. Family life at court came to resemble a bear garden rather than the happy domesticity celebrated by court poets. Queen Caroline gained a reputation for theological heterodoxy which alarmed those who associated the monarchy with ecclesiastical orthodoxy if not with divine right. But this lay in the future: in 1727 the very uneventfulness of the accession was reassuring.

Hanoverian regality was confident but not pretentious, at any rate by the baroque standards of the day. Foreigners were partly shocked, partly impressed, when they witnessed the modest magnificence of the crowned heads of England. The palace of St James's, which George II showed no inclination to rebuild, was an acknowledged source of embarrassment, even of scandal, to Englishmen who cared about the image which their ruler projected abroad. The only splendid statue of a recent king in London was Grinling Gibbons's portrayal of James II in Whitehall, which successive Revolution monarchs had permitted to retain its prominent place. Attempts under George I to offer a fitting Hanoverian competitor had not been very successful. A ludicrous statue surmounted the spire of St George's, Bloomsbury. Another, erected in Grosvenor Square in 1726, was defaced and eventually dismembered by passers-by.[3]

There was no hint that George II's succession would bring a new and alien splendour to the court: pedantic though he was about forms and precedences, his pedantry always smacked more of the German princeling than the rival to the Most Catholic and Most Christian Majesties of the Bourbon monarchies. Yet his court did not give out a sense of insecurity. To all intents and appearances the succession was rock solid. There would be no Twenty-Eight to follow 1727 as there had been a Fifteen to follow 1714. This was not merely the perspective from London. Provincial England exhibited the same stability. It was confirmed by the assurance with which the oligarchs of Whig government in corporation and

[3] G. S. Dugdale, *Whitehall Through the Centuries* (London, 1950), p. 76; E. B. Chancellor, *The History of the Squares of London* (London, 1907), p. 39.

county alike confronted their opponents. In Whittlebury Forest in Northamptonshire, for example, village communities hastened to demand their supposedly ancient right of felling the tallest trees as 'coronation poles'. But when a number of valuable trees vanished overnight, suggesting commercial exploitation of customary privileges, neither the government nor its local supporters were impressed by the claim that the right had been clearly established in 1714, on the accession of George I. Then, in the midst of a succession crisis, it had been prudent to treat such provocation with lenity; in 1727 there was, and was felt to be, no such necessity.[4] In Whittlebury Forest as at Westminster Whig rulers behaved as if the accession of the second Hanoverian King was the most natural thing in the world.

The tranquillity of George II's accession had much to do with the international setting. In Rome the Old Pretender was completely isolated. Since 1716 the Anglo-French alliance had effectively deprived him of the support on which the Stuarts depended for their restoration to the English throne. Without this the promises of aid from Vienna and Madrid were worth little. This is not to say that British ministers were heedless of the Jacobite threat, least of all in the disturbed diplomatic conditions of 1727. Europe was virtually divided into two armed camps, the alliances of Hanover and Vienna. The former, based on Anglo-French collaboration, was dedicated to preserving the uneasy balance of power negotiated at the great peace settlement of Utrecht in 1713. The latter, bringing together Spain and Austria in an unlikely combination, was designed to destroy it. The implications were maritime and colonial as well as continental. In the last year of George I's reign Britain and Spain were on the brink of war. Some of the principal British gains at Utrecht—Gibraltar, Minorca, and a share in Spain's American trade—were at risk. Within days of George II's elevation his ministers assured foreign courts, friendly, neutral, or hostile, that there would be no significant change in the diplomatic posture of the Court of St James, let alone any weakening of its stance towards the Vienna alliance. The will of the King himself was clear on these points. George II was a veteran of the War of the Spanish Succession. His knowledge of European affairs was extensive, his judgement in diplomatic matters generally sound,

---

[4] J. H. Cooke, *The Timber-Stealing Riots in the Forests of Whittlebury and Salcey, In 1727–28* (Northampton, 1885).

if unimaginative. Like his father he valued the interests of his
Electorate at least as highly as those of his British subjects. It was
widely believed in England that the alliance of Hanover was
designed mainly with the security of Hanover in mind. But its
architect, Lord Townshend, had insisted that it guaranteed the
security of the Protestant Succession and the prosperity of British
trade. In any event it seemed prudent to continue the policy of
George I. Cardinal Fleury, the principal director of French foreign
policy, may have been slightly startled to receive a personal letter
from the new King of Great Britain. He can hardly have been
surprised by its assurance of unchanged measures.[5]

Less predictable was the King's decision to continue with the
men as well as the measures of his father. As Lord Hervey, an
acute if acerbic chronicler of court life, recorded in his memoirs,
George II had frequently expressed his dislike for the 'four governors of this kingdom': Sir Robert Walpole, the First Lord of the
Treasury; his brother Horatio Walpole, ambassador to Versailles
and unofficial diplomatic adviser to the Cabinet; the Duke of
Newcastle; and his fellow Secretary of State Lord Townshend.
'He used always to speak of the first as a great rogue, of the second
as a dirty buffoon, of the third as an impertinent fool, and of the
fourth as a choleric blockhead; it was very natural to expect the
reins of power would not long be left in their hands.'[6] Certainly
these men expected short shrift from the new court. George I had
died at Osnabrugh on 11 June. When Walpole carried the news to
his successor on 14 June, he was curtly ordered to report to
Sir Spencer Compton, the new King's political confidant. But
Compton made the fatal mistake of asking Walpole's assistance,
notably in drawing up the official declaration which a new monarch
was required to make to his Council. Such deference gave Walpole
an invaluable opportunity to demonstrate his superior skill and
experience. Later on, both George II's son Frederick, and his
grandson the future George III, went to elaborate lengths to ensure
that on their own accession there would be no such necessity to
rely on their predecessors' ministers. In 1727 the old ministry
continued virtually unchanged. Compensation was found for the

---

[5] W. Coxe, *Memoirs of the Life and Administration of Sir Robert Walpole, Earl of Orford*
(3 vols., London, 1798), ii. 518.
[6] R. Sedgwick, ed., *Some Materials towards Memoirs of the Reign of King George II*, by
Lord Hervey (3 vols., London, 1931), i. 29-30.

leading adherents of the new court—a peerage for Compton, the office of Master of the Horse for the Earl of Scarborough. Apart from this the only significant alterations were those which Walpole succeeded in procuring to demonstrate his supremacy, including the removal of a personal enemy, Lord Berkeley, from the Admiralty.

This extraordinary turn of events gave rise to much speculation. Hervey's account stresses the stupidity of Spencer Compton, who allowed himself to be so easily outmanœuvred by Walpole. But Hervey was incapable of offering a charitable explanation where a malicious one would do. It is at least as plausible that Compton was, as Walpole's Secretary to the Treasury John Scrope believed, 'frighted with the greatness of the undertaking, and more particularly as to what related to money affairs'.[7] The influence of Queen Caroline was also important. She had scant regard for the abilities of Compton, and did not conceal her distaste for his attention to the King's mistress Mrs Howard. Above all, she possessed a shrewd appreciation of Walpole's talents, based on the years which Walpole had spent in opposition with the then Prince and Princess of Wales between 1716 and 1720.

If the Queen was seeking evidence to convince her husband she soon obtained it. Parliament met for a short session on 27 June in a seemingly dazzling demonstration of Walpole's managerial talents. The King was granted a civil list of £800,000. This sum was unprecedentedly generous and carried with it a promise of any surpluses on the duties voted to finance it. The Queen's jointure was fixed no less lavishly at £100,000. The largess was not altogether Walpole's doing. Parliament passed through a brief 'honeymoon-period' in its relations with George II in 1727, before his political preferences were revealed. Tory opponents of the previous King hoped for a less hostile disposition on the part of his successor. Only the Jacobite William Shippen had the temerity to oppose the financial arrangements. Walpole was a skilled parliamentary performer, certainly; but, more important in the summer of 1727, he was lucky.

[7] Coxe, *Walpole*, ii. 520.

THE GROWTH OF OPPOSITION AND THE FALL OF TOWNSHEND

George II's surprising adherence to his father's minister gave rise to a mixture of congratulation and consternation. In a published sermon the Bishop of Gloucester Joseph Wilcocks rejoiced that unlike Rehoboam, 'the Son and Successor of Solomon, he forsook not the Council of the old Men, those who stood before his Father while he yet lived, and who, by their Experience and Success, were most likely to give wholesome Advice, and, by the Blessing of God, to make his Reign glorious'.[8] Wilcocks was duly rewarded with the Deanery of Westminster and the Bishopric of Rochester. Others were less enthusiastic. The price of endorsing George I's choice of ministers was to drive still deeper the resentment of George I's opponents. Some of these were discontented Whigs, men like Lord Carteret and William Pulteney, who had lost the struggle for power with Walpole and Townshend under one Hanoverian King and were now deprived of a second chance to win it under his successor. Their following was not large: in the Commons it was doubted whether more than a dozen MPs would support them. However, they provided the germ of a 'malecontent Whig' party which was to grow to formidable proportions in subsequent years.

No less disappointed and much more numerous were the Tories, whose expectations of a fresh beginning in their relations with the Hanoverian regime proved sadly mistaken. Yet they had some grounds for optimism. There was no logical reason for George II to perpetuate his father's proscription of the Tory party. The precedent of William III clearly demonstrated that a Revolution monarch with Whig antecedents could only gain by refusing to become the property of one party. To those who asserted that the Tories were Jacobites, it could be answered that while the Stuarts remained loyal to Rome there was little danger of their successfully appealing to the 'Church Party', as Tories frequently described themselves. It was plausible, too, to argue that Jacobitism was the resort of men rendered desperate by the antipathy of George I. Given a less hostile atmosphere under his successor it would quickly lose its attraction. Queen Caroline was well known to favour a degree of *rapprochement* with the Tories. Some of her

[8] *The Providence of God, the Preservation of Kingdoms* (London, 1728), pp. 15–16.

clerical friends, including the celebrated Thomas Sherlock, were of Tory or at least High Church background. Yet none of these arguments carried the day. The King listened graciously enough to suggestions that he might begin by relaxing the persecution of the Tory squires in their natural habitat, the Commissions of the Peace. But as the memoirs of Lord Chancellor King reveal, the hopes thus raised were quickly quashed by the opposition of Whig magnates such as the Duke of Grafton in Suffolk.[9]

Possibly the court was confirmed in its attitude by the results of the general election which by law followed a new accession. From a strength of nearly 180 in the Commons the Tories were reduced to less than 130. Nor was this simply a case of fair-weather friends deserting them in the close boroughs, where party loyalty took second place to the personal interests of corrupt borough-mongers or tiny electorates. In the counties, where electorates were large and relatively independent, the Tories had held almost three-quarters of the seats, 58 out of 80. After the election they could muster less than half, 37. The loss of both seats, in Kent, in Yorkshire, in Lincolnshire, and in Cambridgeshire, for example, could not be attributed to oligarchical manipulation. It seemed to court Whigs that Toryism was on its death-bed if not yet in its death-throes. The parliamentary session of 1728 appeared to confirm their view. Austria and Spain were brought to the nego-tiating table, and the prospects for a lasting peace appeared good. On questions which might have been controversial the ministry won massive majorities: 290 to 84 on the size of the army, 280 to 84 on the retention of Hessian mercenaries in British pay, 250 to 97 on the National Debt.

These promising indications proved misleading. The peace-makers made painfully slow progress. There were reports of Spanish attacks on British trade, but the court seemed reluctant to respond in kind. Admiral Hosier's ships were compelled to watch the silver galleons carrying Spain's financial life-blood pass freely under their guns; a still more expensive fleet was kept armed but immobile at Spithead. The war had to be paid for yet it was not to be waged. The land tax stood at an unpopular four shillings in the pound. Walpole was driven to desperate expedients to finance the maintenance of land and sea forces on a war footing.

---

[9] *The Life and Letters of John Locke, with extracts from his Correspondence, Journals, and Common-Place Books. By Lord King* (2 vols., London, 1830), ii. 49–50.

Merchants complained bitterly that the balance of trade was turning against them. The anxieties voiced were not merely those of the bellicose, the interested, and the alienated. Whigs had accepted the French alliance on the grounds that it protected Britain's naval and commercial interests, while offering a prospect of dictating peace to the rest of Europe. But in 1729 this case was beginning to look flimsy: there was a suspicion that the reviving confidence and vigour of the French court, under the kingship of Louis XV and the direction of Cardinal Fleury, would end by making the British the dupes rather than the dictators of Europe. When the opposition ventilated the sensitive issue of 'Spanish depredations' in February 1729, the ministry's majority fell with startling suddenness from over 200 to only 35.

The administration was also weakened by increasingly acrimonious relations between Walpole and Townshend, longstanding though their partnership had been. The death of Lady Townshend, Walpole's sister, in 1726, had removed an important connection between the two men. But the accession of a new King, and the special relationship which Walpole enjoyed with the Queen, made matters much worse. There is no reason to challenge Hervey's judgement. A 'great mortification to Lord Townshend's pride was the seeing and feeling every day that Sir Robert Walpole, who came into the world, in a manner, under his protection and inferior to him in fortune, quality, and credit, was now by force of his infinitely superior talents, as much above him in power, interest, weight, credit and reputation.'[10] No less important, from Walpole's vantage-point, his brother-in-law was becoming a liability. In the Commons it was Walpole's task to raise supplies for a foreign policy of doubtful utility; he also had to bear the brunt of public and parliamentary criticism. The employment of the Hessian troops and the Spanish depredations had the potential to bring down the ministry. Later, in 1730, the opposition found another such issue when it was reported that France was rebuilding the fortifications of Dunkirk, in violation of its treaty obligations. Everything pointed to action against Townshend. The aid of the Queen and Townshend's fellow Secretary of State, Newcastle, was enlisted, and in May 1730 Townshend was compelled to resign.

Walpole had already anticipated this outcome by taking control of foreign policy. In November 1729 the Treaty of Seville restored

[10] Hervey, *Memoirs*, i. 83.

peace with Spain. After protracted negotiation, a *rapprochement* with Austria made possible a more general settlement, confirmed by the Treaty of Vienna in March 1731. Thus was Britain freed from the burden of an undeclared but costly war. The Austrian alliance was a daring stroke. It included a controversial guarantee of the Pragmatic Sanction, by which the Emperor Charles VI provided for his daughter's succession to the Habsburg territories on his own death. It also weakened the Anglo-French alliance, which had transformed the pattern of European relations since 1716. Not least, in retrospect, it concluded forty years of British involvement with the rivalries of the continental powers. Yet Walpole's object, peace, if necessary at any price, seemed secure, and his reward was considerable. During the parliamentary session of 1730 he was able to reduce the armed forces, bring down the land tax, and abolish the salt duty. With Fleury he had retained sufficient credit to extract a French promise rescuing him from the Dunkirk imbroglio. At court he was supreme, in Parliament he was virtually unchallengeable. Abroad he made his master the boasted, if not quite the acknowledged, arbiter of Europe. 'Robin's Reign' had truly commenced.

WALPOLE'S SUPREMACY

Walpole's pre-eminence at the start of a second decade in power had a novelty about it which is difficult to appreciate in retrospect, with knowledge of the long and successful administrations of later Georgian Prime Ministers. Contemporaries, regardless of their political persuasion, were struck by it. The historically minded were driven back to the sixteenth century in search of precedents, and even then few imagined that Tudor monarchs had been so much under the thumb of their ministers as George II seemed to be. Walpole's supporters cited Burghley, risen from unpretentious origins to direct the destiny and save the religion of his country. Opponents preferred the ambition, arrogance, and avarice of Wolsey. It was the second analogy which tended to prevail with the uncertain and the uninformed.

In his own day Walpole enjoyed a unique degree not only of personal power but of personal abuse. This malevolent chorus long affected his reputation. By the late eighteenth century, however, less unfavourable verdicts were being offered. The economist and philosopher Adam Smith saw in Walpole a far-sighted financial reformer, and the elder Pitt publicly regretted his youthful opposition to Walpole. The writer Philip Thicknesse flatly declared that Walpole 'introduced the Protestant succession'.[11] Sir Robert Peel, not the most likely admirer, perhaps, expressed his strong approval. 'Of what public man can it be said with any assurance of certainty, that placed in the situation of Walpole, he would in the course of an administration of twenty years have committed so few errors, and would have left at the close of it the house of Hanover in equal security, and the finances in equal order.'[12] These assessments rightly recognized Walpole's abiding preoccupation with the need, in an age of chronic dynastic instability, to establish the Hanoverian Succession on a lasting foundation. It was generally the Whigs of 1689 who received the credit for securing the Revolution Settlement, but Walpole has a no less impressive claim. Edmund Burke even exonerated Walpole from the gravest accusation laid against him:

He was an honourable man and a sound Whig. He was not, as the Jacobites and discontented Whigs of the time have represented him, and as ill-informed people still represent him, a prodigal and corrupt minister. They charged him, in their libels and seditious conversations, with having first reduced corruption to a system. Such was their cant. But he was far from governing by corruption. He governed by party attachments. The charge of systematic corruption is less applicable to him, perhaps, than to any minister who ever served the crown for so great a length of time.[13]

Cant or not, it was widely believed that Walpole did indeed reduce corruption to a system. In part this was simply because he was the principal dispenser of patronage. The means of corruption did not multiply under Walpole; official patronage and the National Debt, cited by his antagonists as the main sources of improper influence, were both stable during his ministry. Nor was it true that Walpole engrossed all patronage to himself. He never gained that control of the Crown's ecclesiastical preferments which many of his successors came to expect as of right. He also had limited powers of appointment over the armed forces. Even in his own

[11] P. Thicknesse, *Useful Hints to those who make the Tour of France* (London, 1768), p. 198.

[12] N. Gash, *Peel* (London, 1976), p. 304.

[13] *The Works of the Right Honourable Edmund Burke* (8 vols., London, 1854), *Appeal from the New to the Old Whigs*, iii. 50.

fiscal department he could never depend entirely on the servility of the revenue boards, the customs and excise commissioners. What was true, however, was that Walpole's decision to remain in the House of Commons rather than proceeding to the Lords, when he effectively became first minister in 1721, placed him in a unique position to control and channel the patronage which related to the lower house. This included everything which bore in some measure on MPs or their electors. In such matters he made himself the acknowledged conduit for the transmission of applications and favours, even when his actual command of them was less extensive than his supplicants imagined. Previous ministers, Danby and Harley, for example, had aspired to a monopoly of parliamentary patronage; neither approached it as closely as Walpole.

It is easy to see why Walpole was vulnerable to the charge of corruption. He revelled in the wealth which his office brought him, though it was much exaggerated by contemporaries. When he died in 1745 it came as a shock to many that he was reported to have left debts amounting to £40,000. None the less, his ostentatious display of suburban sophistication in Chelsea and aristocratic opulence at Houghton provoked much critical comment. There was also in his character and conversation a degree of coarseness readily mistaken for cynicism. This sometimes irritated his friends, including the Queen, and contributed to his reputation for parvenu vulgarity. A lifetime of politics and high office did not give him, to say the least, an elevated view of human motives. It was easy for his critics to assume that his disparagement of others reflected a want of probity in himself. Certainly he believed that most of his political enemies were hypocrites who pursued him out of spite and party spirit rather than high-mindedness. He had been the victim of such malice in 1712 when a Tory Parliament placed him in the Tower and expelled him from the Commons for peculation which was never proved. Political prosecutions of this kind he always detested: the Atterbury Plot, which he considered a genuine Jacobite conspiracy, was another matter. No doubt he had a shrewd suspicion that such prosecutions were more likely to change the occupants of the Augean stables than to cleanse them. But his defence of men who were manifestly guilty of malpractice and fraud left a damaging impression.

A series of scandals disfigured public life in the early 1730s. Four statutory bodies were affected: the South Sea Company, the

York Buildings Company, the Charitable Corporation, and the Derwentwater Trust. Two of these cases caused uproar. The disgraceful affair of the Charitable Corporation caught public trustees lining their own pockets at the expense of a fund established for the employment and relief of the poor. Yet Walpole went out of his way to defend one of his supporters among the trustees, Sir Robert Sutton. Sutton was nevertheless expelled from the Commons. The revelations concerning the Derwentwater Trust were no less disturbing. It transpired that Jacobite estates forfeited to the State had been plundered by men appointed to supervise their sale in the public interest. Walpole did his best to save one of his City friends who was involved, Sir John Eyles. Such 'screening' recalled his role in the South Sea Bubble when he had shielded the most highly placed villains from parliamentary or judicial retribution, thereby preserving the court of George I from possible ruin, and advancing his own political career.

The image of the 'Skreenmaster' was one of the most enduring associated with Walpole, though he was never proved guilty of such breaches of trust himself. Even his supporters were sometimes dismayed by this aspect of his politics. Sir John Perceval, an independent Whig who usually supported Walpole, observed that 'it is this meanness of his (the prostitution of the character of a first minister in assisting and strenuously supporting the defence of dunghill worms, let their cause be ever so unjust, against men of honour, birth, and fortune, and that in person too), that gains him so much ill will'.[14] Certainly such conduct was a gift to his opponents, for it facilitated the most improbable allegations. There was nothing whatever, for instance, to connect Walpole with Colonel Francis Charteris, convicted perjurer and rapist. But when Charteris received a royal pardon for the rape of a serving-maid in 1730 it was easy to assume that this was yet another case of ministerial protection of vice in high places. Satirists did not hesitate to draw the analogy between Rape Master General and Skreen Master General.

THE CASE AGAINST ROBINOCRACY

Personalizing politics in this way offered an easily identifiable target, as well as a suitable subject, for the popular press. It

---

[14] Historical Manuscripts Commission, *Egmont Diary*, i. 85.

produced some influential cartoons: *Robin's Reign* in 1731, for which the printer William Rayner was successfully prosecuted, and *Robin's Progress* in 1735, a commission which Hogarth, as the brilliantly successful creator of the *Harlot* and the *Rake*, was asked to undertake. He prudently declined, and the result was an inferior product by an unknown artist but one which left no one who saw it in any doubt as to who and what were being satirized. In retrospect it is obvious that Walpole satisfied a deep contemporary need to find a scapegoat for the ills of the day. Opponents hit on his personal vulnerability in this respect almost by accident. Certainly this was true of John Gay, author of the most successful of all supposedly anti-Walpolian satires.

Gay was not so much a proscribed patriot, as a disappointed placeman. His successful edition of *Fables*, published in 1726, had been dedicated to the younger of George I's grandsons, the future Duke of Cumberland; moreover, through Prince George's mistress Mrs Howard he had what he took to be a secure interest in the future. But on George II's accession, Mrs Howard proved to be an injudicious investment. Gay was offered the humiliating position of Gentleman Usher to the infant Princess Louise. To Alexander Pope, he wrote: 'O that I had never known what a Court was! Dear *Pope*, what a barren Soil (to me so) have I been striving to produce something out of!'[15] The *Beggar's Opera*, which he went on to write, was doubtless in large measure a result of his frustration. Whether it was aimed specifically at Walpole is another matter. No one character could clearly be identified with the Prime Minister and the plot had no unambiguously political content. But Walpole, who was present on the first night in Lincoln's Inn Fields, can hardly have been surprised by its uproarious reception. The roll call of criminals in Act I included '*Robin of Bagshot*, alias *Gorgon*, alias *Bluff Bob*, alias *Carbuncle*, alias *Bob Booty*'; the celebrated scene in which the partners in crime, Peachum and his nominal gaoler Lockit, grew to suspect and finally quarrel with each other, was treated as a hit at Walpole's deteriorating relationship with Townshend; and the repeated references to the 'Great Man' in association with unsavoury characters of the criminal underworld was inevitably taken to have a political connotation. At the end the beggar appeared on stage to remind his audience

---

[15] C. F. Burgess, ed., *The Letters of John Gay* (Oxford, 1966), p. 66.

of the 'Similitude of Manners in high and low Life'.[16] But his listeners plainly preferred to make more precise comparisons with the court of George II and the character of his first minister.

The success of the *Beggar's Opera* demonstrated the popularity and profits to be derived from political satire. Rich, the proprietor of the theatre, became richer and, as the contemporary witticism had it, gay. Gay became rich, though he lost the apartment in Whitehall which he enjoyed as a Commissioner of Lotteries, and spent his declining years in the fashionable and opulent company of the Duke and Duchess of Queensberry. Lavinia Fenton, the actress who depicted the one truly innocent character in the piece, Polly, became a celebrity overnight, caught the eye of the Duke of Bolton, and was said to have had £400 a year settled 'upon her during pleasure, and upon disagreement £200 a year'.[17] The government banned Gay's next play, *Polly*, and began waging a ferocious but somewhat ineffectual war against the theatre. The result was merely to intensify the political polarization of the stage and indeed the arts generally. Like Gay, Jonathan Swift had been a disappointed seeker after preferment. In 1726 he also had written a popular work, *Gulliver's Travels*, which was interpreted as a more specific satire than had been intended. The same could be said of the third great masterpiece of these years, Pope's *Dunciad*, published in 1729. Henry Fielding built his early career as a dramatist on uncompromising satire. Even so, his most enduring denunciation of Walpole's politics, one which, like the *Beggar's Opera*, employed the parallel between high politics and low criminality, was published much later, after Walpole's fall. 1743, the year of his *Jonathan Wild*, was also the year in which Pope's *Dunciad* was given a thrust more explicitly directed against Walpole himself. By then there were no dangers in such unequivocal criticism. Indeed the lesser talents of Grub Street had long since thrown caution to the wind in this respect.

This is not to say that the case presented against Walpole's ministry was by any means merely a personal one. Over the years, the *Craftsman*, first published in 1726 to express 'malecontent' views, developed into an influential vehicle of propaganda against the government. Week in and week out it offered an analysis of contemporary ills which forms one of the eighteenth century's

[16] *The Beggar's Opera* (London, 1921), pp. 4, 47, 91.
[17] Ibid., p. 76.

most important statements of the relationship between political ideas and practice. Much of this analysis was provided by Lord Bolingbroke, the disappointed rival of Robert Harley in the last years of Queen Anne's reign and a declared Jacobite under George I before his return from exile in 1725. A conflict which pitted Bolingbroke against Walpole was fascinating. Both were men of the highest intelligence, both born leaders. They were more or less of an age: Walpole was fifty-one at the accession of George II, Bolingbroke forty-nine. Each was a product, in political terms, of the 'rage of party' which had followed the Revolution of 1688 and reached crisis-point in the second decade of the eighteenth century, between the impeachment of Dr Sacheverell in 1710, and the South Sea Bubble in 1720. Both had retreated from the partisan extremism of their youth. Walpole's Whiggism in the 1730s included much that would have been acceptable to the Tories, and Bolingbroke's Toryism was quite compatible with the views of patriot Whigs. Each was a formidable parliamentary performer, though Bolingbroke was prohibited from taking his seat in the Lords after 1725.

In their contrasting fortunes there was doubtless a large element of luck. But there were also some crucial differences between the two men. If Walpole was arrogant, he rarely made the mistake of displaying it in his daily dealings. Bolingbroke did not suffer fools gladly, and left even those whom he flattered resentful of his condescension. Walpole had a core of steel: his political courage carried him through some desperate crises and made him a figure of exceptional personal authority. Bolingbroke had broken under the stress of the disputed succession in 1715; he never recovered the respect of his contemporaries. Not least, Walpole had qualities much admired by backbench MPs: 'bottom', judgement, consistency. Bolingbroke was considered brilliant, erratic, and unreliable. Even so the contest between Bolingbroke's pen and Walpole's parliamentary power in the 1730s was by no means unequal.

In part, Bolingbroke's argument was historical.[18] He discerned in British history a continuing struggle between the spirit of liberty and the spirit of faction, and plundered Paul Rapin's recently

---

[18] This and subsequent quotations are from Bolingbroke's *Remarks on the History of England* and *A Dissertation on Parties* in *The Works of Lord Bollingbroke* (4 vols., London, 1844).

published *History* for appropriate examples. The ancient Britons were not mere slaves. 'This, we know, they were freemen.' Their liberty, consolidated by the Saxons, had survived the fearful damage inflicted by the Norman Conquest, and the civil strife of the later Middle Ages. It had even defied the despotic tendencies of the Tudors. Bolingbroke had read his Harrington and had no doubt that the sixteenth century had witnessed a decisive strengthening of this tradition, a redistribution of property from Church and nobility to commoners, buttressing the parliamentary defence against the tyranny of the Stuarts and Cromwell alike.

It was easy to depict Walpole as a manipulator of faction. Yet he was also a Whig, with libertarian credentials of his own. Bolingbroke's ingenuity in depriving his opponents of this argument made an important contribution to the cause of opposition. The Robinocracy, he pointed out, might signify the rule of the Revolution families, but it did not follow that it embodied Revolution principles. He shrewdly distinguished what he called the means and end of revolution. The means, that is the principle of resistance, had a Whiggish origin; but the end, the limitation of monarchy and the maintenance of civil liberty, had been retarded by the Whigs of the post-Revolution era. Even the Act of Settlement, the historic compact of the British people and the Electors of Hanover, had lost two of its great safeguards. The requirement that a king might go abroad only with the consent of Parliament, had been repealed in 1715, and the stipulation that war might not be waged for the defence of the foreign dominions of the Crown, had been blatantly violated by George I. The idea, increasingly attractive to Whigs of Walpole's kind, that the Revolution was final and needed no reinforcement, was dismissed with Machiavelli's often quoted maxim that liberty could be preserved only if a constitution were constantly restored to its first principles. Frequent revolutions testified to the essential health of the society in which they occurred. Bolingbroke's tainted past might have been supposed to make this a dangerous argument, but he met the objection head-on, with a perceptive assessment of the state of parties in England. The language of party, he claimed, had been redundant even at the time of the Revolution; by the 1730s it was quite without meaning. Non-resistance and divine right had long since been abandoned in theory as well as in practice, and the old religious animosities which had underpinned them dissolved.

Those who claimed exclusive use of the name of Whig were only a tiny faction of what had once been the Whig party. Those they called Tories and Jacobites were an equally tiny portion of the old Tory party. Both these minorities had an interest in perpetuating an ancient and now irrelevant conflict of their own. The real issue was the corruption of the court versus the patriotism of the country.

This argument was vital to an opposition based on an unstable coalition of discontented Whigs and proscribed Tories. But it needed more to bridge the emotional gulf between Whig and Tory. Among the smart intellectuals of Bolingbroke's circle, and in the increasingly cohesive social life of London's parliamentary classes, this gulf might be crossed. In a few counties, too, it could be spanned. In Bedfordshire the Duke of Bedford made a point of courting the Tories and in due course became not so much a Whig magnate as the ruler of an entire region. But in most localities the lingering appeal of a distinctive Tory tradition remained powerful. So did religious differences. Yet the need for collaboration in Parliament, and therefore in parliamentary elections, was obvious. Walpole could not be defeated by Whigs or Tories, only by a combination of both. Hence the emphasis of Bolingbroke and his friends on the priority of forging a true Country Party, capable of overcoming the old enmities. Hence, too, their concentration on issues which served this priority. The opposition's parliamentary tactics closely matched its propaganda in the press. The Hessian mercenaries, the Spanish depredations, and the Dunkirk for-tifications could be depended upon to incense all hot-blooded Englishmen regardless of party; so could the corruption which underlay the Walpole regime and which the opposition attacked with periodic pension bills. These bills were so popular that Walpole had to rely on the House of Lords to defeat them. There was also the annual onslaught on the standing army, as a mercenary, potentially despotic force, and the unremitting war on the National Debt, a product of the Revolution, indeed, but one which dismayed honest Whigs as it did hidebound Tories. In most of these matters Walpole had little room for manœuvre. His ministry needed, and he argued plausibly that the Protestant Succession needed, placemen and pensioners, standing armies and a national debt. But in one respect he offered a hostage to fortune. His excise scheme was a deliberate initiative; it was also vulnerable to the bipartisan approach of the *Craftsman*.

THE EXCISE CRISIS

Walpole's great objective during the early years of the new reign had been to restore a measure of political tranquillity, chiefly by remodelling Townshend's foreign policy and thereby reducing taxation. From the Treaty of Vienna to the general election which was due in 1734, or as he probably planned, in 1733, this remained his priority. It is often said that Walpole had nothing which could be called a social policy. In a sense this is an anachronism; no eighteenth-century minister had a social policy which would satisfy the criteria of the twentieth century. But it would be truer to say, in any case, that he had a social policy which was lacking in appeal to modern audiences. His aim was to relieve the landowners, particularly that class of small country gentlemen who had borne the burden of the State's expenses since the Revolution, and who, in his view, continued to pay a disproportionate share of taxes. Like many politicians Walpole thought that he perfectly understood the aspirations of the class from which he had himself emerged, though his own circumstances had long since removed him from its essential concerns, let alone its social milieu. In this he doubtless exaggerated his own acumen. There were Tory country gentlemen who retained a conviction that it was their duty to shield their inferiors. The price of paternalism was the land tax. Others so detested Walpole that they forgot their own interest as taxpayers. On the other hand, the country gentlemen together exercised vast electoral influence; in the House of Commons those of them who were Whigs held the fate of ministries in their hands. Certainly Walpole's advisers were confident of the political profits which might be realized by his policy. The excise scheme of 1733 promised revenues which would permit a permanent reduction of the land tax to one shilling in the pound. As Charles Delafaye, one of Walpole's senior officials, put it, 'Half the land tax taken off, and no more remaining than 1s. in the pound, which was never known before since the revolution, must be popular in the country, let the Pulteneyans say what they will against it in the house, and must be of service against the next election.'[19]

The excise fitted well with Walpole's fiscal policy. Already he had reduced the land tax to 3s. in 1728 and 1729, 2s. in 1730 and 1731, and 1s. in 1732. Since 1727 he had periodically tapped the

[19] Coxe, *Walpole*, iii. 125.

Sinking Fund surpluses to lighten the load elsewhere. In 1733 he was to go further, taking large sums from the Fund itself to relieve the taxpayer. The policy was controversial: it endangered the much admired strategy for repayment of the National Debt which Walpole himself had initiated in 1716. But the circumstances of 1733 were not those of 1716. Interest payments on the Debt were lower, and the capital burden less pressing. Walpole sought the applause of contemporaries, not of posterity. The same concern marked his revival of the salt tax in 1732. The salt duty had been abolished in 1730 as an objectionable tax on general consumption. In reviving it to help keep down the land tax Walpole was accused of grinding the faces of the poor. He was also charged with providing renewed employment for the salt officers and thereby swelling the fund of patronage at his disposal. There was, however, another consideration. The salt duties had belonged in the Sinking Fund account. When revived in 1732 they were included in the annual budget. This was effectively a means of transferring resources from Debt redemption to the current account. Walpole may also have viewed the exercise as a test of the public acceptability of excises. In 1724 he had introduced excise duties on tea, chocolate, and coffee, but the transaction had meant more to the East India Company than to the ordinary consumer and voter. The salt duty was politically more sensitive. Yet it was carried readily enough in the Commons. In proposing to convert the customs on tobacco and wine into inland duties Walpole was convinced that he would at once benefit the Exchequer, relieve the taxpayer, and reap a substantial political reward.

Walpole's excise scheme came with sufficient notice to permit an orchestrated campaign in the press. The arguments were old, reaching back into the seventeenth century. Excise duties involved giving extensive powers of search to revenue officers, and a wide jurisdiction to magistrates and excise commissioners. The Englishman's right to privacy on his own property, and also to trial by jury, were put at risk. An entire genre of horror stories, retailed in the press and depicted in broadsheets and prints, exploited such fears. But more important were the diverse interests affected. Walpole emphasized the economic advantages of his proposals. Customs duties were notoriously liable to evasion; the excise would eliminate smuggling, stimulate legitimate trade, even transform London into a 'free port', a natural entrepôt for the commerce of other nations. But this optimism was not shared by those chiefly affected. It was not only fraudulent merchants who were wary of laws which provided for more efficient revenue administration. Walpole caused much synthetic outrage but also genuine irritation by describing his opponents in the merchant community, many of them respected figures in the City, as 'sturdy beggars'. Others, lower down the social scale, felt as strongly. Even honest dealers might prefer to keep clear of officious excisemen. The shopkeepers and tradesmen of England were immensely powerful as a class, scarcely less so in electoral terms than those country gentlemen whom Walpole sought to gratify. Whig or Tory, there was no doubt what they thought of more excises. In the spring of 1733 petitions to Parliament and instructions to MPs flooded in from the provinces in support of a vociferous campaign in London itself.

In the Commons, in March, Walpole's initial proposal relating to tobacco was carried by fair majorities, 265 to 204, 249 to 189. But a minority in excess of 200 was cause for concern, and the growing evidence of public alarm as well as private antagonism made it likely that it would increase rather than diminish. That it did so, however, was only indirectly due to the clamour out of doors. Further incursions into Walpole's working parliamentary majority could only be achieved by detaching or at least neutralizing some of his accustomed supporters, including men who held office in the administration. Walpole's personal enemies seized their opportunity. At court a whispering campaign started: it was widely reported that the King himself had lost faith in his minister. There was no truth in the story but the behaviour of some of George II's friends lent it verisimilitude. In the Commons, when the City formally presented its petition against the excise on 10 April, Walpole's majority fell to seventeen. In the Lords there seemed every likelihood of an equally damaging aristocratic revolt. That evening Walpole held a meeting of his supporters, one which was to live in the annals of Whiggism. Though the excise was doomed, he made it clear that he considered the crisis as imperilling the dynasty itself. His appeal for loyalty to the old cause was never forgotten by those who heard it. On the following day he announced the withdrawal of the excise scheme in the Commons.

Tumultous rejoicings and demonstrations ensued, confirming, if confirmation was needed, that perseverance would have been dangerous indeed. On the streets of London Walpole was burnt in effigy, along with Queen Caroline, and also, such was the mob's sense of humour, with Sarah Malcom, a murderess whose bloody crimes had lately enthralled newspaper readers. The violence of the populace caused something of a reaction on the back-benches. But this was not the main reason for Walpole's rapid recovery from a desperate situation. The decisive consideration was George II's fidelity. The Tory diarist Mrs Caesar judged acutely in comparing the excise crisis with the Sacheverell affair of 1710 and concluding that there was one crucial difference: Queen Anne, in 1710, had decided to support her ministry's opponents, while George II refused to do so.[20] To secure this outcome Walpole pushed his influence to the limit. The King felt compelled to remove Lord Chesterfield and Lord Clinton from their posts in the royal household forthwith. There followed further dismissals, the Dukes of Montrose and Bolton, the Earls of Stair and Marchmont, Lord Cobham and his followers. In the upper house the ministry survived with its majority barely intact; it took peerage creations as well as the dismissals to restore it to health.

In the Commons, recovery was swifter and more complete. The ministry's supporters rallied. 'We have been all put to our stumps' wrote the future Prime Minister Henry Pelham, 'but by the steadiness of the Party ... and the firmness of our master in the main point, we are now gott pretty firm in our seats again, and I doubt not in the least but we shall continue so.'[21] Pelham's confidence proved justified. The final session of Parliament in 1734 was relatively quiet, and enlivened only by the opposition's attempt to repeal the Septennial Act. Yet Walpole paid a high price for his miscalculation. The general election which followed was exceptionally acrimonious and violent. It brought into play the votes of countless small men, freeholders, farmers, tradesmen, and artisans, to whom Walpole's excise seemed the acknowledged precursor of a general excise, offering fearful prospects of taxes on bread, meat, and every common necessity. It proved impossible to dislodge this impression from the ordinary voter's mind. Walpole's newspaper the *Hyp-Doctor* admitted the existence of 'our New English Fever, unlike those which have reign'd in former Years. To trace the

[20] Bodleian Library, MS Film 740, Mrs Caesar's Diary.
[21] British Library, Add. MS 27732, fo. 170: Pelham to Lord Essex, 17 May 1733.

Topography thereof would be to go over most of the Counties of England.'[22]

There were 136 contested elections, more than in any other general election before 1832 except 1710 and 1722. In open constituencies, counties and large boroughs alike, the government was trounced. The Tory party returned 149 MPs to Westminster: this was the only election between 1713 and 1760 in which it improved its parliamentary position. But the test applied by the electorate had little to do with party loyalties as such. Printed lists revealing the voting on the excise in 1733 were circulated. MPs who had supported it were severely punished in the large constituencies. More was spent by the Treasury on secret service expenditure in 1734 than in any year between 1688 and 1782, but it made little difference. In Kent, despite its customary bias to the court (thanks to the local influence of the Admiralty and revenue departments), two ministerial men were replaced by two 'Country' candidates; in Hampshire, where government normally enjoyed a similar advantage, one seat was lost, the other only narrowly saved. Two Tories were seated for Gloucestershire, to the pride of Lord Bathurst, 'it being to be observ'd that there have not been two Torys sent out of this County not once since the Revolution'.[23] Above all, in Walpole's own county of Norfolk the Whigs were humiliated.

That the ministry survived these disasters was the result of two special circumstances. Ironically, those of Walpole's friends who had deserted him in the excise debates were rewarded in the election. In Derbyshire the Cavendish family actually gained a county seat, one which they were to hold until 1832, because they were untainted by association with the excise. More important still was the cumulative success of the Hanoverian regime in controlling the smaller constituencies. The close boroughs of the south and west proved invaluable in repairing the damage done elsewhere. John Scrope, Walpole's Secretary to the Treasury, and therefore intimately involved in the planning of the excise, was defeated in the large and prestigious constituency of Bristol. He found a seat instead at Lyme Regis. In such places it proved no disadvantage to have voted for the excise. With the usual ministerial campaign to 'weed the House' in constituencies where

[22] 14 Aug. 1733.
[23] Add. MS 22221, fo. 129: Bathurst to the Earl of Strafford, 13 May 1734.

controverted elections made it possible to unseat opponents, this proved sufficient. In 1735 Walpole was able to secure majorities of about eighty even on controversial questions. It was enough, but it was far from what he had envisaged when planning his excises; nor did it compare with his majority at the commencement of the previous Parliament in 1727.

Like everyone else Walpole was also aware of the psychological damage inflicted by the excise crisis. Before 1734 he had been able to claim the support of a clear majority of the electorate and the propertied public. After it he was manifestly a closet minister, manipulating the court's political machinery against the wishes of most of his countrymen. His supporters were forced to resort to desperate arguments. The election result had been the consequence of a passing infatuation, itself due to the malevolence and mis-representation of the 'malecontents'. Moreover the ignorance and stupidity of ordinary voters made them unqualified to determine affairs of state. The freeholders who had voted so decisively in the counties were 'as unable to express the *Sense* of the Nation about the Conduct of the Ministry, as the *Beasts* they ride on to give their votes'.[24] Such claims revealed the increasingly narrow basis of Walpolian rule. They also reflected the changing character of Walpole's administration. The Parliament of 1727 to 1734 had seen him at the peak of his powers and his confidence. In these years he was a genuinely creative minister, refashioning his coun-try's foreign policy and reforming its financial system. After 1734 he was perpetually on the defensive. This did not affect his under-lying strategy, that of protecting the Hanoverian Succession. It was the constant theme in Walpole's seemingly tortuous political life, and the fact that contemporaries often chose to forget it should not be permitted to obscure its overwhelming importance in his calculations. But even his friends and followers increasingly came to see their leader as an old man in retreat.

NOBILITY AND ROYALTY

The excise crisis and the ensuing election presented the picture of a minister who had lost all credit with the people over whom he ruled in the King's name. Yet the popular uproar which he faced somewhat obscures the extent to which he was the victim

[24] *London Journal*, 15 June 1734.

of a factious aristocracy. By 1734 there remained only a handful
of Tory peers who had not in some measure succumbed to the
temptations of Whig rule after 1714. The influence of King and
court in the upper house was always proportionately more extensive than in the lower. The bishops, the royal household, and not
least the natural affinity which bound so many noblemen to the
prince, provided the Crown's ministers with a built-in advantage.
Yet Walpole, the supposed master of corruption, had come desperately close to losing control of the Lords in 1733. In the general
election he accordingly paid special attention to the elective element
there. The choice of sixteen representatives from a body of nearly
one hundred and fifty Scottish peers, many of them so impoverished as to be barely on a par with the minor English gentry, was
always influenced by government. The 1734 election was evidently
no exception. In the press, and then in the first session of the new
Parliament, the opposition made much of the unconstitutional
means employed at Edinburgh to corrupt and coerce the Scottish
peers. Walpole also strengthened his position in the House of
Lords, partly by exerting more rigorous discipline over his followers there, partly by creating new peers who would add to the
government's debating power. These included Lord Hardwicke,
shortly to be Lord Chancellor, and Lord Hervey, one of his most
faithful supporters at court. But the opposition was certainly not
less entrenched or bitter in the upper house than it was in the
lower.

In this there was not a little snobbery. Walpole was a parvenu
in the eyes of some peers. He was to be the only Hanoverian Prime
Minister before Addington in 1801 who did not inherit blue blood
from either his father or mother. It was well remembered how he
had led the opposition to the Peerage Bill of 1719, that blatant
attempt to establish the British aristocracy as an inaccessible caste.
His decision not to take a peerage in 1721 eased the task of
managing the Commons but made it more difficult to control the
Lords. There was a group of alienated young peers, including the
able Lord Carteret, who had clustered around Sunderland in the
early years of George I's reign and whose hopes of preferment had
been dashed by Walpole. There was another group which had
attached itself to Prince George, in the conviction that the death
of George I must terminate Walpole's influence. Some of these
men, such as Scarborough, remained loyal after 1727; others

rebelled, and were punished, in 1733. The fact that George II
stood by Walpole did not necessarily reconcile them to their fate.
The famous Rumpsteak club, formed by those who had had the
royal back turned on them, knew sufficient of their master both to
despise his reliance on Walpole and to doubt its endurance. Moreover the very extremes to which Walpole resorted in 1733 caused
a stiffening of aristocratic dislike for him. Particular exception
was taken to the thoroughness with which opposition peers were
removed even from their military commands. There was a view in
noble circles that service in the army was the right not the privilege
of a peer, and that it carried no obligations to the minister of the
day.

   Nervousness at court was intensified by the troubles which
afflicted the King's immediate family in the mid-1730s. It is
doubtful whether royalty has ever been the object of more obloquy
than it was during these years. The most innocent pursuits became
the subject of party recrimination. The liking of the King and
Queen for Handel's Haymarket opera led to a state of open war
between the musical 'ins' and 'outs', moving the Princess Royal to
remark that she 'expected in a little while to see half the House of
Lords playing in the orchestra in their robes and coronets'.[25] Queen
Caroline's literary activities proved equally controversial. Her
patronage of the labourer turned poet Stephen Duck brought down
an avalanche of ridicule from the opposition wits. Her building
projects in Richmond Park, notably the grotto and library, which
she entrusted to Duck's care, gave rise to similar mirth. Pope's
famous grotto at Twickenham was evidently another matter, as
was the elaborate tribute to the traditional values of classical
patriotism and English constitutionalism which Cobham was erecting at Stowe.

   Malice had some substance to feed on. George II spent long
periods in Hanover. Ministers experienced acute difficulty keeping
him at home, even when his presence was urgently required, as in
1737. In the gutter press he was treated with open contempt. His
sexual habits were mocked, his personal foibles, especially his
irascibility, derided. In the winter of 1736, when he nearly perished
in a storm *en route* from Hanover to London, there was hardly a
hint of real concern except among his ministers. Anyone who
doubted that the Englishman's hard-pressed loyalty was more to

[25] Hervey, *Memoirs*, i. 273.

the Protestant Succession than the current incumbent needed only to observe the public response to junior members of the royal family. When the Princess Royal married the Prince of Orange in 1734, the first occasion of its kind since the betrothal of James I's daughter to the Elector Palatine, every opportunity was taken to make unfavourable comparisons between the House of Orange and that of Hanover. The Dutch Prince made a highly successful tour of the provinces, including a visit to proscribed Oxford, which gave time for the lesson to sink in. More important by far, however, was the Prince of Wales.

Since his arrival in England in 1728 Prince Frederick had been the object of intense interest and speculation. His relations with his parents, particularly his mother, were disastrous, for reasons which even those intimate with the family never fully understood. Yet he proved an elusive catch for the opposition politicians who made it their highest priority to secure him. In the excise crisis he declined to join them against the ministry, despite pressure from Chesterfield and Cobham to do so. What finally made his mind up is far from certain. Perhaps it was the sheer accumulation of resentments and temptations to which he was subject. In this respect his marriage to Princess Augusta of Saxe-Gotha, reluctantly authorized by the King in 1736, was something of a landmark. The reluctance did not go unremarked in Parliament: one of Cobham's young followers, William Pitt, lost his rank in the army for having the temerity to refer to it. But worse followed in 1737, when the opposition put forward a motion requesting an establishment of £100,000 per annum for the Prince. The proposal was not unreasonable. It was generally agreed, except by the King and Queen themselves, that the civil list arrangement of 1727 had assumed some such settlement. More relevantly, from Walpole's standpoint, the court's supporters in the Commons were likely to be nervous about putting their opposition to the future King on record when the present King was approaching his fifty-fifth year. In the event the motion was defeated by a narrow majority of thirty; but for the abstention of many Tories it would have been carried. Walpole proved characteristically adept at producing a compromise proposal by which the Prince received a guaranteed sum of £50,000, though at the cost of straining his own relationship with the King to its limits.

The 'reversionary interest' represented by a mutinous Prince of

Wales was a recurring problem for Georgian Prime Ministers. With an ageing king on the throne, it created a natural rallying point for opposition. Its strength was its dynastic respectability. Opponents of the Crown could not be accused of disloyalty when they were led by the heir to the throne. Walpole himself had skilfully exploited George II's hostility to his father between 1716 and 1720, and went to great lengths to deny his enemies a similar advantage with Prince Frederick. Excusing the Prince's unfilial conduct was one of the more irritating, but necessary chores which Walpole found himself undertaking in the presence of the King and Queen.

There were limits even to Walpole's tolerance. At the end of July 1737 the Princess of Wales gave birth to her first child. In a manner which seemed as brutal to his wife as it was offensive to his mother, the Prince removed the Princess, on the point of being delivered, from the direct supervision of the King and Queen at Hampton Court to St James's Palace. Even his friends found it difficult to defend this measure. His parents demanded immediate submission or excommunication. The Cabinet found itself in a quandary. But against the advice of Lord Chancellor Hardwicke, Walpole insisted that 'they had now an advantage over the Prince which ought not to be parted with; and that it would be better for the administration to have a total declar'd separation than that things should remain in the precarious doubtful state in which they then stood.'[26] Hardwicke was a good deal younger than Walpole, with a family which had yet to make its way in the world. He naturally viewed the King's formal declaration of war on his son with misgivings. Walpole had passed the age of sixty and could afford to stop worrying about the reversionary interest. He probably hoped to obtain a firmer hold than ever over George II.

Walpole's response to the death of the Queen in September 1737 is of comparable interest. It was a moment of genuine grief for the minister and indeed for the King, notwithstanding his notorious infidelity. The occasion was marked by the presentation of the Queen's 'crystal hunting-bottle, with a golden stopper and cup', one of only two such gifts which Walpole ever received from his master, the other, as his son Horace waspishly noted, being a

[26] P. C. Yorke, *The Life and Correspondence of Philip Yorke, Earl of Hardwicke* (3 vols., Cambridge, 1913), i. 172.

diamond with 'a great flaw in it'.[27] In a political sense the opponents of Walpole thought his loss a major one. But this was far from certain. There was no noticeable slackening of George II's loyalty. Moreover Walpole had previously grumbled to Hervey about the difficulty of having to overcome not one obstinate royal will but two. For all his skill as a parliamentarian, Walpole's supreme talent lay in managing the royal closet. His constant coaxing of George II had been carried out in close collaboration with Queen Caroline. It is possible that the task was easier without the need to persuade his collaborator. On the other hand, there is force in Chesterfield's belief that courtiers would have doubts about Walpole's standing. At a court opinions counted for more than truths, rumours for more than realities. Even so, Chesterfield's colourful optimism on the occasion seems excessive. 'We have a prospect of the Claud Lorraine kind before us, while Sir Robert's has all thehorrors of Salvator Rosa.'[28] Walpole's extraordinary art collection at Houghton had examples of both masters, the favourite land scape painters of the age, and he would have understood the implication all too clearly. But there is no hint that he thought his political position weaker after the Queen's death.

CHURCH AND STATE

Suggestions that Walpole's grasp was beginning to slip received support from the evidence of growing insubordination among his Church supporters. But as in the case of the Prince of Wales, it is difficult to conclude that Walpole was entirely to blame. The religious storms of the mid-1730s had scattered origins, some of them apparently trivial squalls, the full significance of which could hardly have been predicted. One was the restlessness of Protestant Dissenters. On the part of most of them there was no weakening of their support for Whiggism. They felt some uncertainty, however, about Walpole's commitment to their own definition of Whiggism. Perhaps the most alluring prospect in the promised land of Augustan Whigs was the repeal of the Test and Corporation Acts. Walpole never denied its attraction but preferred to treat it as a distant probability rather than an immediate possibility. He

<hr />

[27] *The Yale Edition of Horace Walpole's Correspondence*, ed. W. S. Lewis (48 vols., New Haven, 1937-83), xxv. 464.

[28] M. Wyndham, *Chronicles of the Eighteenth Century* (2 vols., London, 1924), i. 60-1.

pointed to the positive benefits which Dissent had received from the Hanoverian regime; the repeal of the Occasional Conformity and Schism Acts in 1718, and the grant since 1723 of the *regium donum*, a fund provided by the Crown for the support of Dissenting ministers. As for the Test and Corporation Acts, it could be argued that a judicious combination of occasional conformity and legislative indemnity made them a dead letter for the great majority of Nonconformists. But the rank and file of Dissent, especially in the provinces, entertained a growing suspicion that their leaders had swallowed such arguments far too readily.

Samuel Holden, Chairman of the Dissenting Deputies Committee, strongly defended the dealings of the leadership with Walpole. He reasoned that it was by means of this relationship that the celebrated Dissenting educationist Philip Doddridge had been protected against the threat of prosecution by Tory critics in Northamptonshire. Not all his listeners were impressed. The Liverpool Dissenters roundly lectured the Deputies on their 'fundamental Mistake'. 'It is this, Applying to the Great Men privately, and Endeavouring to make them Parties with you against the Bigots ... instead of applying to them in their Legislative Capacity, where such Complaints properly come before them.'[29] There were attempts to make this an issue in the general election of 1734. In the end, however, these fires were damped down by Holden and his colleagues. Not until 1736 was a formal motion for the repeal of the Test and Corporation Acts put before the Commons. It was defeated by 251 votes to 123. Another motion three years later was lost by 188 votes to 89. Nearly fifty years were to pass before Parliament formally considered such proposals again.

The Dissenters were on stronger ground when they were able to appeal to a community of interest with other Protestants, particularly those pious but latitudinarian Whigs who were well represented among back-benchers in the House of Commons. This element included some distinguished names: Sir John Barnard, the most influential and revered of all City politicians, Sir Joseph Jekyll, a prominent lawyer and the very embodiment of independent Whiggism, William Glanville, a resourceful campaigner against corrupt administration. Such men regarded the Dissenters as allies, particularly when real enemies could be identified. One

[29] N. C. Hunt, *Two Early Political Associations* (Oxford, 1961), p. 196.

of those periodic Catholic scares which marked the eighteenth century as much as the seventeenth provided an obvious opportunity for collaboration. The sparks of anti-popery were fanned into flames by the Dissenters in a series of lectures which they commissioned at their London headquarters, Salters Hall, in 1735. The lecturers, all distinguished preachers and teachers, dwelt on the renewed danger from Rome. Samuel Chandler, who was to spend much of his long career urging co-operation with the established Church, appealed in one of these sermons for joint efforts against Roman Catholics. He was not without encouragement. In December 1734 Gibson, as Bishop of London, had issued a circular warning his clergy against the increased activity of popish priests. Parliament recommended the bishops to enquire closely into Catholic proselytizing in their dioceses.

Little was done in the event, largely because little needed to be done. There was no real evidence of rapid growth in the Roman Catholic population, though the press indulged in reckless exaggeration and speculation. The *Old Whig* reckoned, absurdly, that there were 10,000 priests in London alone. It also calculated a total of 600,000 Catholics in the country as a whole, at least four times the true figure.[30] Trivial incidents were seized upon. A fire in St Martin's Lane was attributed to two Irish papists who had long been at odds with their neighbours and landlords. The acquisition of a new altar-piece depicting the Virgin Mary in St James's, Clerkenwell, was treated as clear evidence of the growing incidence of superstitious practices. If the Dissenters played their part in this campaign, they played a still bigger part in doctrinal disputes. One of the Salters Hall lecturers, James Foster, engaged in a gruelling controversy with Henry Stebbing, a royal chaplain. Their dispute turned appropriately on the nature of heresy. Both Foster and Stebbing were to enjoy long and successful careers as polemicists; their encounter in 1735 suggested that not every Nonconformist initiative in ecumenism was guaranteed a welcome even from Whigs.

The affair which precipitated a genuine crisis within the Church was the nomination of Thomas Rundle to the Bishopric of Gloucester in December 1733. Rundle was thought to have deistic tendencies, and in his youth he had been a disciple of the heretical William Whiston. Gibson entertained sufficient doubts about his

[13] 13 Mar. 1735.

orthodoxy to make a strong protest against his elevation. The concrete evidence in the case was slight: it consisted of the recollection by Richard Venn, one of Gibson's diocesan clergy, of a conversation in which Rundle had openly avowed his scepticism. Rundle's proscription probably had more to do with the general sensitivity of the bench at this time than with the specific charge against him. Eventually Gloucester was given to the untainted Martin Benson, and Rundle was found lucrative compensation in the bishopric of Derry, where, it was assumed, his heresy could do little harm.

Gibson's victory proved pyrrhic. His treatment by the press reveals much about the dilemma of Churchmen at this time. Gibson was a good Whig and a loyal supporter of the government. In the common phrase he was Walpole's 'pope'. But he was no Hoadly or heretic: he shared with many Whigs as well as High Church Tories a growing anxiety about the threat posed to conventional belief by Dissent and Deism. His best-known work was the massive *Codex Juris Ecclesiae Anglicanae*, published in 1713. It was a learned and well-documented defence of the jurisdiction of the Church, much cited in the controversies of the 1730s. 'Dr Codex', as Gibson became known, was made a byword in the prints for the unregenerate Laudianism even of a Whig episcopate. Vulgar abuse was reinforced by some telling arguments directed against him, notably by Michael Foster, a Whig lawyer who was later to become a judge. Foster's *Examination of the Scheme of Church Power laid down in the Codex* went through three editions in 1735 and 1736 and was eagerly followed up in the press.

This was no storm in an episcopal teacup. Gibson and his friends had much to be worried about. In 1736, in the case of *Middleton* v. *Croft*, Hardwicke, then Lord Chief Justice of the King's Bench, delivered a judgement which effectively exempted laymen from the jurisdiction of the Church. This came to be seen as the definitive assertion of the supremacy of statute over canon law. In Parliament, too, there was growing evidence of hostility to the claims of the Church, sometimes in seemingly minor matters. In 1736 the House of Commons suspended its financial support for the restoration of Westminster Abbey, after complaints that the Dean and Chapter had permitted the exhibiting of waxworks in the Chapel of Henry VII, one of London's most popular tourist attractions. It is easy to see why Gibson felt beleaguered. His own

Primate, William Wake, was a senile and useless figure, though
not so senile, as the uncharitable pointed out, that he was prevented
from loading his relations with the most lucrative sinecures in the
gift of an Archbishop of Canterbury. At his back Gibson was
conscious of the pressure from his own supporters. There were,
for instance, the stirrings of a lobby to re-establish Convocation.
Since 1718 Convocation had been effectively killed by continued
prorogation, initially to prevent a confrontation between Bishop
Hoadly and his trinitarian critics, thereafter in the cause of letting
sleeping dogs lie. But not all Whigs approved this policy. In 1742
Convocation was to be permitted to sit. The Whig Archdeacon of
Lincoln George Reynolds sought to persuade it to reform the
canons of the Church in a manner which quickly decided his
superiors against continuing with the experiment. In the mean
time there was no mistaking the growing tension and unease within
the Church.

The anticlerical forces in the Commons registered a considerable
victory in 1736. The Mortmain Bill of that year reflected lay
concern about the lands and endowments which the Church
received, particularly as a result of the activities of Queen Anne's
Bounty. Since its charter in 1704, the Bounty had added some
£420,000 to the capital value of the Church. Its object was to
increase the income of the poorest incumbents, but to the secular-
minded the accumulation of property seemed alarming. There
were stories, as old as the Church itself, about death-bed benefactors who bought their way into heaven at the expense of their
heirs. 'Arguments of such Donations will never be wanting when
Men are pinched by the Messenger of Death.'[31] The bill restrained
these legacies by requiring that they be made at least a year before
the death of a testator. Certain bodies were excepted, notably the
universities and their sister foundations at Winchester, Westminster, and Eton. A further provision restricted the right of Oxford
and Cambridge colleges to purchase advowsons for the enjoyment
of their Fellows. The resulting Act was a blow for institutional
charity, but it commanded widespread support in an age obsessed
with property and devoted to the preservation of family estates.

The bishops had more success in their opposition to a companion
measure, the Quaker's Tithe Bill. Quakers could not, in strict
consonance with their principles, contribute freely to the support

---

[31] G. F. Best, *Temporal Pillars* (Cambridge, 1964), p. 106.

of a State church. In practice, they accepted their liability when prosecuted in the courts. By legislation passed in 1696 such prosecutions were normally undertaken before local magistrates acting with summary powers. But it remained possible for tithe owners to pursue their case in the Exchequer and in ecclesiastical courts. These proceedings were costly and objectionable to those who denied the jurisdiction. The issue was a somewhat synthetic one, not least because many Quakers found it convenient and even conscionable to pay their debts without a murmur. But the reaction of the bishops suggests that the Tithe Bill of 1736, which would have enforced summary jurisdiction in such cases, brought together a range of anxieties and insecurities among Churchmen. Clerical petitions were organized and a considerable agitation worked up.

Walpole supported the Tithe Bill in the hope that it would take the edge off the anticlerical feeling with which he had to contend in Parliament. It has been suggested that he positively sought a break with the Bishop of London, but such hazardous malice was out of character.[32] He seems to have been genuinely startled by Gibson's response. The bill passed the Commons, and, after vigorous lobbying by the bishops, was defeated in the Lords. Thereafter relations between Walpole and his 'pope' were never the same. Clerical advice was increasingly taken from others, notably Thomas Sherlock, Bishop of Salisbury, who had, ironically, opposed the Tithe Bill, and John Potter, who was given the Primacy on Wake's death in 1737. The Crown's ecclesiastical patronage drifted into the greedy hands of Newcastle and Hardwicke. The rift between Walpole and Gibson proved less damaging than it might have been, for the opposition was ill-placed to exploit it. High Church Tories had little in common with their Whig allies. It is possible that Walpole's support for the Mortmain and Tithe Bills had been designed to exploit this difference. Significantly, when the Quakers lobbied the Prince of Wales for support, he declined to become involved. In any event, ministerial anticlericalism was short-lived. William Warburton's *Alliance between Church and State* was published at the time of greatest strain in 1736. It offered a realistic defence of the position of the Church, one which abandoned all pretensions to an independent

---

[32] N. C. Hunt, *Two Early Political Associations*, p. 95; but see S. Taylor, 'Sir Robert Walpole, the Church of England, and the Quaker's Tithe Bill of 1736', *Historical Journal*, 28 (1985), 51–78.

authority, and yet laid on the State a clear duty of protection. It was strongly approved by Sherlock and the court. In time it came to be seen as the classic statement of complacent Georgian Erastianism and a mark of the stable relationship between religion and politics in mid-eighteenth-century England.

THE POLITICS OF PROTEST

The anticlerical agitation was not the only threat to Walpole's rule at this time. There were popular disturbances which caused considerable alarm. The King's Speech closing the session of 1737 referred to these convulsions in strong terms: 'You cannot be insensible, what just scandal and offence the Licentiousness of the present times, under the colour and disguise of Liberty, gives to all honest and sober men; ... defiance of all authority, contempt of magistracy, and even resistance of the laws, are become too general.'[33] The general election of 1734 had been particularly tumultuous. In the Welsh marches, for example, troops had to be employed to maintain order. But not all the protest was overtly political. In Gloucestershire and Herefordshire, the erection of turnpikes provoked the destruction of toll-gates. Coastal districts witnessed pitched battles with smuggling gangs. In Cornwall the county bench was so concerned by the mob violence which erupted after some controversial property litigation that they requested the intervention of the judges. In London the disruption ranged from the faintly ridiculous to the downright dangerous. The theatres were subjected to violent disputes, one of them involving the wrecking of Drury Lane by militant footmen. More disturbing were the Rag Fair Riots of July 1736, when the Irish community in East London found itself assailed on account of its competition with English labour, particularly in the building trade. The Gin Act[34] of the same year provoked riots in defence of cheap liquor. The opposition predictably blamed Walpole for popular disorder, the natural result, they alleged, of years of misgovernment, indebtedness, and corruption. Walpole had another explanation. The London riots in particular he blamed on the 'lower sort of Jacobites'.[35]

---

[33] *Cobbett's Parliamentary History*, x. 341–2.
[34] See p. 149.
[35] G. Rudé, *Paris and London in the Eighteenth Century* (London, 1970), p. 218.

With hindsight this is difficult to credit. Walpole's fears of Jacobitism were genuine, and they were not entirely without substance. But the agents and spies whom he maintained were a source of many false alarms. In the shadowy world of the secret services there was always a penumbra of plot and counterplot, information and misinformation, difficult to ignore at the time and equally difficult to assess in retrospect. A dynastically insecure State provided a constant temptation to dabble in Jacobite intrigue. Ministers grew understandably nervous after an incident in Westminster Hall on 14 July 1736. The courts of Chancery, King's Bench, and Common Pleas were all in session, when, in Lord Hardwicke's words, 'A parcel or packet containing several papers, and some sheets of several acts of parliament, and likewise a quantity of gunpowder, ... fired and blew up', scattering seditious libels around the Hall. Hardwicke suspended the business of his court, perused the papers, which contained a denunciation of recent enactments, including the Gin Act and Mortmain Act, instantly defended the 'reasonableness and necessity' of the Acts, and urged magistrates 'to discover and bring to punishment the authors and contrivers of this wicked and abominable insult'.[36] The outcome of this gunpowder plot was somewhat unexciting: it proved to be the work of a non-juring clergyman of doubtful sanity, Robert Nixon, who was duly fined and imprisoned. Any hope Walpole had of discovering a Christopher Layer or a Francis Atterbury to repeat his triumph of 1723 was disappointed, but it is easy to see why he was moved to anxiety by the activities of the mob in the capital.

Worse still occurred in Edinburgh. In September 1736, a highly effective demonstration of mob power ended in the lynching of Captain Porteous, commander of a military detachment which had killed eight rioters during the tumults attending the execution of a local smuggler. Porteous had been convicted of murder but reprieved by the Crown. The King, though in Hanover at the time, took a close interest in the subsequent proceedings. So did the ministers, including Walpole's principal manager of Scottish affairs, Lord Islay. As Islay's own 'minister for Scotland' Lord Milton observed, 'there is an end of government, if such practices be suffered to escape punishment'.[37] Punishment, however, proved

[36] Yorke, *Hardwicke*, i. 137–8.
[37] Coxe, *Walpole*, iii. 364.

no easy matter, in a case where the offenders were public heroes. Eventually, the ministry was forced to obtain an Act of Parliament fining the city of Edinburgh in order to compensate Porteous's widow, and disqualifying its Provost from office. For Walpole the Act was a major embarrassment. Its unpopularity north of the border compelled most Scottish MPs to vote against it. More importantly, it alienated Islay's brother, the second Duke of Argyll. Argyll was no manager, nor was he a natural leader. But as head of the Campbells he enjoyed huge influence in Scotland. He was also arrogant, ambitious, and above all unpredictable. In the Porteous affair he openly opposed his brother and Walpole. The possibility of a more permanent split in the Campbell family held obvious dangers for the ministry.

This was not Walpole's only parliamentary embarrassment in 1737. Sir John Barnard produced a scheme for the gradual reduction of interest on the National Debt from four per cent to three per cent. There were precedents for easing the interest burden, and no Treasury minister could deny the fiscal advantages of conversion. But a twenty-five per cent reduction in income for those dependent on government stock threatened to alienate some of the major interest groups which supported the regime. It was pointed out that the younger sons of landed gentry, as well as 'monied men', would be sufferers. Walpole was compelled to kill the bill. He gained many friends in the City by doing so, as Barnard, the Father of the City, made some enemies.

It was, and is, often said that the Septennial Act of 1716 rendered parliamentary politics more tranquil than they had been during the era of triennial elections. This is not supported by the evidence of the mid-1730s, when a Parliament which had several years to run provided a succession of alarums and excursions. In one sense, indeed, septennial Parliaments intensified debate, with notable effects on the relationship between the press and party politics. An opposition which enjoyed no immediate prospect of an election had an interest in encouraging extra-parliamentary agitation, even violence. Government, equally, had an interest in quelling public concern and confining the political excitement to Westminster. The achievements of the opposition press in the age of the *Craftsman* are well known, but Walpole's Grub Street activities were hardly less important. In some respects he had the advantage. Although government commanded no formal powers of censorship it possessed a formidable arsenal of legal and political weapons. Thanks to the Special Juries Act of 1729, it was the common assumption that ministers could procure complaisant juries when they pressed charges against printers, publishers, and authors. The Crown's lawyers also had the right to prosecute in the Court of King's Bench with none of the usual preliminaries and proofs required in criminal cases. Above all, the Secretaries of State enjoyed considerable powers, including the issue of warrants for the arrest of persons and seizure of papers: these 'general warrants' were to figure in the notorious case of John Wilkes in the 1760s. Few prosecutions for seditious libel were carried to a conclusion, but those that were, such as the actions against Richard Franklin, publisher of the *Craftsman*, in 1730, and Henry Haines, its printer, in 1737, had an intimidating effect where other potential offenders were concerned. For every such prosecution there were many arrests *in terrorem*, and for every arrest there were still more petty campaigns against street hawkers distributing scurrilous broadsheets and ballads.

There was a positive side to Walpole's propaganda campaign. His surviving papers reveal a well-organized and heavily subsidized government press. Admittedly, his writers tended to be of relatively low calibre. They included William Arnall, a barely educated hack who subsisted on Walpole's dole and wrote as Francis Walsingham in the *Free Briton*, James Pitt, a schoolmaster from Walpole's native county, who appeared as Mother Osborne in the *London Journal*, and John Henley, author of the *Hyp-Doctor* and much derided for the 'monstrous jumble of divinity and buffoonery' at his famous oratory.[38] These are not names to conjure with in the history of political journalism, yet their possessors kept up a trenchant and resourceful defence of their master, with the aid of Treasury subsidies and Post Office distribution. By the mid-1730s there were some grounds for supposing that they had at least halted the advance of their more talented opponents. In circulation terms the *Craftsman* probably reached its peak, a substantial twelve or thirteen thousand copies each week, in 1734–5. Thereafter, as Bolingbroke's enthusiasm wilted and his editor Nicholas Amhurst lost something of his edge, it declined steadily. Its more ferocious sister *Fog's Weekly Journal* suffered a similar decline.

In this context the Prince of Wales's defection was especially

[38] G. Midgley, *The Life of Orator Henley* (Oxford, 1973), p. 144.

important. A new journal *Common Sense* was founded in 1737 with the Prince's friend Chesterfield one of its directors. Prince Frederick succeeded in drawing about himself a talented group of young men. Some of them, James Thomson, George Lyttelton, and Henry Brooke, were to enjoy literary reputations of the first order. Together they promoted the vision of Frederick as a constitutional prince of truly old English principles, offering patriotic harmony and reform in place of Hanoverian strife and corruption. Later, it was a vision best known from Bolingbroke's *Patriot King*, the form in which it passed into Whig legend as the source of a sinister creed for tyrants. But in the 1730s it was associated with new and exciting literary talents.

Walpole had many means of combating such forces. His reluctance to buy off an earlier generation of gifted intellectuals, when most of them, including Swift, Gay, and Pope, were plainly prepared to discuss terms, remains mystifying. But there were some notable defections to his cause in his last years of power, not least Henry Fielding. Fielding's early forte was the stage and the stage itself was something of a special case. Since the beginning of George II's reign the theatre had achieved an unprecedented degree of independence. Magistrates found it impossible to repress the activities of unauthorized theatres, and the owners of licensed playhouses proved equally incapable of controlling their actors. The weak point in the law was the Vagrancy Act of 1714, which was generally supposed, along with older legislation, to render actors liable to the same penalties as rogues and beggars. When the law was tested in the case of John Harper, a player at the Haymarket, in 1733, it proved sadly deficient. Harper argued that he was manifestly not a vagrant, but a freeholder and a substantial householder. It was helpfully pointed out by his friends that he was an unlikely vagabond and highly unsuitable for hard labour in the Bridewell, 'he being a Man so corpulent, that it is not possible for him either to labour, or to wander a great deal'.[39] In any event he was vindicated by the Court of King's Bench.

After this, playwrights and actors threw caution to the winds. Anxiety was expressed about the threat which they presented to the industry and law-abidingness of the middling and lower ranks. The activities of one of the unauthorized theatres, in Goodmans Fields, seemed to offer a special danger to the working habits of

[39] *London Magazine*, 1734, p. 87.

apprentices in the business districts of London. Sir John Barnard, on behalf of the City, sought a bill bringing actors clearly within the vagrancy law in 1735. He did not succeed until the second attempt in 1737. Then, however, the bill was carried with a crucial amendment proposed by Walpole, subjecting dramatic productions to scrutiny by the Lord Chamberlain. Such censorship would never have been accepted in other spheres. But Walpole adduced powerful evidence with which to convince back-benchers of the need to curb the stage. He cited a play, as yet unacted, *The Festival of the Golden Rump*, which attacked the King and Queen in offensive and obscene terms. There is a suspicion that Walpole had promoted this piece, which was accompanied by a deliberately objectionable cartoon, in order to strengthen the case for censorship. The result was a landmark in the history of the stage. In future it was impossible legally to produce a play which did not carry the government's approval. Moreover, the unlicensed theatres were rendered technically illegal; when they revived, in the 1740s, it was under perpetual threat of ministerial action if they trespassed on political sensitivities. In short, the Act was the one undoubted and comprehensive victory in Walpole's extended warfare with the intellectuals of his day.

THE POLICY OF PEACE

The King took a close interest in the Porteous Riots and the Licensing Act. But the sternest test of Walpole's capacity to manage him came in matters of foreign rather than domestic policy. In 1733–4 George II was tempted to intervene in the War of the Polish Succession. Ostensibly it was a war to determine the choice of candidate for the Polish throne, a choice which lay between Louis XV's father-in-law Stanislas Leszcynski and the Austro-Russian candidate Augustus of Saxony. In reality it was another struggle between Bourbon and Habsburg, with the additional anxiety, bequeathed by the War of the Spanish Succession, of Spain's involvement on the side of France. Britain was obliged by treaty to go to the defence of Austria. But Walpole declined to treat the Polish succession as a *casus belli*, and gloried in his pacifism. He told Queen Caroline, in a celebrated boast: 'Madam, there are fifty thousand men slain in Europe this year, and not one

Englishman.'[40] This was a powerful argument, though like many of Walpole's measures it smacked more of pragmatic, insular Toryism than principled, internationalist Whiggism. More controversially, Walpole believed that his policy must make Britain the arbiter of Europe. The Continental powers would fight to a standstill and the King of England would mediate a suitably judicious peace. 'If I can keep this nation out of the war a year longer, I know it is impossible but England must give law to all Europe.'[41]

This proved a notable miscalculation. Charles VI of Austria was induced to make peace on terms which owed nothing to the King of England and registered a considerable reverse for the Habsburg cause. In Poland the French candidate was unseated but only at the cost of placing him in the Duchy of Lorraine and alienating that duchy to France on his death. In Italy Spain's attempt to revise the Treaty of Utrecht was finally successful, with the acquisition of Naples and Sicily for the cadet branch of the Spanish royal family. For its part, Austria obtained Bourbon acquiescence in the Pragmatic Sanction. So far as Britain was concerned, Walpole had deprived the Jacobites of a potential opportunity, had protected the British taxpayer, and had preserved his reputation for husbanding the nation's resources. Whether the price of this success, a manifest reduction in British prestige and influence on the Continent, was worth paying, remained to be seen.

The weakness of Walpole's parliamentary opponents during the Polish War was that they found it difficult to argue that he was neglecting genuine British interests. It was all too easy to imagine the anti-Hanoverian rhetoric which they would have employed if English troops had been sent to the aid of Austria. But the situation was quite different when relations with Spain deteriorated in 1738. The formal settlement of Georgia in the 1730s had revived old disputes about the territorial limits of Spanish Florida. The loss of Gibraltar and Minorca remained a continuing cause of Spanish resentment. Above all there were the notorious 'depredations'. British violations of Spanish trade laws in the Caribbean met with a firm response from the Spanish authorities in America. Under the terms of the Peace of Utrecht it was difficult to distinguish between legal and illegal trade. The Treaty of Seville in 1729 had

[40] P. Yorke, 2nd Earl of Hardwicke, ed., *Walpolania* (London, 1781), p. 361.
[41] Ibid.

laid down a workable procedure for settling such disputes. There was a synthetic quality about the hysteria of 1738–9. Stories which inflamed opinion in England, the tale of Jenkins' Ear, and the account of the tortures inflicted on the crew of the *Robert* with 'hand vices and screws', went back some years.[42] None the less, public disquiet, fed with colourful tales of British 'tars' rotting in Spanish gaols, was readily aroused.

In the parliamentary session of 1738 the Commons mounted a detailed investigation. The result was a report demanding strong measures. For Walpole, the issue had all the incendiary potential of the Dunkirk question without much prospect of Spanish compliance in defusing it. Though the Spanish court was not unwilling to negotiate, it had its own grievances. A preliminary agreement in September 1738 involved paying a sum of £95,000 by way of damages, in return for payment to Spain of £68,000 which the South Sea Company owed on its own account. The Company's refusal to co-operate killed this agreement, the notorious convention of the Pardo, in January 1739. A parliamentary clamour forced the ministry to maintain a naval presence in the Mediterranean under Admiral Haddock. War inevitably followed.

It was Walpole's belief that he had been pushed, and his country tricked, into the war by a combination of mercantile self-interest and political malice. Throughout the first two years of the war he stressed the unrepresentative character of those who opposed his policy, compared with those 'men of figure and sense in the kingdom' who took his own view.[43] According to his brother Horace, it was only the 'vulgar, the ignorant, the prejudiced and the disaffected'[44] who favoured the war. Such claims are difficult to adjudicate. Certainly the business community was far from united in support of the war. It was pointed out that Britain's trade with mainland Spain was worth far more than the hypothetical profits which might be gained by a costly struggle for empire in the Americas. In the City those who clamoured for belligerent measures were stigmatized by the ministry's supporters in a paper distributed freely through the Post Office as 'an insignificant Body of Tradesmen and Mechanics'. A respectable Virginia merchant

[42] J. O. McLachlan, *Trade and Peace with Old Spain, 1667–1750* (Cambridge, 1940), p. 107.
[43] *Parliamentary History*, xi. 502.
[44] Ibid. xi. 274.

was listed as a tobacconist, a well-known silk dyer as a 'rag dyer', and the City-bred High Sheriff of Hertfordshire as a 'soapmaker'.[45] This had something of the effect that Walpole's contemptuous remarks about 'sturdy beggars' had had in 1733. In 1739 the Livery went out of its way to veto the choice of a ministerial supporter, Sir George Champion, as Lord Mayor, though by custom he stood next in the line of succession. The following year, the Aldermanic bench retaliated by turning down the popular choice for the mayoralty, a prominent opponent of the ministry, Sir Robert Godschall. It was a reminder that even in the heartland of patriot politics the Robinocracy continued to flourish. Indeed what truly created a consensus against Walpole was not so much his reluctance to go to war as his lack of enthusiasm for waging it. An early success at Puerto Bello in November 1739 inspired the most exaggerated ambitions of plunder in Spanish America. Subsequent campaigns, designed with the capture of Cartagena, Cuba, and Panama in mind, proved costly failures. By 1742 all hope of finally bringing to fruition the dreams of Drake and Ralegh had been abandoned.

For this Walpole got most of the blame. His direction of hostilities was criticized as at best a mockery, a 'Jeu de Théâtre', at worst a disgraceful display of cowardice, 'our long pacifick war against Spain'.[46] Certainly his own heart was not in it. His opponents employed the image of valiant British seamen betrayed by their governors if not their admirals. Richard Glover's highly successful ballad *Hosier's Ghost* recalled the Admiral who had supposedly been condemned to impotence in the face of the Spanish treasure fleet in 1727, in order to plead the cause of his successors. Such criticism was as defective as Glover's sense of history. Warfare in the Caribbean was never what fireside strategists liked to picture it: the devastating toll taken by the climate and the difficulties inseparable from joint operations between army and navy proved too much for more than one eighteenth-century expeditionary force. Nor was the war unaffected by party politics. Vernon, the hero of Puerto Bello, made no bones about his support for the opposition. He blamed his reverse at Cartagena on insufficient support from home and on the commander of the land forces, General Wentworth. Tobias Smollett, who was present at

---

[45] *Common Sense*, 17 Mar. 1739.
[46] *Craftsman*, 24 Jan. 1741; *Common Sense*, 5 Dec. 1741.

Cartagena as a naval surgeon, censured both officers when he gave his own account in his novel *Roderick Random*.

By the time of Cartagena, in 1741, the war had already changed in character. The death of Charles VI in 1740, and the great Continental conflict which it provoked, gave the War of Jenkins' Ear the appearance of a side-show. With the Habsburg empire on the point of dismemberment, Britain was increasingly drawn into the war in Germany. But the War of the Austrian Succession was not without its compensations. In 1740 there was a real danger that France would intervene in the Spanish war. From the British standpoint, this would have converted a buccaneering adventure into a deadly war of survival, raising the possibility of defeat at sea and a Jacobite invasion. 'Nothing but a diversion upon the Continent can save us,'[47] it was said in London, when reports arrived that squadrons at Brest and Toulon were preparing to sail. The Austrian war certainly proved a diversion.

WALPOLE'S FALL

The preliminaries and progress of war made Walpole's parliamentary position perilous. The Convention of the Pardo had been carried in the Commons by the slender margin of 260 votes to 232, an indication of the fate which he would have met later on if he had stood out against the war when the Convention broke down. January 1740 saw a motion for a bill to reduce the number of placemen in the Commons. It was supported by many instructions from the constituencies, reminiscent of the onslaught on the excise in 1733. The ministry defeated it by only 222 votes to 206. In the same session the Seamen's Registration Bill was treated as an attack on civil liberties and met with a furious reception both in Parliament and in the press. Sir John Barnard asserted that it would make a sailor and a slave 'terms of the same signification': the bill was defeated, notwithstanding Walpole's personal support for it.[48] 1740 also marked the open defection of the Duke of Argyll. His journey to Scotland in the summer of that year, portrayed in the prints as a 'State Pack Horse' on the road from London to Edinburgh, was observed with considerable interest, as were his

[47] A. M. Wilson, *French Foreign Policy during the Administration of Cardinal Fleury, 1726–1743* (London, 1936), p. 324.
[48] *Parliamentary History*, xi. 416.

subsequent electioneering activities. Scottish burgh elections were largely determined by electoral colleges composed of municipal representatives. There was no doubt that in many burghs the Argyll interest threatened a reverse for the ministry at the forthcoming general election.

In the final session of the 1734 Parliament it seemed that an election might not even be required to bring Walpole down. Much depended on the Tories. In 1738 the Jacobite William Shippen had had the impudence to announce that the names of Whig and Tory were dead, and that Court and Country were indeed their true successors.[49] This had long been the dream of the patriot leaders: a genuinely united coalition of all parties dedicated to the destruction of a corrupt ministry. It was not to be. In February 1741 motions were put forward in both houses, requesting the King to dismiss his minister. They were heavily defeated, in the Commons by 290 votes to 106. It was the abstention of many Tories which proved decisive. They pleaded, in self-defence, their ancient principles, particularly the impropriety of attempting to dictate to a king his choice of ministry. They also nurtured an entirely justified suspicion that their Whig allies would ditch them once Walpole had been brought down. In any event the second Parliament of George II ended in a state of high excitement and uncertainty. Walpole's supporters in the press revelled in the discomfiture of their opponents. The defeat of the *Motion*, as it became universally known, was indeed astonishing. As it turned out, however, it was only a stay of execution for Walpole himself.

Who killed cock robin? Walpole's fall from power in February 1742 had long been anticipated, and often prematurely predicted. Moreover, Walpole's primacy had been so complete, so unprecedented, that its end could not but prove a sensation. It was easy to suppose that such an impregnable fortress could only have surrendered to treachery within. Certainly there were some potential traitors. Walpole's old adversary Spencer Compton, Earl of Wilmington, had never been a loyal supporter, and it did not go unremarked that his friend George Bubb Dodington, who had joined the opposition in 1740, was to be observed in frequent consultation with him. Walpole believed that the rot had spread closer to the core than this. According to his son Horace Walpole, he blamed Newcastle and Hardwicke, increasingly the dominant

[49] *London Magazine*, 1738, p. 334.

forces within the Cabinet, for his fall. There was also talk of dirty work in Scotland. Islay's career was not such as to inspire faith in his fidelity. He was, after all, Argyll's brother, and it seemed plausible to assume that the Campbell brothers were keeping a foot in two camps. Yet none of this carries much conviction. There is no evidence that any of Walpole's inner circle of supporters lost heart until it became obvious that his prospects of continuing in power were hopeless. Walpole was the first servant of the Crown, not the master of a ministry responsible to himself. He was not entitled to expect, nor in all likelihood did he seriously suppose, that the stability of the King's affairs and the conduct of a difficult and dangerous war, would be endangered for the sake of keeping him in power against the expressed will of Parliament.

In the final drama the general election played a large part, though the space of time which lapsed between the elections themselves in the spring of 1741 and Walpole's resignation nearly a year later somewhat obscured its significance. There was no doubting the view of the electorate. Admiral Vernon, the hero of Puerto Bello, was put up in seven constituencies and returned in three. His narrow defeat in the populous city of Westminster, after a violent contest, had more to do with sharp practice by the ministry than the verdict of public opinion. In the event the open constituencies did not produce a great number of contests (there were only ninety-five contests in all) nor did they determine the outcome of the election. Already, in 1734, the counties and large boroughs had swung so clearly behind the opposition that further substantial gains in such constituencies could hardly be expected. Rather it was in the smaller boroughs, which had saved Walpole in 1734, that the battle was fought in 1741: in this struggle the forces of his more recent enemies, those who had declared themselves since the defection of the Prince of Wales, counted for more than the public debate about his policies, or even than the deficiencies of his war management. In Scotland, traditionally the preserve of government, Argyll's defection took its toll. In the West Country the Prince of Wales led an effective campaign, based on his own Duchy of Cornwall, and supported by boroughmongers who had an eye to the future, to make inroads into Walpole's Court and Treasury support.

Calculations about the results of the election varied considerably and continue to do so. No eighteenth-century Parliament presented a clear-cut party division, and modern assessments of the election take into account the conduct of MPs in the subsequent parliamentary session, something which was susceptible to further influence between the elections themselves and the summoning of Parliament. Certainly Walpole believed, when the Commons met in December 1741, that he still had a chance of securing a working majority, albeit one dangerously close to single figures. In normal circumstances his opponents would have begun by contesting the choice of a Speaker. But Arthur Onslow, the incumbent, was no creature of the court, and resistance to his election would probably have alienated potential supporters. The opposition did, however, secure the appointment of one of their own sympathizers, George Lee, as Chairman of the Committee of Privileges and Elections.

In any new Parliament the earliest and most telling divisions concerned not the great strategic warfare of public policy but the scattered skirmishes of disputed elections. Walpole had appreciably improved his position by such tactics after previous general elections. This time they proved his downfall. The defeat which seems to have decided him was a division of 236 to 235 on the Chippenham election, on 28 January. But it was the deteriorating trend which made his decision inevitable. On 21 January he had won a marginal victory by three votes against William Pulteney's motion proposing a committee of inquiry into the conduct of the war. Walpole's defence of his record on this occasion was perhaps his most brilliant performance in an outstanding parliamentary career. But three votes in a record house of more than 500 MPs left little room for optimism and none for manœuvre. There was no possibility of parleying. Walpole had tried the desperate expedient of a negotiation with the Prince of Wales during the previous Christmas recess. No doubt he had in mind that reconciliation of father and son which he had brought about in 1720 in order to save the Sunderland ministry. But there was to be no repetition in 1742. He took a peerage as Earl of Orford and left the House of Commons, its first undoubted Prime Minister, on 11 February 1742. It was rightly seen as a moment of profound significance, though in widely differing terms. The press resorted to a variety of disgusting metaphors, principally on the theme of evacuation, the necessary purging of a Britannia deeply affected by corruption and putrifaction, and thereby a guarantee of renewed health in the body politic. Walpole summarized his fate less colourfully to the Duke of Devonshire. 'I must inform you that the panick was so great among what I should call my own friends, that *they all* declared my retiring was become absolutely necessary, as the only means to carry on the publick businesse, and this to be attended with honour and security.'[50]

[50] Coxe, *Walpole*, iii. 592.

CHAPTER 3

The Progress of Politeness

*HOWEVER difficult to quantify, the growing afflu-
ence and influence of the middle class were widely
recognized. Luxury and refinement seemed within the
reach even of relatively humble families. The pursuit
of genteel status and the acquisition of polite manners
in some measure united a class which in other respects
appeared diverse and divided. Educational institutions were reshaped to meet its needs, with the
emphasis on the acquisition of useful skills and social
graces. The old grammar schools and universities came
under heavy criticism and were compelled to adapt
to changing requirements. Some of the most notable
cultural developments of the period, for example the
expansion of the market for books and the immense
popularity of novels and histories, reflected the taste
of middle-class consumers. So did the ubiquity of the
assembly as a focus for ordinary social life and the
proliferation of spa towns and seaside resorts for
bourgeois recreation. Middle-class women shared in
the literary and social opportunities of the period, but
found themselves increasingly excluded from gainful
employment. Some of them tentatively adopted a
feminist position. For most, however, marriage
remained the central preoccupation, one which was
regarded by all families as a matter of the highest
priority; the marriage market was regulated by*

*informal moral censorship and even subjected, in
1753, to statutory control. The internal tensions of
middle-class life, social and sexual, did not prevent
its defenders adopting a united front in the face of external dangers. Much attention was paid to the control
and discipline of servants. The alliance of money and
gentility was calculated to maintain the morale and
sense of superiority of propertied people. Politeness
was the mark of an immensely vigorous but also a
remorselessly snobbish society.*

THE MIDDLE CLASS

THE significance of the middle class in eighteenth-century
England is easily neglected in retrospect. It is even possible
to ignore it altogether, such is the poverty of historical
sociology and the limitations of the models of class employed
by twentieth-century historians. Somewhat fanciful accounts of
the social tensions of this period fasten on the colourful but
often theatrical conflict of 'plebeians' and 'patricians'. In such
struggles bourgeois elements are permitted to appear, incon-
sequentially, as occasional leaders of those below and powerless
dependants of those above, a perspective which deprives them of
coherence and incidentally obliterates their overwhelming importance in the social history of the period. Contemporaries thought
the growing wealth and importance of the middle orders of society
the most striking of developments. The Scottish philosopher John
Millar pointed to what he considered an extraordinary change
which had come over British society since the Revolution of
1688. A great body of merchants, moneyed men, and farmers had
transformed the face both of urban and agrarian society.[1]

The view that western society, in its 'commercial' stage of
development, brought particular benefits to the middling entrepreneur, whether in trade, manufacturing, or farming, is supported
by ample historical evidence. This is hardly surprising given the
unequally allocated rewards of rapid economic growth in developing societies, and the reluctance of eighteenth-century legislators
to redress the balance by means of taxation. What was lacking
at the time, however, was detailed statistical enquiry as to the
distribution of the wealth. In its absence, Millar, like many other
commentators, declined to give the emergence of the middle class
the precise lineaments craved by the social historian. It was commoner by far to dwell on the superior moral credentials and
industry of the middle class than to analyse its make-up. The most
elementary generalizations about it are consequently difficult to
sustain.

When contemporaries talked of the 'middle sort', they generally
had in mind a wide range of incomes and a great variety of occupations. In the countryside small farmers, without property of their
own, joined freeholders, perhaps possessing a small patrimonial

[1] W. C. Lehmann, *John Millar of Glasgow, 1735–1801* (Cambridge, 1960), pp. 334–5.

estate, to provide the landed interest with an outlying flank of modest respectability. At least in the eyes of those who claimed such status, it separated them from the great mass of labourers and cottagers. In the towns, too, some of the smallest self-employed businessmen, shopkeepers, tradesmen, craftsmen, even artisans, would for some purposes be counted with their more august mercantile and professional superiors. But the uncertainty of the criteria makes categorization extraordinarily difficult. At the time there was awareness both of the complexity of such calculations and the relativity of most conclusions drawn from them. Partly it was a matter of regional variations in respect of the basic conditions of material life. As the Scottish politician George Dempster admitted to James Boswell, £30 per annum in London made its possessor far better off for the 'little wants of life' than the Laird of Col in the Western Isles.[2] But comparisons were much more complicated than this. Social standing depended on numerous considerations: family (by birth or marriage), property (real and personal), profession or employment, and less definably 'connections', 'politeness', and 'breeding' (which did not necessarily imply good birth or upbringing). All these might be amplified or diminished by the traditions, perceptions, and outlook of the communities in which they were set. Yet these are familiar difficulties in open societies, and they do not normally inhibit historians from venturing on generalizations.

More obstructive are the large margins for error opened up even by tentative attempts to identify the numbers involved. The calculations offered by Joseph Massie and Malachy Postlethwayt in the late 1750s, themselves necessarily little better than guesswork, reveal the dangers. If an income of £50 is treated as the minimum at which it was possible to aspire to membership of the middling rank, then one in five of all families was entitled so to be considered, divided more or less equally between town and country. A figure of £40 would double the proportion to two in five families.[3] Neither of these sums was a fortune, but forty pounds was twice as much

[2] R. W. Chapman, ed., *Johnson's Journey to the Western Islands of Scotland and Boswell's Journal of a Tour to the Hebrides with Samuel Johnson, LL.D.* (Oxford, 1970), p. 435.

[3] Massie's calculations (see Table 1) are reproduced in P. Mathias, *The Transformation of England: Essays in the Economic and Social History of England in the Eighteenth Century* (London, 1979), pp. 186–7; they have been tentatively revised by P. H. Lindert and J. G. Williamson, 'Revising England's Social Tables, 1688–1812', *Explorations in Economic History*, 19 (1982), 395–408; Postlethwayt published the alternative calculations of 'a

as was generally thought necessary for mere subsistence. The champions of the clergy, for instance, would have rejoiced if they had been able to secure it as the minimum provided for the support of country curates. It offered the possibility of essentially 'consumer' spending on better housing, better furnishing and clothing, better medical and educational services, than the ordinary artisan or peasant could normally expect to enjoy. Probably, too, it was at this same level of forty or fifty pounds a year that one of the commonest criteria employed at the time, the liability of ordinary householders to pay the poor-rate, operated. Nothing more clearly created 'two nations' than the line of demarcation between those who paid poor-rates and those who were not only exempted from payment by their poverty but were all too likely to find themselves applying for relief. Estimates of the proportions on either side of this great social gulf varied according to circumstances and locality, and could be affected by some unpredictable practices, including electoral gerrymandering. In some places the poor-rate payers were more than a third of the population, and even in industrializing cities notorious for their populous slums, they were unlikely to constitute less than a quarter. In Birmingham in the late eighteenth century it was reckoned that 4,000 houses paid to the poor-rate, out of a total of 11,000.[4] It was precisely at this margin where spending power was so constricted and social status so uncertain that very large numbers of families were concentrated, rendering almost impossible hard and fast conclusions about their numbers.

Not everyone on an income which rendered him secure sought to spend it on the acquisition of material goods and the pursuit of social status. The skilled worker or craftsman might, in prosperous times, command wages which amounted to sixty pounds a year, but fritter them away on drink or even reduce his working week to enjoy leisure in preference to luxury. He was a commonplace

gentleman of honour in a public character abroad' in his *The Universal Dictionary of Trade and Commerce*, *sub* 'People'. The figures adduced from these tables are as follows:

	Massie	Lindert	Postlethwayt
Families earning £50 p.a.	280,430	239,282	250,874
approx. and above	(19%)	(16%)	(17%)
Families earning £40 p.a.	617,930	631,935	564,426
approx. and above	(42%)	(41%)	(38%)
Total families	1,474,570	1,538,500	1,483,239

[4] W. Hutton, *An History of Birmingham* (3rd edn., Birmingham, 1795), p. 99.

TABLE I. *Social structure according to Joseph Massie, 1759*

Annual family income (£)	Classification				Total families
800+	2,070 esquires and titled				2,070
400–799	4,800 gentlemen	3,000 merchants	2,500 tradesmen		10,300
200–399	11,200 gentlemen	10,000 merchants	5,000 tradesmen	2,500 master manufacturers	28,700
80–199	2,000 clergy 12,000 lawyers 8,000 army and navy officers	30,000 freeholders 15,000 farmers	10,000 tradesmen 2,000 innkeepers	5,000 master manufacturers	84,000
50–79	9,000 clergy 18,000 liberal arts 16,000 civil office	60,000 freeholders 20,000 farmers	20,000 tradesmen 3,000 innkeepers	10,000 master manufacturers	156,000
40–49		120,000 farmers 20,000 cottagers	125,000 tradesmen	62,500 master manufacturers	327,500
25–39		120,000 freeholders		28,000 London manufacturers	148,000
15–24		200,000 husbandmen	20,000 ale sellers 60,000 seamen	20,000 London labourers 200,000 sundry manufacturers	500,000
14 or less		200,000 country labourers	18,000 soldiers		218,000
					1,474,570

Source: adapted from P. Mathias; see note 3.

figure in contemporary social analysis, perplexing and irritating those who worshipped the god of economic growth at the shrine of material possessions. It was possible to take comfort, however, from the apparently limitless appetite of the middling ranks for social status, as powerful a motive to enterprise and industry as the lust for worldly goods. There seemed no shortage of Englishmen, or, as it was often said, of Englishwomen, whose prime ambition in life was to rise higher up the social ladder. Above all, there beckoned the lure of acceptance into that great and growing, yet tantalizingly unattainable, class composed of gentlemen and their ladies. When the most successful of all eighteenth-century monthly periodicals commenced publication, it called itself the *Gentleman's Magazine or Trader's Monthly Intelligencer*. But the alternative title was quickly dropped, 'as too mechanical, and giving the whole a more genteel and elegant Turn'.[5] The fact was that tradesmen did not want to think of themselves as tradesmen but as gentlemen.

Much significance was attached to the matter of title. The Leicestershire clergyman Aulay Macaulay remarked on the extraordinary increase in the second half of the eighteenth century, in the numbers who described themselves as 'Mr', 'Mrs', and 'Esquire'.[6] In principle, the term 'Esquire' continued to be restricted to men of property or professional standing. It was considered incompatible with a trade, though retired businessmen commonly assumed it as soon as they had invested their profits in property or an annuity. In an urban context it was increasingly worthless as an indication of rank. The right to bear arms could be bought by anyone, but in the second half of the century few who claimed the title even bothered to register with the College of Heralds. Similarly, the appellation 'Madam' ceased to represent anything more than a conviction on the part of its bearer that she could sustain it against all comers of her sex. The depreciation of the currency of title proceeded still more rapidly with the 'rank' of gentlemen, thanks to its wider connotations. Technically it continued to be a particular rung on the ladder. Small country squires who did not presume to count themselves among the county gentry used it with pride. Substantial tradesmen and merchants felt

[5] *Grubstreet Journal*, 15 Mar. 1733.
[6] John Nichols, *The History and Antiquities of the County of Leicester* (4 vols., repr. Wakefield, 1971), iv. 131.

free to resort to it where their courage failed them in regard to 'Esquire', especially when, once again, they sold up or retired. At Birmingham, it was said, 'Gentlemen, as well as buttons, have been stamped here; but, like them, when finished, are moved off.'[7] In the countryside a new term had to be invented to describe the pretensions of men who owned little or no property of their own but enjoyed a measure of opulence. Henry Fielding used the expression 'gentleman farmer' in *Tom Jones* in 1749 and Charlotte Lennox did so in *The Female Quixote* three years later.[8] During the following decade it was to become commonplace. Agrarian improvement seemed to be raising a new breed of rural capitalists who demanded equality of status with their landlords. But more significant was the extension of usage which affected everyday forms of address still lower down the social scale. By the reign of George III 'Mr' and 'Mrs' were widely accepted in towns, and increasingly in the countryside, as the automatic entitlement of anyone who owned property, hired labour, or simply laid claim to a degree of rank and respectability.

This debasement of gentility is one of the clearest signs of social change in the eighteenth century, the mark of a fundamental transformation. Paradoxically, its significance was masked by the concern of those who counterfeited the currency of class to have it pass for sound coin. Contemporary analysts were, however, well aware of the process involved. It was a common observation that in England the appearance of a gentleman was seemingly sufficient to make him one, at least in the sense of his acceptance as such by others. The Swiss traveller De Saussure, at the end of George I's reign, noted that any well-dressed person wearing a sword was treated as a gentleman.[9] By the end of the next reign, the novelist Richard Graves could claim that 'Sir' and 'your Honour' were accorded anyone 'that appears in a clean shirt and powdered wig'.[10] The famed political liberties of Englishmen played a part in the process. In a world where patronage counted for as much as power, titles were a cheap form of bribery. As the head of a Whig college in Oxford put it before the great Oxfordshire election of 1754,

[7] W. Hutton, *An History of Birmingham*, p. 31.

[8] *Oxford English Dictionary*; *The Female Quixote*, ed. R. P. C. Mutter (2 vols., London, 1966), i. 99.

[9] Madame Van Muyden, ed., *A Foreign View of England in the Reigns of George I and George II: The Letters of Monsieur César de Saussure to his Family* (London, 1902), p. 212.

[10] *The Spiritual Quixote*, ed. C. Tracy (London, 1967), p. 140.

when canvassing the local gentry it would be sensible to approach tradesmen and farmers as well, 'to whom the compliment of being considered in the rank of gentleman on this occasion, may, I think, not improperly be made'.[11] It was a compliment which they were certainly ready to welcome. Nothing unified the middling orders so much as their passion for aping the manners and morals of the gentry more strictly defined, as soon as they possessed the material means to do so.

This was a revolution by conjunction rather than confrontation, but it was a revolution none the less, transforming the pattern of social relations, and subtly reshaping the role of that governing class which was the object of imitation. The aspirants sought incorporation in the class above them, not collaboration with those below them. Hence the need to condemn in others the very snobberies which they themselves practised. How many of those who applauded Foote's mockery of social climbing in his play *The Commissary* ('These bourgeois are so frightful' his preposterous hero Zachary Fungus pronounced) were themselves bourgeois?[12] How many, too, found themselves engaged in costly pursuit of the fashionable for the sake of status? Fashion was necessarily transitory; as Richard Owen Cambridge noted, 'they are obliged to change [it] continually, as soon as they find it prophaned by any other company but one step lower than themselves in their degrees of politeness.'[13] This was the paradox of Britain's famed social mobility, one often remarked on at the time. As Soame Jenyns put it, in the same paper for which Cambridge wrote, *The World*, life was one continued race: 'everyone is flying from his inferiors, in pursuit of his superiors who fly from Him with equal alacrity'.[14] But the race seemed to have few losers and there was a distinct possibility that everyone might finish by breasting the tape together. The logical result, Jenyns concluded, only partly in jest, was a nation of gentry, with no common people at all. This was a considerable exaggeration. The true conclusion, one substantially

---

[11] Francis Webber, Rector of Exeter College to Lady Susan Keck, 27 Jan. 1753, quoted in R. J. Robson, *The Oxfordshire Election of 1754* (London, 1949), p. 22.

[12] *The Dramatic Works of Samuel Foote, Esq.* (2 vols., London, 1795), i: '*The Commissary*', p. 34.

[13] *The World*, 102, in G. O. Cambridge, *The Works of Richard Owen Cambridge* (London, 1803), p. 439.

[14] *The World*, 125, in C. N. Cole, ed., *The Works of Soame Jenyns* (4 vols., London, 1790), ii. 93.

achieved by the middle of George III's reign, was not a nation of gentry, but a powerful and extensive middle class. This class rested on a broad, diverse base of property, by no means restricted to land; it increasingly decided the framework of debate and the terms of tenure on which the traditional politics of monarchy and aristocracy were conducted.

MATERIAL WEALTH AND POLITENESS

The principal determinant of these changes was prosperity, particularly from the 1750s. Combined with mild price inflation and relatively low taxation, economic expansion had the effect of stretching the social fabric in its middle and upper sections. Population growth prevented the manual labour force from extracting its proper share of the new wealth and enhanced this sense of a world in which the rich were getting richer and the poor poorer. In reality, all those who by their enterprise, skill, or good fortune succeeded in raising themselves above the ruck of the 'labouring poor' (a phrase increasingly used) were getting richer. Every pound of additional spending power made a disproportionate difference in a society in which most expected to achieve little more than subsistence, and in which the State did nothing to redistribute the benefits of commercial expansion. Contemporaries were struck by the apparently inexhaustible demand for superior manufactured goods, something which plainly had much to do with the industrial growth of the period.

It was one of the main aims of government to ensure that such demand was supplied from English sources. Strenuous efforts were made to restrict the flow of foreign textiles, even when they came via the East India Company and helped offset an adverse balance of trade with India. Home-produced silks, calicoes, cottons, and fine woollens provided both the quality and variety of texture and colour which were needed to sustain the market for fashionable clothes. The frivolous and ephemeral nature of polite taste was condemned by censorious patriots. Yet while the pattern books drew heavily on Paris, the fabrics which gave them effect were overwhelmingly the product of English hands. The same combination, middle-class demand, foreign or at least London fashions, and domestic enterprise, boosted the production of many other luxuries. Toys, buckles, buttons, and trinkets made Birmingham a byword for the miracles of new manufacturing processes. Matthew Boulton's Soho factory was a well-established tourist spectacle in the 1770s; by a happy and convenient coincidence, the industrial wonders of Birmingham were exploited at just the same time as the Shakespeare industry at nearby Stratford-upon-Avon.[15]

Access to tropical raw materials was important to sophisticated taste. Mahogany, brought from central America and thereby a cause of conflict with Spain, rapidly conquered early Hanoverian England. In the 1720s and 1730s it was still relatively novel. Visiting the status-conscious Sir Robert Walpole at Houghton, Sir Matthew Decker was startled to find even the water closets fitted with it.[16] But less opulent aspirers after polite taste were not far behind. 'Hearts of oak' was ironically the toast of many homes which preferred mahogany for practical purposes. The English manufacturer was required to learn new technologies as well as import new materials. Perhaps the most spectacular example of the conversion of a taste for the exotic into a staple of domestic industry was the introduction and expansion of china production. English porcelains effectively began their reign with the Chelsea, Bow, and Longton Hall ware of the 1750s. More enduring names, Worcester and Derby, were established soon after. By the end of George II's reign techniques once restricted to the Far East had been effectively mastered at home. It was, however, the mass production of the Staffordshire pottery industry which was to supply the household needs of lower and middle-class England in coming generations. In this respect the surviving evidence of Georgian extravagance can be somewhat misleading, not because it is false, but because it misrepresents the relative importance of conspicuous consumption among the upper classes, and more commonplace but cumulatively no less significant consumer taste among the middle classes.

It often suited contemporaries to dwell on the extremes of social life. Conversation pieces were much in demand, but those who excelled at them, like Arthur Devis, were customarily paid to paint high society: the changing life-style of the small provincial businessman or attorney was rarely recorded in this way. Even those who made their money by satire had little interest in dwelling on the daily life of the 'middling sort'. With certain exceptions,

---

[15] See p. 309.
[16] Wilton House, Pembroke MSS, Decker's tours.

Hogarth's elaborately calculated contrasts portrayed the excesses and hypocrisies of high life and the vulgarity and brutishness of low life. In the middle there was a great mass of households which shared in the new living standards but left less vivid evidence of their pursuit of material well-being. The sheer size of the middle-class revolution of Victorian England was to submerge most of the physical remains of an earlier, in context no less significant, middle-class revolution. It has to be sought in the erratic survival of the middle-brow art of the mid-eighteenth century, and, more reliably, in documentary evidence and the record of contemporary opinion. Legal records—wills, probate inventories, marriage settlements—confirm the impression created by contemporary comment, that the middle ranges of society benefited as much as any by the creation of new wealth, and that their conditions of life changed substantially.

In the most elementary sense of the physical surroundings of the ordinary middle-class family this change was immense. The architect John Wood, writing in 1749, listed the novelties introduced since the accession of George II. Cheap and dirty floorboards gave way to superior deal covered with carpets. Primitive plaster was concealed with smart wainscoting. Stone hearths and chimney-pieces, customarily cleaned with a whitewash which left a chalk debris on the floor, were replaced with marble. Flimsy doors with iron fittings were abandoned for hardwood embellished with brass locks. Mirrors had become both numerous and elegant. Walnut and mahogany, in fashionable designs, superseded primitive oak furniture. Leather, damask, and embroidery gave seating a comfort unobtainable with cane or rush.[17] He might have added the wealth of trinkets, novelties, and knick-knacks, in the French, Chinese, or Indian 'manner', which invaded many homes. Ornament for its own sake was as important as functional design. Useless expenditure was a hallmark of gentility. Very ordinary households were affected by the characteristic combination of self-conscious taste working with money. The carpets, wall-hangings, furnishings, kitchen and parlour ware in the homes of many shopkeepers and tradesmen in the 1760s and 1770s, would have surprised their parents and astonished their grandparents. It is a measure of the transformation that few of them would have been found even in

[17] B. Denvir, *The Eighteenth Century: Art, Design and Society, 1689–1789* (London, 1983), pp. 51–2.

aristocratic households half a century earlier. The change had as much to do with the nature of what could be 'consumed' as its wider availability. In this sense there was no real precedent for the new constituency of consumers and consumption to which Adam Smith so eloquently appealed in his *Wealth of Nations.*

Commentators were as much intrigued by the impact of affluence on manners, as by its material consequences. In a word, they charted the progress of politeness. This was an ambiguous term. It was naturally associated with the possession of those goods which marked off the moderately wealthy from the poor, the trappings of propertied life. It also included the intellectual and aesthetic tastes which displayed the continuing advance of fashion in its broadest sense. But most of all it affected the everyday routine and rules of social life, from matters as trivial as the time at which one dined, and the way one ate one's dinner, to matters as important as the expectations and arrangements of partners in marriage. There was no shortage of manuals and advice on all such questions. The essence of politeness was often said to be that *je ne sais quoi* which distinguished the innate gentleman's understanding of what made for civilized conduct, but this did not inhibit others from seeking more artificial means of acquiring it. Contemporaries often thought of it, disapprovingly for the most part, as the infiltration of metropolitan mores into every corner of the land and every social class. Why, one critic asked in 1767, were pretentious little villas springing up in the countryside? Why were rural folk engaging in the preposterous social custom of formal 'visits' and the consequent pointless chatter? Why did card-playing take place all the year round even in remote districts? The answer must lie in the capital.[18] London fashions, London habits, London affectations were discerned in unlikely places, in obscure Welsh market towns, in Highland cottages, and in the most distant recesses of the empire. But London was the hub of polite transformation, not its motive power. It was visible in every revolution of fashion and taste; it did not determine it.

MIDDLE-CLASS DIVISIONS

Symmetry was not the same as uniformity. All sought to follow the same code and even the same rhythm of social life, but there

[18] *London Magazine*, 1767, pp. 547–8.

remained many distinctions. Regional diversity made for differences which fascinated those who observed the sometimes uneven pace of social change. By the late eighteenth century the 'cotton gentry' of Lancashire were already a distinctively successful class in their own right. Their opulence in the midst of squalor and poverty startled visitors from the south. But it was still possible to be patronizing about their ignorance of southern manners. The rapid accumulation of wealth and the entrenchment of custom created odd mixtures of the fashionable and the outmoded. When she visited Blackpool in 1788, Catherine Hutton, the daughter of a self-made Birmingham man, was intrigued to find that local clannishness extended even to the choice of accommodation. There were only four guest-houses, one occupied by 'rich, rough, honest manufacturers of the town of Bolton, whose coarseness of manners is proverbial even among their own countrymen', the others by Manchester manufacturers, Liverpool merchants, and county gentry. She found 'that the Boltoners are sincere, good-humoured, and noisy; the Manchestrians reserved and purse-proud; the Liverpoolians free and open as the ocean on which they get their riches'. Marked though such distinctions were, Lancastrians as a class differed from her acquaintance elsewhere. 'All ranks and both sexes are more robust than the people of the south. Hysterics and the long train of nervous disorders are unknown in the county.'[19] Significantly she felt at home only with the local lawyers, though, as she noted, the manufacturers were far wealthier.

Lawyers, like other professional men, clergy and doctors especially, could be a divisive influence. They claimed a superiority by reason of their education which seemed to place them above the ordinary merchant or manufacturer. But they also helped to ease the tensions of middle-class life. They might well start from humbler origins than their business colleagues. It was easier to progress from rags to riches in law or medicine than it was in trades which required an expensive apprenticeship and a handsome capital. The two Hunter brothers, William and John, came to London with 'no capital but genius, industry and integrity'.[20] As the most fashionable physicians of their day, in the early part

---

[19] C. H. Beale, *Reminiscences of a Gentlewoman of the Last Century: Letters of Catherine Hutton* (Birmingham, 1891), pp. 56–7.

[20] Joseph Adams, *Memoirs of the Life and Doctrines of the late John Hunter* (London, 1817), pp. 197–8.

of George III's reign, each accumulated a handsome fortune and a formidable reputation.

Professionals provided relatively uniform services, depending on a nationwide coincidence of consumer expectations and commercial practices. Moreover, they often moved more freely among propertied people than men who drew their living from some form of business. There was much agonizing about the social differences within the professions themselves. The gulf which separated the careworn curate from the plump pluralist, the hedge attorney from the circuit barrister, and the country apothecary from the society doctor seemed wide indeed. But even humble curates, attorneys, and apothecaries might have direct dealings with the élite, however deferential their approach to it. The production and sale of goods required little social intercourse with the customer; the provision of professional services often did. Professional men were expected to conduct themselves as gentlemen and knew well the commercial importance of doing so. In many small places they were themselves the élite: in market towns the 'rule of three'—Lawyer Claw, Parson Thrift, and Doctor Lopp, with 'best house, best living, and best pay'—made them the centre of polite society around which shopkeepers and their wives, retired officers, ambitious schoolmasters, neighbouring 'gentlemen farmers', and all the numerous tribe of the marginally middle class might cluster.[21] In larger places they provided a distinct circle of wealth, power, and prestige, between the outer ring of landowners who constituted county society and the inner core of merchants, bankers, and tradesmen who ruled municipal society. Lawyers particularly, with their easy entry to the world of public affairs and political intrigue, were well placed to exploit the social opportunities which their position offered.

One division which could be overcome only with difficulty was that of creed. Religion was in some measure a matter of class. The vast majority of gentry were, nominally at least, members of the Church of England. Within landed society only a dwindling minority of Roman Catholics, and a still tinier residue of that once extensive class, the Puritan gentry, declined to conform. Middle-class religion presented a more diverse and complicated picture. Dissent was in decline in the countryside, though in some regions, for instance the old Puritan heartland of East Anglia, it retained a significant rural presence. But in the towns it proved both more

[21] S. J. Pratt, *Gleanings in England* (2nd edn., 3 vols., London, 1801), i. 332.

resistant to decay and readier to respond to opportunities for expansion, particularly in the second half of the century. Its vigour was commonly associated with middle-class congregations or middle-class leadership of more mixed congregations. In large cities new chapels were numerous. Of the twenty-two places of worship built in Birmingham between 1730 and 1795, only five belonged to the established Church.[22] Birmingham was an extreme example of one of the eighteenth century's substantially new cities. Norwich, still England's third city in point of population in 1750, was much older, with a cathedral and numerous medieval churches. Yet Dissent was a large and important part of its life at all levels, not least that of its municipal rulers. No less than a quarter of its sheriffs between 1718 and 1753 attended the Presbyterian chapel which was rebuilt as the famous Octagon in 1753.[23]

It is difficult to assess the effect of such distinctions. Businessmen did not usually permit their religious views to get in the way of commercial collaboration. The Quakers, though known for their exclusiveness, were active participators in an open society. Those who dropped the old forms of address and adopted the polite manners of the day were denounced as backsliders by their brethren. But even the most conservative, the 'plain Quakers', were often adroit at exploiting commercial innovation. Moreover, some political institutions made genuine partnership across sectarian lines perfectly practicable. The numerous *ad hoc* bodies created by statute to improve the administration of local government were never subjected, like the old corporations, to religious tests. There were also trends in the religious life of the period which positively fostered the co-operation of like minds in different congregations. This was plainly true of much charitable activity. The progress of evangelicalism both in the established and Dissenting churches brought a similar mentality to the solution of social problems. The anti-slavery campaign of the 1780s and the Sunday school movement, at least in its first phase, owed much to this common approach. On the other hand, the political traditions of urban life made it difficult to ignore religious differences. Perhaps the diminishing relevance of party politics in a national setting even accentuated the remaining lines of religious demarcation. Muni-

[22] W. Hutton, *An History of Birmingham*, pp. 172, 193.
[23] D. S. O'Sullivan, 'Politics in Norwich, 1701–1835', M.Phil. thesis (East Anglia, 1975), ch. 9.

cipal oligarchy gave opportunities both to Churchmen and Dissenters to entrench themselves in power. In many places the
resulting strife provided a link between the sectarian conflicts of
the seventeenth century and the renewed religious struggles of the
early nineteenth. If tithes had been more of a reality in the towns
and cities such discord might have been far worse. As it was,
Church rates caused increasing irritation. And when the question
of civil rights under the Test and Corporation Acts came to be
ventilated once more, in the 1770s and 1780s, it was all too easy
to revert to the old lines of battle.

Perhaps as divisive as religion, though in very different ways,
were the obvious disparities of wealth and social standing. The
stratification of the middle class was almost infinite, corresponding
as it did to the innumerable gradations of income and snobbery
on which contemporary analysts frequently commented. But this
was true of all classes. The acrimony invested in trivial quarrels
between different ranks of the peerage, for instance in the periodic
disputes as to the precise status of Irish peers in England, matched
any of the petty social wars which social satirists recorded among
the *nouveaux riches*. It may also be doubted whether any class had
a stronger sense of its own importance than the respectable artisans
and small farmers who dreaded nothing more than descent into
the ranks of the truly poor. There was, however, one particularly
important division within middle-class England which was widely
recognized at the time. When the House of Commons was treated
to an unusually precise analysis of social class in 1734, in this case
in the London parish of Whitechapel, much was made of this
division. On the one side there was a class 'composed of Gentlemen
of Fortune, Sense, Reputation, and good Manners' together with
'Tradesmen of good Credit, great Dealings, and, most commonly,
of good Understanding'. These men did not serve parish offices,
but they were the élite of Whitechapel. On the other side were
'Tradesmen of lower Degree, such as Artificers, Carpenters, Bricklayers, Glasiers, and Painters etc', who did occupy parish offices,
and a 'large unruly Herd of Men' below them who were substantial
enough to be ratepayers but were the terror of the parochial
vestry.[24] This basic distinction, which could easily be neglected in
other contexts, for example when broad questions relating to
poverty were under discussion, or when the affairs of landed society

[24] *Commons Journals*, xxii. 271.

were debated, was crucial. It helped define the ruling body of the great cities on which so much of the economic vitality and cultural development of the age depended. It also bore closely on the process which made it possible for the landed gentry and the upper elements of bourgeois society to collaborate. When they did so they constituted that category of the indisputably 'polite', which in the last analysis forms the closest thing to a governing class in Georgian England.

Government had an obvious interest in this class, or union of classes, for it provided a solution to some pressing fiscal problems. Everyone paid taxes, directly or indirectly, and the middle class in general, through poor-rates, house and window taxes, and increasingly through stamp and excise duties, contributed largely. But one of the most consistent preoccupations of government was to find an effective means of tapping the wealth of the upper middle class, that substantial section of society which was undeniably opulent but which did not place more than a small portion of its wealth in land. Hence the taxes which formed an increasingly important part of wartime budgets from the 1740s onwards, the carriage and coach taxes, the plate tax, the servant taxes, and a whole range of stamp duties. The prime targets were those conspicuous consumers of goods and services whose livelihood, given the prevailing horror of a direct income tax, was largely immune to taxation by traditional means.

MIDDLE-CLASS VULNERABILITY

At this level of society comfort and security seemed assured. But this was not altogether the contemporary perception. The pace of economic expansion and its unstable nature created a sense of the vulnerability of property and politeness, even when expressed in the supposed stability of landed society. Bankruptcy was the nightmare of the eighteenth-century bourgeoisie. Personal liability for business debts was for most purposes unlimited. The law gave extensive powers to creditors. Particularly in respect of imprisonment for debt it subjected the individual to constraints which would have seemed intolerable if exerted by the State for political purposes, and which were the subject of more or less constant public controversy and criticism as they stood. No doubt the great could evade or soften the operation of such laws: the scandalous manner in which aristocratic young men seemingly escaped the consequences of their misdeeds was a popular subject for hostile moralizing. But at most levels of propertied society the instability of property was regarded as a fact of life.

Credit and its mysterious operations ruled all. Defoe compared it to a mistress. A coy lass, she was a 'most necessary, useful, industrious Creature', but also a potentially despotic lady, endangering all who dealt with her.[25] Her victims were those who had relatively little to lose as well as those who valued themselves in hundreds and thousands. The small debtor was seen as presenting a social problem of the first importance. In retrospect he can be viewed bringing up the rear of a great army of the lower middle class. Small tradesmen, shopkeepers, and craftsmen slipped into and out of this class as family fortune and commercial fate dictated, often leaving little evidence of their ascent or descent.

In the literature of the period it is naturally the most literate portion of the lower middle class which has left its memorial. The plight of genteel poverty was often considered more affecting than actual want among the lower classes. Schoolmasters who dispensed learning and the elements of gentility to the children of respectable tradespeople and earned a stipend of £10 or £20 a year were held up as objects for compassion and relief. Poor curates were expected to sustain the authority of their order before opulent and contemptuous flocks. The impoverished clergy were a well-educated and articulate class. No doubt it is for this reason that their vulnerability was endlessly discussed, though the debate also reflected concern with the pastoral consequences. A common complaint was that parents pushed unsuitable sons into a Church which simply had no room for them without radical redistribution of ecclesiastical property. Evan Lloyd's poem *The Curate* rehearsed the arguments in satirical vein, attacking the 'pursy rector' as unbrotherly in his exploitation of the poor curate, and showing how the poverty of the young clergyman made him a despised figure in market towns and villages. Perhaps most telling was his sad incapacity to take advantage of his cloth in the marriage market. Half-digested learning was no substitute for the sophistication which money could buy.

[25] *Defoe's Review in 22 Facsimile Books* (New York, 1938), iii. 17; vii. 461.

Can Harry Stotle teach the Art to kiss?
Can Plato give a Lady real Bliss?
A Lady's Appetite asks rich repast,
To diet on a Scholar, is to fast.

Lloyd, who led a raffish life in London 'as the Welch Parson' and ended in gaol, was hardly a laudable example of his class but his lament on behalf of the curate may have represented their anxieties better than the high-minded concern of senior churchmen.[26] He also had fellow-sufferers in other professions. Half-pay officers who, it was drily remarked in Parliament, 'tho' they hardly live, they never die'[27] were perpetually lamenting their condition. Clerks who lived on a pittance in expectation of a chance to display their talents in a post of responsibility and profit featured in many hard-luck stories. All these victims, as they were so often presented, had in common their pretensions to politeness. But even in a competitive world their numbers always seemed to exceed demand for their services. Before the nineteenth century the bourgeois professions were singularly ineffective at improving their collective power by creating monopoly conditions for what they had to offer. Attempts in this direction were often advocated, usually with suitable assurances that the public could only benefit by regulation. But entry into the professions remained relatively simple, as is indicated by the ease with which ambitious young men tried first one profession then another. Not a few lawyers were failed authors and actors, as not a few actors and authors were failed lawyers. It was possible to move from law to medicine, and if necessary back again. Clergymen were by training and tradition equipped to teach; they could also readily take up medicine. But the price of open access was the existence of large numbers for whom success in career terms was always an objective rather than an accomplishment.

In old age disappointments were even more demoralizing: provision for retirement was one of the rewards of success, not a compensation for failure. Families suffered accordingly. It is no coincidence that much charitable activity and not a little of the growing insurance business was addressed to widows and children whose menfolk had given them certain expectations without the

---

[26] (London, 1766), pp. 45–6; see also D. Garrick, *A Whipping for the Welch Parson* (London, 1773).
[27] *London Magazine*, 1735, p. 319.

means to sustain them. Mothers driven into the grave and daughters into prostitution featured in many appeals for generosity. In fact the supposedly respectable background of London prostitutes claiming to be the daughters of impoverished clergymen was one of the stock jokes of the period. Yet there were many for whom the plight of respectable women was no joke. The story recorded in the diary of the pious Mrs Cappe, of an army officer's widow who was left in poverty by the death of her husband in the Caribbean, matches the theme of many a mawkish novel. Willingly accorded the title of 'Madam' in the Dales village where she settled, she was none the less threatened by humiliating prosecution as a pauper under the Law of Settlements.[28]

At least this lady had her undoubted gentility to comfort her. This was not given to everyone. The sheer pretentiousness of the middle class at its lowest level was a matter of endless comment and much satire. George Colman's exploitation of the subject in a play significantly entitled *The Man of Business* was typical of the genre. He illuminated the aspirations of a whole class of what would later be called 'white-collar' workers. Typical of those he mocked was 'A little shop-keeping mechanick, or one of your dapper city clerks, that draws his pen from under his ear in the evening, to go and drink tea at Bagnigge-Wells or Dobney's Bowling-Green.' He also mercilessly satirized the world of the barely respectable who lacked reliable employment. His hero's landlord boasted five lodgers in a mere two weeks occupying what he called his 'genteel' room: 'An ensign in the guards; a poet-man from Paddington; A Scotch actor-man! An old battered lady from Soho; and a very fine young one from the New Building at Marybone.'[29]

MIDDLE-CLASS SCHOOLING

In nothing was the power of the middle-class revolution seen more clearly than its impact on education. The institutions inherited from an earlier age, especially the grammar schools, the Inns of Court, and the universities, were the subject of growing misgivings. Traditionally they had provided a learning well suited to the gentry, with a view to a life of honourable leisure or a career in

---

[28] *Memoirs of the Life of the Late Mrs Catherine Cappe* (London, 1822), pp. 11–14, 16.
[29] *The Dramatick Works of George Colman* (4 vols., London, 1777), ii. 126, 203.

one of the professions. To humbler Englishmen they also offered, by means of free or subsidized places both at school and college, the possibility of preferment and respectability. In the seventeenth century this system had shown signs of breaking down. It turned out more well-educated young men than the professional opportunities of Stuart England could sustain. In the eighteenth century it simply provided the wrong kind of training for an age which was primarily interested in the practical accomplishments of basic literacy and elementary book-keeping on the one hand, and the polite attainments of fashionable living on the other.

The grammar schools, in particular, were disadvantaged by the very safeguards which earlier generations had erected for their protection and the public good. Deeds of bequest, charters, and statutes laid down rules of government and methods of instruction which proved difficult to adapt to new needs. They encouraged in those who administered and taught in the grammar schools attitudes which satisfied the letter of the law without fulfilling their spirit. Trustees who met the nominal requirements of standards which had long since been overtaken by inflation, and schoolmasters who collected an equally outmoded salary while doing the bare minimum to earn it, were a common cause of complaint. Teaching posts were frequently indistinguishable from sinecures and held by clergy whom it was virtually impossible to discharge. Some of the most scandalous cases of neglect were laid at the door of ecclesiastical bodies which might have been expected to exercise their responsibilities with particular care. At Cambridge the Perse School had been entrusted to the management of Caius College. But the college diverted the growing income of the benefaction to its own profit and treated the Mastership as a sinecure appropriate for its junior fellows. In 1785 the pretence of keeping the school open was abandoned: only a protest from the citizens of Cambridge compelled it to recommence admitting pupils.[30] Individual clergy could be as cynical as clerical corporations. At Farnworth in Lancashire in 1756 the parishioners turned in desperation to their bishop to get rid of their master, on the grounds that he kept the boys in ignorance and rendered them unfit for business: his method was said to consist in putting them to Ovid and Virgil without introducing them to the elements of classical syntax. He was not induced to depart until he had been granted a pension for life

[30] J. M. Gray, *A History of the Perse School, Cambridge* (Cambridge, 1921), pp. 83–6.

equivalent to thirty per cent of his salary.[31] It was often difficult to improve on the terms specified by benefactors without expensive and hazardous litigation which might consume the funds of the foundation. There were sometimes suspicions that trustees and feoffees were as ready to furnish their own pockets as schoolmasters were to neglect their teaching duties. Even without such corruption it was all too easy for ancient endowments to wither away under negligent or incompetent management.

The classics seemed an acquisition of dubious value to many parents. The landscape gardener and architect Humphry Repton thus accounted for his own removal from Norwich Grammar School at the age of twelve: 'My father thought proper to put the stopper in the vial of classic literature, having determined to make me a rich, rather than a learned man.'[32] The basic principle of much grammar school education, the provision of a classical curriculum for scholars of lowly birth at little or no cost, no longer seemed self-evidently desirable. New foundations were rare. Most of the old grammar schools which prospered did so by evading or at least supplementing their inherited prescriptions and practices. The proximity of a promising market was obviously helpful. Previously unpretentious schools in the vicinity of London were able to take advantage of their location. Yet even they usually depended still more on vigorous leadership. The reputation of Kingston in the middle of the century owed as much to its head-master Richard Wooddeson as to its pleasant position close to the capital. During a tenure of forty years Wooddeson's pupils include the historian Edward Gibbon, the poets Edward Lovibond, William Hayley, and George Keate, the classical scholar and con-troversialist Gilbert Wakefield, the Shakespearian commentator George Steevens, and the pamphleteer Francis Maseres. This remarkable list was recorded, with a glowing testimony to Wood-deson's personal qualities, in Wakefield's memoirs.[33] Schools with no obvious advantages flourished under powerful, usually dic-tatorial men. Rugby enjoyed sudden fame thanks to the efforts of Thomas James. Though headmaster for the relatively short period of sixteen years, he laid the basis for the nineteenth-century glories

---

[31] C. R. Lewis, *The History of Farnworth Grammar School* (Widnes, 1905), pp. 113, 117.
[32] G. Carter, P. Goode, K. Laurie, *Humphry Repton Landscape Gardener, 1752–1818* (Norwich, 1982), p. 6.
[33] *Memoirs of the Life of Gilbert Wakefield* (2 vols., London, 1804), i. 43.

of the school and earned the unusual gift of a Crown canonry bestowed by the Prime Minister at the request of the governors.

Admired schools tended to become identified with one man, often enjoying (or perhaps condemned to) a long tenure. Bradford Grammar School had Benjamin Butler as its headmaster for fifty-six years, from 1728 to 1784. In his case longevity was a particular ambition. A weathercock specially erected for the purpose warned him against leaving his house on days when an east wind was indicated, and incidentally alerted his pupils to his immobility.[34] Successful pedagogues, whether by design or necessity, usually depended for their livelihood on their school. (Headmasters who also enjoyed a profitable benefice had little incentive to improve or innovate.) They needed to be known for the traditional magisterial qualities, especially firm discipline and sound learning acquired at university. But they could not succeed without a flexible view of what made for good schooling. Besides the traditional emphasis on the classics, a thoroughly 'modern' education required a grounding in English and mathematics, probably with some attention to history, geography, and even a little natural philosophy; nor were the peripheral but socially valuable attainments of drawing, dancing, and foreign languages to be neglected. The essence of this strategy was to attract fee-paying students, for the most part boarders, whose accommodation might be as profitable as their instruction. It could only be pursued where the rules of the school either permitted such entrepreneurial activities or, if they did not, where they could be safely ignored or evaded. Significantly, James's tenure at Rugby commenced after the school trustees had succeeded in obtaining an Act of Parliament giving them a free hand in such matters in 1777. Disputes were common and in a litigious age could readily lead to legal embarrassments. In 1765 the Skinners Company, which controlled Tonbridge, was forcibly reminded by the local vestry of its responsibility to accept local boys without charge.[35] Enfield Grammar School began both the eighteenth and nineteenth centuries with punishing bouts of litigation, but in between flourished under two resourceful masters, John Allen and Samuel Hardy, who spanned the period 1732 to 1791 and based the fortunes of the school on private

[34] W. Scruton, *Pen and Pencil Pictures of Old Bradford* (Bradford, 1889), p. 80.
[35] R. S. Tompson, *Classics or Charity? The Dilemma of the 18th-Century Grammar School* (Manchester, 1971), pp. 89–90.

boarders.[36] Leeds did not flourish. Thanks to its persistence with classical instruction it decayed steadily in the course of the late eighteenth century. In 1805 it was to be the subject of perhaps the most famous judicial determination in the history of British education, when Lord Eldon ruled that its statutes did not permit commercially useful instruction.[37]

In many schools neglect of their traditional function was obligatory for commercial success. The presence of poor boys from local homes was a grave deterrent to parents in search of a polite, modern education. In choosing schools, parents were influenced by the opinion of their betters. What might be called the social priority of education, the need to make good connections by placing one's child among the rich, the powerful, and the privileged, was paramount. It is this which largely accounts for the ups and downs of school history in the period. Success in terms of fashionable prestige and therefore in terms of numbers, often came and went with startling suddenness. Such rapid changes of fortune were the combined effect of magisterial vigour and parental choice. This was certainly true of the famous public schools, most of which had outgrown, if not altogether shed, their chartered past, and were well placed to exploit the market for learning.

Under George II the leading position of Westminster seemed assured as the training ground of the élite: it boasted bishops and peers, generals and admirals, Lord Chancellors and high society doctors, artists and writers in profusion. Yet under George III it was outshone by its rival Eton. Eton had a headmaster, Edward Barnard, of exceptional administrative ability and social influence, 'the Pitt of masters'. But in this case the patronage of royalty itself may have been the decisive consideration. Long before he admitted that he was an 'anti-Westminster' in 1804, George III had displayed his delight in Eton. He first visited it with the Queen in 1762 and subsequently took a close interest in its pupils: stories of his encounters with boys whom he met while walking in Windsor were legion. 'I wish from time to time', he is said to have remarked, 'to show a regard for the education of youth, on which most essentially depend my hopes of an advantageous change in the

[36] L. B. Marshall, *A Brief History of Enfield Grammar School, 1558–1958* (Richmond, 1958), pp. 28–30.
[37] R. G. Wilson, *Gentlemen Merchants: The Merchant Community in Leeds, 1700–1830* (Manchester, 1971), p. 210.

manners of the nation.'[38] Eton doubtless bore a special burden in this respect but other schools were subjected to the changing expectations and attentions of patrons and parents. Winchester attracted only 35 fee-paying pupils in 1724. This figure rose to 123 in 1734, sank to 10 by 1750, recovered to 105 in 1779, and fell to 38 again by 1788. The close connection between upper-class patronage and the personal qualities of individual headmasters was almost always the cause of such fluctuations.[39]

COMMERCIAL EDUCATION AND ITS LIMITATIONS

The more successful grammar schools are best viewed not as part of the inherited framework of education, but rather as elements in a newer, essentially commercial system. Grammar school masters had to struggle to adapt their inheritance to new requirements. Their rivals were able to offer the modern curriculum without the handicap of outmoded statutes and obstructive governors. In the case of girls this was virtually the only form of schooling available to middle-class parents, for there were hardly any schools of the old kind which provided facilities for daughters as well as sons, other than charitable institutions. There is no satisfactory means of estimating the numbers educated in private schools, or even the number of schools themselves. They sprang up and withered away wherever individual enterprise and public interest dictated. Schools were labour rather than capital intensive, and it required but a small investment to take lodgings, offer tuition to a handful of children, some of them boarded, employ an assistant, and contract for the occasional services of specialist teachers.

Even on their own ground the old schools could be challenged by resourceful interlopers. Before 1773 Manchester Grammar School had to cope with the competition of the so-called Salford Grammar School, a private foundation managed by a controversial Tory clergyman, John Clayton.[40] King Edward VI School at Bath similarly lost ground to the small academy run in the nearby Rectory of Claverton by Richard Graves, better known to posterity as novelist and poet.[41] Whatever the curriculum, these were in the

---

[38] H. C. Maxwell Lyte, *A History of Eton College (1440–1875)* (London, 1875), pp. 324, 347, 348.

[39] A. F. Leach, *A History of Winchester College* (London, 1899), chs. 24–5.

[40] A. A. Mumford, *The Manchester Grammar School, 1515–1915* (London, 1919), pp. 174–6.

[41] K. E. Symons, *The Grammar School of King Edward VI, Bath* (Bath, 1930), p. 242.

strictest sense commercial activities. There were no charters, no rules, no governors: only the individual educational entrepreneur offering his services in a highly competitive but ever-expanding market. Permanent institutions rarely resulted. Even the historical evidence for their existence depends largely on the survival of newspaper advertisements and the occasional childhood reminiscences of those who attended them. In the towns they must have been numerous. In Derby, with a population of less than ten thousand, there were at least eight commercial schools founded or in existence between 1770 and 1789.[42] Because they were so ephemeral it was easy for Victorians to deduce that such schools had scarcely existed at all and to suppose that their Georgian predecessors had been brought up in a state of ignorance and barbarism.

The Dissenting academies have been treated as honourable exceptions, precisely because the requirements of the Dissenters made a more institutional and less commercial approach desirable. Yet even these schools, designed primarily as seminaries for the training of Nonconformist clergy, were typically short-lived. Many were founded by gifted or determined individuals who failed to pass on their torch of learning. This was true of some of the most famous, including Samuel Jones, who was a distinguished orientalist as well as a formidable pedagogue. Thómas Secker, Archbishop of Canterbury, Joseph Butler, Bishop of Durham, and Samuel Chandler, the uncrowned patriarch of Dissent in the latter part of George II's reign, all received their education under Jones at Tewkesbury. Yet the school had perished in 1724, before any of them made a name for himself. The vulnerability of the academies is demonstrated by the attempts made to put some of them on a more permanent footing in the 1770s and 1780s. Warrington, the most celebrated of their number, collapsed ignominiously in 1783. The historian of the Dissenting academies attributes Warrington's decline and fall to the indiscipline of its students and the consequent public discredit. But at the time Gilbert Wakefield blamed its financial weakness. Without resources of its own the burden of a relatively large and expensive staff proved too much.[43]

---

[42] R. P. Sturges, 'The Membership of the Derby Philosophical Society, 1783–1802', *Midland History*, 4 (1977–8), 221.

[43] H. McLachlan, *English Education under the Test Acts* (Manchester, 1931), p. 224; *Memoirs of the Life of Gilbert Wakefield*, i. 215–16.

The two foundations which were partly supported from the proceeds of the sale of the Warrington site both experienced difficulties. Hackney, established by the leading lights of the Unitarian movement, maintained the intellectual tradition of Warrington, but encountered equally embarrassing financial problems and foundered in 1796. Manchester combined 'useful and manly studies preparatory to commercial life' with the more predictable 'liberal and systematic education' for clergy. It survived only by migrating, first to York in 1803, and eventually to Oxford.[44]

How accessible was this essentially commercial system? Only the better off sought an education which would carry their children through adolescence and to the brink of university or marriage. But such were the potential rewards of the basic accomplishments, particularly in reading and writing English correctly, and in arithmetic sufficient to master book-keeping and accountancy, that parents with ambitions for their children could not afford to neglect them. Contemporary worries about 'over-educated' children at least attest to the popularity of schooling. The quality of what was offered was another matter. It was a frequent complaint that towards the lower and cheaper end of the school market, all manner of abuse, neglect, and downright barbarism took place.

Problems arose where costs were being cut in order to attract custom. One of the anxieties about popish proselytizing arose from the popularity which Roman Catholic schools were said to derive from their low charges.[45] Certainly education was kept well within the financial range of the modestly comfortable middle class. At Eton the charge for a year might be as high as £50 under George II. But at most places less than half this sum was required. In the mid-1740s John Aikin, later a tutor at Warrington, was charging £12 per annum for board and study. With additional items thrown in—French instruction, a set of books which included Fables, Cicero, Homer, and a 'Compleat System of Geography', and stationery—the total came to £14. 5s. 3d.[46] With some allowance for Aikin's Presbyterian high-mindedness and a degree of price inflation in the following decades, this was representative of the cost of a polite education. It was roughly the level reported by those who offered satirical criticism of the schooling of the day.

---

[44] *The Works of Thomas Percival* (4 vols., Warrington, 1807), iii. lxxix–lxxx.
[45] B. Porteus, *A Letter to the Clergy of the Diocese of Chester* (London, 1782), p. 18.
[46] C. H. Beale, *Catherine Hutton and Her Friends* (Birmingham, 1895), p. 45.

Charles Jenner's Zachary Birch left his school at York every Whitsun in order to advertise it in London, offering board and instruction from £12.[47] As at many fictitious academies, life for his charges consisted of cold, hunger, and regular beatings. Edward Kimber described a similar Yorkshire establishment, managed by a Mr Prosody. Prosody's career came to an end when he was prosecuted for his Jacobitism by a gentleman whose son he had flogged to excess; though he died of a broken heart when the Archbishop of York stopped him teaching, a lifetime of modest fees for thirty boarders left him in a position to bequeathe £1,500 to his daughter.[48] The supposed secret of such wealth was explained by John Trusler. In the 1780s his Dr Slashem was charging more than his predecessors of the mid-century—£20. But there was also the profit of selling the many incidental items desired by boys and their parents, the lucrative practice of milking pocket-money held in trust for his charges, and the 'presents' evolved by long custom in old schools and eagerly imitated in new ones.[49]

Finding the right school was a perplexing problem. Some looked, optimistically, to a national solution. One suggestion was for a public school in every ward in London, and similar schools, on the model of Eton and Winchester, in every county town.[50] Few parents can seriously have expected the State to intervene but they did have the benefit of a constant flow of advice. Much of this discussion was conducted in terms of a seemingly aristocratic preoccupation with the relative advantages of education by private tutor or by public school. Locke, whose educational theories remained almost unchallenged for most of the eighteenth century, had placed this subject at the centre of the debate. As the space devoted to it by Richardson's *Pamela* suggests, it was by no means exclusively the concern of the upper crust. A private tutor could be hired for approximately twice the cost of a conventional education—less, if he were expected to care for more than one child. But even if this were beyond the parent's budget, it mattered a great deal what richer parents did. Much of the value, especially

---

[47] *The Placid Man: or, Memoirs of Sir Charles Beville* (2nd edn., 2 vols., 1773), i. 44.

[48] *The Life and Adventures of Joe Thompson: A Narrative Founded on Facts* (London, 1783, originally 1750), p. 81.

[49] *Modern Times, or, the Adventures of Gabriel Outcast* (4th edn., 3 vols., London, 1785), i. 42–5.

[50] *A View of the Internal Policy of Great Britain* (London, 1764), pp. 213, 220–1.

the snob value of schooling, depended on the attendance of the well-born and wealthy. At a fashionable school such as Fountaine's in Marylebone the 'best' pupils in point of rank were regularly introduced to enquiring parents, a ploy used by many private schools intent on impressing potential customers with the superiority of their product.[51] Hence the emphasis on the value of 'connections' at school.

There were well-known disadvantages. Life at the great public schools was considered a kind of primitive subculture which nurtured immorality and indiscipline. Even respected masters had to cope with riot and rebellion, as the distinguished literary critic Joseph Warton, during a long but decidedly tempestuous career at Winchester, could testify. The popular press enjoyed an opportunity to censor the gilded youth of the best schools: 'a herd of brutes in human shapes,' one journalist observed in 1779, 'who glory in the violation of decency, of the common rules of society, and are the terror of the neighbourhood in which they reside.'[52] Rowdiness and worse fuelled resentment of their money and privileges. But it also caused disquiet in aristocratic circles. The campaign which commenced in the last quarter of the century to reform public school education took account of this concern. It was epitomized in the educational writings of Vicesimus Knox, like his father before him and his son after him, headmaster of Tonbridge School. Knox's *Liberal Education* was published in 1781 and went through ten editions within the decade. It offered a vision in which traditional values were joined with a new spirit of improvement. Not only did Knox hope to purge the schools of their indiscipline and degeneracy, he also planned to revive a strictly classical education as the suitable medium for training the commercial and professional classes. This ran counter to the practical wisdom of the day, but it was to prove immensely attractive in the coming years.

Higher education was inevitably affected by reconstruction below, though it did not lend itself to radical remodelling. The universities and the Inns of Court filled two distinct functions, the professional education, respectively, of clergy and lawyers, and the 'finishing' of well-bred boys. In the latter respect indeed they were not universally admired. The Inns were less frequently employed

---

[51] *Memoirs of the Life of the Rev. Dr. Trusler* (Bath, 1806), pp. 36–7.
[52] *London Magazine*, 1779, p. 260.

to round off a gentleman's education than they had been in the seventeenth century, partly because English law was no longer viewed in so favourable a light, though Blackstone did his best to defend it in this respect. It may also have been because the Inns themselves were undesirably situated, too close to the increasingly unfashionable City and not far enough from an all too fashionable but also dissolute Westminster. Oxford and Cambridge were known for rising fees and an increasingly aristocratic complexion: nearly sixty per cent of peers born in the mid-eighteenth century were educated there, compared with only thirty-five per cent of those born in the years before 1680.[53] Even so they were not always approved by upper-class parents. If schools sometimes had difficulty controlling the *jeunesse dorée*, it was unlikely that colleges would prove more effective. Moreover, the blue-blooded and well-heeled did not mix well with their poorer colleagues, many of whom attended university with a view to a career in the Church, the one profession for which a degree was virtually obligatory. There was a social gulf between the 'Foundationers' in most colleges and the 'Gentlemen Commoners'. For most the latter was an unattainable status, the former an undesirable one. Numbers at both universities fell markedly in the mid-eighteenth century. Together they admitted about five hundred annually in the 1720s. By the 1760s the figure was not much above three hundred. It rose somewhat to four hundred by the 1780s but hardly in line with the population growth of the period.[54]

Even where the universities seemed well placed to exploit contemporary trends they proved deficient. The medical education which they offered was lengthy, expensive, and unpractical. The huge growth of the medical profession was sustained by universities in Scotland and on the Continent, by the training offered in the hospitals, and above all by the instruction, formal and informal, available in London. Only those who aspired to the pomp of the Royal College of Physicians, itself a body subject to criticism from without and divisions within, derived much obvious benefit from Oxford and Cambridge. Historians have blamed the ancient universities more generally for their religious exclusiveness, their outdated academic rules, and their lethargic teaching. Attempts to open their facilities to Dissenters were notably unsuccessful.

[53] J. Cannon, *Aristocratic Century* (Cambridge, 1984), p. 47.
[54] Ibid., p. 45.

During the subscription debates of the early 1770s, Oxford firmly resisted all change, and Cambridge made only nominal amendments to its statutes. A similar fate met endeavours to tighten academic discipline. John Jebb's campaign to introduce a new system of university examinations in Cambridge was decisively defeated in the Senate in 1774. Pleas for effective professorial instruction generally fell on stony ground. Even the new Chairs of Modern History, founded at each university by George I, degenerated into sinecures. The first occupant of the chair at Cambridge to take his lecturing duties seriously, John Symonds, who was elected to his post in 1771, found little support. Both universities were ruled by men whose careers only partly depended on the quality of the education which they offered, and whose sights were usually on preferment elsewhere, whether by means of a college living or an influential patron. Yet the criticism was often misplaced.[55] The somnolence of university scholarship has been exaggerated. Oxford, the victim of Gibbon's scorn, could boast the Hebraicist Robert Lowth, the jurist William Blackstone, the orientalist William Jones, and the medievalist Thomas Warton. A similar defence might be offered of university teaching. Tutorial vigour at both places depended on college fellows. Individual colleges set testing standards. Oxford's Hertford College, founded on the basis of Hart Hall in 1740, was equipped with statutes which made it a byword for a more serious approach to university education, with consequent appeal even to aristocratic parents. St John's College at Cambridge introduced internal examining requirements which made the laxity of the university irrelevant, and even led its Master William Powell to oppose Jebb's reform on the grounds that the imposition of external standards would merely interfere with internal rigour.[56] Gibbon's verdict was at best highly selective, at worst manifestly unjust.

BOOKS AND THE BOURGEOISIE

Much education was designed with practical results in mind. But its most enduring legacy was somewhat unintended. The growth

[55] L. S. Sutherland, *The University of Oxford in the Eighteenth Century* (Bryce Lecture, 1972).

[56] D. A. Winstanley, *Unreformed Cambridge: A Study of Certain Aspects of the University in the Eighteenth Century* (Cambridge, 1935), pp. 327–8.

of a reading public, expecting and enjoying access to books, as a means both of instruction and recreation, has major implications for the cultural history of the period. Literacy among the labouring classes seems to have improved only slowly. In the mid-eighteenth century about a third of men and two-thirds of women were unable to sign their name, though the local incidence of illiteracy varied widely. But the acquisition of basic reading and writing skills by those on the margin of middle- and lower-class life, for whom they were coming to be an essential working asset, was a notable feature of urban society.[57] In some respects, too, the quality of literacy mattered as much as the quantity. The sheer volume of printed matter produced in the period is striking testimony to the extent of the reading market. The second quarter of the century was particularly significant in this respect. It was a time of much concern about the threat to literary standards presented by an apparently inexhaustible demand for cheap editions and digests.

It was also the point at which the monthly magazines definitively established themselves. Edward Cave's *Gentleman's Magazine* commenced its long career in 1731, plundering the newspaper press for news and comment, as well as featuring articles and reviews of its own. The range of subjects covered was immense. Current affairs, poems and ballads, medical advice and mathematical problems, stock prices and the weather, preferments and obituaries, all jostled for space in its crowded and closely printed pages. The formula proved highly successful. By 1734 Cave was printing 9,000 copies a month: within a decade the figure rose to 15,000.[58] Competitors quickly appeared, the *London Magazine* in 1732 and a number of imitators in the 1740s and 1750s. There were also more specialized ventures, for example the two great literary reviews of the period, the *Critical Review* and the *Monthly Review*. In 1758 the publisher Robert Dodsley began an enterprise which was to endure even longer than Cave's. His *Annual Register*, edited by an impecunious young Irishman, Edmund Burke, extended the principle of the monthly digest to the more relaxed medium of the yearly review. There were many pointers to wide and growing readership in the mid-eighteenth century, including

---

[57] R. S. Schofield, 'Dimensions of Illiteracy, 1750–1850', *Explorations in Economic History*, 10 (1972–3), 437–54; R. A. Houston, 'The Development of Literacy: Northern England, 1640–1750', *Economic History Review*, 2nd ser., 35 (1982), 199–216.

[58] W. B. Todd, 'A Bibliographical Account of *The Gentleman's Magazine*, 1731–1754', *Studies in Bibliography*, 18 (1965), 85.

the proliferation of both metropolitan and provincial newspapers, and the multiplication of new tract and book titles generally. But in the variety of their concerns and the ubiquity of their presence, the magazines remain a peculiarly characteristic expression of the middle-class England of their day.

Though the market for the printed word was transformed, the processes of production were slow to change. There were a few notable innovations in the book trade, most of them identified with enterprising individuals, none altogether successful. John Baskerville's elegant experiments in typesetting made his editions the pride of collectors throughout Europe, but they did not prove profitable. Baskerville, who had had at least three careers before he turned to printing in the mid-1750s, stone-cutting, teaching, and japanning, made far more by his japanning business than by his printing. An equally mixed experience was that of John Walter. Having lost a fortune in insurance during the Seven Years War he eventually made his reputation as the founding father of *The Times* and one of the pioneers of modern journalism. Between these two careers he also launched a 'logographic' press, which was designed to facilitate cheap and rapid printing by the production of type in blocks of three or more characters. Begun in 1784, this enterprise foundered within the decade.

The biggest rewards in the world of books and bookmen went to those who employed existing technology, while resorting to novel methods of promotion and publicity. Booksellers had to be masters of the art of advertising—the 'puff'. Books were by no means their only business: many sold stationery or other commodities. Not a few made their profit from the patent medicines whose sale depended so much on shrewd publicity. In the long run, admittedly, the growth of the book market was to stimulate a high degree of specialization which separated out the distinct trades of publisher, printer, and bookseller. But commercialization did not introduce such differentiation overnight. The mid-eighteenth century was the heyday of the bookseller-publishers. Campbell's *London Tradesman*, published in 1747, confidently stated that 'Their Business is, to purchase original Copies from Authors, to employ Printers to print them, and publish and sell them in their Shops.'[59] Most of this class operated from London, though there were some notable exceptions, such as Benjamin

[59] repr. London, 1969, p. 128.

Collins of Salisbury, who marketed his books throughout the country. Their publishing was often specialized in point of subject. The Rivingtons, one of the best known publishing names to appear in the eighteenth century, had a near monopoly of sermons and sacred literature. Dodsley's literary interests made him the friend of poets and a critically competent editor of his authors. The Newbery firm dominated the production of chapbooks and children's books. Its founder John Newbery was gently satirized by the poet Henry Dell in the *Bookseller* in 1766:

> Next Newbery the muse presents to view
> Bookseller, author and quack doctor too;
> Renown'd for all,—He knowledge can supply,
> To lisping babes, and babes of six foot high

The function of the bookseller was controversial, amounting, as it seemed, to a novel form of patronage in which the author was turned into a hack and the public inundated with meretricious literature. Dr Johnson considered this cant. He was in a position to know, having spent a considerable period of his life in literary poverty. He also wrote the definitive dismissal of aristocratic patronage in his famous *Letter to Chesterfield*, after the Earl had failed to carry out his promise of support for Johnson's *Dictionary*. But on the subject of the booksellers he was open-minded. Of Andrew Millar, he remarked: 'I respect Millar, Sir; he has raised the price of literature.'[60] Millar boasted a remarkable list of authors—Johnson himself, Thomson, Fielding, Robertson, Hume (he took particular pleasure in publishing the products of his native Scotland). Not long after his death in 1768 significant changes in the book trade disrupted the system on which he had thrived. In 1774, following a prolonged battle in the courts, the London booksellers were defeated in their campaign to establish a law of copyright which would give authors and their publishers a guaranteed property beyond the statutory period of twenty-eight years offered by the Copyright Act of 1710. An attempt to bring about by legislation what could not be accomplished by litigation was crushed soon after. These reverses doomed, if they did not immediately destroy, the informal 'congers' or cartels by which the great booksellers had controlled copyright sales and thereby

[60] G. B. Hill, ed., revised L. F. Powell, *Boswell's Life of Johnson* (6 vols., Oxford, 1934–50), i. 288.

monopolized the publishing business, at least in England. It appropriately coincided with a substantial further expansion of the market for popular literature. John Bell's edition of the British poets commenced in 1777, offering pocket-sized volumes at low prices. It stimulated his rivals to commission from Johnson his celebrated edition of the poets with 'Lives', and was succeeded by numerous exercises in mass publishing in the 1780s. Bookselling itself was affected. James Lackington later claimed to have revolutionized the trade. He sold strictly for cash, lowered prices, and brought up stocks of what in modern parlance were 'remaindered' editions for disposal at a discount. He reckoned that in 1784 his catalogue offered thirty thousand volumes. About this time, he thought, began a trend which multiplied the sale of books by four in twenty years.[61]

In the progress of bourgeois bookmanship, a special importance attaches to the provision of libraries. The expression 'circulating library' caught on in the early 1740s. It was often used pejoratively. Commercial subscription libraries dispensed 'low' literature, condemned as the source of polluted morality by the self-appointed censors of the day. They sprang up wherever booksellers found a market for cheap fiction, poetry, and *belles-lettres*. In some places they plainly provided a social as well as literary service. No aspiring spa town could afford to be without a bookshop-cum-subscribing library where morning browsers might meet and chat before the serious business of pump-room and assembly got under way. They were by no means the only libraries which extended the facilities of expanded publishers' lists to those who could not afford to collect on their own account. In fact the best documented libraries of the eighteenth century are those which were primarily designed to provide more learned and improving literature to serious enquirers after knowledge. The object was a library fit for scholars and gentlemen, but supported by the middle-class devices of subscription membership and government by committee. The Bristol Library Society, instituted in 1773, was typical: in its first decade it mustered around 130 members, charged an annual subscription of one guinea, accumulated a list of nearly 600 titles, and recorded over 13,000 loans.[62] The ten most popular books

[61] *Memoirs of the First Forty-Five Years of the Life of J. Lackington* (London, 1792), pp. 219 ff.
[62] P. Kaufman, *Libraries and their Users* (London, 1969), pp. 29, 31.

were travels (Brydone's *Sicily* and Hawkesworth's *Voyages*), the histories of Hume, Robertson, Goldsmith, and Lyttelton, Chesterfield's *Letters*, Raynal's *European Settlements*, and novels by Sterne and Fielding. But such libraries also offered a wide range of scientific, theological, and antiquarian scholarship. In this respect they played a significant part in the flowering of provincial, urban culture which is one of the most notable features of the late eighteenth century.

Libraries of this kind spread rapidly in the early years of George III. In Yorkshire, for example, Leeds acquired one in 1768, Bradford in 1774, Hull in 1775. They were supplemented by institutions which performed a similar service under another name: book clubs, which were cheaper and less pretentious than the learned subscription libraries; school libraries like that at Shrewsbury, which effectively operated as a municipal library; cathedral libraries, which lent readily to the relations and friends (including women) of the clergy. In this last respect the established Church had a built-in advantage. But the prominence of Dissenters in subscribing ventures is a reminder of their civic and intellectual vitality. The same earnest men who built hospitals, workhouses, and churches, who joined together in debating, 'conversation', and philosophical societies, were usually to be found involved in one way or another with the expanding provision of books. In this, as in so many ways, the urban élite of Georgian England, the professional and business classes broadly defined rather than the political oligarchy often taken as representative of municipal life, was the moving force.

Nobody challenged the value of learned libraries. But new books and new readers were controversial in other respects. It became conventional to condemn all but a small proportion of contemporary fiction as frivolous and even malignant trash. James Beattie, the scourge of the deists, also deplored the collapse, as he saw it, of the classical culture on which he had been reared. Its cause he identified in the growing purchasing power of the new, barely literate, who had never been exposed to the civilizing influence of the ancients. The point was not universally conceded. The novel, at least from the pens of its most celebrated champions, could be defended both on cultural and moral grounds. Richardson specifically attacked some of the classics, including the epics of Homer and Virgil, for their preoccupation with brutality and war, their projection of a false code of honour, and their indelicacy in sexual matters.[63] Smollett vindicated his rivals as well as himself in emphasizing the moral force created by the incipient sentimentalism of the 1740s. 'The laudable aim of inlisting the passions on the side of Virtue was successfully pursued by Richardson, in his Pamela, Clarissa, and Grandison; a species of writing equally new and extraordinary, where, mingled with much superfluity, we find a sublime system of ethics, an amazing knowledge and command of human nature.'[64]

Contemporaries were aware of the sociological significance of the novel. The Irish theologian Philip Skelton noted in the 1780s that novels 'for half a century have made the chief entertainment of that middle class which subsists between the court and the spade'.[65] Looking back on nearly forty years of novels in 1778 the *Critical Review* sought to analyse their popularity. It discerned no contradiction in the extent to which lords and ladies, aristocratic scenes, and upper-class fashions figured in them. Why, the reviewer asked, did Fanny Burney's Evelina have to have a rich father and why did she have to marry a lord? The answer was a simple one: the reader's desire to escape from the humdrum routines of middle and lower-class life.[66] Such escapism did not indicate a lack of social envy or moral purpose. Richardson's Pamela, the prototype of many such heroines, had first vanquished aristocratic rakery and then converted it to virtue. The formula was to prove irresistible.

Less contentious than the taste for novels was the attention paid to history. 'I believe', wrote Hume, 'this is the historical Age and this the historical Nation.'[67] In part the rage for historical literature was sustained by the contemporary interest in antiquarianism, largely the work of gentlemen amateurs who depended on inherited wealth or an undemanding profession for their livelihood. The eccentric philanthropist William Hanbury even anticipated the *Victoria County History* by proposing to endow a Professor of Antiquity who would compile the history of every county.[68] Such

[63] I. Watt, *The Rise of the Novel: Studies in Defoe, Richardson and Fielding* (London, 1757), pp. 242–50.

[64] *The History of England, from the Revolution in 1688, to the Death of George the Second* (London, 1827), p. 559.

[65] R. Lynam, ed., *The Complete Works of the late Rev. Philip Skelton* (6 vols., London, 1824), vi. 247.

[66] *Critical Review*, xlvi. 203–4.

[67] E. C. Mossner, *The Life of David Hume* (London, 1954), p. 318.

[68] J. Prophet, *Church Langton and William Hanbury* (Wymondham, 1982), pp. 112–13.

co-ordination was hardly necessary. There were few counties which did not acquire a multi-volume history under George II or George III. Many of them were the work of country clergymen. It was sarcastically observed that 'the clergy *now-a-days* study all history but that of the bible'.[69] Few of these histories could properly be described as popular. Most were expensive and could only be financed by prestigious subscription lists. A few were so lavish and impractical as to raise a suspicion that they were projected to support authors who had no intention of carrying out their promises. Even those that were completed could achieve a middle-class readership only via the library shelf. But the influence of the antiquarians should not be underrated. They sometimes broke completely new ground. John Whitaker's *History of Manchester* greatly disappointed the reviewers when it appeared in 1775. Yet it was one of the first urban histories and revealed the potential in a subject which appealed to the inhabitants of large cities.

Antiquarians enjoyed particular prominence when their concerns coincided with other contemporary interests, for instance in tourism. William Stukeley's investigation of the history of Stonehenge was essential reading for educated visitors, even if it did not discourage them from carrying off 'archaeological specimens' to the detriment of future generations. But most of all, antiquarians helped rescue history from the reckless optimism sometimes generated by complacent faith in progress. Many made a genuine effort to step into the mental world of the inscriptions, monuments, and charters which they scrutinized. John Brand, a pioneering historian of popular customs, put the point gently but persuasively to those who were tempted to treat the past only as reassurance of their own superiority. 'Prejudice may be forewarned, and it will apologize for many seemingly trivial Reasons, assigned for the beginning and transmitting of this or that *Notion or Ceremony*, to reflect, that what may appear foolish to the enlightened Understandings of Men in the *Eighteenth Century*, wore a very different Aspect when viewed through the Gloom that prevailed in the *seventh* or *eighth*.'[70]

Beyond the antiquarians lay the popular historians, who exploited the immense market which was made manifest in the

---

[69] Charles Jenner, *Letters from Altamont in the Capital, to his Friends in the Country* (London, 1767), p. 251.

[70] *Observations on Popular Antiquities* (Newcastle upon Tyne, 1777), p. vii.

1750s. Publishers, indeed, had perceived the potential profits earlier. The *Universal History*, which commenced in 1729 and concluded in 1784, ran to sixty-four volumes on the ancient and modern world. It was the work of a team of authors employed by a combine of enterprising booksellers.[71] But the major rewards went to the historians of the 1750s and 1760s, Hume, Smollett, Goldsmith, and Robertson. All had their critics. Hume's treatment of the Stuart period raised doubts about his objectivity. One of the disadvantages of writing a history of England, as, from very different perspectives, the Jacobite Thomas Carte and the republican Catherine Macaulay also discovered, was that party animosities were almost bound to intrude. But it had long been a cause for complaint that English authors had devoted so little attention to the past of their native country. Translations of Rapin's history were the first resort of those seeking an authoritative source in the 1730s and 1740s. Hume's was much the most successful of the attempts to supply this deficiency. It brought him fame and fortune far beyond what his philosophical writings could bring: he gave as his reasons for not finishing his *History* that he had grown 'too old, too fat, too lazy and too rich'.[72] Smollett proved equally shrewd in his exploitation of the potential history-reading public, though the sophisticated considered him a hack. Horace Walpole thought his popularity 'a reflection on the age sad to mention, yet too true to be suppressed!'[73] Goldsmith hardly pretended that his history was more than hack-work. Robertson, partly because he avoided writing directly about England, received much less criticism. Significantly, his life of Charles V was as popular as his histories of Scotland and America. For most purposes it was assumed that biography was closely linked with the art of the historian. Serious biographies as well as catchpenny lives provided booksellers with some of their most successful lines. Some scholarly productions, like Robertson's own Charles V and Lyttelton's Henry II, had a genuine mass market. Properly treated, history and biography were eminently safe subjects, with none of the moral dangers of more imaginative and perhaps more salacious literature. In the new syllabus of the modern school they could be granted a

[71] G. Abbattista, 'The Business of Paternoster Row: Towards a Publishing History of the *Universal History* (1736–65)', *Publishing History*, 17 (1985), 5–50.

[72] E. C. Mossner, *The Life of David Hume*, p. 556.

[73] Horace Walpole, *Memoirs of King George II*, ed. J. Brooke (3 vols., New Haven, 1985), iii. 97.

secure place as part of the training of a well-informed and liberal mind. The tendency to see history in personal and moral terms accentuated its didactic value. Thomas Holcroft's simple account of the essential value of the discipline reveals this clearly. 'History and biography are the great resources, as these furnish continual and real examples of the effects of the passions.'[74]

By 1783, when Holcroft made this observation, it was commonplace. But it was at about this time that it also came to acquire a tinge of controversy. The fact that history as an intellectual discipline appealed to some of the more daring spirits of the age was found somewhat perplexing. It was the despised deist Bolingbroke who had offered one of the most convincing justifications of the study of history and his spiritual successor Hume who penned one of its most celebrated examples. From the standpoint of moral crusaders history was plainly a double-edged sword. There was no shortage of moral crusaders in the last quarter of the eighteenth century. The evangelical tendencies of the 1770s did not reduce interest in history: they did, however, help to create the sense that the springs of historical knowledge must not be polluted by the unsound principles of historians. Hannah More feared that younger readers of Hume might conclude 'that the Reformation was really not worth contending for'.[75] With Gibbon's famous *Decline and Fall* it seemed that Christianity itself might fall victim to a sceptical historical spirit. The next generation had an obvious mission: to erect on the newly established foundation of serious historical interest, a great superstructure of safe, edifying, unsensational literature, suitable for a devout and disciplined public.

ASSOCIATION AND ASSEMBLY

Libraries and book clubs were partly an indication of the demand for books, partly an example of the proliferation of clubs generally. They served numerous purposes. Many were essentially primitive forms of social insurance. Such were the box clubs, which permitted ordinary wage-earners to contribute to mutual benefit funds with a view to their support in sickness or old age. They were organized by groups as unlikely as Oxford college bedmakers and unemployed black freemen. There was more than a suspicion in

[74] *The Family Picture; or, Domestic Dialogues on Amiable and Interesting Subjects* (2 vols., London, 1783), i. 14.
[75] *The Works of Hannah More* (6 vols., London, 1833–4), iv. 95.

some places, for instance the West Country clothing towns, that they were working men's combinations, to be used for co-ordinating coercive pressure on employers. The Breeches-Makers Benefit Society, which the young Francis Place joined, 'though actually a benefit club, was intended for the purpose of supporting the members in a strike for wages'.[76] The eighteenth century had significant terms for expressing the differences between otherwise similar organizations. 'Association' had overwhelmingly favourable connotations until the political and religious turmoil of the 1780s: before then it went with the individualism, liberty, and self-determination traditionally attributed to Englishmen. People associated to secure some manifestly laudable political object or social good. Combinations were by definition selfish conspiracies against the public weal. Monopolizing businessmen or striking workers were not associating but combining, often in a way which brought them directly into conflict with the law. But the line was a narrow one, as the box clubs themselves demonstrated. In their subversive role they could attract the full weight of upper-class disapproval. But as instruments of social control they came to seem attractive, especially towards the end of the century; shorn of their undesirable connection with the consumption of alcohol ('boxes' were traditionally in the care of tavern-keepers) and supervised by local clergy and magistrates, they received official support as the 'friendly societies' of a later age.

Most clubs were short-lived and informally constituted, essentially the expression of a dynamic, increasingly urban society in which the traditional structures of corporate and communal life were either absent or inappropriate for the full range of contemporary conditions and aspirations. A few with literary or philosophical aspirations, Johnson's Literary Club, the Spalding Gentlemen's Club, the Lichfield Lunar Society, have passed into the conventional image of the Georgian age. But these were merely the most celebrated examples of a universal activity, engaged in by low as well as high. The novelist Edward Kimber reckoned clubs one of the most characteristic products of contemporary society. In London as many as twenty thousand men met every night in this way, he calculated in 1750.[77]

---

[76] G. Wallas, *The Life of Francis Place, 1771–1854* (London, 1898), p. 6.
[77] *The Life and Adventures of Joe Thompson*, p. 111.

Clubs as such were almost by definition meant for men. For the company of women outside the family it was necessary to turn to what Defoe in the 1720s called 'that new-fashion'd way of conversing by assemblies'.[78] The activities of assemblies—cards, dancing, conversation—were less important than the forum which they created for social and sexual mixing. Coffee-houses, taverns, and inns were unsuitable for polite female company. Boarding-houses were usually too small to offer recreational facilities, and when hotels began to come into fashion in the 1780s they were regarded primarily as safe places for family accommodation. The great pleasure gardens which grew and prospered in the 1740s and 1750s, Vauxhall, Ranelagh, and Marylebone, were highly commercial and even impersonal. Because they were the resort not merely of high society but of pickpockets, rakes, and whores, they could hardly be regarded as respectable meeting-places for marriageable women and unmarried men.

Assemblies could be strictly regulated as to size and social conduct. They were open only to those paying a fee or subscription. The 'quality' guaranteed by such payment varied a good deal, depending chiefly on locality. In country districts it was important not to be too fastidious if social intercourse were to take place at all. In Westmorland the assemblies included both tradesmen and gentry.[79] In more populous areas the options became numerous and the gradations subtle. Londoners learned to distinguish between Assemblies with 'uncouth names'—Deptford, Wapping, Rother-hithe, Shad Thames, where the company was not of the politest, and those, the City Assembly, and the London Assembly, for example, where subscriptions were in guineas rather than shillings.[80] Raffish assemblies teetered perpetually on the brink of disaster. Such was the case at Portsmouth in 1768, it was claimed, when 'rather than stand still, a Gentleman may dance with a Wench, who the Morning before, sold him a Pair of Gloves'.[81] Even so, however fragile the conventions, it was recognized that the assembly did provide a degree of protected equality and respectability. Behind the barriers erected by subscription all aspiring to gentility were

[78] G. H. Cole, ed., *A Tour through England and Wales* (2 vols., London, 1927), i. 186.

[79] T. Holcroft, *Alwyn: or the Gentleman Comedian* (2 vols., London, 1780), i. 31.

[80] C. Jenner, *Town Eclogues* (London, 1772), p. 12.

[81] Robert Wilkins, *The Borough* (London, 1768), p. 16.

expected to mix freely, without the crippling respect for rank and hierarchy which was associated with the artificial manners of an earlier age. At Tunbridge it was reported in 1766: 'all ranks are mingled together without any distinction. The nobility, and the merchants; the gentry, and the traders, are all upon an equal footing, without anybody's having a right to be informed who you are, or whence you came, so long as you behave with that decorum which is ever necessary in genteel company.'[82]

SPA AND SEASIDE

Three of the great motive quests of middle-class life, marriage, health, and diversion, came together in one of the most enduring creations of the age, the watering-place. The rage for spa water and sea water had antecedents in the seventeenth century, but as a mass industry, capable of transforming the face of towns and cities, and remodelling the rhythms of propertied life, it belonged to the reign of George II. The philanthropist Jonas Hanway, who was shocked by the ladies' bathing dresses at Southampton, and thereby moved to reflect on the peculiar responsibility of the female sex to keep indecency within bounds, called it 'this reign of Saltwater'.[83] The medical component of the fashion was important. New spas had no hope of establishing themselves without a competent and commercially minded medical authority to certify their merits. Prosperity could start from very small beginnings. The whimsical John Buncle found Harrogate in 1731 a small, straggling village with the best sulphur wells in Britain, no ladies of pleasure, and the chief form of entertainment country dancing.[84] Malvern started to acquire a reputation for its springs a little later, one which induced the famous Dr Addington to send the young son of the wealthy MP George Pitt to die there in 1764.[85] Fifteen years later it still only had one house for accommodation. Cheltenham was another late comer. Visitors considered it 'a poor place' and an 'insipid' one, yet with the help of its much prized waters it was

[82] T. Benge Burr, *The History of Tunbridge Wells* (London, 1766), p. 121.

[83] *A Journal of Eight Days Journey from Portsmouth to Kingston upon Thames* (London, 1756), pp. 17–18.

[84] T. Amory, *The Life and Opinions of John Buncle Esquire*, ed. E. A. Baker (London, 1904), pp. 285–9.

[85] M. Pennington, ed., *Letters from Mrs Elizabeth Carter, to Mrs Montagu, Between the Years 1755 and 1800* (3 vols., London, 1817), i. 213–14.

to be one of the most popular resorts by the early nineteenth century.[86]

Some cynicism was expressed about the health-giving properties of the spas. The tendency of ladies in search of social diversion and sexual dalliance to discover an urgent need for a visit to the 'waters' was a well-established joke. One journalist advised a straightforward stomach-ache as infallible in this respect. 'The Cholick (in the Stomach I mean) is a clean, genteel Distemper, and by no means below Women of the first Condition; and they should always keep it by 'em, to be us'd as Occasion requires.'[87] In his skit *The Spleen* in 1776 George Colman suggested that Islington Spa needed only a learned dissertation and a scheme to extract salts from the New River to make it fashionable once again. However, such scepticism had little effect on the marketability of medical recreation. It is difficult to explain, for instance, why Epsom, once popular, should have fallen from favour, except in terms which take account of the declining reputation of its wells. Moreover, a development of the first importance, the extension of touristic interest to the seaside, owed much to the support which it received from the medical profession.

Dr Richard Russell's tract on the value of sea water, both for internal and external use, *A Dissertation on the Use of Sea Water in the Diseases of the Glands*, was published in 1750 and went through six English editions in twenty years. The middle of the century saw the rapid development of coastal resorts. Scarborough was an established spa, but with the new vogue for sea-bathing it enjoyed a brisk trade, at least until it began to lose favour at the end of the century. Few places were so remote from the sea that they were entirely without access to suitable beaches. Many of the great seaside towns of the nineteenth century were first developed in this period. Blackpool had a flourishing, mainly Lancashire clientele, by the 1780s. Weymouth was patronized by some distinguished visitors, Ralph Allen, the 'Man of Bath', in 1763, the Duke of Gloucester in 1780, the King himself in 1788. Even the remote Welsh coast began to exploit its potential, particularly at Aberystwyth, where there was a regular tourist season by the

---

[86] Richard Joseph Sullivan, *Observations made during a Tour through Parts of England, Scotland, and Wales* (London, 1780), p. 117; Mary Morgan, *A Tour to Milford Haven, in the Year 1791* (London, 1795), pp. 95–9.
[87] *Gentleman's Magazine*, 1737, p. 498.

1780s. But the greatest beneficiary of the new vogue was Brighton. At the time of the Seven Years War, when it received its first 'great resort of company', it was a fishing village with some 2,000 inhabitants, the victim of an old Sussex saying which was soon to be superseded: 'Proud Lewes and poor Brighthelmston'. Its population quadrupled by the end of the century. As a resort it advertised healthy air, clean water, and a good mineral spring. The annual mortality rate was one in sixty-two, compared with one in thirty-two in London.[88] Its progress was not completely untroubled. The jocular *New Brighthelmstone Directory: or, Sketches in Miniature of the British Shore*, published in 1770, pointed to the moral dangers and social embarrassments created by the arrangements for bathing. Men had been banished from the Steine in order to discourage the female crowds which gathered to watch their naked feats, but the price of prudery had been a notable diminution in the numbers bathing. Such discouragements proved temporary. By the early 1780s the once notoriously inaccessible Sussex coast was popular with upper and middle-class Londoners, for whom the turnpike and the chaise made it eminently accessible. The scene was set for the transition from Brighthelmstone to the Prince Regent's Brighton.

Much of the popularity of spa and seaside derived from the need for places to which the polite classes could resort during the summer, when the recess of Parliament and the dust of London gave rise to an annual exodus. There was a sense in which Brighton was merely a summer encampment for West End Society. The same was true of Bath. The consequences for provincial life were sometimes viewed with misgivings. The absentee landlord, who deserted the community which he was meant to serve and govern, was a well-established figure in the social demonology of the late eighteenth century. Traditionally, the county life of the summer— assizes, races, music-meetings, plays, balls—had at least brought the magnates and gentry back for a month or two. The tradition continued, but it was under growing threat from the tendency of polite society to migrate from London to Bath or Brighton (or indeed the Continent) with no more than a fleeting visit to a shuttered country house. In the process the social calendar of the localities suffered severely. It was observed in 1771 that the races at places as diverse as Reading and Ludlow, once major attractions

---

[88] Anthony Relhan, *A Short History of Brighthelmstone* (London, 1761), pp. 15, 36, 38.

for propertied society in the Thames Valley and the Welsh borders respectively, were fading into obscurity as young men and women of fashion took themselves off to the watering-places.[89] So potent a diversion could only be countered in kind. Some of the smaller spas were developed in order to provide provincial society with modern facilities. The fifth Duke of Devonshire's grand design for Buxton, commenced in 1780, served this purpose in his county of Derbyshire, and within easy distance of his house at Chatsworth. The laureate William Whitehead had once spoken of 'the dreary waste of Buxton'.[90] By 1785 the poetess Anna Seward was able to celebrate a very different view while awaiting the completion of 'its beauteous Crescent'.[91]

Controversies about the social consequences of the new re-creations give the impression that the spa and the seaside were essentially part of the scenery of aristocratic life. The snobbery which determined the social round at such places and the terms in which they were customarily advertised reinforces this impression. It is none the less misleading, like so much of the eighteenth-century's seeming passion for aristocratic values. The success of the new fashion was based on its appeal to the broad mass of the propertied public. For the great majority the very idea of a holiday or even a visit to a place of fashionable resort was new and exciting. Aristocratic patronage, commercial exploitation, and the social aspirations of bourgeois England were closely bound up in the new trends. The conjunction was no less to be observed at Bath, the most fashionable of all such places, than among its humbler imitators.

Bath owed its enormous popularity under George II and George III to a remarkable triumvirate. Richard 'Beau' Nash made its social regimen famous: even if the anecdotes of his rebukes to royalty are apocryphal, their currency testifies to his dictation of the social calendar at Bath. The pattern which he established and which took its place as part of a balanced and integrated day, with proper time for the waters and for social mixing, became the model for spa life in many other places. At Tunbridge, where Nash was also employed as the 'arbitrator' of pleasure, his importance was

[89] E. J. Climenson, ed., *Passages from the Diaries of Mrs Philip Lybbe Powys of Hardwick House, Oxon. A.D. 1756 to 1808* (London, 1899), p. 134.

[90] *An Hymn to the Nymph of Bristol Spring* (London, 1751), p. 19.

[91] *Letters of Anna Seward* (6 vols., Edinburgh, 1811), i. 14.

acknowledged by the first historian of the town in naïve terms. He 'first taught the people of fashion how to buy their pleasures, and to procure that ease and felicity they sought for, without diminishing the happiness of others'.[92] Nash's coadjutor Ralph Allen, Pope's Man of Bath, had a reputation for high-mindedness which made him a darling of the moralists and the friend of an influential group of clerics and politicians, led by William Warburton and William Pitt. In retrospect his commercial acumen is just as striking, not merely for the expansion of the postal network which helped make him famous in his own day, but for the shrewdness which he brought to the rebuilding of Bath and the exploitation of his quarries of Bath Stone.

The third of this trio, John Wood senior, helped create perhaps the most lasting of all eighteenth-century images, the Georgian townscape. He finished his masterpiece, Queen Square, between 1729 and 1736. In the subsequent transformation of the city his son played an equally important part. The Pump Room was greatly enlarged in 1751 and completely rebuilt in 1780. One of the first provincial hospitals was opened in 1742, and supervised by Dr Oliver, who gave his name to the Bath Oliver biscuit. The Play-house was opened in 1751. The principal Assembly Room, built by John Wood in 1728, was extended in 1750, and supplemented by the younger Wood's Upper Rooms in 1771. Gay Street was virtually finished by the accession of George III, the Circus by 1766. Against this backdrop were enacted some classic scenes of Georgian life, including Sheridan's conquest of Miss Linley, Lord Chatham's quest for relief from the gout, and Lady Huntingdon's pilgrimages to one of her favourite chapels. Against it too there could be viewed the endless procession of the great, with the bells ringing at their entry, the waits welcoming at their lodgings, crowds flocking after them in the walks. The talk was of politics and court scandal; the pattern of life seemed to make Bath what in some respects it was, the continuation of Oxford Street. But it was far more than this.

Bath's population increased from less than 3,000 in 1700 to nearly 35,000 a century later. Outside London it had the biggest migrant community of all, receiving as many as 12,000 visitors in a season by 1750. According to Dr Penrose, a Cornish clergyman who recorded his impressions of Bath in 1765–6, the money taken

[92] T. Benge Burr, *The History of Tunbridge Wells*, pp. 113, 112.

each week amounted to more than £10,000.[93] Women out-numbered men, but more striking was Bath's social diversity. It is a paradox but not a contradiction that the emphasis on aristocracy assured humbler visitors that they were indeed participating in a truly polite diversion. Bath owed its name to the great but its fortune to the mass of the middling. Critics enjoyed pointing out the resulting ironies. Matthew Bramble was shocked by 'what is called the fashionable company at Bath; where a very incon-siderable proportion of genteel people are lost in a mob of impudent plebeians, who have neither understanding nor judgment, nor the least idea of propriety and decorum; and seem to enjoy nothing so much as an opportunity of insulting their betters'.[94] One of the most successful satires of an age not generally at ease with satire, the 1760s, owed its reputation to acute social observation of the Bath scene. Christopher Anstey's *New Bath Guide*, published in 1766, gently mocked those who sought at Bath, not the health or exercise which ostensibly drew them there, but 'A grace, an air, a taste refin'd, To vulgar souls unknown.' The popularity of the *Guide* was immense; its publisher Dodsley made so much by it that after five years he returned the copyright (originally purchased for £2,000) to the author in recognition of the exceptional profits which it had generated. Anstey himself, an East Anglian country gentleman, showed when he subsequently returned to Bath that he had nothing serious against the city. Nor indeed did his readers. It was exactly the fascination of Bath that it drew both the naïve upstarts like Anstey's Blunderhead family and those apparently unlimited numbers who were quite certain that they did not resemble them in any way.

Bath had many humble imitators, fulfilling a similar social function. In the unlikely environs of the Wash, for instance, James Lackington found a small resort at Freestone, where fenland farmers and tradesmen went for the salt water, with somewhat unfortunate results. Unable to afford a full month's treatment, they none the less contrived to swallow an equivalent amount of water in two weeks.[95] But the most voracious consumers of holiday leisure were undoubtedly Londoners. This was the joke which

---

[93] B. Mitchell and H. Penrose, eds. *Letters from Bath 1766–1767 by the Rev. John Penrose* (Gloucester, 1983), p. 92.

[94] Tobias Smollett, *Humphry Clinker*, ed. A. Ross (London, 1967), p. 66.

[95] *Memoirs*, p. 326.

made Cowper's John Gilpin so risible in 1784. Nobody could take seriously a successful London tradesman, whose life was still bounded by the City. As Vicesimus Knox put it, 'Your true Cockney, one who was never out of the sound of Bow bell, is uncommon in the present age. No persons ramble more than the citizens to Bath, Tunbridge, Brighthelmstone, Margate and all other places of fashionable resort.'[96] George Keate's *Sketches from Nature*, in 1779, described the affectation of those thus transported. Eleven hours in a City hoy brought flocks of visitors to Margate, one of the fastest growing tourist centres of the third quarter of the century. They might boast of preferring the Parades at Margate to the Pantiles at Tunbridge and the Steine at Brighton. Their language was that of fashionable society. 'Every creature at Margate was *monstrously* polite,—every place about it *immensely* pretty,—and the smuggled tea most *extravagantly* cheap.—I might have picked up *anecdotes* and *affectation* to have lasted my life.'[97] For those less ambitious and more impecunious there were still nearer resorts. The capital was ringed by villages which offered matching if less modish delights. 'To be cooped up in the *Row*, amidst the smell of the printing-house, and Dolly's beef-steaks, all the Dog-days?—No, give me fresh air, and Islington—as genteel as Tun-bridge, Brighthelmstone, Southampton, or Margate.'[98] There was little dramatic licence in this. George Cumberland, a government clerk of respectable but not wealthy family, bemoaned his fate in London in August without the wherewithal even for a short holiday:

What Luxury to bathe by moonlight in the Thames! How refreshing the air of Hornsea! How sweet the cows of Islington etc, etc, the suburbian relaxations. How thoroughly does the opulent man despise you—yes—I have felt the insolence of riches, and the proud thoughts which 20 new guineas in the month of July inspire—and now I know not but I may soon be reduced to meet my pleasure in a Skittle ground—admire the Dog and Duck—and go once more to Vauxhall.[99]

[96] *The Works of Vicesimus Knox* (7 vols., London, 1824), ii. 341.
[97] (2 vols., London), ii. 201.
[98] *The Dramatick Works of George Colman*, iv. 281–2.
[99] C. Black, ed., *The Cumberland Letters* (London, 1912), p. 203.

WOMEN IN POLITE SOCIETY

It did not go without notice that the leisure activities of the Hanoverian middle class gave opportunities to women as well as to men. Women not only shared fully in the literary and recreational life of the day but seemed positively to dominate it. The effect on their ordinary lives could be striking. The historian of Scottish manners, John Ramsay of Ochtertyre, who had lived through many of the changes which he described, recorded a 'wonderful change upon female manners, in consequence of playhouses, assemblies and concerts'. Previously, 'the Scottish women made their most brilliant appearance at burials.'[1] When there was controversy about the social and moral consequences of such change, it focused largely on the dangers to the female sex. The immorality supposedly encouraged by the ubiquitous novel was treated as a special threat to the chastity of young women who wasted their days reading it. Freedom of conversation and social mixing at the assembly and the theatre, not to say less approved forms of diversion, masques and gaming, also held dangers for women insufficiently protected by mothers and aunts, fathers and brothers. Even the new educational opportunities proved controversial where women were concerned. Boarding schools were charged with drawing future generations away from their duties as wives and mothers. 'The girls, then, from such schools are totally undomesticated. And undomesticated women have houses without order; servants without discipline; children without instruction.'[2] Most critics preferred the thought of no schooling at all to a polite education. Those who did envisage an alternative received little encouragement. Mrs Montagu conceived of a literary academy which would provide young women with the intellectual foundations for independent development. But her chosen instrument, the famous Mrs Barbauld, who acquired a formidable pedagogic reputation through her extra-curricular work in her husband's school, was reluctant to become involved.[3] Caution in these matters was by no means the preserve of the politically conservative and theologically orthodox. Thomas Day, whose politics were authentically radical and whose religious ideas owed more to Rousseau than Revelation,

[1] A. Allardyce, ed., *Scotland and Scotsmen in the Eighteenth Century* (2 vols., Edinburgh, 1888), ii. 60–1.
[2] R. Polwhele, *Poems* (5 vols., Truro, 1810), v. 65.
[3] L. Aikin, *The Works of Anna Laetitia Barbauld* (2 vols., London, 1825), i. xvii.

thought 'a polite education may be considered as a species of inoculation, which effectually prevents the fair patient from feeling any subsequent attack of shame or timidity during the rest of her life'. He longed, like many of his contemporaries in the later decades of the century, for 'a cargo of plain, honest housewives'.[4]

In principle, women had such little freedom of action that these worries may seem surprising. But it was precisely because the formal disadvantages of women were so extensive that any advance was so important. The growing tendency even for middle-class families to provide married women with guaranteed rights through the use of legal instruments, notably the marriage settlement, was much discussed. Parents had an interest in ensuring that the substantial sums which they often devoted to marrying their daughters were not left entirely at the mercy of a vicious or feckless husband. The superior legal status of unmarried woman may also have served somewhat to modify the status of wives. Women who married were virtually deprived of a share in the property of their husbands and families. They were the *femmes coverts* of legal language, often likened to slaves. But women who were not married enjoyed rights comparable to those of men. Something between a sixth and a fifth of all property was owned by women if the surviving tax records of the period are a reliable guide. Most of them were property-owners as widows, some as daughters and heiresses. Such women enjoyed complete control of their own lives, and unlimited access to the social privileges which property brought, though not, for the most part, its political rights.

Even married women seemed increasingly to live a life of leisure and liberty. Contemporaries were well aware of the trends which made this so. For practical purposes it was possible to have a profession or trade and still live the life of a gentleman. It was much more difficult to do so and live the life of a lady, not just because snobbery made work for profit an unladylike activity but because work suitable for middle-class women seemed increasingly hard to obtain. Shopkeepers' wives played a part in what for many couples was a joint rather than a male enterprise; farmers, too, continued to expect active collaboration from their families. But the diminishing opportunities for respectable female employment,

[4] *Select Miscellaneous Productions, of Mrs Day, and Thomas Day, Esq. in Verse and Prose* (London, 1805), p. 113; *The History of Sandford and Merton* (4th edn., 3 vols., London, 1787), iii. 302.

above the ranks of ordinary labourers and artisans, were much lamented. Some attributed the alleged idleness of the typical farmer's wife to the snobbery and commercialism which had infected rural life. 'The fine lady, his wife, would faint at the idea of attending at market, like her mother or grandmother, with a basket of butter, pork, roasting pigs, or poultry, on her arm.'[5] Paradoxically, the fashion for rural pastimes in the second half of the century made dairy-management the diversion of some aristocratic women. At Hampstead Lady Mansfield and Lady Southampton vied to produce the better butter.[6]

Such affectations did not conceal the diminishing role of women in practical and useful enterprises. 'The middling order of women', noted the clerical essayist John Moir, 'are deprived of those stations which properly belong to them, very often to their utter ruin, and always to the detriment of society.'[7] Milliners, mantua-makers, staymakers, embroiderers, seamstresses, all were exposed to male competition. Hairdressing and peruke-making were coming to be dominated by men. The same was true of medicine, in some branches of which women had traditionally figured. Successful dentists, oculists, above all midwives, tended to be male. The crucial advantage of hospital training was confined to men. Women themselves increasingly sought the services of the professionally trained. Resistance to this trend proved unavailing. The self-taught midwife Elizabeth Nihell fought a rearguard action in defence of her sex, against the celebrated gynaecologist William Smellie. In her *Treatise on the Art of Midwifery* of 1760, she urged the damage done by Smellie's obsession with forceps, the superior manipulative talents of women, and the requirements of female modesty. It was to little avail. Women surgeons disappeared still more quickly. A rare exception, who practised in the remote Forest of Bowland in the 1780s, enjoyed her position only because, unlike her brethren, she advertised no charge without a cure.[8]

The debate about the changing role of women extended readily to their rights. The Blue Stockings of the mid-eighteenth century

[5] Quoted in I. Pinchbeck, *Women Workers and the Industrial Revolution, 1750–1850* (new edn., London, 1969), p. 34.

[6] B. Rodgers, *Georgian Chronicle: Mrs Barbauld and her Family* (London, 1958), pp. 99–100.

[7] *Gleanings; or, Fugitive Pieces* (2 vols., London [1785]), ii. 65.

[8] C. H. Beale, *Reminiscences of a Gentlewoman of the Last Century: Letters of Catherine Hutton*, p. 60.

were not advanced feminists. Yet, with the advantages of education and gentility, they were prepared to voice some challenging ideas. The novelist Samuel Richardson, whose writings centred so largely on the subject of the female psyche, had no intention of unleashing a female rebellion. But he surrounded himself with an admiring circle of women who hung on his every word and proved surprisingly irreverent in exploring their implications. The young Hester Mulso, better known in later years as the learned Mrs Chapone, argued tenaciously against the subjection of daughters to fathers in her 'Letters on Filial Obedience'. She quoted Pufendorf and Locke, claimed that '*women*, as rational and accountable beings, are free agents as well as *men*', and pointed out that the Bible required obedience to mothers as much as fathers. Wives, she claimed, could not be required to obey men who were manifestly not endowed with natural superiority; even those who did meekly submit retained a right to their own opinions and were entitled to be treated by their husbands as equals, not dependants. She later remembered enough of these heretical thoughts to recognize 'some strong sense, amidst many absurdities, improprieties, and odious indelicacies' in Mary Wollstonecraft's *Rights of Women*.[9] Feminism of her kind lacked the robust quality of the very first feminists, the Aphra Behns and Mary Astells, and suggested rather the soft sentimentalism of the age of Pamela. It expressed itself not in strident criticism but in gentle ridicule: the Blue Stockings enjoyed many private jokes about the 'lords of creation'. It was eventually to be all but overwhelmed by the colossal conservatism of the evangelicals. Yet it was broadly based in the new social, literary, and sexual confidence of polite women, and reflected a genuinely changing perception of their influence which was to have wide-ranging repercussions.

However much the role of women changed, the central concern of most of them remained the same. For the middle and upper classes marriage was a prime weapon of the social war. A successful marriage was not merely a means of acquiring property and status; it could transform the prospects of entire families. For women between the ages of fourteen and forty it was a subject of overwhelming interest, and for their fathers and mothers hardly less so. In a stable, closely regulated society it could be treated, no doubt, as a matter of parental direction, with little disturbance to

[9] *The Works of Mrs. Chapone* (4 vols., London, 1807), ii. 115, 202.

family life and no alarming social implications. But eighteenth-century society was neither very stable, nor closely regulated: marriage like many other transactions was a competitive and unpredictable business. In point of social prestige the emphasis was on the upward mobility of women rather than men. Men were free, even encouraged, to marry below them, for money if not for love. As Pamela discovered, perhaps as Pamela calculated, it was possible for a woman to be carried into a higher class of society by a fortunate match. In suitable circumstances, men might similarly be translated to a higher station. But this was much more difficult. It also presented a dilemma for women. A woman who married below her station could hardly expect to regain it. A woman who married above her station was assured of her ascent.

The social mobility of women through marriage was seen by statisticians and social analysts as a critical factor in the differential rates of marriage between the lower classes and their betters. Arthur Young noted that even in the countryside one-sixth of farmers were unmarried compared with only one-tenth of labourers.[10] The demographer John Howlett reckoned that the proportion of labourers to their superiors was three to one. Yet lower-class marriages outnumbered those of the middle and upper classes six to one. In towns the disparity was even greater. The cause, he thought, was 'a certain pride of station; a shame and fear of descending beneath it; a superior, perhaps, a false, refinement of thought; a luxury and delicacy of habit; a tenderness of body and mind, which rendering formidable the prospect of poverty, and thereby checking the impulses of nature, frequently prevent matrimonial connections.'[11] Putting it another way, far too many girls were brought up with expectations which could not possibly be fulfilled given the competition for husbands. Spinsterhood was the fate of countless daughters of small professional men on incomes of £50–£100, clergy, army and navy officers, attorneys, apothecaries. James Lackington condemned 'the stupid pride and ignorance of their parents, who, by the manner of bringing them up, have excluded them from the endearing relations and unspeakable pleasures of wives and mothers'.[12] The hunt for a good husband

[10] *A Six Months Tour Through the North of England* (2nd edn., 4 vols., London, 1771), iv. 247.

[11] *An Examination of Dr Price's Essay on the Population of England and Wales* (Maidstone [1781]), p. 28.

[12] *The Confessions of James Lackington* (London, 1804), p. 200.

often seemed hypocritical. The same boarding school which supposedly made its pupils unsuitable wives and mothers provided them with polite manners, correct accent, good deportment, refined appearance, and elegant accomplishments. With these a girl might achieve a better marriage by far than her parents could arrange. Parents spared no expense to assist her, while deploring the need to do so. Similarly, parents who thought the latest fashions dangerously daring and provocative were apt to suppress their doubts if the daring and provocation could ensnare a young man of good birth. Compromises of this kind were evidently compatible with high-minded disapproval of the same conduct in others.

Individual parents were in no position to resist the demands of social flexibility and an open marriage market. But in the mass there were means of regulating an otherwise undisciplined competition. Controls were concentrated on those aspects of the marriage market which rendered women and their property most vulnerable. The Marriage Act of 1753 will forever be associated with the name of the Lord Chancellor who promoted it, Lord Hardwicke, but its principles had long been debated, and on at least two occasions, 1718 and 1735, similar bills had been projected. It was designed to eliminate the notorious scandal of the clandestine marriage, a source of profit to unscrupulous clergymen, and of anxiety to aristocratic parents. Elopement not only pitched true love against parental authority, it presumed a socially unsuitable match with a woman of higher birth and greater wealth than the groom. The debates in Parliament on the Marriage Bill touched tender spots. Some highly placed men had benefited by a runaway marriage. Henry Fox, who had eloped with the daughter of the Duke of Richmond, and whose marriage was thereby an important part in the making of a successful and political career, bitterly resented the bill, and made periodic attempts to have it repealed, a duty which he bequeathed to his son Charles James Fox. Others saw in the bill a blatantly oligarchical intention to preserve the aristocracy as a caste. Still others considered it a threat to civil and religious liberties, since it effectively required all who sought a legal union, including papists and Dissenters, to marry with due form in a parish church. Some doubted Parliament's right to remodel an institution of divine origin. Not least it was feared that legislation would discourage the lower sort from marrying, endangering the nation's resources of manpower and morality. The passage of the bill was contested with acrimony rather than effect. Once on the statute book, it by no means killed off elopements, as the popularity of Gretna Green testified. Nor, in all likelihood, did it render aristocracy more exclusive than it already was. But as a pointer to contemporary sensitivity on the subject of marriage its importance is undeniable.

Marriage in the proper manner was important, but marriage on any terms was better than none. Worse than a daughter who made a disadvantageous marriage was one who surrendered her virtue before marrying. The obsession with the sexual vulnerability of unmarried women only makes sense in the context of a society which invested high stakes in marriage as an institution. Again the very freedom which was necessary for the marriage market to operate satisfactorily created immense risks. Little could be done about this. Protecting a daughter against all temptation was tantamount to removing her from the game, and was possible only for those fortunate families who were guaranteed a suitable match by their wealth and status. For the rest the game must be allowed to proceed with a careful calculation of the risks involved and an uncomfortable awareness that failure might imperil the stake as well as the prize. All depended on the prudence as well as skill of the players themselves, and in the last analysis parents were onlookers not players. None the less they could do their best to ensure that chastity kept its value until its reward was secure.

It was commonplace to attribute the almost morbid interest in this matter to the overriding need to maintain dynastic succession untainted by the pollution of bastardy or disputed inheritance. The transmission of property depended on maintaining sexual morality while permitting sexual competition. It was a difficult balance to preserve and one which involved a good deal of humbug. Edward Moore's popular *Fables for the Female Sex* of 1744 offered some conventional advice. Beauty must be used to attract men but without coquetry; dress must allure but not in provocative manner; daughters must be allowed an element of free choice but not at the expense of the parental veto. Such uneasy compromises figured in a great mass of literature devoted to the instruction of daughters and the comfort of parents. They required some significant mental adjustments. The well-established view that women were sexually more voracious than men came under attack. Sexual desire on the part of a woman exposed her to appalling dangers, dangers which must be averted by making her a cold-hearted temptress if necessary. Hugh Kelly's *Memoirs of a Magdalen*, published in 1767, was perhaps the most popular of a whole literary genre devoted to this end. Kelly concentrated on the dangers of that time between initial attraction and eventual marriage when a woman might think herself successful and drop her guard. 'Of all the stages in a woman's life, none is so dangerous as the period between her acknowledgment of a passion for a man, and the day set apart for her nuptials.' In the case of the heroine Louisa, this vulnerability defeated even a high-minded fiancé, Sir Robert Harold: 'a cursed sopha lying most conveniently ready to assist the purposes of my rashness, I proceeded from liberty to liberty till she was actually undone!' Such weakness was fatal in every respect. Sir Robert rejected his bride: 'Did these women but know how we worship them for refusing to gratify our wishes.' She was also expelled by her father.[13] With variations this was a recurrent theme of novels and poems. It is unsurprising that the sentimental man of the late eighteenth century professed to find the women of his age unnatural, coquettish, artful, and calculating: these were the qualities which a generation of marriage-makers had fostered.

THE UNITY OF POLITE SOCIETY

The sexual and social tensions of the polite classes can give the impression of a propertied society divided within its own ranks. The intense competitiveness and the fine gradations which separated one stratum from the next added to this sense of an unstable structure. Yet this impression is in some respects misleading. Contemporaries were struck by the extent to which the pursuit of politeness submerged rather than exposed distinctions. The declining importance of regional differences was an obvious instance. High priority was accorded the elimination of local accents. From a Victorian vantage-point Lucy Aikin recalled the importance which her parents had attached to this. 'One circumstance, wholly overlooked in its moral bearings, even by parents vigilant as mine, tended to produce in me a settled conviction of my own superiority to those around me, which I feel to have been permanently injurious. This was the constant attention paid to preserving my speech free from the vulgar and ungram-

---

[13] (London, 1782 edn.), pp. 15, 17, 26.

matical dialect of the place. My own language and pronunciation, I was taught, were right; those of the children my companions were, of course, *very wrong*.'[14] A bishop, like John Green of Lincoln, who had a Yorkshire accent, was mocked by his clergy.[15] The cultural differentiation was no longer that of 'court and country', sophisticated 'cit' versus clod-hopping country squire. Rather it was a question of class.

Local identities were an obvious casualty of this process, as George Colman observed in his occasional paper *The Genius*, in 1761.

It is scarce half a century ago, since the inhabitants of the distant counties were regarded as a species, almost as different from those of the metropolis, as the natives of the Cape of Good Hope. Their manners, as well as dialect, were entirely provincial; and their dress no more resembling the habit of the town, than the *Turkish or Chinese*. But time, which has inclosed commons, and ploughed up heaths, has likewise cultivated the minds, and improved the behaviour of the ladies and gentlemen of the country.[16]

Provincial loyalties were still encouraged for some purposes. The militia, as revived in 1757, was based on the counties. In 1782 the Crown began associating infantry regiments with specified districts, 'so as to create a mutual attachment'. Initially this was an artificial exercise. The Buffs, for example, were allocated East Kent, solely on the grounds that the current commander happened to be a man of Kent.[17] There was also some early tactlessness on the part of the War Office. Enthusiasm for the new policy turned to outrage in Worcestershire, when men recruited for the Twenty-Ninth Foot were then diverted to the Forty-Third, with which there was no connection.[18] But in time the value of county titles was demonstrated to the most sceptical military minds. For the gentry, of course, these loyalties were something to be managed and exploited rather than shared. The county, for all the ancient

[14] P. H. Le Breton, ed., *Memoirs, Miscellanies and Letters of the Late Lucy Aikin* (London, 1864), p. xiv.

[15] F. G. Stokes, ed., *The Bletchley Diary of the Rev. William Cole, 1765–67* (London, 1931), p. 35.

[16] No. V in *Prose on Several Occasions; by George Colman* (London, 1787), pp. 54–5.

[17] C. R. B. Knight, *Historical Records of the Buffs: Part One, 1704–1814* (London, 1925), pp. 237–8.

[18] H. Everard, *History of Thomas Farrington's Regiment subsequently designated The 29th (Worcestershire) Foot, 1694 to 1891* (Worcester, 1891), p. 104.

traditions which it suggested in landed families, was more in the nature of a political and social stage than a natural habitat or a cultural need. They were inevitably patronizing about those for whom the immediate environment was more important. Readers of Mrs Bennett's *Anna* were expected to laugh at her portrayal of the servants of a Somerset bridegroom and a Sussex bride. The union was the product of a national marriage market. But the servants still lived in a local framework. The resulting animosities neatly measured the gap between upper- and lower-class perceptions of the importance of place.[19]

Servants occupied a sensitive position on the line which separated polite from plebeian life. Drawing this line with clarity was a major concern. Architectural historians have observed the tendency in great houses to remove servants from the presence of their employers. Staff accommodation was ideally placed at a distance: corridors and passages which enabled servants to be summoned were as far as practicable distinguished from thoroughfares used by those they served. This need to keep servants not merely in their place but in a suitably remote place was felt just as keenly in less wealthy homes, which lacked the space and resources to make the physical changes possible in larger houses. A common solution was to ensure that servants did not reside with their masters and mistresses. The growing practice of paying 'board wages' in lieu of 'living in' was censured for its effect on the moral well-being of the servants themselves. The *World*, one of those mid-century papers which sought to do for public morality what the *Spectator* had done forty years earlier, described it as a gigantic evil, 'conducive to the universal corruption of the lower part of this nation, and so entirely destructive of all family order, decency, and economy'.[20] An alternative was to encourage servants to keep themselves to themselves. The imprudence of permitting any intercourse with children was constantly emphasized. The avowed danger was the moral degeneracy of servile life. But the real concern was as much the possibility of social contamination. Mary Ann Galton, brought up in a Quaker household in the 1780s, remembered how her mother 'took the greatest pains that we might receive no contamination from ignoble minds, no vulgarism of habits or ideas'. She was particularly prohibited from passing

[19] *Anna; or Memoirs of a Welch Heiress* (4 vols., London, 1785), i. 50–1.
[20] No. 157, *The Works of Soame Jenyns*, ii. 123.

through a lobby contiguous to the servants' offices.[21] Evangelicals feared the threat which servants might pose to paternal authority. The Eclectic Society, founded by the forebears of the Clapham Sect in 1783, advised maternal vigilance where there was any risk of servants criticizing their employers in front of children. 'It is the duty of mothers to be as Sarah was—*much in the tent*.'[22]

There were other dangers, too. Ballads which told of romances between footmen and their mistresses pointed to hazards of a uniquely alarming kind. A disastrous marriage, with its threat to property and social prestige, was almost the worst imaginable result of excessive familiarity between servant and employer, but there were many worrying possibilities which fell short of it. The great majority of servants were female. In the 1780s a maidservant could be employed for as little as three or four pounds per annum, even in London. No middle-class family could afford to be without maidservants, but their very necessity sharpened the sense of the problem which they presented. The immorality of young female servants was a matter of general agreement. John Trusler reckoned there were few servant maids in London, or even in the country, who were not whores. 'It is perhaps an uncharitable supposition, but it is nevertheless true.'[23] The fact that many of them owed their fall to masters or masters' sons did not remove sensitivity on this point. Moralists commonly saw such liaisons as the result of artful, libidinous young women corrupting naïve, untutored boys. The picaresque heroes of puritanical novels did not seduce their parents' maids, they were seduced *by* them; this was true, for instance, of Edward Kimber's Joe Thompson, and Robert Paltock's Peter Wilkins, two of the most popular of their kind. Young men placed in this position were not expected to accept the moral consequences of their actions, unless they were themselves of lowly origin. The antiquarian William Cole relished telling the story of a Buckinghamshire clergyman who found his maid with child and determined on compelling the father to marry her. When he discovered that his brother, a naval officer on leave, was responsible, he became 'more easy in that Respect'.[24]

The one easily agreed solution was to ensure sound supervision

---

[21] C. C. Hankin, ed., *Life of Mary Anne Schimmelpenninck* (2 vols., London, 1858), i. 21.

[22] J. H. Pratt, ed., *Eclectic Notes* (2nd edn., London, 1865), p. 72.

[23] *The London Adviser and Guide* (London, 1786), p. 48.

[24] *The Blecheley Diary of the Rev. William Cole, 1765–67*, p. 275.

of servants. It was stressed that the ultimate beneficiaries of a well-regulated household were the servants themselves. The register offices which sprang up in London in the middle of the century and which acted as employment agencies, emphasized that the happiness and prosperity of society depended on 'each of its members being employed in a station suited to his capacity'.[25] Free-born Englishmen, even those without property, were meant to have significant political and legal rights, but servants were rarely seen in this light. The poet-physician John Armstrong argued that servants had sold their liberty for a certain term. Yet he also observed that they were often born with 'as delicate Sensations as their Superiors', and admired the informality with which he saw them treated in France.[26] In this respect as in others the competing requirements of egalitarian rhetoric and domestic government placed enlightened masters in a perplexing dilemma.

The essential unity of the experience of propertied life was reinforced rather than weakened by some of the inconsistencies which contemporaries thought they observed. It was easy to point to extremes which seemed to indicate the contradictions involved. Gentility without money was embarrassing to all parties. The third Duke of Dorset earned sympathy because he inherited the title but not the estates of his ancestors and could not afford to keep up the great house of Knole.[27] The fallen squire of Moseley Hall, reduced to labouring on a turnpike, and sued for debt in a common court of requests, was pitied rather than despised by the *nouveaux riches* of Birmingham.[28] The poet Richard Savage, who believed himself to be the heir to an earldom, made a beggarly profession of his status. But even he, at his trial for a killing committed during a drunken brawl, had to endure the taunts of the judge, who played on the contrast between his poverty and his standing as a 'gentleman' in addresses to 'gentlemen of the jury'.[29] Money without gentility was a commoner butt of humour, but few doubted that possession of it would soon render the possessor polite. The very uncertainty of origins made it easy for polite society to coalesce

[25] *The Inspector* (2 vols., London, 1753), ii. 62.

[26] J. Armstrong, *A Short Ramble through some Parts of France and Italy by Lancelot Temple* (London, 1771), pp. 94–5.

[27] *Passages from the Diaries of Mrs Philip Lybbe Powys*, p. 149.

[28] W. Hutton, *Courts of Requests* (Birmingham, 1787), pp. 377–82.

[29] C. Tracy, *The Artificial Bastard: A Biography of Richard Savage* (Toronto, 1953), pp. 86–7.

into a largely consistent mass. How, otherwise, could a relatively well-born traveller confuse East Anglian graziers at Stanstead with gentlemen from London?[30] Much interest was displayed in the ease with which it was possible to turn the vulgar into the polite, particularly where the language and letters of politeness were available. Plebeian poets were almost commonplace, from Stephen Duck, the thresher poet who acquired the highest patronage of all, that of Queen Caroline, through James Woodhouse, the shoemaker poet commended by Shenstone and Johnson, to Simon Hedges, the labourer poet, who attracted the attention of the Earl of Chatham. In the case of Robert Dodsley, who began his rise to fame at the level of footman, the result was remarkable literary and commercial success. But the process had its dangers. The poetess Anne Candler, for all the interest which she inspired, was condemned to spend much of her life in a Suffolk workhouse, thanks to a wastrel husband. Her talents and taste merely alienated her from the class to which she belonged. 'Uncultivated, void of sense, Unsocial, insincere, Their rude behaviour gives offence, Their language wounds the ear.'[31] Such was the penalty of politeness for those who could not afford the price of admission to polite society. In the last analysis the middle class which benefited so markedly by the economic changes of the eighteenth century was a class defined by material possessions.

[30] *The Cumberland Letters*, p. 59.
[31] J. Todd, ed., *A Dictionary of British and American Women Writers, 1660–1800* (London, 1984), p. 73.

CHAPTER 4

Industry and Idleness

SOCIAL *problems, the subject of some cynical Augustan satire, were treated in an increasingly serious and didactic manner in the literature of the 1740s. Practically, too, there were new initiatives. Characteristic expressions of early eighteenth-century benevolence, the societies for the reformation of manners and the charity school movement, were less favoured under George II. Institutional charity was concentrated on the rapid expansion of hospitals, in the provinces as well as in London, and on philanthropic experiments in the grand manner, notably the Foundling Hospital and the Magdalen House. This concern with curing disease and saving lives had much to do with the high mortality rates recorded in the second quarter of the century. It was accompanied by acute anxiety about the indiscipline and immorality of the lower classes, supposedly evidenced by the popular taste for gin and the rising level of crime. The emphasis was on heightening the deterrent force of the criminal law rather than reappraising the causes of criminality. A similar inflexibility governed attitudes towards the poor. With real wages at a relatively high level, poverty was attributed to temporary misfortune or culpable fecklessness. 'Luxury' and its demoralizing consequences were also blamed for the economic ills of the day. Yet in retrospect it is possible to discern growth and innovation even where contemporary pessimism was most marked, in agriculture and the textile industry. Within a framework of continuing mercantilism, overseas trade and colonial development were displaying new features, the full significance of which became clear only in the 1750s and 1760s. Though tradition sanctified the old machinery of economic regulation, commercial competition was bringing it to breaking point long before the ideology of free trade removed its theoretical* raison d'être.

MORAL INSTRUCTION

THE most enduring images of early Hanoverian society are those etched on the mind of posterity by William Hogarth. Hogarth offered a break with traditional techniques and also with traditional themes—what he himself called a 'new way of proceeding, viz painting and Engraving modern moral Subject a field unbroke up in any Country or any age'.[1] The twin series of prints which constituted his first manifesto in this cause and also made his fortune as a commercial artist came within the space of two years, *A Harlot's Progress* in 1732, *A Rake's Progress* in 1733. The climax of his campaign, and despite much later work probably his greatest triumph, *Marriage à la Mode*, appeared later, in 1745. These complex narrative compositions represent not only Hogarth's own artistic vision but some of the central preoccupations of the early part of George II's reign. They focused on high life, its vanities, fripperies, and frivolities; also its ultimate futility, degradation, and cynicism. The same targets can readily be identified in other classics of the day, in Gay's *Beggar's Opera*, in Pope's *Dunciad*, and in Bolingbroke's *Craftsman*. They helped define a hostile world in which city, court, and commerce had come together to destroy the moral foundations of the governing order.

In Hogarth the sheer inevitability of the process of corruption appeared more starkly than elsewhere. It was not only the governed who were paraded as helpless captives of their plight rather than as free moral agents. The same was true of most of Hogarth's individuals, whatever their class. The rake was as much a victim as the harlot, though his origins were gentle as hers emphatically were not. Even the unlovable Viscount Squanderfield in *Marriage à la Mode* was easily viewed as the pawn in a cynical game dominated by dynastic arrogance and commercial avarice. There were, admittedly, real villains in Hogarth's world. The very first plate of *A Harlot's Progress* included two, the rapist Colonel Charteris and Mother Needham, a notorious procuress who had died after being exposed in the pillory in 1731. Yet even they were merely the most complete examples of the vulnerability of modern man to the corrosive nature of commercial society. In such satire little by way of practical prescription for amelioration was offered.

[1] *Autobiographical Notes*, printed in J. Burke, ed., *William Hogarth: The Analysis of Beauty* (Oxford, 1955), p. 216.

In this there was an element of politics. The old Tory world-view offered a return to traditional, paternalistic values and supposedly pre-commercial practices. But for Whigs (and Hogarth was such, in so far as he was anything) it was not clear that this was an attractive alternative, even if it could be shown to be a realistic one. Hogarth had no desire to spoil his market by making his satire too pointed. Nor did he have any very constructive view to offer. The public were left to deplore, and to buy.

This relative abstinence from moral didacticism did not persist very long. Even in the 1730s it was not true of all critics of the existing order, and by the 1740s it was coming to seem unnecessary, even objectionable. The sequel to Walpole's fall made it clear that the social and cultural revolution (or rather reaction) which had been expected to follow the passing of the Robinocracy was as remote as ever. War, rebellion, and commercial crisis shifted attention away from the preoccupations of the 1730s. The generation of Pope, Swift, and Bolingbroke, men approaching the end of their lives, seemed increasingly out of touch with contemporary problems. The ethical solutions of the 1740s were unsophisticated, perhaps sloppy and sentimental, but there is no doubt of their appeal. Hogarth's own *Industry and Idleness*, published in October 1747, was as explicit an expression of this new concern as any. In twelve plates it told the contrasting stories of two apprentices, Goodchild and Idle. Goodchild made his way, by means of unfaltering industry and integrity, to opulence and power. Idle fell into godlessness and vice. In the final scenes he was appropriately condemned to the gallows by Goodchild, now arrived at the eminence of Lord Mayor of London. Ingenious commentaries notwithstanding, Hogarth seems to have intended no irony.[2] Here was no condemnation of the possessors of property and authority, only a warning to the young apprentice that failure to observe the virtues of sobriety and hard work led inexorably to ruin and premature death.

The lesson was doubtless as ancient as the City of London itself, but circumstances during the Walpole era enhanced its relevance, as the success of George Lillo's *The London Merchant, or the History of George Barnwell* demonstrated. Unveiled in 1731 and frequently staged thereafter, it was one of the earliest domestic

[2] R. Paulson, 'The Simplicity of Hogarth's *Industry and Idleness*', *Journal of English Literary History*, 41 (1974), 291–320; but see *Autobiographical Notes*, p. 225.

tragedies, taking for its theme not, as the prologue put it, 'the fall of nations or some hero's fate', but a 'tale of private woe' in which an ordinary English business family was ruined by an apprentice's criminal passion. Ironically, the theatres in which it was presented were themselves the object of suspicion, which Walpole exploited with his stage licensing legislation in 1737. Fears that the luxury which had infected the upper and middle ranks of society was fast spreading to those below were commonplace. It was not only Hogarth, acute judge of the saleable that he was, who saw in such concern a growing market for moralistic art.

The moral tone of the popular literature of the 1740s is not in doubt where the education of the lower class was concerned. The lessons transmitted through the columns of the *Spectator* thirty years earlier were remembered and reiterated in the favourite works of the day. Richardson's portrayal of plebeian virtue and aristocratic vice made *Pamela* a work of unimpeachable moral credentials. Fielding, however much he poked fun at Richardson's solemnity and Pamela's hypocrisy, declared his attachment to the same cause. His account of the 'great man' Jonathan Wild, thief-taker, racketeer, and master criminal, whose exploits in the under-world it was tempting to compare with Walpole's in the respectable world, was meant to leave his readers in no doubt that 'a man may go to heaven with half the pains which it costs him to purchase hell'.[3] In *Joseph Andrews*, his first serious novel, Fielding took pains to explain his intentions, likening his purpose to that of his friend Hogarth. Art and letters joined in the war on immorality, and never condoned where they appeared to smile. 'The vices to be found here ... are never set forth as the objects of ridicule, but detestation.'[4] The greatest of his comic novels, *Tom Jones*, published seven years after *Joseph Andrews* in 1749, was introduced with similar gravity. 'Practical morality' was always his object, not least with a view to the needs of the young.

Fielding's sister Sarah carried this concern to its logical conclusion with her novel *The Governess* published in 1749. Set somewhat forbiddingly in the schoolroom ('a little female academy'), it was one of the first novels written specifically for children and heavily didactic in tone. The final words of the conclusion

[3] (London, 1966), p. 186.
[4] *Joseph Andrews*, ed. A. R. Humphreys (London, 1962), p. xxii; see M. C. Battestin, *The Moral Basis of Fielding's Art: A Study of Joseph Andrews* (Middletown, Conn., 1959).

were fitting. 'Never did any young Lady leave Mrs. *Teachum*, but that her Parents and Friends were greatly delighted with her Behaviour, as she had made it her chief Study to learn always to pay to her Governors the most exact Obedience, and to exert towards her Companions, all the good Effects of a Mind filled with Benevolence and Love.' The emphasis on order and obedience was characteristic of such works and was not without political implications. The patriotic concerns of the 1730s vanished from sight in much of the literature of the 1740s, especially that designed with the education of the middle and lower orders in view. Typical in this respect was Edward Kimber's popular tale, *The Life and Adventures of Joe Thompson*, published in 1750. Kimber was a Whig, a Dissenter, and son of Isaac Kimber, a Baptist minister and biographer of Oliver Cromwell. But he was not inclined to encourage a spirit of independence, let alone rebellion. The readers of *Joe Thompson* were urged to defer to superiors, to shun those who were 'uneasy' under any form of government, and to 'cover' rather than 'declare' the faults of statesmen.[5]

THE REFORMATION OF MANNERS AND THE CHARITY SCHOOL MOVEMENT

Renewed enthusiasm for moral standards may partly have derived from a sense that the methods by which previous generations had regulated such matters no longer operated effectively. The London Society for the Reformation of Manners, founded in 1691, had vigorously pursued its purpose of mobilizing ordinary citizens in the enforcement of the laws against immorality for nearly fifty years. Prosecutions of offences such as drunkenness, prostitution, gaming, and profanation of the Sabbath, as reported by the Society, diminished sharply during the first decade of George II's reign. The Society's published report of 1738 was its last. There were spasmodic attempts to revive the movement, usually undertaken by the evangelically minded, but not until the 1780s was the national campaign for moral reform resumed.

Various reasons have been offered for the London Society's demise. It was said at the time that the conviction of a prominent member for murder had destroyed its credit.[6] But there were

---

[5] *The Life and Adventures of Joe Thompson*, p. 168.
[6] *Lettres de Monsieur l'Abbé Le Blanc* (2 vols., Amsterdam, 1751), i. 291.

TABLE 2. *Prosecutions by the London Society for the Reformation of Manners*

PROSECUTIONS for lewd and disorderly practises, keeping bawdy and disorderly houses, sabbath breaking, profanity and swearing, drunkenness, keeping common gaming houses, and gaming

1721	2,199	1727	1,363	1733	487
1722	7,251	1728	778	1734	410
1723	2,224	1729	1,226	1735	590
1724	2,449	1730	734	1736	682
1725	2,506	1731	895	1737	478
1726	1,060	1732	528	1738	545

Source: G. V. Portus, *Caritas Anglicana* (London, 1912), appendix v.

plainly broader considerations. Propertied opinion was affected by deistic tendencies in the 1730s: the pious puritanism of the reformers may have fallen victim to the prevailing scepticism. Critics also stressed the inquisitorial nature of reforming activity. The prosecutors acting for the societies were not meant to profit by their activities, but in the public eye they were tarred with the same brush as criminal informers. The rhetoric of liberty was overworked in the last decade of Walpole's power. The debates on the excise crisis, the Gin Act, and the Smuggling Acts dwelled on the threat which ministerial measures represented to the ordinary Englishman pursuing his own devices, often in his home. Reformers could easily be charged under the same heading. As the *Weekly Register* put it in 1731, 'our constitution allows a set of ruffians to break into private companies, and hurry gentlemen before a magistrate, on a bare suspicion of being criminal; or be committed to prison over-night, at discretion, only to be discharg'd in the morning.'[7]

There were also sectarian implications. From the inception of the Society for the Reformation of Manners, High Church clergy had doubted the wisdom of encouraging laymen to take a lead in what had traditionally been the special responsibility of the clergy and the church courts. 'Lay-Eldership and Fanatacism', the famous Dr Sacheverell had called it.[8] But there were matching suspicions on the other side. Clerical authority was detested by Dissenters,

[7] *Gentleman's Magazine*, 1731, p. 61.
[8] T. Isaacs, 'The Anglican Hierarchy and the Reformation of Manners, 1688–1738', *Journal of Ecclesiastical History*, 33 (1982), 401.

and even lay supporters of the established Church might consider that the work of reformation was best not left to its ministers. Significantly, the bill proposed in 1733 to amend the procedures of ecclesiastical courts was meant to make it harder for private informers to enter suits against laymen. Bishop Gibson's championship of the judicial rights of the Church did much to assist the scaremongers.[9] What was at issue, of course, was not the need to enforce the laws against immorality. Rather it was a question of the appropriate machinery for doing so. The Parliaments of George II were to become notorious by their enthusiasm for extending the powers of the ordinary magistrate. Perhaps the reforming societies were victims of their determination to keep control of the judicial process firmly in the hands of the propertied gentlemen who controlled the county benches just as they dominated the House of Commons.

This was not the only respect in which zeal for social reform seemed to have faltered. Early eighteenth-century philanthropists had prided themselves on the expansion of godly education. How many of the charity schools were genuinely new, and how many merely continued or replaced existing ones, it is difficult to know. What is not in doubt is that the principle of subscribing to schools for the poor, schools supervised not by parochial or by ecclesiastical authorities but by governors responsible to the subscribers, was popular. It was co-ordinated by a well-publicized national campaign in collaboration with the Society for Promoting Christian Knowledge. By the 1730s this campaign was losing momentum. The annual festivals of the London Charity Schools continued, with support from the SPCK, but there was no boasting of new foundations. The total of 1,329 provincial schools recorded in 1723 appeared implausibly unchanged in the printed reports of succeeding years. In London itself, of the 150 or so schools listed in 1760, only nine had been founded under George II, almost all of them in the populous and impoverished parishes south of the river.[10]

The evidence of individual establishments also suggests

---

[9] See p. 41.

[10] They are listed in the accounts published by the SPCK with the annual sermons on behalf of the London Charity Schools. It should be said that in 1753 one authority claimed a general increase in the number of charity schools since 1735, but offered no supporting evidence; see Thomas Alcock, *Remarks on Two Bills for the Better Maintenance of the Poor, etc.* (London, 1953), p. 5.

FIG. 1. Charity schools by county, 1724

Source: M. G. Jones. *The Charity School Movement* (Cambridge, 1938), pp. 364–71

declining interest. A systematic study of Kent has subscriptions falling off in the 1720s and not reviving until the 1770s.[11] Some charity schools, like that established at Southampton in 1713, lapsed altogether, and had to be refounded in the next age of expansion under George III.[12] Some were forced to contract their operations. At Stamford the withdrawal of subscribers compelled the trustees to lower their educational standards and reduce numbers.[13] At Isleworth there had been nearly thirty subscribers in 1715, but there were only seven by 1726. Subscription was accordingly abandoned and the school came to depend on a combination of charity sermons and personal bequests.[14] But dying subscribers were not necessarily more reliable than living ones. In the growing parishes of St Giles in the Fields and St George's, Bloomsbury, the flow of benefactions kept going into the 1730s but diminished in the following decade and almost dried up altogether in the 1750s.[15] Success in this less promising climate depended very much on local circumstances. Liverpool's Blue-Coat School, founded, like that at Southampton, under Queen Anne, did not wither under the Hanoverians. Its treasurer for forty-one years was the redoubtable Bryan Blundell, who turned from shipmaster to educator and philanthropist. Blundell's own account makes it plain that a school which had begun by subscription grew as the result of individual endowments, not least his own. He regarded it as a kind of living family trust. 'I may truly say, whilst I have been doing for the children of this school, the good providence of God hath been doing for mine, so that I hope they will be benefactors to this charity when I am in the grave.'[16] He was duly succeeded as treasurer by two of his sons in turn and the school continued to expand.

The charity schools had never been free of controversy, even in the days of their prosperity. In the early years of George I's reign, when party antagonisms were at their most bitter, it was alleged that they were nurseries of High Church principles, even of treason.

---

[11] R. Hume, 'Educational Provision for the Kentish Poor, 1660–1811: Fluctuations and Trends', *Southern History*, 4 (1982), 133–4.

[12] *The Southampton Guide* (2nd edn., Southampton, 1775), p. 16.

[13] *The New State of the Charity-School at Stamford in the County of Lincoln* (n.d.).

[14] R. Hyam, *A History of Isleworth Grammar School* (Isleworth, 1969), p. 11.

[15] *A Short State of the Charity Schools of St Giles in the Fields, and St George, Bloomsbury* (London, 1795).

[16] *Some Account of the Life and Writings of Mrs. Trimmer* (2nd edn., 2 vols., London, 1816), ii. 319.

Bernard Mandeville, notorious for his argument that luxury was the inevitable, desirable accompaniment of economic growth and social progress, had also aroused controversy with his *Essay on Charity and Charity Schools* in 1723. But it was not necessary to have read Mandeville to believe that poor children were being educated beyond their needs and above their station. On this view it was positively mischievous to encourage children to compete for skilled jobs and better by far to teach contentment with the manual work for which Providence had intended them.

The charity schools were accustomed to defending themselves against such charges. Teachers concentrated on the most basic accomplishments, which were unlikely to provide a ladder to potentially threatening learning; they also stressed the cultivation of sound religions and moral principles, including submission to political authority and social deference. Not only were pupils instructed in good working habits and the elementary techniques appropriate to their class, they were capable of earning their keep and serving local tradesmen. The schoolroom as a form of inexpensive, even profitable poor relief, was a familiar concept in the early eighteenth century, as it was to be again during the industrial expansion of the late eighteenth century. The Poor Law Act of 1723, which provided for the establishment of local workhouses, may have facilitated the supersession of the true 'catechizing' school by something rather resembling a juvenile workshop.[17] But it was probably demographic and economic change which took the edge off controversy and blunted the vigour of the educational campaigners. Minimal population growth, higher living standards, and signs of a labour shortage in the 1730s and 1740s lessened the contemporary fear of a crisis caused by too many children and too few schools, and made it seem unnecessary to establish new foundations on any scale. Significantly, where there was still clearly room for expansion it tended to take place. The daily charity school had never been notably successful in rural Wales, for instance. A paucity of teachers and a scattered population required a different formula. It was found in the late 1730s when religious revival and Griffith Jones's celebrated system of 'circulating schools' provided both the stimulus to action and the means of executing it.

[17] M. G. Jones, *The Charity School Movement: A Study of Eighteenth-Century Puritanism in Action* (Cambridge, 1938), pp. 92–3.

THE HOSPITAL MOVEMENT

The decline of some of the most vital causes of the early eighteenth century did not betoken any lack of interest in good works. Rather the changed concerns of George II's reign reflected particular social needs and vested interests. A notable feature of the age was its enthusiasm for the establishment of new hospitals, for the most part providing free treatment for poor patients. The impulse came predictably from the capital, though the most striking example of metropolitan zeal in this respect was not the most typical. Thomas Guy, a Dissenter who had made a fortune in the book trade, and increased it by a well-timed investment in the South Sea Company, was a benefactor in the grand manner of the great Tudor and Stuart philanthropists. When he died in 1724, his bequests were numerous and diverse: they included almshouses for his native but ungrateful town of Tamworth, where he had been rejected as a parliamentary candidate, a fund for the relief of poor debtors, and legacies to every living relative, even children of cousins to the third generation. But as an active Governor of St Thomas's, his favourite scheme was a new hospital. Guy's was chartered by an Act of Parliament in 1725, and was admitting nearly two thousand patients per annum within the decade. Its founder's memorial in St Thomas's Church, Southwark, was executed later, in 1780, by John Bacon, appropriately a self-made man of Southwark birth. It not unfairly claimed that 'after administering with extensive bounty to the claims of consanguinity, he ... rivalled the endowment of kings'.[18]

Individual exploits of this kind were uncommon. The other general hospitals instituted in London at about this time, the Westminster in 1720, St George's in 1733, the London in 1740, the Middlesex in 1745, were joint enterprises, sustained by that most characteristic eighteenth-century device, the subscription. They customarily derived between a half and two-thirds of their income from such contributions.[19] As an example of what a distinguished medical writer, Thomas Percival of Manchester, called 'the polity of hospitals', the London Hospital, founded in 1740

[18] S. Wilks and G. T. Bettany, *A Biographical History of Guy's Hospital* (London, 1892), p. 61.

[19] D. Owen, *English Philanthropy, 1660–1960* (Cambridge, Mass., 1965), p. 48.

but only so named in 1747, may stand for all.[20] Its principal promoter was its first surgeon John Harrison, whose master-stroke was to get a prominent Whig courtier, the Duke of Richmond, to become the first president. From 1759 it had a purpose-built home, resembling 'a denuded brick-built country house stranded in town'.[21] It was governed by committee, funded by subscription, and served by physicians and surgeons elected by the subscribers. The lives of the inmates were closely regulated and their welfare safeguarded by visitors, whose duty it was to search out uncleanliness, mismanagement, and abuses of every kind. Patients received the assistance of the Church, by means of an established chaplaincy, and were made well aware of their good fortune. Those who were discharged cured, or at least alive, received a printed notice informing them that 'Thro' the charitable assistance of the Governors of the hospital, you have in your late afflictions, without any expence, been provided with comfortable lodgings and proper advice.'[22] The scale of the London, like the other metropolitan hospitals was considerable. By 1785 it was admitting 7,000 patients a year.[23]

Some provincial hospitals benefited by generous benefactions. But even these depended more on continuing public support. Addenbrooke's, at Cambridge, dated its foundation from a legacy of 1719, but the will was implemented only with the aid of subscribers and an Act of Parliament in 1767. In most cases it was the local nobility, gentry, and clergy, who headed the subscription lists and provided the semi-official backing which was needed to stimulate support on a wider scale. This was not always a painless process. A start on Hereford's infirmary was delayed for twelve years, from 1764 to 1776, owing to inadequate support in a county with limited resources. Thomas Talbot, the clergyman who conducted a persistent campaign on its behalf, castigated the 'noble and Opulent' for not imitating their counterparts elsewhere.[24] Lincolnshire, a county with a largely non-resident ruling class and little real sense of community, had to wait twenty-four years from

[20] *The Works, Literary, Moral, and Medical, of Thomas Percival* (4 vols., London, 1807), ii. 565.

[21] D. Cruickshank, *A Guide to the Georgian Buildings of Britain and Ireland* (London, 1985), p. 159.

[22] E. W. Morris, *A History of the London Hospital* (London, 1910), p. 110.

[23] *Account of the London Hospital* (1785).

[24] *Three Addresses to the County of Hereford* (Hereford, 1774).

the first detailed proposals in 1744 until its hospital was eventually approved. But such tardiness was untypical. Beginning with Bristol in 1735, twelve provincial hospitals were founded by 1760, and a further twelve by 1783.

The Georgian hospital movement is usually discussed in terms of its contribution to the progress of medical science. Contemporaries were well aware that the arguments were not all on one side. In the last quarter of the century the criticism directed at the hygiene and healthiness of prisons was sometimes found applicable to the arrangements in hospitals. So far as the saving of life was concerned their effect is unlikely to have been statistically considerable either in improving or worsening matters. It is arguable that the movement is more interesting for the light that it casts on the requirements of the propertied society which financed it. Hospitals were built on a foundation of bourgeois sentiment mixed with solid self-interest. A spirit of benevolence was naturally encouraged by the clergy. The earliest of the county hospitals, in Hampshire, was inspired by a prebendary of Winchester, the friend of Queen Caroline, Alured Clarke. He went on to play a prominent part as Dean of Exeter in the establishment of an infirmary for Devon in 1741. Gloucester Infirmary had the Bishop as its ex officio president, as Newcastle had the Bishop of Durham as its patron. Most hospitals possessed chapels and chaplaincies; virtually all relied on annual sermons and festivals to top up subscriptions and legacies. The clergy who gave their support stressed familiar arguments: the duty of the rich to care for the poor, the uncertain possession of wealth in a commercial society, the political prudence of ensuring a decent standard of medical care for the industrious poor. The requirements of economic prosperity and social stability combined with divine law to make such care the highest of priorities.

These were arguments which could be applied with suitable adjustments to a wide range of good causes, workhouses, schools, dispensaries, and so on. But fundamentally the hospitals served the interests of the individuals who contributed to them. Subscription carried the right, pro rata, to nominate a quota of patients. It offered families on modest incomes a chance to relieve and patronize the poor. It also provided in some cases for their domestic dependants. The proposed statutes of Lincoln Infirmary sought to outlaw this form of medical insurance, no doubt on the grounds that use of a charity for such purposes amounted to a form of petty corruption

Newcastle
1751

York
1740

Leeds
1767

Hull
1782

Liverpool
1745

Manchester
1752

Chester
1755

Lincoln
1769

Nottingham
1782

Stafford
1766

Shrewsbury
1745

Leicester
1771

Norwich
1771

Birmingham
1766

Hereford
1776

Worcester
1746

Northampton
1743

Cambridge
1767

Gloucester
1755

Oxford
1770

Bristol
1735

Salisbury
1766

Winchester
1736

Exeter
1741

0   50 miles

FIG. 2. Provincial hospitals founded before 1783

and would restrict the opportunity to treat the most deserving and destitute cases.[25] Self-denying ordinances of this kind were not widely adopted. They would not have helped engender enthusiasm among those for whom charity began at home. A sick servant was almost always an encumbrance, and often a source of infection. In this sense hospitals sprang up as much to serve middle-class households as lower-class slums, though the needs of the latter were plainly greater. Cornwall, for example, lacked a county hospital until 1799. Yet, as the Cornish antiquarian William Pryce pointed out in 1778, there was no great body of workers more exposed to the danger of accident and injury, and more in need of specialized medical care, than the tin miners of the peninsula.[26]

Pryce was a surgeon as well as a historian. In Worcestershire it was another physician with diverse interests who was instrumental in the founding of an infirmary. John Wall was a Fellow of Merton College, Oxford, an enthusiastic amateur painter, publicist of the waters at Malvern, and an early exponent of the use of quinine in malarial cases. At Northampton in 1743, a similar part was played by the recently arrived doctor James Stonhouse. He was not only a respected physician, but a pious one: the Dissenter Philip Doddridge and the evangelical James Hervey gave him strong support. Stonhouse's *Friendly Advice to a Patient*, published in 1748, was purchased in vast quantities for distribution to hospital inmates. In 1787, by which time he was himself in orders and enjoying a different kind of preferment and prestige as a popular preacher, he was able to announce the fifteenth edition of 6,000 copies, and was still enquiring of a friend at Shrewsbury whether it was given out to patients at the hospital there.[27] His task at Northampton had been an easy one. At Leicester in 1766 it took some notably vigorous propaganda in the *Leicester Journal* by one of the town's doctors, William Watts, to get the local campaign for a hospital launched.

The enthusiasm of the medical profession aroused some scepticism. Opponents argued that doctors used infirmaries for experiments on the poorer members of society, or, as it was put at

[25] Printed *Statutes* (Lincoln, 1745).

[26] G. C. B. Davies, *The Early Cornish Evangelicals, 1735–60: A Study of Walker of Truro and Others* (London, 1951), pp. 15–16.

[27] *Letters to a Young Clergyman, from the late Reverend Mr. Job Orton* (2nd edn., 2 vols., Shrewsbury, 1800), ii. 231.

Leicester, for 'trials of skill'.[28] It is difficult to believe that such suspicions were entirely groundless. But the educational function of the infirmaries was even more important than their scientific value. Although most specifically forbade their medical staff to charge fees for their services, they were permitted and expected to have paying pupils of their own in attendance. Hospitals were in effect a source of considerable profit to established physicians and surgeons, and a training school for future generations of doctors. The profession prized the opportunities offered. Considered strictly as an investment, the handsome donation of £32. 6s. which the first surgeon of the Liverpool Infirmary made to its building fund, proved highly profitable; so did the twenty guineas donated by his junior colleague the first apothecary.[29] The eagerness with which elections to medical posts were contested and the votes of subscribers sought, particularly in the large metropolitan institutions, is sufficient testimony to the professional value of a hospital position.

Provincial hospitals concerned themselves with every kind of ailment. In London the middle of the century saw growing interest in more specialized treatment. Initially, wards were set aside for gynaecology and midwifery. Before long there was a call for separate establishments. It was seceders from the Middlesex Hospital, concerned that what they regarded as the most useful branch of that charity was the least attended to, who founded the British Lying-in Hospital in Long Acre, Covent Garden, in 1749.[30] The City of London Lying-in Hospital followed one year later, the General Lying-in Hospital (later Queen Charlotte's) in 1752, the Royal Maternity Hospital in 1757, and the Westminster Lying-in Hospital in 1765. Two smallpox hospitals were founded in 1746, one for those undergoing inoculation, the other for those suffering 'naturally'. The isolation of such patients was as important as their cure. The Lock Hospital for venereal diseases also commenced in 1746. Its patients received moral instruction as well as medical care. The Lock was closely associated with Lady Huntingdon's 'genteel Methodists'. Her preacher Martin Madan was its chaplain for many years until his public advocacy of polygamy in 1780

[28] Printed *State of the Leicester Infirmary* (1773).
[29] G. McLoughlin, *A Short History of the First Liverpool Infirmary, 1749–1824* (London, 1978), pp. 14, 38.
[30] Printed accounts of Lying-in Hospital for Married Women, 1749–51.

compelled him to resign; for a time his assistant was the equally well-known Thomas Haweis, a prominent evangelical who was to be distinguished by Lady Huntingdon as an executor of her will. Another foundation with more than medical implications was St Luke's Hospital for the insane, founded in 1751. It was established partly because the waiting lists for admission to the Bethlehem Hospital were so long, partly because the Bethlehem's constitution did not allow subscribers to share in its government.[31] There was also polite distress at the practice which permitted public viewing of the inmates of 'Bedlam', as the governors of the Bethlehem themselves recognized when they finally stopped it in 1770, at considerable financial loss to the foundation.

St Luke's represented a form of specialization which offered possibilities outside London. 'Mad-doctoring' was a growing and lucrative profession. Its most successful practitioner William Battie, for many years physician at St Luke's and a prominent writer on mental illness, made one of the largest of all eighteenth-century medical fortunes by it. His was a controversial branch of medicine. Mental illness had a special fascination for the literate and propertied public. Growing numbers of people had the opulence and leisure to indulge a preoccupation with their own mental state. Literary fashions which seemed positively to encourage a state of melancholy (the 'graveyard school' in the 1750s, the cult of 'feeling' in the 1760s, the vogue for 'sensibility' in the 1770s) were charged with engendering hypochondria and hysteria.

Private establishments catering for the insane caused some disquiet. It was believed that they were often prisons by another name. Smollett painted what was plainly not meant to be a fictional picture of such institutions, attended by physicians ready to diagnose 'weakness of the nerves', and containing 'fathers kidnapped by their children, wives confined by their husbands, gentlemen of fortune sequestered by their relations, and innocent persons immured by the malice of their adversaries'.[32] The press reported court cases arising from illegal imprisonment of this kind and in 1774 Parliament was brought to regulate private madhouses, after consulting Battie as the most eminent member of his profession. The legislation did not put a stop to complaints.

[31] *Reasons ... St. Luke's Hospital* (London, 1763).
[32] *The Life and Adventures of Sir Launcelot Greaves*, ed. D. Evans (London, 1973), pp. 187–8.

An alternative solution seemed to be at hand in the form of public hospitals. Three northern cities equipped themselves with lunatic asylums, Newcastle in 1763, Manchester in 1766, York in 1777. These were not merely designed, like other provincial infirmaries, for the poor. Propertied families took quite a different view of mental disease from other illnesses. They did not expect to send sufferers of their own class to general hospitals; they might well, however, wish to incarcerate an insane relation in a public asylum, if comfort and care at the right level were available. But combining public and private facilities in the same institution proved a difficult art. At Newcastle the official physician of St Luke's House, John Hall, found himself involved in a series of controversies about his private patients.[33] York similarly got into a muddle over its fee-paying policies, intricately designed for the needs of different classes of patients though they were.[34] This was not the only respect in which hopes were disappointed. These institutions were founded at a time when it was hoped that enlightened treatment and the latest techniques would prove unprecedentedly humane and effective. Experience did not sustain expectation. The realistic medical course, like the social priority which lay behind the foundation of new madhouses, was custody rather than cure.

The story of the hospitals as told by contemporaries was not one of uninterrupted success. They were expensive to maintain, cumbersome to administer. They were also vulnerable to the winds of economic change and the whim of the subscribing public. Population growth and the associated social problems of the second half of the century suggested the need for less elaborate solutions. Hence the interest in what amounted to out-patient treatment. A succession of charities, beginning in 1757, provided for the delivery of pregnant women in their own homes; the dispensary movement, making cheap remedies available to the poor, commenced in 1769 and rapidly expanded; inoculation societies and even rupture treatment societies were not far behind. But in the 1740s and 1750s the emphasis was on bricks and mortar, charters and statutes.

---

[33] P. M. Horsley, *Eighteenth-Century Newcastle* (Newcastle, 1971), p. 126.

[34] *Sotheran's York Guide* (1796); see also A. Digby, 'Changes in the Asylum: The Case of York, 1777–1815', *Ec. Hist. Rev.*, 2nd ser., 36 (1983), 218–39.

THE FOUNDLING AND THE MAGDALEN

The ventures of this age which most completely caught the contemporary imagination were the Magdalen House and the Foundling Hospital. The Foundling was the brain-child of the eccentric seaman Captain Thomas Coram, who made the plight of London's infant population his peculiar concern until the equally eccentric merchant Jonas Hanway took over from him. Coram was not a Thomas Guy. In old age he had himself to be supported by a public subscription and he died in debt. Nor was he easy to work with. As a vigorous Georgia Trustee he had already quarrelled bitterly with his colleagues; in due course he was to do the same with the governors of the Foundling Hospital. But his importance in paving the way for the new charity is not in doubt. His arguments were rooted in an admitted public scandal, the vulnerability of poor children to murder, exposure, and desertion by parents, and in effect by the parochial authorities whose duty it was to care for orphans. At a time when sentimental interest in children and childhood was growing, the evidence was much attended to, not least by women with charitable inclinations. Coram's success in obtaining a Ladies' Petition, signed by leading figures at court, was thought to have been crucial in securing the patronage of government.

The hospital was chartered in 1739 and its foundation-stone laid on a site in open fields beyond the northern boundary of Holborn in 1742. It quickly became one of the great sights of London. Handel composed an anthem specially for it ('Blessed are they that consider the poor'), was made a governor, and conducted a succession of benefit performances of the *Messiah* to the great profit of the foundlings. Hogarth was also a governor and a benefactor; he began the picture 'hangings' which made the hospital in effect a gallery of contemporary art, and enlisted the aid of some of the most distinguished artists of the day, Francis Hayman, Joseph Highmore, and the sculptor Michael Rysbrack. During its first years the new foundation was held up as the very embodiment of a humane and civilized society. The public was encouraged to identify with its beneficiaries. Children admitted were named after subscribers, or in desperation after well-known figures of romance and history—Clarissa, Tom Jones, William Shakespeare. Happily, the thirty-eighth child admitted, named Thomas Coram, proved a credit to his benefactor, and in later life was to be seen visiting the hospital in a carriage which plainly indicated his worldly success.[35]

The actual record of the hospital hardly matched its propaganda. In its first year of operations, though admittedly in temporary accommodation at Hatton Garden, 56 of 136 admitted died within its walls.[36] These were children in many cases too sick to be sent into the country for nursing (the normal procedure for babies left at the hospital), and the record of parish workhouses was certainly far worse. Even so, keeping infant mortality within defensible bounds proved a difficult task. Funds never matched the ambitions of the governors. Parliament provided financial aid but only on condition that the doors were opened to all. While this policy prevailed between 1756 and 1760, the result was a completely unmanageable flow of abandoned and orphaned children, many of them from the provinces. In 1760 the experiment had to be abandoned: parliamentary grants diminished and ceased altogether in 1770. Thereafter the hospital was again a private establishment, relying on voluntary subscription, and increasingly on shrewd exploitation of the building value of its London estate.

The prostitutes of the capital were as visible in their misery and degradation as its infant children, though it is not entirely clear why they should have aroused particular concern in the 1750s. At the outset of the Seven Years War moral outrage seems to have come into fashion again. John Brown's *Estimate of the Manners of the Times*, a sustained attack on luxury, commerce, effeminacy, and immorality, enjoyed extraordinary popularity. There was also a prevailing impression that prostitutes were not only more numerous (a difficult proposition to prove), but more prominent, more shameless, more obviously a threat to public decency. Saunders Welch, an active Westminster magistrate who campaigned for 'reformation', reckoned in 1758 that matters had grown much worse in recent years. Prostitutes of 'higher rank' had begun parading the Strand and Fleet Street as early as noon each day, making it impossible for modest women to walk the streets: at least a hundred women were to be found between Temple Bar and Charing Cross, either exposing themselves in windows and doors,

---

[35] R. K. McClure, *Coram's Children: The London Foundling Hospital in the Eighteenth Century* (New Haven, 1981), pp. 240–1.

[36] B. Rodgers, *Cloak of Charity: Studies in Eighteenth-Century Philanthropy* (London, 1949), p. 28.

or openly accosting men in the street.[37] John Cleland's acquaintance with the problem was less official but probably more intimate. His description of the Strand girls 'on a Cruize in the Streets or posted at the Doors', often in tawdry clothes likely to lure apprentices and country bumpkins, and his accounts of those 'common bagnios, whose doors are kept open, day and night, for the hospitable entertainment of distressed couples' suggests the same essential lack of concealment recorded by Welch.[38]

The foundation of the Magdalen House for repentant prostitutes in 1758 offered compassion and practical help in place of contempt and prosecution. Its principal proposer was a wealthy merchant, Robert Dingley, who had links with other reformers—Welch, Jonas Hanway, Henry Fielding. A number of businessmen involved in trade with Eastern Europe shared his interest, including representatives of a family, the Thorntons, which in time came almost to define the evangelical ideal of the philanthropic laity. The Magdalen was part of a larger plan. A laundry and a carpet manufactory were suggested as self-supporting forms of honest industry for women who had resolved to change their ways. The Female Orphan Asylum founded at Lambeth in the same year as the Magdalen, was meant, as its enthusiastic supporter Henry Fielding expressed it, to serve as a 'Preservatory', complementing the Magdalen in its role as a 'Reformatory'. Like the Lock, the Magdalen was the object of much interest on the part of the 'polite' classes. William Dodd's sentimental sermonizing made his tenure of its pulpit the foundation of a promising clerical career before he was drawn into the riskier ventures of bribery and forgery.[39]

What practical effect the Magdalen had was debatable. The report of 1761, after two and a half years, boasted of sending 68 reformed whores into domestic service 'with credit', and restoring 25 to their family or friends. But it also had to admit that another 60 had left less satisfactorily, of whom 41 were dismissed for 'want of temper', 10 were 'uneasy under confinement', and 9 did not return from hospital.[40] On the other hand, the Magdalen was not

[37] *A Proposal To render effectual a Plan, To remove the Nuisance of Common Prostitutes from the Streets of the Metropolis* (London, 1758), p. 17.

[38] *The Case of the Unfortunate Bosavern Penlez* (London, 1749), p. 12; *The Surprises of Love* (2nd edn., London, 1765), p. 88.

[39] See p. 491.

[40] *An Account of the Rise, Progress, and present State of the Magdalen Charity* [1761], pp. 7–8.

a nine day's wonder. Queen Charlotte consented to bestow her royal patronage on it in 1765, and in its first thirty-five years of existence some three thousand women were taken in. None the less it suffered much criticism in the late eighteenth century, in the same way as other monuments to the ambitious earnestness of the mid-century. One satirist of 1781 foresaw economic ruin in the mentality which had produced the Magdalen. A future traveller to the London of 1899, he predicted, would find that the exchange itself had become a college for repentant prostitutes. He pictured what was plainly an existing institution: 'every apartment has its weeping inhabitants in public, who laugh in private, to think what fools people must be to give up their money to support it.'[41] The Foundling Hospital came in for similar criticism, including the charge that it encouraged people to rely on public charity rather than their own endeavours.[42]

PATRIOTISM AND POPULATION

Almost every charitable impulse had more than a tinge of patriotic ardour. One of the arguments which united otherwise diverse enterprises was the need to increase the nation's manpower at a time of growing international insecurity. The enormous disparity between French and British resources in this respect and the fact that in the 1730s France ceased to be an ally made this concern one of growing urgency in the 1740s and 1750s. Hence the anxiety of the benevolent to emphasize the national advantages which their projects promised. Hospitals, for instance, preserved labouring lives of real value—they were not meant to be refuges for vagabonds and sturdy beggars. The Foundling Hospital stanched the nation's loss of blood at its critical point, the fearful waste of infants who in time would themselves produce children if preserved long enough to do so. Even the Magdalen and the Lock helped diminish the damage done to childbearing capacity by venereal disease. Welch calculated that of the 3,000 prostitutes who inhabited the Bills of Mortality, 2,500 had been rendered barren by their pro-

---

[41] *Anticipation, or the Voyage of an American to England, In the Year 1899* (London, 1781), p. 25.

[42] James Stuart, *Critical Observations on the Buildings and Improvements of London* (London, 1771), p. 45.

fession. 'Those who understand political arithmetic, must allow this to be no less a national than a moral evil'.[43]

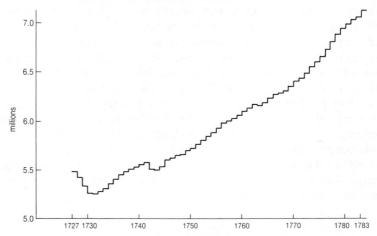

FIG. 3. Estimated annual population of England, 1727–1783

Source: see note 44.

The obsession with manpower (and womanpower) must be viewed in the context of very high mortality rates. The accession of George II coincided with a crisis which in effect removed the entire population gain since the Restoration. The quinquennium 1726–31 reveals the biggest loss of any since 1561. Another major set-back occurred in 1741–2. In effect natural population growth was stunted by natural disasters. The best estimates suggest a total population for England in 1727 of just short of 5.5 million; in 1745 it had risen by barely 150,000. Only thereafter was the upward trend firmly resumed. The figure of 6 million was achieved for the first time in 1757 or thereabouts.[44]

The impact of mortality can only be fully appreciated by means of statistics less grand but in a local context more telling. In Gloucester the decade beginning 1700 had produced a small surplus of 24 births over burials. Between 1710 and 1720 it suffered a net reduction of 19. In the 1720s it experienced a major loss of 448, and in the 1730s of 82.[45] This was not an urban phenomenon.

[43] *A Proposal*, p. 13.
[44] E. A. Wrigley and R. S. Schofield, *The Population History of England, 1541–1871* (London, 1981), pp. 333, 335, and appendix 3.
[45] P. J. C. Ripley, 'The City of Gloucester, 1660–1740', M.Litt. thesis (Bristol, 1978).

In the Bromsgrove area of Worcestershire burials also exceeded baptisms in the fatal period 1725–30.[46] In rural Anglesey the diarist William Bulkeley almost casually explained the reduced numbers of Easter communicants at Llanfechell in 1734: during the previous seven years 'a great Mortality destroyed almost half the parish'.[47] In the case of London the 'Bills of Mortality' offered statistical confirmation of common observation. The Quaker doctor John Rutty, who made a study of such matters, noticed that the monthly total in November 1729 was the highest since 1665, and that the figures for the end of 1732 were the worst for seventy years. The underlying causes were far from clear. Fears that a recurrence of the Plague in Marseilles in the early 1720s would be brought to England via the trade routes proved groundless. Though smallpox was a major concern, some of the epidemics were in the nature of influenza infections or 'catarrhal fevers' as Rutty called them. In Dublin, where he was able to observe their effect at first hand, 16,281 of the deaths which occurred over a period of thirty-one years were due to 'fevers' compared with 13,751 due to smallpox.[48] Disease, in any case, was not the only consideration. There is some evidence that the worst period of all, in the late 1720s, was made much graver by a sudden subsistence crisis. In 1728–9 wheat had to be imported to cope with home demand: chronic shortages heightened the danger represented by infection for the poorest classes. It was certainly a common observation that they were by far the most vulnerable to the epidemics.[49]

It was not only military and naval resources which were potentially depleted by disease. It was also the nation's labour force. The relatively high real wages of the 1730s and 1740s reflected demographic decline or at least stagnation. The sense of plenty in the midst of death and destruction was accentuated by a series of fortuitously good harvests, which swamped the market for agricultural produce during these years. Cereal prices were generally low. The highest prices prevailed in 1740–1, when climatic

[46] D. E. C. Eversley, 'A Survey of Population in an Area of Worcestershire from 1660 to 1850 on the Basis of Parish Registers', in D. V. Glass and D. E. C. Eversley, eds., *Population in History* (London, 1965), p. 408.

[47] G. N. Evans, *Religion and Politics in Mid-Eighteenth Century Anglesey* (Cardiff, 1953), p. 18.

[48] J. Rutty, *A Chronological History of the Weather and Seasons, And of the Prevailing Diseases in Dublin* (London, 1770), pp. 17, 31, 338–9.

[49] A. Gooder, 'The Population Crisis of 1727–30 in Warwickshire', *Midland History*, I (1971–2), 22.

conditions produced two poor harvests in succession. The resulting food riots and crimes against property considerably jarred the contemporary image of the labouring man's life. Starvation was not readily associated with rural society: the bucolic idyll presented by Thomson in his *Seasons* and less felicitously by the peasant poet Stephen Duck in his *Thresher* assumed the possibility of modest material comfort for a labouring population which enjoyed stable wages and falling prices. Until the economic and demographic change of the second half of the century it was tempting to dwell on the poverty of degradation rather than the poverty of immiseration. Where misery occurred, as it did in the cities, it was blamed not on want but on excess and self-indulgence.

Gin seemed to provide the decisive evidence for this thesis. Consumption of spirits soared in the early years of George II's reign, with effects on the urban poor which were memorably displayed by Hogarth. The devices usually employed by the middle class in a mood of social improvement offered little hope of a solution. Voluntary subscription and committee attendance could hardly curb the popular appetite for alcohol at a time when it was so cheaply available. Parliamentary action was called for. But excises on alcohol were dependable sources of revenue. They also contributed to the Crown's civil list, guaranteed to the King by Parliament at the beginning of the reign. This was not the only powerful interest likely to be affected. The raw material for most of the cheap gin drunk on the streets of London was the inferior 'long malt' which was unsuitable for brewing into beer but ideal for distillation, with or without aniseed, juniper, or other cheaply obtained flavours. At a time when farmers were producing more food than the domestic market could absorb, the demands of the distilling industry were particularly welcome. No legislature in which the landed interest was strongly represented could ignore this consideration.

The first attempt to defy these forces was made in response to lobbying by the Middlesex magistracy in 1729. The Act of that year imposed a duty on British spirits and required retailers to take out a costly £20 licence. It led to the manufacture of a liquor known as 'Parliament brandy' since it was said not to infringe the prohibition in the statute. It also coincided with a period of very low grain prices, which farmers were quick to blame on the contraction of the distillers' demand. In 1733, when excises were the subject of almost universal execration, thanks to Walpole's proposals for the introduction of new duties on wine and tobacco, the Act was repealed. Within three years a more draconian solution was attempted. The Act of 1736 imposed a swingeing duty of twenty shillings per gallon, and raised the retailing licence to £50. It provoked serious rioting, proved virtually unenforceable, and was said to have done more than anything else to discredit the use of informers as prosecutors. This experiment in what amounted to prohibition for the poor (but not, as was pointed out, for the rich), was abandoned after seven years.

Subsequent legislation concentrated on the mode of sale. For four years from 1743 to 1747, and permanently from 1751, the small distillers were prevented from selling by retail. So, from 1751, were chandlers, grocers, and others only incidentally engaged in the spirit trade. It was believed that the sale of spirits by shopkeepers who also supplied the necessities of life to poor families was the cause of much of the problem. If so, the Acts of 1743 and 1751 were crucial. The historian of London's poor credits that of 1751 with a notable reduction in the evils of spirit-drinking and terms it a 'turning-point in the social history of London'.[50] But spirit prices were rising anyway. The age of cheap food was over. In the 1730s and 1740s the price of wheat per quarter averaged less than thirty shillings; in the 1750s it was almost a third higher, at slightly under thirty-eight shillings.[51] The value of barley and malt as a fall-back for cereal producers was reduced by the growing food requirements both of humans and horses. Excise statistics provide striking evidence of the result. Total domestic consumption of spirits fell from 7,886,000 gallons in 1745, to 5,453,000 in 1752, and 3,243,000 in 1758. Practically all the reduction can be accounted for by a fall in the volume of British spirits.[52] The obvious conclusion is that Mother Gin was starved of nourishment by the prohibitive price of malt, rather than smothered by a benevolent and paternalistic Parliament.

---

[50] M. D. George, *London Life in the Eighteenth Century* (London, 1966), p. 49.
[51] T. S. Ashton, *An Economic History of England: The Eighteenth Century* (London, 1955), p. 239.
[52] Public Record Office, CUST. 48.17.

POVERTY

The easing of the gin problem did not eliminate complaints about the fecklessness of the class which principally consumed it. John Clayton's published advice to the poor of Manchester in 1755 savoured more of ferocity than its boasted 'friendliness'. Clayton accused them of idleness, extravagance, and mismanagement. Given six days a week by God for their work they took every opportunity to lessen that number, by unnecessary attendance at weddings and funerals, by taking excessive holidays, or merely by spending their time in the alehouse or tea-shop. The English labouring class was guilty of improvidence and indiscipline. 'We are grown infamous for a general Want of good Manners in our Populace.'[53] Clayton's accusation faithfully represented one of the most characteristic concerns of the reign of George II. It was a common fear that the English labourer was too well paid, too well fed, too well clothed, and altogether too pampered for his own and his country's good. The belief that English wage rates put British manufacturers at a disadvantage compared with their Continental competitors was long-standing. But it gained new force at a time when the cost of living was falling. Complaints that workmen preferred to take their enhanced standard of living in the form of reduced working hours and less industrious habits rather than additional pay were also familiar. They were to continue into the late eighteenth century when circumstances were quite different. In the mean time the relative ease with which an ordinary labourer could provide at least the means of subsistence for himself and his family fuelled such criticism.

Rising real wages were not incompatible with the existence of genuine poverty. During the era of low food costs there was persistent pessimism about groups which did not share in the general prosperity, or which suffered in times of dearth. Although George II's reign produced few initiatives to revise the complicated rules and regulations which had been erected on the simple framework of the Elizabethan Poor Law, a substantial piece of legislation enacted under his predecessor commanded much attention. The statute of 1723 in effect endorsed experiments which had previously taken place only in large towns and by means of local Acts of Parliament. It permitted parishes, either singly or in

[53] *Friendly Advice to the Poor*, p. 35.

collaboration with others, to establish workhouses and withhold relief from applicants who refused to enter them. The workhouse had a variety of functions. It was expected to deter the 'sturdy beggar', who might prefer outdoor relief to an honest day's work, but would surely prefer an honest day's work to an austere institutional regime. It also offered the prospect of housing those who were too young, too old, too infirm, or too witless to cater for themselves. The hope was that this could be done at low cost, or even at a profit. There is no means of knowing how many workhouses were actually established as a result of the Act. When the House of Commons ordered a national survey in 1776, about 2,000 houses, with a capacity in excess of 90,000 were identified.[54] But some of these may have existed before 1723, and not a few must have been erected during the worsening conditions of George III's reign rather than as a response to the original legislation.

One of the main aims of the workhouse movement was to stimulate the profitability of such establishments by entrusting their management to private contractors. The example of Matthew Marryott, who boasted of his success in such an experiment at Olney in Buckinghamshire, was cited at the time, and incidentally induced a number of parishes in the Home Counties to offer him contracts. But the economics of workhouse production were always somewhat speculative, and the common experience suggested that contractors were more likely to make their living by exploiting the poor and defrauding the parish, than by enterprise and commercial skill. The story of Marylebone's misfortunes in this respect could be matched in many other places. The parish had experimented with a poorhouse in 1730, but a permanent building, specially commissioned, was not opened until 1754. Its first Master, appropriately named Francis Parent, was in effect a 'farmer' in the Marryott manner. He received a fixed sum for each of his charges, was expected to provide a proper level of care, including instruction for the children, and kept the profits of their labour (principally spinning). Within a very short time he was accused of drunkenness, misappropriating supplies, and permitting his son to seduce one of the female inmates. His successor was strictly an employee, receiving a salary of £20 a year for carrying out the instructions

---

[54] J. S. Taylor, 'The Unreformed Workhouse, 1776–1834', in E. W. Martin, ed., *Comparative Development in Social Welfare* (London, 1972), p. 61.

of his parish.[55] It is significant that the mode and scope of management rather than the principle of indoor relief were blamed for such failures. Most of those who advocated reform in the middle and later eighteenth century envisaged workhouses on a larger scale, controlled at county or hundred level by committees composed of propertied men, as remote as possible from the petty corruption and incompetence which were frequently associated with vestries, overseers, and contractors. A systematic programme of this kind was never executed but in an urban setting, at least, larger institutions inevitably developed. Marylebone itself acquired a new workhouse in 1776, regulated by a local Act of Parliament and ruled by a rotating committee of substantial citizens. It started with 300 inmates and was built (prudently as it turned out) to house 1,000; its predecessor, now converted to a subsidiary infirmary, had opened with an intake of about 40.

The first systematic student of poor relief history, Sir Frederick Eden, near the end of the century, thought at least that the 1723 Act had succeeded in reducing poor-rates. It is a contestable judgement. Eden admitted that indoor relief was by no means synonymous with low rates.[56] However, since it is difficult to establish firm statistics, proof is unlikely to be forthcoming either way. Information collected for Parliament in 1748–50 suggests annual expenditure on poor relief from the rates of about £700,000. This figure is not completely dependable, and there is nothing to compare it with, beyond the guesses of contemporary commentators. On the whole these imply a degree of stability from the 1720s to the 1750s, as does local evidence.[57] But long-term trends are compatible with sharp short-term variations. This was partly why poor relief levels were a matter of such abiding interest. Perhaps no other tax was so unpredictable. Tithes were levied as a proportion of produce. Taxes laid by Parliament varied little in peacetime. But the poor-rate might rise or fall suddenly in response to harvest, disease, or any number of trivial, local accidents. Small parishes were particularly vulnerable to unexpected eventualities. Even on a national scale, temporary set-backs could be misleading. They provoked jeremiads which need treating cautiously as his-

---

[55] A. R. Neate, *St Marylebone Workhouse and Institution, 1730–1965* (London, 1967), p. 4.

[56] A. G. L. Rogers, ed., *Sir F. M. Eden, The State of the Poor* (London, 1928), pp. 48 ff.

[57] e.g. D. R. Mills, 'The Quality of Life in Melbourn, Cambridgeshire, in the Period 1800–1850', *International Review of Social History*, 23 (1978), 395.

torical evidence. For instance, the controversialist Thomas Carte, writing in 1742, cited unprecedentedly high poor-rates and spoke of 'an universal Face of Poverty upon the common People'.[58] But Carte, as a Jacobite, was bent on proving that the Hanoverian age had brought nothing but disaster. Moreover, the early 1740s were years of unusual cold and hunger. Emergencies of this kind were met with voluntary subscription to purchase food and fuel, a steep increase in outdoor relief, and some ventures into institutional experiment on the lines of the workhouse. But none of the crises of this period lasted long enough to yield permanent changes of policy, let alone any parliamentary legislation which would have altered the basis of a long-established Poor Law.

If the statute-book is considered a reliable guide to contemporary anxieties, it was vagrancy rather than destitution which caused the most concern. Vagrancy was inseparable from the problem of poverty, though the connection was not always accepted at the time. The emphasis was on the nuisance, disorder, and crime to which vagrancy gave rise rather than the unemployment or deprivation which helped produce it. It can hardly be coincidence, however, that the two most important statutes, of 1740 and 1744, dated from a time of dearth aggravated by the disruption of war. These Acts were partly intended to speed the traditional process by which wanderers were returned to their parish of settlement. But they also applied sanctions which included hard labour and transportation as well as the familiar whippings and short spells in a house of correction. Perhaps significantly, it was migrant Irish workers who came in for some of the harshest treatment under these laws. Of real strain on the established system of poor relief there was little sign.

In some parts of the country, indeed, there was nothing which could properly be described as a system. In North Wales neither the rating law nor the law of settlements was observed. In their place an ancient reliance on charity and communal support continued in defiance of English legislation. Not until the 1760s and 1770s was the need to levy rates and appoint overseers of the poor felt. In the mean time, even in England there was little sense of the urgency of reform. Self-appointed experts were not wanting to point out the deficiency of the existing laws, but Parliament remained largely unmoved. In 1751 Sir Richard Lloyd, one of the

[58] *A Full Answer to the Letter from a By-Stander* (London, 1742), p. 177.

few MPs who took a close interest in such matters, was given an opportunity to address the attention of a major Commons Committee to the question. The Committee was set up not to consider poverty, but rather to investigate the post-war crime wave: poverty was added only for the bearing which it was supposed to have on criminality. None of the resulting recommendations bore immediate fruit.

The commonest complaints about the Poor Law concerned its management. Criticism of private contracting was only part of a wider campaign against the whole structure of parochial admin-istration. It was alleged that neither the officers responsible for the execution of the law nor the vestries to which they were account-able acted in the public interest. In urban areas especially, men of property did their best to avoid serving as churchwardens and overseers, leaving such offices to those who saw them primarily as an opportunity to feather their nests. Critics pointed out that many vestries were composed of an illiterate rabble easily manipulated by demagogues. The commonplace eighteenth-century principle that democratic rule meant gross corruption and inefficiency drew not a little of its support from observation of parish government. Typical was a popular tract of 1744 denouncing the social injustice of a system which perverted the intentions of Elizabethan legis-lators. 'In the stead of substantial Householders, according to the real Intention of the Law, you have a continual Succession of mean People in Office, whose Study and Interest it is, to lay the Burthen of their Levies more particularly upon the Lands, although their own numerous Occupations increase the Poor Twenty to one.'[59] Here was a perceived social conflict of the first importance, between the families of real property and the shop-keeping, even artisan class, which in the cities had a considerable share in local govern-ment. There were two obvious solutions. One was to divert import-ant powers to bodies other than the vestries. The tendency of Parliament to give a large measure of both judicial and admin-istrative authority to magistrates, not least in matters of Poor Law administration, derived in part from the belief that parishes were no longer to be trusted with their own affairs. More radical, but more difficult to implement, was the notion of reorganizing parochial administration in favour of 'select vestries' of powerful

---

[59] *A Short View of the Frauds, Abuses, and Impositions of Parish Officers, with some Considerations relating to the Poor* (London, 1744), p. 9.

but respectable oligarchs. The idea was controversial and local Acts of Parliament generally avoided using the term even when they effectively accepted the principle. In the long run, however, it was to be widely adopted, with important consequences for the nineteenth-century debate about the nature of local government.

CRIME

Criminality, like poverty, is never at an acceptable level from the perspective of propertied society. There is no certain means of knowing whether, in the age of Walpole, crime was on the increase, but modern estimates suggest that the overall reduction or at least stabilization of crime levels which appears to have occurred in the late seventeenth century continued until population growth pushed it up in the second half of the eighteenth.[60] This was most clearly the case in rural areas, somewhat less so in urban. Estimates are necessarily based on the evidence of indictments, but if, as seems likely, they reflect the actual incidence of crime and not merely the propensity to prosecute, they fit ill with the common belief of the time that crime was growing beyond control. In the resulting debate politics, though not straightforward party politics, had a way of intruding. Defenders of the Hanoverian regime sometimes shared with their Tory enemies a belief that the general tendency of English society since the Revolution of 1688 had been away from order and in the direction of indiscipline, if not anarchy. These unlikely allies parted company when they considered the remedies offered by governments since 1714. From the standpoint of court Whigs, measures such as the Riot Act, the Black Act, and the Smuggling Acts, were a stern but rational rebuke to manifest lawlessness and treason. To their opponents they were part of the same distempered world, despotic responses to a crisis which would not have arisen but for the rule of Whig despots. Opposition Whigs could in theory reject the premises of both. But not a few of those who opposed Walpole in the 1730s were implicated in the now objectionable policies of the earliest Hanoverian ministers, and still more found it embarrassing to join in Tory anathema against everything that had occurred since the Revolution. The one common view to which all these parties could subscribe was that crime was increasing. It was, none the less, a view which owed

[60] J. M. Beattie, *Crime and the Courts in England, 1660–1800* (Oxford, 1986), Part I.

more to the changing character of crime, and also to the way in which a literate and semi-literate public was made aware of crime, than to any real increase in its incidence.

Public interest in the deeds and misdeeds of criminals seemed limitless. Reports of the Old Bailey Sessions and other courts in the vicinity of London, published for a popular readership, remain one of the best sources for the legal history of the period, notwithstanding their obvious sensationalism. The Newgate Ordinary's lives have passed permanently into the vulgar literary canon of the age. Fascination with the dying and dead, enhanced by the publicity which attended the execution of capital convicts, was fed with numberless dying speeches and penitent lives. As the satirist Sir Herbert Croft pointed out, a convict reprieved from the gallows at the last moment was likely to return to Newgate to find his own dying speech already being hawked about the streets.[61]

The literary interest doubtless reflects exceptional crimes and criminals. Mysteries attracted particular attention. Hence the publicity which attended the case of Eugene Aram, who carried out a callous murder at Knaresborough in 1745 but was convicted only in 1759 after an accomplice had confessed to the crime. Aram was caught as a result of a chance identification in King's Lynn, where he had fled to take up a career in schoolmastering. His learning, his eloquent defence, and the fact that his conviction turned entirely on the suspect evidence of a turncoat gave rise to sympathy before his execution and forensic speculation after it. His career was not forgotten. Andrew Kippis caused controversy by including a life of Aram in the first volume of his *Biographia Britannica* in 1778. The cave in which his victim's bones had been discovered continued to be shown to visitors to Knaresborough well into the nineteenth century and Aram himself was later the subject of one of Bulwer Lytton's forays into historical fiction. A similar mixture of sympathy, scepticism, and enduring mystery was aroused by Elizabeth Channing: her story of kidnap and torture in an Enfield bawdy-house kept newspaper readers enthralled in 1753. The most distinguished victim of her perjury was Henry Fielding, whose gullibility led him to accept her story and join in a public subscription for her relief. When it turned out that one of her brutal assailants had been in Dorset at the time of the alleged offence, Fielding came in for predictable mockery. But what exactly had

[61] *Love and Madness* (London, 1780), p. 107.

happened during the twenty-seven days when Elizabeth Channing disappeared from view continued to be a matter of speculation and public interest.

Some criminals earned a permanent place in the rogues' gallery by their sheer notoriety. Jane Webb, alias Mary Young, alias 'Jenny Diver' after the cant name for a pickpocket and the character in the *Beggar's Opera*, was one such. She ran a bawdy-house until the extortion of 'Civility money for Bridewell men' diverted her attention to pickpocketing, her true *métier*, which was terminated only with her transportation in 1738 and execution three years later. Her story was so popular that it was told in one of the penny histories sold by travelling chapmen; the fact that it included some useful hints about practical self-defence measures against the pickpockets no doubt enhanced its popularity.[62] Real glamour, however, attended only a small band of criminals. Highwaymen enjoyed more than most. Their victims were by and large the relatively well off who could afford to travel on horseback or by coach, and they did not frequently have to resort to violence. Partly for this reason they were viewed quite differently from the footpads for whom physical force and even murder might be necessary to ensure escape and safety. Some highwaymen acquired a reputation for politeness which earned them a degree of romantic interest, especially in retrospect, when their menace was forgotten and travel on dark roads had come to seem dull rather than dangerous. Few of the stories which accumulated about the name of Dick Turpin, executed at York in 1739 after some narrow escapes, had anything of substance about them. What was undeniable was that this branch of crime was potentially lucrative. One Scottish gang boasted that they 'practised in the higher walks of crime; for they observed that more could be made on the highway in one night than by sneaking about the country for twelve months'.[63]

Most crime was committed against men and women of small property, precisely the class which provided a mass readership for the popular press. Even when unusual circumstances or an unhappy human situation drew tears of sympathy from this class it was unlikely to challenge traditional morality or the legal

[62] *Drury Lane in Tears*, n.d.; *Select Trials at the Sessions House in the Old-Bailey* (4 vols., London, 1742), iv. 335–60.

[63] J. Thompson, *A New Improved, and Authentic Life of James Allan, the Celebrated Northumberland Piper* (Newcastle, 1828), p. 447.

status quo. Its superiors were increasingly concerned in the mid-eighteenth century at the way in which some punishments, particularly the ultimate sanction of the gallows, seemed as likely to promote compassion for the victim as a sense of just retribution. But the gross theatricality of public executions and the festival atmosphere which sometimes accompanied them did not necessarily imply popular dissent from the justice of the process. In the last analysis the law depended on relatively humble people—small tradesmen, craftsmen, and artisans—for its implementation: they were both prosecutors and jury. Without their active collaboration the judicial system would never have worked.

Concern at the level of crime as opposed to interest in its more sensational aspects reflected changing circumstances. Such anxiety increased markedly in the years following the War of the Austrian Succession. The peace brought problems which had not been experienced for more than thirty years. Massive demobilization released into civilian society men of an age, disposition, and brutality, so it was said, to commit crime on an unprecedented scale. Parliament sought to ease the process of adjustment by permitting ex-soldiers and sailors to exercise a trade without formal apprenticeship. At a time when the traditional machinery of trade regulation was in any case breaking down, this relaxation of the law made little difference.

More could be done about punishment than prevention. The Commons Committee established under the chairmanship of Sir Richard Lloyd in 1751 made proposals which would significantly have changed the direction of penal policy. It suggested more systematic use of imprisonment and offered a scheme for hard labour in royal dockyards. The notion was not completely novel. In 1737 a writer in *Fog's Weekly Journal* had advocated perpetual hard labour for capital convicts, principally on the grounds that execution was not a harsh enough penalty for serious crime. 'We are condemn'd to death by Nature.'[64] In 1751 the Committee's interest in labour had more to do with the deficiencies of alternative penalties for felons. It was a weakness of the penal system that it provided little between the ultimate punishment of death and the relatively mild sanction of branding or whipping inflicted on many first-time offenders. Prison was used extensively for debtors, and

[64] 23 July 1737.

of course for the detention of those awaiting trial. Also, in the shape of the house of correction, it had a place in the treatment of lesser offences. But major changes in the administration and funding of prisons would have been required to make them viable as the principal form of retribution and deterrent. Instead it was customary to resort to the use of transportation. As authorized by the Act of 1718, deportation to the American colonies had been the previous generation's solution to another post-war crime wave. But it did not commend itself to everyone. Given the compensations of life in the colonies, it seemed less than intimidating. Moreover, illegally returned transportees were thought to be responsible for some of the worst crimes at home. Conviction for a further offence rendered them liable to inevitable execution, a consideration which promoted desperation and ruthlessness. None the less, Parliament, or rather the House of Lords, declined to act on the Lloyd Committee's recommendation. Doubts on the part of the judges and fear of the financial consequences on the part of government militated against it.

Not every proposal was ignored. One of the arguments accepted by the Committee and urged in the press, notably by Henry Fielding in his *Enquiry into the Causes of the Late Increase of Robbers*, was the desirability of enhancing the deterrent effect of capital punishment. By the Murder Act of 1752 a convict's corpse might be permanently hung in chains, or handed over to the surgeons for anatomical dissection. It was supposed that superstitious fear of gibbeting and dissection, and the disgrace which either brought upon the malefactor's family, made such a sentence more terrifying than death itself. Short of extending more unpleasant forms of execution, such as those in theory applied to traitors (hanging, drawing, and quartering) and to women who murdered their husbands (burning) there was little more that Parliament could do in this gruesome department of the law. Judges, however, had considerable power to adapt penal policy to circumstances. A sharp increase in the resort to hanging, by means of less liberal use of the prerogative of pardon and commutation, took place after 1748, as it did later, during the crime waves which followed the Seven Years War and the War of American Independence. It was indeed one of the standard defences of a ferocious but discretionary criminal code that it made possible such flexibility in sentencing policy. The doctrine was to become increasingly controversial in the last quarter of the century, but in the 1750s it remained largely unchallenged.

Capital punishment was not the only aspect of the judicial process to which the authorities addressed themselves. Under English law the detection and prosecution of crime were more a matter of private action than public responsibility. The trouble and expense involved were considerable discouragements to the ordinary citizen. In 1752 Parliament authorized the granting of compensation to those who prosecuted criminals at their own expense, and two years later it agreed to reimburse the costs of poor witnesses. At the same time the Crown was offering unprecedentedly handsome rewards for information leading to the conviction of particularly dangerous or irritating criminals. In the short run this policy secured some notable convictions. But in the long run it exposed alarming legal anomalies. Large rewards offered the criminal fraternity powerful inducements to betray their own number. A well-organized concern could in effect make a double profit by commissioning crimes and then delating those they had employed to execute them. At the very least there was a grave danger of perjury and injustice in evidence procured by such mercenary means.

The most notorious of such cases was that revealed in 1755–6. The four principals tried on this occasion, M'Daniel, Berry, Eagan, and Salmon, were alleged to have received upwards of £1,720 from the Treasury by way of reward for their 'thief-taking'. They were convicted of conspiracy after arousing the suspicions of a resourceful Kentish Chief Constable who had heard them give evidence in a case which ended with the execution of their victim. Justice of a kind was eventually done, though in a bizarre way, as John Rayner, the first historian of the penal legislation of George II's reign, pointed out.[65] This 'hellish' case was, he thought, the worst instance of perjury in a hundred years or more. Yet it could only be prosecuted under the Forgery Act of 1729, resulting in a sentence of seven years' imprisonment and two sessions in the pillory. In the event this proved sufficiently severe. Eagan, exposed at Smithfield, was killed by an enraged mob; Salmon, who suffered with him, was seriously injured by the hail of stones and oyster shells. The two remaining malefactors, having survived the pillory

---

[65] *Readings on Statutes, ... Passed in the Reign of his late Majesty, King George the Second* (London, 1775), pp. 194–203.

once, were excused a reappearance there. With Salmon they died of 'natural' causes in the unhealthy environment of Newgate. The case was not reassuring to those who gave thought to the problems of criminal administration. It arose because the State had unintentionally promoted the commission of crime and even murder; it yielded a sentence which seemed eccentrically light, but which, thanks to the unpredictable brutality of the pillory, ended by being distinctly terrifying.

Crime wave or no, it was reasonable to entertain doubts about the rationality of the means used to combat it. Yet the period is not primarily remembered for the confusion and inconsistency which it engendered in such matters. On the contrary, it offers something of a landmark in the history of criminal prosecution, thanks to the activities of the Fieldings. Henry, appointed to the Westminster magistracy in 1749, and his blind brother John, who joined him in 1751, were to the fore in the campaign to make the capital a law-abiding city. Henry died in 1754, John not until 1780. Between them they made the name Fielding synonymous with peace-keeping for a generation of Londoners. The financial aid which they received from the Crown in effect turned them into salaried officials responsible for the policing of a vast conurbation, though technically their only legal powers were those which they enjoyed as magistrates of Middlesex and Westminster. Their role was not a completely new one. Westminster had long been a special concern of government. It was a great and growing city, yet one which lacked the chartered corporation and elaborate self-governing machinery of London, Bristol, Norwich, or Liverpool. It was the seat of legislature, executive, and judiciary: all three were potentially vulnerable to its undisciplined inhabitants. More than any other place in the British Isles, perhaps the western world, it brought immense wealth into highly unstable proximity to manifest destitution and potential disaffection.

Sir Thomas De Veil, Henry Fielding's predecessor as uncrowned Chief Justice of Westminster during the early years of George II, carried out similar functions. But the Fieldings had a gift for publicizing themselves and their work. Some of their activities, for example their enterprise in founding an employment and general advertising agency, the Universal Register Office, aroused controversy. But the gathering and disseminating of information were crucial: intimate knowledge of the underworld was a large part of their success. More palatable in the eyes of posterity was the seemingly progressive aspect of their system. Their constant availability as magistrates anticipated the establishment of rotation offices and stipendiary justices; equally their systematic use of 'pursuers' and peace officers (later to be known as Bow Street Runners) in the detection and arrest of criminals looked forward to the emergence of a paid police force. Their methods were not necessarily applicable outside the capital, and their contemporary influence can be exaggerated. But their prominent part in the war on crime between 1750 and 1780 is not in doubt.

RECESSION OR RECOVERY?

Most analyses of the causes of crime emphasized the influence of luxury. This diagnosis was quite consistent with a deep-rooted pessimism about commercial prospects. There were two diametrically opposed views about the relationship between luxury and the economy: one, increasingly fashionable in intellectual circles, held that luxury was both the expression and in some sense the cause of economic growth; the other, traditionally more influential, treated luxury as evidence of a congenitally diseased commercial system, which substituted vulgar extravagance for solid worth. Of the two the second was more widely accepted in the 1730s and 1740s. Statistical support for either view is difficult to establish in retrospect. Modern 'macro-economic' calculations necessarily employ crude and unreliable estimates to arrive at disarmingly precise conclusions. They are expressed in annual averages calculated over long periods of time, rendering it difficult to make 'micro-economic' deductions. The most recent of them suggests modest growth between 1700 and 1760, sufficient, indeed, to make the gains of the succeeding period less spectacular than they once appeared to historians of 'industrial take-off' in the late eighteenth century.[66] Other assessments based on the most promising production statistics, the excise collections and the overseas trade figures, also imply growth for much of the period, interspersed by short-lived recessions, the worst of them caused by the French war of 1744–8.[67] The prevailing view at the time was much more

[66] N. F. R. Crafts, *British Economic Growth during the Industrial Revolution* (Oxford, 1985), ch. 2.
[67] T. S. Ashton, *Economic Fluctuations in England, 1700–1800* (Oxford, 1959), ch. 6.

gloomy, mainly because there was disturbing evidence of disruption and decline in two crucial sectors, agriculture and the woollen industry.

At the heart of the concern about agriculture, or husbandry, as contemporaries still preferred to call it, was an understandable preoccupation with the extremely low prices of the period. In retrospect they can be seen as part of a distinct pattern of relatively stable rents and prices which endured throughout the century between the 1650s and 1750s, and which was plainly connected with relative demographic stagnation. But there is no doubt that the first twenty-five years of George II's reign caused peculiar problems in this respect. A series of abundant harvests, interrupted only briefly in 1728 and 1740–1, drove prices far below what most contemporaries could recall. It was easy to suppose that the relative advantage this brought to the urban population in particular and the labouring classes in general was achieved by penalizing others: the landlord, who found himself having to cope with rent arrears, and the tenant farmer, whose livelihood itself was threatened by vanishing markets. The fact that both were expected to raise their standard of living to compete with the way of life enjoyed by professional and business people made their own perception of their plight all the sharper.

Walpole's policy of reducing the tax burden on the landed interest was designed to exploit this discontent, or rather to divert it from his own partial reliance on the offending commercial interests. Paradoxically, the very grimness of conditions in the 1730s made it difficult to transmit this message to the intended beneficiaries. The excise scheme came at a time of intense rural depression and found the ordinary farmer or freeholder more disposed to vent his unthinking rage than grasp the proffered relief. The diarist William Stout noted the contrast in Lancashire between the easy living which labouring people enjoyed, thanks to plentiful provisions, and the severe hardship suffered by poor farmers who were driven by low prices to slaughter their most precious assets, their cattle.[68] Yet, particular seasons, and particular places apart, it is not clear that the agrarian picture was as dark as some painted it. One of the few systematic studies of estate management, based on the records of the Gower family estates, mainly in Staffordshire,

[68] J. D. Marshall, ed., *The Autobiography of William Stout of Lancaster, 1665–1752* (Manchester, 1967), p. 211.

confirms the impression that the early 1730s and mid-1740s were difficult but finds no evidence of a continuing recession. The clearest signs of more sustained depression come from the open field agriculture of the Midland Plain, which was to be revolutionized by the parliamentary enclosure movement after 1760. On the light soils of East Anglia and in the pastoral regions of the west and north-west there were more grounds for optimism.[69]

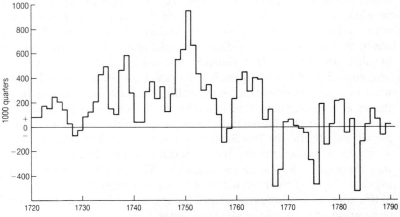

FIG. 4. British imports and exports of wheat (net), 1720–1790

There is evidence of investment in agricultural improvement under George II. Rising prices offer a strong inducement to extend land under cultivation and improve the productivity of existing tillage. But stable prices, accompanied as they were in the 1730s and 1740s by favourable climatic conditions, also provide a spur to reduce the costs of production. Particularly in cereal-growing regions this appears to have been happening. The great opportunity of the period lay overseas. By any standards the rise in grain exports was dramatic. The commentators who anxiously scrutinized customs statistics to estimate the health of the national balance of trade traditionally directed their attention to manufactures. But in the mid-eighteenth century agriculture came to

[69] J. R. Wordie, *Estate Management in Eighteenth-Century England: The Building of the Leveson-Gower Fortune* (London, 1982), pp. 164–74; B. A. Holderness, 'The Agricultural Activities of the Massingberds of South Ormsby Lincolnshire, 1638–c.1750', *Midland History*, 1 (1971–2), 24; J. V. Beckett, 'Regional Variation and the Agricultural Depression, 1730–50', *Ec. Hist. Rev.*, 2nd ser., 35 (1982), 35–51.

play a comparably important part: in the peak year of 1750 it contributed one fifth of all British exports by official values.[70] Perhaps more than at any other time in its history the England of George II was the granary of western Europe. This state of affairs owed something to geographical advantage: the British Isles were well positioned to undercut the price of the cereals traditionally exported from the Baltic region to southern Europe even when they were carried by Dutch merchantmen, famous for their competitive rates. It owed something, also, to the bounties which Parliament offered on grain exports, whether wheat for milling, or barley for malting.

The bounty, established in 1689, had long been seen as compensation for the burdens placed on the landed classes by the Revolution. Certainly under George II a considerable portion of the land tax was returned to its payers in the form of the bounty: appropriately, the regions most highly rated to the land tax, the east and south-east of England, were those which benefited by the continental market for grain. It was in this part of the country, too, that some of the most progressive husbandry was practised. 'Turnip Townshend' no longer receives the credit for agricultural innovation once accorded him; but the widespread adoption of the new techniques which Arthur Young was later to trumpet on behalf of East Anglian farming undoubtedly coincided with Townshend's lifetime. At the time when William Stout was lamenting the plight of Lancashire farmers, their Norfolk colleagues were enjoying an export bonanza. They were also unconsciously preparing British agriculture for its crucial role during the following century, that of maintaining the supply of domestic foodstuffs to a population expanding faster that at any time in the history of production.

Woollens were not less regarded than agriculture. They were part of the Englishman's inherited image of his history and nationhood. Successive governments supported them regardless of party. They enjoyed remarkable privileges, including a monopoly of home-produced wool, and protection against competition from the sister kingdom of Ireland. None the less their representatives complained bitterly in the 1730s and 1740s. One problem was the growing strength of the linen industry, which in Scotland enjoyed

[70] A. H. John, 'English Agricultural Improvement and Grain Exports, 1660–1765', in D. C. Coleman and A. H. John, eds., *Trade, Government and Economy in Pre-Industrial England: Essays presented to F. J. Fisher* (London, 1976), p. 51.

similar status to woollens in England: though woollens and linens did not compete for the same markets, Scottish production was increasingly reducing British demand for Continental linens. On the reciprocal sale of these linens a large European market for English wool depended.

A further difficulty was the decline of the Levant trade. In 1725 southern Europe was the most important market for English cloth, and within it the Levant was its biggest customer. Levant merchants were famous for their wealth; they were prominent both in the government of the City and in its great financial corporations. The early eighteenth century was their heyday. The term 'Turkey merchant' was often applied to wealthy businessmen, even when their connection with the Levant was slight. The essence of the Levant trade proper was the exchange of English broadcloth for Middle Eastern silk. It was at its peak after the War of the Spanish Succession, remained vigorous for much of the 1720s, but thereafter began a decline which was to reduce it to insignificance by the reign of George III. Various causes were assigned. The Levant Company was accused of monopolistic practices which militated against the competitive pricing of English goods and penalized merchants who did not enjoy its privileges. In response the Company stopped commissioning its own ships for the voyage to the eastern Mediterranean in 1744, and threw open the carrying trade. In 1753 it was compelled to admit traders on payment of a minimal £20. (Later on Adam Smith was to consider even this nominal membership fee unjust.) These measures did nothing to arrest the decline. The truth was that changing terms of trade rather than monopoly explained the downward trend. The French advantage in the Mediterranean, once the Bourbon government and Languedoc businessmen fully exploited it, in the 1730s, made English cloth expensive. Worse, Levant silk fell victim to the new and cheaper charms of its Bengal rival, brought in by a concern more monopolistic than the Levant Company, the East India Company. In the early 1720s three-quarters of all imported silk came from the Levant; forty years later the proportion had fallen to a quarter.[71] In 1753 Jonas Hanway, whose own life before he became a full-time philanthropist was spent largely in the trade of the Middle East, was prompted to Miltonic musing on its collapse:

[71] R. Davis, *Aleppo and Devonshire Square: English Traders in the Levant in the Eighteenth Century* (London, 1967), p. 139.

'our Turkey merchants, who some years since figured at the top of the commercial world, now bow their diminished heads.'[72]

It was natural enough in trying times to suppose that the depression in the Levant trade was representative of a general trend. In fact it was not. There is no evidence that woollen production was in fundamental decline. In some instances it positively flourished. The early years of George II saw the consolidation of the West Riding as a cloth-producing region of the first importance, a position on which it was to build its immense prosperity in the late eighteenth century. Even within the Levant trade it was ousting the West Country in cheaper goods, and in other markets, it was already far ahead. The ups and downs of regional competition were themselves relative. Except for some specialized producers, notably in Worcester, where the loss of the Levant trade proved disastrous, the mid-century sufferings of the western counties were short-lived.[73] The West Country remained a major centre of cloth production for many years. But from the standpoint of a Gloucestershire clothier there was seeming cause for concern. Those to whom he appealed in London were impressed. The industry was well-established in the west, it had parliamentary influence by means of the over-represented boroughs of the region, and it was structured in a way which generated violent conflicts between capitalist clothiers and well-organized weavers' combinations: its voice was duly heard. Yorkshiremen who saw West Riding production of broadcloths soar from 32,000 pieces in 1730 to 41,000 in 1741, and again to 60,000 in 1750, were content to join in protesting at the diminution of those markets which the industry as a whole was losing; they were understandably less vociferous about their own continuing prosperity.[74]

THE ATLANTIC ECONOMY

Woollen production was a sensitive economic indicator in part because of its historical importance. But its continuing value in the sector which caused most controversy, that of exports, is clearly demonstrated in the overseas trade statistics. As a proportion of

---

[72] *An Answer to the Appendix Of a Pamphlet, entitled Reflexions upon Naturalization, Corporations and Companies, etc.* (London, 1753), p. 32.

[73] J. de L. Mann, *The Cloth Industry in the West of England from 1640 to 1880* (Oxford, 1971), ch. 2.

[74] T. S. Ashton, *An Economic History of England*, p. 249.

total exports woollens steadily diminished. But the underlying trend in terms of volume was upwards. Moreover, textiles as a whole retained their dominating position in overseas trade, as the growth of the linen and cotton manufactures offset the comparative decline of wool. Like other industries, textiles profited by the opening of new markets. Changes in the direction of trade mattered more than shifts in the relative importance of different commodities. Traditional markets in Europe were notably sluggish between the accession of George II and the outbreak of the Seven Years War. Within the empire the story was quite different. The East Indian export multiplied nearly sevenfold, the West Indian more than doubled, and shipments to Ireland increased markedly. Imports into the continental American colonies almost quadrupled.[75] This switch from European to colonial markets can be discerned before the 1720s, and it was to continue long beyond the 1760s; but as a development of unmistakable importance it belongs to the mid-eighteenth century.

There were internal implications to the changing patterns of overseas commerce. Not the least was the effect on shipping and the ports it used. London's mighty share of international trade remained much the biggest but proportionately it was falling. The beneficiaries were principally the ports which looked west towards the Atlantic and overseas empire. Bristol was the longest-- established of them but not the fastest growing; Whitehaven, from a standing start, enjoyed remarkable growth until reaching the limits imposed by its dependence on the Irish coal trade; Glasgow and Liverpool were the most complete success stories of all, eighteenth-century creations *par excellence*, the former on the basis of the tobacco trade, the latter with the emphasis on slaves. Both were dependent on the new Atlantic economy. Both, too, had rich industrial hinterlands which carried them into an era of nineteenth-century growth exceeding even their eighteenth-century experience. But the expansion of all four during the reign of George II at a time of relative stagnation and decline in other places, is clear evidence of the vitality and flexibility of overseas trade.

It is also a reminder of the economic importance of empire. Colonial demand extended to a range of British manufactures, but provided a special boost to some of the newer ones. This was notably the case in the iron industry. Exports of iron nails, for

[75] E. B. Schumpeter, *English Overseas Trade Statistics, 1697–1808* (Oxford, 1960), p. 17.

TABLE 3. *Destinations of exports (including re-exports) from England and Wales: Average annual values, 1726–1785* (in £ thousands)

	1726-30	1731-5	1736-40	1741-5	1746-50	1751-5	1756-60	1761-5	1766-70	1771-5	1775-80	1781-5
Europe (West) i.e. France, Flanders, Holland, Germany	3,570	3,441	3,701	4,275	4,593	4,945	3,354	4,880	3,921	4,410	3,715	3,510
Europe (South) i.e. Spain, Portugal, Straits, Turkey, Venice	2,400	2,861	2,868	1,920	2,748	3,136	3,380	2,831	1,572	2,790	2,002	1,728
Europe (North) i.e. Sweden, Denmark, and Norway, Russia, Poland, and Prussia	254	247	269	339	353	376	329	494	472	525	555	565
Ireland, Channel Islands, Isle of Man	545	701	788	875	999	1,203	1,052	1,672	2,086	2,092	1,825	1,867
British West Indies	473	383	494	728	732	710	952	1,119	1,174	1,353	1,244	1,272
North America	524	595	758	771	1,025	1,301	2,052	2,065	2,135	835	1,291	2,268
Africa	198	161	207	130	180	227	217	399	569	775	244	513
East Indies	112	154	262	455	522	787	817	976	1,100	912	906	930

Source: E. B. Schumpeter, *English Overseas Trade Structure, 1697–1808* (Oxford, 1960), Table V.

instance, rose from 14,442 cwt. in 1725 to 36,971 in 1750; virtually the entire export went to British colonies, fully two thirds of it in 1750 to the thirteen American colonies. In the same period wrought iron exports nearly trebled from 42,014 cwt. to 122,527; their market was a wider one, but British possessions, together with Africa and the East Indies, commanded over two-thirds of the total. Even among textiles it was the newer branches of the industry which most effectively exploited the overseas opportunities. Four-fifths of linen exports went to North America and the West Indies.[76] Both before and after 1760 there was a natural connection between the newest and most dynamic manufactures and the newest and most dynamic markets.

The success of the colonial trade should have come as no surprise to those who believed that economic growth could be achieved by wise legislation and efficient administration. Yet the reign of George II later came to be seen as an age of 'salutary neglect' where the colonies were concerned, to be contrasted with the provocative and eventually self-defeating interventionism of George III's ministers. It is certainly the case that early Hanoverian government showed little interest in proposals to impose new taxes on their more distant subjects. This probably had more to do with their innate conservatism than any solicitude for the colonists. The management of the empire was considered, not least by George II and his ministers, peculiarly a matter for the Crown. Occasionally, for example in 1734 when the House of Lords was alarmed by the American claim to a distinct, legislative authority based on colonial charters, Parliament was permitted to make threatening noises. But the interesting possibility of a full-blooded confrontation between the imperial and colonial legislatures did not materialize. Had ministers of this era been less preoccupied and more aware of the growing insubordination of representative bodies in the colonies, they might have resorted to this threat more readily.

Parliament did none the less exercise its right to make laws for the empire as a whole. What history knows as the mercantilist code, already well established by the early eighteenth century, expanded steadily, multiplying the restrictions on the freedom to trade and manufacture. Not a few of them had to do with America. The most controversial of these was the Molasses Act of 1733, which sought to restrain trade between the thirteen colonies and

[76] E. B. Schumpeter, *English Overseas Trade Statistics, 1697–1808* (Oxford, 1960), pp. 64, 66–8.

the foreign West Indies, principally with a view to preserving the imperial market for British sugar; statutes which prevented Americans from competing with British manufactures, notably of hats in 1733 and iron in 1750, also came to seem oppressive. Whig apologists of a later age treated these measures as insignificant gestures to special interests; salutary neglect in this sense consisted of government's refusal to execute the objectionable laws which Parliament insisted on enacting. There was some truth in this contention, but it had more to do with the inherent limitations of George II's government than its deliberate policy. Given a powerful political imperative the early Hanoverian regime could demonstrate legislative urgency and executive rigour, as Scotland discovered in the wake of the Forty-Five. But under normal circumstances, it took more than an Act of Parliament obtained by a noisy interest group to command determined administrative action. Even where commercial regulations had a bearing on public revenue, the effectiveness of government outside London and the Home Counties was less than impressive. The Isle of Man's smuggling activities, for instance, were as uninhibited as those of the American colonies. When circumstances and fiscal priorities changed in the 1760s, the former were tackled in the same spirit as the latter. What was different about the 1730s and 1740s was not the enlightened and liberal imperialism of Walpole and Pelham, but the domestic distractions which ministers of George II faced, the limited public and political consensus which they were able to call on in the implementation of policies, and the limitations of the administrative process.

Even to speak of colonial policy before the Seven Years War is somewhat misleading. In the Board of Trade the government had a department specially charged with oversight of colonial as well as commercial matters. But the Board lacked political weight. Its president did not normally have a seat in the Cabinet, and executive authority throughout the Empire, in so far as it was lodged in any minister, lay with the Secretaries of State. Lord Halifax, who headed the Board of Trade from 1748 to 1761, fought hard to increase its influence, with important results after his retirement. Under George III the colonies came to have a Secretary of State of their own, an acquisition of which they were not, however, much enamoured. The innovative climate of ideas which seems to have prevailed at the Board in the 1750s had a considerable impact

on the making of American policy a decade later. Charles Townshend's controversial American measures in 1767 derived largely
from his thinking as a junior minister at the Board of Trade under
Halifax. But all this was very much in the future. The men who
sat at the Board of Trade were aware of the crucial developments
taking place in Britain's western empire under George II. Some
of them had an understanding of the importance which America
was acquiring as a market for British manufactures. Their close
scrutiny of colonial legislation also led to an appreciation of the
dangerous trends emerging in the character of provincial politics,
especially in so far as the authority of the executive suffered.
Martin Bladen, who sat on the Board for twenty-nine years from
1717 to 1746, kept up a long, if at times lonely campaign for a more
systematic and authoritarian approach to colonial government.
But without direction or even much interest from above, junior
ministers like Bladen were in no position to introduce a coherent
policy for a rapidly expanding empire. It was said that the common
talk of Walpole and his circle was that 'It would be better for
England if all the Plantations were at the Bottom of the Sea.'[77]
This, rather than the Whig genius for pragmatic government, was
the essence of salutary neglect.

Extra-parliamentary pressures might have made a difference.
But public interest in North America did not exceed that of
Cabinet ministers. The apparent exception to this rule, the chartered foundation of Georgia in 1732, actually proves it. It was the
brain-child of a group of philanthropic enthusiasts for colonization,
who indulged in a potent mixture of patriotism and piety. Georgia
was to be a territorial buffer and human buttress protecting the
Carolinas against the still expanding Spanish empire in Florida.
The first settlers were to be English debtors released from gaol
and Protestant Salzburgers fleeing from the popish intolerance of
the Habsburgs. The strategic importance of the new colony led
James Oglethorpe, the principal promoter, to devise a scheme for
land allocation which operated on quasi-feudal principles, offering
property in return for military service and restricting the rules of
inheritance so as to ensure a continuing capacity for self-defence.
In contrast with earlier schemes of the kind, Parliament was asked
to foot part of the bill, by means of annual grants towards the
expense of settlement and defence. But most significant of all was

---

[77] *Common Sense*, 1 Aug. 1741.

the hesitant, almost hostile attitude of the ministers of the day. The Board of Trade put the Georgia Trustees on a par with the proprietors of other colonies, and considered them inimical to the rights of the Crown and the requirements of good government. Walpole offered only grudging aid in the Commons, and made it clear that he was doing the Trustees a favour which he expected to be repaid in political and electoral currency. Only in 1752 did the Crown assume full responsibility for the province.

In due course Georgia was to join in the revolt against Britain, though its record was more ambivalent than some, and its role in the American Revolution slight. But it looked south rather than north, and its founders were primarily concerned with its Spanish neighbours. In this respect it belonged truly with the characteristic preoccupations of English empire-builders in the mid-eighteenth century. Again, there is a crucial distinction between the handful of administrators who gave time and thought to problems of empire and those they served at court, in Parliament, and among the public at large. Bladen, for instance, had well-founded doubts about the old obsession with tropical empire, and the lure of gold, silver, and sugar. His view was not shared by many of his contemporaries, as the early years of the War of Jenkins' Ear revealed. Anson's voyage around the world, celebrated by posterity as evidence of a power poised to assert global supremacy, was in origin an old-fashioned buccaneering expedition, intended to singe beards and scupper treasure fleets in the approved Elizabethan manner, at little cost in terms of men and material. Those who sailed on it were thoroughly imbued with this mentality, as Anson's chaplain recorded in his published memoirs of the voyage. Rounding Cape Horn before the full horrors of storms and scurvy struck them, he recalled the 'romantick schemes' and expectations of 'opulence' with which they had entertained themselves. The 7 March 1742, was, it transpired, 'the last chearful day that the greatest part of us would ever live to enjoy'.[78] By June 1744, when Anson's expedition arrived back in England, the costly campaign to devastate Spain's empire in the Caribbean had failed still more comprehensively, dragging down with it the reputation of British arms.

The time was ripe for a shift of attention to more profitable

[78] *A Voyage round the World In the Years 1740–4 By George Anson* (2 vols., London, 1748), i. 75.

parts of the globe. Yet it came only slowly and with little help from the politicians. In India the East India Company was left largely on its own. The consequence was the loss of Madras in 1746 and the disaster which befell the British in Bengal in 1756. Nor did Clive's recovery in 1757 owe much to support from home: that came retrospectively rather as a result of his triumph, than as a contribution to it. Genuine public interest in India also grew later, the product not of informed appreciation of its utility but of the almost accidental acquisition of a territorial empire there. The story was similar in North America. The capture of Louisburg in 1745 owed something to new doctrines which were being heard in Cabinet at the time, thanks to the Duke of Bedford. But it owed more to the unexpected vigour and resourcefulness of the New England force which took it; without that the boasted prowess of Admiral Warren would have signified little. Grand plans for a full-scale invasion of Quebec came to nothing thanks to the pre-occupation of the King, the Duke of Cumberland, and the Pelhams with the Continental war. In the Seven Years War it was to be a very different matter. Even then it is doubtful if public interest and political attention would have been directed northwards but for the ambitious activities of the French there. The public appetite for basic information about the North American colonies, indicated by the great popularity which attended William Douglass's *Summary, Historical and Political* in 1749, and by the positive torrent of journalistic publications on the subject which followed it, derived from patriotic alarm at expansive French imperialism. An empire desired by France must be an empire worth keeping British.

THE DECLINE OF ECONOMIC REGULATION

The same spirit which informed colonial policy affected other kinds of economic regulation. At no point under George II was there a noticeable movement away from the traditional faith in what Adam Smith was to stigmatize as the 'mercantile' system, though contemporaries did not normally call it that, let alone employ the term 'mercantilism'. Trade with European powers was essentially a form of undeclared warfare, the object being to maximize the benefits to the home country while minimizing those to competitors. The prime weapon was the customs duty, which, despite its fiscal consequence to government, was increasingly seen as a means of protectionism rather than a revenue-raising device. This was demonstrated by the way export duties fell into disfavour. After Walpole's revision of the Book of Rates in 1723 virtually none remained: the odd exception, such as the duty on coals exported, applied only where it was believed that the foreign customer had no choice but to buy from Britain, to the relief of the taxpayer as well as the profit of the producer. In fact the export account was run at a huge deficit from the standpoint of the Treasury. Not only did it produce hardly any income, it swallowed up subsidies in the form of bounties designed to make British exports competitive in unfavourable markets and 'drawbacks' on imports of colonial goods intended for re-export.

Import duties were also seen principally as a species of economic regulation. Though many remained in being because ministers were reluctant to experiment with funds which had become a part of budget calculations, new ones were rarely introduced with a view to revenue. They were not the only means of protecting the home market for domestic manufactures, but the alternative, outright exclusion, was losing favour. Tradition has it that the foundation of the modern cotton industry was laid by the prohibition placed on imported calicoes in 1700 and 1721. Similarly, in 1722, Parliament prohibited the use of cloth buttons in order to encourage the silk and mohair industries, and in 1748 it forbade the wearing of French cambrics.[79] Such regulation did not always work. The metal button rapidly superseded its embroidered rivals, to the loss of Coventry and Macclesfield and the gain of Birmingham. Nor were French cambrics so easily recognized that it was practicable to identify their unpatriotic wearers. Measures which smacked of sumptuary legislation were, in any case, somewhat controversial. Though they might appeal to moralists and mercantilists, they conflicted with another favourite principle of the age, the desirability of inhibiting State interference in the ordinary life of the individual.

Mercantile warfare was conducted against adversaries who commanded similar tactics, sometimes with better disciplined forces. It could therefore not be pursued *à outrance* without cost. The

---

[79] N. B. Harte, 'State Control of Dress and Social Change in Pre-Industrial England', in D. C. Coleman and A. H. John, eds., *Trade, Government and Economy in Pre-Industrial England*, pp. 152–3.

effective embargo on Anglo-French trade maintained by both sides until the Eden treaty of 1787 not only protected the English silk and cloth industries against French competition, but also deprived English drinkers of cheap French wines and spirits, and English hardware manufacturers of a handsome market for their wares. It generated a vast smuggling trade. States less permanently alienated, such as Austria and Prussia, had to be treated cautiously. A new duty or a new bounty injudiciously authorized by a Parliament attentive to its electors' interest, might readily provoke retaliation from Continental competitors. Some states were capable of out-gunning the British government in this respect. Denmark and Sweden, for example, succeeded in imposing discriminatory tariffs on British goods, against their treaty obligations and without suffering retaliation. This impunity derived from recognition that Swedish iron ore and Norwegian timber were vital to the British economy in general, and the Royal Navy in particular.[80]

Diplomacy and commerce were inextricably mingled, not just at the consular level but also for the Ambassadors and Secretaries of State who had constantly to weigh dynastic and strategic inter-ests in a balance which responded to commercial considerations. It is almost impossible to say in some cases which counted for most. The struggle with France was political, military, imperial, commercial: moreover, inherited prejudice was perhaps as instru-mental as anything in preventing attempts to modify such a deep-seated rivalry. Perhaps this was why, when Britain and France made peace in 1713, Bolingbroke's ambitious plan for a commercial *rapprochement* was rejected; perhaps too, it explains the reluctance of the Whigs, when they became advocates of alliance with France, between 1716 and 1731, to revive it. The Portuguese trade, which opened the way to a lucrative relationship with Brazil, was sus-tained partly by the famous Methuen Treaty of 1704, partly by a continuing coincidence of strategic interests, principally with regard to Spain. The pattern thus set acquired a certain enduring, prescriptive form of its own, embodied not least in the human contacts involved. Lisbon was host to a resident community of British businessmen, who played a large part not merely in trade between the two countries but also in Portugal's own trade with

[80] H. S. K. Kent, *War and Trade in Northern Seas: Anglo-Scandinavian Economic Relations in the Mid-Eighteenth Century* (Cambridge, 1973), ch. 1.

other partners, notably in the Mediterranean. Not surprisingly the French came to consider Lisbon an English colony.[81]

Adherence to traditional doctrines of empire and trade was perfectly compatible with less monopolistic practices at home. In a sense free trade had long been a fundamental principle of domestic economics, to be deployed in a rhetorical way as part of the Englishman's inheritance. It was used, for instance, to defend the naturalization of Jews in 1753: making them equal competitors in trade and manufacture was apparently in accord both with English tradition and natural rights. 'A free trade, a free government, and a free liberty of conscience, are the rights and the blessings of mankind.'[82] Monopoly served the national interest in foreign trade, but at home it militated against it. Combinations, whether of merchants intent on maintaining high prices or workers concerned to maintain high wages, were in most cases illegal. If they did not contravene specific legislation, they were likely to fall foul of the common law of conspiracy. This at least was the theory, though the practice was somewhat different. Many businessmen were determined to restrict rather than extend competition. Cartels were a feature of not a few industries. Parliament regularly sought to curb them in the interests of the consumer, or, more likely, to meet the demands of other interests which deemed themselves hurt by such combinations. The Newcastle coal trade, for example, was notorious for its price-fixing at every point from the pit-head to the retailer. Though MPs were naturally concerned about the price of fuel in London and the south-east, it was the clamour of the diverse groups involved, coal-owners, shippers, and coal-merchants, which made it possible to identify and tackle monopolistic practices on the part of one or other of them.[83] Legislative intervention usually complicated such problems; it rarely solved them. In the course of the eighteenth century some 200 acts or ordinances were promulgated on the subject of the coal trade.

Trades which did not come into such direct contract with the ordinary householder were easier to protect against external regulation. The copper and brass industry, which grew considerably

[81] H. E. S. Fisher, 'Lisbon and its English merchant community and the Mediterranean in the eighteenth century', in P. L. Cottrell and D. H. Aldcroft, eds., *Shipping, Trade and Commerce: Essays in Memory of Ralph Davis* (Leicester, 1981), pp. 23–44.

[82] Quoted by J. Hanway, *An Answer to the Appendix*, p. 11.

[83] M. W. Flinn, *The History of the British Coal Industry*, vol. ii: *1700–1830: The Industrial Revolution* (Oxford, 1984), ch. 8.

in the eighteenth century and made an important contribution
to economic growth, was a blatant case of price-fixing. The
smelters and manufacturers systematically used their power to
dominate both the miners who supplied their raw material and
the customers who bought their products. They never succeeded
in resolving all the tensions in a diverse and scattered industry,
but by the reign of George III they rather resembled one vast
combine than capitalist competition at its most vigorous. The most
celebrated entrepreneur in this line, Thomas Williams of the
Anglesey Copper Company, made his name and his fortune by his
success in the mixture of bullying and coaxing needed to maintain
a common front against foreigners and the consumer alike.[84]

Informal cartels permitted collaborative investment. The South
Sea Bubble had left a prejudice against the joint-stock company
which was embodied in the Bubble Act of 1720. Subsequent
scandals concerning public trusts, notably the Charitable Corporation and the York Buildings Company, drove the prejudice still
deeper. The temper of the age was deeply opposed to corporations.
Samuel Madden's *Memoirs of the Twentieth Century*, printed but
never published because of its subversive implications, included a
prediction that three centuries hence two great companies, the
Royal Fishery and the Plantation Company (supposedly founded
by Frederick I and George III respectively) would be dominant
forces.[85] His anxiety says much about the fears of the time, less
about its dangers. The Georgia Trust had more of impractical
high-mindedness about it than oligarchical conspiracy. Projects to
secure the home fishing interest had a comparable record of good
intentions and limited results. The Royal British Fishery, a patriotic endeavour which attracted much interest in the 1750s, was
meant to break the monopoly of the existing fishing interests, not
to reinforce it. In the event the attempt to establish a genuine
mass market in a highly perishable commodity proved excessively
optimistic.

Existing corporations, inherited from an earlier age, were not
noticeably more menacing. The Royal African Company no longer
had a real commercial role. The Muscovy Company provided
useful diplomatic and managerial services in a market where com-

---

[84] H. Hamilton, *The English Brass and Copper Industries to 1800* (London, 1926),
chs. 6–8.
[85] (London, 1733), pp. 369 ff; copies are accordingly very rare.

pletely independent enterprise would hardly have flourished, as did the Levant Company. The decaying Hudson's Bay Company went to great pains to disarm criticism of its relatively insignificant activities in North America. The South Sea Company was merely a pawn of the other financial corporations of the City and the Treasury. The East India Company enjoyed relative commercial stability in a region where interlopers were, for the moment at least, easily bought off; its share in the National Debt also made it the object of solicitude on the part of Treasury ministers. Until the territorial expansion associated with the Seven Years War it enjoyed a relatively tranquil political life. There remained the Bank of England, a uniquely favoured corporation. Even with due allowance for its reputation for efficient management, its immunity must be attributed largely to the place which it occupied in the fiscal calculations of government, and the Revolution system of finance. It was too important to be permitted to become a political football; perhaps, as well, it was too remote from the accidents and adversities of ordinary commercial life to behave like one.

By modern standards neither capital nor labour was widely or intensively organized. But capital had little to fear from contemporary conditions, whereas labour was in a decidedly weaker position. None the less labour enjoyed more cohesion and greater power than the formal record might suggest. The early nineteenth-century historian of the working class, Gravenor Henson, observed that under George II 'a system of riot, respecting wages, was continually in motion.'[86] He presumably had in mind the convulsions in the woollen and hosiery industries which occurred in that period. But riot was only the extreme manifestation of a bargaining power which had many tactics at its command in a time when population growth was minimal and competition for jobs restricted. The prehistory of the trade unions remains obscure, mainly because they lacked anything like a national organization— not surprisingly, given the regional character of most commercial and industrial activity. But there is evidence that more or less formal combinations were widespread in the larger manufacturing concerns. Nor were they altogether excluded from political power. Parliament showed considerable interest in the doings of the

[86] S. D. Chapman, *Henson's History of the Framework Knitters* (Newton Abbot, 1970), p. 245.

clothing workers, and even, briefly, intervened in their favour, with an Act of 1756 designed to protect West Country weavers' wages.

Important changes were taking place in the terms on which employers and employees dealt with each other, though most of them were not the product of conscious policies. Wage regulation, in theory the duty of a paternalistic magistracy, lapsed in the course of the eighteenth century. The number of wage tables approved by the county benches declined steadily. By the beginning of George III's reign those still being issued were more in the nature of a mechanical ritual than a meaningful activity.[87] This was doubtless bound up with a matching diminution in other branches of economic regulation. Guilds, as corporations with commercial functions, were generally in rapid decline in the early eighteenth century. The collapse appears to have begun in the years following the Revolution, initially among those which supervised the distributive trades: it affected manufacturers in the 1730s and 1740s, and the service and construction industry, in the first years of George III.[88]

The story of apprenticeship as an institution was more complicated but the trend similar. In declining industries the advantage of engaging in a prolonged form of training seemed increasingly dubious; in new and developing trades it was positively irrelevant. Even where apprenticeship remained the norm, its nature was changing. Masters were increasingly accused of no longer accepting apprentices on the old basis, effectively as members of their family: it was feared that they used them merely as a cheap form of manpower which could be boarded out and treated much as if it were wage labour. The practice of reducing apprenticeship terms from the traditional seven years to five or even three helped create the impression of a bastard institution which no longer fulfilled its historic function. The repeal of the Act of Artificers had to wait until 1814 but as early as the beginning of George III's reign there were calls for its discontinuance. Apprenticeship took a very long time dying and its vitality varied from locality to locality. Spirited efforts were made to save it. At Leeds the guilds had lost their economic significance by the early eighteenth century, but the

---

[87] W. E. Minchinton, *Wage Regulation in Pre-Industrial England* (Newton Abbot, 1961), pp. 20–1.
[88] K. D. M. Snell, *Annals of the Labouring Poor: Social Change and Agrarian England, 1660–1900* (Cambridge, 1985), ch. 5.

apprenticeship laws continued to be observed until about 1770.[89] At Exeter there was a series of attempts, increasingly desperate by the 1760s, to enforce apprenticeships.[90]

A related institution which came under intense pressure was the 'freedom', the right to exercise a trade or craft within an incorporated town. Corporations did their best to arrest its decline, but appeals to the law were less than effective. This was not because judges and juries were prejudiced in favour of free trade or hostile to the principle of regulation—probably the contrary was true of both. Rather it was because the complexities and uncertainties of charters, by-laws, and traditions gave grounds for dispute in an age when the communal spirit which had previously underpinned them was weak. Leicester, an intensely conservative corporation, took its struggle to defend the freedom to the highest level, losing a case which it brought against a recalcitrant watchmaker, in 1749.[91] At Bath the critical setback occurred when it was defeated in a similar contest in 1765.[92] Smaller boroughs could not afford the burden of litigation and gave up the struggle earlier. At Wallingford there was a flurry of fines for not taking up the freedom in the early years of George II, succeeded by reluctant recognition of the futility as well as unpopularity of the practice.[93]

The economic uselessness of the freedom was offset by its political utility. Where municipal freedom carried the parliamentary franchise it came to be prized principally for its electoral value. The power of corporations to create or sell freedoms, regardless of the experience, qualifications, and family of those enfranchised, made a farce of the institution and transformed the image of the ordinary freeman. In many places the once proud counterparts of the county freeholders were reduced, so it seemed, to a municipal rabble. The approach of a general election was the signal for sudden creations of freemen *en masse*, in line with the political affiliation of the dominant body on the corporation. At Gloucester in 1727, no less than 469 freemen were created in one year, with

[89] R. G. Wilson, *Gentlemen Merchants: The Merchant Community in Leeds, 1700–1830*, p. 164.
[90] W. G. Hoskins, *Industry, Trade and People in Exeter, 1688–1800* (Manchester, 1935), pp. 50–3.
[91] J. Thompson, *The History of Leicester in the Eighteenth Century* (Leicester, 1871), pp. 77–9.
[92] S. C. McIntyre, 'Towns as health and pleasure resorts: The development of Bath, Scarborough and Weymouth, 1700–1815', D.Phil. thesis (Oxford, 1973), p. 73.
[93] Berkshire Record Office, Wallingford Borough Records.

a view to the general election.[94] In the great city of Norwich the freedom was effectively a form of political property rather than a licence to trade by the early eighteenth century, and nothing occurred thereafter to revive its commercial significance.[95] This trend should be seen as part of a wider process which weakened the ancient framework of regulation, not merely in municipalities. A critical defeat was the reverse suffered by the London Framework Knitters Company in its attempt to enforce its apprenticeship regulations on the provincial hosiery industry. The Company was defeated twice before the courts, in 1725 and 1731, and although the verdict was given against it only on a technicality in both cases it did not venture a further test until 1745. On this occasion the ground was carefully prepared and it received the support of the Lord Chancellor and the Chief Justices. The result was a storm of protest from the main hosiery districts, the East Midlands and Surrey, uniting workers, employers, and ratepayers, in an appeal to Parliament. Under threat of legislation the Company backed down without further struggle.[96] It was, in a way, a fitting emblem of an age in which institutional regulation was giving way before the requirements of private enterprise and commercial expansion.

[94] R. Sedgwick, *The History of Parliament: The House of Commons, 1715–1754* (2 vols., London, 1970), i. 246.

[95] See P. Millican, ed., *The Freemen of Norwich, 1714–1752* (Norfolk Record Society, xxxiii, 1952): the admission of freemen before elections was a regular feature.

[96] F. A. Wells, *The British Hosiery Trade: Its History and Organization* (London, 1935), ch. 2.

CHAPTER 5

Patriotism Unmasked, 1742–1757

WALPOLE'S *fall was followed by demands for constitutional reform and the punishment of Walpole himself. They were effectively blocked by the new ministry. The patriot cause seemed comprehensively to have foundered. George II and Carteret were the principal beneficiaries of the crisis of 1742, but their foreign policy provoked an outburst of anti-Hanoverianism, and the King was forced to experiment with a Broad-Bottom coalition of Whigs and Tories. Open war with France preceded a Jacobite rebellion which was quelled only with difficulty. The Tory party showed little interest in a Stuart Restoration but remained alienated from the court of George II. In the midst of this crisis Henry Pelham was able to construct a lasting ministry. He used it to carry through an ambitious legislative programme for Scotland, and to bring the war to an end. The Pelhamite peace was somewhat marred by factious disputes within the government. It also suffered from the dynastic tensions created by the Prince of Wales, until his death in 1751, and by his brother the Duke of Cumberland. A series of controversial naturalization bills culminated in the unpopular 'Jew Bill' of 1753, but the ministry's readiness to bow to extra-parliamentary opinion saved it from serious damage. The essential stability of the regime was threatened first by Pelham's death in 1754, and then by the difficulty which Newcastle experienced in managing the ministry from the House of Lords. The rivalry of William Pitt and Henry Fox led the former to invest in a patriot programme of a kind which had not been seriously pressed for ten years or more. Even so it was the misfortunes of war and the influence of the new Prince of Wales which gave Pitt his opportunity to practise his principles in office. It remained to be seen whether he would prove truer to his promises than Pulteney in 1742.*

PULTENEY'S PATRIOTISM

I T would be difficult to exaggerate the significance attached by contemporary opinion to the resignation of Walpole. Many years of reiterating the proposition that he was personally to blame for his country's ills had created an expectation that his fall must surely bring about a change in its fortunes. More was involved in this expectation than the revival of the war effort. Many MPs received well-publicized instructions from their constituents, demanding what the City of London called 'a speedy and effectual reformation'. The desired reforms were those which had figured so much in the propaganda of the *Craftsman* school. Place and pension bills, the repeal of the Septennial Act, a reduction in the standing army, all seemed within reach at last. There was also a determination that posterity must be left in no doubt of the proper lesson to draw from Walpole's fall. Due punishment for Walpole himself was not just the vindictive wish of his personal enemies among the Whigs and his party opponents among the Tories. In remote North Wales a loyal Hanoverian Whig like William Bulkeley felt it as fervently as his more typically Jacobite countrymen. In his diary under 18 February 1742 he noted: 'the grand Corrupter laid down all his places and retired to his house in Norfolk. May God grant them honesty and resolution to pursue the Enemy of their Countrey to the Scaffold.'[1]

These hopes were quickly disappointed. In the midst of a great Continental war, the idea of reducing the standing army was soon dropped. Enthusiasm for triennial elections was not feverish among MPs only recently elected to a new Parliament. The Place Act procured in 1742 hardly matched the rhetoric which had preceded it. It prohibited a number of junior officials in government departments from sitting in the House of Commons, but ministerial influence was only marginally diminished. An attempt to reform electoral procedure, mainly by restricting the Crown's legal powers over corporations, made progress in the lower house but was defeated in the upper. Above all, that signal act of vengeance which would demonstrate once for all that no minister could with impunity monopolize power, enfeeble both legislature and electorate, and make the cause of the Crown indistinguishable from

---

[1] G. N. Evans, *Religion and Politics in Mid-Eighteenth Century Anglesey* (Cardiff, 1953), p. 129.

that of corruption did not materialize. Though a Secret Committee of the Commons was established to investigate Walpole's dealings, its scope was restricted to the previous ten years. This excluded some promisingly murky episodes under George I. The resulting report produced chapter and verse for the charge of corrupting electors with public money, principally in the constituencies of Wendover and Orford. But it offered little that could be used to legal effect without the evidence of Walpole's immediate dependants, especially the Solicitor to the Treasury Nicholas Paxton. Unsurprisingly, this was not forthcoming. A bill which guaranteed personal indemnity to those who incriminated themselves by giving testimony against Walpole passed the House of Commons, but was defeated in the Lords. When the session of 1742 ended, nothing had been achieved to bring Walpole to justice. An attempt by the Tories to revive the investigation at the start of the following session, wanting 'to *reform* their own *reformation*', as a future Lord Chancellor, Charles Pratt, put it, was easily rebuffed.[2] Paxton lost his office; so did another of Walpole's henchmen Joseph Bell, who as Comptroller of the Post Office paid the price for many years of political interference with the postal service.

As in 1727, so in 1742, what did not happen was as important as what did happen. Liberal constitutionalists of the nineteenth and twentieth centuries were to look back to Walpole's fall as the nation's coming of political age. A crisis of exceptional severity had passed and a minister, reviled by most of those whom he governed, had been permitted to retreat with his life and his property, even his dignity. In the evolution of a civilized code of political conduct, ensuring the orderly succession of governments, Walpole's immunity thus took on a special significance. An alternative view is that it demonstrated the hypocrisy of a corrupt oligarchy intent on deceiving its inferiors. As an early historian of the Georgian working class put it, 'With Sir R. Walpole began the practice of selecting members in opposition to act the part of sham patriots, to deceive and cajole the people, by pretended speeches for liberty.'[3] In 1742 the emphasis was also on the cynicism of patriots rather than their enlightened humanity and political tolerance.

---

[2] G. Hardinge, *Biographical Memoirs of The Rev. Sneyd Davies* (London [1816]), p. 141.
[3] S. D. Chapman, *Henson's History of the Framework Knitters* (Newton Abbot, 1970), p. 256.

How far was the leading patriot, Pulteney, to blame for the failure of 'speedy and effectual reformation'? The case against him bears an appropriate resemblance to the charges laid against Walpole twenty years before. It was alleged that in the negotiations which preceded Walpole's fall, Pulteney sold his friends down the river, saved the King and most of his ministry from wholesale reform, and preserved Walpole from retribution. The claim that Pulteney had served himself and Carteret at the expense of his allies was difficult to deny, though it could be countered with the suggestion that their allies would have behaved in the same way if the King's preference had fallen on them. At issue was a very real difficulty, George II's unrelenting hostility towards the Tories. A number of leading opposition Whigs who had learned to live with them, the Duke of Argyll, the Duke of Bedford, the Prince of Wales himself, insisted that the leaders of the Tory party must be included in the new administration. At a meeting in the Fountain Tavern in the Strand on 12 February 1742, this question was thrashed out between the principals. Argyll and his colleagues advocated 'the establishment of a ministry on a broad bottom, as the term was, by which they meant to take the Tories into the Administration. They talked of extinguishing parties with their names, and having but one party. And Pulteney came into the same thing, but he said he was for doing it by proper degrees as occasion should happen. He was not for forcing the King into it.'[4] Argyll accepted the restoration of the offices which he had resigned in 1741 in the belief that concessions would be made on this crucial point. They were not, and he resigned on 10 March, in effect declaring war on those 'New Whigs' who had followed Pulteney into government. Pulteney may have been justified in his view. Whatever the reason, the crisis of February 1742 was as important as any, perhaps more important than those of 1727 and 1744, in preventing that great Country Party coalition which had been the hope of so many Whigs and Tories throughout the period of Walpole's primacy.

Walpole's immunity was a separate matter. Pulteney's plea of innocence was recorded for posterity in the memoirs of his protégé Thomas Newton, who eventually became Bishop of Bristol thanks to Pulteney's influence at the court of George III. Newton denied

---

[4] Dudley Ryder's Diary, quoted in R. Sedgwick, *The History of Parliament: The House of Commons, 1715–1754*, i. 52.

that his patron had given any guarantees. When the King, through Newcastle and Hardwicke, requested his protection he replied that he was not the leader of a party and that he would in any case be no 'screen'. At a second meeting he was simply asked not to 'inflame' feeling against Walpole. Pulteney answered that he was not 'a man of blood' but that some parliamentary censure was unavoidable.[5] This was tantamount to a tacit agreement to let Walpole off lightly. In Parliament Pulteney blamed his failure to obtain majorities against Walpole on the misleading directions given out by his friends. On the motion of 9 March 1742 for a secret committee with powers to investigate the preceding twenty years, Pulteney and his intimates were mysteriously absent. The Duke of Newcastle wrote to the Duke of Richmond, 'Joy, Joy, ten thousand Joys to you my Dear Duke, we have flung out the Secret Committee by two Noes 244, Ayes 242. The 244 all old friends, but our new ones prevailed upon *some* to be absent.'[6] Later, in 1745, Pulteney admitted, 'I contented myself with the honest pride of having subdued the great author of corruption.'[7]

What incriminated Pulteney most in some minds was his decision to accompany Walpole to the House of Lords, as Earl of Bath. Pulteney was a vain man, and his wife a snobbish woman. A peerage had its attractions. None the less, it looked like pusillanimity. Before Walpole's decision to stay in the Commons in 1721 it would not have been thought odd at all. But by 1742 it was assumed that prime ministerial power was difficult to combine with a peerage. Moreover, Pulteney was a formidable orator who seemed to belong naturally in the lower house. His friends put about a story that Pulteney had been duped by the King into taking a peerage. Newton has him accepting a peerage because of the thanklessness of his position. This is one way of putting what was probably true, that Pulteney could not bear the psychological pressures exerted on him at this time.

The expectations of the opposition in 1742 could not have been met without a wholesale change of ministry. But Pulteney had become enmeshed in a negotiation premised on the assumption that the Old Corps of Whigs would remain in office, albeit without

---

[5] *The Works of the Right Reverend Thomas Newton* (3 vols., London, 1782), i. 29.

[6] T. J. McCann, ed., *The Correspondence of the Dukes of Richmond and Newcastle, 1724–1750* (Sussex Record Soc., lxxiii, 1982–3), p. 82.

[7] *Works of Thomas Newton*, i. 40.

their head. Though Pulteney made various pleas on behalf of the Tories, and subscribed to the cant of a broad-bottom, patriotic ministry, he had no desire to be the Whig who undermined Hanoverian Whiggism. Moreover, as he said, he was not the leader of a party. His personal following was small, his ally Lord Carteret was pushing him towards compromise, and the war demanded firm, united government. He was also dealing with a cunning cabal of politicians: Hardwicke as Lord Chancellor, Newcastle as Secretary of State, Henry Pelham as Walpole's obvious successor in the House of Commons. They did not hold all the cards in 1742, but they had a shrewd idea of how to play them, and an understandable anxiety about their personal stake in the game. They were preserving their own careers, ensuring Walpole's personal safety, and protecting their master. George II remains a shadowy figure in the negotiations, but a crucial one. Pulteney had initially demanded a direct negotiation with the King himself. It was the kind of demand which came naturally to powerful opposition leaders at the moment of their triumph. Pitt was to insist on it in 1766, Rockingham in 1782, Fox in 1783. On these occasions George III was forced to parley directly with his conquerors. George II, usually charged with weakness, never did so. He dealt at one remove, through ministers who protected him from personal humiliation, and ensured that any promises made could subsequently be broken or explained away as not being the King's own. Pulteney was reduced to dealing with Newcastle, Pelham, and Hardwicke: it was an underrated triumvirate at the time, but before very long it would govern the country.

CARTERET AND CONTINENTAL WARFARE

In the short run the King was the real victor of 1742 and 1743. The decision to place the Earl of Wilmington, the former Spencer Compton, at the Treasury, absurd though it seemed in respect of Wilmington's political weight, was a sign of George II's influence on the disposition of offices in 1742. He had been loath to lose Walpole, but Walpole's fall had paradoxically removed the one effective brake on his Hanoverian ambitions. Even with Walpole in power a Continental war would have presented a considerable challenge in terms of domestic politics. In 1741, to the horror of his ministers, the King had concluded a convention of neutrality on behalf of his Electorate. This had committed him to give his electoral support in the imperial Diet not to the Habsburg candidate for the Empire, Maria Theresa's husband, but to the French candidate, Charles Albert of Bavaria. In effect there were two foreign policies in the autumn of 1741: that of the King of England, subsidized by Parliament, and that of the Elector of Hanover, unrestrained by his English ministers.

This potential conflict of interests may have contributed as much as anything to the deterioration of Walpole's position in the opening weeks of the new Parliament. Though the convention was repudiated, in return for ministerial assurances of support for Hanover, there remained the underlying problem of how to restrain the power of France, succour Maria Theresa, and keep George II's Hanoverian interests under control. After Walpole's fall the prime responsibility for solving it lay with Newcastle's new colleague as Secretary of State, Lord Carteret. Carteret presented more of a threat than Bath to the Old Corps Whigs. His congenial, convivial manners were relished by the King; his diplomatic experience, albeit somewhat dated, gave him a knowledge of Continental affairs and an insight into their springs, which he exploited to the full. Less happily, he displayed a notable lack of interest in parliamentary management. The arts of patronage were the most important of any in the making of eighteenth-century ministers. Those who affected to neglect them for the sake of popularity, notably the elder Pitt, covertly employed them with great adroitness. Those who really did ignore them could not prosper for long. Carteret was in this category, though in the short term it made little difference. He seemed to value those things which the King valued, and despised those men whom the King seemed to despise. For a while this was sufficient to make him undisputed first minister.

In the bitterly anti-Hanoverian atmosphere generated by the events of 1742 and 1743, Carteret was blamed for allowing Hanover's interests to take precedence over those of his country. William Pitt's reputation as a patriot orator was made denouncing his services to the 'despicable electorate'. In retrospect, an impartial assessment of Carteret's merits is rendered difficult by two contrary temptations. One is to bow to the contemporary propaganda and subsequent historiography which make him a squanderer of British men and money in Continental adventures. The alternative is to recognize him as a brilliant failure, an intellect of exceptional power, a statesman of European stature, who was maligned and brought down by men of no vision.

Nobody has ever accused Carteret of intellectual confusion: if for this reason alone, some caution is needed in condemning his so-called Hanoverianism. He had a clear understanding of strategy and tactics and his apparent complicity with George II's prejudices was more in the nature of tactics. If anyone could carry the King with him while redesigning the politics of Europe to remove the threat of Frency hegemony, it was Carteret. Newcastle blamed the ineffective manœuvres of the allied army in 1742 on Carteret's acquiescence in a royal plot to protect Hanover at the expense of more important objectives. But the army was led by generals, British, Dutch, and German, who could not agree on what to do with it. Moreover, the bitterly criticized decision to take George II's Hanoverian troops into British pay in 1742 was approved by Newcastle and his friends as much as it was by Carteret. The best news of 1742, the Treaty of Breslau between Maria Theresa and Frederick of Prussia, owed something to Carteret's shrewd management of the Austrians. It was followed by an Anglo-Prussian treaty which held out the promise of a new Grand Alliance against overweening French power. The best news of 1743, the battle of Dettingen in June, less justly, also redounded to his credit. It was a victory in the tradition of Marlborough, a victory by a motley allied army confronting a superior French force under the command of a famous general, Noailles, in a crucial strategic position, on the Main. To the King's unbounded delight, he was in command himself, with Carteret present to advise and congratulate him.

Dettingen was unquestionably a historic battle. As Carteret boasted to his Cabinet colleagues, 'The honour of the English nation is now higher than ever it was since my Lord Marlborough's time.'[8] The reluctance of the King to authorize a full-scale pursuit of the defeated French army made the victory less complete than it might have been in a strategic sense, but it presented George II with the initiative in Continental politics, and offered a fair opportunity to test the metal of Carteret's statesmanship under favourable conditions. The result was not reassuring. The summer of 1743 was a heady time for King and minister: it produced what

[8] Yorke, *Hardwicke*, i. 325.

some of their friends as well as their enemies regarded as hare-brained schemes. The first, the Project of Hanau, was meant to detach the Emperor from the French alliance and restore lasting peace to central Europe. It ignored the underlying Prusso-Austrian conflict which had given rise to the war in 1740, and it took for granted Austrian compliance in Bavaria's aggrandizement. It was dropped before Parliament was given an opportunity to debate this remarkable diplomatic revolution. Instead the Treaty of Worms was negotiated, offering large subsidies to Britain's allies, Austria and Sardinia, and implicitly guaranteeing support for continued warfare in support of the Habsburgs. 'No peace without Spain' had been the millstone about the necks of Queen Anne's Whigs; 'no peace without Silesia' seemed likely to perform a similar function for George II's. Hanau had been meant to give peace to Germany: Worms bade fair to give war to all Europe. In October 1743 France and Spain formally activated the Family Compact so long feared by British opponents of the Bourbon claim to Spain. By the spring of 1744 Frederick of Prussia had renounced his alliance with George II and rejoined the Emperor and Louis XV for a renewed onslaught on Maria Theresa.

The British part in Dettingen produced rejoicing at home. It may seem surprising that growing immersion in Continental warfare proved so patriotic a cause. But the war in the Caribbean had turned sour after Puerto Bello, anti-French sentiment was given scope in the circumstances of 1741 which it had lacked since 1713, and the plight of Maria Theresa appears to have aroused a degree of sentimental support for the old Austrian alliance which would have startled those who could recall the hostility to Vienna in the last years of George I. Popular bellicosity was intense during the early 1740s. It is notable that two patriotic songs of enduring popularity, Thomas Arne's *Rule Britannia* and Henry Carey's *God Save the King*, date from this period. For ceremonial pomp Handel's Dettingen *Te Deum* proved almost as long-lasting.

If patriotic spirit was strong, patriotic unity was another matter. It is doubtful which was stimulated more by the War of the Austrian Succession, 'anti-Gallicanism' or anti-Hanoverianism. The growing sense that ministers were merely serving the interests of the Electorate was a gift to the men who had been left out of the coalition government of 1742. In December 1742 a motion in the Commons approving the ministry's readiness to take Hanoverian troops into British pay for the defence of Austria, was carried by 260 votes to 193; during the subsequent session, in January 1744, a similar motion registered 271 votes against 226. For a reconstructed ministry, on an issue of exceptional importance, these were adequate rather than reassuring majorities. Instead of relieving this pressure, Dettingen had made matters worse. In retrospect it remains unclear how far the stories of George II's mistreatment of the English forces before and during the battle were justified. They closely resemble the indignation voiced at William III's preference for his Dutch troops half a century earlier; in a mixed army under battle conditions tensions of this kind were doubtless inevitable. What can be said is that if the duty of an allied commander is to promote co-operation in the face of the enemy, if necessary at the expense of his personal prejudices and his national predilections, George II manifestly failed in it. There was intense bitterness among the British officers and troops which was transmitted to their correspondents at home. It played a part in the Earl of Stair's decision to resign his command of the army, a damaging blow in view of Stair's long career and considerable prestige. It also contributed to the difficulties which the administration faced in Parliament.

The Old Corps ministers were understandably dismayed by the sequel to Dettingen. As it seemed to them, they bore the brunt of the King's unpopularity in London; yet they were expected to find the money with which to sustain his ambitions and Carteret's schemes. The prospect of a long, expensive war after the Treaty of Worms brought relations within the Cabinet to breaking-point. Though Carteret was compelled to renege on his apparently open-ended subsidy commitment to Maria Theresa the fortunes of war offered little comfort. Hostilities with France formally commenced in February 1744, after three years of war conducted nominally as auxiliaries. The immediate threat of a French invasion was dispersed by the accidents of the weather in the Channel rather than the intrepidity of the British navy. A promising action against the Bourbon fleets off Toulon in the same month was vitiated by the acrimonious rivalry of the principal officers involved, Mathews and Lestock. There ensued the inevitable and long-drawn-out controversies which always resulted from a naval reverse: eventually, Lestock was court-martialled and cleared, while Mathews was court-martialled and disgraced. On land the war had switched, as in the last great war against France, from Germany to Flanders. But there was no Marlborough in 1744, and the window of opportunity opened at Dettingen would not remain open for very long. Carteret, or Granville, as he became on his succession to an earldom in October, remained breezily, even drunkenly (as his colleagues complained) complacent.

The point of crisis was reached in November, when the Old Corps Whigs formally demanded the dismissal of Granville rather than face a further parliamentary session with him. There followed some desperate negotiations in which Granville sought to form his own administration. He had the aid of the Prince of Wales and expected support from the Tories. But the cohesiveness of the Old Corps proved remarkable, a tribute to the solidarity which Walpole had built up in the course of twenty years of shrewd management. Walpole himself was summoned to London to provide the King with moral support but instead advised him to co-operate with Pelham. Parliament was due to meet on 27 November. On the 24th Carteret resigned. For the second time in two years the King was compelled to part with the minister of his choice.

BROAD-BOTTOM

It was far from certain that the new arrangement would last longer than its predecessor. From the beginning there were doubts about the sincerity of George II's repentance, epitomized in the appointment of the Earl of Harrington as Granville's successor in the Secretary of State's office. Harrington was an avowed supporter of the Pelhams, but he was also an old friend of the King's, and might be expected to continue Granville's policies, no doubt with Granville advising behind the scenes. The Old Corps leaders were well aware of the risks which they had taken by humiliating the King. But they had their own strategy, one which in most respects was realistic. The new plan was announced not as a revival of the Old Corps but as a Broad-Bottom of the kind for which Argyll had agitated in 1742. Some of the Whigs left out in the cold then were brought in: these 'New Allies' were satisfied at the expense of the 'New Whig' friends of Granville. The newcomers included some powerful magnates: the Duke of Bedford, who was placed at the Admiralty, the Earl of Sandwich, appointed to serve under him on the Admiralty Board, Lord Gower, a Tory who had been given a taste of office in 1742 only to resign it the following year, and who was now made Lord Privy Seal again.

There were bitter pills for George II to swallow. Lord Chesterfield, a long-standing enemy, was made special Ambassador to the Dutch and Lord-Lieutenant of Ireland. The advantage of these posts was that they at least kept him at a safe distance from the King. The inclusion of Pitt, whom Pelham was particularly anxious to detach from opposition, was flatly refused by George II, not unnaturally, after Pitt's offensive speeches against Hanover. He did not, however, veto the treaty which was made with the Tory party and followed by the conferment of office on two of its leaders in the Commons, Sir John Philipps and Sir John Hynde Cotton. Cotton's enormous physical bulk gave cartoonists their chance to provide the Broad-Bottom with an identifiable image. Sceptics were assured that the historic compact had at last taken place. That prince of turncoats Lord Bolingbroke put in an appearance, having retreated from his French retreat, to give unsolicited advice about the terms on which the Tories should be conciliated.

Yet the coalition did not succeed. The King had accepted it in the most grudging spirit. He had no intention of abandoning Granville. His relations with the ministers proved acutely uncomfortable for all those involved, and incidentally yielded some remarkable documents, now preserved among the papers of Newcastle and Hardwicke. Long lectures were read to the King on the nature of his duties. In response he offered robust abuse. Remonstrating with him in January 1745, Hardwicke said: 'The disposition of places is not enough, if your Majesty takes pains to shew the world that you disapprove of your own work.' The King answered: '*My work!* I was forc'd: I was threatened.' 'Your Ministers', Hardwicke pompously, if correctly, observed, 'are only your instruments of Government.' 'Ministers', the King replied, 'are the Kings in this Country.'[9]

Convincing George II that he must give unqualified support to his Cabinet proved impossible; convincing the Tories that they were now full partners in Hanoverian government was not much easier. The King displayed no interest in making them welcome. The Tories themselves were hesitant allies, and not overly impressed by a handful of offices. What did attract them was rehabilitation

[9] Yorke, *Hardwicke*, i. 382–3.

in the counties, where in many cases they represented a majority of the squirearchy. Pelham undertook to restore substantial numbers of them to the Commission of the Peace in six counties which were specified as a test of his goodwill. This was a sensitive matter. The magistracy had extensive powers, frequently used for electoral advantage. Actual proscription, in the sense of dismissing magistrates for their political views was almost unknown, after the numerous removals made during the first four or five years of Hanoverian rule. It was also unnecessary. From the standpoint of the government it was sufficient to ensure that any new names added belonged to dependable Whigs. Twenty years of this policy rendered the county bench a quiescent body; those few Tories who remained rarely troubled to attend for the pleasure of being outvoted. Stability bred complacency in their opponents, and in due course a matching reluctance to carry out duties which seemed onerous without being politically urgent. Increasingly the Whig rulers of rural England turned to the lesser gentry, to men of business, even, in the 1740s and 1750s, to clergymen, to act on their behalf. The Broad-Bottom threatened to upset this process of stabilization, almost of depoliticization. Substantial additions to the magistracy from the ranks of Tory families would revive party conflicts and imperil entrenched Whig oligarchies. Pelham was prepared to take this risk for the sake of peace at Westminster, but his local supporters brought a different perspective to bear. There was much haggling about the details of the new commissions, and Pelham found it difficult to deliver what he had promised. In the end he did sufficient, with Hardwicke's collaboration as Lord Chancellor, to fulfil the letter of his undertakings. Whether it was enough to disarm the suspicions of the Tories seemed more doubtful, and even if it was, the manner of its doing had created some bitterness.

The *rapprochement* with the Tories might have worked better in peacetime or in a war which did not intensify dynastic difficulties. But the Broad-Bottom was negotiated at the very time when anti-Hanoverianism was at its height. This presented an inescapable dilemma for Pelham. The Old Corps's hostility to Carteret's Continental politics had created an expectation that his fall would bring about a radical change of policy. The capture of Cape Breton, the key to French Canada, in June 1745, seemed promising. It could be portrayed as a concession to the 'blue-water' strategy advocated by the Tories and the New Allies. But in reality it did not signify a new vision of empire in London. For the most part the foreign policy of the Broad-Bottom was difficult to distinguish from that of Carteret. Diplomacy remained a matter of holding together an unstable coalition. War continued as a contest of attrition fought out between Continental armies. The new ministry did not fare better than its predecessor, though it drew comfort, in January 1745, from the Emperor's death and his son's decision not to dispute the succession of Maria Theresa's husband Francis II. The Habsburgs accordingly regained their throne at Frankfurt in 1745. But Bavarian calculations had little effect on grand strategy. What happened in Flanders mattered more. There, in May 1745, rather less than two years after Dettingen, a still greater battle was fought before the important garrison town of Tournai, at Fontenoy. The young Duke of Cumberland, in command of the allied forces, was widely commended for his courage, and the British infantry made an advance in the face of enemy cavalry which rendered the day heroic in the honours of their regiments. It was, none the less, a crushing defeat, rendering the defence of the Low Countries highly problematic.

THE FORTY-FIVE

Within a few weeks of Fontenoy, on 23 July, Prince Charles Edward landed in the Western Isles with a handful of supporters: he quickly collected an irregular army. The King, appropriately, was in Hanover, and returned only on 31 August. He was not disposed to take the threat very seriously. Nor did Cumberland see any need to divert troops defending Belgium against the flower of Louis XV's armies to the preservation of England against a Highland rabble. Father and son were soon forced to revise their view. On 17 September Edinburgh surrendered to the rebels; on 21 September, at Prestonpans, the main body of loyal troops in Scotland, under Sir John Cope, was put to flight. The Young Pretender was convinced that the wonders which his name had wrought in the north would be repeated in the south. In a practical sense his best hope was the generalship of Lord George Murray, his most valuable recruit on the march through Scotland, and representative of one of the greatest Scottish magnate families, the house of Atholl.

By this time Cumberland had not only detached troops but had returned to supervise operations against the invaders himself. None the less the Prince evaded both Cumberland marching from the south and the force under General Wade which pursued him from Newcastle. By 4 December he had reached Derby. Between his own army of about 5,000 and London there was nothing to stop him but a small body of Guards and a hurriedly assembled force of militiamen from the capital, gathered together at Finchley, and later rendered immortally farcical in Hogarth's *The March to Finchley*. The ministry was in some disarray, with the King openly displaying his contempt for the Old Corps, and Bath and Granville parading their restored credit. A panic in the City was arrested only with difficulty and thanks to a morale-boosting subscription to defend the government's credit. Along the Prince's expected line of march, and indeed in many other places, there was much burying of gold, rattling of arms, and nominal harrying of papists. But at what seemed the critical moment the Prince, disappointed of the support which he had been led to expect, decided on retreat. A self-proclaimed double agent, Dudley Bradstreet, subsequently boasted that he had been instrumental in this fateful decision, presenting himself to the Prince as a Jacobite nobleman who had information of substantial forces waiting to ambush the invading army. Bradstreet was actually an Irish papist who had spent a time in gaol for keeping a disorderly house, and the authorities were unimpressed by his services to the cause of Hanover. His curious story, appropriately published along with an account of his other 'adventures' and 'amours' in 1755, is no more bizarre and unbelievable than many others to be found in the history of Jacobitism.[10]

What is clear is that the Prince was reluctant to retreat but was overborne by the opinion of his council. His last stronghold in England, Carlisle, was surrendered on 31 December. On the return march northwards, at Falkirk, he enjoyed a further victory, or what passed for such, over a force under General Hawley. Shortly afterwards Cumberland was sent to Scotland to display his professionalism as a soldier. The denouement on Culloden Moor near Inverness took place on 16 April. At Prestonpans the Highlanders had shown what the broadsword could achieve against well-trained troops. At Culloden it was not enough against the artillery and

---

[10] R. C. Jarvis, *Collected Papers on the Jacobite Risings* (2 vols., Manchester, 1972), ii. 94–106.

numerical superiority which Cumberland brought to bear. There followed the much embroidered story of the Prince's flight to France, and the often exaggerated but none the less harrowing tale of Cumberland's campaign of terror in the Highlands.

How real a threat was the Jacobite rebellion of 1745? Hardwicke, whose judgement was always measured, did not share the early complacency, but neither did he give way to panic later on. His main anxiety was that the French might time an invasion to coincide with the rebellion. The forces at the command of government were sufficient to cope with one or the other, he thought, but not both together.[11] An effective militia might have done something to offset the limitations of the standing army. But in most places the militia was moribund, a victim of Whig reluctance to maintain a force in which Tory country gentlemen must of necessity play a large part. There was also confusion about the precise powers which the Crown could employ to levy forces for defensive purposes. The volunteer regiments raised by Whig peers in the course of the rebellion, and subsequently authorized by Parliament, took time to assemble. Many Whigs as well as Tories viewed them as blatant jobbery on the part of the magnates who commanded them. On the other hand, the army which they confronted was not formidable in point of numbers and arms, whatever its spirit. Its prospects depended less on intimidating or defeating the ministerial forces in open battle, than on attracting the support of Tory Englishmen. The Forty-Five was unquestionably a civil war in Scotland, as the presence of large numbers of Scots in the victorious army at Culloden testifies. But a Stuart Restoration was difficult to envisage without a matching civil war in England, and this showed little sign of materializing.

Jacobite agents always spent much of their time calculating the strength of their covert support in England. Inevitably these calculations contained a good deal of incorrect information and still more of wishful thinking. Tory families which had persistently demonstrated their dislike of the Hanoverian court were often assumed to be enthusiastic advocates of unseating it in favour of its Stuart rivals. What would have happened if a substantial body of French troops had been landed is a question which has long engrossed historians of the Stuart cause. It is, however, hypothetical. The only foreign troops to arrive in England were the

[11] Yorke, *Hardwicke*, i. 482.

6,000 Dutch troops supplied in accordance with long-standing treaty obligations, and placed under the command of Wade. The French, foiled by the weather in the spring of 1744, were unprepared for a further attempt in 1745. Their support for Prince Charles was less than lavish, and certainly gave English Jacobites little cause for hope.

A more useful and altogether unhypothetical question concerns the attitude of the Prince's alleged friends to an expedition which lacked the assistance of a foreign invasion or foreign diversion. It is answered by the evidence of what happened during the Prince's march south. Though he picked up a number of supporters on his progress through the north-west, very few were of a rank to impress propertied opinion. His army went out of its way to avoid alienating English opinion by indiscipline or brutality, and most of the subsequent complaints concerned their conduct on the retreat northwards rather than the advance southwards. He succeeded in collecting taxes in a number of places, but the evidence of willing collaboration is slight. The Welsh gentry were expected, under the leadership of Sir Watkin Williams Wynn, to rise in the Pretender's favour, yet notably failed to do so. The old Lord Barrymore was one of very few major figures to incriminate himself at this time, though even in his case the government did not trouble to prosecute him. 'Now is the time or never,' the Prince wrote to Barrymore as he prepared to march south from Carlisle.[12] On the basis of his subsequent experience the answer was clearly never. Whatever their private preferences, men of property were not prepared to risk either their property or their lives for the Stuarts.

The facts of what happened in 1745 will never completely disperse the belief that English Jacobitism was a potent force, capable of bringing about a second Restoration. The hopes of the exiled court continue to sustain historical illusion as they sustained the exiles themselves. In the Stuart papers, appropriately united with the royal archives at Windsor, thanks to the interest of George IV in the romantic cause of his cousins, there is a great mass of 'evidence' which can be deployed to support the proposition of widespread Jacobite conspiracy. Most of it is highly unreliable, except as a pointer to the state of mind of the Stuarts and the men who spent their lives working on their behalf. The difficulty of

[12] Quoted in R. Sedgwick, *The History of Parliament: The House of Commons, 1715-54*, i. 442.

estimating the quantitative extent of disaffection is not, however, the only one. There is also the problem of assessing its qualitative significance. Expressions of support for the Stuart family could be the product of many things: temporary disappointment or irritation with the status quo, an investment in some form of political reinsurance against the unpredictability of dynastic fortunes, and, not least, a degree of alienation from the Hanoverian regime which did not necessarily entail a sincere disposition to help bring it down.

Sentimental Jacobitism was commonplace. Its main public expression, as the novelist Richard Graves put it, might be a 'harmless pun once a year: in wearing a sprig of rue and thyme on the Eleventh of June (the accession of his late Majesty), as the Tenth was honoured with a white rose.'[13] Its prime function was to create a measure of solidarity among those who opposed the government, and who needed some sense of a viable alternative to reinforce their cohesion: Jacobite clubs were mostly of this variety rather than actively subversive. A Pretender whose remembrance was preserved by emblematic drinking glasses, buckles, bracelets, and garters, more than by musket and bayonet, was unlikely to prove much of a threat. Significantly, this alienation was felt most strongly by young men of Tory background who could not recall the early years of the Hanoverian accession, let alone the Revolution of 1688. It expressed their resentment at their continued exclusion from power except on terms which amounted to total surrender of their identity. To translate even this degree of animosity towards George II into enthusiastic support for James III was a formidable task.

Defenders of the regime believed that the Forty-Five had conclusively demonstrated the Pretender's failure in this respect. The requirements of propaganda induced a shift of Whig attitudes which in time was to do much to heal party rifts. Walpolian Whigs had insisted that the Tory party was essentially a Jacobite party. On many occasions this claim had been used to enforce the loyalty of those wavering Whigs who showed signs of joining the Tories in opposition. Thus had Walpole rallied his supporters during the historic crises of early Hanoverian England, after the South Sea Bubble, and after the failure of his excise scheme. But in 1745 and 1746 Whigs preferred to emphasize the unity of the response to

[13] *The Spiritual Quixote*, p. 24.

the Young Pretender's invasion. 'Not one *English* nobleman, or gentleman of any distinction, joined the rebellious crew.'[14] This was substantially true. It is difficult to believe that anything could have changed it, short of a dramatic collapse of confidence within the regime itself, for instance by an act of folly comparable to James II's conduct in 1688. Whatever else he was, George II was no coward. To Hanover he customarily went in prosperity; in adversity he did not hesitate to return from it.

Alternatively, a change of faith on the part of James III might have brought considerable rewards. But this was not on offer. All kinds of inducements were held out by the Pretender, many of them extremely attractive. An end to the Hanoverian entanglement and Continental warfare would have gained the votes of an overwhelming majority of Englishmen, both Whigs and Tories. Promises of a new era of constitutional government, free from the taint of corruption and the scourge of party, were also difficult to resist whatever scepticism was entertained about their practicality. But none of this cut much ice while those who made the promises remained papists. Assurances of support for the ancient rights and legal privileges of the established Church hardly helped; there was always the hideous precedent of James II, a king who had taken his coronation oath to defend the Church and then set about undermining it. Whig propaganda constantly returned to this argument. Anti-popery, increasingly shunned by the polite classes, lived again as an expression of national unity in 1745. In truth it provided the decisive argument against the legitimate line of Stuarts, as it had done ever since 1689. There were many diverse reasons for opposing the Young Pretender in 1745, and not a few for supporting him. But the one thing which almost all Englishmen and most Scots shared was detestation of his religion.

This is not to say that Tories rushed to demonstrate their loyalty to King George. The associations and subscriptions to support the Crown were the government's principal means of galvanizing opinion in its favour. The earliest and most celebrated of the county associations was that initiated by the Archbishop of York Thomas Herring, two days after Prestonpans, on 23 September. His rousing speech on the occasion, all the more remarkable coming from a cleric, captured the patriotic imagination as nothing previously had. It was to remain long in the collective mind of

[14] George Benson, *Sermons on the Following Subjects* (London, 1748), p. 444.

patriotic Protestantism and did something to enhance the York-shireman's perception of his special place in English history. There followed a country-wide movement on similar lines, and a spate of loyal addresses, quickly printed in the government's official paper, the *London Gazette*.

In the absence of a systematic study of the associations in the context of county and urban communities it is difficult to be sure that they represent very much more than Whig demonstrations designed to sustain Whig morale. Some Tories joined in them, but many did not. In a few counties, for instance Oxfordshire, there was a concerted refusal on the part of the Tory peers and gentry to have anything to do with them. The constitutional argument that it was improper to make free grants to the Crown without parliamentary authority (an argument to be repeated during the War of American Independence) provided a respectable defence of their position, but it is difficult to believe that it was the motivating one. It is much more likely that for many Tories positive support for George II was as repugnant as it was for James III. If political passivity can ever be said to rest on profound principles and deep feelings then it did so in the case of many Tories at this time. The sums subscribed were not as impressive as they might have been. Yorkshire's total of nearly £33,000 was substantially less than one year's contribution to the land tax. The satirist Macnamara Morgan unkindly alleged that Herring's own donation of £200 was not in proportion to his patriotic ardour.[15] But money was not what was required. Many of the promised donations were never taken up. Cash collected was not necessarily spent. The balance of the London subscription had to be given to charities in 1748.[16] If ever a beleaguered government needed to convince itself that it was something more than a mere oligarchy it was in 1745. The value of the associations and subscriptions was that they permitted it to do just that, not much more.

THE PELHAMITE SUPREMACY

The Pretender was not the only loser in 1746. In February the ministry repeated their demonstration of November 1744, but with greater boldness still. Resigning in a body, they dared the King to

---

[15] *The 'Piscopade: A Panegyri-Satiri-Serio-Comical Poem* (London, 1748), p. 31.
[16] W. Maitland, *The History and Survey of London*, i. 661.

form a ministry on his own. He seemed genuinely surprised. Granville later claimed to have been altogether ignorant of any plot, and received the King's summons sitting by his fireside over Demosthenes. He spent two days attempting to form an alternative administration before announcing his total failure. 'Family circumstances which have lately detained me at home, shall now engross me. I will go home, into the country, to my books, to my fireside. For I love my fireside.'[17] Bath was less philosophical but equally impotent in the face of Old Corps unity. It remains astonishing, a unique demonstration of an eighteenth-century government's resolve to act in unison. On other occasions of comparable upheaval, 1714, 1782, 1783, it was dismissal by the Crown, not voluntary resignation, which united those concerned. Even the City threatened to withdraw the funds which it had promised for the following year's borrowing requirement. 'No Pelham, no money.'[18]

When the Old Corps returned to office they completed the work begun in November 1744. Those friends of Bath and Granville who had remained then were expelled now; those 'New Allies' whom it had been necessary to neglect then were appeased now. In particular Pitt was admitted to office, first in the lowly if remunerative post of Joint Vice-Treasurer of Ireland, then as Paymaster-General, another lucrative position. If Pitt had died at any time during the next eight years he would have gone down in history as a canting patriot concerned only to raise his purchase price. His elevation seemed to provide the conclusive proof of George II's humiliation. But Pelham was not vindictive in his hour of triumph. He permitted the King to retain the services of the two brothers, Edward and William Finch, who had been instrumental in maintaining communications between their royal master and Granville, on the grounds that offices in the royal household were not to be interfered with against the King's wishes. Magnanimity was an important aspect of Pelham's management. So was timing. Granville was quick to point out to Hardwicke that the Old Corps had displayed selfishness tantamount to treachery in resigning during a rebellion which threatened the Hanoverian line and the Protestant Succession. The allegation has often been repeated since. In reality it is a mere debating point. When the

---

[17] Yorke, *Hardwicke*, i. 507.
[18] J. B. Owen, *The Rise of the Pelhams* (London, 1957), p. 296.

Old Corps resigned in February 1746 the suppression of the rebellion was a foregone conclusion. They had refrained from such action under considerable royal provocation in the summer of 1745 precisely to avoid precipitating a political crisis at a time of real emergency. However, Pelham did pick his moment carefully. George II's one hope of success in sustaining Bath and Granville was to dissolve Parliament and give them a free hand in a general election. But the risks of a dissolution at such a time would have been very high and would effectually have made the King appear even more irresponsible than his ministers. As the shrewd Duke of Richmond put it, in the midst of the crisis, 'My Lord Granville must have a new Parliament, and that I fear will be a Jacobite one.'[19]

The mass resignation of February 1746, unlike the negotiation of February 1742, and the *démarche* of November 1744, created a viable successor to Walpole's system of government. The first major parliamentary test, the periodic motion to employ Hanoverian troops, in April 1746, was passed with ease by 255 votes to 122. The contrast with the earlier divisions on the same subject in 1742 and 1744 was striking. Subsequent developments confirmed the ministry's basic security. Pelham was the only eighteenth-century Prime Minister whose career was terminated by death rather than dismissal or resignation. In large measure the achievement was a personal one. Pelham had always been Walpole's candidate to succeed him. His experience in financial affairs as a former Lord of the Treasury and Paymaster-General made him master of those fiscal questions in which mastery earned the most respect from back-bench MPs. His coolness under fire, his gift for conciliating his enemies, his solid debating technique, and his capacity for relevant, incisive argument earned him both goodwill and admiration.

The standard contemporary history, Tindal's continuation of Rapin, described Pelham's greatest assets as his transparent honesty and decency: 'no man was ever more, than he was, what he appeared to be.'[20] But there was more to him than an amiable and uncomplicated personality. 'Harry the Ninth', as the press sometimes called him, was an authentic political and parliamentary

---

[19] *Correspondence of the Dukes of Richmond and Newcastle*, p. 205.
[20] N. Tindal, *The Continuation of Mr Rapin's History of England* (21 vols., London, 1759), xxi. 488.

heavyweight; his right to the title of Prime Minister matches that of Walpole, North, and Pitt. It was natural to bracket him with his brother, the Duke of Newcastle. But Pelham did not share power to a greater extent than Walpole, North, or Pitt. His command of patronage was extensive. When Newcastle took over as First Lord of the Treasury on Pelham's death in March 1754, he had to learn the business of managing elections from a standing start, with the help of Pelham's secretary John Roberts. In matters of policy, no Prime Minister could dictate to his Cabinet colleagues. But the fact that Pelham was Newcastle's brother made it easier for him to stand up to him as Secretary of State than it would have been if they had not been related. There were frequent quarrels between the two, most of them made up by the indefatigable Hardwicke, who, as he confessed, sometimes grew tired of carrying water between them. To the extent that Cabinet authority was genuinely shared it was between this trio rather than between the two Pelhams. But it was Newcastle who was neurotic on the subject of authority, not Pelham. Newcastle had a succession of colleagues as Secretary of State after Walpole's fall, Harrington from 1744 to 1746, Chesterfield from 1746 to 1748, Bedford from 1748 to 1751, Holderness thereafter. All but the last found it acutely difficult to put up with Newcastle's interference and insecurity.

Pelham's most complete triumph was his success in drawing into one government disparate, even divided forces. He came close to reuniting the Whigs as a governing party. A few of the Bath–Granville group remained in opposition, but Granville was not one to force his way to office by parliamenteering. He characteristically stopped his friends opposing Pelham's budget in 1746 on the grounds that doing so would offend the King. Eventually, in 1751, he was once more incorporated in the ruling coalition, with the important office of Lord President of the Council. The only substantial Whig enclave in opposition was that associated with the Prince of Wales, who had his own sources of patronage with which to sustain a parliamentary party as well as the promise of more when he succeeded to the throne. He was effectively leader of the opposition to Pelham from the middle of 1746 until his premature death in 1751. As Walpole had found, political acumen could not prevent a vain and ambitious heir to the throne resorting to opposition if he chose. Pelham has traditionally been awarded high marks by comparison with Walpole, notably for his skill in winning over dangerous enemies like Pitt, Chesterfield, Bedford, and Granville. The comparison is not entirely fair. Walpole was temperamentally more combative than Pelham, but he did not always go out of his way to drive his rivals into opposition. The aristocratic obstruction which he faced at court was a consequence of the novelty of his own dominance. The faction dismissed after the excise crisis, for instance, could not have been permitted to remain in office without bringing him down, as the King and Queen recognized. Pelham was never in this position. Walpole had blazed a trail as first minister, minister in the House of Commons, and supreme director of patronage, which Pelham was able to follow with far less controversy. Pelham's own managerial skills are not in doubt, but it is assuming a lot to assume that the way in which he employed them in the 1740s would have worked equally well in the 1720s and 1730s.

The sense that Pelham had reunified the Whigs, on lines of interest if not ideology, was enhanced by his failure to carry the Tories with him. The Broad-Bottom had always been a speculative project. Provoked by Granville's supremacy, it did not survive his humiliation. Of the leading Tories taken in since Walpole's fall, only Lord Gower, related by marriage to the Duke of Bedford, stayed in office after 1746. The Forty-Five had tended to revive party distinctions at the very time when a period of quiet in this respect was needed to cement the work of the architects of the Broad-Bottom. The Tories themselves were an almost impossible party to lead and direct, such was their innate sense of individual independence, and their divisions on family and regional lines. Pelham found it difficult to compel his own supporters to cooperate with the Tories, and the King did nothing to help. The circumstances of 1745 cried out for an imaginative, even a romantic gesture from the Crown. An appeal for Tory aid, reinforced by all the tactics which a court had at its disposal, might have worked wonders. But George II was incapable of imaginative or romantic gestures, even those which were manifestly in his interest. The conciliation of the Tories in the wake of the Forty-Five would have done much to strengthen his power and his dynasty, as his grandson George III, was to discover. Instead the Tories were left to make an alliance with the Prince of Wales.

The political pattern created in the later years of the Pelham ministry came to have a distinct appearance of *déjà vu*, with Pelham enjoying a personal pre-eminence very similar to Walpole's, the Whigs more or less united in an impressively solid alliance, the Tories and the heir to the throne acting together in opposition. But there was one unusual feature: the growing power of the King's second son. Cumberland was only twenty-five when he made his name as the victor of Culloden (his birthday was the day before the battle). What he longed for most was the respect of his comrades and adversaries on the battlefields of Europe, but there he was never able to repeat his triumph over the Highlanders. None the less, as a prince of the blood, as Captain-General of the Army (a title not conferred since the War of the Spanish Succession), and not least as an intelligent and resourceful politician, he was in a powerful position. He acquired his own political following, led by Henry Fox in the House of Commons. The Tories, with their long-standing horror of militarism, feared that he was fashioning his influence in the army into a weapon with which to destroy the civil constitution. The Prince of Wales naturally played on these fears but they are not to be dismissed simply as the prejudices of Cumberland's enemies. Even Pelham remarked that Cumberland did not conduct himself 'prudently with regard to the temper of this country and constitution'.[21] There was also more than a hint of concern in the King's attitude towards his younger son. Pelham judged it prudent to conciliate Cumberland, partly as a counter-balance to the Prince of Wales, partly because, in the last analysis, Cumberland's advice was usually sound. But Cumberland's relations with the ministers, especially Newcastle, were not invariably good and he certainly complicated Pelham's political life.

There was another presence not far removed from the King. Lady Yarmouth had first attracted the admiration of her sovereign on one of his visits to Hanover in 1735. After the Queen's death she resided in England as *maîtresse en titre*. She became an important channel of communication between the King and the politicians and seemed to work equally well with all of them. The impossible Pitt found her as helpful as did the amiable Pelham and the neurotic Newcastle. She seems never to have been suspected of intrigue or double-dealing. It is remarkable that she should not have given way to temptations to which other royal mistresses had succumbed. Without a diarist like Lord Hervey to reveal the

21 M. Wyndham, *Chronicles of the Eighteenth Century*, i. 258.

intimate secrets of the court in the 1740s and 1750s, and without a body of royal correspondence such as exists for George III, it is difficult to know whether she was quite so impartial and disinterested as the absence of accusations against her suggests. But as one of those who kept the machinery of state running smoothly during the last two decades of the King's life, her role has surely been underestimated.

THE PEACE OF AIX-LA-CHAPELLE AND THE LEGACY OF THE FORTY-FIVE

Pelham's skill was seen most completely in the adroitness which he showed in dealing with the major questions of policy confronting him after the consolidation of his power in the spring of 1746. The first priority was to bring to a close a war which had proved expensive, damaging, and inconclusive. His was the only ministry which negotiated a peace and survived it for more than a few months between the Revolution of 1688 and the comparable success of Lord Liverpool's ministry in 1815. Yet the chances of doing so seemed remote. In most respects the war situation was deteriorating rapidly. In Flanders the armies of Louis XV at last achieved the territorial gains which had proved beyond the prowess of the Sun King. Belgium was effectively in French hands by the end of 1746. In the United Provinces a *coup d'état* in favour of the Orange family produced a reinforcement of the allied armies but made little difference to the outcome. In June 1747 Cumberland's forces were decisively defeated at Lauffeld, and when the fortress of Bergen-op-Zoom fell three months later, Holland lay helpless before the French army. The fall of Madras in September 1746 did not suggest that the British East India Company could long hold out against its rival. On the other hand, German politics had stabilized with the Anglo-Prussian alliance of August 1745 and Maria Theresa's recognition of the need to abandon Silesia at the Peace of Dresden in December of the same year. Most promising of all were the naval victories of 1747, which, if they had only occurred earlier in the war, might have transformed the strategic outlook. Anson's victory off Finisterre in May and Hawke's off Belle-Île in October gave the navy effective control of the Channel and the Atlantic.

The way was open for France in the Low Countries and for

Britain in the Americas. The result was an awkward stalemate. Whoever made peace was likely to be accused of throwing away a crucial advantage. Whoever refused to make peace might be saddled with the blame for a disastrous sequel. The diplomats took some time to hammer out a settlement, but its outlines were obvious enough: a return to the status quo, modified to take account of the gains which had been made at the expense of the Habsburgs, by Prussia in Silesia and by Spain in Italy. Pelham's main anxiety was the restoration of Cape Breton. 'Our people', he observed, 'are so mad upon it that it requires more spirit and conduct to get the better of, than I doubt our present Government are masters of.'[22] His technique for making it palatable was none the less effective. He called a general election in 1747, a year before it was due under the Septennial Act, and kept the issue of a pusillanimous peace in the background. The Prince of Wales, who had planned a repetition of his triumphs in 1741, was humiliated in his own Duchy of Cornwall. The Tories lost a fifth of their parliamentary strength. If the evidence of elections meant anything in Hanoverian England, 1747, like 1715, signified the loyalty of the British electorate to the Protestant Succession. With a secure majority, Pelham made his peace at Aix-la-Chapelle and reduced the armed forces as speedily as possible. Newcastle did his best to claim the laurels for concluding the tortuous diplomatic negotiations which had begun at Breda in the summer of 1746 and took fully two years to reach completion, but in reality the credit for ending a divisive and difficult war was his brother's. If there is truth in the story that the wily Bishop Sherlock was responsible for advising an early election, perhaps he deserves a share too.[23]

The immediate post-war situation was not without its problems. The Forty-Five left a legacy of bitterness which took a while to dissipate. The treatment of those identified as traitors was intended as a judicious mixture of firmness and compassion. About 120 were executed, a third of them deserters from the British army. Public attention was concentrated on the fate of the four peers who were tried by the House of Lords, three, Kilmarnock, Cromarty, and Balmerino, under the Treason Act of 1696, the fourth, Lovat, by impeachment. Only one, Cromarty, was reprieved, on the

[22] Sir R. Lodge, *Studies in Eighteenth-Century Diplomacy, 1740–1748* (London, 1930), p. 134.
[23] A. Hartshorne, ed., *Memoirs of a Royal Chaplain, 1729–1763* (London, 1905), p. 127.

grounds of a large family and his wife's pregnancy with her tenth child. Sympathy rather than severity was in the air. The fashionable Dissenting minister James Foster published an account of his last interview with Kilmarnock, exculpating the peer and proclaiming his sincere repentance and new-found loyalty. Even Lovat, executed in April 1747 after a long career of tergiversation, attracted some compassion on account of his advanced age and his stoicism. The romantic haze which eventually settled irremovably over the last desperate adventure of the Stuarts seems to have appeared very early. Within days of Culloden the adolescent Edmund Burke was recording 'how the minds of people are in a few days changed, the very men who but awhile ago, while they were alarmd by his progress so heartily cursed and hated those unfortunate creatures are now all pity and wish it could be terminated without bloodshed'.[24] The poet William Shenstone wrote a haunting ballad, lamenting the sad necessity of the fate of one young volunteer in the Prince's army, Jemmy Dawson.

> Distorted was that blooming face,
> Which she had fondly lov'd so long,
> And stifled was that tuneful breath,
> Which in her praise had sweetly sung[25]

The Lowland Scot Tobias Smollett also wrote a famous ballad, *The Tears of Scotland*. It was later compared with *Lillibulero, Hosier's Ghost*, and *Hearts of Oak* for its popular impact: it 'made every tender-hearted Whig feel himself for moments a Jacobite'.[26]

In a party sense the Forty-Five had reverberations which took some years to die away. In places where Jacobitism had been a force its passing was not without pain. In Manchester the daily spectacle at the Exchange of the heads of three followers of the Young Pretender executed in 1746 provided a vivid reminder of the reality of what had occurred in 1745. One of them belonged to a son of Thomas Deacon, physician, non-juring bishop, and founder of a chapel called 'The True British Catholic Church'. There were bitter clashes between Deacon's supporters and his Whig opponents in the town. Not until 1750 did Manchester's

[24] T. W. Copeland *et al.*, eds., *The Correspondence of Edmund Burke* (10 vols., Cambridge, 1958–78), i. 63.
[25] *The Works in Verse and Prose of William Shenstone* (3 vols., London, 1764–9), i. 187.
[26] 'Essay on Ballads', *London Magazine*, 1769, p. 580.

party strife show signs of subsiding.[27] Elsewhere, too, the strains were considerable. Gower's desertion to the Old Corps had violent repercussions in the West Midlands. In 1747 Staffordshire had its only contested election between 1715 and 1832: it was marked by mobbing which culminated in an attack on Gower's son-in-law the Duke of Bedford at Lichfield Races. The region was known for displays of political intemperance. As late as Restoration Day 1750, Walsall was the scene of a Jacobite riot which required a detachment of dragoons and prosecutions at the subsequent assizes to deal with it.[28]

A similar atmosphere prevailed at Oxford, where undergraduates resorted to drunken revels of a relatively harmless kind, but found themselves subjected to a full-scale inquisition. The university's failure to take these disturbances seriously was followed by proceedings in the courts in London and provoked Newcastle to talk of what had once been mooted under George I, a statute which would bring the universities under royal supervision. No doubt he had in mind the interesting patronage possibilities which Crown control of all fellowships and scholarship would create. However, this plan was dropped. The Prince of Wales leaped to the defence of learning and made a formal compact with the Tories which threatened more than usually tiresome parliamentary obstruction. Moreover, the ministry could hardly proceed against Oxford without taking similar steps against Newcastle's own university of Cambridge. But the episode was an unpleasant reminder that Tory acquiescence in the defeat of the Young Pretender was not at all synonymous with submission to Hanoverian rule.

A controversial election at Westminster in 1749–50 also owed much to the Tory sense of betrayal after the failure of the Broad-Bottom. The election itself resulted from the appointment of Gower's son Lord Trentham to a seat on the Board of Admiralty: the costs of his re-election far exceeded any profit he made from his new office. The 'Independent Electors of Westminster' put up a wealthy City financier, Sir George Vandeput, as Trentham's opponent. Westminster was an exceptionally large, open constituency, a mixture of seething populism and dire corruption. One of the charges against Trentham was that he had given his

---

[27] W. E. A. Axon, *The Annals of Manchester* (Manchester, 1886), pp. 86, 89.
[28] F. W. Willmore, *A History of Walsall and its Neighbourhood* (Walsall, 1887), pp. 368–9.

support to a troupe of foreign actors: he had to contend with the
slogan 'No French Strollers'. His supporters among the Westminster magistracy and in government were also attacked for the severity
with which they responded to a seamen's riot against bawdy-
houses.[29] There followed a riotous contest, a prolonged scrutiny
of the poll, and a vituperative parliamentary debate before Trentham was seated, by a handful of votes. The sequel was enlivened
by Alexander Murray, brother of the Jacobite Lord Elibank,
and an enthusiastic promoter of mayhem during the election.
Summoned before the Commons, he was accused of seditious
conduct and imprisoned in Newgate. Thanks to the Sheriffs of
London he was released at the end of the session, and there was
talk of securing him a second time. In the interim the capital rang
to cries of 'Murray and Liberty'. In retrospect his experience
suggests a foretaste of what was to occur later when Wilkes engaged
in his memorable contests with the House of Commons. But for
Murray's alleged Jacobitism and the caution which it induced in
many Whigs, the resemblance might be still more marked.

This was not to be the only evidence that electoral contests
could still stir deep party controversies. The Tories had suffered
severely in the general election of 1747, but they demonstrated
their continuing capacity to irritate on more than one occasion
during the years which followed. In the metropolitan county of
Middlesex in 1750 the Tory George Cooke decisively defeated
his opponent at a by-election which contrasted strangely with a
conclusive Whig victory at the previous general election. In 1751
Oxford University displayed its anger at a by-election caused by
the decision of one of its MPs, Lord Cornbury, to accept a peerage
from Pelham. Cornbury was heir to the Earldom of Clarendon:
his treachery as last male representative of the main branch of the
Hyde family was punished by the success of a high-flying Tory
country gentleman, Sir Roger Newdigate, at the expense of two
moderate candidates. By the time of the next general election, in
1754, the Prince of Wales was dead and the waves of discontent
created by the Forty-Five seemed little more than ripples; even so
the election for Oxfordshire, when the Duke of Marlborough
challenged Tory control of a county long known for its hostility
to Whiggism, provided perhaps the most infamous of all county

[29] N. Rogers, 'Aristocratic Clientage, Trade and Independency: Popular Politics in Pre-
Radical Westminster', *Past and Present*, 61 (1973), 70–106. See also p. 298.

contests under the unreformed Parliament, and like the Westminster election, dragged on through the subsequent session of parliamentary proceedings. A few years later these great conflicts of Whig and Tory were to acquire a somewhat dated and unreal air; had George II been capable of burying his prejudices they would have lost their *raison d'être* much earlier. In the mean time the bitterness of party politics remained seemingly undiminished.

CONCILIATION IN ENGLAND AND COERCION IN SCOTLAND

Pelham was sometimes choleric under pressure, especially that exerted by his brother. But his politics were ultimately the politics of compromise and conciliation. This was indicated most clearly by his readiness to disown the oligarchical forces generally supposed to sustain the Whig regime. In 1746 he supported the repeal of the clause in Walpole's Act of 1725, which had given the Court of Aldermen a veto over all corporate acts. The statute of 1725 was regarded with extreme dislike in the City. Rightly or wrongly, it seemed to confirm the belief that Whiggism in London was indistinguishable from plutocracy. Pelham's willingness to appease the critics suggested greater confidence in his public reputation. It was only part of what has been called a 'diplomatic revolution in the City'. In 1747 Pelham permitted open bidding for shares in the government's borrowing requirement in place of the usual backstairs bargaining.[30] Three years later he propelled through Parliament a revolutionary scheme to reduce the effective interest rate on the National Debt from four per cent to three per cent within the space of eight years. In 1737 Walpole had toyed with a similar project, only to withdraw his support when threatened by the opposition of the moneyed interest. Pelham was less pusillanimous. Notwithstanding the burden of borrowing added by the war, and in the face of determined opposition from the financial corporations, the Bank, the South Sea Company, and the East India Company, he succeeded in carrying the great majority of subscribers to the National Debt with him. In this Pelham was encouraged, as indeed Walpole had been, with less effect, by Sir John Barnard, a figure of immense prestige with the mass of

---

[30] L. S. Sutherland, 'Sampson Gideon and the Reduction of Interest, 1749–50', *Ec. Hist. Rev.* 16 (1946), 24.

liverymen who made London politics so volatile. But it was not mere populism which moved Pelham. He owed equally valuable support to the great Jewish financier Sampson Gideon, who was no more representative of the small stockholder than the companies who opposed him. Pelham was a believer in the political attractions as well as intrinsic virtues of cheap, efficient government, regardless of party animosities. He was a peculiarly difficult minister for 'patriots' of the old school to oppose.

Not all Pelham's measures were conciliatory. In the wake of the Forty-Five Parliament was asked to approve a series of bills which were designed once for all to eliminate the Highlands as a breeding ground of disaffection. These statutes present a striking contrast to Parliament's customary treatment of local immunities, and indicate something of the determination and rigour which could seize Hanoverian Whigs given sufficient provocation. It is notable that they were not the work of Cumberland, for all his supposed lead in oppressive measures, but the considered policy of the Cabinet, in large measure devised by Hardwicke as Lord Chancellor. In Scotland as in other parts of the realm the traditional Whig concern had been not how it was governed but who governed it. Only when confronting open defiance, in the Malt Tax riots at Glasgow in 1723, and the Porteous Riot in Edinburgh in 1737, had ministers resorted to direct intervention in the affairs of Scotland, and then with a degree of circumspection forced on them by the need to appease their own Scottish supporters. The Union, as defined in 1707, had bestowed sweeping legislative powers on the Parliament at Westminster while protecting Scotland's ecclesiastical and judicial institutions against interference. The possible tensions in this arrangement had been glimpsed in the years immediately following the Union but rarely showed themselves under the early Hanoverians. In Scotland, as in Ireland and the American colonies, and indeed in English counties and corporations, Whig ministers preferred not to unleash the full power of Parliament, lest it provoke a popular reaction which might threaten their own hegemony. Scottish government under George I and George II was essentially about patronage. From the perspective of London, the question was how to ensure that Scottish peers and MPs played their part in maintaining the Hanoverian regime; from that of Edinburgh, it was how to ensure that Scotsmen and Scottish interests obtained their due regard. The successful Scottish

politicians were those who succeeded in balancing these not necessarily incompatible requirements.

The past masters at this exacting but rewarding game were the
two Campbell brothers, the second and third Dukes of Argyll. The
third Duke, who as Earl of Islay had been one of Walpole's most
useful allies, and who succeeded his mercurial brother in 1743,
was a particularly adroit manipulator of Anglo-Scottish relations.
The play of factions and changing political circumstances occasionally interfered with the Argyll supremacy but for the most part it
was the central fact of Scottish politics throughout the reign of
George II. So far as the ordinary government of Scotland was
concerned the Forty-Five made little difference. Indeed its main
effect was to correct a minor divergence from the prevailing system
which had been permitted at the fall of Walpole. In 1742 a separate
Scottish department of state had been established with the Marquis
of Tweeddale at its head. A similar experiment had been brought
to a close by Walpole in 1725: this one was terminated in 1746.
Tweeddale had refused to take the rebellion seriously in its early
stages, and when he resigned at the beginning of the year, he was
not replaced. Thereafter, with periodic irritations and interruptions
from his English colleagues or his Scottish rivals, Argyll was
effective viceroy of Scotland until his death in 1761.

But the kingdom which Argyll ruled was not left as it had been
before 1745. To the rediscoverers of the romance of the Highlands
in the late eighteenth century it was the Disarming Acts of 1746
and 1748, especially the prohibition on traditional dress, which
struck the most poignant note. More important in reality were two
Acts of 1747, one abolishing heritable jurisdictions, the other
appropriating confiscated estates to the use of the Crown, instead
of permitting their sale to third parties in line with precedent. Both
belonged with an elaborate scheme thrashed out in Edinburgh as
well as London, with Argyll's long-standing 'sousministre' Lord
Milton, playing a leading part. Milton had an interest in social
regulation which went far beyond the political emasculation of the
Highlands. As a member of the Board of Trustees, the body which
since 1727 had done much to encourage Scotland's increasingly
important linen manufacture, he had a strong sense of the connection between commercial progress and political stability. His
summary of his prescription for the Highlanders was 'civilising
them by introducing Agriculture, Fisherys, and Manufactures, and

thereby by degrees extirpateing their barbarity, with their chief marks of distinction, their language and dress, and preventing their idleness, the present source of their poverty, Theift and Rebellion'.[31] Like many other progressive Scots Milton believed that it was the feudal structure of Highland life which constituted the underlying problem. The aim was to abolish the judicial rights and pseudo-military authority of the clan chiefs, and to remove their tenants or 'tacksmen', regarded as a useless and parasitic layer of rural society. By these means the peasantry of upland Scotland would be liberated and converted into a prosperous, property-loving tenantry on the English model. Estates forfeited by attainder were designed as the nucleus of a great Crown estate which would serve as a model for the new agricultural economy. The abolition of heritable jurisdictions, the great body of legal, administrative, and fiscal rights which underpinned the eccentric independence of Scottish magnates, was essential if a uniform society comparable to other parts of the empire was to be created.

This project could hardly be carried out in its entirety. The forfeited estates were burdened with debts which had to be cleared before they could be used to initiate a new era of agrarian capitalism. Not until 1752 did Parliament set up a trust to administer the estates, and not until the early years of George III was progress made with the problem of the debt. The most ambitious part of Milton's scheme, the purchase of additional lands to provide government with a dominating influence in the Highlands, was never undertaken. Heritable jurisdictions also presented difficulties. They were guaranteed by Article Twenty of the Treaty of Union, and were by no means restricted to the Highlands. Many Scottish Whigs objected to their extinction, and even English Whigs accepted that infringement of property rights on this scale must be compensated at a generous rate. The government attached high importance to these matters. In the Commons, what Newcastle described as 'this Battle for our Constitution' proved a testing one.[32] At the same time Hardwicke told the Duke of Cumberland, 'how deeply we are engaged in Scotch Reformation'.[33] In the Lords, Hardwicke himself delivered a speech which was regarded with something like awe at the time, and which remains fascinating

---

[31] C. S. Terry, *The Albemarle Papers* (2 vols., Aberdeen, 1902), ii. 447.
[32] *Correspondence of the Dukes of Richmond and Newcastle*, p. 244.
[33] British Library, Add. MS 35589, fo. 211: 16 Apr. 1747.

for the light it casts on the legal radicalism of a Whig customarily regarded as the embodiment of oligarchical conservativism. Hardwicke did not deny the antiquity of the rights which he was proposing to abolish at a stroke. They were simply indefensible because they conflicted with a sacred principle. 'I look upon the administration of justice as the principal and essential part of all government.'[34] Unless the judicial power was vested fully in the Crown as the ultimate representative of the public, there could be no guarantee of the individual's liberties. This was not the only instance of Hardwicke's thoroughgoing Whiggism. An Act of 1746 took stern measures against the non-jurors, and Hardwicke used his influence in the Lords in 1748 to reinforce it with a provision which inhibited the clergy of the episcopalian Church from officiating in Scotland without the approval of English or Irish bishops. This assumed that Scottish episcopalians were Jacobites unless proved otherwise to the satisfaction of English Whigs. It was one of the rare occasions when the bishops in the House of Lords rebelled against their political masters, in this case in vain.

The effect of this legislation is difficult to determine. The first generation of Englishmen to take a serious interest in the subject from a cultural and anthropological viewpoint, in the 1770s, thought it crucial. But it does not follow that the disintegration of Highland civilization should be attributed to Harwicke's programme. Agrarian improvement was not unknown before 1745. 'Gentle Lochiel', whose early adherence to the Young Pretender helped ensure that the invasion was not aborted at the start, and who was wounded at Culloden, has been described as 'a brisk and enterprising business man'.[35] Contact with England and its commercial empire had already transformed Lowland society and it is difficult to believe that it would not soon have had a comparable impact in the Highlands. It may be that the statutory incursion into Scottish life of the Pelham Ministry is of more interest for what it reveals about English Whiggism than for what it did to Scotland.

---

[34] Yorke, *Hardwicke*, i. 594.
[35] B. Lenman, *The Jacobite Risings in Britain, 1689–1746* (London, 1980), p. 245.

NEWCASTLE'S DIPLOMACY AND LEICESTER HOUSE POLITICS

Englishmen had gone to war in 1739 to win an empire from Spain; they went out of it in 1748 on the point of a prolonged struggle for another empire with France. The mutual restoration of conquests in 1748 did not remove the basic cause of Anglo-French conflict. In India, jockeying for position by the rival East India Companies continued. The fact that the governments at home were not technically involved as principals did not lessen the consequence of what was being fought. In the Caribbean there were interminable disputes over the status of the so-called Neutral Islands. In America French activity around the Great Lakes made it obvious that the ambition of creating a great empire running from the St Lawrence to New Orleans was by no means dead. Contrary to the view subsequently propagated by the followers of Pitt, Newcastle had a clear understanding of these menaces. He saw, as Pitt came to see, that they could not be neutralized without blocking French power in Continental Europe. Pitt's celebrated boast in the next war that he had conquered America in Germany was better evidence of his own hypocrisy than Newcastle's inadequacy. This is not to say that Newcastle brought quite the same clarity of vision to his schemes which Pitt did; but the real criticism of his foreign policy is of a different kind.

Newcastle's main object was so to buttress the Old System that France would be deterred from meddling in Germany or threatening Hanover. The Old System as such was not what it had been. The Austrians were quick to remember the inconsistency of British policy between 1735 and 1748, and quicker still to forget Britain's part in the preservation of the Habsburg empire in the early 1740s. The Dutch were manifestly incapable of offering the kind of support which they had provided in the age of Marlborough. The Franco-Prussian alliance was as menacing as ever. Newcastle sought additional allies, if necessary by means of peacetime subsidies. His treaties with Bavaria and Saxony went through Parliament in 1750 with relative ease; but in the Cabinet they aroused opposition, not least from his own brother.

Worse was to come. Newcastle adopted a scheme for securing the election of Maria Theresa's son the Archduke Joseph as King of the Romans; if successful, it would have guaranteed the succession to the Holy Roman Empire, and averted a repetition of the contested election which had set Europe alight in 1740. In Newcastle's mind it would also cement Anglo-Austrian relations after a difficult period, show the Bourbons the futility of further intrigues in the Empire, and display the King of England in that role which most appealed to him, the arbiter of Habsburg and Hohenzollern fortunes. This was not, in origin, the hare-brained project which it later came to seem. However, it quickly got out of hand. Newcastle treated the Electors of the Holy Roman Empire much as he would have treated the electors in a rotten borough. It was a rational mode of procedure, but the rules of the game made the Empire a trickier, and infinitely more costly affair. There was no fixed period for the election, nor even any necessity for such an election to take place. (It was eventually conducted in 1764, without fuss or fanfare.) Nor was it certain whether the rules of election required a bare majority or an 'eminent' (two-thirds) majority. Naturally enough, the Electors themselves took every opportunity to raise the bidding and postpone a determination on these points. By 1752 when he travelled to the Continent with the King to supervise this great affair, Newcastle had spent large sums of money, infuriated his brother, made George II look foolish before the powers of Europe, and, crowning folly, alienated the Austrians by his failure. The ultimate irony was that Vienna declined to co-operate further without a guarantee from Versailles of its acceptance of the election. The French court refused to oblige without concessions from Britain in America. Even Newcastle saw the absurdity of making sacrifices in America to implement a plan whose ultimate object was to avoid making such sacrifices, and the scheme fizzled out.

There was no parliamentary crisis to accompany these manœuvres. The election of 1747 had been exceptionally quiet and the subsequent Parliament was correspondingly submissive for the most part. 'In the memory of England', observed Horace Walpole, 'there never was so inanimate an age: it is more fashionable to go to church than to either House of Parliament'.[36] Walpole also noted when Pelham died at the end of this Parliament, in March 1754, that he had been a remarkably lucky minister.[37] One piece of good fortune, in a political sense, was the premature death of the Prince

[36] *Horace Walpole's Correspondence*, xx. 357–8.
[37] Ibid. 411.

of Wales in 1751. It changed the calculations of a generation of politicians. Also, like the last such instance, the death of Prince Henry in 1612, it provoked a great number of patriotic laments and poetic effusions, not least by men who had lost their own as well as their country's saviour. In Parliament it further strengthened the ministry's position. The death of the heir to the throne could not lengthen the reign of his father, but it rendered its likely consequences less predictable. The Princess Dowager of Wales hastened to offer her duty to George II. Her adolescent son was utterly dependent on his grandfather's will. The uncertainty inseparable from a court in which the King was approaching seventy years of age remained but in its new form it promoted circumspection rather than risk-taking. It was not a time to make strong speeches in Parliament, speeches which might be remembered and used against their authors.

This is not to say that dynastic tensions were eased by Frederick's death. The Regency Act of 1751 made the Princess Dowager Regent in the event of the King dying before her son attained his majority. Cumberland was appointed President of the Regency Council, to which she would be responsible for the exercise of her powers. The Duke professed to be deeply offended that he was to be denied the Regency. Relations between Cumberland and his sister-in-law were even worse than those which had formerly obtained between Cumberland and his brother. The spectre of Jacobitism, which should have been laid to rest in 1746, still haunted this somewhat unreal scene. Rumours of conspiracy abounded, culminating in the Elibank Plot to assassinate the King in 1752, and a Prussian plot of 1753. In both, Newcastle's *agent provocateur* 'Pickle the Spy' played a large part in exaggerating expectations and fears on either side. When Lochiel's outlawed brother Archibald Cameron was foolish enough to be caught in Scotland in 1753, the ministry thought it necessary to have him executed.

In 1752 there was a ludicrous but damaging scandal in the household of the young Prince George. The Prince's governor Lord Harcourt and his preceptor Thomas Hayter, Bishop of Norwich, accused their immediate subordinates, Andrew Stone and George Lewis Scott, of teaching their charge Jacobite doctrines. Stone was a close associate of Newcastle, having acted for many years as his secretary; his political influence was considerable, and it was easy to attach a sinister connotation to his activities. The fact that Scott was a protégé of Bolingbroke's also exposed him to the malice of envious Whigs. Harcourt was replaced by Lord Waldegrave, and Hayter by his brother Bishop of Peterborough, John Thomas. This did not put a stop to the innuendo. In 1753 Lord Ravensworth made public a story about some Jacobite revels of twenty years before, allegedly involving Stone, his friend William Murray, now Solicitor-General, and James Johnson, now Bishop of Gloucester. What passed for evidence among Jacobite-hunters gave the story some support. Stone had been accused of treachery by Hayter the year before. Murray, a brilliant lawyer and a loyal servant of the Pelhams, was also brother of Lord Dunbar, at one time virtually chief minister of the Pretender. Johnson had been proposed as a possible successor to Hayter in 1752 but vetoed on account of his upopularity. All three had been at Westminster under its supposedly Jacobite headmaster Robert Freind, and all three had gone on to Christ Church, Oxford. School and college loyalties were well to the fore in the resulting parliamentary debates. The administration took the matter seriously and held a formal Cabinet Council investigation. Ravensworth's evidence, a statement by the Recorder of Newcastle Christopher Fawcett, had looked impressive, but before this tribunal Fawcett caved in and the accused were triumphantly vindicated. None the less the belief that there was no smoke without fire ensured that the story was not forgotten. Its historical significance was very slight, but its historiographical importance much greater. The notion that the future George III had been indoctrinated at a tender age by a set of crypto-Jacobites fitted too well with later perceptions of his 'prerogative' tendencies to be dropped. The link with Bolingbroke, through Scott, was particularly useful in this respect. Bollingbroke's tract *The Idea of a Patriot King* originally written some years earlier but published without his authority from a manuscript among the papers of Pope, could be interpreted as the blueprint for a new form of kingship to be proclaimed on behalf of Frederick, Prince of Wales, and, after his death, Prince George. A promising conspiracy was at hand when the Whig opponents of George III cast about for damning evidence of his subversive upbringing.

FACTION AND THE 'JEW BILL'

There was no eighteenth-century ministry which could not be called factious in some sense, and hardly any Cabinet genuinely united for any period of time. But the ministry of 1746–54 seemed riven by faction because its arguments were not translated into great conflicts in and beyond Parliament. The continual disputes between Pelham, Newcastle, and Cumberland never threatened Pelham's own pre-eminence and made little difference to the measures adopted; yet they inevitably affected the daily life of courtiers and ministers. They were also complicated by wider Cabinet rivalries. The Duke of Bedford and his ally the Earl of Sandwich were prominent in these until their ejection in 1751. The troubles thereby caused reveal the way in which essentially personal differences could threaten the stability of the government. Bedford's quarrel with Newcastle in 1748 was the predictable one that he was not permitted as Secretary of State to direct his own office, but was treated in effect as a junior minister responsible to Newcastle rather than to the King. Cumberland's current contempt for Newcastle, based on earlier disagreements about the conduct of peace negotiations in 1747–8, led him to support Bedford. In due course the King was induced to take their side, and before very long Newcastle was warning his brother and Hardwicke that he would resign rather than be humiliated by a combination of the King, Cumberland, and Bedford.

The pettiness of these quarrels stands out clearly in the voluminous documentation to be found in the Newcastle and Hardwick papers. In part they were a product of the internalized politics of the Pelham government: a ministry which set out to comprehend all the talents must inevitably be subject to their rivalries. In part, too, they were a result of Newcastle's temperament, as Pelham and Hardwicke themselves well knew. But Newcastle spent almost thirty-three years of his life in high office under George II and much of the blame attaches to the monarch rather than the minister. The King relished a quarrel between his own ministers, provided it did not threaten his Electoral interests or his personal prejudices. Unlike his successor he was almost completely lacking in personal loyalty to those who served him, and while he often wanted the courage to stand up to them, he never unwaveringly committed himself to support them. He rarely missed an opportunity to annoy

the Duke. In this instance the eventual outcome was predictable.
Newcastle was humoured, Bedford and Sandwich were forced out,
and a measure of temporary harmony was restored to the Cabinet,
but only after prolonged and acrimonious disputes. From the
outside Pelhamite politics looked placid; from the inside they seem
peevish.

In due course Bedford had an opportunity to take his revenge.
With a general election due in 1754 a Jewish Naturalization Bill
was put before the penultimate session of the Parliament. It was a
relatively modest measure, in effect authorizing Parliament to
naturalize individual Jews. It belonged with previous attempts, in
1747, 1748, and 1751, to attract foreign immigrants whose skills
and capital seemed more than usually valuable at a time when
there was much concern about population decline and labour
shortage. These earlier proposals had given rise to strong
opposition, which Pelham might have done well to recall. But
opinion of a kind which he respected was in favour of relaxing the
legal restrictions. Malachy Postlethwayt gave considerable space
to the arguments for going so in his *Universal Dictionary*, pointing
out that in London some 30,000 foreigners were crammed into
two quarters of the City, with no prospect of assimilation into the
community around them unless they were granted a minimum of
rights to acquire property. His only restriction would have been a
ban on voting in elections for first-generation immigrants.[38] None
the less, naturalization was unpopular, especially in corporate
towns where freemen feared open competition for employment. In
London anxiety on this point was heightened by legal contests
between employers bent on hiring non-freemen, and journeymen
determined to protect their traditional monopoly of work. Outside
Parliament the debate was prolonged but inconclusive. As the
Gentleman's Magazine put it, 'The argument for it is—to fill our
island with industrious people; that against it, our manufacturers
will then want work.'[39] The Bill of 1751, supported by the ministry,
provoked tumultuous demonstrations and was defeated by the
narrow majority of 129 votes to 116.

The Jew Bill of 1753 began in the House of Lords and was not
expected to be as controversial. Its peculiar weakness was that it
permitted a junction between two elements which had often been

[38] *sub* 'People'.
[39] 1747, p. 45.

kept apart by the problem of Jacobitism: popular, patriotic, xeno-phobic Whiggism, and High Church Toryism. Initially the min-istry held out for the bill. It passed the Lords with little difficulty, and the clamour which it provoked in the Commons was overcome by sheer weight of numbers. But when peers and MPs departed from London for the summer they were left in no doubt of the unpopularity of what they had done. The bishops, whose lines of communication with popular opinion by the medium of the parochial clergy were in some ways more reliable than those maintained by party politicians, were especially appalled by the response. A torrent of anti-Semitism flowed from the press. The threat which it bore to court Whigs who were shortly to face their electors at the polls seemed to justify retreat. In the following parliamentary session the Act was repealed. Bedford sought to make an issue of an older statute of 1740, which naturalized Jews who settled in the colonies, but found little support. If Pelhamite government was an oligarchy, it was evidently one which was remarkably sensitive to the opinions of those whom it governed.

THE NEWCASTLE MINISTRY

Pelham's death in March 1754, advanced if not caused by one of the bouts of gluttony to which he was prone, opened the way to an intriguing constitutional experiment. It is a question whether the eighteenth-century system could ever permit a successful min-istry to be controlled from the House of Lords. Peers did not make enduring Prime Ministers until Lord Liverpool broke the pattern in the early nineteenth century. Newcastle had the chance to do so if any could. His assets included long experience of government, an unaristocratic devotion to politics as a way of life, an underrated gift for managing George II, and lifelong identification with the ruling body of Whigs. There were, indeed, commoners who seemed well fitted to assume the mantle of Walpole and Pelham. Fox, protégé of Walpole himself, friend of the Duke of Cumberland, experienced Secretary at War, and powerful speaker in the Commons, was the obvious choice. Pitt, a fiery orator who had proved his pragmatism by loyal service under Pelham, had sufficient ambition and arrogance for the highest office, and personal ruthlessness beyond any politician of his age. Murray, Solicitor-General, had the best legal mind of his generation and the most complete all-round debating talent of his time. But Murray did not aspire to ministerial responsibility, and was besmirched with the mud which had stuck to him during the Jacobite scare of 1753. Pitt was not much liked by Old Corps Whigs and remained uncongenial to the King. Fox, like other Tories who had been converted to Walpolian Whiggism for the sake of office, was never altogether trusted by his colleagues, and his association with Cumberland was a decidedly mixed blessing. Above all he was *persona non grata* with Hardwicke, a dangerous enemy indeed. Like many Lord Chancellors, Hardwicke expected to be exempted from party politics even when he engaged in them himself. He never forgot the personal attack which Fox had made on him in opposition to his Marriage Bill in 1753, though it was not more bitter than his own on Fox. Hardwicke took the credit for dishing Fox and installing his friend Newcastle at the Treasury. But George II may have had his own reservations about entrusting everything to Cumberland and Fox. Later, in 1757, he was to give them a chance. But that was in wartime when Cumberland's role was more important, and when the only alternative was the unpalatable one of a ministry headed by Pitt. In 1754 the arguments were nicely balanced, but in the end they all seemed to point to Newcastle.

The Newcastle administration was not a success. It would be wrong to lay the exclusive blame for this on its director. Newcastle had integrity, industry, judgement, and common sense. He was a better manager of men than it suited most of his contemporaries to admit. No minister could have borne so much responsibility and disposed of so much patronage over so many years without making enemies. His peculiar misfortune was that while his deficiencies were minor, they were mostly ridiculous. He was perpetually anxious and perpetually excited. He completely lacked either *gravitas* or bravado, or indeed any other impressive exterior qualities which might conceal his lack of confidence in himself. He was not so much disliked as mocked: had he been more feared he would also have been more respected. Many ministers suffered more from the brutality of the press, but perhaps none provoked more ridicule, both private and public. This did not make him a worse minister, but it certainly made him a less effective one. What mattered most, however, was the difficulty which he experienced in managing the House of Commons at a time when it required firm and persuasive leadership. Initially he offered Fox the chance to defend the government's measures there, but when Fox discovered that he was to have the responsibility without the disposal of patronage, he soon declined. Newcastle fell back on Sir Thomas Robinson, an experienced diplomat but a lightweight parliamentarian. The result was disastrous.

The new Parliament met in November 1754 with an ample ministerial majority, but it did nothing to raise the minister's morale. Pitt and Fox, still occupying the offices which they had held under Pelham, pounced on Robinson and Murray. Robinson could not stand up to them; Murray would not. The sense that Newcastle could not survive for long was enhanced by the drift to war in America. A Virginian force under Colonel George Washington, ordered to warn off the French forces entrenching themselves on the Ohio, was defeated in open battle in the spring of 1754. Newcastle threw himself into the hands of Fox by asking Cumberland to join the Cabinet and provide the benefit of his military expertise. Hardwicke later identified this as one of crucial weaknesses of Newcastle's ministry: 'The not refusing to carry on the King's Business, but on Condition, that the Army shall be subservient to the Ministers and in effect to the Civil Power.'[40] The decision to send an expeditionary force to America under General Braddock was virtually taken by Fox and Cumberland, with Newcastle unable or unwilling to exert his authority. The spectacle of a government with a massive majority in Parliament, in a state of total disarray, was certainly bizarre.

That Newcastle could not survive without sharing power was obvious. Pitt and Fox were the only men with both the stature and ambition to determine the fate of Newcastle's ministry. Fox seems to have decided at this juncture that he must throw in his lot with the Duke. In retrospect this is usually considered a miscalculation. He was offered little more than a promise of a place in the Cabinet, and a say in the management of the Commons. But it is likely that Fox was acting on Cumberland's orders. The alternative, thoroughgoing opposition, was hardly possible when Cumberland was so publicly committed to the ministry. Pitt took a riskier course, dictated by desperation. He had evidently decided to cut loose after Pelham's death, in the belief that he was unlikely to get a better opportunity to improve his standing. Submission

[40] British Library, Add. MS 35595, fo. 4.

to Pelham had meant accepting the authority of a man thirteen years his senior and infinitely more experienced. Acquiescing in the priority given to Fox would have been tantamount to surrendering for good. As always, Pitt, an underrated tactician and an overrated strategist, made some shrewd tactical decisions. He had nothing to gain by shoring up the power of Fox and Cumberland. Moreover, there was credit to be earned with the Prince of Wales by opposing his uncle. Pitt was also beginning to see the value of conciliating the Tories. This required hypocrisy on an impressive scale. As late as December 1754, he had publicly berated Oxford University for its lingering Jacobitism. Before very long he was cultivating the friendship of William Beckford, one of the new generation of Tory leaders, and a man with useful connections in the City. By 1756 he was poised to project himself as the latest patriot leader capable of abolishing Whig and Tory distinctions.

The political process begun during the session of 1754-5 intensified in the months which preceded that of 1755-6. In May 1755 a squadron was dispatched under Admiral Boscawen to prevent French Canada being reinforced from home. What constituted a formal act of war was the subject of much disagreement in the eighteenth century, but even in Britain resort to naval force without a declaration of war was criticized. In the event Boscawen failed in his object and the ministry reaped the odium but not the advantage of a pre-emptive strike. There followed an onslaught on commercial shipping, and French preparations for counter-attack, notably with an assault on Minorca. The need for allies on the Continent (Newcastle's treaties of 1750-1 had lapsed by the time they were needed, in 1755) led to the hasty conclusion of subsidy treaties with Hesse-Cassel and Russia. The prospect of a parliamentary session dominated by the old wrangles about Continental alliances and Hanoverian influence was all too near. Worst of all, the defeat of Braddock's expedition and the death of its leader promised a punishing time for the minister deputed to defend Newcastle's military record. Who would it be? Hardwicke would have gone to any lengths to foil Fox, but the King seemed ready to go to any lengths to keep out Pitt. Fox was duly installed as Secretary of State and acknowledged leader of the Commons.

The session was as stormy as anticipated. At its beginning the ministry had a majority still in excess of 200. But Pitt was in majestic form. His speech likening the junction of Newcastle and Fox to the confluence of the Rhône and Saône was one of the classic orations of the unreformed Parliament. Still more interesting debates seemed promised when Pitt and his friends were formally dismissed for their insubordination. As at the beginning of the previous Continental war, Hanover provided the central theme. In January 1756 the Convention of Westminster, a defensive alliance with Frederick of Prussia, was announced. In retrospect the Convention has a special importance because of its part in precipitating the Diplomatic Revolution. Neither party intended it to have this effect. Frederick was pushed into it by Newcastle's subsidy treaty with Russia the previous year, a treaty which held the alarming possibility of a triple attack on Prussia, by Britain from the west, Austria from the south, and Russia from the east. He was perhaps over-hasty in his apprehension but he certainly did not intend his reinsurance policy with London to endanger his prior engagement with Versailles. For Newcastle the Convention was a logical means of safeguarding Hanover; for this purpose Prussia was always the preferred candidate, a point on which English ministers were agreed.

The consequences were none the less momentous. In Vienna there was a shrewd appreciation that if the main object of Habsburg policy was to be the recovery of Silesia and the reduction of Prussian influence in Germany, there was much to be said for a radical reappraisal of relations with the Bourbons. In Paris there was a less shrewd but understandable anger that Frederick had precipitately allied with his own ally's enemy. In May 1756 the First Treaty of Versailles was signed, initiating a defensive alliance between France and Austria; before very long, the Russians, equally offended by the Anglo-Prussian accord, joined this pact. An offensive alliance of the three powers did not follow until a year later, but in effect the diplomatic pattern of the Seven Years War had been set. In Britain the political consequences were predictably narrower. The Convention of Westminster was interpreted as another example of Hanoverian measures. When Hanoverian and Hessian troops were brought to England in the spring of 1756 in case of a French invasion this impression was enhanced. The Prussians had been paid to protect Hanover and expose England to invasion. Now Hanover must be paid to provide aid which would not have been necesssary if a less craven attitude towards the Electorate had been adopted. This line of reasoning was naturally a popular one.

PITT AND PATRIOTISM

There was little that was original about Pitt's campaign in the Commons in 1755–6. The arguments and emotions, the latter more in evidence than the former, were those which had figured so much in 1742 and 1743. Nor did Pitt's opposition yield immediate results. The ministry was in no danger of losing its parliamentary majority. MPs rightly considered that Newcastle's diplomacy was the proper and practical means of dealing with a threatening situation. The real significance was that Pitt was staking out ground which had been left vacant by the politics of the previous years. 'Patriotism', extinguished by Pulteney's pragmatism, Pelham's skill, and an authentic challenge to the Protestant Succession, was viable once again. Intelligent observers found this difficult to believe at first. Horace Walpole remarked in August 1755 that 'there is not a mob in England now capable of being the dupe of patriotism; the late body of that denomination have really so discredited it, that a minister must go great lengths indeed before the people would dread him half so much as a patriot.'[41]

Pitt himself must have been aware of the dangers and difficulties of his enterprise, on which, indeed, he would hardly have embarked but for the novel situation created by the death of Pelham and the rise of Fox. He did his best to inject new life into the patriot programme. The Militia Bill of 1756 was the work of the Townshend brothers, Charles and George, but Pitt gave it his full support. It had strong backing from the Tories and it was difficult for Whigs to oppose at a time of crisis. The militia was viewed as a constitutional force, officered by men of property, manned by Englishmen drawn from the plough and the loom: it had none of the low, mercenary characteristics of the standing army. The government preferred to defeat it in the Lords rather than bear the odium of opposing it in the Commons, and it was obvious that in some form it was likely to pass into law before long. Pitt's astuteness went beyond the militia. There was talk of the need for economy and efficiency in government. Pitt himself, as Paymaster-

---

[41] *Horace Walpole's Correspondence*, xx. 493.

General, had refrained from profiting by the considerable balances which passed through his hands. He was not in fact the first Paymaster to act thus, but he was the first to parade his virtue. It was doubtless convenient to forget that this man of the people in the making had shown a lamentable want of 'patriot' consistency in the 1740s. Even now, while he belaboured the Newcastle ministry, he sat for a pocket borough of the Duke of Newcastle.

Pitt's investment in patriotism was mere speculation: he can hardly have foreseen what profit it would bring, or how quickly. Everything went wrong for Newcastle and Fox in the spring and summer of 1756. In the Mediterranean the unfortunate Admiral Byng opted to save his fleet, after a brief encounter with the French navy, rather than risk it to preserve Minorca. There was endless debate about the extent to which he was personally responsible for this critical reverse. There were other candidates, the Governor of Gibraltar, who refused to reinforce Byng, and the ministers themselves, accused of giving him an inadequate force. In the event he paid the price of court martial and execution himself. In North America Fort Oswego fell to a new French commander, Montcalm. In India Calcutta had to be surrendered to the professed enemy of the East India Company, Siraj ud-Daula. Notwithstanding their parliamentary majority, Fox and Newcastle felt increasingly isolated. In May 1756 the Prince of Wales came of age and promptly used his new status to choose his own first minister or Groom of the Stole. He selected Lord Bute, a Scottish peer with little political experience, and a close friend of the Prince's mother (some said her lover). Lest anyone doubt the direction in which he was moving, Pitt made it clear that he had a high opinion of Lord Bute, and infinite respect for his future sovereign.

It is difficult to be sure which of these developments played the decisive part in bringing down the Newcastle administration. Probably it was Minorca, which reduced Fox to a state of utter panic and put Newcastle in a position from which there was no escape. The combination of a naval defeat followed by a major territorial loss was devastating. The Tories were privately jubilant, and busy preparing a campaign of protest in the counties to demonstrate the existence of a national movement in favour of political change. It proved unnecessary. Fox resigned in October, shortly before the new parliamentary session. Murray had already given up his political duties to be appointed Lord Chief Justice of the King's Bench; a judicial career had always been his prime ambition, and his elevation was the result of a long-standing promise by the reluctant Newcastle. Newcastle himself resigned shortly after Fox. For the King there remained no alternative but to treat with Bute and Pitt.

Leicester House and some undefined public opinion, largely composed of the Tories and those they represented, were no basis for an enduring government. Pitt's ministry was a partnership with the Duke of Devonshire, a Whig uncontaminated, from Pitt's standpoint, by close association with the Pelhams. But without the Old Corps it was manifestly weak. Unlike his son in 1784, Pitt was unable to build up sufficient parliamentary support to defy his opponents. No doubt it would have helped if George II, like George III, had made plain his confidence in the new minister and shown his willingness to call a general election to sustain him. It was an odd situation. Newcastle had resigned with a massive parliamentary majority on paper; Pitt governed with a negligible parliamentary minority on paper. His strategy at Westminster was a characteristic piece of pragmatism dressed up as principle. He did not hesitate to continue Newcastle's Continental policy. An Army of Observation was to be sent to protect Hanover, but like Pulteney's Pragmatic Army of 1742 it was somehow not to be spoken of as an authentic Continental army. On the other hand, the Hanoverians and Hessians were to be sent home, and Highlanders recruited in their place.

Pitt was prostrated for much of his short-lived ministry. As at other critical points in his career his health, mental as much as physical, seems to have collapsed under the pressure. Government and Parliament alike were rudderless. In April 1757 Cumberland delivered the *coup de grâce*. The King dismissed Pitt and summoned Fox to form a ministry, with Lord Waldegrave acting the part of Devonshire to Pitt, and Cumberland as its real head. This proved a difficult undertaking. Neither Bute nor the Duke of Newcastle would have anything to do with Fox. Not for the first time, George II found himself without a Cabinet at a time of crisis. The comedy quickly acquired the elements of farce present when Granville had sought to construct a ministry in 1746, but Byng's trial lent a tragic dimension to it. Newcastle and Fox were anxious to sacrifice Byng as a scapegoat. Pitt and the Tories had no desire for Byng's political masters to be left off so lightly. However, Pitt's supporters in the City took the uncomplicated view that a British admiral who allowed a French fleet to escape from beneath his guns must be guilty of some offence which justified execution. When Pitt sought the support of the House of Commons for a royal pardon, the King's rebuke to him was devastating: 'Sir, *you* have taught me to look for the sense of my subjects in another place than in the House of Commons.'[42]

Byng was duly executed. In the confusion the Tories set about glorifying the martyred Pitt–Devonshire Ministry. Pitt and his former colleague as Chancellor of the Exchequer, Henry Bilson Legge, were honoured with the freedom of a number of towns and cities, suitably conveyed in 'gold boxes'. The gold boxes did not fool many Whigs but they have led historians to suppose that Pitt's public support at this time was overwhelming. It was not. What saved Pitt was the general hostility to Cumberland, Newcastle's interest in returning to office at almost any cost once the embarrassment of Byng's trial had been surmounted, and Bute's anxiety to demonstrate his influence on the making of ministers. The result, at the end of June 1757, was a ministry which combined the forces of Pitt and Newcastle, with the former as Secretary of State and the latter as First Lord of the Treasury. Almost everyone who could cause trouble was included. Pitt's Grenville 'cousinage' was given ample representation, Pelhams and Yorkes and their connections returned in abundance, Fox resumed his old office of Paymaster-General, Bedford was made Lord-Lieutenant of Ireland, Devonshire became Lord Chamberlain. The Tories and Bute were nervous about the very comprehensiveness of this Whig coalition but Pitt was full of assurances that it also comprehended them. In a sense it suited Pitt well that the ministry began with a considerable set-back for British arms. Cumberland, having set off for Germany in the belief that the government was to be entrusted to the safe hands of his friends, met with defeat as soon as he encountered the French, at the Battle of Hastenbeck. He was compelled to negotiate a humiliating convention to save Hanover from the ravages of a victorious French army. Even the King, an earlier negotiator of Hanoverian neutrality, but not in the wake

<hr />

[42] Horace Walpole, *Memoirs of King George II*, ii. 223.

of military disaster, was appalled. Cumberland was recalled and deprived of his office as Captain-General. Whatever else interfered with the success of Pitt's second ministry, it would not be a combination of the King and his second son.

CHAPTER 6

Salvation by Faith

THE evangelical revival had its origin in a period when conventional religion was under pressure from fashionable deism. The doctrine of justification by faith permitted a rebellion against the early eighteenth century's attachment to 'natural', 'reasonable' religion. It attracted diverse groups, including parish clergy who accepted the authority of the established Church. Wesley himself was an opponent of those who wished to separate from the Church and also of those who could not accept its Arminianism. None the less he was often seen as a threat to the forces of tradition and order. His appeal to the poor aroused much suspicion of his motives. Neither the Church nor the Dissenting sects could readily match the dynamism of the revivalists. Resistance to Methodism was often violent, reflecting popular hostility as well as genteel disapproval. The Church used its episcopal powers and legal privileges to combat Methodist influence. Clerical dislike of the evangelical model of the priesthood was heightened by Wesley's reliance on lay preachers and encouragement of pious women. Lady Huntingdon's Connection came in for similar censure. Uniting the enemies of the evangelical movement was a profound distrust of its emotionalism and 'enthusiasm'. Polite literature was steeped in the Newtonian view of the world: between the enlightened empiricism *of the educated and the primitive superstition of the uneducated there was a widening gulf. The popular reception of reforms like the repeal of the Witchcraft Act and the introduction of the Gregorian calendar confirmed the belief of polite society in the barbarity of its inferiors. Yet the process of scientific discovery provided some uncomfortable moments for rationalists, and even when they condemned the forces of unreason they were less than confident of vanquishing them.*

THE DEIST THREAT

PERHAPS no doctrine is more characteristic of the eighteenth century, at least in the sense that it throve the more it was opposed, than the evangelical doctrine of justification by faith—what John Venn called 'the capital doctrine of the Gospel'.[1] Those who advocated it in the second quarter of the century believed that they had made a profound rediscovery, one which matched the achievement of the Reformation. They also claimed to be shocked by the need for such a rediscovery. The eleventh of the Thirty-Nine Articles subscribed by every clergyman of the established Church and in theory by every Dissenting minister clearly laid down, as the evangelical John Berridge pointed out, that 'we are accounted righteous before God, only for the merits of our Lord and Saviour Jesus Christ by faith, and not for our own works and deservings, and that we are justified by faith only'.[2] Yet most clergy preached, in varying proportions, a mixture of faith and works; in Berridge's view they were more or less indistinguishable from papists.

Works, of course, were not the main target of the new reformers, only the strongly defended flank of a vast body of doctrine which they characterized as 'natural religion'. They believed that it commanded as much support in the commonplace views of clergy and Churchmen as in the speculations of philosophers and free-thinkers. They also believed that it had taken a sinister, perhaps a fatal, hold on the minds of their elders and betters. The first generation of revivalists were mostly men born soon after the turn of the century. They were not the first to encounter the hideous and many-headed hydra of heterodoxy; Socinianism, deism, Arianism, even atheism, all were known to their fathers. But they were the first to face these horrors at the point when they seemed about to engulf English society. The fact of their own inexperience did not lessen their indignation at what they considered a fearful act of betrayal by many of the leading intellectual lights of the day. The authorities whom they confronted in the early years of Hanoverian rule were men of the seventeenth century. Matthew Tindal had

---

[1] M. Hennell, *John Venn and the Clapham Sect* (London, 1958), p. 72. The same expression was used by John Berridge; R. Whittingham, ed., *The Works of the Rev. John Berridge* (London, 1838), p. 308.

[2] R. Whittingham, ed., *The Works of the Rev. John Berridge*, p. 360.

been born before the Restoration, in 1657. His allies in scepticism, both inside and outside the Church, were all in middle or old age at the time of their greatest influence in the 1720s. The reawakening was in a real sense a revolt of the young against the irresponsibility of their elders.

For all kinds of churchmen the 1720s and 1730s were a testing time. 'I truly think,' wrote the Dissenting minister Nathaniel Lardner, 'that the Christians of this nation are at present under a great trial.'[3] The fact that the enemies of Christianity had been brought up to defend it naturally increased the loathing which they incurred. Tindal, whose *Christianity as old as the Creation*, published in 1730, was a particularly skilful defence of deism with arguments frequently used to sustain Revelation, had started his university education at Lincoln College, Oxford (the College of which Wesley was later to be a Fellow) and went on to a Fellowship at All Souls. Thomas Woolston, whose *Six Discourses on Miracles*, which appeared between 1727 and 1730, and offered a daringly allegorical interpretation of everything that was miraculous in the Gospels, was a Fellow of Sidney Sussex College, Cambridge. Lardner was shocked by Woolston's scepticism, but his own anxieties reveal the dilemma of those subjected to this historic test: he deprecated the use of the law against Woolston, and found himself involved in a public controversy with Edward Waddington, the Bishop of Chichester, as a result. Disputes of this kind weakened the fight against heterodoxy; they also had a large element of party politics in them. It was not unreasonably supposed that a Whig government was a reluctant prosecutor in these cases. Convocation had been suspended in 1717 to prevent it pursuing the notorious Whig controversialist Benjamin Hoadly, when he had the temerity to impugn the apostolic credentials of the Church of England. Moderate Whigs in the Church would have been glad to resuscitate it as a means of combating heresy and maintaining ecclesiastical discipline. Every general election up to 1741 was accompanied by bitter electoral contests among clergy who hoped for its revival, but there was no sign from Whig politicians to encourage them.

The court of George II had a reputation for unorthodoxy which reinforced the conviction of many Tory High Churchmen that a Hanoverian Lutheran was no better than a rank Socinian. Queen

---

[3] *Memoirs of the Life and Writings of the late Reverend Nathaniel Lardner* (London, 1769), p. 21.

Caroline, in particular, was the object of much suspicion. It was hardly justified. The truth about the Queen was that she was genuinely fascinated by things of the mind, without always having a complete grasp of them. Horace Walpole's story that she had recommended Bishop Butler to Sir Robert rings true. 'She never could make my father read his books, and which she certainly did not understand herself: he told her, his religion was fixed, and that he did not want to change or improve it.'[4] The impression was certainly given that she was a dependable patron of the free-thinkers. Samuel Clarke, detested for doctrines which seemed unpleasantly close to the Unitarianism he claimed to combat, she dared not make a bishop, but it was rumoured that she would have dearly loved an opportunity to do so. Hoadly himself was a friend of Lady Sundon, one of Queen Caroline's closest confidantes, and was protected by the court of George II as by that of George I. In 1734 he received his fourth episcopal promotion, to the rich see of Winchester: he retained it until his death, appropriately one year after George II's. Robert Clayton, a protégé of Clarke, and a relative of Lady Sundon, received two Irish bishoprics in succession, Killala in 1730, Cork in 1735, thanks to the Queen's influence (and a third, Clogher in 1745, thanks to the King's). His *Essay on Spirit* of 1751 provoked a renewal of the Arian controversy and seemed particularly shocking from the hand of a bishop.

The Rundle affair of 1734[5] also provided evidence of the court's unreliability in religious questions. It was observed that the King and Queen were slow to reward the defenders of orthodoxy. Daniel Waterland, the most persistent opponent of Clarke, thought that the Queen was responsible for blocking his promotion: certainly he seems to have owed his principal preferments to Bishop Gibson, and the offer of a bishopric did not come until after the Queen's death in 1738.[6] On the other hand, the evidence that she actively opposed the orthodox is not impressive. Hoadly's principal enemies in the Bangorian controversy had been Francis Hare, Andrew Snape, and Thomas Sherlock. All three were removed from their royal chaplaincies by George I in 1718. But they did not suffer under his successor. Hare received first the Bishopric of

---

[4] *Horace Walpole's Correspondence*, xx. 167.
[5] See pp. 40–1.
[6] R. T. Holtby, *Daniel Waterland, 1683–1740: A Study in Eighteenth Century Orthodoxy* (Carlisle, 1966), pp. 6–7.

St Asaph in 1727 and then that of Chichester in 1731. Sherlock underwent similar rehabilitation with the Bishopric of Bangor in 1727 and the Bishopric of Salisbury in 1734. Snape, as Provost of King's, Cambridge, was highly regarded at Windsor and enjoyed further preferment in the 1730s. Jacobites, perpetually at a disadvantage on account of the Pretender's Catholicism, sought to identify the rule of the Hanoverian family with atheism and infidelity. In this as in other respects it is important to distinguish between the courts of George I and George II. The trial of Edward Elwall of Wolverhampton for heresy and blasphemy in 1726 had suggested that even the judicial bench had become infected with fashionable scepticism.[7] But efforts were made to remove this impression in the new reign. Woolston himself, threatened with prosecution in 1725, had been permitted to escape; but he was prosecuted successfully in 1729 and spent his last years within the 'rules' of the King's Bench prison.

In some ways the attitude of the State was less worrying to defenders of the faith than the attitude of the Church itself. Some clergy were proud to avow their support for Hoadly and Clarke. Men like Arthur Ashley Sykes, John Jackson, and John Balguy came to be regarded by late eighteenth-century Unitarians as guardians of a sacred tradition of candid dissent. One such, John Disney, dubbed them 'rational and liberal christians'.[8] By many of their contemporaries they were viewed in a different light. Richard Bentley portrayed the deistic threat both within and without the Church in dark colours. 'That the soul is material, Christianity a cheat, Scripture a falsehood, hell a fable, heaven a dream, our life without providence, and our death without hope—such are the items of the glorious gospel of these evangelists.'[9] But the starkness of contrasts implied in this list of outrageous propositions is misleading. Much of the offensive thought was couched in terms designed to make it compatible with what was considered defensible in Christian doctrine. 'Natural religion' was a battleground on which the real differences could be narrowed, and it was often difficult to tell the warriors apart. Christianity might be defended as the religion of nature, as well as the religion

[7] J. L. Cherry, *Stafford in Olden Times* (Stafford, 1890), p. 37.

[8] J. Disney, *Memoirs of the Life and Writings of Arthur Ashley Sykes* (London, 1785), p. 240.

[9] Quoted in C. J. Abbey, *The English Church and its Bishops, 1700–1800* (2 vols., London, 1887), i. 234.

of Revelation. Even the mystic William Law appeared to accept it in these terms, to the alarm of John Wesley, one of his admirers. Its dangers seemed obvious to later readers. William Jones, a High Churchman of the reign of George III, observed that 'natural religion' had 'produced the deistical substitution of naked morality, or Turkish honesty, for the doctrines of intercession, redemption, and divine grace'.[10]

The defence of conventional theology was not without its own difficulties. The defenders conceded positions which they thought dispensable, only to find that their brethren regarded them as essential. An incautious admission, an argument which cut two ways, a generous acknowledgement of a powerful point, could readily involve men of good faith in controversy with their own supporters. Sherlock's *Tryal of the Witnesses* of 1729 raised eyebrows because it employed the judicial technique of cross-examining the apostles before a jury.[11] But Sherlock shared his predicament with many others; it was that of conceding either too little or too much. His abandonment of a literal interpretation of the Old Testament before the telling criticism of Anthony Collins seemed prudent, leaving the way open for a typological interpretation of scripture which was to have many followers in the late eighteenth century.[12] Yet it earned him few friends. The magisterial Bishop Butler was subsequently accused of adopting a negative tactic, counter-attacking natural religion rather than shoring up Revelation from within. Later generations found it difficult to appreciate how men of sincerity could have engaged in a debate on terms which seemed necessarily to put them at a disadvantage. Even in victory they were criticized for condescending to dispute with unworthy antagonists. Some, indeed, thought their victories were pyrrhic. Thus John Venn put it: 'They have confuted to the entire satisfaction of every admirable mind the objections of the infidels, and yet strange to tell infidelity has never been more prevalent than during that period and has even been gaining ground considerably.'[13]

[10] W. Jones, *The Works of the Right Reverend George Horne* (2nd edn., 4 vols., London, 1818), i. xx.
[11] C. J. Abbey, *The English Church and its Bishops*, ii. 51.
[12] In *The Use and Intent of Prophecy in the Several Ages of the World*, H. W. Frei, *The Eclipse of Biblical Narrative: A Study in Eighteenth and Nineteenth Century Hermaneutics* (New Haven, 1974), pp. 70–1.
[13] M. Hennell, *John Venn and the Clapham Sect* (London, 1958), p. 14.

The vantage-point of the late eighteenth and early nineteenth centuries is not the best from which to assess the strengths and weaknesses of Christianity's defenders during this period. Venn's generation had lost the deep sense of disarray which afflicted believers in an era of rational and scientific scepticism. A fairer test might be the comparison with other countries. In this respect it is the limited damage done by rationalism which seems remarkable. England had most of the features of the Enlightenment in the Continental sense, some of them in unusual prominence. It had a large, literate middle class, with a marked interest in the intellectual speculations and findings of the age. In London an exceptionally free and flourishing press transmitted a wide range of sceptical influences from the capitals of the European Enlightenment— Paris, Edinburgh, The Hague. Anticlericalism was fashionable in politically influential circles. Freemasonry, which emphasized religious tolerance and belief in God but no particular God, was essentially a product of the England of George I and George II, though one which was exported with spectacular success. The first Grand Lodge was established in 1717: offshoots quickly multiplied. Early Grand Masters testified to the religious and political diversity of the movement. They included the Huguenot mathematician J. T. Desaguliers, the sceptical and learned Duke of Montagu, the Whig magnate turned Jacobite the Duke of Wharton, and the leader of English Catholicism, the Duke of Norfolk. Freemasonry was not intended to be either anti-Christian, or anti-Catholic, though on the Continent it was to be interpreted as both. But it expressed some potent early Hanoverian preferences. Assimilating such preferences to the traditional pattern of churchmanship was no simple task. Nor was it easy to cope with the religious pluralism and the sense of almost boundless intellectual choice which marked the period. Yet the morale of the established Church in England survived in surprisingly good order. It may be that its latitudinarian friends under George II brought a timely flexibility as well as resourcefulness to the task of supporting it.

High Churchmen often thought that the safest way to respond to natural religion was to ignore it. The historic authority of the Church, from the Fathers to the Reformation and beyond, offered a haven for those determined to resist the new rationalism without engaging it on its chosen field of battle. The writings of the non-juror Charles Leslie provided an invaluable guide to this form of tactical retreat. The Hutchinsonians[14] used it repeatedly, with more success than they enjoyed when they ventured to attack the scientific case against the Old Testament. In this respect they doubly exemplified the wisdom of leaving natural religion well alone. When High Churchmanship regained its confidence in the late eighteenth century it prudently ignored the Hutchinsonian onslaught on Newtonianism while continuing its reliance on Leslie. There was, however, an alternative strategy, one which had more consistent support throughout the period, and also the advantage that it was not associated with party politics or dynastic disputes. This was the thoroughgoing reliance of evangelical churchmen on Revelation, not merely in the sense of the saving message of Christ as revealed in the Scriptures, but in the sense of every individual's opportunity, by means of 'experiential religion', to receive his personal assurance that he was saved.

THE EVANGELICAL AWAKENING

The English 'awakening' had its origins in the early part of George II's reign. A succession of events during these years were to pass into history, even into legend, for their special significance in the revival of the evangelical tradition. 1728 saw the arrival of the Moravians in London: their piety quickly attracted interest. A year later the Holy Club was formed at Oxford, with the Wesley brothers, Benjamin Ingham, and James Hervey pursuing their remorseless routine of personal devotions and charitable works. They were joined at Oxford by George Whitefield in 1732. There followed the Wesleys' voyage to Georgia in the service of Oglethorpe and the Georgia Trustees, and their return in 1738, after three years of frustration and controversy. In May of that year Wesley attended a meeting of the pious in Aldersgate Street, and felt his heart 'strangely warmed'. If Wesley was the St Paul of evangelical Protestantism, this was the road to Damascus. The young Welshman Howell Harris had had a similar experience in 1735, when he 'felt a strong impression on my mind'; he turned to religion at much the same time that his fellow countrymen Daniel Rowlands and Howell Davies were doing so. He started teaching at Trevecca soon after, and founded his own society. At Bideford similar activities were being undertaken by Wesley's

[14] See pp. 279–80.

Oxford friend James Hervey. In 1739 Harris clashed with the law for the first time when the Riot Act was read against his hearers at Pontypool.

Field preaching was already familiar to Welshmen. Griffith Jones had been employing it for some years. It came to be the authentic hallmark of early Methodism, after it was attempted by Whitefield. Whitefield had also been to Georgia but came back without Wesley's sense of failure. The orphanage which he left behind him at Savannah was one of the earliest institutional expressions of the new evangelicalism. His initial campaign in England got under way before he went to America, in the West Country in 1737 and early 1738; when he returned, it was resumed, with sensational results, first in Bristol, then in the capital. 1739 was to be the *annus mirabilis* of the evangelical awakening. Denied the pulpit at Islington by the churchwardens, he cheerfully resorted to the churchyard, and then to open spaces best known for high-waymen and horse-races, Moorfields, Kennington Common, Hackney Marsh, Marylebone Fields. Wesley followed his example, at first somewhat hesitantly, then with enthusiasm. If polite society had contrived to miss the extraordinary scenes produced by field preaching it did not remain ignorant of the new phenomenon for long. By the end of the decade Bishop Gibson had published his first anathema against the novel practices, in his *Pastoral Letter*, and two robust opponents of Wesley, Henry Stebbing and Joseph Trapp, had launched the campaign against him in print.

Methodism came to play such a large part in the story of evangelicalism, that it is tempting to view the evangelical revival in its early years as a stage in Methodist history. The very term Methodist has many advantages, not least its use by contemporaries. However, it carried a good deal of ambiguity about it. Wesley himself defined a Methodist cautiously in his Dictionary (characteristically described by him as 'the best English dictionary in the world') as 'one that lives according to the method laid down in the bible'.[15] Those who were not themselves Methodists used it of anyone who seemed a religious crank or fanatic. Fellow labourers in the vineyard did not like it. Howell Harris expressed his preference in 1763 for 'not taking the name Methodist. The name I had and do take still is exhorter, and the people in Wales

---

[15] G. H. Vallins, *The Wesleys and the English Language* (London, 1957), pp. 26, 31.

were called the Society People.'[16] If these were the alternatives it is easy to see why the expression went on being used. It indicated commitment to a particular way of life without sectarian associations. One of the boasts of the evangelicals was their appeal to a rich diversity of faiths and sects. Harris himself wrote of the London community which he attended in 1742, 'We have Churchmen, Presbyterians, Scottish and English, Lutherans, Calvinists, Independents, Baptists, Quakers, Papists, Jews, Arians, and Arminians, and we all live in sweet harmony.'[17]

There is an obvious danger in giving Wesley and his followers more significance in the second quarter of the century than they deserve. Though his Methodist society at Oxford was later considered by many the commencement of the English Revival, it is not a very appropriate starting-point. In the field Wesley was certainly not first, being preceded by Harris and Whitefield. In the eyes of onlookers, Whitefield was the more prominent of the two for some years. In point of organization, one of Wesley's manifest strengths, it is difficult not to concede to the Welsh Calvinists the prior claim to a distinct, institutional structure within which to promote revivalism. Originality was not Wesley's special claim. Even his religious societies had (as he himself knew) precedents in the Woodwardian societies of the early eighteenth century, some of which survived for many years. Moreover, in Wesley's youth, evangelical ministers, friends and comrades of Wesley in many cases, but often his critics, collaborated in the promotion of 'vital' religion. There were, in particular, a number of parochial clergy who remained firmly within the established Church, and who constituted a kind of advance guard for the evangelical army of the late eighteenth century. The most memorable in the light of subsequent events was Henry Venn, firstly curate of Clapham, where he made the momentous acquaintance of John Thornton, then Vicar of Huddersfield, where he acquired his reputation for godly preaching to multitudes of people, and finally Rector of Yelling in Huntingdonshire, where he came into contact with earnest young Cambridge men, including Charles Simeon.

Venn formed a living link between the early revivalists and the Clapham Sect, but there were many others whose only memorial

[16] E. Evans, *Howell Harris Evangelist* (Cardiff, 1974), p. 41.
[17] G. M. Roberts, ed., *Selected Trevecka Letters (1742–1747)* (Caernarvon, 1956), p. 42.

was the sheer vigour of their labours. Yorkshire had not a few such. 'How is that county blessed with faithful laborers', exclaimed the pious Earl of Dartmouth in 1762.[18] Apart from Venn he listed Venn's curate at Huddersfield, George Burnett, and his friend Richard Conyers. It was Conyers who earned a notorious reprimand from Archbishop Hay-Drummond of York, one in which his friends gloried: 'Were you to inculcate the morality of Socrates, it would do more good than canting about the new birth.'[19] Dartmouth also mentioned Thomas Adam, Rector of Wintringham, though it was technically in Lincolnshire rather than Yorkshire. Adam was an opponent of Wesley, and afterwards remembered by evangelicals for his posthumous works, especially the 'Private thoughts'. There were also Wesley's old friend Benjamin Ingham, by this time leader of the northern Moravians, Samuel Furley, famous for his thunderous preaching, and Thomas Clarke, another of Venn's friends. With the exception of Ingham, all these men worried about the Methodist threat to the integrity and discipline of the Church, and all were sooner or later enabled to preach the evangelical message from their own pulpits, as incumbents of parochial livings. Clarke was a particularly striking case of the capacity of the established Church to accommodate this breed of revivalist. Hounded out of his curacy of Amersham, on account of his unpalatable sermons, he found a temporary refuge with Venn, but in due course, thanks to the religious leanings of the Duchess of Bedford and her son the Marquess of Tavistock, returned to the Amersham neighbourhood as Rector of Chesham Bois.

The early evangelicals included some potent names in other parts of the country. Samuel Walker of Truro took the lead in a Cornish awakening. The clerical club which he and a group of like-minded colleagues formed about 1750 has some claim to be considered the first of a model which was to prove popular in later years. Walker was his own man, and at times a blunt, though amiable critic of Wesley. He was deeply concerned at the separatist tendencies which were all too clear among Wesley's flock, even when their shepherd rebuked them on that account. He disliked lay preachers, opposed itinerancy, had doubts about Wesley's doctrine of assurance, reservations concerning Wesleyan Armi-

---

[18] E. Sidney, *The Life of Sir Richard Hill* (London, 1839), p. 185.
[19] A. C. H. Seymour, *The Life and Times of Selina Countess of Huntingdon* (2 vols., London, 1844), i. 280.

nianism, and in 1756 roundly condemned the 'mysticism, Moravianism, and Methodism' which he found in Bristol.[20] Ironically, his own congregation felt compelled to separate from the Church when his successor at Truro after his death in 1761 proved a very different kind of minister. William Grimshaw of Haworth was another parish incumbent who welcomed the activities of the Wesley brothers without sharing their views. So were the outspoken John Berridge, Vicar of Everton in Cambridgeshire for nearly forty years, the hell-fire preacher William Romaine, for awestruck Londoners the principal resident representative of revivalism, and William Talbot, founder of an enduring evangelical tradition at Reading. None of these men was more than a few years younger than Wesley. They were contemporaries and equals, not acolytes or dependants.

Wesley's distinctiveness is not diminished by an appreciation of the work of his brethren. Nor is his significance to be judged by the numbers of members of the Wesleyan connection recorded in his own lifetime. These reached just over 26,000 on the eve of the great controversy with the Calvinists in 1771, and nearly 57,000 by the time of his death in 1791. But there were many who were influenced by his teaching or affected by the Methodist movement without aspiring to formal membership. In biographical terms the critical decision on his part was perhaps a negative one, his decision not to take a parochial living. Wesley was plainly reluctant to take on such a responsibility when it became an obvious possibility in the early 1730s, and was somewhat disingenuous in his justification for not doing so. In part his Georgian adventure was an escape from an English curacy or incumbency. The consequences were of the first importance. With a parish he could not possibly have performed the extraordinary labours and travels which he continued almost to the time of his death in 1791. Unremitting attention to detail and an indefatigable capacity for hard work were crucial to the prosperity of the Wesleyan connection. His vivid recollection of congregations and the individuals who composed them, together with his clear judgement of the men who served him, sustained a national organization which remained to a remarkable extent, at least until the 1780s, the creation of one man. But behind this astonishingly effective dictatorship, there were skills

[20] G. C. B. Davies, *The Early Cornish Evangelicals, 1735–60: A Study of Walker of Truro*, p. 105.

especially suited to the age. Not the least was his manipulation of the media.

Wesley was not only a powerful preacher, he was also a fluent writer, with a shrewd appreciation of the techniques of mass communication. Both he and Whitefield published their spiritual experiences very early in their evangelical career, with predictably controversial consequences. There is a sense in which Wesley's most complete triumph was as a hack author. His plagiarism was notorious and in most cases unconcealed. Since the object was joy above all earthly riches the infringement of copyright was not something Wesley felt embarrassed about: arguments which tended to the defeat of Satan were worth using wherever they came from. The vanity of authors doubtless got what it deserved at his hands. The sheer quantity of his writing and publishing remains remarkable. His collection of devotional works and saintly lives abridged would alone have occupied the energies of many an assiduous compiler. The 'church library', a potted version of the classics of religious literature in fifty volumes, was a formidable editorial achievement. The only surprise is that it took him so long to found a regular periodical with which to nourish the faithful. His *Arminian Magazine*, the first official journal of Methodism, did not commence publication until 1778. It was by no means the first in the field. Wesley's own cause had suffered much at first setting out, in the late 1730s, from the critical attention of the *Weekly Miscellany*, a newspaper which proclaimed itself the guardian of orthodoxy and establishment. In the 1760s and 1770s there was a spate of such publications, including William Dodd's *Christian Magazine* and Augustus Toplady's *Gospel*. Wesley's latecomer predictably placed the emphasis on popular consumption. In addition to some unsophisticated sermonizing, it offered confessions and pious deaths redolent of popular 'crime literature', accounts of all manner of supernatural occurrences, and 'no news, no politics, no personal invective'.[21]

EVANGELICAL ANIMOSITIES

Internal conflict marked the evangelical revival almost from the beginning. By 1740 the Moravian James Hutton was gloomily

[21] F. E. Mineka, *The Dissidence of Dissent: The Monthly Repositary, 1806–1838* (Chapel Hill, 1944), p. 43.

reporting to his leader Count Zinzendorf the tensions which had begun to affect an initially coherent movement of spiritual renewal and reform. The 'poor and simple' Charles Wesley was unwary of those whom he cultivated in Bristol, and in London his brother John was proving difficult to control: 'He will have the glory of doing all things.' The Methodists and Moravians were in fact on the brink of separating for good.[22] Hutton approved the labours of James Hervey in the West Country, Benjamin Ingham in Yorkshire, and Howell Harris in Wales, but they were highly uncoordinated. The early history of Welsh evangelicalism provides much evidence of vigour, little of harmony. Welsh Calvinism was rent by a great rift between Harris and Rowlands in 1746. It had started as a relatively polite difference of opinion on the doctrine of assurance, but degenerated into a personal squabble which extended to accusations of sexual misconduct on Harris's part. In 1750 Harris retreated to Trevecca to pursue his own vocation: periodic emergences thereafter maintained the magic of his name but did not regain (nor did he really seek) the leadership of a unified Calvinistic connection.

English Methodism was dogged by two divisive questions almost from its inception: Calvinism and separatism. Wesley is usually presented as having clear and consistent views on both, but as an ecclesiastical politician he was not without the capacity to compromise. Though he broke for practical purposes with Whitefield on the issue of predestination in the 1740s, their relationship long continued one of mutual respect and regret rather than enmity. It may be significant that the real crisis of Calvinistic Methodism came soon after Whitefield's death in 1770. In that year Wesley produced a minute of the proceedings at his annual conference, on this occasion held at Bristol, which was interpreted as a public rebuke to the Calvinistic followers of Lady Huntingdon. Uproar followed. Wesley was abashed enough to authorize concessions, but not in time to prevent a damaging public debate. It was begun, more or less accidentally, by John Fletcher of Madeley, who was unaware, when he penned his first defence of Wesley's position, that the dispute was on the point of being resolved, or at least compromised. Fletcher, a young Swiss who had settled in England, was a supreme example of the impact which an evangelical minister could make on a rapidly industrializing community. (Madeley was

[22] D. Benham, *Memoirs of James Hutton* (London, 1866), p. 47.

close to Coalbrookdale in Shropshire.) He was also a pivotal figure in the early history of Methodism, a devoted friend of the Wesleys, but sufficiently respected by Lady Huntingdon to have been made visiting superintendent of the Calvinist college at Trevecca. Yet he had no hesitation in siding with Wesley in defence of Arminianism.

Fletcher's pamphlet *Checks to Antinomianism*, written to justify the Bristol minutes, commenced a controversial war which continued for nearly a decade. On the Calvinist side it produced some brutal polemic, much of it from the pen of Wesley's former adherent Augustus Toplady, who showed no mercy to his mentor. Nor was chivalry to the fore in the writings of the Hill brothers, Richard and Rowland, Shropshire gentry formerly on close terms with Fletcher. The elder brother Richard, who later inherited the family baronetcy, and became a whimsical speaker in the House of Commons, had exhibited a taste for controversy at an early stage in his evangelical enthusiasm. His first tract was a robust assault on a member of his own university, John Allen, Vice-Principal of St Mary Hall, for denying the doctrine of salvation by faith alone. It was followed by a series of diverting and damaging pieces denouncing the expulsion of the St Edmund Hall Methodists in 1768. The Calvinist controversy found him at his most vitriolic. Aristocratic connections gave him a special perspective on Methodism. It was, for instance, on the strength of a conversation with the Superior of the English Benedictines at Paris, that he observed that 'Popery was about the midway between Protestantism and Mr. J. Wesley.'[23] Not even the spiritual version of the Grand Tour was practicable for many of Wesley's followers, unless it be a pious pilgrimage to the Moravian headquarters at Herrnhut.

These exchanges left both sides bloodied but unbowed. Their only indisputable effect was to bring the evangelical cause into disrepute. Ridicule was a more sinister enemy of salvation by faith than rational criticism, and the spectacle of the bringers of brotherly love engaged in acrimonious combat exposed all those involved to mockery. In this respect the mid-1770s were generally rather trying. An incident at the Trevecca anniversary meeting of 1776 was the occasion of some ribaldry. When Toplady announced the hymn 'Blow ye the trumpet blow', the scaffolding on which he and his brethren were standing collapsed, carrying with it forty

[23] Sidney, *Sir Richard Hill*, p. 185.

ministers. None was hurt and Toplady resumed with some aplomb, singing 'Salvation, O thou bleeding Lamb, To thee the praise belongs'.[24] There were also the antics of Sir Harry Trelawny, a young baronet entranced by evangelical preaching. He proved an unstable convert, passing rapidly through a variety of doctrinal persuasions before taking refuge in the established Church, where he had begun. Political differences were also an embarrassment. Wesley's famous *Calm Address to our American Colonies*, essentially plagiarized from Dr Johnson's tract *Taxation No Tyranny*, nailed the colours of Arminian Methodism to the mast of empire. But the Hills were quick to express their sympathy for the colonial cause. All in all it is not surprising that the numerical growth of Methodism slowed during this difficult period.

The question of separation was a perpetual affliction for Wesley. It was proposed publicly at the Bristol conference of 1756. Charles Wesley and Samuel Walker believed that John's encouragement of lay preaching made the formation of a distinct, dissenting church, inevitable. 'It has been a great fault all along,' Walker observed, 'to have made the low people of your council.'[25] Wesley's tactics of pacifying, some would say fobbing off, his mutinous supporters, while calming the anxieties of his clerical colleagues, were broadly successful but required constant attention. In 1758 he opined that it might be lawful but not expedient to separate. Charles insisted that nothing could make it lawful; to John Nelson he became distraught on the subject. 'Rather than see thee a Dissenting minister, I wish to see thee smiling in thy coffin.'[26] The Rolvenden case of 1760,[27] threatening Methodist congregations with prosecution as illegal conventicles, perturbed Wesley not because it amounted to persecution, but because it increased the danger that he would be forced to secede by the intolerance of his own Church. In 1766, at the Leeds conference, separation was vigorously debated, with the additional irritation for Wesley, that his own authority was brought into question. Thereafter he was rarely free from anxiety on this score. Disputes about the appointment of preachers and the powers of chapel trustees became increasingly serious. In 1784 a model deed was produced which

[24] E. Sidney, *The Life of the Rev. Rowland Hill* (5th edn., London, 1861), p. 170.
[25] L. Tyerman, *The Life and Times of the Rev. John Wesley* (3 vols., London, 1870–1), ii. 251.
[26] Ibid. ii. 383.
[27] See p. 294.

bestowed authority on the 'conference of the people called Method-ists'.[28] The conference was virtually Wesley's mouthpiece but its potential to speak for itself was obvious long before he departed. Lay preachers inevitably put considerable pressure on their clerical colleagues, not least because they sought the full priestly authority that would allow them to celebrate holy communion. This was what Charles had dreaded, and it worried Wesley. But in 1784 he took the revolutionary step of ordaining a number of ministers for service overseas. He also appointed Thomas Coke, already in orders, Superintendent in America. This looked very like making bishops: in fact Coke soon began terming himself such. Wesley was determined not to separate while he lived, but he surely had a shrewd understanding of the necessity for doing so once he was dead.

THE EVANGELICAL REVIVAL AND THE PEOPLE

From the beginning Methodism was identified with the religious life of the lower and middle classes. Its ministers made no apology for concentrating their energies on the poor. Whitefield gloried in doing so and even received the grudging approval of Dr Johnson on that account. 'He had devoted himself to the lower classes of mankind, and among them he was of use.'[29] Wesley's talent for organizing as well as inspiring the poor makes him a figure of overwhelming interest to sociologists of religion. His record in this respect needs treating with some caution, however. If mere poverty had been sufficient to guarantee success, Wesleyanism would have become what it never was, a genuinely national force, uniting town and country, industry and agriculture, north and south. In many districts the Methodists believed that they were prevented from spreading their message by the hostility of the squirearchy and the clergy, not least when united in the formidable figure of the 'squarson'. Certainly it is notable that when they did eventually make some headway in such areas, it was in upland or woodland zones, where the forces of genteel property were represented ill or not at all, and where a genuine tradition of independence existed. Methodism found its most promising environment in semi-industrial communities which had outstripped the capacity of pat-

---

[28] Tyerman, *John Wesley*, iii. 417.
[29] *Boswell's Life of Johnson*, iii. 409.

ernalistic landowners and parish clergy to cater for them. Especially where the parochial structure was flimsy, in large northern parishes or in places of rapid urban development, opportunity offered and need dictated. On the other hand, it is somewhat dangerous to characterize the breeding ground of Methodism as the outcast, the degraded, the lawless, and the undisciplined. There were few such communities in eighteenth-century England, though there were many which lacked the familiar ethos imparted by landed gentry, beneficed clergy, and prosperous tenantry. The 'new nation' of the mining and manufacturing areas already had its own hierarchy and its own forms of social control. Part of the evangelical success lay in its appeal to a ruling class which was less confident and less polite than that which governed by a combination of property and prescription in agricultural districts and in old municipalities. But its influence was none the less far-reaching and Methodism would not have progressed very far without its approval.

Wesley wanted to vanquish sin, not social deprivation. The poor were suitable cases for treatment primarily because they lacked the diversity of opportunity for sin available to the rich. They were not intrinsically healthier in a spiritual sense, but the prospects of a cure were better when so many sources of foulness were cut off from them. In Wesley's case there was also an element of personal preference. He was not very good at preaching to the rich, though he did not blame himself for his deficiency in this respect. 'Oh how hard it is to be shallow enough for a polite audience', he confided to his journal on one occasion.[30] In fact it was perfectly practicable to preach revival and renewal to polite congregations. Lady Huntingdon's preachers proved this, at least to their own satisfaction. They, too, were seeking out sin, and not unreasonably thought that it should be attacked most vigorously where it was strongest, in polite society. The early chapels of the Huntingdon Connection were often in places of fashionable resort, Bath, Tunbridge, Margate, or at least in towns with assemblies, balls, and the regular attendance of the upper crust. The meetings held at the Countess's London house, at the height of her fashionable appeal, near the end of George II's reign, included four duchesses and over a dozen peers or their wives. Some aristocrats, Lord and Lady Dartmouth, the Marquess and Marchioness of Lothian,

---

[30] N. Curnock, ed., *The Journal of the Rev. John Wesley* (8 vols., London, 1909–16), v. 429.

Lady Chesterfield, Lady Glenorchy, two successive Earls of Buchan, proved more than fair-weather friends. 'Oh! how far below his grace is his nobility!' exclaimed Fletcher of the eleventh Earl of Buchan.[31]

This aristocratic component of the evangelical revival was small, and dependent on family relationships: the Ferrers, Hastings, and Shirley families, at the centre of Lady Huntingdon's Connection, were closely linked by consanguinity. But blue-blooded support had the important effect of reassuring middle-class men and women, especially in London, that evangelicalism might be embraced without social stigma. The Lock Hospital was notable for the dissemination of Calvinistic evangelicalism, and preachers at other charitable foundations were often expected to imitate the manner of the revivalists, with due allowance for the sophistication of their audience. The fashionable cleric William Dodd was dubbed a Methodist because he relied on similar rhetorical techniques. Wesley, of course, was entitled to point out that preaching to people of property was not at all the same thing as convincing them. He sought evidence of transformed lives, not applauding congregations. But the poor were not invariably better at transforming their lives than their betters, and it is difficult to believe that there was not a measure of inverted snobbery in Wesley's make-up. His contempt for 'genteel Methodism' was barely concealed: it may have had its origins in the social ambiguities of his own background, and in the prejudices and egotism of the young Tory don.

Wesley's appeal to the poor disturbed many contemporaries. The social conformity of nineteenth-century Methodism should not be read back into the mid-eighteenth century, though it is true that its radical potential was often exaggerated. Alexander Jephson's attack on the Methodists in 1760 charged them with levelling, because they taught denial of the riches of the world. Excessive austerity and rigour were wrong, he argued. It was better to urge the rich to find employment for the poor than to encourage them to give away their wealth, for no amount of such charity could ever satisfy the poor.[32] Pooling of money by communally minded Methodists aroused suspicions of a contempt

---

[31] Seymour, *Selina Countess of Huntingdon*, ii. 18.

[32] *A Friendly and Compassionate Address, To all serious and well disposed Methodists* (London, 1760), pp. 31–9.

for the values of commercial society. Not very consistently, there were also anxieties about the readiness of evangelical groups to offer financial support to co-religionists who needed funds to maintain themselves in trade. Such loans were not uncommon. George Cussons, founder of the Navy and Army Bible Society in 1779, was enabled to start his own business in 1774 by a personal loan of £50 from John Thornton.[33] Contrariwise, it was claimed that lay preaching deprived the country of useful craftsmen and workers. Evan Lloyd, whose satire *The Methodist* of 1766 landed him in prison because it included an incautious reference to an evangelically inclined squire, listed mechanics, bricklayers, bakers, tinmen, weavers, brewers, gardeners, footmen among the occupations affected. In a broader sense Wesley's conception of the devout life could be viewed as a revolt against the world of property and patronage in which most of his educated contemporaries lived. His societies fitted none of the approved models of ordinary association. They did not belong in the familiar structure of vestry, churchwarden, and parson. They did not acknowledge the social stratification and common conviviality embodied in so many clubs. They utterly rejected the ethos of the tavern, the alehouse, and the coffee-house, which dominated working-class friendly societies as it did polite societies and gentlemen's clubs. They had their own rules and rituals, which seemed as mysterious as those of the Freemasons, but made them far more objectionable in their intercourse with the rest of mankind. The wild rumours about love-feasts and 'amorous' classes aroused both prurience and prudishness in others, and promoted the belief that they offered a challenge to the patriarchal values and family sense of middle- and lower-class life. Their refusal even to be considered as rebels and dissenters in any conventional way made their peculiar form of rebellion and dissent especially irritating.

> Is there a *Tribe* who boast *peculiar Light*,
> *Dissent* from all, and yet with all *unite*?[34]

Wesley was accused of many things, including both Puritanism and Popery. Posterity has found some force in the claim that he revived the zealous spirit of the previous century. A majority of the writings which he abridged for his 'complete body of Practical

---

[33] *Memoirs of Mr George Cussons of London* (London, 1819), p. 50.
[34] *The Saints: A Satire* (London, 1778), p. 1.

Divinity' or Christian Library could be classified as the work of Puritan authors.[35] In his own Dictionary he defined a Puritan as 'an old, strict Church of England man'.[36] Most contemporaries considered the Dissenting sects as repositories of the Puritan tradition. Why, it might be wondered, did they not achieve the same galvanizing effect as Wesley, a Puritan, if he was such, with a High Church background? Up to a point, the answer is that they did. Risdon Darracott, Nonconformist minister of Wellington in Somerset from 1741 until his death in 1759, was celebrated for the inspiration of his preaching and the magnetism of his ministry: Whitefield called him 'a flaming successful preacher of the gospel', the 'Star in the West'.[37] The Methodists had admirers among the Dissenters, the most notable of them Philip Doddridge. None the less, compared with its North American counterpart in the era of the Great Awakening, Old Dissent in England was slow to respond to the evangelical challenge. Not until the 1770s did the Rational Dissenters become alarmed by its inroads. In 1779 Richard Price expressed his fear that 'the most valuable part of the dissenting interest is likely to be ground to death between enthusiasm on the one hand, and luxury and fashion on the other.'[38] Congregationalism and Baptism almost doubled their membership between 1750 and 1790, in line with the expansion of Methodism. But in the crucial early decades of the evangelical revival Nonconformity could do little to match the appeal of Wesley and Whitefield.

It was often observed that Dissent was almost as much part of the establishment as the Church itself. The Toleration Act permitted freedom of worship to all who could assent to the central doctrines of Protestantism. Most Presbyterians, Baptists, and Congregationalists, the three main sects, came under this heading. Whig rule offered a standing guarantee that this historic settlement would endure. The compact between Dissent and mainstream Whiggism was confirmed by the repeal of the Occasional Conformity and Schism Acts in 1718 and by the *regium donum*, which had a symbolic significance far beyond its financial value.[39] The

[35] R. C. Monk, *John Wesley: His Puritan Heritage* (London, 1966), pp. 32–42.

[36] G. H. Vallins, *The Wesleys and the English Language*, p. 33.

[37] J. Bennett, *The Star in the West* (London, 1813), p. 65.

[38] *A Sermon, Delivered to a Congregation of Protestant Dissenters, at Hackney, On the 10th of February last* (2nd edn., London, 1779), p. 28.

[39] See p. 39.

relationship was shaken but not fundamentally endangered by the failure of Whig Parliaments to repeal the Test and Corporation Acts, and the difficulties which Walpole experienced in managing the Dissenting interest in the 1730s. A certain air of complacency settled over some congregations. Dissent was retreating into its urban heartland under George II, but even there the emphasis was on its appeal to prosperous businessmen and their families rather than the poor and unprivileged. Where it was successful, it was almost too successful for its own good. Distinguished ministers found themselves subject to temptations which resembled those of their rivals in the Church. When Hugh Farmer, one of Doddridge's ablest pupils, took up his ministry at Walthamstow in 1737, he found himself in a quiet country parish: yet before very long, he was lionized by the 'genteel and opulent class of dissenters' who resorted to the Essex countryside for the summer. His move to Salters Hall, the most famous of all Dissenting chapels, in 1761, to take the afternoon lecture, cannot have made much difference to the composition of his congregations.[40] Even when they went beyond their meeting-houses into the fields, Dissenting ministers were at a disadvantage: technically it was legal for them to officiate only in chapels licensed under the Toleration Act. The clergy of the established Church were not penalized in this way. Though their legal rights to preach at large were somewhat uncertain, particularly where ecclesiastical jurisdiction was concerned, they were not liable to prosecution by the civil authorities.

Dissent was also hampered by its internal divisions and doctrinal disputes. If natural religion sapped the will of the parochial clergy to preach the Gospel, it must have had a similar effect on Nonconformist ministers. The Trinitarian controversy caused secessions from many congregations; Presbyterianism, in giving birth to what became virtually a separate Unitarian movement, was divided and almost destroyed by the turmoil which it caused. Old disputes about the doctrine of election and the theology of baptism remained unresolved. The growing revulsion of moderate Dissenters of the Doddridge kind against hard-line predes-tinarianism was particularly damaging. It divided many meet-ings, and drew ministers and laity alike either into Methodism or back to the security of latitudinarian Churchmanship.

[40] M. Dodson, *Memoirs of the Life and Writings of the late Reverend and learned Hugh Farmer* (London, 1804), p. 16.

THE ESTABLISHED CHURCH

The established Church was not less divided. Its inherited political conflicts were particularly daunting. When Thomas Secker surveyed his new diocese of Bristol in 1735 he found occasion to enter the word 'Whig' or 'Tory' by the name of each of the parochial incumbents, alongside brief descriptions of their pastoral and personal qualities.[41] There was no diocese in early Hanoverian England which was not divided on Whig–Tory lines. Whig patronage directed through the Crown and the bishops gradually turned the cathedral chapters into Whig monopolies, but the parochial influence enjoyed by the country gentry ensured that it did little to dilute the Toryism of the inferior clergy. The universities were divided against each other and within themselves. Oxford maintained its predominantly High Tory complexion, notwithstanding the gradual conversion of the mighty Christ Church into a Whig preserve. Cambridge was essentially Whig by the beginning of George II's reign, but a tenacious and embittered Tory presence remained a force in several colleges. Party politics were slower to change in the Church than in the State. There was no significant 'country party' among the clergy and it was precisely on ecclesiastical questions that parliamentary Whigs and Tories found it most difficult to find common ground. It is not a coincidence that the revival of the confidence and coherence of the Church as a political institution took place in the early years of George III, when the old party loyalties finally evaporated.

Hanging over the history of the eighteenth-century Church is a question which continues to haunt its defenders. Why was it unable to develop that unifying sense of missionary zeal which would have enabled it to take full advantage of the religious impulse of Georgian England, in the process becoming truly a national church? The question says more about the mentality of Churchmen than the peculiarities of the age. The Church had never provided a truly national religion. Even when reinforced by a State determined to command the religious allegiance of its subjects, it had rarely exerted more than partial and uncertain control. Its acquisition of a formal monopoly of civil office under Charles II was more in the nature of a confession of failure than the prelude to a triumphant assertion of authority. The Toleration Act confirmed

[41] Bristol Record Office, Diocesan Archives.

this state of affairs, initiating an era of voluntarism and pluralism in religious matters, which made the retreat into sectarian Anglicanism inevitable. The fact that the new religious enthusiasts saw themselves as loyal sons of the Church, appears paradoxical in this context, but it offers no contradiction. Whatever the source of their inspiration and however complete their orthodoxy, they were unrepresentative of the great body of the clergy, opposed by many of their superiors, and unsupported by the institutional structure of the Church.

Modern scholars have sought a clear view of the strengths of the Church principally by disposing of the obstructive prejudices of their predecessors. Piety and pastoral efficiency can be found in sufficient measure to disprove the grosser charges of clerical corruption and incompetence laid by Victorian censors of the Georgian Establishment. Bishops, one of the favourite targets of reformers who identified an oligarchical Whig regime with a corrupt Whig episcopate, have acquired a new respectability. There is evidence of scrupulous attention to the responsibility of ordination, and conscientious execution of the duties of visitation, confirmation, and diocesan administration. Even Hoadly, the very type of episcopal cynicism and Erastianism, is in danger of being rehabilitated.[42]

What weight should be given to this kind of revision is a matter for debate. Not every bishop can plausibly be presented for re-accreditation as a representative of a selfless and serious-minded profession. The correspondence of John Butler, one of the most influential bishops of the 1770s and 1780s, was not known to Victorian critics, but it confirms their worst suspicions. 'Is there a yard of lawn more dirty than Butler?' enquired Horace Walpole.[43] Butler was a political hack employed by the Onslow family and by Lord North: his rewards included the bishoprics of Oxford in 1777 and Hereford in 1787. He was a furious opponent of Wilkes and an unforgiving enemy of America. His letters were punctuated by bitter outbursts against the colonial rebels: 'mankind cannot suffer by their extirpation', he remarked at one point. He was a poor scholar, confessing his inadequacy in Hebrew, and had no high view of his creed. Deputed to write in defence of the Thirty-

---

[42] W. M. Marshall, 'Episcopal Activity in the Hereford and Oxford Dioceses, 1660–1760', *Midland History*, 8 (1983), 106–20.
[43] *Horace Walpole's Correspondence*, xxix. 134.

Nine Articles when they were under attack in 1772, he reported
to his patron Lord Onslow: 'I am busy, considering, why I subscribed to the 39 Articles thirty years ago'. His conclusion was
merely that they were tolerable, 'without trying your patience by
reading them'. As a beneficed clergyman much of his time was
spent promoting his claims first to a canonry then to a bishopric.
As a bishop he devoted his attention to the complex actuarial
calculations required to maximize his personal profit from his
episcopal leases. He was unimpressed by criticism of pluralists: 'Is
it any respect more material, how many sinecures, than how many
estates a man has?' Towards the end of his life his opinions became
unashamedly reactionary. He was a fervent admirer of Burke's
Reflections and conceived a bizarre scheme to immortalize George
III on the newly restored façade of his cathedral at Hereford. He
was not much enamoured by the evangelical fashion which affected
many of his contemporaries in the last years of the century. He
defended both the slave-trade and slavery against the abolitionists.
Yet he was not, *pace* Horace Walpole, regarded in his own day as a
particularly bad bishop or a scandalous priest. He is not necessarily
more representative than a saintly bishop like Benson of Gloucester, a scholarly bishop like Hurd of Worcester, or an executive
bishop like Porteus of Chester and London. But any generalization
about the episcopate has to take account of the Butlers, of whom,
indeed, there were not a few.[44]

Nineteenth-century strictures were the product of a potent but
noxious mixture of evangelicalism and the Oxford Movement.
They made anachronistic assumptions about the conditions
required for spiritual renewal. The fact that the Church was a
thoroughly inegalitarian institution did not itself inhibit its effectiveness in an evangelical sense. The impoverished curate was
not bound to be less effective pastor than a well-fed parson.
Redistributing the income enjoyed by non-residents and pluralists
might have seemed a supreme act of justice but it would not
necessarily have strengthened the missionary zeal of the clergy.
Nor is it certain that a universally admired episcopate would have
been able to fend off the diverse threats to its authority. The
decline of ecclesiastical courts was a blow to the status and power
of the bishops. So was the robust independence enjoyed by the
parish clergy at a time of respect for all property, including the

[44] Surrey Record Office, Guildford, Onslow MSS, Butler Correspondence.

parson's freehold. Above all, the sheer secularism of the times bred a contempt for sacerdotal pretensions which was shared even by loyal sons of the Church. Papists were not entirely immune from it, as the memorable remark of a leading Roman Catholic, Sir Robert Throckmorton, during the negotiations between the Catholic gentry and Lord North for a measure of parliamentary relief, testifies: 'we don't want bishops.'[45]

Some bishops made strenuous efforts to recruit ordinands capable of meeting the challenge of the age. The tests required by canon law were applied with growing consistency: the increasing difficulty of entering the Church without a university training was one result. Bishops were not the only men concerned to maintain standards. Church patronage was the critical determinant of the quality of the clergy and it could be employed in surprising ways. The republican Thomas Hollis, who owned an advowson in Dorset, made his chosen candidate in 1754 sign a statement of support for the late 'happy revolution' and the system of toleration. He was also required to undertake that he would accept no other benefice or employment. 'It is amazing how much even one ingenious worthy man of character can change a country place in a few years,' Hollis noted.[46] Hollis was idiosyncratic in both his political and religious views. But there were other reformers with similar ideas. The evangelical John Thornton purchased advowsons with the intention of promoting the right kind of clergymen. At his death, he left a trust charged with continuing and extending this scheme. However, such projects were exceptional. Somewhat more than half of all livings belonged to lay patrons, the great majority of them determined to use them for their own interest, either by selling them exactly as if they were estates, or by using them to reward relations and dependants.

The Church offered an increasingly attractive career to men for whom it was nothing else but a career. Many clerical incomes rose markedly in the second half of the century, as tithes claimed their share of agricultural improvement. The parish clergy benefited as a result. But those of their brethren who depended on fixed incomes or the generosity of their betters, in a word the curates, found their stipends falling behind the rate of inflation. This

---

[45] N. Abercrombie, 'The First Relief Act', in E. Duffy, ed., *Challoner and his Church: A Catholic Bishop in Georgian England* (London, 1981), p. 180 n.

[46] F. Blackburne, *Memoirs of Thomas Hollis, Esq.* (2 vols., London, 1780), i. 55–7.

widening gulf in terms of real remuneration made access to the patronage which commanded an income derived from tithes additionally valuable. The landed families with younger sons naturally took a close interest in this state of affairs; demographic change in the mid-eighteenth century considerably increased the number of such families. The matching rise in the cost of an Oxford or Cambridge education played into their hands. It took a good deal of determination to attempt a career in the Church without access to funds and the secure prospect of a living. Not surprisingly, the proportion of parish clergy who were themselves the sons of clergymen fell markedly in the second and third quarters of the century. Nor is it very strange that the laymen who took their place were increasingly genteel, and even aristocratic. The Velvet Cushion, eponymous subject of a famous evangelical novel, was appropriately occupied in the mid-eighteenth century by the second son of a noble family 'whose want of talents had early designated him, willing or unwilling, to spend the tithes of a considerable living'.[47] The products of this system were not known for their spiritual dynamism, though there were exceptions. One such was the second son of the Earl Cadogan, William Bromley Cadogan. Presented before he was of an age to be ordained to the living of St Giles, Reading, 'as being near the family seat', and subsequently appointed to St Luke's, Chelsea, he startled his fashionable congregation at Chelsea by taking Sabbatarianism and charity schools seriously. 'The train of coaches that first attended his church soon drew off.'[48] He went on to become a prominent evangelical, and biographer of William Romaine.

Aristocratic dominance of the upper reaches of Church preferment was not unopposed. George Grenville, as Prime Minister, is reported to have 'considered bishoprics as of two kinds, bishops of business for men of abilities and learning, and bishops of ease for men of family and fashion'.[49] Throughout the period some bishoprics were kept out of aristocratic hands and bestowed on men, who, if they were not necessarily of humble origin, at least had both talent and industry to recommend them. London, the most obvious case of a bishopric of business, was held in succession by the immensely powerful Gibson from 1720 to 1748, and by the

---

[47] J. W. Cunningham, *The Velvet Cushion* (London, 1814), p. 135.
[48] J. Pratt, *The Works of the Rev. Richard Cecil* (3rd edn., 2 vols., London, 1827), i. 138.
[49] *Works of Thomas Newton*, i. 85.

equally formidable Sherlock from 1748 to 1761. After two very brief tenures, Richard Terrick's promotion from Peterborough to London in 1764 was attributed to his connection with Bute and openly despised by Warburton, principally on the grounds that Warburton should have been given it. But Terrick was no cipher. Nor was Lowth, his successor from 1777 to 1787 and a scholar whose interests extended far beyond his library. None of these was nobly born. Gibson's origins were genuinely poor, and the others were all sons of clergymen, none noted for his fortune. In Lowth's day several of his colleagues on the bench were indeed men of high birth. But appearances could be misleading. Not all aristocratic Cabinet ministers were lightweights, nor were all their cousins in the Church. Thomas Newton, Bishop of Bristol, thought Cornwallis an excellent Archbishop of Canterbury, though he was the son of an earl, on the grounds that he had ability in large measure and pride in none. Newton himself was not above a little pride. At Warburton's episcopal consecration in 1760 he took the occasion to state that while the apostles were of undoubtedly low birth, 'yet times and circumstances are so changed, that persons of *noble* extraction by coming into the church may add strength and ornament to it.'[50] Warburton, with no university education and an attorney's training, was indubitably a self-made man, and Newton himself was no more than the son of a cider and brandy merchant. The young curate of Broxbourne in Hertfordshire, William Jones, was surprised by the uncouth country accent of Bishop Law of Carlisle.[51] The truth was that noble prelates remained a minority.

The Church had an obvious function as the appendage of a relatively liberal, decentralized State, and the preserve of a landed class which had a strong hold on the political institutions of the day. Its spiritual effectiveness is more difficult to assess. Much episcopal attention was devoted to maintaining frequent services, including weekday prayers and 'double service' on Sundays: regular communion was also a high priority. The evidence of visitation records suggests that the Church was more successful in these respects than its critics claimed. It was not only pastoral apathy which impeded it. Attendance at church was in effect voluntary. Congregations were inevitably influenced by the

---

[50] Ibid. ii. 601.
[51] O. F. Christie, *The Diary of the Revd. William Jones, 1777–1821* (London, 1909), 92.

practices of their richer members, which did not invariably coincide with clerical preferences. The tendency to 'plain religion' and rational preaching was quite compatible with individual piety but it did not always promote the communal devotion on which the Church relied in many rural parishes. The parish clergy of the mid-eighteenth century were particularly concerned about the difficulty of securing the religious allegiance of the poor at a time when polite society had its own distinctive patterns of worship and seemed little interested in galvanizing the spiritual life of its inferiors.

To the requirements of the propertied classes, the Church was notably responsive. Generalizations about its inadequacy in the face of urban expansion can be misleading. In some places there were too many churches for a static or declining population, not too few. Many parishes were unable or unwilling to maintain them in good order. None the less there was much rebuilding and much restoration. Nor was it as difficult to create new parishes as is sometimes claimed. Populous parishes in London's suburbs and Westminster were divided and redivided. Private chapels sprang up within the established Church as in Dissenting sects. Provided they did not interfere with the authority of an incumbent or encroach on his tithes, they were easy to establish. Financed by pew rents or congregational contributions they were eagerly sought by fashionable preachers, more particularly since they were often filled by election rather than nomination. They were emphatically not designed to serve the poor. In this respect the claims made on behalf of Richard Cecil, an evangelical who took over the Church's largest London chapel at Bedford Row in 1780, and made a point of providing free seating as well as rentable pews, were distinctly unusual.[52] Such chapels were essentially a response to middle-class needs. In this sense at least the Church was by no means lacking in creativity.

THE WAR ON THE METHODISTS

The fact that evangelical enthusiasm found its main audience among the poor does not mean that it was invariably well received by them. In the early annals of Methodism violent persecution was common. Riotous resistance to the word of God usually had

[52] J. Pratt, *The Works of the Rev. Richard Cecil*, i. 17.

the opposite effect to that intended so far as its principal victims were concerned, since it promoted a validating sense of martyrdom and encouraged public sympathy for those victimized. None the less the suffering of travelling preachers was genuine. Wesley himself received a physical battering on a notorious occasion at Colne in 1748, when the local curate, a former papist, advertised for volunteers as 'commander-in-chief' of a force dedicated to 'the defence of the Church of England, and the support of the manufactory in and about Colne, both of which are now in danger, ... let them now repair to the drumhead at the cross.'[53] Perhaps it is not surprising that itinerant preachers were given to military metaphors. John Smith, the Irish Methodist, spoke of Wesley's *Hymns* and *The Pilgrim's Progress* as his 'small arms' and the Bible as his 'artillery'.[54] He was subjected to some particularly vicious treatment by Irish mobs.

Ordinary worshippers suffered along with their exhorters, in some respects with longer-term consequences. Wesley was acutely aware of the physical and psychological pressure exerted on congregations exposed to the full weight of communal censure. The war waged on Staffordshire Methodists in 1743 and 1744 was perhaps the most bitter of all such campaigns of intimidation. After the middle of the century physical violence became less common, as Methodist societies established themselves in the familiar structure of local life, and earned the respectability associated with regular habits, orderly chapels, and prominent converts. Even so, intimidation of one kind or another continued. At Congleton, which acquired a Methodist chapel in 1760, opponents tried a variety of tactics short of actual physical assault. These included kicking a football, playing a hurdy-gurdy, and beating drums outside the chapel during divine service, letting dogs loose among the congregation, and hurling dirt and rotten eggs at its members. Wesley did not approve much of Congleton. Of neighbouring Burslem, a rough pottery town, he remarked 'Even the poor potters here are a more civilised people than the *Better sort* (so called) at Congleton.' But Congleton's lack of sophistication may have stood it in good stead. Under the guidance of a local apothecary as preacher, the chapel flourished: the opposition was silenced with

---

[53] Tyerman, *John Wesley*, ii. 15.
[54] C. H. Crookshank, *A Methodist Pioneer: The Life and Labours of John Smith* (London, 1881), p. 16.

a display of physical force, and by 1767 a new chapel was being constructed.[55]

It was commonly said by evangelical preachers that when they suffered for their preaching, even at the hands of a mob, it was usually because they had offended people of property, squires, clergymen, and 'some of the stupid and intemperate farmers', rather than the poor as such.[56] The bringers of salvation liked to think that their hearers were obstructed only by their betters. It is far from clear that this was always the case. Methodists brought the promise of heavenly joy, not earthly enjoyment. Their hostility to pastimes which figured in everyday life did not make them many friends. Anything that savoured of drink, gaming, or mere frivolity, was condemned and forbidden to the faithful. In Wales, and later in other regions, the Methodists were credited with transforming the lives of ordinary working-class people. This, after all, was their boast from the beginning. In his early travels Howell Harris made a point of denouncing cock-fighting; he was assured that one of his listeners had gone straight home and cut off the heads of his cocks.[57] All manner of popular revelry came under the censorious scrutiny of the new reformers. Eventually polite society was to grasp the advantages of a creed which contributed to the control of undisciplined elements. At the time there was less appreciation of the point, partly because evangelicals made it clear that their strictures applied to everybody, not merely those whom they harangued on the streets and in the fields. William Seward, the first Methodist martyr, who died at Hay on Wye in 1742 after being struck on the head by a stone, had gone out of his way to irritate his superiors. The riots which he caused at Monmouth in 1740 occurred at the races, where the local magnate, the Duke of Beaufort, was dining; Seward preached against 'horse-races, balls, assemblies, whoredom, and drunkenness'.[58]

Not only humble field preachers were unpopular. Clergymen who took themselves with extreme seriousness were an irritating and uncomfortable presence in any place. Joseph Milner had this demonstrated to him in clear terms at Hull, where he was a former local schoolmaster, a well-liked figure in the town, a not

[55] R. Head, *Congleton Past and Present* (Congleton, 1887), p. 261.
[56] G. Redford and J. A. James, ed., *The Autobiography of the Rev. William Jay* (2nd edn., London, 1855), p. 38.
[57] T. Rees, *History of Protestant Nonconformity in Wales* (London, 1861), p. 374.
[58] Ibid., p. 397.

inconsiderable string-puller on behalf of his family, and high in favour with the corporation. In 1770 he experienced his 'revolution', acquiring 'what he afterwards used to call vital, practical, experimental religion'. Not surprisingly, when he began carrying a bible in his pocket, and shunned cards, theatre, and the assembly, he found the genteel and convivial class of Hull decidedly hostile: when he went on to reform the lives of their inferiors he got into even more trouble. 'Embarrassing and difficult cases were frequently proposed to him, where heads of families or superiors insisted on their dependents leaving off their religious practices.' Milner's martyrdom was not very testing, and it moderated after seven or eight years in which his middle-class parishioners increasingly came to share his earnestness.[59] Men like Milner carried with them an utter conviction of their own rightness, which, even when expressed in the rhetoric of humility and accompanied by good temper and tolerance, was profoundly annoying to those who did not share or wish to share their vision. Opponents thought them a disruptive, antisocial force, imperilling communal harmony. This was what Richard Darley, the most prominent gentleman in Bishop Wilton, told the Yorkshire lay preacher Nicholas Manners, when he first set out in the early 1750s. 'As your sort of preaching is apt to breed quarrels amongst neighbours, I have agreed with my neighbours to hear you no more.'[60]

In theory persecution could be reinforced by prosecution. But the law had its limitations. Partly this was because the climate of opinion in which it actually operated, a climate of fragile but widely accepted tolerance, made it difficult to enforce even the laws which were available. But more important was the legal uncertainty of proceeding against unauthorized preachers. Howell Harris worked out a thorough defence of his activities, arguing that conventicles which offered no challenge to the doctrines or discipline of the Church of England could not be brought within the statute of Charles II designed to catch Dissenting meetings. At worst they might be arraigned before an ecclesiastical court as a breach of canon law, something which would have given rise to endless wrangling and was not likely to find favour with Whigs who distrusted Church courts. The law of riot could not, Harris

---

[59] I. Milner, *An Account of the Life and Character of the late Rev. Joseph Milner* (new edn., London, 1804), p. xxiv.
[60] *Some Particulars of the Life and Experience of Nicholas Manners* (York, 1785), p. 19.

thought, carry conviction when used against a religious meeting. The failure of a number of attempts to employ it against the revival in Wales suggests that he was right.[61]

The most effective sanctions were those brought to bear within the Church. Ironically these depended on evangelical concern to obtain its approval. Ordination for young men who had displayed their 'enthusiasm' was problematic. Many popular lay preachers sought ordination early in their careers only to be disappointed. Joseph Benson was typical. Educated by a Presbyterian minister, he became a teacher at Kingswood School and Trevecca, resigned from the latter as a result of his adherence to Wesley during the quarrel with Lady Huntingdon, attended St Edmund Hall, Oxford, was disowned by his tutor ('I could not help seeing the hand of God in this affair'), and was refused orders by the Bishop of Worcester. He went on to become one of Wesley's most valued preachers and a leading figure in the separation which followed Wesley's death.[62] The young Howell Harris claimed to have been rebuffed four times, three of them by the Bishop of St Davids. Rowland Hill was refused ordination by three bishops: one of them, the Bishop of Carlisle, agreed to ordain him priest, if one of his brethren would make him a deacon. But the Bishop of Bath and Wells refused to do so even when the Archbishop of Canterbury so instructed. Withholding orders was not the only sanction. Thomas Haweis, disciple of Berridge, author of *The Evangelical Expositor*, and in time executor of Lady Huntingdon's will, found the testimonials on which his ordination depended blocked by Bishop Lavington of Exeter, one of the most determined episcopal opponents of the revivalists. Happily ordained, none the less, by Secker, he was the subject of complaints for his activities in a club at Oxford, and was forbidden to preach there in 1762 by Bishop Hume.[63] The licensing of curates was an important episcopal function. Haweis's friends William Talbot and Joseph Jane sought to test the validity of Hume's action by demanding that Talbot be licensed as curate of St Mary Magdalene in place of Haweis. They failed.[64] The bishops as a body became increasingly adroit at co-ordinating their activities in such matters under George III. They

[61] G. M. Roberts, ed., *Selected Trevecka Letters (1742–1747)*, pp. 84–7.
[62] R. Treffry, *Memoirs of the Rev. Joseph Benson* (London, 1840), p. 39.
[63] A. S. Wood, *Thomas Haweis, 1734–1820* (London, 1957), pp. 79–82.
[64] Sidney, *Sir Richard Hill*, p. 83.

I (*a*). The Robin Hood

I (*b*). St Monday

The independence of the ordinary Englishman was much discussed and often censured. Above is the most famous of all popular debating societies; below, a diverse body of tradesmen celebrating a long weekend.

2. The House of Lords and House of Commons

Parliament was thought notably lacking in architectural grandeur. On the right the unpretentious appearance of the House of Commons is displayed, on the left the unassuming entrance to the House of Lords, as depicted in *A New and Accurate History and Survey of London* (London, 1766).

BOREAS.

I Promise to pay seventeen Millions in ten Years—of I am Minister.

3 (b). Boreas

3 (a). The Stature of a Great Man

Personal political caricature was slow to develop. 3 (a) purports to represent Lord Bute, but is actually an old print of Sir Robert Walpole, with the caption suitably altered. Lord North, in 3 (b), was the first Prime Minister widely caricatured with some verisimilitude.

6 (*a*). The Norman Conquest, or the Battle of Hastings

6 (*b*). The Massacre of the Britons at Stonehenge

Popular interest in history was intense, if not always very scholarly. Hayman's depiction (1752) of the Battle of Hastings featured fifteenth-century armour, Flaxman's (1783) of the exploits of Hengist, a curious neo-classical celebration of the verse of Thomas Chatterton on the subject.

7. (*a*). A garden chair
made of roots

7 (*b*). Two Gothic chairs

English furniture reflected the frequently faddish taste of the period: above, a
rococo self-parody made of roots, 1754; below, chairs in the Gothic manner,
1766.

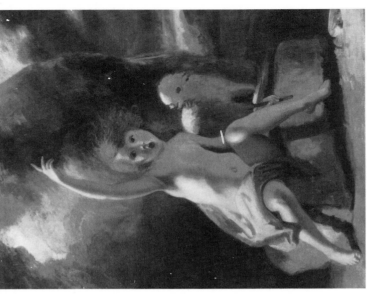

8 (a). Master Crewe as Henry VIII

8 (b). The Child Baptist in the Wilderness

Interest in children was strongly reflected in fashionable art. Reynolds exploited it frequently, here in a costume study of a juvenile Henry VIII, and in a devotional subject, St John the Baptist as a child.

deeply irritated John Thornton, a man with aristocratic connections of his own and by no means a friend of Methodists and lay preachers. 'I am every day more sick of our bench's abominable opposition to the serious clergy', he confessed in 1774.[65]

Considering that the Methodists and evangelical clergy were generally staunch defenders of the historic authority of the Church against the internal subversion of Unitarians and the external attacks of the Dissenters, episcopal victimization was hard to suffer. But it was not only the bishops who brought their power to bear. Wesley's university proved a vigorous opponent of his doctrines. The expulsion of six undergraduates from St Edmund Hall in 1768, on grounds which had no better foundation than their religious views, was readily portrayed as vindictive intolerance, at a time of much interest in questions of toleration. It was not something of which everyone in Oxford was proud: even in their own society the men expelled had support, not least from their Principal. But it was only the most extreme instance of commonplace harassment, albeit much of it of a minor order. The young Peard Dickinson, one of Wesley's well-born followers, found St Edmund Hall an uncomfortable berth in 1779 and migrated to Hertford College to avoid the worst of it.[66] But in the university at large neither he nor his friends found more than grudging tolerance, and not always that.

There were other ways in which the Church could harry its less favoured sons. A sensitive issue was the legal status of the chapels founded by the evangelicals. For the most part they were not licensed as Dissenting meeting-houses. The men who officiated in them were either clergy of the established church or not clergy at all. The framers of the Toleration Act had not foreseen this development. Even so, it is remarkable that the legal standing of the chapels (as distinct from the legality of conventicles held in them) was not tested before the courts for many years. When it was, the results were momentous. The occasion was Lady Huntingdon's decision in 1779 to take over a prominent hall in north London, the 'pantheon'. This building, known henceforth as the Spa Fields Chapel, lay in the parish of St James, Clerkenwell and was treated by the vicar of the parish as a dependent chapelry. Appropriately for a secular and propertied age, the evangelical cause was

[65] S. Meacham, *Henry Thornton of Clapham, 1760–1815* (Cambridge, Mass., 1964), p. 8.
[66] J. Benson, ed., *Memoirs of the Life of the Rev. Peard Dickinson* (London, 1803), ch. iii.

challenged not by an authoritarian bishop but by an incumbent defending his right to the patronage and profits of his parish. In the Consistory Court of London his claim to control the chapel was upheld, and the Huntingdon ministers appointed to it were forbidden to officiate. The Countess had always assumed that at least those of her clergy formally nominated her chaplains as a peer of the realm were immune from prosecution. This belief was widely shared: even Wesley had accepted a chaplaincy from the pious Countess of Buchan. But the decision of the courts was that the chaplains of peers could act only in the private chapels of their patrons. This judgement forced the Huntingdon Connection to begin licensing its chapels as Dissenting meeting-houses, a process which alienated many loyal members of the Church, and put the Connection firmly on the road to separation. A similar predicament shortly faced the Methodists. The Church, it was increasingly obvious, was ready to amputate an offending limb over which it had no control. Or, as Bishop Porteus made clear to one of his evangelical clergy, it was necessary to choose between the discipline of the Church and the freedom of Dissent. There was to be no middle way. 'Let him not be a Methodist in the morning, and a Church-of-England man in the afternoon.'[67]

THE EVANGELICAL CHALLENGE TO CONTEMPORARY VALUES

The men who made the evangelical revival did not set out to be comfortable. As the bluff Sir George Savile, father of Yorkshire Whiggism and a shrewd commentator on his times, remarked, 'the Methodists acted as a blistering plaster upon the backs both of the clergy and people'.[68] It is tempting to explain the resistance which they encountered in terms of a somewhat paradoxical conflict of authority. Wesley was an avowed High Churchman. For the Church as an apostolic institution he had the highest veneration. Its civil rights he did not question. His politics were thoroughly conservative, even reactionary. But Methodists did not always follow where he led. Evangelical ministers who were not of his persuasion certainly felt free to disagree with him, though like him, most of them regarded any political question as a matter of relative

---

[67] R. Hodgson, *The Life of the Right Reverend Beilby Porteus* (London, 1811), p. 270.
[68] I. Milner, *An Account of the Life and Character of the late Rev. Joseph Milner*, p. xxxii.

insignificance. Wesley's politics did not, in any case, reassure his opponents in the Church. Even when he employed it to ends of which they approved, Wesley assumed a degree of authority which was interpreted as a challenge to his ecclesiastical superiors and to the governors of lay society. The Methodists claimed to go wherever souls needed saving, but few of their enemies believed that they were interested only in souls.

Methodism offered a revolutionary perception of social relationships which was bound to seem subversive to much contemporary opinion. A central issue was the place of religion in society, a subject on which the rulers of the established Church were understandably touchy. The Church's part in a propertied world included tithes, sinecures, pluralism, lay patronage, and a whole ecclesiastical economy which, to say the least, seemed remote from the scriptural models recommended by evangelicals. It had, none the less, powerful vested interests to protect it, and articulate voices capable of speaking in its defence. The restraint observed by the Methodists in this respect is in some ways remarkable. They did not, for the most part, directly assail the irrational, hierarchical, and inegalitarian character of the Church polity, in the way that many Dissenters did. What they did do, implicitly and explicitly, was to criticize the spiritual torpor which it seemed to have promoted. This was more irritating to many of the clergy than a straightforward attack on Church abuses, since in many cases they would have joined in a demand for some measure of reform, particularly where lay rectorships and patronage were concerned. But the spiritual superiority claimed by the evangelical clergy was found thoroughly offensive and brought forward some bitter ripostes. Bishop Gibson's measured criticism of the Methodists in 1739, and Bishop Lavington's angry onslaught on them a decade later shared a resentment of this alleged arrogance.

William Warburton's attack on Wesley, in his *Doctrine of Grace* of 1762, was not only typical of the indignation felt by many of the clergy, but suggested the somewhat desperate polemical straits to which they could be reduced. Warburton had stoutly defended the alliance of Church and State, at a time when Wesley was no more than an obscure and frustrated missionary in Georgia.[69] Now he disposed quickly of the apostolic ideal of the priesthood. In modern times, he noted, the extraordinary operation of the Holy

[69] See above, p. 43–4.

Ghost was no longer necessary. 'Now the profession of the Christian Faith is attended with ease and honour.' To the young satirist William Mason, who never allowed his cloth to stand between him and the world, Warburton expressed his view that every candidate for orders must have 'a *call*; by which I meant, I told him, nothing fanatical or superstitious; but an inclination, and, on that, a resolution, to dedicate all his studies to the service of religion, and totally to abandon his poetry.'[70] This was firm advice but it was not excessively demanding.

The evangelical model of priesthood offered an implied rebuke to the beneficed clergy. Poor, itinerant, condemning secularism as well as sin, Methodists were infuriatingly unworldly. It was possible, of course, to hit back at their own peccadilloes. The financial arrangements which sustained them were scrutinized with understandable interest by defenders of the established order. In truth there was not much to discover. A system which supported preachers by means of small, weekly contributions and kept most of them in a minimum of comfort could not be criticized very severely. But a casual approach to the keeping of accounts inevitably brought accusations of corruption. Whitefield got into trouble on this score, as did the Moravians. Wesley, with a large organization to maintain, was unceasingly vigilant, lest the shepherds be accused of fleecing their flock. He was also aware of the threat of jobbery even in a godly community. The letter read to the Manchester conference after his death was a fair description of his own conduct as well as a prudent direction for the future: 'to have no respect of persons in stationing the preachers, in choosing children for Kingswood school, in disposing of the yearly contributions, and the preachers' fund, or any other public money.'[71]

Wesley's lay preachers were viewed with loathing by many Churchmen. There may not have been much of the sacramental character of the priest left in latitudinarian England, but what remained was all the more cherished in some quarters. Wesley seems to have had no doubts about laymen, however: as early as 1742 he pronounced them as well qualified as clergymen in 'substantial, practical, experimental divinity'.[72] Their use was

---

[70] A. W. Evans, *Warburton and the Warburtonians: A Study in some Eighteenth-Century Controversies* (London, 1932), p. 198.

[71] R. Treffry, *Memoirs of the Rev. Joseph Benson*, p. 142.

[72] Tyerman, *John Wesley*, i. 370.

controversial among those of Wesley's fellow evangelists who remained wedded to the discipline of the established Church. They were particularly annoyed when Methodists invaded their own parishes. Grimshaw and Venn in Yorkshire both remonstrated with Wesley on this point. The humble origins of lay preachers heightened the objections to them. It was one of the formal accusations laid against three of the St Edmund Hall sufferers that they were 'bred to trade'.[73] Part of the magic of Methodism was that it not only held out the assurance of redemption to men of modest birth and education, but permitted them to offer the same assurance to others. For those of a certain temperament this commission to convert had manifest attractions. Such men often came from families of conventionally religious background yet one which seemed inadequate to their children. Thus 'Frankie' Barr, a formidable Yorkshire evangelist of the early nineteenth century, recalled his farming parents of the 1780s: 'They were miserable formalists, attending regularly the services of the Established Church, but were awfully destitute of the power of saving grace.'[74] This level of society, the yeoman farmer, the small tradesman, or artisan, produced many who were moved to preach justification by faith. It had a sturdy sense of independence, perhaps tinctured with a contempt for superiors and an urge to leadership, and enough, but not too much education, to make it an ideal breeding ground for lay preachers.

Clerical hostility to the bearers of the evangelical message sometimes had sexual undertones. The clergy of the established Church stressed their debt to the Reformation in respect of clerical marriage, an institution which they saw as peculiarly fitting them to complement and lead lay society, by contrast with their popish counterparts. Sermons addressed to the Sons of the Clergy, the charity which supervised the distribution of alms to the widows and orphans of the parish clergy, rarely missed an opportunity to endorse this view. The ideal clergyman was immersed in the same domestic problems as his parishioners, sharing the same daily concerns. It is no coincidence that the most popular clerical story of the age, *The Vicar of Wakefield*, was one in which the trials and tribulations of the hero had to do with his family, not least his

---

[73] Sidney, *Sir Richard Hill*, p. 114.
[74] W. Smith, *The Village Cooper: Memoirs of The Life, Character, and Labours of Francis Barr, Local Preacher, etc.* (Leeds, 1849), p. 14.

daughters. Some critics of latitudinarianism were tempted to
associate it with a distracting domesticity and a corrupting
carnality. William Law, author of the influential *Serious Call to a
Devout and Holy Life*, was one such. Early Methodism entertained a
certain ambivalence about the married state. Women and Wesleyan
preaching did not go very well together. 'No trap so mischievous
to the field-preacher as wedlock,' observed John Berridge, 'and it
is laid for him at every hedge corner.' It had, he added, maimed
the uxorious Charles Wesley, and would have had a similar effect
on John Wesley and George Whitefield, 'if a wise Master had not
graciously sent them a brace of ferrets' for wives.[75]

Wesley's own relations with women were certainly not happy.
His humiliation in Georgia resulted from his unsuccessful courtship of a girl whom he then sought to prevent marrying his rival.
A not dissimilar tussle with one of his own ministers over Grace
Murray, an orphan keeper who had tended him while he was ill
in 1748, ended similarly and embarrassingly with the triumph of
his supplanter. His eventual marriage to Mary Vazeille, the widow
of a London merchant, in 1751, was approved by some of his
friends, in the belief that it would save him future awkwardnesses
of this kind. It proved an unhappy marriage, and failed in its
principal objective. Wesley's outpourings about his domestic
life to Sarah Ryan, a woman whom he made housekeeper at
his school at Kingswood, and who was alleged to have three husbands alive, raised a good many eyebrows. The view which
he had early expressed, that celibacy was preferable in a priest,
would appear to have been prudent in his own case, whatever its
merits in point of principle. Critics enjoyed nothing more than
a juicy scandal. Wesley's followers did not oblige with many of
these, but when they did the results were predictably damaging.
Richard Graves, whose novel *The Spiritual Quixote* is a lucid
summary in satirical form of the case against Methodism, was
careful to include a jibe against Methodists who supposedly had
two wives.[76]

More horrifying still than the sexual enticements of women
were their spiritual advances. Quaker women were traditionally
unique in the equality which they enjoyed with respect to religious
testimony. They were well placed to take advantage of the feminism

[75] Seymour, *Selina Countess of Huntingdon*, i. 388–9.
[76] p. 123.

which flourished in some quarters in the late eighteenth century. As Thomas Clarkson boasted, 'The Quaker-women, independently of their private, have that which no other body of women have, a public character. This is a new aera in female history.'[77] Methodist women were not formally authorized to preach on the same footing as men, but there is no doubt that their ministerial role was a real one. In the local societies whose weekly meetings played a crucial part in the early establishment of Methodism women were much depended on to sustain communal fervour, a feature of evangelical devotion which aroused ribaldry and suspicion in equal measure. A satire of 1778 described 'obstetrical female saints' who supervised the 'new birth' of converts and acted as spiritual spies for their male superiors.[78] Some women were effectively lay preachers enjoying the same function as their male counterparts. Sarah Crosby, who set off for Derby in 1761 and found herself beginning to preach to her assembled classes, 'as my Lord has removed all my scruples respecting the propriety of my acting thus publicly', was perhaps the best known.[79]

One woman was a continual source of irritation to the Church, though the bishops were reluctant publicly to admit it. Lady Huntingdon was as much head of her Connection as Wesley was of his, and not less dictatorial. 'A *leader* is wanting', Whitefield had told her in 1749. 'The honour hath been put upon your Ladyship by the great Head of the Church.'[80] She was certainly equal to this honour. In a formal sense her chapels were administered by trustees established for the purpose, but there was no doubt of the driving force behind them. Her displeasure was dignified but terrifying. Offended by her followers at Reading, she pronounced excommunication with stinging disdain. 'Should the souls of Reading find better care or more faithful services (as I have nothing in view for any but their spiritual blessedness), so we will turn to our other calls.'[81] Her preachers did not lightly ignore her directions. John Berridge had the courage to do so when declining her order to go to Brighton in 1762, and protested: 'You threaten me, Madam, like a pope, not like a mother in Israel.'[82]

[77] T. Clarkson, *A Portraiture of Quakerism* (3 vols., London, 1806), iii. 288–9.
[78] *The Saints: A Satire*, p. 2.
[79] Tyerman, *John Wesley*, ii. 398.
[80] Seymour, *Selina Countess of Huntingdon*, i. 117.
[81] Ibid. ii. 404.
[82] Ibid. i. 324.

She took such bluntness, from friends and enemies alike, in her stride. One enraged cleric, Dr Nicholas Carter (father of the Blue Stocking Elizabeth Carter), sent a letter to 'Old Mother Huntingdon' in which he roundly lectured her for her temerity. 'A woman of your rank and education I should have thought would have known better than to be guilty of any such rashness. Pray who gave you leave to send your *preaching-fellows* into my parish?'[83]

As a woman the Countess had to work at second hand, but it rarely impeded her effectiveness. She proved a redoubtable opponent of Wesley in the Calvinist controversy of 1771. In the same year she denounced the wife of the Archbishop of Canterbury, Cornwallis, for making Lambeth Palace the scene of unseemly 'routs'. Cornwallis received two preliminary remonstrances from Lady Huntingdon, one via her cousin Lord Townshend, who was related by marriage to the Cornwallis family, the second via the evangelical Martin Madan, who was also connected with the Archbishop. Both having failed, she organized a powerful deputation to the King, consisting of herself, the Duchess of Ancaster, and Lord Dartmouth. The result was a discomforting royal rebuke in writing to Lambeth.[84] She represented a somewhat different kind of threat from Wesley. Wesley despised the system of patronage which underpinned Church, State, and their alliance. Lady Huntingdon cheerfully used it for her own ends. When the ageing Bishop Hoadly refused to ordain the evangelical poet Moses Browne, later curate to James Hervey and in his turn the employer of John Newton as his curate at Olney, it was the Countess who procured the favour. She did so by getting her relative Lady Gertrude Hotham to approach her nephew, the politician Welbore Ellis.[85] She was a remorseless puller of unlikely strings. The male Chesterfields were not known for their piety, but the fourth Earl was bullied into giving her £20 for her Tabernacle at Bristol in 1749, on condition that his name did not appear, and the fifth Earl was chivvied into investigating the alleged abuse of charitable funds at Repton School in 1782.[86]

[83] Seymour, *Selina Countess of Huntingdon*, ii. 133.
[84] Ibid. ii. 280–3.
[85] Ibid. i. 167–8.
[86] Ibid. ii. 451–2 ff.

ENTHUSIASM AND REASON

The faith of which Wesley and Whitefield talked was obnoxious to many of their contemporaries. They were particularly disturbed by the suddenness of the conversion experience. The young William Jay, in time a powerful Methodist preacher, was acutely conscious of its dangers, though he was reluctant to condemn those who claimed greater certainty. 'Some persons love to talk of their being born again, and of their being made new creatures, with a kind of physical certainty and exactness.'[87] The assurance of being saved was a perilous tightrope to tread, and it is far from clear that Wesley himself had the intellectual sophistication to walk it with confidence. It was easy to fall into antinomianism, a familiar terror to seventeenth-century Calvinists, and one of which Wesley was all too aware. Throughout his life he insisted that sinless perfection was practicable as an earthly condition, though he did not claim to have met with it often, and certainly did not number himself among those who enjoyed it. Some of his followers had every intention of enjoying it, often with troublesome consequences for Wesley himself. One such was James Wheatley, whose scandalous personal life led to his expulsion by Wesley at Bristol in 1751. He went on to Norwich and enjoyed an astounding success which compelled Wesley to resume relations with him. But his spiritual labours were almost as vexing as his sexual lapses. The Norwich congregation was highly undisciplined and was eventually abandoned to the Huntingdon Connection. Still more annoying was the notorious George Bell, a former corporal in the Life Guards, who was converted by Wesley's insubordinate preacher Thomas Maxfield, and proclaimed himself a prophet. His prediction of the end of the world on 28 February 1763 caused a panic in London and forced Wesley to publish a stern disavowal in his *Cautions and Directions*. Bell spent what he expected to be his last day on earth in prison, having been arrested for unlicensed preaching, while taking his last look at the capital before it was consumed by flames. His prophecy unfulfilled, he abandoned his faith. Maxfield renounced all connection with Wesley. The whole affair was deeply embarrassing.

Critics and satirists treated the emotional extravagance of revival as its most vulnerable point. The two most successful dramatic

[87] G. Redford and J. A. James, *The Autobiography of the Rev. William Jay*, p. 21.

assaults, Foote's skit on Whitefield in *The Minor* and Bickerstaffe's *The Hypocrite*, dwelt heavily on it. The fact that those who made this criticism were manifestly unfair in their accounts of what was involved should not obscure the real concern to which they appealed. It was not necessary to be a cold-hearted rationalist or a hedonistic liver of the good life to have doubts about the techniques employed by Wesleyan preachers. The extraordinary manifestations of popular faith witnessed in the early years startled even those who were instrumental in promoting them. At Haworth, the year when 'our dear Lord was pleased to visit my parish', Grimshaw noted amazing 'weeping, roaring and agonies'.[88] It was difficult to know where these cavortings should properly stop. The Welsh were stigmatized as 'Jumpers', a charge to which Daniel Rowlands responded by accusing the English of being 'Sleepers'.[89]

The testimony of some of those subjected to these techniques was particularly damning, though lapsed converts were hardly impartial authorities. James Lackington, in his much read memoirs, gave an account of his own experience which was typical of this kind of back-stabbing. He had been converted by Thomas Bryant, an early Wesleyan and forceful 'damnation-preacher'. The prayer-meetings, inner circles, and love-feasts to which he was invited gave him little chance to use his own reason, or even his own will. 'At last, by singing and repeating enthusiastic amorous hymns, and ignorantly applying particular texts of scripture, I got my imagination to the proper pitch, and thus was I born again in an instant, became a very great favourite of heaven, ... had angels to attend all my steps, and was as familiar with the Father, Son, and Holy Ghost, as any old woman in Mr Wesley's connection.'[90] Wesley did not attach great value to enthusiasm in the sense which his enemies spoke of it; nor was it at all what he meant by 'experiential religion'. But he never succeeded in dislodging the impression that it was the central element in his message: neither, in a lifetime of rational argument, did he convince the sceptics that he was anything but an enemy of reason.

Every road taken by educated people seemed to be lighted by reason. Mysticism was considered decidedly eccentric, though

---

[88] G. G. Cragg, *Grimshaw of Haworth* (London, 1947), p. 22.
[89] E. Evans, *Howel Harris Evangelist*, p. 61.
[90] J. Lackington, *Memoirs of the First Forty-Five Years of the Life of James Lackington* (new edn., London, 1793), pp. 85–6.

Swedenborg had an English following which included his trans-
lator Thomas Hartley, Rector of Winwick, Northamptonshire, and
the Quaker businessman William Cookworthy. The Moravians
were often accused of mysticism, but they had more in common
with Wesley's 'practical divinity', in which there was little that was
metaphysical. The virtues of empiricism were axiomatic for the
generations educated under the spell of Newtonianism. A rare
challenge was offered by Henry Brooke's *Universal Beauty*, published in 1735. 'Yet infinite that Work, beyond our Soar, Beyond
what *Clarkes* can prove, or *Newtons* can explore.' Brooke, whose
epic novel *The Fool of Quality* was admired and abridged by
Wesley, has been hailed as 'a mystic isolated in an age of reason'.[91]
Yet even he was confused in his rejection of materialism: his praise
for God's cosmic craftsmanship seems to have derived primarily
from his appreciation of the Deity's handiwork as expressed in
the laws of science and the evidence of reason.

John Hutchinson's critique of Newton, developed in the last
years of Newton's life, was later, in 1748–9, approved by a prominent group of Oxford dons and theologians and celebrated by the
poet Christopher Smart in his *Jubilate Agno*.[92] Smart, like Brooke,
was highly unrepresentative, for all the interest which he aroused.
If most creative literature serves to satisfy rather than challenge
the conventional requirements of its market, there is not much
doubt what readers of the eighteenth century wanted to be told.
They were heavily bombarded with middle-brow science. In the
wake of Newton's death in 1727 there came a spate of works
designed to popularize his achievement, the most celebrated of
them Henry Pemberton's *View* in 1728, Algarotti's version for
ladies, translated from the Italian in 1739, and Maclaurin's
posthumous *Account* in 1748. Benjamin Martin's introduction to
general science for the layman, the *Philosophical Grammar*, went
through forty editions in as many years after it came out in 1733.
The fact that these men, especially Maclaurin, were themselves
respected mathematicians is an indication of the significance
attached to the work of public education in such matters, as well
as the profit to be derived from it. It was noted with pride that

[91] (London, 1735), Part II, p. 20; L. Stevenson, 'Brooke's Universal Beauty and Modern
Thought', *Proceedings of Modern Languages Association*, 43 (1928), 209.
[92] K. Williamson, ed., *The Poetical Works of Christopher Smart*, i: *Jubilate Agno* (Oxford,
1980), pp. 131–2.

one of the principal media for the setting and solving of difficult mathematical problems was the *Ladies Diary*, a periodical avowedly intended for pleasure rather than professional scholarship, and 'sent abroad in the poor dress of an almanac'.[93]

The vogue for scientific idiom was exploited by poets, but not with a view to irreverence or atheism. Pope's unwary secularism in his *Essay on Man* showed the danger of linking Newtonianism with questionable theology. It was a danger which the Newtonians themselves for the most part ostentatiously avoided, and Pope's successors were careful to distance themselves from his example. Thomson was one of those who took the opportunity of Newton's death to praise him in verse, and the imagery of *The Seasons* owed not a little to his reading of the master. The aesthetic interests of the mid-eighteenth century made the alliance of science and spirituality all the more popular. Milton's epics and Newton's optics provided a rich source of inspiration for the scientific school of the sublime. Subsequently the layman's interest in science moved away from mathematics, physics, and astronomy in the direction of natural history. But this made no difference to the theological orthodoxy of what was offered. A torrent of verse after 1760 displayed the beauties of animal and vegetable creation in a way which reinforced admiration of the wisdom of their creator. If the verse has generally been found wanting in merit by literary critics, it none the less assisted the process by which scientific innovation could be rendered compatible with traditional religious belief.[94]

'Enlightened' Churchmen did more to preserve the cause of godliness than Wesley supposed. Outright resistance to the empirical method earned either ridicule or contempt, as the history of the Hutchinsonians demonstrated. But the flexibility of much Establishment thinking eased the tension between a revolutionary view of creation and a Christian model of the Creator. By the late eighteenth century it was easier to absorb scientific novelties into a conventional theology than had seemed possible a century earlier. The prominence of Rational Dissenters, in the debates on this point, is somewhat misleading. It was not necessary to follow Priestley into materialism in order to incorporate his scientific

[93] *Critical Review*, 41 (1776), 387.
[94] W. P. Jones, *The Rhetoric of Science: A Study of Scientific Ideas and Imagery in Eighteenth-Century English Poetry* (London, 1966), ch. 7.

discoveries into the divine plan of a Christian God. Orthodox
Churchmen cheerfully did so, as did Roman Catholics. Charles
Walmesley, Vicar-Apostolic of the Western district from 1764 to
1797, and author of a *General History of the Christian Church* in
1771, was no challenger of established authority. In the later years
of his life he opposed the Cisalpine movement among English
Catholics. But in his readiness to fit scientific advances into a
Catholic world-view, he was typical of his time. He was a con-
tributor to the *Philosophical Transactions* of the Royal Society and
brought his Newtonianism to bear on sacred subjects, ingenuously
calculating, for instance, the precise measurements of the New
Jerusalem.[95]

SUPERSTITION

Conventional religion and scientific research had a common enemy,
common superstition. That Wesley was a practical student of
exorcism surprised few of his opponents. Enthusiasm and superstition went naturally together, and the fact that many of his
followers were uneducated merely reinforced the identification of
the two. Popular literature seemed to confirm the attachment of
its readership to discredited patterns of thought. Almanacs were
'seen and believed in almost every cot and pot-house in the kingdom'. It was said that in this respect Francis Moore had provided
the 'creed of the common people of England'.[96] In Wales almanacs
were much the most successful form of Welsh language publishing; Welsh bibles, by contrast, had to be provided on a non-
profit-making basis by the SPCK. Chapbooks maintained the
appeal of stories and myths in which magical happenings played a
large part. Enlightenment and established religion together (in
England no strange alliance) reinforced middle and upper-class
contempt for superstitious practices. It was widely assumed that
superstition went with a Papist's faith, not a Protestant's. The
foremost authority on popular customs, John Brand, roundly
condemned belief in ghosts, fairies, and exorcism as the residual
rubbish of Romish superstition.[97]

---

[95] G. Scott, ' "The Times are Fast Approaching": Bishop Charles Walmesley OSB (1722–
1777) as Prophet', *Journal of Eccesliastical History*, 36 (1985), 597.
[96] S. J. Pratt, *Gleanings in England*, iii. 78, 75.
[97] *Observations on Popular Antiquities*, chs. x, xi.

The resources of polite society were increasingly deployed against popular superstition. The best-known example is the repeal of the Witchcraft Act of James I in 1736. It was seen as confirming an existing trend. The last conviction had occurred in 1712, the last indictment in 1717. Uprooting the communal prejudices which sustained belief in witchcraft was hardly to be achieved by statutory means, however. The witch convicted in 1712, Jane Wenham, had been protected from further victimization after her pardon by the family of Lord Chancellor Cowper. But her death and burial in 1729 provided a reminder of the powerful emotions involved. The unfortunate curate of Hertingfordbury, instructed by Lady Elizabeth Cowper to deliver a sermon suitable for the rational education of a poor congregation in such matters, decided that discretion was the better part of valour when confronted by his irate parishioners.[98] Lady Elizabeth had a down-to-earth explanation of Jane Wenham's offensiveness, based on her treatment of an enthusiastic suitor: 'She had a peevish Virtue, and I suppose not only denied the Inamorata but exposed him.' Her explanation was typical of upper-class determination to attribute primitive beliefs to ordinary human malice. Addison's observation that witches were usually old women chargeable to the parish had a comforting rationality about it which appealed to educated minds confronted with the superstition of their inferiors.[99]

Periodic outcries against witches were accordingly received with indignation. The most notorious, the case of Thomas Colley, occurred in 1751. Colley was executed for his part in murdering an alleged witch whom he had taken a leading part in ducking, with fatal consequences to her and himself. The affair seems to have originated not with Colley, but with a publican who conducted a vendetta against the supposed witch after she abused him for unneighbourly meanness. She was evidently a Jacobite as well as a sorcerer, 'telling him, that the pretender would have him and his hogs too'.[1] Educated incredulity at the credulousness of the uneducated was marked. The learned Elizabeth Carter was not amused to find in 1760 that she had acquired a reputation for foretelling the weather, predicting high tides, and even conjuring,

[98] Hertfordshire Record Office, D/ED, F234.

[99] P. J. Guskin, 'The Context of Witchcraft: The Case of Jane Wenham (1712)', *Eighteenth Century Studies*, 15 (1981–2), 58.

[1] W. B. Carnochan, 'Witch-Hunting and Belief in 1751: The Case of Thomas Colley and Ruth Osborne', *Journal of Social History*, 4 (1970–1), 393.

among the poor of Wingham. 'I really thought there had been no such nonsense left even among the lowest of the people at present.'[2]

The elimination of superstition had to do with class, and with economic progress. One of the features of life on the Celtic fringe which English visitors found so fascinating was its propensity to maintain untenable beliefs. The Manxman's stories of mermaids and mermen were thought ludicrous but diverting.[3] The Welsh also had a reputation for outlandish gullibility. Joseph Cradock, an early popularizer of the Welsh tour, considered them 'not inferior in supersitition to the Laplanders'.[4] The controversy concerning Scottish second sight, promoted by the travels of Pennant and Johnson, assumed similar tendencies among the benighted inhabitants of the Highlands and Islands. Such examples were reassuring to the reader. They suggested that as commercial society developed and popular education improved, the residue of irrationality would inevitably wither away. While it lasted it was possible to laugh, to patronize, and perhaps to pity those whose credulity made them easy to exploit. Laughter there certainly was after a remarkable happening in 1738. When two large birds alighted on top of St Paul's Cathedral and declined to be frightened away it was popularly supposed that they had come to warn Englishmen of the acute peril in which Spanish atrocities placed them. The response of a resourceful press-gang, in placing a turkey on top of the Monument and pressing the crowd which gathering to observe it, seemed appropriate as well as ingenious.[5]

Laughter was also the usual response when the introduction of the Gregorian calendar in 1752 encountered opposition on account of the eleven days of September 1752 which disappeared to accommodate it. The reform of the calendar had a certain symbolic significance in terms of the conflict of enlightenment and bigotry. It was initiated by the Earl of Macclesfield, President of the Royal Society and exemplar of the scientific nobleman, and championed in Parliament by the Earl of Chesterfield, who considered himself the very embodiment of modern politeness. The hostility which it aroused was not merely unreasoning atavism. The Act caused complications for the celebration of birthdays and anniversaries

[2] M. Pennington, *Memoirs of the Life of Mrs Elizabeth Carter* (London, 1807), p. 167.
[3] S. Markham, ed., *John Loveday of Caversham, 1711–1789: The Life and Tours of an Eighteenth-Century Onlooker* (Salisbury, 1984), pp. 77–8.
[4] *Letters from Snowdon* (London, 1770), p. 66.
[5] William Maitland, *The History and Survey of London*, i. 589–90.

and irritated many who saw no necessity even for a minor incon-venience in the cause of conformity to Continental practice. It also worried Churchmen for whom the non-juror Robert Nelson's *Companion to the Festivals and Fasts of the Church of England* was more in the nature of a sacred text than a liturgical guide. There were political undertones. Because the King was in Hanover in 1752 it was alleged that his Regency Council had arbitrarily intro-duced the change in his absence.[6] In the notorious Oxfordshire election of 1754 the issue was raised because one of the Whig candidates, Lord Parker, was Macclesfield's son and burdened with vicarious responsibility for it.

Minor comedies like the calendar affair reinforce the notion, well established among historians, of a dislocation between popular and patrician culture, brought about by the impact of economic growth and the development of class. The idea is not without its dangers. Cultural confusion tends to invalidate such simple categories. Educated people themselves found it difficult to draw a clear line between rational and irrational belief. Contempt for an inferior's absurdity could turn to discomfort when events exposed one's own naïvety. Rational theologians did their best to take the conjuring out of Christianity, but only the most daring altogether denied the everyday role of Providence, and once admitted, evid-ence of divine intervention was not always easy to distinguish from superstitious nonsense. The long controversy concerning the historicity of miracles, culminating in the outcry caused in 1749 by Conyers Middleton's *Free Enquiry* and David Hume's essay on the subject, confirmed the importance of the question of the Deity's capacity to suspend divinely ordained laws of nature.

The London earthquakes of February 1750 understandably caused anxiety on this point. It was raised to extraordinary heights by a lunatic trooper's prediction of a further, apocalyptic earth-quake, scheduled to take place two months after the first. The opportunity was too good for Churchmen to neglect. Indeed it presented a rare occasion when clerical enemies could combine. The hell-fire preacher William Romaine and his episcopal opponent, Thomas Sherlock, both urged their countrymen to reform their moral conduct before divine punishment was visited on them. Sherlock's pastoral letter of 1750 must rank as one of the most popular of all ephemeral publications. Smollett recorded the

[6] *Sermon on Old Christmas Day, 5 January 1753* (London, 1753).

outcome in his *History*: 'In after ages it will hardly be believed, that on the evening of the eighth day of April, the open fields, that skirt the metropolis, were filled with incredible numbers of people assembled in chairs, in chaises, and coaches, as well as on foot, who waited in the most fearful suspense until morning, and the return of day disproved the truth of the dreadful prophecy.'[7]

It was not only in the presence of God that scepticism might prove injudicious. Medical speculation exploited a very human weakness. No figure was more laughable than the mountebank parading his nostrums before ignorant folk at country fairs. But the distinction between quackery and scientific enquiry was not always clear, and it was easy to be caught out. The Oratory which John Henley, disappointed of Church preferment, erected to disseminate eccentric opinions to a fee-paying audience, attracted serious interest, until it degenerated into one of the tourist spectacles of the 1730s. The notorious imposture of the Godalming woman Mary Tofts, who claimed in 1726 to have given birth to rabbits, fooled a number of doctors, including the anatomist to the royal household Nathanael St André, before it was exposed. Miracle cures throve on the mass marketing of medical prescriptions: who could tell whether the claims made for them were justified, and who could ridicule sick patients who grasped at the prospect of recovery? Most medical controversies were guaranteed to find authorities on both sides of the question and it was asking a lot for the inexpert layman to choose between them.

In this medicine was not unrepresentative. Part of the wonder of science was the constant discovery of new features of the physical world which astounded and baffled men of judgement and sense. Self-appointed experts were prone to show off their knowledge by explaining phenomena which puzzled ordinary minds. Why, it was wondered in 1772, had the otherwise unremarkable Mary Clues, taking to her bed in an advanced state of intoxication, and upsetting her candle, burnt herself almost to obliteration without doing the least damage to the bed or the room in which she slept. The answer, according to the travel-writer Thomas Pennant, was to be found in the newly unlocked mysteries of chemistry: she had expired insensibly in the same manner as her candle, her veins full of spirits, the flames nourished by her own 'phlogiston'.[8] The

[7] pp. 317–18.
[8] T. Pennant, *The Journey from Chester to London* (London, 1782), pp. 165–6.

very readiness of defenders of faith to use scientific evidence enhanced this tendency. Sherlock himself somewhat desperately resolved the conundrum of the Trinity by appealing to Benjamin Franklin's scientific discoveries as Pennant appealed to Joseph Priestley's. 'The operation of our Saviour in the Unity he compared to electricity.'[9] Samuel Horsley, known to posterity principally for his uncompromising attack on the materialism and heterodoxy of Priestley, had also been Secretary of the Royal Society, and saw no conflict between empirical scholarship and traditional theology. His first published work was 'The Power of God, deduced from the Computable Instantaneous Productions of it in the Solar System'. This ingenious argument was devoted to a proposition of particular value in the struggle against deism, the assertion that Creation provided evidence of a constant divine impulse, not merely an initial, once for all act of creation.[10]

The more miraculous the natural world seemed, the harder it became to dismiss new miracles as irrational. The chemist James Keir lectured his free-thinking friend Erasmus Darwin to some effect on this point. 'You are such an infidel in religion, my dear doctor, that you cannot believe in transubstantiation; yet you can believe that apples and pears, hay and oats, bread and wine, sugar, oil and vinegar, are nothing but water and charcoal, and that it is a great improvement in language to call all these things by one word—oxide hydrocarbonneux.'[11] Every remarkable discovery confirmed the matchless ingenuity of the author of all things. Employing reasoning familiar to many deists, the Dissenter Thomas Amory thought 'the plain argument for the existence of a Deity, obvious to all, and carrying irresistible conviction with it, is from the evident contrivance and fitness of things to one another, which we meet with through all the parts of the universe.'[12] The process was exemplified by the great explorations as well as by experimental advances. Patagonian giants did not seem more remarkable than the completely new species of flora and fauna discovered in the Southern Hemisphere. In short, the progress of knowledge promoted a certain circumspection on dismissing the seemingly fanciful. The Cock Lane ghost of 1762, one of the more

[9] D. Benham, *Memoirs of James Hutton*, p. 106.

[10] H. H. Jebb, *A Great Bishop of One Hundred Years Ago* (London, 1909), pp. 17–18.

[11] H. Pearson, *Doctor Darwin* (London, 1930), p. 105.

[12] T. Amory, *The Life and Opinions of John Buncle, Esquire*, ed. E. A. Baker (London, 1904), pp. 85–6.

ingenious impositions in the history of the supposedly supernatural, attracted the interest of distinguished men of learning.
Few of them rushed to believe it; equally few of them were prepared
to discount it without careful enquiry. In retrospect the fact that
Methodists had played a considerable part in publicizing the ghost,
with the pious Earl of Dartmouth being brought in to vouch for
its authenticity, gave rise to predictable mirth. But there was always
a measure of caution in dismissing those who believed without
hesitation in spirits, evil or otherwise. In the pursuit of truth it
seemed as unwise to adopt an impenetrable scepticism as it might
be to give in to unthinking enthusiasm.

CHAPTER 7

The Fortunate Isle

In the middle of the eighteenth century Britain enjoyed remarkable prestige among other Europeans. The British themselves considered their reputation entirely deserved. Religious tolerance and liberty under the law were much prized. But reality did not always accord closely with expectations. The rights of religious minorities were variable and uncertain. The execution of the laws was lax and discretionary rather than liberal. There was bitter criticism of lawyers and the judiciary. The legal privileges treasured by propertied Englishmen were not all available to their poorer compatriots. New legislation and administrative procedures put strains on traditional assumptions about civil liberty. Anxiety on this score was matched by concern about Britain's less impressive reputation in cultural matters. The arts seemed disturbingly dependent on foreigners for their excellence, and even for their existence. Englishmen sought solace in the glories of their language and literature, in the triumph of the 'natural' garden, and in the adoption of Italian and classical models with which to express the native English genius. Under George II they received little encouragement from the court. But George III provided well-intentioned patronage, including an important part in the foundation of the Royal Academy. English xenophobia complicated the adoption of Continental tastes. It also caused problems within the British Isles themselves. Celts seeking a share in the new prosperity of the period suffered greatly from the national prejudices of Englishmen. Scots, in particular, found themselves victimized thanks to the political influence and unpopularity of Lord Bute during the early years of George III. There were clearly defined limits to the enlightenment and liberality which commentators commonly identified as hallmarks of British life.

RELIGIOUS LIBERTY AND TOLERANCE

THE accolade of 'The Fortunate Isles' was claimed by the author of a piece entitled 'Great Britain superior to any other Country' in 1774. He also approvingly quoted the poet James Thomson's description: 'Island of Bliss'.[1] No doubt some of his readers would have demurred. Yet these terms did express the complacency of the British when contemplating their place in creation. They also reflected the admiration which most things English aroused among foreigners in the grip of Anglomania. For all the industrial and imperial achievements of a later age, it is doubtful whether the British have ever had such a good press among the opinion-makers of Continental Europe as they enjoyed during the middle decades of the eighteenth century, between an age of religious conflict and an age of revolutionary crisis. A stream of visitors, the most famous Voltaire and Montesquieu, came, saw, and were conquered. Many arrived with favourable impressions already formed, and returned home with them merely confirmed. Some wrote of their pleasure, and had it translated into English, a form of compliment which was gratifying to their hosts. The naïve enthusiasm of P. J. Grosley, whose *Tour*, published in 1772, was particularly popular, was typical. Like others, he voiced the occasional criticism, condemning the insolence of working men, and deploring the melancholic spirit found at all levels of society. But such complaining was rare. For Grosley, as for most visitors, the emphasis was on the civilized character of English society, signifying its emergence from an era of barbarism and strife. Tolerance without cynicism, moderation without apathy, liberty without licence, these were the keynotes: for a generation of enlightened men, not to say women, who had many Continental examples of superstition, fanaticism, and despotism to denounce, they sounded enticing indeed.

Toleration had a special significance, partly because the Enlightenment was so preoccupied with the civil consequences of religious belief. In some respects it was rather misleading. Hostility to religious minorities remained an abiding characteristic of many Englishmen and Scotsmen, especially uneducated ones. The reaction against the 'Jew Bill' of 1753, the Gordon Riots in 1780, and the onslaught at Birmingham on Priestley and his fellow Dissenters

[1] *Sentimental Magazine*, 1774, p. 357.

in 1791, testified to the prejudice which lay barely concealed beneath the surface of eighteenth-century tolerance and sometimes burst above it. Some found comfort in the unrepresentative nature of such outbursts. Priestley himself blamed the persecuting spirit of the West Midlands, where 'every thing narrow and illiberal' seemed to originate.[2] Others blamed the Gordon Riots on the turbulence of life in the capital. But Warwickshire was not the only seat of disturbance after the 'Jew Bill', and during the French Revolution. Nor was anti-popery in 1780 restricted to London. If distinctions were to be drawn the most plausible related to social rank. Toleration was increasingly seen as the virtue of the polite classes. It progressed as the political tension inherent in religious conflict relaxed, especially with the decline of Jacobitism; it was easy, therefore, to connect it with the enhanced sense of security enjoyed by a ruling class primarily interested in the preservation of its political power. Toleration also reached down through layers of middle-class opinion, as, it was presumed, education and enlightenment made themselves felt against ancient prejudices. There were exceptions. Country gentlemen of traditional cast of mind retained a residue of anti-popish prejudice. In some provincial towns religious strife continued to be a feature of municipal life. But even this was regarded as remediable. The Unitarian John Disney was embarrassed by the views of some of his own mentors, men such as Francis Blackburne and Thomas Hollis, who remained bitterly hostile to Catholicism while many of their friends among the Rational Dissenters were committed to toleration in its fullest sense. Yet he took solace from the thought that this was a matter of generation. It was an 'error of the times', not of the men who, 'had they lived some few years later, would have survived these prejudices'.[3]

The religious liberalism of English society was deduced in part from the benevolent negligence of the State. Hanoverian government showed no desire to interfere in the spiritual life of the ordinary citizen. Walpole was sceptical in his private beliefs and correspondingly pragmatic in his attitude towards religion. The Duke of Newcastle, of all ministers the most interested in the business of the Church, was concerned rather with promoting

---

[2] *Familiar Letters, addressed to the Inhabitants of Birmingham* (Birmingham [1790]), Part V, p. 63.

[3] J. Disney, *Memoirs of Thomas Brand-Hollis* (London, 1808), p. 9.

dependable men than controversial measures. He showed no more interest than his predecessors in reviving Convocation. Nor did his successors take a different view. George III and Lord North were devout defenders of the Establishment. Yet it was they who granted extensive privileges to Roman Catholics, in Canada and to a lesser extent in England, and they who resisted attempts to impose episcopacy on America. North, as Chancellor of Oxford University, supported it in the theological controversies of the 1770s but proved a reluctant opponent of Dissenters seeking a greater measure of toleration. This is not to say that governments were not committed to what they saw as the civil constitution of the Church. Walpole supported the Test and Corporation Acts by guile and prevarication, North and George III did so with conviction. As the ideological climate changed in the last decades of the century such inflexibility proved controversial. But nobody accused them of seeking to turn the clock back. Their belief that they were defending the constitution which they had inherited was incontestable.

Religious freedom was extensive by Continental standards. Protestant Dissenters worshipped in meeting-houses which bishops had no option but to license. The psychological difference which this made not only to conscientious Dissenters but also to those of less deep-rooted convictions was crucial. In theory, Church courts retained considerable powers, but it proved increasingly difficult to exercise them. Custom and convention counted for more than the coercive power of canon law. There were many rural parishes where the writ of parson, archdeacon, and bishop still ran and where the ancient forms of pronouncement, penance, and excommunication had some meaning. But once defied or violated such authority was difficult to enforce. As the High Churchman William Cole put it in 1766, 'The discipline of our Church, thro' the Practices of the Dissenters, is now so relaxed as to come to nothing, there is no parlying with your Parishioners on any Point of Doctrine or Discipline: for if you are rigid, they will either abstain from all ordinance, or go over to the Dissenters.'[4] Even against unlicensed preachers and congregations, the legal machinery depended on the readiness of the civil authorities to operate it. The Cornish clergyman John Penrose was enraged to discover in 1766 that a Baptist preacher in his parish was effectively immune from

[4] F. G. Stokes, ed., *The Blecheley Diary of the Rev. William Cole, 1765–67*, p. 9.

prosecution.[5] Significantly, co-ordinated attempts to defend the rights of the Church were made chiefly against its own mutinous sons, the Methodists, and then with limited success.[6] In 1760 at Rolvenden in Kent a group of 'enthusiasts' were successfully prosecuted under the Conventicle Act, with the connivance of local JPs. But the verdict was reversed on appeal to the King's Bench. The case was reported nationally and aroused much controversy. The war on the Methodists was indeed a prolonged one, and sometimes involved extraordinary manœuvres, such as the use of impressment in the notorious persecution of the Yorkshire mason John Nelson.[7] It was, none the less, a losing war.

The Roman Catholics were more vulnerable: their legal disabilities far exceeded those which applied to Protestant Nonconformists. But it was a matter of commonplace observation that the laws in question were rarely executed. Public chapels were in danger only at times of extreme political tension. In Lancashire, where the papists were numerous, they enjoyed practical immunity comparable to that of Dissenting meeting-houses. Much use was also made of private chapels, provided in London by foreign embassies, in the country by Catholic gentry. Foreign commentators stressed that the discrimination which was practised in England was essentially a matter of choice not merely on the part of those who practised it but also for their victims. Roman Catholics were not subject to legal distinctions as such, any more than English Jews were required to wear badges of their race. It was refusal to take the oaths ordained by the State which disqualified them from the enjoyment of official privileges. This was a rather naïve view of the situation. The legal status of Roman Catholics as 'recusants convict' (and indeed of Jews) was a complex matter, but few subjected to it can have considered themselves in any sense the equals of their Protestant fellow citizens. Yet there was no doubt that by comparison with religious minorities in many European countries their relative security was real and prized.

Papists and Jews were debarred from public life and political rights, but this was by no means true of Protestant Dissenters. Although the Test and Corporation Acts had survived the Hanoverian Accession, the Dissenters who were penalized by them

[5] *Letters from Bath 1766–1767 by the Rev. John Penrose*, p. 168.
[6] See above, p. 251.
[7] *John Nelson, The Yorkshire Stonemason* (London, 1903), pp. 32 ff.

were to some extent protected by statutory indemnity. The precise effect of the annual Indemnity Acts remains somewhat obscure, though the mere belief that they provided full protection had an influence regardless of the legal technicalities. More important, particularly for the Presbyterians who played so large a part in urban Dissent, was occasional conformity. Prohibited by law between 1711 and 1718, occasional conformity subsequently permitted the full enjoyment of municipal rights to those prepared to take the Anglican sacraments once a year. The practice had enraged High Churchmen in the difficult years following the Revolution of 1688 and continued to anger them throughout the eighteenth century. Yet the gap which it bridged between Dissenters and their brethren in the Church was in many instances narrow.

A 'comprehensive' national Church had seemed a real possibility in the 1690s, and when Samuel Chandler pursued the idea with the Bishops of Norwich and Salisbury in 1748 it briefly seemed so again. Chandler's hope for a simpler, more strictly scriptural definition of faith than the Thirty-Nine Articles proved over-optimistic, but even Herring, the Archbishop of Canterbury, endorsed his claim that on most questions of doctrine there was little to separate them. Indeed, divisions within the Church and within the sects themselves were in some respects far greater. The convulsion in the Presbyterian community which produced a distinct Unitarian movement was matched by Trinitarian controversies in the established Church. The strains created by the evangelical revival also affected conformists and nonconformists alike.

The political power wielded by Dissenters could be considerable. In some towns Dissenters were firmly entrenched, with powers which rendered 'Anglicans' oppressed majorities. Coventry and Nottingham were well known for their Dissenting oligarchies. At Bridport there was 'a kind of anti-Test for no man is admitted a Member of that corporation who is not a Dissenter'.[8] It is easy to see how, in self-perpetuating corporations, a combination of careful organization and occasional conformity could being about such a state of affairs. Power of this kind did not lessen the religious and political polarization which characterized many boroughs. Dissenting Coventry, like High Church Leicester, suffered the most bitter conflicts, impeding efficient administration and civic

[8] B. Short, *A Respectable Society: Bridport 1593–1835* (Bradford-on-Avon, 1971), p. 32.

progress. There is a sense, indeed, in which Dissent in the eighteenth century can only be defined in political terms, that is to say by reference to its legal subordination to a State Church. Under George III various circumstances conspired to sharpen the resulting sense of alienation. The growing confidence and conservatism of the Church under a true Defender of the Faith as supreme governor, the intellectual vigour of the Rational Dissenters, and not least the ideological implications of popular resistance to government both at home and in the colonies, combined to transform the political face of Dissent. It is possible to exaggerate the unity of the Nonconformist experience and dangerous to generalize about its place in national life. But there were not a few who believed, with Edmund Burke, that the 1770s and 1780s were a landmark in its history, replacing the grateful beneficiary of a tolerant, pluralist State, with a resentful, even revolutionary force.[9]

LAWYERS AND THE LAW

The fact that Dissenters owed most of their freedom to the non-implementation of the laws which penalized them, rather than to their removal, has a significance beyond the history of religious toleration. It was often said that while England was greatly overburdened with laws, much the greater part of them were not executed. This was perfectly in tune with Montesquieu's maxim that in despotic states the laws must be few, but strictly administered. Oliver Goldsmith wove it into a self-congratulatory commentary on the Englishman's liberty which was guaranteed to appeal to his readers. 'Scarce an Englishman who does not almost every day of his life, offend with impunity against some express law ... Gaming houses, preaching at prohibited places, assembled crowds, nocturnal amusements, public shews, and an hundred other instances are forbid and frequented.'[10] These examples were well chosen. It was the potentially intrusive supervision by the State of the ordinary citizen's life which in practice proved most ineffectual. The periodic gusts of moral outrage which impelled Parliament to action were rarely followed by systematic prosecution. On the subject of illicit gaming no less than four

---

[9] See p. 532.
[10] *Citizen of the World, Letter L*, in A. Friedman, ed., *Collected Works of Oliver Goldsmith* (5 vols., Oxford, 1966), ii. 211–12.

statutes were approved in the six years 1739–45, as a result of public pressure to purify the night-life of the capital. They had little effect. Such negligence reflected the want of an effective police force. No figure was more detested than the private informer, on whose mercenary instincts so many laws depended for their enforcement.

Yet there was more to erratic implementation of the laws than this. Even those laws which were enforced were often applied in a bizarre and arbitrary manner. The criminal code, for all its seemingly ferocious resort to capital punishment, was notorious for its unsystematic operation. Between the preferment of a charge and the execution of sentence on a convicted criminal there were many opportunities for the exercise of discretion. This state of affairs gave rise, and continues to give rise, to accusations of personal partiality and class bias on the part of those entrusted with such discretion. The use of judicial leniency and the royal pardon for political purposes was an admitted scandal. More ambitious allegations seem to rest on unverifiable assumptions about the nature of commercial society rather than on demonstrable historical truth. They also neglect the extent to which those who enjoyed authority in this ramshackle system of justice, not least the juries which had so large a say in the fate of malefactors, were remote from the 'ruling class', however defined. The simplest explanation of the irrationality which marked the administration of the law may be found in the strains which contemporary trends were placing on traditional values and procedures. The rapid but uneven growth of affluence, together with urban expansion, made for an unprecedented incidence of crime, or at least for an unprecedented sensitivity to crime. Multiplying capital offences was a natural response on the part of propertied opinion and the power which it exerted in the legislature. But few who advocated it expected the utmost rigour of the law to be exerted in every case, and the traditional premisses of penal policy were modified only with extreme reluctance.

The law was supposed to deter by unpredictable example rather than by certainty of detection or punishment. Its operation, like less awesome but equally characteristic expressions of communal wrath, the ducking-stool, the skimmington, and the village stocks, depended on the publicity attending the potential consequences of crime. Hence the continuing employment of the pillory, a form of sentence which effectively handed the criminal to the mob for its own verdict. Hence, too, the burning of libels, the parading of penitents, the branding and whipping of offenders. Hence, above all, the heightened theatricality of the most solemn retribution of all, public execution followed by public dissection, or in some cases, permanent public display of the corpse. The most extraordinary of all such spectacles, the hanging of Lord Ferrers for the murder of his servant in 1760, was also peculiarly satisfying, for it subjected a peer of the realm to the most public of humiliations. Ferrers himself dreaded this aspect of his ordeal most of all. By 1760, indeed, voices were raised against this as against other features of contemporary justice. Yet public execution was defended as one of the rights of Englishmen, not less necessary than public trial. In 1769 when a hanging was transferred from Tyburn to Bethnal Green, the Sheriffs of London protested that it would 'make way for private executions, and for all those dreadful consequences with which private executions are attended, in every country where they have been introduced'.[11] Tyburn's notorious 'Tree' was moved to Newgate in 1783, principally to safeguard the sensibilities of polite West End householders. At their new venue the executions themselves remained open to all comers. Public concern about the use of capital punishment was most likely to arise when the victim selected was manifestly a scapegoat. Such a case was the uproar which accompanied the fate of Bosavern Penlez, executed for his part in a riotous attack on a bawdy-house in 1749. It incidentally provoked a pamphlet war between Henry Fielding and another novelist, John Cleland. There was genuine doubt as to Penlez's guilt, as indeed there was, in somewhat different circumstances, about the justice with which Admiral Byng was dispatched in 1757. More fundamental reappraisals of the function of the law in the community required a completely fresh perspective, and there was little hint of that until the last quarter of the century.

Implemented or not, the sheer quantity of law exasperated many commentators. Law-making as an activity was growing rapidly, especially after the middle of the century. Then, the increasing volume of local legislation, such as turnpike bills, enclosure bills, and improvement bills, became a positive torrent to join the only slightly less impressive flow of private Acts and the continuing

[11] Sheriffs of London to Lord Weymouth, Nov. 1769, *Gentleman's Magazine*, 1769, p. 613.

inundation of public statutes. Demands for co-ordination and standardization went largely unheard by the legislators, responding as they were to the pressures of interest groups and local communities, rather than to the rational requirements of public policy. The administration of the law was no less the subject of criticism. Lawyers are rarely popular as a class, but the expense as well as complexity of the judicial process in the eighteenth century made them particularly vulnerable. Attention focused on the ubiquitous attorney, one of the main beneficiaries of the litigious nature of the period, and also of the remarkably wide variety of activities, fiscal, commercial, agricultural, and electoral, which were touched by the law. A rare attempt to regulate the legal profession, emanating from Yorkshire in 1729, resulted in an Act which required the registration of those practising as attorneys and scrutiny of their qualifications. It seems to have done little to diminish the volume of complaint about their exactions and impositions. The 'pettifogger' or 'hedge attorney' was one of the most execrated stereotypes of the age.

The courts themselves were exempt from statutory intervention, though criticism extended to the highest courts of King's Bench, Common Pleas, Exchequer, and Chancery, where, as the satirist Macnamara Morgan put it, 'four ancient Rook'ries, invested with Pow'r, All the Gold in the Nation and Silver devour'.[12] Chancery, the principal arbiter of property, was the target of much hostile comment. 1725 had witnessed a spectacular attempt to control some of its most disquieting features, when the Lord Chancellor Lord Macclesfield was impeached and unseated for selling judicial offices. Periodic efforts to regulate Chancery, particularly its scales of fees, and its management of the properties which it held in trust, continued to be made. Yet little was done to combat the central criticism of the courts, that their procedures were outmoded, cumbersome, and above all fiercely expensive, in effect the resort of the rich, often against the poor. It is not difficult to see why Parliament was loath to do more than tinker with the judicial machinery of the State. The dual obsession of the age with property and customary rights made radical reform unthinkable. The common law, especially, had a revered place at the centre of the Englishman's inheritance; it also had powerful vested interests to protect it. Even manifestly sensible changes encountered

[12] *The Processionade* (London, 1740), p. 3.

resistance. The introduction of English as the language of legal proceedings in 1731 proved a great success but was none the less accompanied by much grumbling.

This is not to say that the law in England resembled that of the Medes and Persians. The role of the judiciary in the development of legal doctrine was considerable. Lord Mansfield, the greatest legal luminary of the age, and Lord Chief Justice of the King's Bench for thirty-two years until his retirement in 1788, was the hero of those who looked to lawyers for enterprise befitting an era of commercial expansion. Even the patriot poet Robert Lloyd, boon companion of Wilkes and Churchill, praised him extravagantly in his *Law Student*: 'Alone from Jargon born to rescue Law, From precedent, grave hum, and formal saw.'[13] Mansfield's reputation was based on his readiness to extend and occasionally overturn traditional common law principles in order to offer legal protection to a wide range of commercial properties, transactions, and practices. Among common lawyers he provoked predictable alarm, particularly when he seemed to encroach on the sacred law of land tenures, truly the Ark of the Covenant in the English Temples. But he had few imitators. When William Blackstone set out to explain the principles of English law in his *Commentaries* of 1765–9, his standpoint was that of a conservative Oxford lawyer. Yet he found much to complain about, both in the legal antiquarianism of his profession, and the practical abuses to which the law seemed so prone. It was plainly not necessary to be a Beccaria or a Bentham to have doubts about the accumulated wisdom of centuries of legal tradition.

When ordinary Englishmen spoke of the law, they had in mind the historic safeguards of civil liberty rather than the obscure profundities which Blackstone delighted in explaining. Trial by jury and the writ of habeas corpus enjoyed a reverence similar to that bestowed on parliamentary representation. Neither came under direct attack, though there was some concern over the Jury Act of 1729, which provided for special juries in certain cases and awakened suspicions that they would be packed in the interests of property and authority. Otherwise it was necessary to look to rather remote menaces, like the Quebec Act of 1774, which legalized the use of summary jurisdiction in Canadian civil litigation, and thereby provoked talk of a ministerial conspiracy against the

---

[13] W. Kenrick, ed., *The Poetical Works of Robert Lloyd* (London, 1774), i. 29.

common law. Habeas corpus was suspended only once between 1727 and 1783, during the Forty-Five; the fear, at the start of the Seven Years War, that it was under threat from judicial obscurantism and the requirements of naval conscription proved short-lived.

There was no shortage of alternative causes for concern. The constant addition of new capital offences to the statute-book had important implications, particularly when judicial construction seemed to multiply them still further. The Black Act of 1723 was deeply mistrusted. It had been directed against the poaching gangs operating in the royal forests under George I. In time, as interpreted by the courts, it was applied to a much wider range of offences. Similar controversy was provoked by the Smuggling Acts of 1736 and 1745. Given the ambivalence of contemporary attitudes towards the violation of revenue laws, almost any regulation was likely to be controversial. The Smuggling Act of 1736, by making the carrying of arms a ground for arrest, attacked a long-standing English tradition. Even in the House of Lords it provoked the assertion that 'The wearing of Arms is an Act, not only innocent but highly commendable'.[14] This continued to be a defensible view. The campaigns of the 1750s to revive the militia and those of the 1780s to establish a citizen police force owed much to it. It was also one of the counts against the hated game laws. Support for the criminal law in general could be found at most levels of society. But the game laws, condemned even by Blackstone, offended many of middling status, not least the tenant farmers who found themselves potential law-breakers on their own farms. At times, as in the 1750s when landlords promoted game associations to protect their rights, there was even the threat of a countryside class war with their tenants.

Other restrictions, if more readily justified, aroused resentment. Naval impressment gave rise to agonized debate, partly because those who were most concerned about civil liberties were also the most vocal advocates of a 'blue water' strategy and the 'wooden walls of England'. Proposals for a more rational system of recruitment came from naval officers worried by its inefficiency. Temple Luttrell's bills to this end during the American War of Independence, though supported on humanitarian grounds, derived from suggestions made within the service. Parliament, however,

[14] *London Magazine*, 1736, p. 718.

despaired of alternatives which would prove more effective or more economical than the press, and there was no assistance from the courts. Indeed, the definitive judgements in *Rex* v. *Broadfoot* in 1743 and *Rex* v. *Tubbs* in 1776 firmly established the Crown's right to impress on grounds of immemorial usage. The judge in the Tubbs case was Mansfield, often suspected of authoritarian tendencies. But in the Broadfoot case it was Michael Foster. Foster was a good Whig: he penned a scorching attack on Bishop Gibson's claims for Church courts, and differed with Mansfield himself about the judicial extension of the Black Act. Yet he was unmoved by the arguments against impressment. It was left to municipal corporations to offer bounties which would remove the press-gang from their locality, and to individuals to argue about the terms of the exemptions granted from time to time by the Admiralty. On the other hand, there were some notable victories against the State in the reign of George III, principally in defence of the freedom of the press and as a result of the activities of John Wilkes.[15] But even here some important limitations were strengthened rather than weakened. Mansfield's doctrine that in cases of libel the determination of guilt was effectively a matter for judges rather than juries, was not new but by the end of the American War had acquired enhanced standing. It was not to be modified until Fox's Libel Act of 1792.

The underlying tendencies of eighteenth-century justice also gave rise to concern. The extension of summary jurisdiction was rarely discussed without being condemned. Parliament placed more and more responsibility on the shoulders of ordinary JPs. In this respect it is easy to understand why defenders of trial by jury were worried: whole ranges of offences were determined, sometimes without appeal, by magistrates sitting on their own, or in 'petty sessions' with a colleague. Neither the judicial impartiality nor personal integrity of such judges could be taken for granted. The iniquities of those in Westminster and Middlesex were notorious. At best they were 'trading justices', dependent on fees for their livelihood; at worst they were implicated in the criminal underworld of the metropolis. Addressing a metropolitan audience in 1775 William Pell thought it necessary to assert that 'although a Middlesex Justice, no man could say he had ever fouled his

---

[15] See pp. 357-8.

fingers by the receipt of a dirty shilling in the way of business.[16] In the capital and in many provincial boroughs it was assumed that the requirements of justice were subordinated to the personal or political interests of those responsible for dispensing it. But the superior moral credentials of the countryside did not guarantee higher standards there. Some of the most damning satirical indictments were of rural JPs. Smollett's Justice Gobble was one such: sycophant to a local magnate, Lord Sharpington, a 'low fellow thrust into the magistracy without sentiment, education, or capacity'.[17] Confronted with his misdeeds, Smollett's knight errant Sir Launcelot Greaves was driven to question his own assumptions about the nature of the Englishman's legal heritage. 'Oh! If such a despicable reptile shall annoy mankind with impunity, if such a contemptible miscreant shall have it in his power to do such deeds of inhumanity and oppression, what avails the law? Where is our admired constitution, the freedom, the security of the subject, the boasted humanity of the British nation? Sacred Heaven!'

Gobble was caricature, but less colourful portrayals of the work of the early Georgian justice confirm the extensive and controversial nature of his activities. Nor is there any doubting the contemporary concern. The proscription of the Tory gentry, which was not fully lifted until the death of George II, put severe strains on the impartiality and respectability of the magistracy as a class. An Act of 1732, setting a property qualification of £100 per annum in real estate for county justices, was designed to ensure that landowners of genuine independence would man the rural benches. But this figure was too low to achieve its object and no Whig government was prepared to raise it to one which would. In mid-century, accusations of personal venality and political bias became less common. The country clergy were admitted to the magistracy in numbers while Lord Hardwicke was Lord Chancellor, principally to offset the shortage of suitable candidates. They became prominent and in some counties dominant during the last decades of the century. Their introduction was generally thought to have improved the quality of local justice and administration, though it also created controversy about the wisdom of entrusting secular powers to the spiritual guardians of the rural community. There was also a matching seriousness of purpose about many lay

---

[16] *London Chronicle*, 26 Sept. 1775.
[17] *The Life and Adventures of Sir Launcelot Greaves*, ed. D. Evans (London, 1973), p. 98.

magistrates in the 1770s and 1780s, as the cause of reform, in matters as diverse as prison management, the reformation of manners, and poor relief, became more fashionable. But this did nothing to lessen the power which they exercised, however much it altered the nature of the accusations made against them. Shortly, by the time that William Godwin penned his *Caleb Williams* in 1793–4, it was to be class oppression rather than corrupt self-interest that was at issue.

ARTISTIC BACKWARDNESS

Britain's famed liberty sat uncomfortably with its insignificance as a centre of the arts. Considerable pains were taken to explain England's artistic backwardness. Climate was given prominence in such analyses, in line with fashionable interest in the social and political influence of the natural environment. It could be cited either in the general terms which made a fertile land and a sun-blessed agriculture the obvious foundations of cultural pre-eminence, or more specifically to explain some of the advantages which Providence had bestowed on the countries of southern Europe, not least the quality of light which was thought by some to have made Italy the inevitable home of Renaissance art. Climate was a discouraging solution to the problem of cultural regression, since it was inherently unalterable. More promising was the belief that the classical inheritance of the Mediterranean peoples had given them a head start, though one which a northern society with vigour, wealth, and education could readily make up. Equally reassuring was the notion that Englishmen had gratuitously hampered their own progress in earlier times. The Irish artist James Barry blamed the religious confusion of the sixteenth and seventeenth centuries for killing off the natural creativity of the English. In his own day, he supposed, the rational temper of the age offered no such impediments.[18]

Comforting though such reflections may have been, there were still grounds for pessimism. Religious attitudes continued to dismay those artists who hoped for the support of an enlightened Church establishment. Plans for the embellishment of the nation's churches, beginning with a controversial scheme for the adornment

[18] *An Inquiry into the Real and Imaginary Obstructions to the Acquisition of the Arts in England* (London, 1775), ch. v.

of St Paul's, foundered on Protestant asceticism and austerity.[19]
There was also thought to be a connection between English
philistinism and English patriotism. It seemed all too possible
that the very spirit which accounted for a robust libertarian tradition prohibited cultural sophistication. 'We shall not', remarked the essayist Vicesimus Knox, 'easily find a Hampden in a
connoisseur.'[20]

Whatever the cause, it was not the absence of a market for
works of art. Foreign artists poured across the Channel to furnish
Continental refinement. Some otherwise promising developments
in native art were all too dependent on this continuing migration.
The enthusiasm of the English gentry and nobility for immor-
talizing themselves, their friends, and their heroes, offered much
employment to sculptors and monumental engravers. But to critics
it seemed that most of the resulting work went to foreigners.
Giovanni Guelfi, brought from Italy by Lord Burlington in 1714,
throve on his patron's immense influence during the twenty years
which he spent in Britain. Michael Rysbrack, who arrived from
Antwerp a little later, in 1720, and owed his early success to another
influential architect, James Gibbs, became for a while the most
popular of all sculptors, serving 'court and country' alike. He
executed busts of Bolingbroke and Walpole with equal verisimilitude and impartiality in 1737–8. He was also responsible for
an evocative statue of William III on horseback, erected in Bristol's
new Queen Square in 1735. But by then he was already in danger
of being eclipsed. His rival Roubiliac came via the court of Dresden
from Lyons. His statue of Handel for the new Vauxhall Gardens
enjoyed more public exposure and perhaps more fame than any
other eighteenth-century work. No less telling was the success of
a countryman of Rysbrack's, Peter Scheemakers. He made his
name with his Shakespeare in Westminster Abbey, a commission
which he owed principally to the high society physician and patron
of virtu, Richard Mead. It seemed that even in glorifying their
own history, Englishmen were reliant on imported talent.

In this plight some were reduced to the desperate argument
that the second-rate must be patronized in order to maintain the
national honour. John Cleland had his fictional aristocrat the
Marquess of Soberton display inferior paintings at his country seat

[19] *Works of Thomas Newton*, i. 105–8.
[20] *The Works of Vicesimus Knox*, i. 61.

in order to encourage his compatriots, 'seeing not the last shadow of a reason to imagine, that the British genius could not, with due encouragement, take as high a flight in any art as any other nation whatever'.[21] There was a certain irony in Cleland's championship of English art. His own accomplishment was to have made pornographic literature a truly native genre. His *Memoirs of a Woman of Pleasure*, published in 1749–50, brought down the wrath of the authorities, and made a small fortune for his publisher Ralph Griffiths. Cleland disingenuously claimed that his intention had been to point up the dangers of such literature. He did not argue that *Fanny Hill*, as it subsequently became known, was a valuable addition to the national stock of cultural refinement: it did, however, prove one of the most enduring achievements of the mid-eighteenth-century mind.

LANGUAGE AND LETTERS

From a patriotic standpoint the disadvantages suffered by Englishmen started with the most obvious characteristic that they shared, their tongue. The *Encyclopaedia Britannica* contrasted Britain's prestige in the world with the insignificance of its language. 'It is the language of a great and powerful nation, whose fleets surround the globe, and whose merchants are in every port; a people admired, or revered by all the world;—and yet it is less known in every foreign country, than any other language in Europe.'[22] In part, this was seen as a matter of educating foreigners to a better understanding of the virtues of this newcomer among contenders for the prize of lingua franca. But the negligent manner in which Englishmen treated their language was also at issue. It is perhaps significant that the *Encyclopaedia* was a Scottish enterprise, for this concern was perhaps felt most strongly by Celts seeking to achieve cultural assimilation. One of the most insistent propagandists for 'fixed and stated rules' against the 'chance and caprice' which seemed to have governed the evolution of the English language, was an Irishman, Thomas Sheridan, father of the playwright and an influential lecturer on public speaking.[23] But Eng-

---

[21] *The Woman of Honor* (3 vols., London 1768), ii. 119–20.
[22] (3 vols., London, 1773), ii. 879.
[23] J. Barrell, *English Literature in History, 1730–80: An Equal, Wide Survey* (London, 1983), p. 111.

lishmen were also perturbed. There was a continuing debate about the advisability of establishing a national academy on the French model, with a view to purifying the language. Such proposals foundered on understandable anxiety as to the composition of such a body. They were also open to the objection of linguistic absolutism: it was said that an academy would represent a fatal departure from that reverence for custom which marked the unique inheritance of the Englishman.

What could not be achieved by formal institutions must be accomplished by informal means. The nationalism implicit in attempts to standardize usage, orthography, and pronunciation, was displayed in the most popular dictionaries of the period, Nathaniel Bailey's *Universal Etymological Dictionary*, which was published in 1721, and went through many subsequent editions, and Johnson's famous dictionary of 1755. Johnson denied any intention of 'embalming the language' but did not conceal his concern to 'fix' the conventions which he validated. Nor was his patriotic aim in doubt: unworthy Gallicisms and other foreign intrusions were to be eschewed. Even so Johnson saw himself elucidating the existing rules of the English language rather than creating new ones. He sought a formula, 'by which its purity may be preserved, its use ascertained, and its duration lengthened'.[24] The same caution was displayed by the grammarians. Robert Lowth, in his *Short Introduction to the English Grammar* of 1762, firmly defended the language against the imputation that it was ultimately irrational.

Both Johnson and Lowth were, in matters political and ecclesiastical, staunch friends of the established order. But some of the most influential and controversial students of language in the late eighteenth century were dissenters in both religion and politics. Most of them declared their faith in tradition, just as they asserted the legitimacy of their political principles with reference to the 'ancient constitution' of Englishmen, but they were also conscious of the attractions of a more rationalistic approach. Joseph Priestley entered this debate in the same year as Lowth with his *Course of Lectures on the Theory of Language and Universal Grammar*. John Ash, who published an introduction to Lowth's grammar in 1766 and a fully fledged dictionary in 1775, was also a Dissenter, as was John Fell, whose *Essay towards an English Grammar* was produced

[24] *The Plan of a Dictionary of the English Language* (London, 1747), p. 32.

with a preface by his pupil Richard Sharp in 1784. So, too, was Thomas Spence, who published his *Grand Repositary of the English Language* on phonetic principles in 1775. Spence was to be a hero of republicanism in the 1790s; even in 1775 he was busy with a revolutionary scheme for the nationalization of land. Like other writers on the language, his thinking exhibited a tension between rationalism and libertarianism which it was impossible altogether to resolve. But this was equally true of the political speculations of late eighteenth-century reformers. Patriotism was, after all, a confusing and potentially contradictory creed.

It was easier to celebrate literary men than linguistic measures. The revival of Shakespeare clearly suited the need for a heroic figure in the history of letters. It also touched a sensitive nerve in respect of Britain's standing abroad. Hume sarcastically noted in English veneration for the giants of an earlier age, Shakespeare, Spenser, and Bacon, 'that national spirit, which prevails among the English, and which forms their greatest happiness'.[25] Voltaire had contrasted Britain's prowess in the prosaic worlds of politics and science with its barbarism in the realm of the creative imagination. His English admirers were embarrassed by his contempt for Shakespeare's neglect of the classical rules of drama. One of those who had worshipped at the shrine of Ferney, George Keate, attracted attention by publicly remonstrating with his idol on this point in 1768.[26] By this time Shakespeare's special standing in Britain itself had been decisively confirmed by a famous partnership. Johnson and Garrick, schoolmaster and pupil, had set out from Lichfield for London in 1737, with, according to literary legend, only a few pennies between them. Johnson's *Shakespeare*, published after a lengthy delay in 1765, was the latest in a line of Augustan editions and commentaries, but its textual rigour put Shakespearian scholarship on a new footing. Above all, its magisterial defence of Shakespeare's dramatic technique in the context of sixteenth-century conventions helped secure his unchallengeable place as *the* national poet.

It cannot be said that Garrick showed the same respect. His modernization of the plays for the stage was insensitive in the extreme. The verdict of the player whom the Vicar of Wakefield encountered—pantomime under the sanction of Jonson's or

---

[25] See J. Towers, *Observations on Mr Hume's History of England* (London, 1778), p. 139.
[26] *The Poetical Works of George Keate* (2 vols., London, 1781), ii. 136–8.

Shakespeare's name—could well have been applied to some of these productions, though it is notable that the pictorial representation of the murder of Shakespeare which the artist Philip Dawes exhibited in 1765 was set at Covent Garden, notorious for its vulgarity, rather than at Garrick's Drury Lane.[27] In any event Garrick's enthusiasm made up for much of the critical dismay which he caused. As was noted on his retirement in 1776, he had restored Shakespeare to the very centre of the English stage.[28]

Garrick's career had begun in 1741, at a time when the theatre was thoroughly demoralized following the turmoil of the 1730s and the censorship imposed by the Act of 1737. In an era of famous actors and actresses, Macklin, Quin, Foote, Clive, Cibber, Woffington, his peculiar combination of talents made him the acknowledged master. He was the first actor-impresario who brought the glamour of the London stage to the attention of a national audience. When he went abroad in 1765 it was observed that his absence was treated 'as one of the greatest national calamities that could befal us'.[29] Few who saw him in his tragic roles, beginning with his astonishing early success as Richard III, doubted that they had seen the greatest English actor in the greatest English dramas. This process of identification, almost of fusion, was completed by the Shakespeare Jubilee in 1769. The Jubilee itself was not an unqualified triumph. Wet weather and a shortage of accommodation at Stratford made it uncomfortable for those attending. But it created the Shakespeare industry. Busts, medals, engravings, porcelain and pewter mementoes followed in profusion. So did the wooden souvenirs carved from the inexhaustible mulberry tree which Shakespeare himself had supposedly planted. Keate was awarded an inkstand from this venerable source by the corporation of Stratford in 1769, in recognition of his doughty defiance of Voltaire. From Henry Cooper, the executor of this work, he received further offers, notably of two small heads of the great bard. 'I have add the pleasure of carving things of one sort or another ever since the Jubilee, ... and if you should be anyways dubeious as it's not the tree, I will come upon oath that it his of the real tree.'[30]

[27] *Collected Works of Oliver Goldsmith*, iv. 96.
[28] 'The British Theatre', *London Magazine*, 1776, pp. 230–1.
[29] Ibid., 1765, p. 635.
[30] P. M. Horsley, 'George Keate and the Voltaire-Shakespeare Controversy', *Comparative Literature Studies*, 16 (1945), 7.

ENGLISH ARTS AND FOREIGN INFLUENCES

It took a little longer for Shakespeare to become an international industry. This, after all, was the trickiest of all undertakings: to promote general acceptance of those features of their cultural tradition which Englishmen themselves valued. Moreover, try as they might, the champions of home-produced art found it difficult to boast of a manifest success which did not owe something to imported aid. George Vertue, the historian of engraving, thought that he could identify in the artistic and technical achievements of his time an especially important native development.[31] But Hogarth's manner was not readily exported, and caricaturists, notwithstanding the master's attempts to prove their superior credentials, retained a reputation for vulgarity and a certain insularity. His successors, Rowlandson, Bunbury, Gillray, were appropriately at their best as satirists of the political and social scene at home, as Hogarth had made his own name by depicting London life. Vertue was not mistaken about the expansion of the artistic press. But in the refined engraving tradition which he most respected it was far from clear that his countrymen had achieved the permanent independence for which he hoped. Francesco Bartolozzi, brought from Venice in 1764 on the promise of a formal appointment to the King, had no rival worthy of the name during the last decades of the century. Even Robert Strange, who thought himself such a rival, was hardly evidence of English superiority. Strange was an Orcadian whose bizarre career included service in the army defeated at Culloden, and a long period in Italy.

Horace Walpole shared Vertue's ambitions but looked for their fulfilment in a different place. 'We have discovered the point of perfection. We have given the true model of gardening to the world; let other countries mimic or corrupt our taste; but let it reign here on its verdant throne.'[32] The most enduring legacy of the hegemony of the natural English garden was the familiar landscape of woodland, vale, and water which Capability Brown made obligatory on country estates in the third quarter of the eighteenth century. But the origins of the movement belonged at least a generation earlier. William Kent, famous for his Palladian interiors, was also responsible for a string of the most praised

[31] *Vertue Note Books (Walpole Society)*, xxx. 199; xviii. 15.
[32] *On Modern Gardening* (London, 1785), p. 81.

gardens of early Hanoverian England, many of them associated with the Whig governing class—Pelham at Esher, Newcastle at Claremont, Dormer at Rousham, Burlington at Chiswick, the royal family itself at Richmond. Joseph Spence, who reckoned Kent 'the sole beginner of the national taste', also praised Pope for his articulation of the principle behind it. 'All garden is landscape-painting. Just like a landscape hung up.'[33] Others deserved a share in the copyright. There was Stephen Switzer, the horticulturist, who publicized criticisms of French and Dutch gardening current in the early eighteenth century. More importantly, there was Charles Bridgeman, who was credited with the invention of the ha-ha, that ingenious device by which the acquisitive Englishman could conceal his garden boundary and 'appropriate the landscape' without either endangering his shrubs or injuring his agriculture.

By the 1730s the new taste was well established. In the early stages it was compatible with a richly emblematic, even a manifestly political, design. Cobham's complex essay in classical patriotism at Stowe, where Brown learned his trade, was the most celebrated of such experiments in the first half of George II's reign, though his relations the Lytteltons were hard on his heels at Hagley. In the 1750s the creation of the poet William Shenstone, a short distance from Hagley at the Leasowes, became equally famous. Shenstone's *Unconnected Thoughts on Gardening* embodied a complete justification of the essential principles of natural gardening: rejection of formal layout, especially the straight lines of hedge and shrub which had been universal in 'polite' gardens a few years before; awareness of the sentimental and picturesque possibilities of well-sited ruins and memorials; above all, total integration of garden and landscape, extending to the planning of the humblest cottages as well as the grandest prospects.[34] The natural garden was itself an evolving concept. It required defending against the Gothic and Chinese fads of the 1760s, notably by William Mason in his poetic onslaught on the Oriental taste recommended by Sir William Chambers. Mason's *English Garden* in 1772 and his *Heroic Epistle to Sir William Chambers, Knight* in 1773 unhesitatingly championed the legacy of Kent, Shenstone, and Brown. In the long run, however, the legacy needed adapting to new times.

---

[33] J. M. Osborn, ed., *Joseph Spence: Observations, Anecdotes, and Characters of Books and Men* (2 vols., Oxford, 1966), i. 252, 405.

[34] *The Works in Verse and Prose of William Shenstone, Esq.*, ii. 125–47.

It was repeatedly pointed out in the late eighteenth century that in some respects the 'natural taste' was a highly artificial concept. The picturesque vogue of the 1780s and 1790s was to bring considerable changes. By then, however, one thing was certain: in the garden the Englishman had found his artistic *métier*. Foreigners might admire and emulate, but hardly excel.

In other respects nationalism and the requirements of cultural sophistication fitted very ill together. French influence was important in inverse proportion to the permanence of the objects affected. In things ephemeral, clothes, fabrics, food and drink, it seemed all powerful. Furniture also owed something to foreign fashions. Daniel Marot, the Huguenot designer who had been a favourite at the court of William III, continued to act as a conduit of baroque taste well into the reign of George II. Parisian pattern books remained popular in England until Chippendale's *The Gentleman and Cabinet Maker's Director* took the furnishing world by storm after 1754. Matthias Lock, who contributed many of the plates in the *Director*, was himself one of the pioneers of *rocaille* in England. Silverware was similarly affected. In the same period, the Huguenot masters, Paul De Lamerie and Paul Crespin, made the tradition initiated by Meissonier under the French Regency the dominant one among London gold and silversmiths. Here, if anywhere, were traces of the rococo revolution which swept over France and Germany before the neo-classical reaction of the late eighteenth century.

The most permanent monuments to the wealthy Englishman's taste, the country houses which he erected and the paintings which he hung in them, proved more resistant to cross-Channel influences, with one or two notable exceptions, for example the extraordinary popularity which attended the works of Claude Lorraine. Englishmen turned most naturally in the direction of Italy when they looked beyond their own shores. Italy was neither a nation state, nor a political rival. In this respect Rome seemed an entirely appropriate exile for the Stuart pretenders. Italy's peculiar combination of inherited glory and political feebleness made it highly suitable for a form of colonization. 'Italy was become, in a manner, our own,' it was observed in 1771.[35] It was the obvious destination of those Grand Tourists who could afford

---

[35] James Stuart, *Critical Observations on the Buildings and Improvements of London* (London, 1771), p. 36.

the time and money to go beyond Paris, and overwhelmingly the favourite market-place for works of art and 'antiquities'. For most of the period it was undisturbed by warfare: even in the War of the Polish Succession, when the life of visitors might have been rendered uncomfortable, the French government, for reasons of state, was careful to instruct its generals against giving provocation to English tourists.[36] There were small English colonies in many parts of Europe, if only for the purpose of conducting trade, but it is difficult to suppose, for instance, that the third Earl Cowper, who went to Florence on the Grand Tour and stayed there until his death, could have spent so tranquil a lifetime in many other Continental cities.

The dominant architectural fashions of the age owed much to the Italian vogue. The reign of George II was practically conterminous with the English reign of Palladio, proclaimed by Colen Campbell, enthroned by Burlington and Kent, and accepted as lawful sovereign by a whole generation of architects. In effect the ruling class appropriated the Venetian Renaissance as the proper model for a truly national style. Its most complete expression was the erection of the great houses of the Whig families: Burlington's own Chiswick, Walpole's Houghton, Coke's Holkham, Castlemaine's Wanstead, Lyttelton's Hagley, Rockingham's Wentworth Woodhouse. In due course it came to seem slavish in its wholesale adoption of one style; it was also possible to criticize its dubious practicality, particularly in its employment of lighting conventions better adapted to Italian conditions than the weak sun and hazy skies of England. But at the time there were only occasional undercurrents of hostility. The much repeated tale that the City of London refused its sanction to Burlington's design for the new Mansion House on the grounds that Palladio was not a freeman, even if apocryphal, suggests that there were reservations among the City fathers about a style which Hogarth had memorably pilloried as alien and effeminate.

The early Hanoverian age left few public buildings in the Palladian manner, but this is largely because it was relatively unmarked by public building at all. When the inevitable reaction came, in the 1760s, it was not so much a patriotic rejection of an Italianate taste, as a natural extension of enthusiasm for the Renaissance to its classical antecedents. There was no British

[36] J. Black, *The British and the Grand Tour* (Beckenham, 1985), p. 89.

Winckelmann, but Englishmen and Scotsmen played a part in the process of rediscovery. Robert Wood's *The Ruins of Palmyra* was published with the support of the Society of Dilettanti in 1753, while James Stuart and Nicholas Revett were on their famous expedition to Greece. The first volume of their *Antiquities of Athens* appeared in 1762. It came at precisely the right moment for those who were jaded with Palladianism and had begun to learn that Rome itself must not be considered the paragon of classical perfection. Just two years later there was published a further work of unusual importance: Robert Adam's *The Ruins of the Palace of the Emperor Diocletian at Spalatro in Dalmatia*.

It is possible to exaggerate the hegemony of the Adam brothers in the 1760s and 1770s. Throughout that period the Gothic and Chinese tastes were scarcely less popular than the neo-classical. The Gothic, in particular, had obvious patriotic appeal, for its evocation of a medieval past in which England could claim a full part. Moreover the brothers themselves felt that they did not receive sufficient recognition. Their great Adelphi scheme foundered in the credit crisis of 1772. The same year saw the triumphant completion of James Wyatt's Pantheon. Wyatt was to establish his reputation at the expense of Robert Adam's. The most prestigious public building of the day, Somerset House, was entrusted to Sir William Chambers, who considered himself rather than Adam, the originator of neo-classical ornament. Yet it is difficult to deny the claim made by Robert and James Adam in their *Works in Architecture*, the first volume of which appeared in 1773. They boasted in the preface of having 'brought about, in this country, a kind of revolution in the whole system of this useful and elegant art'. Certainly, their grotesques and arabesques remain among the most evocative images of the third quarter of the century. Much of their success was owed not to the principles of their designs but to the thoroughness with which they were executed. The same care which went into embellishing the orders was put into everything, down to door-handles, fire-irons, and wine-coolers. Moreover, their work, for all the grandeur of the great show-pieces like Syon House, Osterley Park, and Kedleston, could be scaled down to the requirements of bourgeois town-dwellers. In fact the cheap materials and vulgar craftmanship which increasingly extended the scope of the Adam taste were also responsible, eventually, for discrediting it.

By the time of Robert Adam the intensity of the debate about patriotic art had diminished. The passing of the generations which seemed to be symbolized by the crowning of George III in succession to his grandfather had real significance. Attacks on the cultured Englishman's liking for all things Italian showed signs of letting up at this time. Italian opera, not to say the lower forms of theatre which derived from it, had always been a subject of acute sensitivity since its rapid conquest of the London stage early in the century. The steady importation of Italian singers was an enduring source of delight to the *cognoscenti* and of contempt among the philistine. The contempt was not lessened by the fortunes thus made. During the reign of George II the most successful men, Monticelli and Farinelli, as well as the idolized women, Faustina and Cuzzoni, enjoyed earnings unmatched on the English stage until the age of Mrs Siddons. Perhaps it was not surprising that one of the last imported talents of this era, Manzuoli, went out of his way to compliment his English listeners as 'a rational, and attentive assembly' not to be met with on the Continent.[37] Some of the knowledgeable meekly accepted that while home-produced ballads had a certain naïve charm, nothing of English growth could rival the success of the Italians. Others watched for signs of genuine improvement. When Cecilia Davies ('L'Inglesina') was introduced to her audiences, including the relatively sober Three Choirs Meeting, she was described as the first Englishwoman who had been tolerated on an Italian stage.[38] Resignation seems to have become the prevailing tone even among the critically minded. George Colman's comedy of 1762, *The Musical Lady*, included the usual complement of ludicrous foreigners, but his conclusion did not suggest the desirability of encouraging native competitors.

> Now for the moral! Ye, that love to roam
> For taste abroad, learn common-sense at home!
> For arts and arms a Briton is the thing,
> John Bull was made to roar—but not to sing.

At the time Colman was writing, the stream of artists who made their way to Florence and Rome to learn or polish their art, was swelling rather than diminishing. This was as true of the most

---

[37] 'The Lyric Music Revived in Europe', *London Magazine*, 1768, p. 222.

[38] C. L. Williams and H. G. Chance, *Origins and Progress of the Meeting of the Three Choirs* (Gloucester, 1895), p. 51.

'English' of the English school as it was of the most self-consciously cosmopolitan. Wright of Derby, whose genius for lighting effects owed nothing to Correggio or Italian skies, went late, after his masterpieces rather than before, but he went none the less. By the time the young James Barry arrived in Rome, in 1766, to find what he called 'a fairyland', such a trip seemed an essential part of the artist's education.[39] The commencement of Barry's career dovetails neatly, in historical retrospect, with the end of Hogarth's. Hogarth died in October 1764, without ever having crossed the Channel or prejudiced his uncompromising insularity. His own art owed more to Continental influences than he liked to admit, but he never relaxed his campaign for a native school, rooted in 'natural' rather than inherited or adopted traditions. With his friend Henry Fielding he had waged war on the affectation and effeminacy of Italianate Englishmen. More constructively, he offered his compatriots an artistic theory which might sustain their cultural confidence. His *Analysis of Beauty*, published with characteristic self-advertisement in 1752, expounded the superior merits of the serpentine curve and championed the virtues of 'movement'. This brave attempt at artistic self-determination never really carried conviction, and it suffered severely from the satirical pen of Paul Sandby. In his last years Hogarth himself was a deeply embittered man: his celebrated curve had come to seem decidedly cranky, and his nationalism appeared narrow-minded. Not long after his death Sir Joshua Reynolds was to begin delivering the famous *Discourses* in which he swept aside such provincialism and openly gloried in the universal legacy of the classical masters.

THE ARTS AS NATIONAL INSTITUTIONS

How was it possible to give institutional shape to the national revival of the arts in the mid-eighteenth century? Some looked to the Crown. But the record of George II was not very encouraging. It was a common complaint that he did not sufficiently encourage the creative talents of his adopted country. Smollett, the first historian of his reign, regretted that an era which had finally settled the succession and raised British prestige abroad to unprecedented heights, had seen the greatest English writers of the day, Richardson, Young, Thomson, neglected by the court. Genius had flour-

[39] W. L. Pressly, *James Barry: The Artist as Hero* (London, 1983), p. 10.

ished but only 'under the culture of a public which had pretensions to taste'.[40] The fate of the poet laureateship seemed symptomatic of the *malaise* affecting relations between the Hanoverian regime and men of letters. The long tenure of Colley Cibber (1730–57) almost matched that of his royal master. Cibber plumbed new depths of banality in his celebrations of official occasions and provided a perpetual butt for satirical opponents. The verse in which he proclaimed Providence's peculiar benevolence to Protestant Englishmen was all too readily derided.

> The word that form'd the world
> In vain did make mankind;
> Unless, his passions to restrain,
> Almighty wisdom had design'd,
> Sometimes a William, or a George should reign.[41]

Critics made honourable exception for Queen Caroline's interest in matters of the mind, and allowance was granted for the court's musical bent, though some time was to pass before Handel could be decently claimed as a triumph of the English spirit. In this, as in so many other ways, a new reign offered the possibility of an exciting new beginning.

George III made a point of patronizing indigenous talent. His support of William Boyce promised well for English musicians. When the Queen sought to provide a fitting celebration of her husband's birthday at the conclusion of the Peace in 1763 she did so with an illuminated concert of music composed and conducted by Boyce. Joseph Wilton's early commission to decorate the new coronation coach in 1761 suggested that English artists would also receive encouragement. Wilton was to become a highly successful sculptor, but these propitious beginnings were in some ways misleading. The patriot King found some of his aspiring protégés as difficult to deal with as their less cultured compatriots. The painter Richard Wilson lost favour at an early stage when he haggled over the price of a view of Syon House which had been commissioned by Bute for the King. Wilson caused particular irritation by offering to accept payment from the Crown in instalments. In such squabbles the complications of Bute's special relationship with the King inevitably caused problems. The engraver Robert Strange became

[40] *The History of England, from the Revolution in 1688, to the Death of George the Second,* 'George II', pp. 59–60.

[41] E. K. Broadus, *The Laureateship* (Oxford, 1921), p. 125.

embroiled in a quarrel with Bute after refusing to engrave a portrait by Allan Ramsay of Bute and the King as Prince of Wales. As a result he found himself shunned at court.

There were also doubts about the breadth of the new court's artistic interests. By 1772 it was being alleged that the Augustus of 1760 had turned to trivial pursuits, and become the prey of miniaturists, bookbinders, and toymen.[42] This was not entirely fair, but there was something in the view that George III had inherited his father's artistic aspirations without his conceptual range. He depended heavily on others for advice. His most striking achievement was undoubtedly the magnificent collection of books which eventually passed on to the British Museum as the King's Library. When John Adams, the first minister of the United States, saw this collection in 1783, he was deeply impressed. 'The books were in perfect order, elegant in their editions, paper, binding, etc., but gawdy and extravagant in nothing. They were chosen with perfect taste and judgment; every book that a king ought to have always at hand.'[43] This was high praise but it is significant that the actual purchase of the books was carried out on the advice of an informal panel of experts and with the assistance of a network of agents both in Britain and on the continent.

What no critic could take away from George III was his part in establishing the Royal Academy; with the British Museum, it was one of two great cultural institutions founded in the mid-eighteenth century. The Academy represented the latest of several attempts to provide a national forum for the arts which would also serve as a training centre for artists. The best known of its predecessors, the Society of Artists, which received a royal charter in 1765, had grown out of the informal schooling and exhibiting associated with Hogarth's generation. Its first officers were a powerful group by any standards: George Lambert, often accounted the founder of the modern landscape school, Francis Hayman, after Hogarth the most successful of early Hanoverian artists, Paul Sandby, whose 'views' had considerable influence on the first wave of romantic landscape painters, as well as Wilson and Wilton. The Society's exhibitions were a regular feature of the artistic calendar. But it was racked by personal dissensions, and lacked both the backing and organization which made the Royal Academy, founded in

1768, so successful. Thanks to the influence at court of Sir William Chambers the Academy had unstinting support from the King. It was established on an elaborate plan, with detailed schemes for teaching and examining, funds with which to assist indigent artists, annual exhibitions which quickly became an important social as well as artistic event, and handsome accommodation, in due course, in the newly rebuilt Somerset House. Sir Joshua Reynolds initially showed little enthusiasm for the Academy. He was none the less prevailed upon to become its first president. The choice was wise. He had precisely that mixture of qualities which made for effective administration of the Academy during its early years and simultaneously rendered it an object of interest to polite metropolitan society. Even so it seems unlikely that it would have enjoyed such success without the active encouragement of the court.

If it had been founded under George III the British Museum would perhaps have been known as the Royal Museum. It was established in 1753 in distinctly unpromising circumstances. George II was uninterested in the project and the Prime Minister, Henry Pelham, opposed it. It was initially financed by means of a public lottery, and quickly engendered a depressing controversy about the allegedly corrupt manner in which the lottery was administered. Moreover it did little more than recognize the national obligation to preserve two great collections, the Cotton collection, acquired in 1722 and since stored unsatisfactorily in Westminster School, and Sir Hans Sloane's collection, sold by his trustees on preferential terms in 1753. Grandiose plans for a specially commissioned building had to be abandoned in favour of a modest scheme for the conversion of Montagu House in Bloomsbury. The early years of the new institution did not inspire confidence. Its officials seemed more concerned to quarrel and carp than collaborate in the consolidation of an important scholarly venture. Viewing the exhibits was a tiresomely protracted business. A proposal to charge an entrance fee was only beaten off with difficulty in 1784. Even the reading room proved less than satisfactory. Its first keeper, Peter Templeman, resented his duty of attending on the needs of readers. When Thomas Gray paid a visit he found only the antiquarian William Stukeley, gossiping with acquaintances, two visiting Prussians, and the amanuensis of a peer with an amateur interest in history, Lord Royston.[44] The Museum

[44] E. Miller, *That Noble Cabinet: A History of the British Museum* (London, 1973), pp. 66–7.

and its library survived these difficulties but it was natural enough
to contrast them with the blaze of fashionable glory which initially
attended the Royal Academy. This is not to say that George III
did not prove a loyal supporter of the Museum. It was he who
purchased on its behalf one of its most important collections of
printed works, the Thomason Tracts. None the less, it was tempting to speculate what might have transpired if the Museum had
been the product of royal munificence.

ENGLISH NATIONALISM AND THE FOREIGNER

Whether they were prouder of their traditional liberties, or their
more recent cultural sophistication, Englishmen revelled in what
William Wilberforce unhesitatingly described as the special privilege of being born an Englishman.[45] The xenophobia of the English
was a subject of repeated comment on the part of visiting foreigners.
At moments of national crisis, notably in wartime, it was predictably unrestrained. The paranoid poet Christopher Smart half-
consciously satirized the patriotic mania of the Seven Years War
in his *Jubilate Agno* with a celebration of his cat Jeffrey—'For the
English Cats are the best in Europe'.[46] It was customary to blame
the illiterate and uneducated for the cruder manifestations of
xenophobia, such as the Noverre riots in 1755, when a company
of Swiss actors was driven from the stage of Drury Lane and the
theatre severely damaged in the process. But it is not obvious that
literacy made very much difference in this respect. The literature to
which ordinary Englishmen did have access, for instance the widely
disseminated chapbooks, did nothing to challenge entrenched
prejudice and bigotry. Popular penny histories rehearsed the
triumphs of English arms and the humiliations of England's French
and Spanish enemies. They also perpetuated vulgar racism. The
Hull Tragedy told the tale of a Yorkshire knight Sir Peter Symonds
who found himself involved in a ghastly cycle of domestic strife
and murder thanks to the satanic nature of black servants. It was
typical of a genre which reinforced commonplace prejudices against
almost everything and everyone alien and unfamiliar.[47]

The mentality of the polite classes was more complicated. A

---

[45] R. Anstey, *The Atlantic Slave Trade and British Abolition, 1760–1810* (London, 1975),
p. 174.
[46] *The Poetical Works of Christopher Smart*, i: *Jubilate Agno*, p. 88.
[47] (London, 1748).

few radical spirits systematically denied the validity of national prejudices and blamed them on the influence of politicians who throve on pointless rivalries. There was also a more general tendency for educated men and women to congratulate themselves on their superiority in this respect. Self-conscious displays of magnanimity were almost as much a feature of the wars of the period as unrestrained chauvinism. Hence the public subscriptions to relieve starving French prisoners of war during the Seven Years War and the American War.[48] Hence, too, the outburst of indignation when the French envoy sent to negotiate peace terms in 1762, the Duc de Nivernois, was fleeced by a Canterbury innkeeper on his way from Dover to London: the result was a boycott which drove the landlord out of business. But such demonstrations were apt to appear synthetic and short-lived. Nor was it altogether clear that the means by which middle and upper-class Englishmen thought themselves liberated from old prejudices actually operated in the way they supposed. The Grand Tour may well have made them more knowledgeable about other societies, but it did not necessarily spread tolerance. There was some scepticism about the value of an experience which involved young aristocrats disgracing themselves and their country in front of their hosts. As a public critic of the notorious Lord Lyttelton remarked in 1775, 'it is said, my Lord, you have made the *grand tour*, and have seen Europe: Europe, it is certain, hath seen your Lordship.'[49]

Even serious-minded travellers tended to find only support for their preconceptions. The letters and diaries of the Grand Tourists, not to say the guides and travel literature which they took with them, were in many cases marked by condescension and complacency. A traveller like Joseph Cradock, musician, littérateur, gentleman amateur in a whole range of avocations, was proud of his enlightened views, yet constantly made comparisons, profound and trivial, with England. Lyons was Matlock in an urban setting; the prospect from Westminster Bridge excelled any Continental competitor, not excluding the Bay of Naples and the view from Bordeaux; even the famed French ortolans tasted less well than Dunstable larks.[50]

---

[48] See p. 625.

[49] *The Boat Race* (London, 1775), p. xii.

[50] Joseph Cradock, *Literary and Miscellaneous Memoirs* (4 vols., London, 1828), ii. 140, 221, 217.

For apprehensive defenders of the Roast Beef of Old England mentality it seemed reassuringly clear that a nation of shopkeepers, or even a nation of genteel merchants, was unlikely to depart from the traditional attitudes which they cherished. The same spirit which had animated fox-hunting squires and High Church mobs alike lived on among the prospering middle ranks of society in the age of commerce. Their patriotic enthusiasm was confirmed by the popular art of the period. It took an American, John Singleton Copley, fully to exploit the interest in historical and contemporary scenes, with his unashamedly commercial exploitation of the market for high quality engravings. 'History painting' under Copley's influence became a vigorously patriotic art form, with strictly national subjects to the fore and the prejudices of ordinary households in mind. His portrayals of heroic moments during the American War, the siege of Gibraltar, Major Peirson's defence of the citadel at Jersey, Chatham's last speech in Parliament, were a world away from the classical themes on which his predecessors had dwelt.

There was, however, a paradoxical flavour to the nationalism of propertied as well as unpropertied Englishmen. The same classes which maintained their commitment to the special status of all things English also displayed their dedication to foreign fripperies. The snob appeal of imported luxuries, from Parisian fashions to French governesses, was one of the most obvious manifestations of the middle-class purchaser's modishness. At the same time it was subject to unremitting criticism as being incompatible with the moral standards and patriotic duty of Englishmen. 'In former days our forefathers disdained to receive any improvement from a stranger.'[51] This was the tone of much contemporary comment. Because it combined lofty disapproval of the pursuit of materialism and insular dislike of foreigners, the campaign against imported finery was one of the safest subjects for the guardians of the Georgian conscience. It also offered almost limitless opportunities for the ridicule of those who were its targets. This is not to say that it had much perceptible effect. No doubt the same purchasing public which approved Parliament's periodic attempts to restrict imports of foreign cambrics and silks, and which applauded the royal family's readiness to patronize domestic products, cheerfully

51 *London Magazine*, 1768, p. 546.

continued to buy whatever was suggested by the requirements of bourgeois taste.

There were important political implications to this conflict of theory and practice. Patriotism as usually defined signified both adherence to the ancient constitution and vigorous defence of the national interest. Parliamentary oppositions relished nothing more than a chance to charge government with neglect of the latter. Their enthusiasm in this respect showed no signs of letting up in the years following George III's accession, as the Falkland Islands[52] dispute proved. Outside Parliament there was matching agreement on this point. John Wilkes missed no opportunity of linking his own cause with loyalty to the flag. Even in his prolonged and acrimonious dispute with Hogarth he made a point of digging up the old controversy about Hogarth's *March to Finchley* in 1746, in which Hogarth had represented the defenders of the Protestant Succession as a drunken rabble. Later on, during the Middlesex election crisis, there was a notable identification of the Antigallican Society with Wilkesite Londoners. At what point reformers first began to be embarrassed by the connection between patriotism at home and bellicosity abroad, it is difficult to say. Enlightened commitment to the fraternal interests of the peoples of the world was beginning to look uncomfortable by the side of old-fashioned emphasis on the virtues of the ancient constitution during the 1770s and 1780s. Later on, the French Revolution was to bring about the bifurcation of the patriotic tradition in spectacular circumstances. But long before then signs of the forthcoming strain were apparent. In 1783, for instance, Thomas Holcroft, himself a prominent actor in the drama that unfolded with the onset of the Revolution, was already complaining that the long-standing Anglo-French rivalry was the artificial contrivance of statesmen rather than the true expression of what Englishmen and Frenchmen felt.[53]

ENGLISH NATIONALISM AND THE CELT

The most controversial, and also the most corrosive, effects of English nationalism were felt at home. Popular animosity towards the remaining nations of the British Isles was deeply entrenched.

---

[52] See p. 525.
[53] *The Family Picture* (2 vols., London, 1783), ii. 14–15.

It manifested itself wherever Englishmen found themselves afflicted by Irishmen, Welshmen, and Scotsmen. Often the form which it took seemed relatively harmless. Contempt for what was taken to be the Welshman's characteristic of deviousness, not to say his practice of downright theft, was maintained by chapbook stories of dishonest drovers and the vagrants and tinkers who came with them. Very often, the object was merely to point fun at the relative backwardness of Celts who found themselves in superior and unfamiliar English surroundings. Hence no doubt the story of *Taffy's Progress to London*, the cartoons of Sawney kilted in the boghouse, and the endless succession of Irish jokes which appeared in jest books marketed for an English audience.[54] Less droll were the ugly outbreaks of violence provoked by the belief of artisans and peasants alike that Irish labour was competing with them on unfair terms. The most notorious of such outbursts occurred when anti-Irish sentiment became mingled with the confused politics of the London mob, as in the mid-1730s and the late 1760s.

Just as polite society was dismissive of prejudice towards foreigners, so it tended to treat such incidents as the consequence of lower-class ignorance. But the pretence that similar attitudes did not extend higher up the social scale was difficult to maintain. Polite patriotism of this kind was much more marked in relations with the Irish and Scots than the Welsh. Invasions from Wales seemed relatively innocuous. Welsh clergymen, like their counterparts from the backward north-west of England, continued to find the poorer curacies and livings of the Church of England an adequate inducement to leave their native land and suffer the poverty and indignity of a servitor's life at Oxford. A handful of Welsh gentry, such as the Wynns, Mostyns, Vaughans, and Edwardes, enjoyed a full share of the privileged life which their estates and parliamentary influence brought them, particularly after 1760, when their predominantly Tory politics were no longer an impediment to their advancement. In London they maintained a Welsh school, and kept up a degree of sentimental attachment to their native culture through the Society of Ancient Britons, with the nominal assistance of successive Princes of Wales. But there was no swarm of immigrant Welsh doctors, lawyers, or army officers to irritate English rivals, nor any marked invasion of

---

[54] J. Ashton, *Chap-Books of the Eighteenth Century* (London, 1882), p. 475.

Welsh labourers to incense the working Englishman. It was a very different story with the Irish and Scots.

Both Ireland and Scotland possessed a large landed class, impoverished by comparison with its southern English counterpart, but all the more anxious to share its opulence and imitate its life-style. In each case there was a tension between the traditional role of this class and the commercial practices which it increasingly imposed. Both countries, too, possessed a vigorous urban life, making Dublin and Edinburgh partners, albeit junior partners with London, in the spreading of an anglicized culture. Both had ambivalent political relationships with England. In Ireland the retention of parliamentary institutions at Dublin ensured a powerful and at times acrimonious response to anything that smacked of imperial imposition, from Wood's Halfpence under George I to the money bill disputes of the later years of George II. Most impressively of all it made possible a potentially revolutionary brand of Irish nationalism during the War of American Independence.

In Scotland there was nothing like this. The Scottish gentry were fully committed to the imperial system and, during the American War, proved themselves enthusiastic defenders of its authority against another 'colonial' society. Apart from occasional genuflections in the direction of Scottish nationalism, for example in opposition to the Porteous Bill in 1737, and in hesitant support for a Scottish militia under George III, they did little to encourage a sense of independence. Nor indeed, was there evidence of restiveness among the business classes, for whom, by and large, the prosperity of the west of Scotland was synonymous with unrestricted access to British markets. This is not to say that political life north of the border simply withered away. It was particularly marked in the context of the national church. Unlike the Church of England, which had been deprived of its Convocation, the Kirk in Scotland retained a General Assembly, in some measure supplying the place of a Scottish Parliament. The prolonged and at times bitter struggle between Moderates and Evangelicals in the middle decades of the century revealed the continuing vitality of domestic Scottish politics. The issues were not entirely new. Moderate insistence, for the most part successful, on the maintenance of rights of patronage in the Kirk continued an ancient conflict between gentry and congregational elders. But the

Moderate offensive also reflected the extent to which the lesser gentry, lawyers, and academics who for practical purposes dominated Scottish social, religious, and academic life in a period of exceptional intellectual vigour, were themselves being drawn into a supranational culture. In their case, of course, it left them with the actual business of governing Scotland while their superiors enjoyed their newly transplanted life as part of a British ruling class largely resident in London.

Transplantation was also an option for middle-class Scotsmen and Irishmen, especially if the term is permitted to include the younger sons of the gentry. No doubt it was these who accounted for the continuing hostility which so many Britons encountered in Britannia's capital. The Irish made a substantial contribution to the legal, literary, military, and political life of the metropolis, aside from those absentee Anglo-Irish landlords, such as the Ponsonbys and Fitzwilliams, who were English in all but name, and those powerful Irish families, like the Luttrells and Connollys, who retained a strong sense of their Irish background but periodically immersed themselves in English society. The most successful of their lowlier compatriots, without benefit of an English education or connections, were naturally those who proved most adroit at adapting to their adopted environment. The worst affliction and the most ineradicable was a strong accent. Irish actors and actresses played a part on the London stage out of all proportion to their number, but not a few suffered if, like Ann Dancer, they were 'rendered disgusting' by their brogue.[55] The most famous of all Irish statesmen at Westminster, Edmund Burke, endured much mockery on account of his accent, notwithstanding his oratorical gifts. In his early days in Parliament he appeared in the press as Edmund Bonnyclabber.[56]

Irish eccentricities and Irish tempers were inexhaustible topics of conversation. The stereotypes were so firmly established that no individual could hope to overcome them, though he might nurse the hope of anglicizing his sons and daughters so completely that their origins would never be suspected. Protests were regularly made against this state of affairs, usually in terms designed to make the Irish fit English models of what constituted an appropriate national character. Their nobles were superior, their people brave

[55] 'The British Theatre', *London Magazine*, 1767, p. 324.
[56] e.g. *Public Advertiser*, 1 May and 27 Aug. 1770.

and genteel.[57] It was also repeatedly pointed out that English criticism was dishonourable and unfair. The poet Hugh Kelly deplored 'the meanness of national reflections'.[58] Interestingly, Kelly's remonstrance was addressed to the 'patriot' Lord Mayor of London, Brass Crosby. There were many resemblances between opposition politics in London and Dublin but they evidently did not prevent the Wilkesites exploiting English hostility towards the Irish.

The Wilkesites played a still bigger part in the campaign against all things Scottish. Indeed, it is difficult to account for the extent and depth of anti-Scottish feeling in the 1760s and 1770s without reference to political circumstances. It is often remembered that George III was the first Hanoverian to declare his patriotism as a native-born monarch, but sometimes forgotten that he was proud to call himself a Briton, not an Englishman. Junius shrewdly castigated him on this point: 'you affectedly renounced the name of Englishman'.[59] At issue, of course, was the power of Lord Bute and the patronage which he supposedly directed into the acquisitive hands of his countrymen. There was also the obvious convenience of linking George III's allegedly authoritarian tendencies with the Scottish ancestry of the Stuarts. The web which was fashioned from this material could hardly have been more flimsy yet it served to trap many Englishmen, especially opponents of the regime. National prejudice was strengthened by the sensitivity of London opinion to the sheer numbers of newcomers. In 1787 it was reckoned that a century before, there had been no more than 50 Scots and 28 Irishmen in the capital, whereas it now seemed that there were almost as many as its English inhabitants.[60] This implausible calculation was at least significant for its assumption that there had been a huge increase in the interim.

The swarm of Scotsmen offended English susceptibilities and annoyed envious English competitors. An influx of Scottish doctors focused resentment on peculiarly sensitive relationships, commercial, medical, personal. It was believed that Bute's patronage was merely the most prominent expression of a national tendency: Scotsmen always favoured their own, to the detriment

---

[57] John Cleland, *Memoirs of a Coxcomb* (London, 1751), p. 272.
[58] *London Magazine*, 1770, p. 306.
[59] J. Cannon, ed., *The Letters of Junius* (Oxford, 1978), p. 161.
[60] J. Ashton, *Men, Maidens and Manners a hundred years ago* (London, 1888), p. 83.

of native-born Englishmen. Philip Thicknesse bitterly attacked Scottish families who refused to employ English physicians and apothecaries.[61] In the same spirit David Garrick made a famous remark about Robert Adam's use of Scottish labourers on his building projects: 'Come, come, don't deny it: they *are* really national.'[62] Yet Adam, when commissioned to erect an important public building in his native capital, firmly told his employers that local bricklayers would not do: they must be brought from London.[63] The truth was that almost nothing the Scots did, regardless of the circumstances, would satisfy their hosts. Under the English Poor Law Scots who had not gained a legal settlement had no entitlement to relief. Hence the need of Scottish (like other alien) communities to provide for themselves. Yet when they did so they were criticized for encouraging national prejudices. No doubt for this reason, the celebrated Scots Society at Norwich renamed itself the Society of Universal Goodwill in 1787.[64]

Englishmen evidently had a deep and continuing need to preserve their prejudices. The extent to which they carried them remains startling. Dr Johnson's reflections on the Scots, perhaps the most remembered of all such, were mild and good-humoured compared with those of many of his compatriots. Lord Shelburne, who considered himself a standard-bearer of enlightened cosmopolitanism, was savage in his denunciation of Scots. 'That nation is compos'd of such a sad set of innate, cold-hearted, impudent rogues,' he told Richard Price, 'that I sometimes think it a comfort when you and I shall be able to walk together in the next world, which I hope we shall as well as in this, we cannot possibly then have any of them sticking to our skirts.'[65] Not surprisingly, many Scots despaired of changing such views. David Hume, who suffered a lifetime of English condescension, asked Sir Gilbert Elliot, a prominent Scottish MP, 'Can you seriously talk of my continuing an Englishman? Am I, or are you, an Englishman? Will they allow us to be so? Do they not treat with Derision our Pretensions to that Name.'[66] Many of Hume's countrymen had taken particular

[61] *Useful Hints to those who make the Tour of France* (2nd edn., London, 1770), p. 22.
[62] *Boswell's Life of Johnson*, ii. 325–6.
[63] J. Lees-Milne, *The Age of Adam* (London, 1947), p. 134.
[64] *An Account of the Scots Society in Norwich* (2nd edn., Norwich, 1787), p. 48.
[65] 'The Price Letters', *Proceedings of Massachusetts Historical Society*, 2nd ser., 17 (1903), 359.
[66] E. C. Mossner, *The Life of David Hume*, pp. 405–6.

pains to make themselves acceptable. Literate Scotsmen were obsessed with the need to eliminate those Scotticisms which made them a figure of fun to Englishmen. The mid-eighteenth century seemed something of a watershed in this respect. As John Ramsay of Ochtertyre put it, 'Nobody now doubted the possibility of a Scotsman writing pure, nay, even elegant English, while he spoke his native dialect a little diversified.'[67]

Ironically, polite society in England was quite capable of indulging an enthusiasm for Scottish letters, as the success of John Home's *Douglas* on the English stage, and the extraordinary popularity of Ossian testified. Scots hoped to make literary success a basis for Anglo-Scottish co-operation. The blind Scottish poet Thomas Blacklock rather plaintively appealed for such harmony in his ballad *The Graham* in 1774. Occasionally Englishmen expressed similar views. Richard Cumberland was thought adventurous indeed in inserting a generous Scot into his play *The Fashionable Lover*. Yet such ploys had little effect. Shortly after Cumberland's production the world of books and bookmen was torn in two by a bitter quarrel between the publishers and booksellers of Edinburgh and London, with the latter seeking to obtain an extension of the copyright laws to fend off the superior commercial competition of their Scottish rivals.[68] Even in this, English cultural superiority was deployed against North British presumptuousness: Edinburgh books, it was observed, were 'incorrect, and not fit for a gentleman's library'.[69] Gentility was the most prized of all possessions in eighteenth-century Britain. It surprised not a few of those Celts who pursued it that it was compatible with the expression of extravagant and intolerant national prejudices.

[67] A. Allardyce, ed., *Scotland and Scotsmen in the Eighteenth Century*, i. 310.
[68] See pp. 93–4.
[69] *Parl. Hist.*, xvii. 1087.

CHAPTER 8

Patriotism Restored, 1757–1770

THE years between the formation of the Pitt–Newcastle ministry and the appointment of Lord North as Prime Minister had a shattering effect on the political stability associated with the early Hanoverian reigns. The dominant personalities of these years, Pitt, Bute, and George III, were all in some measure committed to the patriot creed evolved by the opponents of the Walpole and Pelham regimes. They did not, in the event, succeed in initiating a new era of patriotic harmony; they did, however, transform the nature of party politics. Initially, the public response to their declared ideals was euphoric. No less striking was the popular enthusiasm for the military successes of the Seven Years War. Thereafter, disillusion and dissent set in. The accession of a new king resulted in the humiliation of the Whig magnates who had dominated government for half a century. It also fed fears of royal favouritism and a sinister influence 'behind the curtain'. The ensuing years were marked by recurrent political controversy and an almost permanent sense of instability and crisis. In America and in India the legacy of the war and the imperial intervention which it stimulated brought a host of problems. At home the turbulent career of John Wilkes testified to a new spirit of challenge and criticism, threatening to render Englishmen as ungovernable as their colonial com-

patriots. The aim of the well-intentioned patriots who had created this state of affairs was to restore the ancient liberties and conventions which the corruption of early Hanoverian government had supposedly violated; paradoxically their achievement was to change the language and the substance of politics in directions that were very largely novel, and for most of those involved by no means welcome.

PITT'S POLITICS

THE Pitt–Devonshire ministry had been meant to break the mould of British politics: in this it seemed to have failed. Yet an important change had taken place in the climate of opinion which determined the priorities of political debate. Patriotism before 1757 had been the creed of opposition, whether 'patriots' were considered as high-minded friends of their country (their own view), or factious fomenters of popular discontent (the ministerial view). Government had been about making things work, maintaining the status quo, heading off disaster, both foreign and domestic. Newcastle was the living relic of this age, with his vacuous rhetoric and his reputation for wheeling and dealing. But his new colleagues in 1757 were committed by inclination and circumstance to a more positive view of politics: they necessarily subscribed to the patriotic programme which had been evolved over so many years of opposition to Walpole and the Pelhams. This mentality survived the accession of George III. There were eight ministries between 1757 and 1770. All were influenced by it, not least that of Rockingham in 1765–6, which in theory was the true heir to the Pelhamite inheritance.

In personal terms three men stand out, for their commitment to patriot policies and for their influence on the shape of politics: Pitt, Bute, and George III. In 1757 all three were united, as they were never to be again. Bute and Prince George had been instrumental in installing Pitt in power and looked forward to his ministry as a kind of curtain-raiser to the glorious reign of patriotism which must commence when George II died. They were compelled to revise this view, when Pitt declined to play his allotted role, especially in the matter of Bute's attempts to guide the disposal of patronage. Relations gradually cooled until by 1759 a deep bitterness had set in. Deprived of an active part in the ministry, the Prince and Bute could only brood on their discontents and lay plans for the future. Bute's control over his royal protégé became ever more complete; he found that he could even afford to neglect the Princess of Wales, as he replaced her in her son's affections. The talk at Leicester House was of a naïvely fastidious kind. The Prince, whose grandfather and great-grandfather must often have wondered whether they would be allowed to retain the Crown of Great Britain at all, debated with himself and his mentor the terms on which he would be prepared to accept it. Bute, whose political experience was slight and whose parliamentary education was still slighter, considered whether he would condescend to take the formal responsibility of the Prime Minister's office as First Lord of the Treasury. All this was going on while Pitt governed, Newcastle fussed, and the British empire became the mightiest of its age, or indeed of any earlier age.

Pitt did not forget his patriotism for it was crucial to his political survival. The ministry seemed secure, almost unopposed as it was in Parliament, and firmly entrenched in the royal closet. But it was only a coalition, and one made up of the most disparate parts. The old guard had lost its nerve with the fall of Minorca, but it had not mislaid its malice. The King grudged and grumbled, Cumberland sulked in his disgrace, Fox was temporarily content to count the profits to be made by a Paymaster-General in wartime; Newcastle and Hardwicke collaborated for the purposes of war, more loyally than Pitt deserved, perhaps, but suspicious of his intentions and fretful at his imperiousness. Everything depended on the success or failure of British arms. Without victory Pitt knew that his alliance with Newcastle would prove as short-lived as Fox's two years earlier. The Grenville clan on which he personally relied was well represented in the administration but proved more adroit at provoking conflicts with the Pelhamite block than strengthening Pitt's position. Their leader Lord Temple had a disconcerting habit, for one of such limited talents, of placing his own interests before his brother-in-law's political strategy. The Tories were crucial: without them Pitt had no effective support of his own at all. But they were not by nature government supporters and they were slow to understand the need for compromise. At least until he got the victories which he confidently expected Pitt needed more than words to keep his faith with them.

The result was a patriot programme which, though it often divided the ministry, was essential for the maintenance of Pitt's personal position. The Militia Act had gone through in the session of 1757, and needed determined support thereafter. Newcastle and his friends continued to regard it as a device for the restoration of Tory influence in the counties. Its military value was a matter of debate. During the invasion scare of 1759 all but a handful of counties, such as Oxfordshire, where party animosities made co-operation impossible, raised their quota of troops; there was much marching and exercising, and Pitt was able to release regular troops for duties elsewhere. Whether the milita would actually have stood up to an invading force seems doubtful. It was deeply unpopular with ordinary Englishmen who, for the first time in two generations, found themselves balloted and conscripted for service. The militia was a grossly unfair measure in class terms: exemption from the ballot required payment of a sum of £10 to hire a substitute, a figure which applied equally to the greatest magnate and the humblest labourer. The officers were largely Tory country gentlemen who fancied themselves patriotic defenders of hearth and home in the manner proclaimed by 'country' ideology. The men whom they commanded turned out to be not the sturdy yeomen envisaged by militia enthusiasts, but much the same ragtag and bobtail who kept the army supplied. Popular opposition was put down, but only after some alarming riots and a regular siege of some country houses, including the Duke of Bedford's Woburn. Horace Walpole sarcastically commented that 'the standing army was employed to impose upon the people a constitutional force'.[1]

Pitt staunchly defended the militia and the amending acts needed to make it work. He also backed his brother-in-law George Grenville, whose Navy Bill had been defeated by Newcastle in 1757 but was let through in 1758. The bill was designed to speed up the payment of seamen's wages, thereby enhancing the minimal attractions of service in the navy. It proved modestly successful. A matching effort to create a fair system of conscription for merchant seamen, rendering the hated 'press' redundant, proved too radical, or perhaps too unpopular with merchant shipowners, to gain similar support. Other patriot initiatives were proposed, only to be blocked, mainly by the Newcastle wing of the ministry. The extension of the militia to Scotland provoked some uncomfortable debates both in England and Scotland before being ruled out. A proposal to grant judges unlimited security of tenure was discussed but made little progress. In 1758 there was a determined effort to reform the law of Habeas Corpus, matching the famous Act obtained by the Whigs in 1679. The new Act would have made it more difficult for legal vacations to be used by way of evasion of the law and would have reduced judicial discretion, particularly in cases resulting from naval impressment. But George II viewed it as an encroachment on his prerogative. Hardwicke and Mansfield,

[1] H. Walpole, *Memoirs of King George II*, ii. 271–2.

the legal luminaries of the age, affronted by Pitt's assertion that he 'would force any judge who nibbled at the liberties of the people to hide his head', made short work of his arguments.[2] Pitt came near to breaking up the coalition for the sake of the bill, but eventually acquiesced in its extinction in the House of Lords, perhaps content to have made clear to the Tories his own commitment to it. Two years later he compensated them with a new Qualification Act, designed to strengthen the statute of 1711 requiring MPs to be substantial landowners. But even this proved a doubtful victory. Parliamentary candidates who lacked the requisite qualification continued to evade the law with impunity.

PITT AND THE SEVEN YEARS WAR

This patriotic programme was hardly complete but it showed sceptical supporters that Pitt was no Pulteney. 'I have been charged', he boasted to the Commons, 'with striking a bargain with the Tories, but I know of no bargains or demands which it is uncandid for me to name.'[3] He did not, however, admit publicly his dilemma in respect of grand strategy. Patriotism required a 'blue water' policy, to defeat France at sea and in the colonies, while leaving Germany in general and Hanover in particular to their own devices. But Newcastle had made a heavy commitment to the European mainland. Moreover, Pitt knew that it was a commitment which made sense. In political terms, it secured George II's support. In diplomatic terms, it pre-empted the great advantage which France would derive from uncontested control of Germany at any peace negotiations. Less predictably, but in restrospect most importantly, it encouraged the French to divert more resources to the Continent than they could afford while they were also heavily engaged overseas.

Pitt wriggled on this hook. Negotiations for the renewal of the Prussian subsidy in 1758 were conducted with caution. Prince Ferdinand of Brunswick was employed in the role which Cumberland had so completely failed to sustain, that of protecting Hanover and Frederick II's right flank. Troops were another matter. In December 1757 Pitt imprudently told the Commons

[2] A. F. B. Williams, *The Life of William Pitt, Earl of Chatham* (2 vols., London, 1913), ii. 38.
[3] Ibid. ii. 62.

that he would not send 'a drop of blood to the Elbe, to be lost in that ocean of gore'.[4] Yet within a few months he bowed to Prussian demands for clearer evidence of Britain's commitment and promised, in the Second Treaty of Westminster, a first detachment of British troops to garrison Emden. Within a few months more he was sending English regiments to campaign with Prince Ferdinand. The strategy of which he was later to boast, winning North America on the plains of Germany, was in place.

Its success owed much to the limited objectives of the Anglo-Prussian alliance. Britain's aim was the defence of Hanover: Frederick's was protection of his own domains, retention of Silesia, and control of Saxony. The allies had in effect to defend a great circle of central European territory against an onslaught by French, Austrian, Russian, and Swedish armies. The Russians were particularly menacing, but co-operation between the courts of Paris, Vienna, and Moscow was not invariably effective, nor were their generals always in tune. Frederick's survival, and indeed Ferdinand's resourceful campaigning against the French, remain astonishing feats of generalship. There were some low points, notably in August 1759 when the Russians slaughtered half of Frederick's army at Kunersdorf and brought him to contemplate suicide, and in October 1760 when Berlin itself was briefly occupied. But there were also some brilliant victories, Rossbach and Leuthen against the French and Austrians in 1757, Zorndorf against the Russians in 1758, and Torgau against the Austrians in 1760. Sceptics were amused by the way the British newspapers treated the cause of Frederick, the self-confessed deist, as the cause of Protestantism, but there is no doubting the enthusiasm which his German victories aroused. Nor was there any restraint in celebrating Minden in August 1759 when Ferdinand and his British allies combined to inflict a humiliating defeat on the army of Louis XV, effectively guaranteeing the preservation of the Electorate, and rendering French victory in the German war improbable.

By the time of Minden Pitt was in a position to turn embarrassed acknowledgement of the need for British action in Germany to unashamed bragging of it. But during the intervening years he desperately needed something to quell the grumbling of the Tories and to pacify his friends in the City. That something was a

[4] Ibid. i. 355.

succession of audacious descents on the French coast, intended
to inflict damage on enemy fortifications, shipping, and communications, and also to divert French troops from more important
stations in Germany or overseas. Not least, they were meant to
provide evidence of Pitt's fidelity to his 'blue water' professions.
In a military sense they proved almost useless. They were expensive to mount and their objectives were relatively unimportant:
Henry Fox memorably described them as breaking windows with
gold guineas. The first of these expeditions, to Rochefort in
September 1757, was a costly farce, producing mirth in Paris,
embarrassment in London, and a court martial for its commander.
The following year an attack on St Malo misfired; a further landing
at Cherbourg at least permitted the army to return with some
captured French guns for display at the Tower. A final descent,
on St Cast, was rebuffed with heavy losses. If this was the price
of patriot strategy it was a high one, higher than Pitt could afford
to pay for long, though he concealed his chagrin with exaggerated
claims about the numbers of troops which France had been forced
to bring home. But by the time of the St Cast disaster in September
1758, the first really good news of the war in the west had arrived.
Louisburg, the key to the St Lawrence, had been taken by a
combined naval and military attack, and the way to Quebec was
open.

Louisburg transformed Pitt's morale. When Parliament met in
November 1758 he astonished the Commons by boasting of the
millions of pounds devoted to the war, and by extravagant remarks
about the terms on which one day he might make peace. The new
year began with 95,000 troops and 80,000 seamen in British pay.
In Germany, in America, in the West Indies, in Africa, in India,
extraordinary efforts were promised. The results were startling.
In India Clive's crucial victory against Siraj ud-Daula at Plassey
had been achieved in 1757. The dispatch of troops to assist him
was to provide the means by which the French could be driven
down the Coromandel Coast; their decisive defeat at Wandewash
in January 1760 effectively destroyed them as a power in Asia.
Goree on the West African coast was taken shortly after Christmas
1758. In the Caribbean a rebuff at Martinique was amply compensated by the capture of Guadeloupe, second only to Cuba
among sugar islands. In August 1759, soon after Minden, the
French Toulon fleet, which had led a charmed life for so much of

the preceding war, was decisively defeated off Cape Lagos; three months later the Brest fleet was dealt a matching blow at Quiberon. These naval victories secured British control of the Mediterranean, fatally weakened French attempts to reinforce Canada, and made an invasion of England itself impossible. In the North American Lakes the forts which had defied successive British commanders, Loudoun in 1757 and Abercromby in 1758, fell to Amherst in 1759. Above all Wolfe's direct attack on Quebec up the St Lawrence secured the route to Montreal and the final conquest of French Canada. 1759 was a remarkable year, a 'South Sea Year' for expenditure, an *annus mirabilis* for victories. When Pitt met his third parliamentary session, in November 1759, his familiar egotism, expressed in neurotic brooding in 1757, in arrogant assertiveness in 1758, was unrestrained. Proposing a monument to Wolfe's memory, he boasted that he had himself done more for Britain that any orator for Rome. 'And for the Grecians, their story were a pretty theme if the town of St Albans were waging war with that of Brentford.'[5]

Pitt was entitled to claim some credit for the success of the war, if only because he had kept his own nerve and sustained that of many others. More extravagant assessments of his leadership must be treated cautiously. There were, in a sense, two decisive battles in the Seven Years War, the battle of Germany and the battle of the Atlantic. In the former his own share was limited; moreover, it is not clear, after the rhetoric and vanity are scraped away, that he did more than Newcastle would have done, let alone Fox. In the Atlantic the critical consideration was the success of a navy which, though its numerical superiority was slight, achieved a stranglehold on the French fleet. However, naval historians no longer attach great weight to Pitt's direction of the navy: more was owed to the activities of a notable Navy Secretary, John Clevland, and a famous First Lord of the Admiralty, Anson. During the last stages of the preceding war the navy had been on the brink of the success which it achieved in 1759, but the opportunity had been lost by the rout of the army in the Low Countries. If men needed a dynamic force at the helm, or even as a figure-head, in Pitt they had one, but whether they needed either remains uncertain.

Much the same is true of the army. Pitt certainly recognized the

[5] R. C. Simmons and P. D. G. Thomas, eds., *Proceedings and Debates of the British Parliaments Respecting North America, 1754–1783* (New York, 1982–), i. 305.

claims of Amherst and Wolfe; but he had no share in Clive's appointment. Nor were all his generals great ones. Sir John Mordaunt was widely censured for the Rochefort fiasco, and the Duke of Marlborough did not impress at St Malo. (The French, it was observed, were not to be conquered by every Duke of Marlborough.) The Earl of Loudoun and James Abercromby, as commanders in America, were heavily criticized for the inactivity which marked the campaigns of 1757 and 1758. Not all these men were Pitt's original appointments, but one who was his undoubted personal choice failed him in spectacular fashion. Whether Lord George Sackville was guilty of imprudence or cowardice at Minden, when the British cavalry under his command omitted to follow up the success of their own and Prince Ferdinand's infantry, remains a matter of dispute. Modern authorities tend to the former view; Pitt himself took the latter and contributed substantially to Sackville's disgrace. Pitt's special achievement was essentially political and personal; neither as diplomat nor as grand strategist did he display exceptional qualities. The result, however, was the same. Victory made him what he had long claimed to be, the tribune of the people. It also made him the most powerful figure in British political life.

THE NEW REIGN

1760, the centenary of the Stuart Restoration, not only saw the empire extended beyond the dreams of seventeenth-century Englishmen, but also the accession of the third Hanoverian who claimed the throne by parliamentary title. George II died, as the obituarists recorded, of a ruptured coronary ventricle, on 25 October 1760. The occasion was marked by extraordinary rejoicing, not, indeed, at the expense of George II's memory, but rather in recognition of the promise which the accession of a young prince seemed to offer. The euphoria of the occasion was soon to be overclouded by faction and recrimination, but there is no doubting its initial effect. Even in remote parts, as the Scottish historian of manners Thomas Somerville later recalled, 'transports of loyalty bunrst forth'.[6] The keynote was patriotic harmony. When he met the Privy Council at Carlton House the new King referred proudly to 'this my native country', a boast echoed in the addresses of

6 T. Somerville, *My Own Life and Times, 1741–1814* (Edinburgh, 1861), p. 52.

	British possessions
	French possessions
	Spanish possessions

FIG. 5. European possessions in North America and the Caribbean at the outbreak of the Seven Years War

Sources: M. S. Anderson, *Europe in the Eighteenth Century* (London, 1961), p. 245

congratulation which flooded the columns of the newspapers. Poets, actors, novelists cashed in. Typical was the affecting tale of *Angelicus and Fergusia*, which was given a finale requiring lines of 'Henrys and Edwards' to appear in homage to the new monarch; above them there rose the spirit of Prince Frederick, 'the friend of human kind', declaring: 'To you, for heaven, how chearful I resign a crown! which Britons once concluded mine'.[7] Cheerful resignation had not beeen a marked characteristic of the Prince of Wales, but there was no doubt that his heir, in the fullest sense, was George III. The omens seemed unreservedly propitious. Even those who noticed that 25 October, in the new-style calendar, was the date of the Battle of Hastings, could be reminded that old style it was the anniversary of Agincourt.

If contemporaries thought of the new reign as a watershed, historians have not been wanting to confirm their view, albeit in a somewhat different sense. It is particularly tempting to see it as a historic moment in the evolution of the ruling class, substituting unity and coherence for division and conflict. Certainly the new regime placed much emphasis on the extinction of ancient animosities. For the first time the Tory country gentlemen were welcomed at court, not grudgingly, but with open arms. Peerages and honours were distributed among those who valued such things. More to the point, the process of relaxing proscription in the counties, begun by Pelham and hastened by Pitt, was completed. The Whig oligarchies of shire and borough were finally compelled to give up some of their local influence. In Oxfordshire a new Commission of the Peace was printed with the long proscribed families helpfully identified by asterisk. In the Welsh marches the bitter pill of Tory restoration was even forced down the throat of the 'Shropshire gang', who for decades had monopolized both the parliamentary representation of the region, and the disposal of local patronage.

There was an emotional home-coming for many Churchmen. Though the early Hanoverian Church had never been the exclusive preserve of latitudinarians, Cambridge, and the Duke of Newcastle, as its enemies claimed, 1760 proved a considerable reverse to all three. Lord Lichfield, the Tory Chancellor of Oxford, paraded his university's loyalty to the new King; hopes that a Hanoverian monarch might appear in the Sheldonian Theatre were raised.

[7] (London, 1761), pp. 65–6.

Many parched mouths in college and parsonage watered at the prospect of the royal chaplaincies, canonries, and livings suddenly open to Tory, High Church, Oxford men. Such expectations were not altogether compatible with patriotic consensus, however. It was not possible to reward Tories without offending Whigs, as repeated disputes over Lord-Lieutenancies and Commissions of the Peace demonstrated. In time the new forces released by the accession of George III were to divide the political nation as much as ever, though along new lines. The reconciliation of the backwoods squirearchy doubtless made the process of county government somewhat easier, and possibly prepared the way for the enlightened local administration which was one of the boasts of the age of John Howard. Yet the twenty years following George III's accession produced forty-eight county election contests, compared with only twenty-eight in the two decades preceding it. Nor was the Church restored to a confident sense of its own coherence without awakening a certain uneasiness in other quarters. Perhaps it was significant that the most extravagant and controversial obituary of the dead King, likening him to King David, was penned by Samuel Chandler.[8] Chandler was a living representative of the toleration and moderation, even co-operation, which had marked relations between highly placed Churchmen and Dissenters under George II. By the time he died, in 1766, he already seemed slightly out of place under George III.

Tobias Smollett had one of his fictional characters pronounce George III 'too good for the times'. From a very different standpoint his Whig rival Laurence Sterne praised the King for attempting to 'stop the torrent of corruption and laziness'.[9] It was claimed in the press that the King had personally instructed the Treasury not to involve itself in corrupt bargains with borough-mongers at the next general election. The generous civil list arrangement of 1727, by which surpluses on the civil list duties were credited to the Crown rather than the Exchequer, was revoked, though George III had doubts about the prudence of taking his patriotism this far. Within the decade he was compelled to return cap in hand to Parliament for payment of his debts. The judges were granted security of tenure overriding even the accession of a new monarch,

---

[8] *The Character of a Great and Good King* (London, 1760).
[9] *The Expedition of Humphry Clinker*, ed. A. Ross, p. 128; L. P. Curtis, ed., *Letters of Laurence Sterne* (Oxford, 1935), p. 126.

though in 1760 there had been no intention of turning out Whig judges. The Durham Act of 1763 made it illegal for non-resident freemen to vote in parliamentary elections within a year of their appointment; massive creations of such votes had been customary not merely at Durham but in many boroughs where the franchise went with corporate freedom. An Act of the same year sought to regulate the granting of forty-shilling annuities, in order to obstruct the creation of block votes in county elections. It was made clear, notwithstanding murmurs of protest from old Whigs, that the new militia would be extended and made permanent. The promise of Frederick Prince of Wales that all landed gentlemen with £300 per annum would automatically be placed in the Commission of the Peace, though not implemented by statute, was effectively honoured by a substantial increase in the size of the county benches.

Was this at last the new dawn of patriotism for which so many had hoped in vain in 1742 and 1756? George III's intentions have been the subject of much disagreement. Historians necessarily depend on their sources. Whig historians were guided by the evidence which the diarist Horace Walpole mustered to support his malice, and by the arguments which Edmund Burke levelled against the court. They consequently saw only an avowed absolutist, intent on restoring the patriarchal authority of the Stuarts. But Walpole was not an impartial historian, and Burke did not pretend to be. Sir Lewis Namier had the advantage of access to the personal correspondence of the principal figures. He was struck by the pettiness of Newcastle's preoccupations, and impressed by the sincerity of the King as revealed in his youthful letters. Since Namier wrote it has been impossible to believe that George III consciously sought to make his kingship absolute, or indeed that his constitutional ideas were anything but platitudinously conventional, truly those of a Revolution monarch. Yet Namier did not adequately recognize the extent to which the programme of a patriot king must give rise to legitimate concern about the new policies adopted. Nor was he altogether frank about the attitudes and language which prevailed at court during Bute's supremacy. A corrective is available in the form of a newly unveiled source, the diaries of the fourth Duke of Devonshire.[10]

Devonshire was a senior Whig statesman imbued with good

[10] P. D. Brown and K. W. Schweizer, eds., *The Devonshire Diary* (Camden 4th ser., vol. 27, 1982).

sense and judgement; he was no pawn of the Pelhams, nor was he overly impressed by Pitt. He had no animus against either the King or Bute initially. He saw clearly that they were bent on taming Pitt and controlling Newcastle. This may have been imprudent but it was hardly unconstitutional. The problem as Devonshire saw it was to reconcile the interests of Pitt, Newcastle, and Bute, without alienating a young prince of extreme inexperience, even ignorance.

That young man's sensations of honour were more delicate; that I was apprehensive if any attack was made on Lord Bute, the King would run great lengths to support and the attempt might so sour the King's temper at the first out set of his reign, as might make him both himself and his people unhappy; that therefore I was much for moderate measures, and by giving his Lordship a reasonable share of power prevent him from grasping at the whole.[11]

This was a remarkably prophetic judgement but it did not diagnose overreaching kingly ambition as the cause of political *malaise* in the early 1760s. Devonshire had none of Pitt's unreasonable insistence on unlimited powers, nor Newcastle's neurotic conviction that a king not prepared to accept the shackles of the Pelham family must be an enemy of Revolution principles. Rather there was a shrewd appreciation of a simple human situation: an adolescent monarch, an ambitious favourite, and two over-mighty ministers. There was something more, however. Devonshire was worried by the sheer naïvety of the King and his adviser. 'I was surprised to find they knew mankind and the carte de pays so little.'[12] They seemed, above all, to have little sense of the distance which separated rhetoric from reality. Lectured by Bute on the kind of language which Privy Councillors might employ in advising a monarch, Devonshire blew his top. 'I answered: "Not bear it! he must bear it, every King must make use of human means to attain human ends or his affairs will go to ruin." '[13] Such a combination of innocence and haughtiness was alarming. But worse still was the King's attitude to the war. Devonshire was as much a 'patriot' as any of the new men, and more than anything he was shocked by their apparent neglect of their country's interests.

The war was a brilliant one yet it was not Bute's war and both he and his master felt that deeply. The victories accumulated, but

[11] Ibid., p. 82.   [12] Ibid., p. 79.   [13] Ibid., p. 52.

they were victories for Pitt. Canada was finally surrendered in 1760. The following year the last operation against the French coast succeeded in taking Belle-Île, and in the West Indies Martinique and St Lucia were seized. But from the beginning of the new reign it had been made clear that such triumphs were not unmixed blessings. There was some undignified haggling between Pitt and Bute over the terms in which the war should be described. This quickly got into the newspapers. When the City of London addressed the Crown by way of congratulation on the capture of Montreal it spoke of this 'just and necessary war'; back came the royal reply referring to this 'necessary and expensive war'. This was more than sour grapes on the part of the new court, for it reflected mounting public concern about the price paid for Pitt's victories. Depressing statistics could be produced. The average cost per annum of the Nine Years War and the War of the Spanish Succession had been slightly more than £5 million; during the War of the Austrian Succession it had risen to £6.6 million. In the Seven Years War the corresponding figure was £13.7 million. The taxation needed to support war loans bore heavily on land and affected trade. The tribune of the people was not against taxing the populace, and when the beer excise pushed the price of strong beer from $3d.$ to $3\frac{1}{2}d.$ per quart, there was rioting in London. William Godwin, in a less well-known role as one of Pitt's earliest biographers, recalled the effect of war on the public mind and identified the year of George III's accession as the turning-point. 1759 had dazzled the people of England; 1760 restored them to their senses.[14]

Anxiety about the moral consequences of war matched the dismay at the expense. The dramatist Samuel Foote later produced a brilliant caricature of the war profiteer in his portrait of Mr Fungus, a tradesman of 'mean extraction and low education' who went to Germany as a commissary with the army and returned wealthy, corrupt, and powerful. It was significant that he had made his fortune in Germany. There was a growing sense that this war of Pitt's, like earlier wars, was in the last analysis conducted for the benefit of foreigners. All the doubts of the Tory squires, partly quieted by Pitt's rhetoric of 1757 and by the initial effect of his victories, revived under the pressure of financial exhaustion and with the encouragement of the new court. Israel Mauduit's pamphlet,

[14] *The History of the Life of William Pitt, Earl of Chatham* (Dublin, 1783), p. 84.

Considerations on the Present German War, caught this mood perfectly, and belongs with Swift's *Conduct of the Allies* as one of the most influential tracts in the history of diplomacy and war. Mauduit argued that Hanover had never been at risk; it had only been attacked because France knew that Great Britain would defend it. 'They always will go thither, as long as the English councils resolve to oppose them there.'[15] As for Frederick of Prussia, he had been of no assistance to Hanover, and by his cynical perfidy towards Austria had bedevilled British relations with the Continent. Why should Englishmen contemplate an annual budget of £20 million to save him? Why was it necessary to consider the fate of Hanover when the Elector of Hanover himself no longer seemed interested in doing so? These were debatable, even tendentious arguments, and they could be answered. But Pitt must have been conscious in the early months of the new reign that the national mood was not disposed to listen to the answers.

THE PEACE OF 1763

By 1763 the war was over and both Pitt and Newcastle were in opposition. This was partly a measure of George III's determination, partly a consequence of the support which he attracted both in and out of Parliament. At an early stage Devonshire had warned that Pitt and Newcastle together 'can easily get the better of a Favourite'.[16] But Pitt and Newcastle had never been more than reluctant allies, and not even the rivalry of Bute was sufficient to unite them for long. Pitt departed first in October 1761. In a sense he had most to lose, for Bute had been made his fellow Secretary of State, in place of the pliant Holderness, in March, and plainly expected to play a full part in the determination of policy. At issue were both the conduct and the conclusion of the war. In the peace negotiations which got under way in the spring of 1761 there was agreement on the principle of restoring Britain's gains in the Caribbean in return for the cession of Canada and the restoration of Minorca. But Pitt placed much weight on the need to exclude the French from the North American fisheries. Cod, he claimed, was Britain's gold: through the maintenance of a great fishing fleet, it provided a continuing source of recruits for the

[15] (Dublin, 1761), p. 29.
[16] *Devonshire Diary*, p. 44.

royal navy. Pitt's Cabinet colleagues throught his demands unrealistic. The discussions failed for another reason, however:
Choiseul, with what he regarded as a trump card up his sleeve,
proved an implacable negotiator. That card was the Bourbon
family compact, revived by the accession of Carlos III to the
Spanish throne in 1759. The prospect of a Spanish war promised
all kinds of new hazards, a further Continental front in Portugal,
an assault on Gibraltar and perhaps Jamaica, even an invasion of
England.

Pitt was never one to refuse a challenge. He proposed an immediate pre-emptive attack on the Spanish treasure fleets, and war *à
outrance* against the combined Bourbon powers. When the Cabinet,
including Newcastle, demurred, he resigned. His motives were
doubtless mixed. He said himself that he would not be responsible
for what he did not direct. By this time he had a clear appreciation
that Bute, for all his denials, was bent on ruling rather than
adorning the new court. He was also conscious that making peace
could prove a difficult, unpopular business, with which the hero
of the Seven Years War might prefer not to be associated. It did
not help in this respect that he obtained a peerage for his wife and
a pension for himself when he resigned. His prestige was too deeply
established after 1759 to be severely shaken, but he was much
criticized in the City and in the press. And if he expected that an
appalled people would indignantly thrust him back into power he
must have been deeply disappointed. On the other hand, his
judgement was proved right in one respect. Regardless of the
British Cabinet, Carlos III sought glory and revenge. War was
declared in January 1762 without the advantage, for Britain, of the
naval initiative.

Newcastle was nervous. At the beginning of the new reign he
had talked of resigning to make way for Bute; the latter's reluctance
to challenge him had seemed puzzling. He expected more difficulty
with the general election, held in March 1761. Yet there was little
about it to disturb him. There were only fifty-four contested
elections and nothing resembling a national contest on party lines.
In Scotland Bute was in charge, but elsewhere Newcastle was left
to manage the election; for all his anxious listing of friends and
enemies he found little to sustain his fear of a campaign of subversion. In this respect at least Bute had a shrewder appreciation of
political realities. 'The new Parliament', he observed, 'would be

the King's let who will chuse it.'[17] Thereafter, relations became more strained, as Bute's confidence grew, and Newcastle found himself without even Pitt's doubtful support. Spanish aggression provided the new court with an opportunity to indulge its own version of a patriotic war. Cuba might be attacked; Portugal must be protected; above all Prussia could be abandoned, all the more now that a change of regime in Russia had rendered Frederick II's position less precarious. Newcastle decided to make the Prussian subsidy an issue of confidence, and resigned in May 1762. There followed a lull while he and his opponents considered tactics. Bute was conciliatory, even offering Newcastle a role in his Cabinet as a kind of sleeping partner. Newcastle was in agonies of uncertainty. 'I don't know, *who are my friends*', he had said in April.[18] Were they so numerous as to repeat the triumph of 1746, or was the last of the great Whig ministers to be humiliated by his own followers?

The suspense was broken by George III. In an injudicious but understandable fit of irritation with Devonshire, who declined either to attend the Cabinet or resign, the King dismissed him with every mark of contempt. This was certainly a mistake. The Cavendishes were not a family to be humiliated. For the moment, however, the power of the Whig clans was broken. When Newcastle called out his forces against Bute's Peace Preliminaries he could muster minorities of only sixty to seventy in the House of Commons. Many of his so-called friends signalled their adherence to the new regime. There was evidently a great difference between Carteret and Bute, and between George II and George III. Those who remained loyal to Newcastle suffered. The Slaughter of the Pelhamite Innocents came to be exaggerated in due course, but it was a substantial blood-letting none the less, the most extensive since 1714. Some of Newcastle's lowliest supporters, those Sussex men who had found the reign of George II a propitious time for a career in customs or excise, were dismissed, to mark the disgrace of the greatest of all Hanoverian magnates. For Newcastle, with his memories of the accession of George I, the mobs of 1715, the South Sea Bubble, and the Atterbury Plot, it was a traumatic time. Nobody was more surprised to find himself in opposition to a Hanoverian King than Newcastle himself.

[17] Sir L. Namier, *England in the Age of the American Revolution* (2nd edn., London, 1966), p. 156.
[18] Ibid., p. 365.

TABLE 4. *Peace of Paris 1763: British gains and losses*

Africa	Senegal retained, Goree restored to France.
W. Indies	Grenada, St Vincent, Dominica, Tobago retained. Martinique, Guadeloupe, St Lucia restored to France. British logwood rights in Honduras confirmed, without fortification.
North America	Canada and all territory east of Mississippi retained; French right of fishing in Gulf of St Lawrence and off Newfoundland restored, with unfortified possession of islands of St Pierre and Miquelon. Florida ceded by Spain in return for restoration of Cuba; Spanish renunciation of claims in Newfoundland fishery.
Europe	Minorca regained in return for restoration of Belle-Île to France. Germany evacuated by France, Portugal by Spain.
The East	France restored to Indian possessions of 1749 on an exclusively commercial basis. Manila restored to Spain without territorial compensation.

In the mean time the Peace went through. Bute's 'ridiculous, popular war' as Newcastle had christened it, proved both as expensive and as successful as Pitt's.[19] Portugal was saved, Cuba captured, and Manila in the Philippines taken. With his last card trumped Choiseul came to terms. The resulting settlement, negotiated by the Duke of Bedford in Paris, with more freedom than most ministers would have given him, but with enthusiastic support from Bute and the King, was approved by Parliament in December 1762 and signed in February 1763. It quickly generated two enduring myths. One was the supposed unpopularity of the Peace. Bute had bullied the King into employing Henry Fox as his agent in the House of Commons. Fox's unsavoury reputation embarrassed George III and made it easy enough for opponents to claim that he corrupted the Commons into supporting peace. But this was nonsense. Parliament overwhelmingly supported the Peace. Independent MPs were horrified by the cost of the war and found the peace terms honourable. Outside Parliament, there was opposition in London, but little elsewhere. Pitt's own constituency of Bath, a respected and independent corporation, indicated its support for the treaty. Pitt was furious, and parted company with

[19] Namier, *England in the Age of the Revolution*, p. 314.

his supporters there, including the 'Man of Bath', Ralph Allen, who had been instrumental in getting him elected and was now shocked by Pitt's factiousness. Even Newcastle was publicly humiliated when his beloved University of Cambridge sent up an address of congratulation.

It remained only to pretend that the people of England were deluded and that the Peace was indeed a disastrous one, a true successor to the Peace of Utrecht. Certainly Bute had not extracted the full advantage from his Spanish war. His evident dismay when a British force captured Havana sickened even some of his supporters. For restoring it he gained only Florida; for returning Manila he obtained no territorial equivalent at all. But the notion that more could be extorted from France was debatable. Pitt argued that France emerged strong enough both to seek and obtain revenge, Bute that greater demands would alienate the French beyond all hope of future co-operation or even coexistence. In a sense both were wrong. France could not have been reduced further without exhausting conqueror as well as conquered. On the other hand kid gloves were unlikely to impress Choiseul and his successors. There was one central aim in French diplomacy after 1763: to reverse the humiliation of the Seven Years War. Faced by some ministers, Grenville when he rebuffed French attempts at aggrandizement in the Bahamas in 1764, and North when he was prepared to go to war over the Falklands in 1770, they backed down. With others, notably Grafton over Corsica in 1768, they were more fortunate. But in the long run they would seek advantage from any British embarrassment, as the War of American Independence was to demonstrate.

Bute was charged with perfidy as well as pusillanimity. The accusation seems excessive. Frederick II had neither a moral nor legal claim to perpetual British subsidies; nor did his own record suggest respect for international obligations. It is arguable that the Anglo-Prussian alliance had worked more to his advantage than Britain's, especially after Minden, when the main function of British troops became the protection of Frederick's flank. But the opposition in England saw some political profit in the slighting of the Protestant hero by the Elector of Hanover; they also argued that the new court was dangerously isolated in Europe. Whether this had much to do with the Prussian rupture in 1762 is another matter. Prussia had joined with Britain in 1756 to counter the threat of Russia; from 1762 to 1781 this requirement was obviated by the Russo-Prussian alliance. Significantly, when Pitt and Newcastle eventually returned to power, their attempts to cultivate the friendship of Prussia proved futile. Theirs were not the only plans for diplomatic realignment. Grenville and George III hoped for a revival of the ancient Austrian alliance. All ministers between 1763 and 1783 sought to negotiate a Russian alliance. But the truth was that none of the powers of eastern Europe had an interest in aiding Britain without some equivalent commitment, for instance to the aggrandizement of Russia in the Balkans. There was no hope of creating such a community of interest.

Before 1763 the European network of alliances had depended on the central place of Germany in diplomacy and war. The Eastern powers had competing interests there; so did France, and even Britain, with its Hanoverian connection. As it turned out George III was not as negligent of his Electorate as the first days of his reign had suggested. But none of the great powers was ready to disturb the stability of Germany, least of all France with her bitter experience of the Seven Years War. The Eastern states were left to themselves. Between Britain and the Bourbon monarchies there continued a series of fluctuating, ill co-ordinated battles for diplomatic supremacy on the European periphery, in the Mediterranean, in Sweden, in Holland. But the real conflict was overseas, and it was there, in the American War, that the issue was finally to be joined. No minister, in 1763 or after, could have changed these realities of post-war politics, let alone have lessened Britain's isolation.

BUTE, THE EMPIRE, AND THE GROWTH OF OPPOSITION

There was nothing of the little Englander about Bute, Scotsman as he was. The post-war period was one of ambitious, even visionary plans. The world's greatest empire must now be ruled. The Royal Proclamation of 1763 envisaged a new era of American expansion. Canada and the Floridas would be settled. The latter were at once granted self-government on the old colonial model. Canada, with its population of French Roman Catholics, could not be treated similarly until Anglo-Saxon immigration had adjusted the ethnic balance; instead it was offered toleration and the prospect of some allowance for the distinctive political and legal traditions of the French 'habitants'. The West was reserved for the Indians and the fur trade. A brief but bloody Indian rising in 1763 seemed to confirm the wisdom of prohibiting unrestrained colonial settlement up to the Mississippi. Many more things were talked of: a thoroughgoing reform of the intricate and often unenforceable Navigation System; a more regular and better managed colonial administration; the possibility of raising revenues in the colonies capable of supporting the imperial commitment.

Most of what was proposed had often been discussed in the past, usually within the Board of Trade, a body burdened with much information but little executive power. Under the Earl of Halifax in the early 1750s the Board of Trade had acquired an enthusiasm for imperial reform which had a marked influence on some of the men at Cabinet level in the 1760s, including George Grenville and Charles Townshend. Not less important was the transformed climate of opinion in which they operated. There remained widespread ignorance about North America, notwithstanding the flood of publications which had sought to spread enlightenment from the early 1750s. But there was also understanding, perhaps even exaggeration, of its importance to Britain. This was the effect of five years of North American battle reports, from Braddock's defeat to Wolfe's victory. In a sense it was what the colonies had pleaded for. But America had sought security, not a new spirit of intervention and supervision. Even before the war was over it was made clear that British troops would be maintained in the colonies. In London the need to keep the French and Spaniards at bay seemed obvious, and new locations for garrisons, distant from Britain itself, were not without their convenience. But a large military establishment required support, perhaps even the taxation of Americans. It was also noted that one of the functions of the military was to safeguard the western lands against irresponsible colonists. Was it beyond the bounds of possibility, some wondered, that it might also be used to enforce the will of the imperial authorities in the thirteen colonies themselves?

The empire in the east was hardly less important than the empire in the west. The peace treaty gave the French a trading presence in India, comparable to that of the Dutch and Portuguese. It also made the British masters of Bengal, reducing its nawabs to ciphers. Clive had come back to England in 1760; he was sent out again in 1764 to secure a lasting settlement of the East India Company's affairs. The resulting treaty with the Great Mogul took the form of the grant of the diwani, in effect a part of the civil administration of Bengal and more importantly a large share of its revenue. In retrospect the grant was a critical step on the road which took Englishmen from being traders in India to its rulers. In the short term it was to endanger the commercial base of the East India Company and raise questions of the first importance about the political and moral responsibilities of empire in India. It was also to attract the attention of the Crown, its ministers, and Parliament.

None of this was strictly Bute's doing; most of it flowed naturally from the war. Moreover, Bute's ministry was brief. He had become First Lord of the Treasury on Newcastle's resignation in May 1762: he resigned, in favour of George Grenville, in April 1763. This startled many contemporaries. But those who knew Bute were less surprised. He had always said that he might not remain long in office, though it would have been easy to attribute this to self-deception. Lord Shelburne, who knew him well, recorded a devastating verdict on his political character.[20] He was 'proud, pompous, imposing' yet 'the greatest political coward I ever knew'. He had 'much superficial knowledge' but 'false taste in everything'. He planned 'great reformations', yet was 'entirely incapable' of dealing with mankind. He saw himself as a kind of British Sully, the partner, even the patron of his monarch. In Parliament he had huge majorities. There were, admittedly, some uncomfortable decisions to be taken, including the introduction of a controversial cider excise to assist fiscal recovery from the effects of the war. But Bute was his own worst enemy. This is not to say that he did not suffer severe criticism from others. Indeed the torrent of virulence which flowed in the early 1760s exceeded what most contemporaries could recall. Much of it came not from Pitt or Newcastle but from Grub Street and City 'patriots'. These included a group of discontented young Whigs, several of them educated at Westminster in the generation which also produced William Cowper and Warren Hastings. Two of the most vitriolic were impecunious clergymen-poets: Charles Churchill and Robert Lloyd. Both were to die prematurely in 1764, the latter in debtor's gaol; but in 1762 and 1763 they were among Bute's most effective critics, in company with their common friend, John Wilkes. Their

[20] Lord E. Fitzmaurice, *Life of William, Earl of Shelburne* (2nd edn., 2 vols., London, 1875–6), i. 110–11.

political satires were not sophisticated. They accused Bute of plotting an Eleven Years Tyranny matching the design of Laud and Strafford and promising a new era of Tory rule. They throve on deep-laid prejudices, especially the detestation of Scots and all things Scottish.

A more robust temperament than Bute's would have borne these attacks, as Walpole had done. Nor was there much danger of respectable propertied opinion responding. Only in the gutter press was it supposed that Bute's friendship with the Princess Dowager of Wales was improper: the climate of court life under the new King actually verged on the puritanical. On Bute's advice, George III sacrificed his love for an aristocratic young woman, Lady Sarah Lennox, in order to marry a German princess, Sophia Charlotte of Mecklenburg, for whom he felt no initial attachment. This seemed in notable contrast with the moral standards of previous kings. Moreover Bute had able and articulate defenders. Hogarth, who had disdained party politics in a long career as the prince of print-makers, was ready to deploy his talents on behalf of Bute. His cynical comment on the factious politics of Pitt and Newcastle, *The Times*, was succeeded by scorching satirical portraits of Churchill and Wilkes which remain classics of political caricature. Samuel Johnson was also an enthusiastic supporter of the court, like other alienated Tories of George II's reign, a reborn royalist. And the *Briton*, the antagonist of Wilkes's *North Briton*, was edited by Tobias Smollett. Walpole had never had defenders of this stature.

Yet Bute proved unable to withstand the strain of incessant public exposure and criticism. Viewed objectively, his resignation seems a cynical act of betrayal. He did not see it as desertion, of course. Indeed he thought more in terms of yielding responsibility than power. His role would be one of guidance from behind the scenes, offering the superior wisdom of a statesman for whom the actual conduct of office would merely have been tedious. He was to persist in this dangerous and impracticable ambition for two, perhaps three, years. Fortunately, the King, growing in confidence and coming to understand the limitations of Bute's advice, gradually emancipated himself. By the summer of 1765 Bute's influence was slight. A year later it was completely at an end. But the dark legacy of the original design lingered on. There grew up that pervasive myth of a sinister influence 'behind the curtain', which proved almost impossible to eradicate. Interested men could pretend, and some disinterested men could believe, that true authority was wielded by Bute, whatever the nominal responsibility of the ministers of the day. In the short run this had a destabilizing effect. Bute had collected a substantial body of followers in the first two years of the reign. Some were close adherents, Scotsmen like Gilbert Elliot and James Oswald; others were merely Court and Treasury men who saw Bute as the true successor to Walpole and Newcastle, men such as Jeremiah Dyson, the foremost authority on Commons procedure, and Lord North, son of a former Tory, but also cousin to the Duke of Newcastle, and a future Prime Minister. These were the King's Friends: the term was not new nor was the mentality which went with it, the mentality of the courtier-placemen. But Walpole and the Pelhams had managed to integrate this type into the conventional politics of the Whig establishment. While Bute maintained a shadowy political presence his friends were under a constant temptation to remain a body apart, ever watchful for an opportunity to separate the King from his ministers.

The King's Friends were not exclusively responsible for the political instability which marked the 1760s. Pitt bore a measure of blame: after 1761 he would co-operate with none, yet his political prestige and parliamentary weight made it almost impossible to form a lasting ministry without him. More important still was the controversy which marked the reappearance of party divisions, albeit in a new form. Newcastle, by temperament and experience unsuited to opposition, was forced by the young men who had followed him out of office to take an increasingly belligerent stance. In this he was supported by the King's uncle, the Duke of Cumberland. Cumberland's passion for horse-racing kept him in close touch with the Whip grandees, for some of whom Westminster and Newmarket were more or less interchangeable venues of social and political life. A club was formed, Wildman's, to provide the kind of focus which the Cocoa Tree had given the Tories in past decades, and some tentative parliamentary pacts were negotiated. William Dowdeswell, as leader of the West Country campaign against the cider excise, was eventually to become a close friend of the most promising of the Whig magnates after the death of Devonshire in 1764, the Marquess of Rockingham. Rockingham was a descendant of Strafford, and Dowdeswell was accounted an old-style Tory. Yet the party which they were to lead felt itself to be the true inheritor of Revolution Whiggism.

These self-proclaimed champions of the Whig tradition characterized the court and its supporters as Tories. This was an artificial distinction in the circumstances of the 1760s. Most of George III's supporters were of impeccable Whig background, and Toryism no longer represented a coherent creed, let alone a party organization. To many the Whigs seemed more like an aristocratic clique than the lineal descendants of Shaftesbury and Sidney. Yet the sheer repetition of party polemic gradually lent the force of custom to the distinction. It was years, decades even, before these divisions hardened sufficiently to resemble the old Whig–Tory conflict, but in retrospect it is plain that the process was begun in 1762. Perhaps party more than ever needed justification at this time. With a young King on the throne there was no 'reversionary interest', no Prince of Wales capable of forming a natural rallying point of opposition. Nobody in his right mind would have looked to a future reign for political advancement. This deprived opposition of something of its legitimacy, and injected a measure of frustration and bitterness into the activities of the young Whigs. More important still, the disappearance of Jacobitism changed the terms on which government and opposition operated. It was no longer possible for the court to dismiss opposition as a dynastic threat; criticism of a Hanoverian regime had ceased to be tantamount to treachery.

WILKES, GRENVILLE, AND THE AMERICAN COLONIES

The career of John Wilkes clearly demonstrates the importance of these changes. Wilkes's journalism was certainly brutal, and as MP for Aylesbury and a dependant of Lord Temple, he could readily be identified with the opposition leaders. His activities would probably have provoked a hostile reaction from government at any time in the previous two reigns, and the fact that Wilkes was known both for his moral failings and disreputable friends made him seem an unlikely hero of the populace. Against him the ministry issued a 'general warrant', permitting the arrest of any of those involved in the publication of Wilkes's paper, the *North Briton*. The offending issue, Number 45, had directly criticized the King in connection with the supposed deficiencies of the Peace of Paris. There followed a series of arrests and Wilkes himself was committed to the Tower. The resulting storm of protest, in and out of Parliament, startled the ministers. But in retrospect it seems less astonishing. General warrants had a shaky legal basis, deriving ultimately from the Licensing Act of Charles II, which had lapsed in 1695. In due course, the courts were to pronounce them illegal. Ironically they had been utilized by Pitt, Newcastle, and other 'Revolution Whigs' under George I and George II. But what had seemed legitimate when employed against alleged Jacobites was now seen by Whig eyes in a new light.

The summer of 1763 proved boisterous, especially in the City. 'Number 45' became the symbol of the Englishman's liberty under threat from the malignity of Bute. Wilkes himself pleaded his parliamentary privilege as an MP against his imprisonment and even obtained damages against ministers for the seizure of his papers. Thereafter his fortunes changed. The discovery of an obscene and blasphemous 'Essay on Woman' which could be laid to his authorship made him vulnerable to renewed prosecution. He was also wounded in a duel to which he had been cynically challenged by a supporter of the ministry. His flight to France and subsequent outlawry made it easy for Grenville to secure his expulsion from the Commons. None the less, many MPs, including some of the Tory country gentlemen who now supported the court, were dismayed by the authoritarian implications of the general warrants. On opposition motions to make them unlawful forthwith, Grenville was hard put to maintain his parliamentary majority.

The fate of the warrants was decided in a series of judicial determinations arising from actions brought by those of Wilkes's associates who had suffered along with him. In one of these cases, *Entick* v. *Carrington*, in 1765, Pitt's friend Camden, Lord Chief Justice of the Common Pleas, gave a crushing and decisive verdict against their legality. They were not employed again until their revival by statute in 1936. There was much distaste among propertied men for Wilkes, and it is possible to exaggerate both the extent of public support for his views, and his importance in the radical tradition. However, his case remains striking testimony to the novel form of political controversy evolving in the new reign. It also reveals how comprehensively George III had failed in his desire to unite the politicians and initiate a new era of patriotic harmony. Paradoxically it was his enemies Newcastle and Pitt and his grandfather George II who had come closest, during the years of wartime coalition, to the prize of which he and Bute dreamed. But perhaps George III did not dream for long. The rearing experience of the early years of his reign meant that he grew up quickly as a politician. The politics of George II's reign had vanished forever; and if the politics of George III's were not what the King intended neither were they to be determined by his over-mighty subjects.

Bute's successor George Grenville will forever be remembered as the author of the American Stamp Act and thereby the initiator of that fateful train of events which led to the dismemberment of the first British empire. Yet the stamp tax was only a part of a coherent body of legislation for the colonies, most of it expressing conventional wisdom about the principles on which the empire enlarged in the Seven Years War was to be governed. The Currency Act of 1764 extended to the colonies of the southern American seaboard restrictions on the emission of paper currency which had been applied to New England in 1751: it primarily served the interest of British merchants with bitter experience of giving long credit to customers who paid their bills with a depreciating currency. It could also be portrayed as a necessary restraint on the fiscal irresponsibility of colonial assemblies reluctant to tax their own constituents. The American Mutiny Act of 1765 provided for military discipline in the colonies; it was meant to solve a problem which had vexed governments even before the Seven Years War and which had previously been dealt with on an *ad hoc* basis. It proved controversial, especially in New York, where many troops were based; it would have proved still more controversial if George III's advice and the pressure of the opposition had not led ministers to drop a plan for quartering army officers and soldiers on private householders. The Sugar Act of 1764 could be seen as bringing a new realism to the regulation of foreign trade with America. The Molasses Act of 1733 had set a prohibitive duty on foreign sugar, and positively stimulated that illicit trade which had offended British administrators during the Seven Years War. The Act of 1764 reduced the duty from 6d. per gallon to 3d. with the clear intention of collecting it. Even the Stamp Act was but the practical application of notions of taxation which had been in the air for some years, and which had been closely studied by government since the beginning of the new reign.

Whether Grenville should have foreseen the consequences of his legislation is debatable. The Sugar Act began with a preamble, unlike its predecessor of 1733, which included the 'give and grant' formula of taxing legislation rather than the conventional formula of commercial regulations. This did not go unnoticed in New England. The Stamp Act itself was the clearest possible assertion of the right to tax, though it was an impost on legal transactions, newspapers, and dice, rather than a direct tax on property. It provoked one of the great debates in the history of political thought, which began as a discussion of parliamentary representation, and eventually turned into a controversy about the basis of civil association and sovereignty. Grenville proposed the stamp tax in 1764 but postponed its implementation for a year, a concession which later gave rise to dispute about his intentions. It seems unlikely that he was seriously concerned to give the colonies or their agents in London an opportunity to suggest an alternative. The tax itself was not expected to bring in more than £60,000 per annum, but he was plainly aware of its importance as a precedent. In his speech introducing it on 6 February 1765 he claimed that Parliament had unlimited powers of legislation and taxation and that arguments about representation were irrelevant. 'The Parliament of Great Britain virtually represents the whole Kingdom.'[21] Here was a claim which was to have widespread repercussions, not merely in America, where few even of Britain's friends were much impressed by the notion that in some mysterious way the colonists were comprehended in the constituent body which Parliament represented, but in Britain itself, where, as Grenville candidly admitted in the same speech, 'not a twentieth part of the people are actually represented'.[22]

Grenville was a lawyer. In a famous characterization Edmund Burke later identified his legal and administrative training as unconducive to enlightened government. 'Mr. Grenville thought better of the wisdom and power of human legislation than in truth it deserves. He conceived, and many conceived along with him, that the flourishing trade of this country was greatly owing to law

---

[21] P. D. G. Thomas, ed., *Parliamentary Diaries of Nathaniel Ryder, 1764–7* (Camden Miscellany, xxiii, Camden 4th ser., vol. 7), p. 254.
[22] Ibid.

and institution, and not quite so much to liberty.'[23] The criticism was just. One of the features of Grenville's tenure of the Treasury was the new impetus which he gave to the collection of customs duties and the enforcement of trading prohibitions. Not merely in America, but also in the West Indies, where his instructions were blamed for bringing to a halt a highly profitable but technically illegal trade with Spanish America, his measures caused much irritation. He had no sense that there was more to the government of a great empire than rules and regulations.

Ironically, in view of his historical reputation, Grenville's American programme was not controversial in parliamentary terms. Only a handful of opposition MPs opposed the stamp tax in 1765, and even these went out of their way to express their approval of his other measures for the colonies. Where controversy did occur, Grenville showed skill, determination, and courage, qualities which made the conduct of Bute a little earlier seem all the more pusillanimous. Wilkes's expulsion in January 1764 had been carried by a majority of 162; thereafter his absence in France permitted opposition to concentrate on the constitutional aspects of his predicament, particularly when it became clear that the judiciary itself would not support the legality of general warrants. In the two successive sessions of 1764 and 1765 the government was hard pressed when motions were put condemning such warrants. That of 18 February 1764 was defeated by only 232 votes to 218; that of 19 January 1765 by 224 to 185. There were uncomfortable consequences. Opposition scrutinized the powers of the Crown's law officers, as well as those of the Secretaries of State. The Attorney-General's right to initiate prosecutions in the Court of King's Bench was singled out for attack. The King's vindictiveness in dismissing army officers who voted against general warrants in Parliament involved one of the heroes of the Seven Years War, General Conway, and gave rise to criticism closely resembling that which Walpole had provoked by his action against military men in Parliament in 1733. Yet Grenville endured these attacks with aplomb.

His success was built on long experience of the House of Commons and evident competence in administrative matters.

[23] P. Langford, ed., *The Writings and Speeches of Edmund Burke*, ii: *Party, Parliament, and the American Crisis, 1766–1774* (Oxford, 1981), p. 432.

Grenville's dual attention to patronage and policy recalled the regimes of Walpole and Pelham, and seemed to offer something of the same order of stability. Particularly striking was his appeal to the independents, many of them former Tories. For a stalwart Whig with the name of Grenville to attract the support of knights of the shire who, only a decade before, might still have been accounted Jacobites, was not quite as surprising as it seemed. The Grenvilles had spent much of the reign of George II in opposition and were used to co-operating with Tories. But it was also a matter of policy. Grenville was sober, solid, and conservative. He had an obsession with thrift and economy which made him the darling of the country gentlemen, and which proved invaluable in the aftermath of the war. The Peace had reduced expenditure, but not so rapidly as Parliament and public expected. There was also a greatly expanded National Debt, serviced by an alarming proportion of the peacetime budget: in 1763 there were many unfunded debts, run up on votes of credit, and requiring unpopular new taxation or economies to bring them under control. The Seven Years War had added as much to the national indebtedness as the entire accumulation from 1691 to 1727. The peacetime budget of 1764 was almost exactly twice that of 1739. Grenville survived by an exercise in good housekeeping rather than by fiscal innovation. He also took some controversial decisions, notably to retain the unpopular cider excise and to introduce American taxation. In any event both in the press and in Parliament his political stature grew.

How did a minister with sterling personal qualities and broad-based political support find himself out of office within two years of assuming it? Grenville suffered from a crucial deficiency: he had none of the arts of the courtier. His relationship with the King, revealed in remarkable detail in the diary dictated to his wife, was disastrous.[24] He constantly lectured and upbraided; the King, who had freely taken much of both from Bute, was not prepared to take either from a minister whom he had been reluctant to accept in the first instance, and whom he found pedantic and tedious. This animosity was made worse by Grenville's conviction that George III's hostility was to be explained by the influence of Bute. In fact Bute's increasingly sporadic correspondence with the King scarcely represented a threat to the ministry. None the less, it was hardly

[24] Printed in W. J. Smith, ed., *The Grenville Papers* (4 vols., London, 1852).

surprising that Grenville and his principal Cabinet colleagues, the Duke of Bedford, the Earl of Halifax, and the Earl of Sandwich, feared the Favourite. In Parliament their authority seemed increasingly secure; yet trivial disputes over patronage with the friends of Bute kept them in a fever of anxiety about their standing at court. To men of their generation the situation resembled that which had prevailed just twenty years earlier. Then, too, the Pelhams, secure in the House of Commons, had been challenged in the closet by one who claimed a special relationship with the King.

Events in the spring of 1765 seemed positively to conspire to recreate the crisis of 1745. The King fell gravely ill, with the first onset of the porphyria which modern medical diagnosis suggests was his genetic inheritance, and which later produced symptoms of mental derangement. Though he recovered, it seemed prudent to guard against a recurrence of his illness by providing for a regency. The King wished to determine his own choice of a regent; his ministers infuriated him by publicly endorsing the exclusion of his mother the Princess Dowager of Wales for this purpose. In the end George III had his way, but with the Act barely on the statute-book Grenville presented a ministerial ultimatum. He required the King to demonstrate once for all that Bute was no longer a power at court, by dismissing his brother James Stuart Mackenzie from his office of Keeper of the Scottish Privy Seal.

Extraordinary scenes ensued. On the part of the King there were tears and anguish. Such was his desperation that he appealed to the men whose subjugation had been his aim shortly before, in particular to Pitt. But Pitt had his own suspicions, of Bute, and also of his old adversary, the Duke of Cumberland. In this sudden crisis at court Cumberland found himself not only reconciled to his royal nephew but in some measure his intermediary. Negotiations broke down and for a few days Grenville revelled in his triumph. 'George the Third', wrote Horace Walpole, 'is the true successor of George the Second, and inherits all his grandfather's humiliations.'[25] But George III was not George II. On 23 May the King had accepted Grenville's demands. On 12 June he wrote once again to his uncle, with a plea to let 'the World see that this Country is not at the low Ebb that no Administration can be

[25] *Horace Walpole's Correspondence*, x. 153.

form'd without the Grenville family'.[26] Meetings were held at Newcastle's house in Surrey, and at Newmarket and Ascot, where Cumberland's young friends, men such as the Duke of Grafton, the Marquess of Rockingham, and the Duke of Portland, were to be found. After anxious debate the decision was made to form a ministry of 'Persons called from the *Stud* to the *State*, and transformed miraculously out of Jockies into Minister', as a hostile pamphleteer put it.[27] They were also, of course, the representatives of the great Whig families who had ruled England from 1714 to 1762 with barely a break. After only three years out of office the natural rulers of Hanoverian England were back.

ROCKINGHAM AND THE STAMP ACT CRISIS

The Rockingham ministry, or the Cumberland ministry as it might more appropriately be described during its first months in office, commenced in July 1765. It offered a new beginning for the King in his relations with the Old Whigs and raised hopes of an enduring political system. Yet the ministry lasted only twelve months. Partly this was a matter of its constitution. With the exception of the Duke of Newcastle, who was given office as Lord Privy Seal, the Cabinet manifestly lacked weight. Rockingham himself at the Treasury, his Secretaries of State the Duke of Grafton and Henry Conway, and his Chancellor of the Exchequer William Dowdeswell, were all inexperienced in affairs of state. George III eventually came to despise Rockingham's team, describing it as 'an administration of boys'.[28] But he gave it a fair wind to begin with, and never altogether forgot the debt he owed it for ridding him of the detested Grenville. It was policy rather than personnel which made the ministry so short-lived. Rockingham's strategy, revered by later generations of Whigs as a triumph of high principle, was regarded by contemporary observers as dangerously misconceived. Despite the appeals of the King and the warnings of Cumberland, Rockingham made it plain that Grenville's proscription of Bute's friends was to continue, with the additional animus deriving from the Slaughter of the Pelhamite Innocents in 1762. By no means all

---

[26] Sir J. Fortescue, ed., *Correspondence of King George III, 1760–83* (6 vols., London, 1927–8), i. 118.

[27] 'Anti-Sejanus' (James Scott) in *Public Advertiser*, 21 Sept. 1765.

[28] British Library, Add. MS 32976, fo. 325: Newcastle to Charles Yorke, 29 July 1766.

those contaminated by association with the Favourite were ejected, however. His most outspoken and therefore most vulnerable supporter in the royal household, Lord Denbigh, was relieved to discover as Master of the Harriers that his 'Bow wows' were safe, as he put it.[29] More importantly, experienced parliamentarians such as James Oswald and Gilbert Elliot were permitted to remain in office, strengthening the debating power of the administration. But Bute's former Chancellor of the Exchequer Lord Le Despenser was dismissed, and no attempt was made to reinstate Bute's own brother Stuart Mackenzie, whose victimization by Grenville had so infuriated the King. The result was inevitable: the King's Friends continued to regard themselves as a distinct party. Some of them, those out of office, felt free to oppose the ministers in Parliament; the remainder, still in office, were all too liable to mutiny on a signal from Bute or the King himself.

The Rockinghams remained suspicious of Bute's influence in the closet, though all the evidence available suggests that it was in decline. They were also fearful of the public opprobrium which they might incur by making an accommodation with men whom they had systematically opposed since 1762. If this was indeed high principle, they paid a high price for it. While Cumberland lived he contrived to limit the damage done at court. But after his death at the end of October 1765, the mutual suspicion, and even acrimony, which marked relations between the Whig ministers and the King's Friends grew until they finally destroyed the administration. Rockingham was not unaware of the danger in which he stood, but his own remedy was hardly the right one. By persuading Pitt to join him he hoped to defy both King and King's Friends alike. No doubt he assumed that the extraordinary prestige which still attached to Pitt's wartime reputation, as well as his overpowering oratory and his executive experience, would make the ministry's position impregnable. He was also well aware that there were many in his own party, including some of the most familiar names in the history of Hanoverian Whiggism, the Pelhams, the Onslows, the Townshends, who had little faith in the continuance of the government without the support of the Saviour of 1757. But courting Pitt proved as futile as persecuting Bute. Having refused to accept office under Cumberland, Pitt had no intention of doing so under Rockingham or Newcastle.

[29] British Library, Add. MS 35374, fo. 245: John Yorke to Lord Hardwicke, 20 July 1765.

Rockingham's repeated enquiries and approaches were rebuffed, merely enhancing the public impression of a ministry which was not only weak but conscious of its weakness.

It did not help that Rockingham found himself in the midst of an unprecedented imperial crisis within weeks of taking office. America's response to the Stamp Act took almost everyone by surprise. The defiance began in Virginia as early as May, turned to violence in Boston in August, and spread rapidly throughout the thirteen colonies and to the West Indies, rendering the authorities powerless to collect the stamp tax. A congress of colonial representatives met to co-ordinate an embargo on trade with Britain, designed to secure the repeal of the offending legislation. Nothing like it had occurred in the history of the British empire. Cumberland, who had a short way with rebels, thought of repressing American opposition by force. But neither the numbers nor disposition of troops in the colonies made this very practicable. Moreover, Rockingham had an instinct for compromise which chimed well with growing concern among merchants and manufacturers. 1765 was a year of diminished trade overseas and recession at home; it was easy to blame Grenville's pettifogging customs regulations for the former, and easier still to assert that colonial non-importation would aggravate the latter. By late December Rockingham was convinced of the advisability of repealing the Stamp Act, and gave every encouragement to the merchants who campaigned to persuade Parliament to that end. But the violence of the 'Sons of Liberty' in America made concession difficult. Over Christmas the ministers sought some device by which repeal might be conceded without provoking the charge that they were surrendering parliamentary sovereignty to a colonial mob. The resulting bill, suggested by the Attorney-General Charles Yorke, was modelled on the Irish Dependency Act of 1720: it involved a statutory declaration of Parliament's right to legislate for the colonies 'in all cases whatsoever'. This, then, was the formula to be put before Parliament: repeal, based on evidence that the Exchequer would gain little and British trade lose much by the stamp tax, accompanied by a face-saving assertion of legislative supremacy.

The King had doubts about the wisdom of repeal, and the King's Friends shared them, especially when Bute made a rare appearance in the Lords to denounce it. The King's Friends were by nature courtiers, their mentality formed by years in office; many of them were Scots, not a few were military men. All these categories were to support the authority of the mother country throughout the Anglo-American conflict. Rockingham tried hard to get the King on his side, but it was obvious that many placemen would vote against their own government's proposal. Against this, the mighty Pitt placed his weight behind repeal. In what turned out to be his last great speech in the House of Commons, he made an extraordinary attack on the Stamp Act in particular and on the taxation of colonies in general. He must, wrote one observer, be 'king William the Fourth, for he holds in the greatest contempt a law enacted by all the powers of the Legislature'.[30] His tirade was certainly not meant to assist the ministry. None the less he strengthened Rockingham's hand, making the minister's solution seem all the more of a compromise which avoided either of the extremes—enforcement of the stamp tax on the one hand, or complete surrender of Parliament's authority on the other. His impassioned and characteristically theatrical plea for repeal must also have influenced some wavering votes.

An ingenious campaign of persuasion was mounted in the House of Commons. In January and February a mass of evidence, oral and documentary, was presented to prove the close connection between the fate of the stamp tax and the well-being of the British economy. Country gentlemen were invited to believe that unemployment, dearth, and spiralling poor-rates were already in prospect thanks to Grenville's measures. If this were so it had more to do with the post-war slump than with American non-importation, which had barely commenced. But the case was skilfully orchestrated and featured some remarkable talents. Edmund Burke, as Rockingham's private secretary and newly elected MP for Wendover, was making his political début: he was responsible for much of the organization. Benjamin Franklin was one of the witnesses called to give evidence, and made a considerable impression. In the crucial division in the early hours of 22 February repeal was carried by 275 votes to 167, with independent MPs overwhelmingly in the majority, and a large number of placemen in the minority. Burke later remembered this as a heroic day in the history of Parliament, recalling the tumultuous

---

[30] *Selection from the Family Papers preserved at Caldwell* (Glasgow, 1854), Part ii, vol. ii, pp. 60–1: William Rouet to Baron Mure, 16 Jan. 1766.

scenes in the lobbies when victory was announced. 'We did fight that day and conquer.'[31] Rockingham boasted to the King of having been vindicated by 'Publick Opinion'.[32] From around the country came reports of rejoicing in the trading towns and congratulations for the ministers. They were repeated in America with one difference; there it was Pitt who was credited with the victory. The colonists also chose, for the most part, to ignore the Declaratory Act. It was subsequently argued in England that the repeal of the Stamp Act had represented a fatal step towards imperial downfall, creating in America the impression that Britain would never stand up to blackmail and intimidation by the colonies. Rockingham and Burke, on the contrary, always maintained that it had offered a sensible and enduring solution to the American problem, but for the folly of their successors in meddling with further schemes of taxation. On both sides the argument was hypothetical; it will never be resolved by any historical evidence.

In other respects the ministry's record was less controversial but also less impressive. Its foreign policy was more show than substance. Neither Prussia nor Russia displayed much interest in Rockingham's diplomatic overtures. There was some ritual posturing over the issues unresolved with the Bourbon powers, in particular the status of Dunkirk's fortifications. This was mainly for domestic consumption. With a knight of the shire for Worcester as Chancellor of the Exchequer, the objectionable elements in the cider excise were repealed and replaced by additional window duties. Some easy popularity was procured by the passage through the Commons of resolutions which condemned general warrants. More importantly, and largely owing to the pressure exerted by the ministry's new mercantile friends, the last weeks of the parliamentary session of 1766 saw some innovative commercial legislation. Grenville's notorious sugar duty was reduced to 1d. per gallon but was extended to British molasses imported into the colonies as well as foreign. This had the unnoticed consequence of turning a commercial regulation into a straightforward revenue measure. Americans, doubtless relieved to have the duty reduced, were slow to pick up this point. There was also a significant experiment in imperial commerce. In an attempt to meet complaints about the trade depression in the Caribbean, free ports were

[31] Writings and Speeches of Edmund Burke, ii. 443.
[32] Correspondence of George III, i. 275.

established, in Jamaica to open the trade with Spanish America, in Dominica to trade with the French islands. The object was to increase Britain's share of West Indian markets, and to attract much needed Spanish bullion. The practical results were limited, but it could be seen as a significant break with traditional mercantilist policy. Grenville indeed denounced it as an attack on the Navigation System.

Far from building on his parliamentary success, Rockingham allowed his political position to crumble. If anything he became more incensed than ever with the King's Friends, pressing the King for the expulsion of those who had failed to support him in Parliament. But George III was in no mood to humour his ministers further. He had been humiliated by Grenville, disregarded by Rockingham. Cumberland was dead, Bute was broken. It remained only to throw himself into the arms of Pitt. This proved less uncomfortable than he had feared. Pitt, too, needed no longer to think of Cumberland or Bute, let alone of Newcastle. Shorn of personal animosities his own rhetoric could be made to look very like the King's. It was born of the same disillusion with the politics of Pelham and Walpole, and had been nurtured by the same ideological climate of the 1750s: measures not men, the end of party under a patriot king. Above all it meant power for Pitt, for the first and only time, on his own terms. To his friends he trumpeted of his triumph; before the King he abased himself in letters of fawning obeisance. It was a bizarre spectacle, yet the ministerial arrangements made political sense. The King's Friends were reassured: Stuart Mackenzie was reinstated and Bute's relation by marriage, the Earl of Northumberland, received a dukedom, the highest honour which a Prime Minister could recommend or a King bestow. Rockingham left office with dignity at the end of July 1766. He remained unrealistic to the end, taking with him only the inner core of his party and encouraging the rest to serve under Pitt. He apparently expected to govern the new ministry from behind the scenes, a veritable Whig Bute. Newcastle, also out of office, in his case for the final time, was foolish enough to go along with this scheme, in the hope that by such means the Whig families to whom his long political career had been devoted might remain united. It was a forlorn hope.

THE CHATHAM MINISTRY

Pitt's power seemed complete in the summer of 1766. Certainly those who fancied themselves his rivals were quickly disillusioned. Bute took exception to the way in which the new minister and the King restored his friends to favour without consulting him personally, and penned the kind of tutor's reprimand which he had been accustomed to address to the young prince for a decade and more. He was stunned by George III's irritated reply and bitterly promised 'for your sake as well as my own, will never be thus importunate again'. 'As for my party, as it is termed that also is at an end.'[33] In later years the King came to look back on their relationship with loathing and more than a touch of self-contempt. His indoctrination by Bute had occupied perhaps five years: his re-education in the school of politics a further five. By 1766 he was emancipated from the former and capable of graduating from the latter. Rockingham's disenchantment followed shortly after Bute's; by the beginning of the parliamentary session, in November 1766, it was clear that Pitt would neither consult nor conciliate his predecessor in office. The banner of opposition was raised but it proved even more disappointing as a rallying point than Newcastle's unfurling of the Old Corps flag in 1762. Most of the young Whigs who had returned to office with Rockingham in July 1765 showed little inclination to leave it at his bidding. Many of them, indeed, were to become loyal supporters of George III and in time of Lord North, resuming their true place as Court and Treasury men. Rockingham's decision to oppose the ministry was not a negligible matter; his party included powerful magnates and some capable parliamentarians, led by Burke and Dowdeswell. It was also psychologically important, signifying a fateful division of what was left of the Whig tradition between the parties of Pitt and Rockingham. But it was hardly sufficient to bring down the new administration.

The main source of ministerial weakness proved to be internal. Pitt had a grandiose vision of the way in which he would command, deciding the grand lines of policy, infusing a spirit of confidence into the Cabinet, and delegating the detail of government to his juniors: Grafton, who had replaced Rockingham at the Treasury,

[33] R. Sedgwick, ed., *Letters from George III to Lord Bute, 1756–1766* (London, 1939), p. 258.

Shelburne, whose attachments in turn to Henry Fox, Bute, and now Pitt had already made his name a byword for treachery, and Conway, who remained leader of the House of Commons. Pitt himself took a peerage as Earl of Chatham. The resemblance to Pulteney's notorious translation to the Lords in 1742 had unpleasant reverberations in the press and in the City. Its main significance was that it left the management of the Commons to the irresolute Conway, the unstable Charles Townshend, as Chancellor of the Exchequer, and William Beckford, Pitt's dependable supporter in the City. Beckford held no office himself but on occasion startled the House by behaving as if he were the personal emissary of the Prime Minister. Perhaps Pitt's decision was based on self-knowledge; he would never have made a Treasury minister, nor could he have coped with the daily requirements of Commons debate and management. On the other hand, he proved far from comfortable in the Lords, where his old rival Mansfield consistently outpointed and occasionally overpowered him. More-over, his health needed more than a respite from the hurly-burly of the lower house to save it. As in 1756, he suffered some kind of nervous collapse, euphoria giving way to depression and inactivity. Worrying rumours were spread about his mental state. It became plain that his recovery would be long delayed. Much of the next two years was occupied by anxious debate among his friends and excited speculation among his enemies about the prospects of his ever wielding the power which he had grasped.

The magic of Pitt's name did not compensate for his absence. The re-establishment of the Anglo-Prussian alliance on which he placed so much dependence proved impossible; Frederick's claim that he had kept Britain at arm's length only because he had been treated so treacherously by Bute in 1762 was exposed as the fraud it was. From across the Atlantic came alarming news. At Boston attempts to secure compensation for the sufferers in the Stamp Act riots met with violent resistance; at New York the implementa-tion of Grenville's Mutiny Act provoked still sterner opposition. Even the elements seemed to conspire against the administration. A disastrous harvest at home, and the hiatus caused by the change of ministry, found the government unequipped with legislation to prevent the exportation of home-grown grain and keep supplies of food flowing. The Cabinet's decision to impose an embargo by means of Royal Proclamation was prudent. But it was imprudent to claim, as they did when Parliament met, that they had good legal grounds for employing the royal prerogative in this way. Their arguments recalled that dispensing and suspending power which, as used by James II, had served to provoke the Revolution of 1688. This came oddly from a supposedly 'patriot ministry'. The Lord Chancellor, Camden, conqueror of general warrants, was now the apologist for what he described as 'but a forty days tyranny', referring to the time which elapsed between the Proclamation and the meeting of Parliament. There were sufficient doubts among independent MPs to force the ministers to bow to the pressure and accept an Indemnity Act endorsing their action while implicitly denying its legality.

The great issue of the session quickly dwarfed such troubles. The latter part of 1766 was marked by hectic activity on the London stock-market, most of it connected with the speculations of East India investors, as the financial implications of Clive's decision to turn the Company into a territorial power were fully worked out. The directors raised dividends in anticipation of windfall profits, public enthusiasm for the stock became uncontrollable, and there followed the inevitable cycle of reckless overconfidence succeeded by sudden collapse. As in the South Sea crisis, losses were spectacular and involved small investors as well as great. As in 1720, too, it was plain that Parliament would have to intervene. Chatham envisaged a sweeping assertion of the State's right to control the Company's Indian possessions, followed by a settlement which would preserve the commercial prospects of the East India trade while bringing handsome subsidies to the Exchequer. But neither he nor Beckford put up a detailed scheme for the consideration of MPs and the Company's proprietors, the latter body more numerous and not less factious than the former. Rockingham and Grenville, in an unlikely but effective alliance, were able to step forward as the defenders of chartered rights against the prerogative of the Crown and the corrupt designs of its ministers.

The Cabinet drifted: in the Commons, Conway and Townshend seemed to offer contradictory proposals. This disarray was exploited both by the Company and the opposition. After prolonged debate and clandestine negotiation, a settlement was agreed, and propelled, or rather paddled, through Parliament. The Company was compelled to restrict its dividend and discourage speculative investment in its stock; it was also required to contribute £400,000 per annum to the Exchequer in return for its commercial and propertied privileges. In retrospect, this was a landmark in the history of the empire, the first formal intervention in the affairs of India by the British State. At the time no one supposed that it represented a permanent answer to the problem created in the East by the Seven Years War. Nor did it exhibit the grand conceptions, the firm direction, and the incisive action expected of Chatham.

These qualities seemed to be noticeably lacking in general. The ministry's colonial measures, which scarcely fitted Chatham's reputation as a friend of America, have long puzzled historians. They signified the limited nature of the Chathamite commitment to colonial liberties in the sense that the colonists themselves conceived them. They also revealed the Cabinet's lack of cohesion and the strong tide of anti-Americanism running in the House of Commons. The back-bench country gentlemen had voted to repeal the Stamp Act, not to abandon British authority, nor even to drop the idea of a colonial revenue. Townshend, a political weathervane but also a former member of that Board of Trade which Halifax had induced to take America seriously in the early 1750s, devised an ingenious scheme. It involved taxing a number of commodities imported into the colonies from Britain: glass, lead, paint, paper, and tea. He also established an American Board of Customs at Boston, to collect the duties, and allocated the resulting revenue to the payment of official salaries in the royal colonies. The duties were cunningly devised to meet American objections. Benjamin Franklin had given the Commons the impression, during his influential testimony against the Stamp Act, that the colonies would not oppose taxes which arose from the regulation of trade, only those directly levied on American property. Though their plain intention was revenue, Townshend's duties could be presented as commercial regulations. They aroused little controversy in Parliament.

More interest attached to Shelburne's policy for disciplining recalcitrant colonies. Massachusetts Bay legislation to indemnify those involved in the Stamp Act riots of 1765, as a condition of compensating their victims, was disallowed. New York was ordered to comply with the terms of the Mutiny Act or have its assembly suspended by Act of Parliament. Feeling ran high in the Commons as evidence of colonial insubordination mounted. The ministry needed all its resources to fend off sterner measures still, including Grenville's suggestion of a Test Act which would force all American office-holders to declare their allegiance to Parliament. Nor did the end of the parliamentary session bring respite. Townshend died suddenly in September 1767. Without him the Cabinet was dependent on Conway, whose enthusiasm for ministerial responsibility was ebbing fast. The newspapers were filled with rumours of a change of administration. Rockingham, Grenville, and Bedford engaged in a series of inconclusive negotiations. These stood little chance of success, however much they alarmed the ministers. There were no less than four former Prime Ministers more or less active in politics in 1767, Newcastle, Bute, Grenville, and Rockingham, and of these the last two were both intent on office. Neither would serve under the other. The King would have fought hard to resist both but found himself under intense pressure from Grafton to strengthen his administration before the general election which was due in 1768. The solution, adopted in December 1767, was a junction with the Duke of Bedford and his friends. They were not very numerous in either House but they were disciplined and dependable. They also included at least one powerful, bullying Commons speaker, Richard Rigby. Above all their leader was not a candidate for the premiership; he sought only a share of the spoils for his followers. Both King and Cabinet accepted the need for the Bedford alliance, *faute de mieux*. But Chatham's supporters, Shelburne and Conway, were less enthusiastic than Grafton. Everyone knew that without the captain Chatham on the bridge their vessel was adrift. A crew which included a number of Bedfords, supporters of the Peace, of general warrants, and of the Stamp Act, seemed likely to provide direction but not to the desired destination.

THE MIDDLESEX ELECTION

The general election in the spring of 1768 proved to be a quiet one. A lead from the Treasury was largely wanting. Grafton had not called an election to strengthen the ministry or to take his opponents by surprise, but because the Septennial Act required him to do so. Moreover his electoral management was incompetent. Three men, Walpole, Pelham, and Newcastle, had between them managed every election since 1722. In the 1760s the successive changes of ministry and the inexperience of some of the men who had to preside over the Treasury damaged the continuity and coherence of political strategy. Grafton himself was distracted by his affair with Anne Parsons: 'the prime minister of Great Britain', his critic Junius later wrote, 'in a rural retirement, and in the arms of faded beauty, had lost all memory of his Sovereign, his country and himself'.[34] His wife publicly humiliated him by eloping with the Earl of Upper Ossory. After divorcing her, later, in 1769, Grafton was to marry Elizabeth Wrottesley, significantly a relative of the Duke of Bedford. In any event Grafton found little in the political implications of a general election to disturb him. From a party standpoint, indeed, it was a confused election. Since 1767 the Rockingham and Grenville parties had found themselves collaborating in opposition, after five years of bitter hostilities. In administration there was also a curious alliance of Chathamites, Bedfords, and King's Friends, each at one time or another enemies of the other two during the previous Parliament. When issues of principle cropped up as they did in Norfolk, where the questions of general warrants and the Stamp Act were aired, they divided both opposition and government, making it impossible for the party leaders to mount a systematic campaign.

The security which Grafton had gained by his alliance with the Bedfords was unaffected by the results from the constituencies. There were, none the less, eighty-four contested elections, more than in any general election since 1741. Almost all were essentially local struggles for supremacy, but a number arose from the intervention of outsiders in boroughs known to be particularly vulnerable to bribery. In the most widely publicized of these cases the intruders were so-called 'nabobs', men who had made their fortunes in India. Nineteen such candidates were returned to Westminster in 1768. This was not a large number, but the incursion of the nabobs, like so many carpet-baggers before them, provoked a storm of protest from the established interests with which they interfered.

Even the nabobs seemed less worrying than the activities of Sir James Lowther. Lowther, as a son-in-law of the Earl of Bute, automatically attracted notice. It did not help that he was a

---

[34] J. Cannon, ed., *The Letters of Junius* (Oxford, 1978), p. 63.

megalomaniac. By dynastic accident, he represented the coming together of three distinct branches of the Lowther families of Westmorland and Cumberland, a fusion which brought him immense wealth and influence. In 1768 his object was nothing less than a monopoly of the parliamentary representation of his two home counties. With friends in the ministry, and, as others said, secret influence in the shape of Bute, he naturally turned to the Treasury for assistance. It was forthcoming in the form of a lease of certain Crown estates in Cumberland. These lands had been granted to the Portland family by William III but it was alleged that the grant had been technically invalid. Lowther's concern was with the electoral influence which they carried. His opponents claimed that the royal prerogative was being used to invade the propertied rights of the subject and advance the power of the Favourite. On the score of property at least, this argument had some support. When Sir George Savile, friend of the Duke of Portland and the very embodiment of independent Whiggism, laid a bill before the Commons in February 1768 to safeguard the rights of Crown lessees, he was defeated only narrowly, by 134 votes to 114. In the elections which followed a few weeks later Lowther employed his new influence in the most high-handed and brutal way. This proved counterproductive. In his own bailiwick he provoked a reaction which reduced his following in Parliament; he even suffered the humiliation of being unseated in his own constituency of Cumberland. In 1769 Savile's bill was successful and in 1776, after extended legal proceedings, Portland's claim to the disputed estates was vindicated by the courts. In the mean time, remote though they appeared, the affairs of Cumberland and Westmorland seemed likely to present the main focus of interest in the general election. Certainly they would have done so, if John Wilkes had not returned from France at this moment.

This was Wilkes's last throw. His ignominious exile had provided him only with occasional hand-outs from loyal friends and nervous patriots. That he would achieve a greater return from the election seemed unlikely. Yet his decision to stand for the City of London aroused much interest, and perhaps a little apprehension. The result seemed to confirm the view of those who believed that his day was over. London was pre-eminently the home of popular politics but its government was highly structured and its electoral machinery carefully controlled. Even a Wilkes would need time and the assistance of established figures to break into this turbulent but by no means undisciplined world of great oligarchs and small tradesmen. But he did not give up. The City result was declared, with his name at the bottom of the poll, on 25 March. Almost immediately it was put forward for Middlesex. There, three days later, he was returned with a large majority over two more conventional candidates with property in the county.

Wilkes's election was marked by riotous celebrations in the streets of London. There was some surprise at his success. The expelled member for the corrupt borough of Aylesbury had become knight of the shire for 'the first of counties', hitherto represented by dignified and wealthy country gentlemen. Middlesex had none of the regimented politics of the City. Instead it had a few substantial landlords who could answer for handfuls rather than hundreds of votes (though one of them, the Duke of Northumberland, aspired to control its destiny by such means), and great numbers of forty-shilling freeholders who were as remote from the ancient concept of the English freeholder as they could be. By accident or design Wilkes had found the only county which might elect him, as well as the one that mattered most. In any other he would have been shunned by the county community, and ignored by the great mass of rural tenantry. In Middlesex freeholders were likely to be tradesmen, shopkeepers, innholders, craftsmen, small businessmen, even labourers—anyone, in short, owning a small freehold in an essentially urban county, where property was widely distributed and at a time when inflation had rendered the qualification of forty shillings derisory. And there were no wards, no common councilmen, no elaborate organization for delivering votes. Wilkes polled well among the small men, especially those from the riverside districts just to the east of London and from the urban parishes which crowded the City on every side. He offered no political programme—only the memory of general warrants and the rhetoric of liberty. But these proved sufficient. It was perhaps the most famous single election result in the history of British parliaments, and the Middlesex freeholders who brought it about did so in a spirit of plebeian libertarianism which confounded respectable opinion. It was conventional in the eighteenth century to pay lip-service to the broad base of propertied politics. In practice, men of very small property rarely found their way on to the political stage. In 1768 for a short, tempestuous time they crowded it out, with chastening effects on those accustomed to play the principal roles.

In retrospect it is obvious that the ministry would have done well not to involve itself in a new Wilkesite controversy. Even at the time of Wilkes's election for Middlesex there were heads wise enough to grasp this. Horace Walpole, writing on 31 March, thought 'the House of Commons is the place where he can do the least hurt, for he is a wretched speaker, and will sink to contempt, like Admiral Vernon, who I remember just such an illuminated hero'.[35] The most coherent account of the ministerial discussions by any of those directly concerned comes from the pen of the Prime Minister himself. But Grafton's autobiography was written long after the event, and was influenced by a natural desire to escape censure for the mishandling of the Middlesex election. According to him the King did not press proceedings against Wilkes, the Cabinet entertained no disposition to persecute him, and it was only the threat of perpetual popular disorder which compelled the government to take action.[36] This does not quite carry conviction. Side by side in the published correspondence of George III are two crucial letters. One, from Grafton to the King on 22 April, announced the Cabinet's decision 'that Mr. Wilkes should not be allowed to sit in Parliament if it could be avoided by any Means justifiable by Law and the Constitution'. The second, from the King to Lord North three days later, insisted that, despite what he described as North's 'hatred of Lawless proceeding', Wilkes's expulsion was 'very essential and must be effected'.[37] In fact to the extent that the ministry held its hand in the spring and summer of 1768, it was guided not by prudent political tactics and an innate moderation, but rather by uncertainty about the legal position, succeeded by a loss of initiative in confronting the popular opposition out of doors. Probably it was Mansfield, shortly to face Wilkes in the Court of King's Bench, who warned against action in Parliament before the legal questions had been clarified. For the worsening of the position out of doors the ministry only had itself to blame. The precedent it had in mind was that of John Ward, an MP expelled after conviction for gross

---

[35] *Horace Walpole's Correspondence*, xxiii. 8.
[36] Sir W. R. Anson, *Autobiography and Political Correspondence of Augustus Henry Third Duke of Grafton* (London, 1898), pp. 195–6.
[37] *Correspondence of George III*, ii. 20–1.

corruption in 1726. This was a highly inappropriate parallel. Ward had no talent as a demagogue, was convicted of an offence detested by the mob (he was seriously injured in the pillory), and did not attempt to regain his seat in the Commons.

The ministers should have foreseen that Wilkes would not behave like Ward forty-two years earlier. They might be forgiven, however, for failing to anticipate the adroitness with which he exploited his legal rights. Before Mansfield and his colleagues on the bench Wilkes was magnificently insolent: he openly gloried in his 'North Briton 45', and brushed aside his blasphemous obscenity in the 'Essay on Woman' as a 'mere *Ludicrous production*'.[38] He was assisted by the delays and anomalies of the judicial process. On his first day in court, 20 April, he surrendered himself to justice. However, Mansfield, to the consternation of the Crown's lawyers, ruled that his outlawry could only be brought before the court by the Attorney-General: Wilkes himself was temporarily a legal nonentity. Eventually the outlawry was reversed on a technicality, thereby removing at least one ground for immediate expulsion from Parliament. In the mean time proceedings were protracted. On 18 June, he was fined and imprisoned for the two offences of seditious and obscene libel; on this occasion and to the fury of the King, 'He Affected Ease and Indifference by picking his Teeth and talking to those near him while Mr Justice Yates was animadverting upon the Nature of His Crimes.'[39] By this time he had had ample opportunity to organize his friends and supporters. Popular disorder during the Middlesex election itself had stayed largely within the bounds of conventional electoral boisterousness; a more sinister note marked the riots which followed the election in the City. The Lord Mayor Thomas Harley, a supporter of the court, showed resourcefulness in suppressing them, but the animus against government was marked.

Thereafter, matters grew steadily more serious. Some of the worst excesses were committed by the rioting coal-heavers of Shadwell and Wapping: in their murderous attack on the house of the coal 'undertaker' John Green, they linked the name of Wilkes with their cause. In reality Wilkes's stand had little connection with the grievances of the coal-heavers and the other discontented trades which resorted to violence at this time, let alone with the

---

[38] Ibid. ii. 21.
[39] Ibid. ii. 30.

riotous assault on a brothel in Goodman's Fields which also alarmed Londoners in April 1768. None the less the ministry was understandably nervous. The Westminster magistracy had first requested troops as early as 31 March, and detachments were present in Shadwell and Goodman's Fields. A succession of orders in the latter part of April brought reinforcements, some of them from as far afield as Canterbury and Lewes. It was a fair prediction that they would be needed at the King's Bench Prison where Wilkes was committed during his trial, and where, indeed, he was eventually to serve his sentence. On 10 May, the date on which the new Parliament was to be opened, and with rumours current that Wilkes would be released to take his seat, large crowds gathered in St George's Fields, outside the prison. Accounts of the numbers involved vary wildly. But it is certain that many thousands of enthusiastic supporters of Wilkes were present, and that the military were provoked to drastic action. In the resulting 'massacre' some ten or twelve 'rioters' were killed by the fire of a company of grenadiers; at least one of them, William Allen, was said to be entirely innocent of any involvement in the violence which had gone on. After this there were renewed riots in the City, and a newly erected sawmill owned by a court merchant, Charles Dingley, was destroyed. The shock of the massacre subsequently brought about a reduction in mob activity, but against this background the decision to imprison Wilkes was merely a signal for renewed hostilities, with Wilkes adopting a pose of triumph rather than defeat. His 'Address to Middlesex', issued immediately after Mansfield had passed sentence, contrived to be vacuous but inspiring. Revelling in his outlawry and his campaign against general warrants, he promised his electors that on his release he would spend the rest of his life as a 'freeman among you', defending their rights in 'this Glorious cause'.

The rhetoric of Wilkes was an important feature of his appeal. The liberties which he defended were not those of the European Enlightenment but those of the ancient English constitution. His emphasis on resistance to oppression rather than incitement to innovation appealed to the patriotic tradition of the capital. The horrors of militarism came in for predictable censure. Lord Barrington, as Secretary of War, was imprudent enough publicly to thank his troops for their part in suppressing disorder; more damaging still was the letter of 17 April which Lord Weymouth as Secretary of State had addressed to the Surrey magistrates, urging the use of troops to control public disturbances. Wilkes got hold of a copy of the letter and published it as evidence of calculated preparation for 10 May: this achieved the dual purpose of provoking the government and rallying his supporters.

Wilkesites, backed by subscriptions and collections in the clubs, coffee-houses, and taverns of London, made shrewd use of the law. The money thus raised was employed to mount an impudent prosecution of one of the magistrates who had called in the troops on 10 May, Samuel Gillam. Gillam proved a doughty antagonist and there was little likelihood that he would be found guilty of murder for doing his duty as a magistrate. But it was easy to allege that he was being corruptly protected by government. The same was said with still more plausibility when the troops accused of killing Allen were tried at Guildford in August. The evidence proved inadequate to convict, but it did not help that all those involved were Scottish grenadiers, nor that one of them thought to have been responsible for shooting Allen had vanished without trace before he could be arraigned.

In much of this the court was distinctly unlucky, and the year ended on the same note of unpredictable misfortune. Wilkes's colleague as knight of the shire for Middlesex, the country gentleman George Cooke, died in June, exhausted by the strains of the general election. At the resulting by-election, held shortly before the next session of Parliament in early December, there was an opportunity to make new propaganda for Wilkes. The Chathamite lawyer Sergeant Glynn was elected against a little-known courtier, who had also been Wilkes's opponent at the general election, Sir William Beauchamp Proctor. But the election mattered less than the ferment which accompanied it. As in March, there were violent scenes on the road from London to Brentford, culminating in some rough-house tactics by Proctor's mob, in which a supporter of Wilkes was killed. At the resulting trial, two Irish chairmen were found guilty of murder, but after a series of respites, on the basis of doubt about the medical evidence in the case, they received the King's pardon. Wilkes's friends were duly cynical about this exercise of the royal prerogative; among them was a correspondent of the *Public Advertiser*, in the issue of 21 November, who signed himself 'Junius'. In this, the first of a series of vitriolic attacks on ministers, he discussed the eagerly awaited parliamentary debate on Wilkes. 'In the present instance', his letter ended, 'the Duke of Grafton may possibly find that he has played a foolish Game. He rose by Mr. Wilkes's Popularity, and it is not improbable that he may fall by it.'[40]

THE FALL OF GRAFTON

Grafton's problems were not restricted to Wilkes. Since the junction with the Bedfords in December 1767 his Cabinet had been an uneasy coalition. Grafton saw himself as Chatham's standard-bearer but increasingly seemed to be coming under the influence of the Bedfords. With Shelburne his relations were especially bad. Shelburne's mixture of personal insecurity and intellectual pretentiousness made him a difficult colleague and he was concerned more to safeguard his own future as Chatham's heir than to co-operate with his colleagues. He quarrelled with them about the appointment of an envoy at Naples, and also about the supersession of Sir Jeffrey Amherst, absentee Governor of Virginia. Chatham chose to interpret Amherst's dismissal as an insult to himself. Grafton's object was to prevent him resigning his office of Lord Privy Seal while simultaneously provoking Shelburne to give up as Secretary of State. The predictable result, in October, was that both resigned. Since Chatham's presence in the ministry had for some time been an embarrassment and Shelburne's an irritation, the King was not perturbed; but the remainder of Chatham's friends in government grew restive, and Grafton became increasingly concerned that they might resign. In the event, most of them remained, in a state of twittering uncertainty and nervousness. Grafton clung to the Lord Chancellor, Camden; Camden clung to Grafton. Such leadership cannot have inspired confidence in those who looked for firm handling of Wilkes.

Matters of state also posed problems. In the Mediterranean Chatham's old rival Choiseul was moving cautiously but deliberately towards annexation of Corsica. It was not a new French ambition but it was made feasible by the moribund state of Corsica's masters, the Republic of Genoa. Corsica's native defenders, led by General Paoli, were a match for the Genoese but not for the French. From the British standpoint, it could be argued that any Bourbon accession of territory was dangerous, and

[40] *Letters of Junius*, p. 456.

particularly so in the Mediterranean, where the strategic defence of Gibraltar and British trade routes to Italy and the Levant were at risk. On the other hand, it was not clear that the French naval challenge was decisively strengthened by the transfer of sovereignty over Corsica, and Grafton's ministry showed little inclination to make an international issue of it. The opposition at the time, and modern authorities since, have argued that the threat of war, especially the arming of a naval squadron, would have been sufficient to deter Choiseul even after he had dispatched his troops to the island in June 1768. This was a matter of nice judgement. If it had proved wrong, and the government had found itself involved in a new war for the defence of Corsica, the consequences would have been costly. In any event, in Parliament there was a clear majority for Grafton's action (or rather inaction) and opposition attempts to beat the patriot drum proved ineffective. Claims from Bristol that British trade was threatened now as much as it had been in 1739 rang hollow. The most damaging aspect was perhaps the lack of thought which seemed to have gone into the ministers' planning. On the floor of the House of Commons the First Lord of the Admiralty Sir Edward Hawke made a somewhat half-hearted defence of the Cabinet's policy, which enhanced the impression of disarray.

The session of 1768–9 began, in November, with the Corsican problem; it also brought America to the fore again. By this time it was abundantly clear that Townshend's ingenious attempt to exploit the supposed inconsistency of colonial thinking on the subject of direct and indirect taxation had failed. In February 1768 the Massachusetts Bay Assembly protested in the strongest terms against Townshend's Act and circulated the other colonies with a request for joint action. In June Townshend's new Customs Commissioners found themselves at the mercy of a mob when they seized a vessel belonging to one of Boston's best-known patriot merchants, John Hancock. Soon afterwards a full-scale non-importation campaign was adopted in the three major ports of Boston, New York, and Philadelphia, to take effect by the spring of 1769. The ministry's response in this rapidly deteriorating situation was typically confused. Lord Hillsborough, Secretary of State for the Colonies since the junction with the Bedfords, engaged in a futile war of words with the colonial assemblies. He also began thinking in terms of strong action against New England. Troops were sent to reinforce the Governor and the Customs Board. A plan to amend the Massachusetts Charter was discussed, but vetoed by the King and Cabinet, though it was to be enacted in substance five years later by North. In the mean time Hillsborough obtained parliamentary approval for the use of the law of treason against American malefactors. This was a draconian threat if carried out, a mere gesture if not: in the event it was not.

The cause of these difficulties, Townshend's duties, remained. The new leader for the ministry in the Commons was Lord North, heir to a peerage and therefore himself a courtesy 'lord', though a member of the lower house. He had no enthusiasm for enforcing Townshend's grand design. The Cabinet saw the need to defend the British position in principle, but the duties, which largely applied to British exports, were not expected to yield a great sum. The only point of Townshend's Act was to trap the Americans into accepting some kind of revenue-raising taxes; if it failed to achieve that, it was useless. The eventual solution involved substantial concessions. The Americans were offered repeal of the offending duties, at a future date, in return for good behaviour in the interim. However, at the crucial Cabinet meeting on this question, on 1 May 1769, it was decided, by a narrow majority of five votes to four, to retain the tea duty as a reminder of Parliament's right to tax. The majority were all Bedfords, the minority all Chathamites. This decision, though not executed until the following year, was to have momentous consequences. In the mean time opposition attempts to repeal all the duties, including tea, were heavily defeated.

The friends of liberty sought to put these disparate grievances together. General Paoli was brought to England and publicly fêted. His champion James Boswell appealed for funds and appeared at the Stratford Jubilee in colourful Corsican costume. The American community in London stressed the unity of interest between the colonies and Middlesex; their arch agitator, Arthur Lee, made strenuous efforts to associate the two causes in the propaganda of the Wilkesites, with limited success. Wilkes himself had little interest in America, though he received with gratitude the handsome donation dispatched to him from South Carolina. His main concern, naturally, was with parliamentary tactics. Even if it had wished to maintain its relatively inactive policy of the spring the government could not have ignored Wilkes when Parliament met.

In the first place, Wilkes insisted on petitioning Parliament for redress of his supposed grievances, a deliberate act of provocation. In the second, his friends in the Commons were determined to raise the question of his privilege as an MP. Finally, before very long, he would be discharged from prison and the matter of his taking his seat must arise.

The bull was taken by the horns in February 1769. After a series of preliminary legal arguments Wilkes was expelled from the House by a large majority of 219 to 137. Predictably, his name was put forward for the resulting vacancy and he was re-elected, and expelled again. On 8 March an attempt by Burke to get a serious investigation of the St George's Fields Massacre was defeated by 245 votes to 39. The government's majority was holding very firm indeed. When the Middlesex electors next met, on 16 March, there was a feeble attempt to put up a court candidate, that Charles Dingley whose sawmill had been demolished in the riots of a year before: it failed hopelessly, and Wilkes once again had to be unseated by the Commons. Finally, on 13 April a more determined ministerial challenge took place. This was made by Henry Lawes Luttrell, who resigned his own seat at Bossiney to stand in Middlesex and obtained 297 votes against Wilkes's 1,143. On 19 April the historic motion giving Luttrell Wilkes's place as knight of the shire for Middlesex was approved by 197 votes to 143. It was highly controversial in anyone's terms.

There were precedents for expelling MPs, and the need to reaffirm such an expulsion had occurred before, most memorably in the case of Robert Walpole, unseated for alleged corruption in 1712. But the Commons was now presuming to go further, incapacitating Wilkes as a parliamentary candidate and selecting another candidate in his stead. At the very least such a disqualification might have been thought to require an Act of Parliament rather than a mere resolution of the Commons; at worst it was tantamount to a claim by the Commons to use its authority in election disputes to determine its own membership, in effect at the bidding of the government. Grafton in his *Autobiography* stressed the inevitability of what was done: once Wilkes had been expelled, the mounting excitement out of doors made Luttrell's election the only logical conclusion. Wilkes's friends proved resourceful organizers, or rather resourceful organizers saw the value of Wilkes to their own purposes. The famous Society of Supporters of the

Bill of Rights was formed in February 1769. Its initial purpose was to assist with Wilkes's debts, but in the long run it was to give a precision and coherence to demands for reform which would have been beyond Wilkes himself. By this time Wilkes had been elected an alderman and his pursuit of place and power in the City was well under way. At the same time electors both in the metropolis and in some provincial cities were drawing up instructions to their representatives to vote in favour of Wilkes. There was a matching attempt by the friends of government to organize a loyal campaign but it met with much difficulty. In the Battle of Temple Bar on 22 March a procession of merchants supporting Parliament made its way through the City to St James's to address the King. An element of farce was lent to the proceedings when the address was temporarily mislaid *en route*; a more alarming note was struck by the mob, which assailed the procession and brought it to a halt in the Strand. Only a bedraggled remnant succeeded in delivering the address. It is easy to see why the ministry, more out of desperation than deep-seated design, resorted to Luttrell.

The summer of 1769 was one of the great landmarks in the history of extra-parliamentary activity. There was no doubting the strength of support in London and Middlesex for Wilkes. Many provincial towns also displayed signs of enthusiasm but in retrospect the evidence is difficult to quantify, let alone validate. The manipulation of newspaper reporting was a regular feature of political organization. Even authenticated demonstrations or celebrations in Wilkes's favour cut little ice when the numbers were small or the occasions trivial. The widespread petitioning organized by the Wilkesites was another matter altogether. Around sixty thousand signatures were collected for such petitions. They represented a broad spread of counties and large boroughs, and, according to their spokesmen, a quarter of the total electorate. Against this it was easy to express scepticism about the origin of some of these petitions. Many of them were initiated by opposition groups with an axe to grind. Counties where the Rockingham party was influential, Yorkshire, Derbyshire, Worcestershire, were prominent. In Buckinghamshire the full weight of the Grenville connection, Grenville himself, his brother Temple, and their brother-in-law Chatham, was exerted, with the aid of Burke. In parts of the West Country some of Wilkes's allies in the metropolis had influence: John Glynn in Devon, William Beckford in Wiltshire.

Naturally the court utilized its own provincial friends. In Essex and Lincolnshire, for example, attempts at petitions were quickly crushed. The wording of the petitions also gave rise to diverse interpretations of their significance. The protests from the London region tended to be anti-ministerial in tone. But in most of the counties the need to conciliate moderate opinion made it prudent to restrict the scope to the Middlesex election itself. Some petitions were rag-bags of local grievances, including, in the case of Canterbury, the decayed state of the local leather manufacture. A further complication was added when Westminster, instead of merely requesting the Crown for redress of grievances, specifically demanded a dissolution of Parliament. This was a logical development. If the men who had voted Wilkes out of Parliament were so clear about their legal grounds and political support, why should they not face their electors with equanimity? On the other hand, the royal prerogative of dissolution was a sensitive matter—was it wise to encourage its use against a House of Commons majority, and, alternatively, was it quite proper to advise the King about its employment? Nervous noblemen like Rockingham detected echoes of seventeenth-century controversy in such debates, and had doubts about giving them a wider hearing. In none of this, it should be stressed, was there much evidence of commitment to a root and branch programme of parliamentary reform. That would require more intensive political education than had hitherto been devoted to the subject.

What effect did the petitions have? When Parliament met in January 1770 they were the main subject of debate. Yet the ministry seemed secure. In the 1768–9 session the lowest majority registered by government on the Middlesex election question had been 50; in the key debate on the Address on 9 January 1770, when North made a devastating attack on the provenance of the petitions, the opposition was outnumbered by nearly a hundred, 254 to 158. Thereafter the ministry's position deteriorated. This occurred only indirectly as a result of the petitioning movement, for if ever a government collapsed from within, it was Grafton's. The weak link in the Cabinet was the presence of the Chathamites, especially Granby and Camden. They were often accounted respectively the foremost English soldier and lawyer of the day; but neither had a political will worthy of the name, and both stood in awe of their leader. Chatham had shown little interest in the Middlesex election initially. But by the summer of 1769, with his health or at least his mental equilibrium restored, he was well aware of its significance. His return to opposition was soon being trumpeted in the newspapers. When he came to town in July he made a point of calling on the King (their last interview) to lecture him on the failings of his ministry. George III was polite but unimpressed; his tolerance of Chatham's conduct between 1766 and 1770 remains remarkable.

By this time the Chathamites in the ministry were wavering. They finally broke when Chatham took the opportunity of the new session to deliver a denunciation of the ministers' treatment of Middlesex, Corsica, and America. Camden and Granby recanted publicly and resigned. Grafton, already weakened by almost two years of crisis and a brutal campaign against him in the press, and now deprived of his props, did not persevere long. He made a disastrous attempt to secure the services of Charles Yorke, the Rockinghams' lawyer, and son of the famous Earl of Hardwicke, as Lord Chancellor. Yorke accepted, but in a fit of remorse at his betrayal of family and party took his own life. Grafton dithered long enough to see his majority in the Commons fall to 44, and finally resigned at the end of January. In opposition the jubilant triple alliance of Rockingham, Grenville, and Chatham seemed about to carry all before it. The King talked somewhat wildly, as he was to do in a similar crisis in 1783, of his crown being at stake. But the Bedfords remained steady. In the Commons the King's Friends rallied. Above all, Lord North, an experienced minister with friends on all sides of the House, agreed to take the Treasury. In a sense, he was the true beneficiary of the Middlesex election, and his long period as Prime Minister Wilkes's most substantial achievement.

CHAPTER 9

New Improvements

PARLIAMENTARY *sovereignty was employed for commercial benefit and material improvement, as well as in constitutional controversy. Turnpike legislation created a national transport network, which, in addition to its economic effects, was perceived to have social and cultural consequences. A series of inland navigation acts made the 1760s and 1770s the first, formative decades of the canal age, and added to the wonders of the English world. 'Improvement Acts' were used on a wide scale to transform the amenities of towns and cities. On the land there was a great increase in the use of parliamentary enclosure bills. The entrepreneurial activity with which this mass of legislation was associated caused considerable heart-searching, complacent though much of the commercial spirit of the age may seem in retrospect. The rapid growth of towns, and especially the suburban expansion of the metropolis, gave rise to debate about the social and moral repercussions of urban change. Agricultural investment, praised for its impact on productivity, was also criticized for its corrosive effect on rural paternalism. The traditional economy of the open-field village, and the old sense of harmony which bound together hierarchical communities, seemed to be vanishing together. Such concern was increased by the food shortages and price inflation of the period. The price rise, especially, had grave consequences for those sections of society which depended on fixed incomes or were unable to maintain their real wages. This included some professional groups, such as the inferior clergy and junior officers in the armed forces, as well as rural labourers. Unrest among groups of workers, notably in London, was sufficient to force employers to make some concessions. But in the end there was little doubt about who gained and who lost by the prosperity of these years.*

TURNPIKES

THERE is a common belief that the economic growth of the late eighteenth century had its origins in the unfettered enterprise of early industrial society, and its most systematic theoretical expression in the liberal economics so confidently adumbrated by Adam Smith in 1776. It is easy to forget how important the intervention of the State (in its widest sense) was to economic development. Particularly from the 1750s and 1760s the full potential of Parliament's legislative authority was unleashed. The same sovereignty which aroused such controversy when its victims were the electors of Middlesex or the citizens of the American colonies, was employed no less extensively in the cause of economic innovation and social regulation. There were no grand statements of constitutional doctrine; moreover, the process was initiated at regional or even parochial level and enforced by means of statutes which were often avowedly 'local' or 'private' in scope. But the revolution thus wrought was not less profound for its relatively smooth and silent progress. Its dependence on Parliament was a natural consequence of the legal uncertainty associated with so much commercial expansion. Under the Bubble Act of 1720 joint-stock companies required the support of a specific statute; it was difficult and legally dangerous to raise large sums of capital without such resort to legislation. Many projects involved collaboration with public authorities and interference with private property. Unless projectors and their financial backers were prepared to run the risk of expensive and obstructive litigation it was prudent to obtain the secure protection of an Act of Parliament.

The construction of a national road network was one of the first achievements of the resulting statutory activity. Turnpike trusts had a seventeenth-century prehistory. The first dated back to 1663, though it was over thirty years before Parliament ventured to approve a second. Highway development gathered pace in the early eighteenth century, fell back in the 1730s, but then accelerated dramatically. There were 25 turnpike acts in the 1730s, 37 in the 1740s, 170 in the 1750s, and 170 in the 1760s. The succeeding decadal totals fell to 75 and 34 respectively.[1] The mid-eighteenth century was truly the age of turnpike mania. Fifty-two per cent of

[1] J. R. Ward, *The Finance of Canal Building in Eighteenth-Century England* (Oxford, 1974), p. 164.

the total mileage constructed between 1696 and 1836 was authorized between 1750 and 1770.[2] In part this reflected the inad-
equacies of existing highway law. The requirement laid on parishes
to provide for the maintenance of public roads which lay within
their boundaries, using 'statute labour' provided by ratepayers,
was insufficient to cope with great thoroughfares carrying traffic
on a regional or even national basis. Turnpikes did not, however,
supplant the traditional system; rather they supplemented it. Even
so, the principle that new roads should be built or old ones
improved by means of a capital programme, serviced by tolls on
travellers, was novel and initially controversial. In the early years
of the turnpikes there were outbursts of popular resentment,
notably in the Bristol, Gloucester, and Hereford areas in the 1730s.
One offender was hanged under the Black Act for his attack on the
Ledbury turnpike in 1736. Turnpike destruction was itself made
a capital offence in 1735.[3]

There was an understandable suspicion that turnpikes primarily
served the interests of the better off. This was doubtless the case,
though not necessarily in the sense implied. Turnpike administration was entrusted to men of property named in the relevant
statute or co-opted by those who were. In practice it was managed
by the small minority who troubled to attend committee meetings.
In their proceedings it was often the vested interests of farmers
and carriers which were most attended to, rather than those of a
selfish landed class. The quality of the roads was disputed. Despite
the interest of the age in technical innovation there was no breakthrough in the mechanics of road construction. Nor was there any
mid-eighteenth-century McAdam, though there were some well-
known road-builders, for example the blind John Metcalf of
Knaresborough, who worked on many Yorkshire roads from about
1765.[4] The advantage of turnpikes arose from the quality of
materials used, the regularity of maintenance, and the relative
professionalism of their administration by the trusts. But there
were constant complaints about deteriorating surfaces on turnpiked
roads. The dilemma of the highway engineer, the new traffic

[2] E. Pawson, *Transport and Economy: The Turnpike Roads of Eighteenth-Century Britain* (London, 1977), p. 114.

[3] W. M. Albert, 'Popular Opposition to Turnpike Trusts in Early Eighteenth-Century England', *Journal of Transport History*, 5 (1979), 6.

[4] C. G. Harper, *The Great North Road* (2nd edn., London, 1922), pp. 10–13.

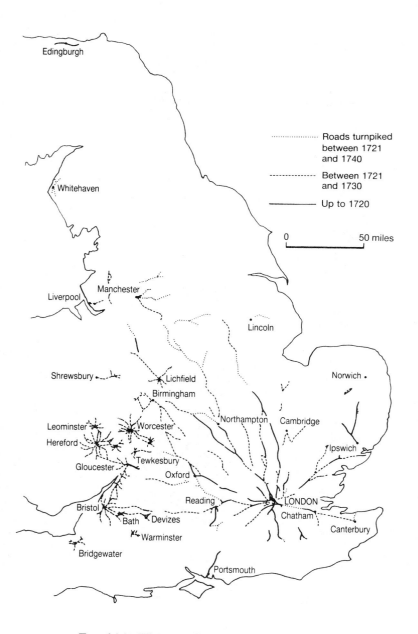

FIG. 6 (*a*). The turnpike road network in 1740

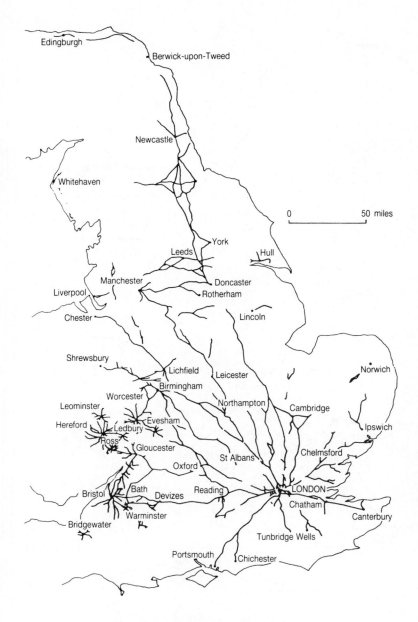

FIG. 6 (*b*). The turnpike road network in 1750

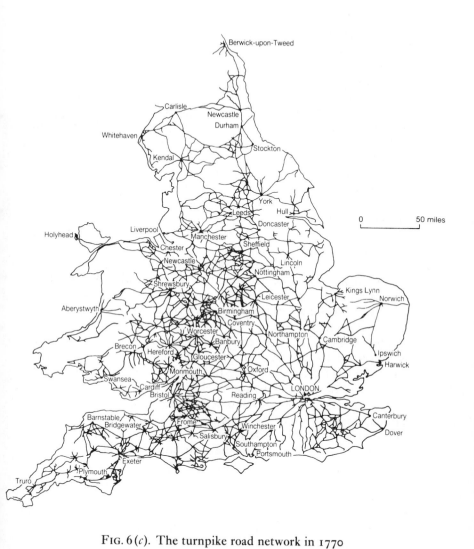

FIG. 6(c). The turnpike road network in 1770

Source: E. Pawson, *Transport and Economy: The Turnpike Roads in Eighteenth Century Britain* (London, 1977), pp. 137, 139, 140

generated by improvement designed to cater for existing excess demand, was already familiar.

Matters were not improved by the multiplicity of highway authorities, and the consequent difficulty of enforcing common standards. Rational discussion moved towards the adoption of wider wheels and better-distributed loads. This was the principle behind the Broad Wheel Act of 1753. But the interests affected were diverse and numerous, Parliament was bombarded with partial advice, and the prospect of a national transport policy remained remote. Nor were the finances of the trusts necessarily healthy. Turnpike debts came to resemble the National Debt in that any notion of paying off the capital was soon forgotten. Tolls were a complicated matter, and rendered problematical by the various exemptions enjoyed by users. Some schemes were plainly imprudent. Light traffic in rural areas did not always justify the optimism of gentry seeking fast roads to carry them to urban civilization. Trusts were most viable in industrial areas. The rapid development of the road network in the West Midlands, Yorkshire, and Lancashire is as striking a feature of turnpike construction, as the better-known appearance of an arterial system linking London with provincial centres.

The economic significance of the turnpikes is difficult to assess. Compared with the canals of the succeeding age they remained a costly form of bulk transport. But given the great quantities of freight traditionally carried on pack-horse and cart, they fulfilled a vital function in the development of regional economies and a national market. Contemporaries readily assumed that they were commercially beneficial. Defoe in his *Tour*, first published between 1724 and 1726, was excited by their galvanizing effect, and devoted a special appendix to a description of their consequences. In the reissue of the *Tour* edited by Samuel Richardson in 1742, further encouragement was offered. 'No Publick Edifice, Alms-House, Hospital, or Nobleman's Palace, can be of equal Value to the Country with this.'[5] Thereafter their value was rarely challenged.

A commonplace observation was that nothing worked like a turnpike to bring local prices into line with the national pattern and promote local production for a wider market. This was particularly the case for products which had a relatively high value to

[5] *A Tour Thro' the Whole Island of Great Britain* (3rd edn., 4 vols., London, 1742), iii. 249.

weight ratio. But heavy goods could be carried profitably over short distances. Development of coal-seams which essentially served a local economy was often connected with highway improvement. The commercial implications were endless. Even the economy of crime was affected. The cash held by turnpike keepers proved a tempting target on the busy roads around London, and armed protection had to be provided on occasion. Fast roads provided a rapid means of escape from the scene of a crime, making the ancient hue and cry seem peculiarly obsolete; desperate remedies, for instance the use by turnpike keepers of loud hailers to warn each other of approaching fugitives from justice, were suggested. Actual robbery on turnpikes was more hazardous since few of them answered the definition of a lonely road, but it was by no means unknown.

The glory of the turnpikes, much trumpeted by travel writers, was the difference which they made to the comfort and speed of ordinary travel. The lumbering stage-coaches of the early eighteenth century, venturing on long journeys which took several days to pass from one region to another, and hauled by teams of horses barely capable of coping with roads often indistinguishable from bogs, featured in many nostalgic memoirs written at the safe distance of the late eighteenth century. They were superseded by the famous flying machines of the 1750s and 1760s: journey times between major centres were slashed more dramatically during this period than at any time before the railway age. A two-day trip like that to Gloucester could be managed in one day with the aid of a 'flier' and willingness to sleep on the road. Many new passenger services opened at this time, and existing ones were rapidly extended. Manchester acquired its first direct link with London in 1754, followed quickly by other northern towns, and eventually, in 1773, by Glasgow. Previously only the old provincial centres had been able to boast a direct connection with the capital. By the 1780s every region in England, and some of Scotland and Wales, had a turnpike network of its own, part of a larger national system. The sheer quantity of services, local, regional, and national, passenger and freight, which can be seen in the weekly timetable of departures from a relatively small provincial city like Salisbury in 1769, gives some idea of the vitality of the transport trade, a major industry in its own right.

It was small wonder that those who lived through this age

TABLE 5 (*a*). *Salisbury carrier and coach services, 1769: Departures*

	Operator	Inn	Destination
Monday			
3.00	SALISBURY MACHINE	Red Lion and Cross Keys	London
a.m.	LONDON AND EXETER POST-COACH	Three Lions	London
Noon	Grey	Running Horse	Semley
1.00	White	Milford Street	London via Stockbridge
4.00	LONDON AND EXETER POST-COACH	Three Lions	Blandford, Exeter
7.00	Avery and Co.	Cross Keys	Oxford
7.00	Avery and Co.	Cross Keys	Dorchester
Evening	EXETER–LONDON COACH	White Hart	Blandford, Exeter
Evening	EXETER–LONDON COACH	White Hart	London
Evening	Brewer and Co.	Red Lion and Cross Keys	Bristol
9.00	Tanner and Combs	Winchester Street	London
Tuesday			
6.00	Brown	Goat	Bath, Bristol, Devizes via Pottern
6.00	BATH MACHINE	Red Lion and Cross Keys	Bath
6.00	GOSPORT STAGE-COACH	White Hart	Southampton, Gosport
a.m.	Harvey	Vine	Wincanton, Mere, Hindon
a.m.	Pound	Vine	London
a.m.	BLANDFORD STAGE-COACH	Antelope	Blandford
a.m.	LONDON AND EXETER POST-COACH	Three Lions	London
a.m.	White	Milford Street	Fordingbridge
a.m.	Halcombe	Lamb	Bath, Bristol, Devizes via Pottern
8.00		Sun	Marlborough via Wilest, Milton, Alton, etc.
9.00	George	Chough	Marlborough
10.00	W. Hayward	Cartwheel	Bath, Bristol, Devizes
10.00	Iliffe	White Hart	London
10.00	J. Hayward	Maidenhead	Bath, Bristol, Devizes via Melksham
10.00	Tarrant	Three Swans	Andover
10.00	Morgan	Red Lion and Cross Keys	Ringwood, Poole
11.00	Iliffe	White Hart	Exeter, Plymouth
Noon	Read	Maidenhead	Shaftesbury
Noon	Brown	Goat	Poole via Cranbourne, Wimbourne
Noon	Edwards	White Horse	Ludgershall, Tidworth, etc.
Noon	Alford	Maidenhead	Chiltern, etc.
Noon	Hayter	Maidenhead	Amesbury
Noon	Payne	Running Horse	Wallop, Amport, Sarson, etc.

TABLE 5 (*cont.*)

	Operator	Inn	Destination
Noon	Short	Chough	Shaftesbury
Noon	Cove	Three Swans	Amesbury
Noon	Maton	Chough	Bulford, Durrington, Everley
Noon	James	Three Swans	Ashcomb, Berwick, Sapson, etc.
Noon	Wiltshire	Chough	Netheravon, Uphavon, Hoxon
Noon	Barton	Six Bells	Broughton
Noon	Wansborough	Chough	Bulford, Durrington, Everley
Noon	King	Lamb	Bishopston, Chalk, Alvedistrey
Noon	Short	Chough	Donhead, Wardour, Shaftesbury
1.00	Barton	Six Bells	Waller, Amport, Sarson, etc.
1.00	Alford	King's Head	Boyton, Codford, Stockton
1.00	Alford	Maidenhead	Shaftesbury
1.00	Brown	Feathers	Christchurch
1.00	TAUNTON COACH	Antelope	Taunton
2.00		Three Swans	Fordingbridge
2.00	Penny	Saracen's Head	Witton
4.00	LONDON AND EXETER POST-COACH	Three Lions	Blandford, Exeter
Evening	EXETER–LONDON COACH	White Hart	Blandford, Exeter
Evening	EXETER–LONDON COACH	White Hart	London
Wednesday			
3.00	BLANDFORD STAGE-COACH	Antelope	London
3.00	SALISBURY MACHINE	Red Lion and Cross Keys	London
7.00	Bury	Cross Keys	Frome, Hindon, Shepton Mallet
a.m.	LONDON AND EXETER POST-COACH	Three Lions	London
a.m.	Whitcher	Goat	Fordingbridge, Ringwood, Christchurch
10.00	Iliffe	White Hart	London
11.00	Iliffe	White Hart	Exeter, Plymouth
11.00	Woolcott	Cart Wheel	Crookham, Chard, etc.
11.00	Figes	Cart Wheel	Southampton, Romsey
Noon		Red Lion and Cross Keys	Cranborne
1.00	White	Milford Street	London via Stockbridge
4.00	LONDON AND EXETER POST-COACH	Three Lions	Blandford, Exeter
Evening	EXETER–LONDON COACH	White Hart	Blandford, Exeter
Evening	EXETER–LONDON COACH	White Hart	London
Evening	Judd	Red Lion and Cross Keys	Romsey, Southampton, Isle of Wight
Evening	Brewer and Co.	Red Lion and Cross Keys	Bristol
9.00	Tanner and Combs	Winchester Street	London

TABLE 5 (*cont.*)

	Operator	Inn	Destination
Thursday			
7.00	Andrews	Three Swans	London
7.00	Andrews	Three Swans	Chard, Crookham, Yeovil, Sherborne, Milbourne Port, Shaftesbury
a.m.		Sun	Taunton, Sherborne, Yeovil, Wincanton, etc.
a.m.		Sun	London
a.m.	Meades	Cross Keys	Blandford, Wareham, Corfe Castle
a.m.	LONDON AND EXETER POST COACH	Three Lions	London
Noon	Grey	Running Horse	Semley
2.00	King	Red Lion and Cross Keys	London via Andover, Newbury
2.00	Penny	Saracen's Head	Witton
4.00	LONDON AND EXETER POST-COACH	Three Lions	Blandford, Exeter
7.00	Avery and Co.	Cross Keys	Oxford
7.00	Avery and Co.	Cross Keys	Dorchester
Evening	EXETER–LONDON COACH	White Hart	Blandford, Exeter
Evening	EXETER–LONDON COACH	White Hart	London
Friday			
3.00	SALISBURY MACHINE	Red Lion and Cross keys	London
6.00	GOSPORT STAGE-COACH	White Hart	Southampton, Gosport
6.00	BATH MACHINE	Red Lion and Cross Keys	Bath
a.m.	Halcombe	Lamb	Bath, Bristol, Devizes via Lydeway
a.m.	BLANDFORD STAGE-COACH	Antelope	Blandford
a.m.	LONDON AND EXETER POST-COACH	Three Lions	London
10.00	Love	Three Swans	Stockbridge, Winchester
10.00	Iliffe	White Hart	London
10.00	TAUNTON COACH	Antelope	London
11.00	Iliffe	White Hart	Exeter, Plymouth
Noon	Short	Chough	Shaftesbury
Noon	Short	Chough	Donhead, Wardour, Shaftesbury
1.00	White	Milford Street	London via Stockbridge
4.00	LONDON AND EXETER POST-COACH	Three Lions	Blandford, Exeter
Evening	EXETER–LONDON COACH	White Hart	Blandford, Exeter
Evening	EXETER–LONDON COACH	White Hart	London
Evening	Brewer and Co.	Red Lion and Cross Keys	Bristol
9.00	Tanner and Combs	Winchester Street	London

TABLE 5 (*cont.*)

	Operator	*Inn*	*Destination*
Saturday			
3.00	BLANDFORD STAGE–COACH	Antelope	London
a.m.	Pound	Vine	London
a.m.	LONDON AND EXETER POST–COACH	Three Lions	London
10.00	Morgan	Red Lion and Cross Keys	Lymington, Ringwood
1.00	Figes	Cart Wheel	Southampton, Romsey
Noon	Cove	Three Swans	Amesbury
Noon	Buckingham	Draghal Street	Oxford
Noon	King	Lamb	Bishopston, Chalk, Alvediston
Noon	Maton	Chough	Bulford, Durrington, Everley
Noon	Edwards	White Horse	Ludgershall, Tidworth, etc.
2.00	Penny	Saracen's Head	Witton
4.00	LONDON AND EXETER POST–COACH	Three Lions	Blandford, Exeter
Evening	EXETER–LONDON COACH	White Hart	Blandford, Exeter
Evening	EXETER–LONDON COACH	White Hart	London
Evening	Gibbons	Goat	Shaftesbury
Also, day uncertain	Duke	Vine	Mere, Hindon
Sunday			
Evening	Judd	Red Lion and Cross Keys	Romsey, Southampton, Isle of Wight

Source: The Salisbury Guide (1769).

TABLE 5 (b). *'Polite' towns and the turnpike system*

Towns are ranked according to the number of households paying the silver plate duty in 1757, not according to population. Particularly at the lower end this emphasizes genteel and middle-class residence rather than commercial or industrial vigour, though the two often coincided. 'Turnpike' signifies that the town in question was on or in close proximity to a turnpiked road by the date specified.

Town	Plate duty payers	Turnpike by 1750	by 1770	Town	Plate duty payers	Turnpike by 1750	by 1770
Bristol	790	✓	✓	Beverley	56	✓	✓
Norwich	245	✓	✓	Rochester	53	✓	✓
York	231	✓	✓	Dover	51		✓
Exeter	218		✓	Colchester	51	✓	✓
Manchester	198	✓	✓	Chatham	50	✓	✓
Bath	193	✓	✓	Whitby	50		✓
Newcastle	192	✓	✓	Hereford	46	✓	✓
Liverpool	178	✓	✓	Newark	45	✓	✓
Oxford	143	✓	✓	Stockton	44	✓	✓
Plymouth	142		✓	Boston	42		✓
Hull	140	✓	✓	Chichester	42	✓	✓
Portsmouth	137	✓	✓	Coventry	42	✓	✓
Chester	125	✓	✓	Croydon	38		✓
Shrewsbury	117	✓	✓	Scarborough	42		✓
Nottingham	116	✓	✓	Stamford	42	✓	✓
Worcester	115	✓	✓	Grantham	40	✓	✓
Birmingham	109	✓	✓	Lancaster	39		✓
Yarmouth	101		✓	Deal	38		✓
Leeds	98	✓	✓	Sheffield	38	✓	✓
Durham	96	✓	✓	Sunderland	38	✓	✓
Canterbury	92	✓	✓	Gainsborough	37	✓	✓
Ipswich	82	✓	✓	Peterborough	37	✓	✓
Gosport	73	✓	✓	Doncaster	36	✓	✓
Lincoln	70	✓	✓	Halifax	36	✓	✓
Wakefield	70	✓	✓	Maidstone	36	✓	✓
Southampton	68		✓	Preston	36		✓
Bury	67		✓	St Albans	35	✓	✓
Windsor	67	✓	✓	Poole	34		✓
Winchester	65		✓	Sandwich	34		
Leicester	61	✓	✓	Whitehaven	34	✓	✓
Reading	61	✓	✓	Bideford	32		✓
Gloucester	60	✓	✓	Guildford	32	✓	✓
Northampton	59	✓	✓	Dorchester	31		✓
Derby	58	✓	✓	Pontefract	31	✓	✓

Town	Plate duty payers	Turnpike by 1750	by 1770
Barnstaple	30		✓
Hertford	30	✓	✓
Kendal	30		✓
Ludlow	30		✓
Cheshunt	29	✓	✓
Lichfield	29	✓	✓
Taunton	29		✓
Wisbech	29		✓
Lewes	28		✓
Louth	28		✓
Ripon	27	✓	✓
Wells	27		✓
Marlborough	26		✓
Richmond, Yorks.	26	✓	✓
Bridgwater	24		✓
Devizes	24		✓
Falmouth	24		✓
Truro	24		✓
Faversham	23		✓
Newport IoW	23		
Totnes	23		✓
Henley	22	✓	✓
Wolverhampton	22	✓	✓
Harwich	21	✓	✓
Bridgnorth	20	/	✓
Chelmsford	20	✓	✓
Chippenham	20	✓	✓
Romford	20	✓	✓
Warwick	20	✓	✓
Berwick	19		✓
Carlisle	19		✓
Newmarket	19	✓	✓
Trowbridge	19		✓
Huntingdon	18	✓	✓
Tewkesbury	18		✓
Tiverton	18		✓
Warminster	18	✓	✓
Blandford	17		✓
Bradford, Yorks.	17	✓	✓
Cirencester	17	✓	✓
Newbury	17	✓	✓
North Shields	17	✓	✓
Penrith	17		✓
Topsham	17		✓
Whitchurch	17		✓
Witham	17	✓	✓
Bishop Auckland	16	✓	✓
Malton	16		✓
Newport	16	✓	✓
Stafford	16	✓	✓
Swaffham	16		✓
King's Walden	16	✓	✓
Ware	16	✓	✓
Warrington	16	✓	✓
Bradford	15	✓	✓
Chesterfield	15		✓
Dartmouth	15		✓
Frome	15	✓	✓
Gateshead	15	✓	✓
Lymington	15		✓
Penryn	15		✓
Sherborne	15		✓
Stockport	15	✓	✓
Weymouth	15		✓

considered improved communications one of the great transformations of their lifetime. Thomas Pennant's praise of progress
contrasted the speed and comfort of what was a two-day journey
from Chester to London in 1780 with the journey which he recalled
as a child when his parents took him from his Welsh school and
placed him in one near London in 1740. Then, the first day could
carry him only twenty miles to Whitchurch, and after a tiring
three days' travel he was still only at Coventry. At Meriden in
Warwickshire it took six or even eight horses to drag the stage-
coach through the mire. A further day was consumed in reaching
Northampton, and another to arrive at Dunstable. London was
attained a full six days after setting out.[6] Genteel life was affected,
not always, it was thought, with desirable consequences. That
hardy race of gentlemen who travelled on horseback, unrecog-
nizable in their heavy frocks, trousers, and jackboots, covered in
dust or mud after a hard day's ride, had vanished. Replacing it
was a new, wild, yet somewhat effeminate breed of dandies, for
whom driving in a light chaise was a recreation and horse-riding
the accomplishment of a boorish hunting set.

Desirable or not, a new age of speed had dawned, arousing
intense interest. Richard Graves had his fictional Columella make
much of it in 1779.

Columella ... observed, that the most remarkable phaenomenon which
he had taken notice of these late years, in his retirement, was the surprising
improvement in the art of loco-motion, or conveyance from one place to
another. 'Who would have believed, thirty years ago,' says he, 'that a
young man would come thirty miles in a carriage to dinner, and perhaps
return at night? or indeed, who would have said, that coaches would go
daily between London and Bath, in about twelve hours; which, twenty
years ago, was reckoned three good days journey?'[7]

Racing and record-breaking by fast chaises became a regular topic
both in polite society and the newspaper press. Not only young
men with money to spare, an inclination for adventure, and a love
of gambling, were involved. Feats became possible which would
have been out of the question a few years earlier. The celebrated
jockey Joseph Rose used the turnpikes to maximize his earnings
and impress his public in 1764, when he rode at Lincoln on
5 September, Richmond on 6 September, and Manchester on

---

[6] *The Journey from Chester to London*, p. 137.
[7] *Columella; or, the Distressed Anchoret* (2 vols., London, 1779), ii. 44–5.

7 September.[8] Even a sedate clergyman like John Penrose might be impressed by a post-chaise journey from Bath to Oxford in 1767, setting out at eight p.m. and arriving in Oxford the following morning, a distance of 71 miles, covered at nearly seven miles an hour.[9]

Widely available public transport opened up intriguing new possibilities of social intercourse, the amusement of which depended on indiscriminate mixing. Many a novel exploited the chance meetings thereby permitted, to the extent that critics complained of such hackneyed openings. But the experience of this extreme and temporary proximity to strangers was so commonplace that it was bound to generate recognition of its human interest. In 1743 when the *London Magazine* incautiously published a poem entitled the 'miseries of a Stage Coach' it was deluged with similar efforts. The resulting images, fat and malodorous grannies, belching and farting innkeepers, cursing troopers, snotty-nosed, travel-sick schoolboys, passed into the stock literature of travel.[10] Class was an important element in the comedy of coach travel. Even on the road there was one obvious form of social discrimination. Those who travelled uncomfortably 'on top' were likely to be doing so with a view to economy and had to contend with the 'pride of inside ones'. No doubt it was Thomas Holcroft's innate republicanism which led him, on the Manchester Commercial Coach in 1788, to forsake the company of his inside passengers, 'an ignorant Cambridge scholar, a boorish country attorney, a pert, travelled officer, a vain, avaricious, rheumatic old woman, and a loving young widow' for the pleasures of dining at Hockliffe with the outside passengers.[11]

The rich and well-born, of course, did not travel by such means. Charles Johnstone's satire on mid-eighteenth-century manners, *Chrysal*, selected private transport as the very emblem of a polite existence. 'In this age of delicacy and refinement the first thing thought of in genteel life is a carriage, which is so indispensably necessary to procure respect, that no eminence in science, no practice of virtue, is held in esteem, where that is wanted.'[12] Private

[8] J. Orton, *Turf Annals of York and Doncaster* (York, 1844), p. 672.
[9] *Letters from Bath 1766–67 by the Rev. John Penrose*, p. 189.
[10] *London Magazine*, 1743, pp. 148, 200–1.
[11] W. Hazlitt, ed., *Memoirs of the late Thomas Holcroft* (London, 1852), pp. 186–7.
[12] E. Baker, ed., *Charles Johnstone: Chrysal or the Adventures of a Guinea* (London, 1908), p. 442.

chaises and carriages multiplied and were identified as a suitable target for taxation by the Treasury in 1747. They were owned overwhelmingly by the urban classes, but their attractions would have been much lessened without the access to and from country roads which they enjoyed, thanks to the turnpikes. The French tourist Saint Fond was staggered by the number of carriages which he passed while travelling a stretch of only twenty miles to Windsor on a Sunday night in 1784 when Londoners were returning from a weekend in the country. He took it as clear evidence of 'a degree of wealth and extent of population, of which one has no notion in France'.[13] In 1765 there were 15,403 private coaches and chaises maintained privately, aside from the 4,392 kept for hire, and excluding stage-coaches and hackneys. In 1779 it was reckoned that post-chaises alone numbered more than 4,000.[14] These were the luxurious form of travel *par excellence* carrying one or two passengers at great speed and maximum expense. Lord North accordingly subjected them to an additional tax.

In London it might be permissible to take a hackney carriage, but for the most part a private coach was an essential feature of comfortable and snobbish living. It is easy to see why: privacy is the first privilege of the rich. Jeremy Bentham was not a little embarrassed at having to travel by public coach to visit his aristocratic patron Lord Shelburne at Bowood. He was even more discomforted to find that his companion as an inside traveller was one of his host's chambermaids. Only the appearance of another genteel visitor to Bowood, Alexander Popham, barrister and MP, brought a measure of relief. Together they took refuge in the excuse that a stage-coach well serviced was quicker even than a hired post-chaise.[15]

Turnpike travel was blamed for many things. It stimulated a great increase in the use of a valuable and not unlimited resource, horsepower. Horses were expensive to maintain, and, it was argued, in times of high prices and shortages, took food from the mouths of the poor. It was reckoned in 1767, one such time, that a stage-coach travelling 200 miles in 6 days had formerly required 18 horses; now, in less than two days it employed 70 horses. All

---

[13] Sir A. Geikie, ed., *B. Faujas de Saint Fond, A Journey through England and Scotland to the Hebrides in 1784* (2 vols., Glasgow, 1907), i. 62.

[14] PRO, CUST. 48. 17, p. 413.

[15] I. R. Christie, ed., *The Correspondence of Jeremy Bentham*, vol. iii: *1781–8* (London, 1971), p. 52.

this because people expected to travel at absurd speeds. 'There is scarce a cobbler in the counties of York and Lancaster, but must now be conveyed to his cousin german in Wapping in two days time.'[16] Speed itself was thought reprehensible by some. Charles Jenner had his benevolent hero Sir Charles Beville denounce

> flying; a practice with which he always found great fault. He has often observed to Norris, that it was a great pity there was not some officer whose business it should be to stop every man travelling post, and inquire whether his business was such as could justify his killing a horse or two, risquing the necks of half a dozen post-boys, throwing three or four servants into fevers, from excessive exercise in keeping up with their master's chaise, and forty other like accidents, which happened more or less every day, from the fashionable mode of travelling ... [all for] ... the mere satisfaction of saying at York, *I was in London this morning*.[17]

Accidents were indeed a common cause of complaint, as was traffic congestion. Turnpikes, by making ownership of a private vehicle advantageous, caused chronic congestion in cities, where most of them were kept at least for part of the year. In 1762 one third of the twenty thousand or so carriages paying duty were based in London, with predictable effects for the safety and tranquillity of the capital's streets.[18]

The turnpike also had political and moral implications. It could be blamed for facilitating the flight of the gentry from their patriarchal responsibilities in the countryside. This indictment extended to women as well as men.

> 'Wives staid at home, but now the turnpikes bring,
>   All to learn vice, buy pins, see the king;
> 'Tis on the turnpikes that we ought to rail,
>   The turnpikes, where sin runs upon the nail[19]

One of the standard clichés of the late eighteenth century was the coupling of circulating libraries with turnpikes. The communication of extravagance, idleness, and a host of other failings, across boundaries of class and locality, was considered characteristic of an age of unprecedented opportunities for immorality. It seemed reasonable to suppose that the sheer expansion of

---

[16] *London Magazine*, 1767, p. 22.
[17] *The Placid Man: or, Memoirs of Sir Charles Beville*, i. 136.
[18] PRO, CUST. 48. 17, p. 413.
[19] E. Thompson, *The Demi-Rep* (2nd edn., London, '1756', actually 1766), p. 35.

the facilities for travel must be connected with the consequent weakening of the nation's moral fibre.

In one respect highway improvement brought indisputable advantages. Complaints about the postal service were traditionally every literate citizen's birthright. By any standards it was expensive. The rates laid down in 1711 and effectively unaltered until 1765 specified a minimum of 3d. (the price of a good meal in a respectable inn or eating-house) for the shortest journeys. Only London had a penny post service until a change in the regulations permitted other cities to emulate it after 1765. Speeds were laid down according to formulae calculated under Charles II.[20] The administration of the service was marred by private profiteering and political corruption. Postmasters had been given a monopoly of 'posting' travellers in 1660 and did their best to exclude competitors. Strictly speaking, it was illegal for one not of their number to hire out a horse with a guide. So far as the mail itself was concerned, postmasters were entitled to charge (at their own rates) for local delivery of letters beyond the network provided by the Post Office, until an important court case in 1772 found these exactions unjustified by law.

The mail was notoriously open to inspection for reasons of State. These included party politics as well as national security. The men involved served every government with impartial, patriotic cynicism. There were only two heads of the Foreign or Secret Office between 1718 and 1787, John Lefebure, who died in 1752, and his successor Anthony Todd. Even where military intelligence was involved, the procedures which they and their underlings followed could readily seem exceptionable. The curious case of Florence Hensey, who was tried for espionage at the beginning of the Seven Years War, on a charge of revealing Boscawen's sailing and the details of the Rochefort expedition to the enemy, opened many eyes to some of the questionable practices of the Post Office. He would not have come before the courts, it transpired, but for an inquisitive postman, whose suspicions had been aroused solely because Hensey was a Roman Catholic and lived a genteel life. Hensey was found guilty of treason, though there was no evidence that his information, culled from newspaper paragraphs, had

---

[20] B. Austen, *English Provincial Posts, 1633–1840: A Study based on Kent Examples* (London, 1978), ch. 2.

actually been sent. He was eventually released without further punishment.[21]

MPs and peers used their parliamentary privilege of franking covers to favour family, friends, and political connections. The revenue potential of the postal service was largely unexploited. Profits reached a peak of £110,000 in 1727, and failed to rise again until after 1764. Net receipts rarely exceeded £100,000 in the intervening period. Then they rose dramatically, to nearly £175,000 by the eve of the American War.[22] Highway improvement and economic expansion generally offered the opportunity of growth and also stimulated thoughts of change. The post was traditionally carried by post-boys riding in all weathers and risking many hazards, both natural and man-made. They aroused increasing concern at a time when sympathy for the young was in fashion. Animal lovers could conveniently join in this anxiety. The American Quaker John Woolman, visiting England in 1772, was so shocked by the cruelty which the postal system inflicted on boys and horses alike, that he advised his correspondents at home not to write to England by means of the public post except in dire necessity.[23]

Had Woolman lived to make a later trip to England, he would have noticed major changes. Mail-carts were introduced in the 1770s, and in 1784 there came a great landmark in postal practice. In that year John Palmer introduced his first mail-coach on the road to Bath. Dover followed a year later and the days of the post-boys were numbered. Postmasters increasingly ceased to be innkeepers and became public servants. Riding was contracted out where possible, and revenues rose steeply, from £160,000 in 1783 to more than half a million by 1797. It is significant that the pressure for change came from outside the Post Office. Palmer was in effect a private contractor. Anthony Todd, for a long time Secretary to the Post Office, as well as head of its interception department, used all his personal influence and not a little trickery to foil Palmer. His motive, to safeguard the inefficient but lucrative practices which he had spent a lifetime promoting, was shared by his colleagues and clerks. Only Pitt's insistence that Palmer be

[21] L. A. Parry, *Some Famous Medical Trials* (London, 1927), ch. x.

[22] K. Ellis, *The Post Office in the Eighteenth Century* (London, 1958), pp. 44–5.

[23] P. P. Moulton, ed., *The Journal and Major Essays of John Woolman* (New York, 1971), pp. 183–4.

permitted a fair trial and Palmer's own tenacity defeated this campaign of resistance and subversion by the paid servants of the State.

CANALS

Interest in inland waterways was not new. Much had been done in the late seventeenth and early eighteenth century to improve river navigation, partly by increased investment in dredging and widening, partly by co-ordination of reclamation schemes with the needs of water transport. However, there were few technical innovations, apart from the gradual adoption of the pound-lock in place of the wasteful flash-locks incorporated in many ancient weirs. Navigation schemes were among the 'bubbles' of George I's reign but most of them proved as insubstantial as the South Sea Bubble itself. The navigable mileage of inland waterways had increased from nearly seven hundred in 1660 to more than eleven hundred in the mid-1720s. Progress proved extremely slow thereafter.[24] The effect of the new spirit abroad at the end of George II's reign was accordingly all the more startling.

The first canal of the canal age was the Sankey Brook improvement, authorized by Act of Parliament in 1755, and designed to provide Liverpool with cheap coal. But the Duke of Bridgewater's canal from his coal-mines at Worsley, initiated in 1759 and by 1761 carried to the outskirts of Manchester, was a completely new waterway and attracted more attention. Most of the canals were the work of joint-stock companies financed by a broad spectrum of the investing public—landowners, businessmen, the professional middle classes. Bridgewater's was one of the very few such ventures launched as a private speculation. Not many even of the greatest landowners had the resources for commercial activity on so heroic a scale. In other respects Bridgewater's canal was more typical of what was to become a familiar pattern, especially in the mixed feelings which it aroused.

Bridgewater's plans for pushing on beyond Manchester to connect with the route to Liverpool quickly aroused the hostility of the rival Sankey Brook proprietors. Competition was to provide one of the keynotes of the canal age, as old and new interests fought to preserve what were essentially monopoly profits masquerading

[24] T. S. Willan, *River Navigation in England, 1600–1750* (London, 1936), p. 133.

as commercial enterprise. Two of these contests raised local competition to the level of national controversies: they even dominated the proceedings of Parliament. One was the battle over the Selby Canal in 1774 in which a new company sought to give Leeds direct access to the Humber at Selby. It was bitterly opposed by the old Aire and Calder Navigation, originally established in 1699, and well aware that its command of freight from the West Riding textile district to the sea would disappear at a stroke. The Aire and Calder eventually won after prolonged and costly arguments before the House of Commons, but only at the expense of building a new canal to improve its own navigation. Still more spectacular was the conflict of 1783 which arose from the alarm of many West Midland industrialists when it seemed that Birmingham might be left out of a great design to link Oxford and Coventry with Staffordshire and thereby with the Severn, the Mersey, and the Trent. Eventually Birmingham's voice was heard, but only after a House of Commons, preoccupied with grand strategy and the peace treaty with America, had been brought almost to a halt by the length, complexity, and contentiousness of the canal controversy.

In this form of legislative and entrepreneurial warfare the stakes were very high. The distribution of waterways in the early eighteenth century makes obvious the opportunities which awaited investors. Inland towns in the eastern counties from Kent to Northumberland were relatively well served by existing facilities. Some of them, such as Bedford and Cambridge, were many miles from the sea. But the dynamic ports of the eighteenth century, Bristol, Liverpool, Whitehaven, and Glasgow, were on the west coast, where, except in the Severn Valley, freight met with more obstructions and higher costs. In local terms, for instance among the burgeoning coal and cotton towns of south Lancashire, there were huge rewards for direct access to the sea and to other industrial centres. In broader, regional terms, there were large areas, particularly in the Midlands, where major manufacturing centres were denied water transport. Hence the ambitious schemes which followed on the pioneering work of Bridgewater and his engineer James Brindley.

Typical of these, and the master plan of Brindley himself, was the Grand Trunk or Trent and Mersey, designed to link the Trent at Wilden Ferry near Burton with the Mersey in Lancashire, thereby joining the east and west coast from Hull to Liverpool.

FIG. 7 (*a*). Navigable waterways, 1724–1727

Source: T. S. Willan, *River Navigation in England, 1600–1750* (Oxford, 1936), p. 32

FIG. 7 (*b*). The waterway system, 1789

Source: C. Hatfield, *British Canals* (Newton Abbot 1969), p. 80

This scheme, settled in 1766, after furious opposition from the old river projectors, required £150,000 starting capital and represented the coming together of diverse interests, including ironmasters in the West Midlands, landowners in Staffordshire, Warwickshire, and Derbyshire, Josiah Wedgwood, whose potteries were to be among the principal beneficiaries, and Bridgewater himself, whose operations in Lancashire and Cheshire were closely co-ordinated with the Midlands schemes. The ninety-four miles of waterway, some of it involving complex and costly engineering, was substantially complete by 1777. This vital arc of communication became the basis for grander projects still. In 1768 Coventry obtained parliamentary approval for a junction with the Trent and Mersey, and in 1769 Oxford followed suit in a design which was eventually to link the Thames with the great river estuaries of the north. The remaining leg in this mighty quadruped spanning the Midlands and linking Severn, Thames, Trent, and Mersey had already been the subject of legislation in 1766. The Staffordshire and Worcestershire was second only to the Trent and Mersey in breadth of conception; when it was completed in 1772 it connected Staffordshire with the Severn and generated a number of tributaries to manufacturing towns in the region.

Enthusiasm for canal development seemed boundless at its height between 1768 and 1776. In retrospect the limitations and qualifications are none the less obvious. The first three decades of George III's reign added approximately a thousand miles of navigable waterway to achieve a total of 2,223 by 1790; this was a large increase but left much potential for further expansion. In the later 1770s interest rates rose and trading conditions deteriorated under the impact of the American War and the government borrowing associated with it. It needed some years of peace to bring adequate supplies of commercial blood to the new arteries and to demonstrate just how vigorous they could be. The result was the great canal mania of the early 1790s. In the mean time some of the earlier projects encountered problems, raising doubts about the viability of further development. The Leeds–Liverpool canal, projected in 1770, was a particularly ambitious scheme, defying the watersheds of the Pennines and offering a link between Hull and Liverpool which would take in all the manufacturing districts of west Yorkshire and south Lancashire as the Trent and Mersey had incorporated those of the Midlands. But there was much dispute over the line to be adopted. The emphasis in York-shire was on rapid access to the west coast, in Lancashire on integration of each manufacturing town into the network. York-shire won the argument but the inevitable result was the diversion of Lancashire interest into other proposals. By 1774 twenty-four miles were complete on the Liverpool side, thirty on the Leeds. Money ran short, as it did on many early projects which rashly offered investors dividends during construction work, and the canal had to wait until 1816 before it was finally finished at a cost of £8,000,000.

Two other long-distance schemes made erratic progress. The Forth–Clyde waterway to connect Scotland's west and east coasts moved slowly from its commencement in 1768. The first Thames and Severn project also encountered difficulties. The vital Stroud-water from the Severn to the centre of the Gloucestershire textile industry at Stroud had been long planned, but was not opened until 1779. In 1783 work began on an extension to join the Thames at Lechlade. It included the celebrated Sapperton tunnel which was visited by the King and Queen in 1786 and pronounced a great feat of underground engineering. However, geology, poor financial organization, and the vagaries of the river authorities made the London to Bristol waterway less successful than anticipated.

Notwithstanding these difficulties the benefits of the first canals were obvious. The two most spectacular achievements concerned the essential raw materials of the agricultural and industrial rev-olutions. It is easy to neglect the importance of the canals to the landed interest; in parliamentary debates and pamphlet contro-versies landowners seemed mainly concerned to protect their parks and perspectives, while obtaining a good return on their own investment in the new ventures. But they also benefited from the carriage of fertilizers and access to new markets. The former were especially valuable. It was a truism much repeated by agricultural authorities of the late eighteenth century that most soils were capable of higher productivity with the application of materials available in profusion in distant farming regions. Land carriage made liming and marling hopelessly expensive beyond a few miles: cheap freight by water brought the price within the farmer's budget. Rural communities also derived a profit from canal build-ing, if only on a temporary basis. The local labour force provided manpower in the early years, before the navigator or 'navvy', became a familiar figure. It has been suggested that the first canal boatmen, often on vessels financed by the canal companies or other substantial industrial proprietors, were not the Romanies of folklore, but small farmers who found employment for their carts during canal excavation and subsequently took to the water.[25]

More than anything else the canals carried coal. Coal had always depended on water transport for competitive pricing, as the importance of the east coast trade from Newcastle demonstrates. Carriage by land for more than ten or fifteen miles raised its price to twice or three times what the market, let alone the pockets of the poor, would bear. On the canals coal could go wherever it was needed, heavily reducing the fuel costs of manufacturing districts. It was also widely available as domestic fuel, and not merely for middle-class households. The Oxford–Coventry link was welcomed for bringing coal to senior common rooms; more important, it fuelled the poor villages of the Banbury and Northampton countryside. In these areas timber and hedgerow destruction for firewood were commonplace 'crimes'. Now it was possible to defend canals on grounds of social benefit as well as economic productivity. This argument was particularly useful against rival, obstructive interests. 'And they must not have fire forsooth,' one pamphleteer observed, 'to keep them alive, for fear Cheshire cheese should go to London by way of Oxford, or coals should be raised by 1d. a hundred in Warwickshire!'[26]

Canals aroused great interest. Brindley, the best known of the new breed of engineers, became something of a cult figure in the 1760s. His origins were low, his literacy doubtful, his mechanical experience that of a millwright's apprentice. He seemed to epitomize the new classlessness and practical-mindedness of the times. 'As plain a looking man as one of the boors of the Peake, or one of his own carters; but when he speaks, all ears listen, and every mind is filled with wonder, at the things he pronounces to be practicable.'[27] His talents, it was said, deserved the pen of a Plutarch. They were, however, overstretched. He allowed himself to become involved in too many projects and the resulting need for delegation provoked bitter complaints from those who expected the personal attention of the master. He died, a victim partly of

---

[25] H. Hanson, *The Canal Boatmen, 1760–1914* (Manchester, 1975), ch. 1.
[26] T. Bentley, *The History of Inland Navigations* (2nd edn., London, 1769), p. 101.
[27] Ibid., p. 88.

diabetes, partly of his strenuous working life in sometimes dangerous conditions, in 1772, before his favourite Grand Trunk was
complete. But his fame was secure. Arthur Young found 'a scenery
somewhat like enchantment' at Barton Bridge, where the canal was
carried over the River Irwell on an aqueduct, and at Worsley where
subterranean access by barge to the mines created one of the most
evocative images of the early industrial landscape.[28] Accounts
of these marvels were quickly absorbed into the Englishman's
perception of his own place in the history of progress. Thomas
Pennant, something of a specialist in such image-building, portrayed the advances of civilization without hesitation or misgiving.
On the Trent and Mersey he saw majestic convoys of barges, each
loaded with twenty-five tons of coal, offering the canal proprietors
a well-earned rate of $1\frac{1}{2}d.$ per ton per mile. But how much greater
was the veritable cornucopia of benefits which flowed to the communities through which the canal passed: smart new slate from
Wales or Cumberland replaced primitive thatched roofs; coal could
be burned by humble villagers at London prices (this was one
commodity which *was* desirable at London prices); corn, butter,
and cheese monopolies were smashed for ever by the healthy
competition of remote farming regions; fields on the verge of utter
sterility were made green and productive once again with fertilizers
brought from further away still.[29]

URBAN GROWTH

Where the new canals had disruptive effects on the local economy
they were likely to prove worse for town than country. It was
claimed that some historic centres, Newbury and Guildford for
instance, had been disastrously affected by the impact of water
navigation on the corn trade, which could now hurry its produce
direct to the great merchants and distillers of London.[30] Sensitivity
to urban change in general, though 'urban' was not yet an adjective
in common use, was marked. There was widespread awareness,
particularly after 1760, of the growth of provincial cities, most
notably those manufacturing centres which depended neither on
the privileges of old corporations nor on the commercial vitality

[28] *A Six Months Tour Through the North of England* (4 vols., London, 1770), iii. 266.
[29] *The Journey from Chester to London*, pp. 50–6.
[30] *A View of the Internal Policy of Great Britain* (London, 1764), p. 279.

associated with the great ports. By the early 1770s Birmingham had a population of nearly 37,000, Manchester 27,000, Leeds 17,000, Sheffield not many less. All four had at least trebled in size since 1700. Birmingham was the first to reach 50,000, about 1780, and Manchester followed within the decade. In 1700 there were only seven towns with more than 10,000 inhabitants, all ports (Newcastle, Bristol, Yarmouth) or great regional centres since at least the late Middle Ages (York, Exeter, Norwich, Colchester). By the middle of the century there were nineteen places of this size, by its end nearly fifty. In 1700 one in five Englishmen (approximately a million in all) lived in something which contemporaries might have called a town, or closer to one in six in a settlement of 2,500, big enough to impress urban historians. But on either count the proportion reached about one in three by 1800.

London grew rapidly and remained in a class apart from all other urban areas; it had half a million inhabitants at the beginning of the century, some 900,000 at the end. But its growth rate was slower than that of many other towns and it seems even to have suffered a degree of stagnation at times, notably during the 1730s and 1740s, when more vigorous places were forging ahead. As a result it housed larger numbers but a smaller proportion of all town dwellers, less than a third in 1800 compared with about half in 1700. Moreover the urban hierarchy was changing rapidly. Two old regional capitals, York and Exeter, were overhauled by formerly insignificant towns like Bath and Sunderland. Some historic centres continued to flourish. Bristol and Newcastle remained major ports notwithstanding the rise of Liverpool and Glasgow. Norwich's worsted manufacture still made it a large and important city, certainly the country's third, perhaps its second until the 1770s. But before very long it was to wilt under the withering competition of the West Riding. If there was a pattern to relative decay, it was to be found in localized textile industries in the south. Tiverton, Worcester, Salisbury, Canterbury, and Colchester were casualties of specialization and concentration elsewhere. Significantly, some highly specialized cases among smaller towns flourished: Witney for blankets, Kidderminster for carpets. But the decline which Defoe noted in his inspection of southern manufacturing towns in the 1720s was irreversible fifty years later.

Despite such examples it must be emphasized that few towns declined in population over the eighteenth century as a whole, though erratic development before 1750 may occasionally have registered a net loss over short periods. In a context of overall population growth, urban failures tended to be relative, not absolute. Gloucester and Lincoln, for example, were county towns with a magnificent past. Gloucester entered the eighteenth century with a prime commercial position on the Severn, a thriving nail-making industry offering potential for future expansion, and obvious importance as a service and distribution centre. Something went wrong. Despite the prosperity of the Severn Valley in the early eighteenth century, most of the industrial enterprise migrated up it to the West Midlands, and most of the commercial enterprise down it to Bristol. Yet Gloucester continued to expand, from under 5,000 in 1715 to well over 7,000 in 1801. In any earlier period this would have been spectacular growth. Lincoln was already in decline as an industrial and communications centre, isolated as it was from the main arteries of eighteenth-century growth. John Mells, a customs officer posted to the area in the 1780s, described it as 'the meanest city this day in all England; many small compact towns have a much greater trade'.[31] Yet it almost doubled in size to about 7,000 during the hundred years before 1801.

Population growth was not the same as prosperity, but there were underlying tendencies that sustained even cities missing out on rapid economic development. Agricultural expansion assisted towns which were required as centres for commercial and professional skills. The middle class of rural and urban England alike needed provincial towns for their social and recreational life, often closely associated with an administrative and judicial function. Many a city which might have foundered on its manufacturing gained a living from its shire hall, its assembly room, its theatre, not to say its clergy, its lawyers, its doctors, and its retired gentlefolk. It was not only the Baths and Brightons, the Buxtons and Cheltenhams, which profited from the expansion of leisure. Dr Johnson's boast on behalf of his Lichfield was only partly bravado: 'We are a city of philosophers: we work with our heads, and make the boobies of Birmingham work for us with their hands.'[32]

Urban growth did not always mean physical expansion. Some ancient cities continued to grow without spilling over into the

---

[31] Lincolnshire Archives Office, Diary of John Mells, p. 77.
[32] Boswell's Life of Johnson, ii. 464.

surrounding country. Norwich's 40,000 inhabitants in 1786 remained more or less within the walls built by their ancestors, mainly at the cost of the gardens for which the city had been known. Elsewhere there was less evidence of containment. In industrial areas the march of the housing terraces into the country-side became a matter of common observation; small villages swelled into substantial townships with none of the institutional structure of old boroughs but all the bustle of new commercial confidence. In a town such as Ashton-under-Lyne, which expanded from 8,000 in 1775 to 16,000 in 1801, the names of new streets clearly reveal the building boom of the American War period: Charleston, Boston, Botany Bay.[33]

The term 'suburbs' crept into use, particularly in London. The lower-class districts south and east of the City vied with each other in squalor: '*Gravesend*', wrote one guide, 'is a detestable exhibition of the worst out-skirts of London.—It is *Wapping* in miniature.'[34] Londoners were embarrassed by the sordid sights on the great roads which led to the capital, but they were proud of the smart and prosperous appearance of neighbouring villages, formerly noted only for the occasional villa or country house. In 1744, John Armstrong, in his popular *Art of Preserving Health*, had celebrated the salubrity of London's half-developed country villages: 'Umbrageous Ham', 'sun-burnt Epsom', 'Chelsea low', 'high Blackheath, with wintry woods assail'd', Hampstead 'courted by the western wind', Greenwich 'waving o'er the water', Dulwich 'yet by barbarous arts unspoil'd'. Only in Richmond ('that sees an hundred villas rise') did he detect alarming urban expansion.[35] Thirty years later all these villages were growing fast, mainly to accommodate middle-class housing rather than upper-class retreats.

Social geography was inevitably affected. The most ancient centres were the slowest to change. In Norwich in the 1780s the greatest business families still lived in the central parishes of Mancroft Ward which had always been associated with the mer-chant oligarchy. A hint of future trends was provided by one of Humphry Repton's earliest commissions to build a villa in the

[33] E. Butterworth, *An Historical Account of the Towns of Ashton-under-Lyne, Stalybridge, and Dukinfield* (Ashton, 1842), pp. 94, 96–7.

[34] Arthur Young, *A Six Weeks Tour through the Southern Counties of England and Wales* (London, 1768), p. 75.

[35] *The Miscellaneous Works of John Armstrong* (Dublin, 1767), pp. 5, 13.

outskirts for the city's wealthiest mayoral family, the Ives.[36] In Gloucester the same pattern of riches in the centre, poverty on the fringe, persisted. The streets in which Robert Raikes was inspired by the spectacle of idle and impoverished children to conceive his Sunday school plan, lay in the out-parish of St Catherine's, where Gloucester's poor had lived for centuries. But where there was rapid expansion of housing the priorities of social snobbery and superior services asserted themselves. Leeds acquired its Parks, Birmingham its Crescent, Sheffield its Paradise Square. These new bourgeois settlements were quickly overrun by the need for cheap working-class tenements around the inner cities in the early nineteenth century; none the less, they represented an important stage in the evolution of suburbia.

The effects were most marked in London. The growth of the slum parishes of east London, Shoreditch, Hackney, Bethnal Green, Stepney, Ratcliff, Shadwell, Limehouse, Wapping—aroused much concern. Urban visionaries planned cheap lower-class housing in the vicinity of smart middle-class development, in order to ensure a proper social balance. Such visions were not shared by building speculators. Even in the City there were signs that the old harmony and hierarchy were disintegrating. The new breed of City businessmen and their families had no desire to live over their premises, in paternal proximity to their servants, apprentices, and poor. 'Oh,' cried Colman's Miss Sterling in his highly successful play *The Clandestine Marriage*, 'how I long to be transported to the dear regions of Grosvenor-Square! far, far from the dull districts of Aldersgate, Cheap, Candlewick, and Farringdon Without and Within.'[37] That prince of bankrupt bankers, Alexander Fordyce,[38] was thought distinctly eccentric to have maintained a lavishly furnished *pied-à-terre* in the City, behind an unprepossessing façade in a dingy lane; his aristocratic wife Lady Margaret was teased by the King himself about it.[39] There were diverse consequences. One of the reasons the court found it so difficult to get its friends to play a leading part in City politics against the Wilkesites was their reluctance actually to reside

[36] G. Carter, P. Goode, K. Laurie, *Humphry Repton Landscape Gardener, 1752–1818,* p. 110.

[37] *The Dramatic Works of George Colman* (London, 1777), i. 173–4.

[38] See pp. 569–71.

[39] *Memoir of the late Mrs Henrietta Fordyce, Relict of James Fordyce* (London, 1823), pp. 37–8.

there. The absence of social regulation became even more worrying, as the great migration to Marylebone got under way in the 1760s and 1770s. Was it any wonder, critics asked, that apprentices were unruly, that the City militia had been reduced to a band of undisciplined ragamuffins, or that fine City houses were left empty or turned over to tenement housing? Such pleas had little impact on the social imperatives of Georgian London. In the *World* in 1787, it was remarked that 'No family of ton can breathe eastward of Berkeley Square; and Turnham Green, Finchley, and Barnet are considered within the smoke of London.'[40]

The march westwards did not stop in fashionable West End squares or even in Marylebone streets: the advance guard was already to be found in villages and market towns further afield. The eighteenth century had yet to find a word for commuting, but it knew the practice. John Howlett described this kind of businessman: 'The greater part of his family are chiefly in the rural mansion, where he himself passes his nights, and only repairs to the city for the transaction of his commercial affairs by day.'[41] There were weekenders too, described with derision by the novelist Richard Graves:

Every little clerk in office must have his villa, and every tradesman his country-house. A cheesemonger retreats to his little pasteboard edifice on Turnham Green, and when smoking his pipe under his codling-hedge on his gravel walk rude with coal-ashes, fancies himself a Scipio or Cincinnatus in his retreat; and returns with reluctance to town on Monday night, or perhaps defers it till Tuesday morning, regardless of his shop, and his inquisitive and disgusted customers.[42]

Mr Diaper in Edward Kimber's novel *The Life and Adventures of Joe Thompson* spent half the week in London but left his wife in his country house.[43]

The new trends gave rise to problems. Colman depicted some of them in *The Spleen; or, Islington Spa*, the story of a tailor who retired to the 'country' with his family and found it unbearably dull. Garrick wrote the prologue and enquired, 'Would not he Islington's fine air forego, Could he again be choak'd in Butcher-Row?'[44] Vicesimus Knox devoted an essay to the difficulties

[40] Quoted J. Ashton, *Men, Maidens and Manners a hundred years ago*, p. 84.
[41] *An Examination of Dr Price's Essay on the Population of England and Wales*, p. 88.
[42] *Columella*, ii. 173–4.
[43] (1783 edn.), p. 25.
[44] *The Dramatic Works of George Colman*, iv. 269.

experienced by businessmen who sought rural retreat but found themselves beset by a resentful, envious, and interfering community, far removed from the bucolic harmony described by the poets.[45] The situation could be reversed of course: in 1768 a writer styling himself Jerry Jonquil censured those city ladies, who, retiring to the country, brought with them social punctilios and precedences which set female society hopelessly at odds.[46] (Given the enthusiasm of the rural middle class for London fashions, this is a less plausible story than Knox's.) The effect on the appearance of London's immediate environs was said to be considerable. The ideal situation was wittily described by Robert Lloyd in his *Cit's Country Box*, of 1757.

> Some three or four miles out of town,
> (An hour's ride will bring you down),
> He fixes on his choice abode,
> Not half a furlong from the road:
> And so convenient does it lay,
> The stages pass it ev'ry day:
> And then so snugg, so mighty pretty,
> To have an house so near the city!
> Take but your places at the Boar,
> You're set down at the very door.[47]

The suburban box sprang up first in places such as Clapham, Fulham, Camberwell, Newington Butts, and Kentish Town. It was embellished in the contemporary taste, sometimes with startling results: Chinese railings, temple façades, tiny ha-has to distant prospects, level lawns to ensure the admiration of travellers. There was much mockery of so-called country boxes. They were often built in rows like the London streets from which their occupants had fled, their gardens and summer houses were all too visible from busy thoroughfares, and their 'prospect' might include sights as unappealing as the gallows on Kennington Common and the cupola of St Paul's shrouded in smoke. By the 1770s these novel residences were appearing further afield. Essex, Hertfordshire, Buckinghamshire, and Surrey began to sprout rural retreats, many of them, by the 1780s, in the new cottage manner.

[45] *The Works of Vicesimus Knox*, ii. 469–74.
[46] *London Magazine*, 1768, pp. 652–3.
[47] W. Kenrick, ed., *The Poetical Works of Robert Lloyd*, i. 42–3.

URBAN IMPROVEMENT

Urban growth required a degree of mental adjustment. The arguments against cities were old. They were premissed on the assumption that metropolitan mores, especially metropolitan monopoly and luxury, sapped the simple patriotism and honest integrity of rural society. This kind of criticism did not soften in the eighteenth century. Indeed it was somewhat sharpened by the success of Richard Price and his friends in causing a panic about population trends.[48] They found it easy to prove that death-rates in cities were much higher than in the country. The obvious conclusion was that the health and labour of the countryside were being drained into an urban 'sink of mortality'.

Price's opponent John Howlett insisted that it was perfectly feasible to render cities healthy, by measures like those pursued in Chester to raise immunity against smallpox. He also went on the offensive by claiming that cities had a beneficial effect on the country around them. Provocatively, in view of contemporary alarm about London's expansion, he ventured to voice his delight at the prospect of further growth, even to the extent of twice its existing size.

All around neat and elegant country houses would be taking possession of every pleasant hill or vale; and gay villages would be rising on every side, which would soon become rich and populous. That this is not mere speculation or fancy, the amazing growth of the towns of Liverpool, Manchester, and Birmingham, within these 60 years past, and the correspondent increase, in populousness, beauty, and significance, of the towns, villages and houses in their respective neighbourhoods, are strong presumptive evidence.[49]

Enthusiasts for the architecture of London also pressed home the economic arguments. According to James Stuart, London was not the swollen head of a drained body, but the very heart, pumping new life into every rural limb. Lopping it off would 'reduce this numerous, flourishing, busy succession of men, called the British nation, to the small number of inhabitants, which the soil, rather ungrateful in itself, could naturally maintain, planted here like

---

[48] See pp. 636–7.
[49] *An Examination of Dr Price's Essay*, p. 6.

cabbage-stalks, and vegetating through the utmost length of years, without wants, and without enjoyment.' Stuart also put some ingenious moral arguments. If the temptations of life in London were considerable, so were the gains. In cities there was more charity, humanity, and 'social virtue' than elsewhere.[50] How many of the improving societies and associations formed by benevolent Londoners would have sprung up in the provinces? Was it even true that the morality of the countryside was superior? One of London's defenders claimed that in the rural arcadia of the north, churches had broken-down communion tables and filth on the floor, prayer books and devotional literature were notable by their absence, and not 10 girls in 50 were still virgins at the age of 17: 'I will stake my credit, that the metropolitans will have by far the majority of vestals.'[51]

A few blemishes on the urban record might be admitted. Churlish Londoners, hardened by the pressures of living in such a crowded environment, made a bad impression on foreigners. But no more than minor improvements in everyday civilities were needed to put this right. *Rules for Behaviour for this populous City* in 1780 advised citizens not to walk arm in arm in the street, to give oncoming strangers the wall without squabbling, to step aside to converse with acquaintances, to use elbows but not hands when pushing through a crowd, to pick up only one paper at a time in the coffee-house, never to whistle in public, and always to treat strangers respectfully, not indeed with a view to French 'complaisance' but rather to making one's fellow citizens 'easy'. It seemed a simple enough formula to complete the moral triumph of metropolitan society.[52]

Readiness to defend city life was by no means synonymous with complacency about its material conditions. The very suddenness of urban expansion made demands for better planning more insistent. In London there was a notable building spurt after some years of relative inactivity. Many of the great squares associated with London's more opulent class had been laid out in the late seventeenth century: this was true of Leicester Square, Bloomsbury Square, St James's Square, Soho Square, and Golden Square.

[50] James Stuart, *Critical Observations on the Buildings and Improvements of London*, pp. 41, 42, 47.
[51] *London Magazine*, 1778, p. 395.
[52] Ibid. 1780, p. 197.

More recent developments in the West End—Berkeley Square, Grosvenor Square, Cavendish Square, and Hanover Square— belonged to the first quarter of the eighteenth century and progressed only slowly under George II. The great thoroughfare of Oxford Street remained for much of its length an unsavoury haunt of footpads and prostitutes after dark. To either side it displayed a curious mixture of urban splendour and semi-rural squalor. After 1760 the pace noticeably quickened. North of the City, Finsbury was growing fast and acquired its polite seal of approval with Finsbury Square, begun in 1777. Further to the west the Bedford estate at last started to exploit the huge potential of its Bloomsbury holdings, with the historic decision to build Bedford Square in 1776. In Westminster the Adam brothers began their ambitious and perilous speculation, the Adelphi, in the Strand. Most extensive of all was the furious activity which took place in the parish of Marylebone. Much of it was concerned with relatively cheap housing intended for middle-class buyers: it was often commenced on an unstable basis with ground landlords selling long leases in small plots. The builders who took up such leases were notoriously vulnerable—'Marylebone bankruptcies' became something of a catch-phrase in the 1770s. None the less it was this housing which supported the great migration of bourgeois Londoners to new and more fashionable surroundings, 'those vast spaces of Ground', as one observer put it, 'which from Bond Street were so lately green fields, and are now Covered with almost Numberless buildings, forming the New Squares and Streets extending even to Mary-Le-bone.'[53]

Building on this scale generated both problems and possibilities. There was a well-established tradition of criticizing London's layout and architecture, since, as it was argued, the opportunities created by Wren after the Great Fire had been wilfully wasted. The litany of laments was rehearsed by James Ralph in his *Critical Review of the public buildings ... in and about London and Westminster* of 1734. John Gwynn put similar points to a more receptive audience in his *London and Westminster Improved* in 1766. The great public buildings of London, compared with the baroque splendours of Paris and Vienna, were a scandal. The House of Commons, House of Lords, and lawcourts in Westminster Hall, while they reflected England's venerable past, suggested an

[53] *Correspondence of George III*, ii. 595.

abysmal want of aesthetic taste in the governments and parliaments of post-Revolution times. The river, a magnificent natural highway, was grossly misused. London Bridge, with its tottering skyline of houses and workshops, loved by narrow-minded Cockneys, belonged more in the sixteenth century than in the eighteenth. Westminster Bridge, begun in 1739, took nine years and nearly £400,000 to construct; its elegance merely whetted the appetite of the improvers, who looked to embankment of the Thames and further bridges, to give the capital a waterway matching its importance.

Dry land was not less depressing. The City was a labyrinth of ill-kept streets and unsafe alleys, rendered offensive by cattle markets, slaughterhouses, and the thoughtless driving of every species of livestock along public roads. Ancient gates and narrow streets created bottle-necks. Charing Cross and Temple Bar were notoriously congested, and around Westminster Hall the traffic kept ministers of state, peers of the realm, even royalty, in their carriages for hours at a time. Those who looked to the opulent west found little to impress them. Where, asked James Stuart in 1771, were the radial avenues, the gardens, fountains, and statues required to set off the elegance of the newly built squares and terraces? In Red Lion Square four watch houses surveyed a wilderness of rubbish and rank grass; in Cavendish Square an attempt at pastoral effect resulted in 'cooping up a few frightened sheep ... with sooty faces and meagre carcases, ... starting at every coach'. Oddly, in such a plutocratic society, Gwynn remarked, the grandest buildings were public hospitals—Greenwich, which, with its decrepit paupers, seemed 'intended merely to put real elegance out of countenance', Bethlehem and, most recently, the Foundling Hospital. There were other notable products of the reign of George II and Palladio, some of them eccentric as well as impressive, like Kent's Horse Guards and Dance's Mansion House. But where was the sheer grandeur of conception which had transformed Berlin and Nancy? If the price of English liberty was tawdry muddle, perhaps there was something to be said for Continental absolutism.[54]

Rescue was at hand, but in pen and ink, not bricks and mortar. Magnificent royal palaces and senates were planned; so were great

[54] James Stuart, *Critical Observations*, pp. 7–8, 10, 13; John Gwynn, *London and Westminster Improved, Illustrated by Plans* (London, 1766), p. 119.

new throughfares running east and west along Cheapside and
Oxford Street, north and south from Finsbury to Southwark, each
lined with grand town houses, gardens, grottoes, and statuary
galore. Such visions were unlikely to be realized. There was nothing
resembling a planning authority for the capital as a whole, and
government resisted demands to take a lead, for example by
investing the proceeds of one or two of its lotteries to set an
architectural example. The only large project in which the State
took an interest, Sir William Chambers's essay in learned conservatism, Somerset House, provoked debate but hardly suggested
an enterprising approach to centralized planning. The City, which
might have co-ordinated planning within its walls, had a reputation
for unyielding narrow-mindedness and commercialism. It did its
best even to obstruct schemes for improvement beyond its jurisdiction, including a widely admired project of 1771 for the
Durham Buildings Embankment on the Strand. Private landlords
were capable of enforcing uniformity and did so to some effect on
the Bedford and Portman estates. But critics were unimpressed by
planning of this kind, designed more with a view to the convenience
of the landowner than the edification of the public.

More determined efforts were made to improve everyday conditions of life in the capital. Unlike the grand manner desired by
the architects, this had a practical logic which gave it a better
chance of success. The main problems were well known. London
and Westminster were both notoriously ill-paved, and since the
widespread introduction of piped water in the early eighteenth
century even new paving was soon wrecked by reconstruction or
repairs. Most streets continued to have a central watercourse, at
times a torrent of sewage and rubbish. Few streets were properly
cambered, and householders intent on keeping the dust at bay
outdid each other in raising their doors and pavements ever higher,
creating bizarre variations in street levels. Guttering ended in
spouts which poured water directly on to the street, regardless of
its users; those who escaped water above and filth below stood an
excellent chance of injury from the colourful, but often dilapid-
ated, signs which indicated shops, trades, or merely private residences. Lighting was variable and, like watching, depended on the
attitude of individual parishes or even individual residents. In most
of these matters the existing municipal authorities had neither the
legal authority nor political weight to improve them. Within the

City attempts at concerted action ran into obstruction at parochial level and found householders reluctant to carry out their ancient duties of paving, lighting, and watching. Outside the City a bewildering array of parishes and other authorities lacked the will as well as the power to impose unity. But by the 1750s the case for reform was overwhelming, and even the benighted authorities of a custom-encrusted metropolis were ready to act.

John Spranger's published scheme of 1754 for paving Westminster had a particularly powerful effect on metropolitan opinion, but the first steps were taken by the City, which formally requested special powers to improve its streets by Act of Parliament in 1760.[55] A commission was set up with full authority for rating householders and supervising construction, repairs, and maintenance. The City's gates were dismantled in 1761; one of them, Ludgate, had been renovated and beautified for centuries of further service as recently as 1733. There were other sentimental casualties. The historic Holbein gate in Whitehall, a cause of chronic traffic problems, was at last removed in 1759. Temple Bar, however, survived periodic appeals for its demolition. The commencement of Blackfriars Bridge in 1760 and the prospective competition which it offered compelled the City to improve London Bridge. Its quaint superstructure disappeared to much lamentation. The work of paving and lighting on a uniform plan proceeded apace. Spouts gave way to drain-pipes; signs were replaced by house numbers— a symbolic as well as practical assertion of the new orderliness and rationalism. Westminster was not far behind. In 1762 Parliament set up the Westminster Paving Commission, charged with bringing the populous parishes of Westminster to co-operate in street improvement. The Commission proved controversial, particularly among vestrymen who saw their money spent without parochial control, and amendments were later made passing some of the powers in the Act of 1762 back to parish committees. The expense of the new paving proved high, and progress was necessarily spasmodic. None the less the transformation of much of the urban landscape of London and Westminster astonished contemporaries, as did the hidden but no less gratifying extension of the piped water system which accompanied it. George Keate celebrated the new British triumph in 1779:

[55] *A Proposal or Plan for an Act of Parliament* (London, 1754).

The good order preserved in our streets by day,—the matchless utility
and beauty of their illumination by night—and what is, perhaps, the most
essential of all, the astonishing supply of water which is poured into every
private house, however small, even to profusion!—the superflux of which
clears all the drains and sewers, and assists greatly in preserving good
air,—health,—and comfort!—[56]

What London does today the provinces do tomorrow. In fact some
provincial cities had obtained 'Improvement Acts', as they came
to be called, before London. Such statutes included the planning,
rating, and co-ordinating powers required to replace cluttered
medieval townscapes with neat terraces, open spaces, and adequate
lighting, sewage, and watching services. After the London experiment this trickle turned to a flood. A few cities, mainly those with
corporations jealous of entrusting new powers to independent
commissions composed of local ratepayers, declined to participate.
Leicester was perhaps the biggest to turn down the opportunity;
it was also significantly one of the last manufacturing towns to
obstruct the use of new industrial machinery, thereby condemning
itself to relative stagnation. But elsewhere there was no shortage
of interest in municipal improvement. One waggish writer, Marcus
Ironicus, predicted in 1768 that lamps would soon appear every
thirty yards along the main roads to the capital, and that carpet
would be laid to ensure genteel travelling.[57]

Pride in cleaning up towns and cities went beyond the new
authorities, as the various self-help schemes of the period indicate.
Churches and their surroundings were included, contrary to the
belief of later generations of censorious Victorians. Again the accent
was on order, hygiene, and comfort. Churchyards and burial
grounds often suffered from insanitary conditions and unsavoury
reputations which galvanized the municipal improvers into action.
At Newcastle, for example, the churchyard, according to the
incumbent, was typical of many in the north-east, which suddenly
ceased to be 'the Receptacles of Filth, or Haunts of nightly
Lewdness'.[58] Those who lived through this era had no doubt
that they had witnessed astounding changes in urban conditions.
Chichester, for instance, was by no means one of the industrial
success stories of eighteenth-century England. Yet its Baptist

---

[56] *Sketches from Nature* (London, 1779), ii. 209.
[57] *London Magazine*, 1768, p. 23.
[58] J. Brand, *Observations on Popular Antiquities*, p. 81.

diarist James Spershott, writing at the age of seventy-four in 1784, observed:

This Century I think may be called the Golden Age. I have seen almost the whole city and Town, new built or new faced, a spirit of Emulation in this way having run through the whole. And that from the Beauty, Elegancy, and new taste in Building, Dress, etc. it would appear to an ancient inhabitant, if reviv'd, as if another Cissa had been here.[59]

Commercial interest was to the fore in the new planning. In small towns reorganizing markets was a high priority: ramshackle 'shambles' and stalls gave way increasingly to superior trading centres financed out of the rates. The agriculturalist William Marshall reported on typical improvements in the 1780s in Gloucester, Tewkesbury, and Cheltenham, condemning the old network of market booths often situated in the middle of main thoroughfares, 'Whereas, in a square, inclosed with shops, shades and penthouses; with shambles in the center, and a corn market at the entrance—the whole are brought together, rendering the business of market commodious and comfortable.'[60]

Apart from practical considerations the new taste had strong aesthetic support. Industrial cities which had grown rapidly in the middle of the century had an advantage in this respect. They were built spaciously in the first instance and often with the elegant brick terraces now favoured. Smollett's Matthew Bramble found Glasgow 'one of the prettiest towns in Europe', while the young William Hutton, in 1741, marvelled at the sight of Birmingham, 'in all the pride of modern architecture. I was charmed with its beauty.'[61] Even old towns might have encouragingly smart new streets. Newark delighted Arthur Young: 'each side of the whole street forms but one front, and in a very neat taste. How much is it to be lamented, that it is not the method in all the towns of *England*.'[62] Young's wish, judged by subsequent developments, was by no means ambitious. There is no way of knowing just how much of the medieval heritage vanished in this, the first age of systematic urban improvement, but it must have been considerable.

[59] 'Spershott's Memoirs of Chichester (18th Century)', *Sussex Archaeological Collections*, xxx. 159.

[60] Quoted D. Alexander, *Retailing in England during the Industrial Revolution* (London, 1970), p. 51.

[61] *The Expedition of Humphry Clinker*, p. 283; L. Jewitt, *The Life of William Hutton, and the History of the Hutton Family* (London, 1878), p. 133.

[62] *A Six Months Tour through the North of England*, i. 102.

Ironically, it was at this time that scholarly gentlemen with country houses to fashion were discovering the glories of Gothic: Horace Walpole at Strawberry Hill, John Chute at The Vyne in Hampshire, Sanderson Miller at Radway in Warwickshire. More significantly still, middle-class tourists were exploring the delights of England's medieval past in ruin and romance.[63] No doubt they failed to see the contradictions. At home the business and professional families who dominated urban society wanted space, cleanliness, order, regularity, neatness; in their tours, as in their journeys of the mind, they sought a somewhat different experience. The Gothic Revival offered historical fantasy without pain, discomfort, or squalor; in the town and city centres where they worked it was another story altogether. The hard-headed bourgeois citizen knew how to distinguish between the pleasures of imagination and the demands of improvement.

AGRICULTURAL IMPROVEMENT

Improvement was a favourite word of the 1760s and 1770s, carrying with it a great mass of material aspirations and moral assumptions. In nothing is this seen more clearly than in the immense resources devoted to the exploitation of the most basic of national assets, the land. In the tax records of the late eighteenth century the term 'improvement' appears again and again, signifying a new enclosure or enterprise, with an appropriate tax to reflect the increased profit of its undertaker or proprietor. But in a wider sense improvement meant a range of innovations, transforming the face of the landscape, and the structure of rural society. It has become fashionable to deride the concept of an 'agricultural revolution', principally by emphasizing that most of the practices recommended by improvers had been introduced long before. Enclosure, intended to promote more flexible use of land, and to introduce that convertible husbandry beloved of enthusiasts for mixed farming in the great Midland Plain, was a regular feature of the period 1560 to 1760. Fen drainage was as vigorously undertaken in the early seventeeth century as in the late eighteenth. The use of root crops to grow winter forage, a crucial condition of the expansion of stock which represented so important an element in higher production, was well known to seventeenth-century Englishmen. The famous

[63] See pp. 473 ff.

turnips which Lord Townshend was supposed to have brought to Norfolk were commonplace not merely in East Anglia, but in much of southern England in the latter part of the seventeenth century, as was clover. Knowledge of the value of fertilizers, and especially of the liming and marling praised in the agricultural reports of the 1790s, was widespread as early as the late sixteenth century. Stock-breeding had its devotees long before the age of Bakewell, as did experimental interest in course rotation and regional specialities like the technique for floating meadows.

Part of this case for an agricultural revolution which preceded the eighteenth century rests on terminological hair-splitting about what comprises a 'revolution', at the best of times a somewhat arid debate. Much, too, depends on contentious guesses about the growth of production in a period for which there are no national statistics, and little hard evidence even at local level. Still more involves claims about the late eighteenth century which are either false, like the assertion that Britain depended on imports for its growing food needs after 1770, or debatable, like the notion that nutritional standards went down. Major aspects of production, such as the expansion of cereal consumption for a growing population of horses, needed for transport and industry as well as recreation, are easily forgotten. It is obvious, too, that establishing the date of an innovation is no guide to the general adoption of a practice. At the very least the late eighteenth century's interest in agricultural improvement, on the part of both the State (government as well as legislature) and the literate public, suggests that the period was particularly important in the dissemination of techniques which had previously depended on individual enterprise.

The confidence of this age of endeavour is conveyed nowhere more clearly than in the travels of Arthur Young. His *Tours* belonged to the period 1768–71 and served as the introduction to a lifetime of publishing, much of it controversial. But Young was nothing if not a controversialist, and perhaps in retrospect the chief value of his work is the prominence which his overblown claims and colourful language impart to those aspects of a changing rural economy which contemporaries found most important. Young's central beliefs concerned the need to treat agriculture simply as a form of entrepreneurial activity. For tradesmen as such he had a certain contempt, but he was aware that the primacy of land could only be preserved by treating it in commercial terms. He stressed the 'necessity of distinguishing between the practice of agriculture as a mere means of subsistence—and practising it as a trade. The former is of no benefit to a modern state, the latter of infinite importance.' He had no sympathy with peasants who bemoaned extortionate rents or landlords who sought popularity at a 'hedge alehouse' by keeping their rents benevolently low. Nothing was better for an estate than a profligate heir whose need for money forced his stewards to ever more rigorous exactions, thereby compelling tenants to draw the full value from their land. 'Thus is the dice-box in this instance of ten times more value to the nation than the sleeping, dronish state of vegetation in which so many landlords are ever content to drawl on, and not raise rents, because their grandmothers did not.'[64]

Enclosure he took every opportunity to praise, rhapsodizing at the thought of what might be done, for instance, as he crossed the waste of Salisbury Plain. 'What an amazing improvement would it be, to cut this vast plain into farms, by inclosures of quick hedges, regularly planted with such trees as best suit the soil!' Of the new techniques in fertilizing he was an avowed enthusiast. One of many purple passages occurs at the very beginning of his first *Six Weeks Tour*, when he describes with wide-eyed wonder the gains made in Norfolk thanks to the practice of marling; any hint of experiment, however small, was praised, and the interest of public figures used in its favour. At Beaconsfield, he was delighted to find Edmund Burke seeking relief from his parliamentary labours with a carefully controlled enquiry into the beneficial effects of pigeon's droppings compared with rabbit's dung. Course rotation and breeding experiments he reported with special enthusiasm. Peasant ignorance infuriated him: in Derbyshire, he observed, one might as well have got the farmers to use an orrery as a hand hoe. In more sober mood, however, he could defend husbandmen whose total dependence on their annual crop made them cautious of taking risks with their livelihood. Some of his passions aroused hostility, particularly his attack on the extravagant horse in favour of the economical ox as a draught animal, and his campaign against the disastrous effects of tea-drinking on the labour force. His own farming credentials were also, it has to

[64] *Political Arithmetic* (London, 1774), p. 48; *The Farmer's Tour through the East of England* (4 vols., London, 1771), i. 161-2.

be said not unfairly, questioned. But as a repository of all that was most naïvely enterprising about the new spirit abroad in the 1760s, he remains a reliable guide.[65]

ENCLOSURE, ENGROSSING, AND RURAL PATERNALISM

Agricultural improvement depended in part on the collaboration of the legislature. There was no general parliamentary enclosure in the eighteenth century, though at times, notably in 1773, the House of Commons grew so concerned by the complexity of the local conditions with which it was asked to deal, that attempts were made to lay down certain rules of procedure. Enclosure was authorized by the private enclosure acts, private in the sense that they were promoted and paid for by private parties, but all too public in the sense that they involved changes in the organization of property and in the social structure of rural areas. They were not unusual in this respect. A high proportion of eighteenth-century legislation was private or local. Nor was the process itself new. Enclosure had two quite different meanings: the appropriation by individuals of land held by the community as a whole for its common use, and the parcelling out of 'open fields' previously held either in common for co-operative farming or in 'severalty' for more or less separate husbandry. In each sense it was an established feature of agrarian life. In some parts of the country, especially the south-west, and to some extent the south-east, open-field farming had never been widespread; in others, for example areas of East Anglia, the rapid progress of enclosure in the sixteenth and seventeenth centuries had left the open field a relative rarity.

Even in regions which retained open-field patterns of farming on a large scale, enclosure by informal private agreement, or by legal contract enrolled in Chancery, was not uncommon. None the less, the impact of parliamentary enclosure was considerable. Nearly four thousand enclosure acts were passed between 1750 and 1810, affecting roughly twenty per cent of total acreage in England and Wales. Most of these acts fell within two distinct

---

[65] *A Six Weeks Tour through the Southern Counties of England and Wales*, p. 167; *The Farmer's Tour through the East of England*, iv. 82, i. 159; *The Farmer's Letters to the People of England* (2nd edn., London, 1768), p. 355.

periods, the 1760s and 1770s, and 1793–1815.[66] Any hypothesis designed to account for this sudden enthusiasm for parliamentary enclosure therefore has to explain a loss of interest in the 1780s as well as an initial burst in the 1760s. It also has to incorporate regional variations. Enclosure in the third quarter of the eighteenth century was largely enclosure of open field. Enclosure of waste, in and about large cities, was highly controversial and has aroused the interest of historians of popular protest. But it was more characteristic of the early nineteenth century. The first generation of parliamentary enclosures was also concentrated in counties with ample open-field arable available for development. Its heartland was Warwickshire and Leicestershire, but many other counties were affected: the East Midlands including Cambridgeshire; the north-eastern counties of England's corn belt, especially Nottinghamshire and the East Riding of Yorkshire; the south Midlands—Oxfordshire and north Buckinghamshire, parts of Gloucestershire and Worcestershire.

Viewed in the long perspective of agrarian history, enclosure was the final stage in the evolution of flexible farming. The rigidity of open-field systems, which tended to require the establishment of permanent arable and permanent grass, was such that in favourable market conditions enclosure acquired an irresistible logic. Population growth and the bounty on grain exports put a premium on more efficient cereal production as well as better stock management; wheat prices stayed relatively high in the 1760s and 1770s at a time when interest rates were generally low enough to justify greater investment in agriculture. Both conditions were partially reversed in the 1780s.

Parliamentary enclosure could be employed by way of coercion when voluntary efforts had failed. The Commons generally refused to legislate without the assent of at least four-fifths of property-owners affected. Some bills had a far from easy passage, and not a few were thrown out. Even so there was an obvious element of compulsion in many enclosure bills, used principally against small owners fearful of change and lacking the capital to contribute their share of investment. The Church was in a strong position to block enclosure, and made tough terms, but ordinary freeholders and copyholders were less well placed to resist. With or without a conflict of interests, parliamentary enclosure had evident attrac-

[66] M. Turner, *English Parliamentary Enclosure* (Folkestone, 1980), ch. 3.

tions. Simple convenience and the desire for a watertight legal title ensured that a statutory device, once created, would regularly be employed in preference to other methods. Expensive though it was, in terms both of parliamentary fees and the cost of fencing, reorganizing, and new investment, it compared very well with the unlimited potential expense of litigation in case of disputes in the future.

Enclosure acts are sometimes seen in apocalyptic terms, transforming the landscape to create the modern English image of the countryside, a patchwork of meadow and hedgerow, and wrecking ancient village communities in the process. Such accounts tend to exaggerate the communal harmony of pre-enclosure days, and underrate the opportunities offered to all ranks by the new regime. It was argued at the time that enclosed land called for more labour, not less. On the other hand, the seasonal distribution of farm work, particularly where the object was increased grain production, might well have disruptive effects; certainly the tendency to replace resident farm servants with wage-paid labour hired for the purpose gained pace during this period. A still more vexed question is that of ownership. Attempts to depict the English yeoman of rural legend as the victim of capitalist enterprise, founder on the overwhelming evidence that small owners and owner-occupiers generally seem to have maintained their numbers after enclosure. Unfortunately the scarcity of land-tax records before the 1770s and 1780s makes it difficult to know with equal certainty what had been happening in the decades immediately prior to parliamentary enclosure, though there are hints that at least in some areas the trend may have been upwards from about the middle of the century.

Contemporaries were less worried by enclosure than by the related practice of engrossing. At its simplest engrossing meant reorganizing agricultural tenancies to create larger farms. Enclosure facilitated engrossing but it was not by any means a prerequisite of it. The beauty of engrossing was that it lay within the power of a single landowner to bring it about. Its advantage consisted in the economies of scale achieved with larger units of production, and in the greater scope for innovation which it provided. The economic benefits were not seriously contested by contemporaries. The social consequences were highly controversial. One was the enrichment of a new breed of tenant farmer, increasingly the most visible power in rural society. The poet Christopher Anstey in his *Speculation* of 1780 deplored the rise of this sinister figure:

> Proud tenants with rapacious hand
> Engross the produce of their land,
> Usurp the empire of the plains,
> And lord it o'er the humbler swains.

Behind this investment and the wealth which it created, were the high food prices of the 1760s and 1770s, some of which were thought to be associated with monopolistic farming. The growth of country banks was one of the features of the period: by 1785 there were well over a hundred in existence, the great majority established during the previous twenty years. It was alleged that one of their objects was to finance farmers who stockpiled their produce: the resulting scarcity brought prices to a level capable of supporting high rents, bank interest, and an inflated standard of living. Even so there would have been less complaint if it was not generally supposed that the main victims of this development were the rural lower classes. Once, it was suggested, hard-working labourers and the sons of yeomen could aspire to a small but self-sustaining farm of their own. Now only men with capital could provide the stock and meet the rent demands for large undertakings. All others were forced downwards into the pool of wage-paid labourers. Moreover, the new farmers often had pretensions of gentility (and their wives especially so), which corroded the old domestic economy and the old sense of community. No longer did master and mistress find it convenient for farm labourers to live directly under their supervision in the family home. Even worse, farmers who had a reduced need for labour and dreaded the poor-rate which accompanied unemployment, were often accused of systematic persecution of the poor. Cottages were destroyed and the settlement of married men prevented. In short, everything possible was done to drive the landless poor to other, less 'respectable' parishes, where the rates rocketed and whole communities of impoverishment and degradation sprang up.

This picture was not universally accepted. Young challenged the claim that larger farms meant less employment. In an exhaustive analysis he showed that small farmers of the traditional kind provided less work for the village labour force than their grander

successors. Large farmers were 'the greatest of all improvers;
Nature takes a new face under their hands; whole counties are
converted at once from deserts, into finely cultivated countries'.[67]
Plausibly enough, in the light of modern research, he suggested
that the superior capital and techniques of the great farmer required
more labour; certainly it was easy to show that improvements such
as marling and liming, greater reliance on winter forage crops,
more intensive use of hedging, ditching, and farm buildings, all
created extra work. Turning conventional wisdom on its head he
also argued against the resident farm servant or farm maid. The
new farms wanted wage labourers with families capable of increasing the rural population and supporting more hands for the economic and military service of the State. The old system favoured
by the sentimentalists had merely encouraged the employment of
childless men and women. The confrontation characterized by
critics as a 'sort of open war between farmers and the working
hand', was for Young and for other optimistic commentators like
the demographer John Howlett, a highly productive relationship
which worked ultimately to the advantage of both parties.[68]

Claims of this kind would have obtained greater credence if
observers had not suspected a more systematic onslaught on the
traditional values of rural society, led by landowners as well as
their tenants. The ultimate guilt of engrossing, after all, lay with
the proprietor, not the man who leased his land. The complaint
was commonplace in the economic tracts and literary laments of
the period, but the popular novelist Frances Brooke put it as
powerfully as any in her *History of Lady Julia Mandeville*, one of
the most successful novels of the early 1760s:

It is with infinite pain I see Lord T— pursuing a plan, which has drawn
on him the curse of thousands, and made his estate a scene of desolation;
his farms are in the hands of a few men, to whom the sons of the old
tenants are either forced to be servants, or to leave the country to get
their bread elsewhere. The village, large, and once populous, is reduced
to about eight families; a dreary silence reigns on their deserted fields;
the farm houses, once the seats of cheerful smiling industry, now useless,
are falling in ruins around him; his tenants are merchants and ingrossers,

---

[67] *A Six Months Tour through the North of England*, iii. 115.
[68] *London Magazine*, 1765, p. 37; J. Howlett, *An Examination of Dr Price's Essay*,
pp. 29–34.

proud, lazy, luxurious, insolent, and spurning the hand which feeds them.[69]

The motors of this degenerative social process were not simply economic. Landlords increasingly sought privacy from their own communities; country houses were remodelled (often with a view to relegating employees to a safe distance), parks extended, footpaths, bridle-ways, and even highways diverted, farmhouses and labourers' cottages demolished. Occasionally, entire settlements were relocated. Village architecture was subjected to the aesthetic as well as economic requirements of a pretentious class of landlords and gentlemen farmers. As Humphry Repton, who made his living out of advising this class, put it, if labourers' cottages 'can be made a subordinate part of the general scenery, they will, so far from disgracing it, add to the dignity that wealth can drive from the exercise of benevolence'.[70] Experts sought to convince the rural rich that it was in their commercial interest to provide for their inferiors. Nathaniel Kent, an enthusiast for agrarian experiments, including those of the King and Queen at Windsor, took a close interest in the practical value of benevolence, and offered the Windham family as an outstanding example of what could be achieved. At Felbrigg in Norfolk, he claimed, the Windhams had bought out every other freeholder and re-allocated the whole parish to small tenants farming on a joint plan, simultaneously meeting the needs of the new agriculture and the ordinary villager.[71] The result was not merely higher production and profit but an increase in population. Arthur Young offered similar examples, including Nicholas Styleman of Snettisham in Norfolk, who obtained an enclosure act for his parish, abolished rights of commonage 'which totally prevented the use of turnips and clover', but carefully preserved the existing forty-one houses, providing each with adequate gardens and pasture, thereby reducing the poor-rate from 1s. 6d. to 1s., and increasing the population from 500 to 600.[72]

Idylls of this kind remained unconvincing. The picture conveyed by more impressionistic evidence, artistic and literary alike, was a

[69] (2nd edn., 2 vols., London, 1763), i. 222–3.
[70] G. Carter, P. Goode, and K. Laurie, *Humphry Repton*, p. 116.
[71] Ibid., p. 114.
[72] *A Six Months Tour through the North of England*, ii. 112; *The Farmer's Tour through the East of England*, ii. 24–6.

distinctly darker one. Gainsborough's landscapes were peopled with subdued, industrious peasants rather than the cheerful rustics of rococo art.[73] The novelist John Cleland presented a morbid image of the nobleman's annual journey from London to his country seat as a kind of cortège making its way through a lifeless landscape.[74] Attempts to find the original of Goldsmith's deserted village range from the poet's Irish home at Lissoy, to the Earl of Harcourt's wholesale displacement of Nuneham Courtenay in Oxfordshire. Goldsmith's portrayal caught the contemporary imagination, not least because it fitted some important pre-conceptions of the time. It is not too much to speak of a crisis of paternalism in the 1760s and 1770s. It was thought that men whose ancestors had been content with the rural round, the company of tenant and parson of an evening, regular entertainment of tenantry and villagers alike, above all the Christmas orgy of patriarchal feasting, now preferred life in London, Bath, and Brighton. They were sternly lectured on their duties, mostly by those who had little acquaintance with the countryside. The Dissenting schoolmaster James Burgh, who spent much of his adult life at Stoke Newington, endorsed a calculation that one 'modern polite supper in town, with a set of Italian musicians to entertain the company' would have once entertained 'a whole country for a week'.[75]

Inspiring models of country hospitality were offered by novelists: in Henry Kelly's *Memoirs of a Magdalen*, there was Sir Robert Harold, whose benevolent rule in Devon made every peasant for twenty miles around ready to venture his life on his behalf.[76] There were even some living exemplars of such paternalism. Mrs Cappe, wife of an eminent Dissenting minister in Leeds and herself a considerable social reformer, tells the story in her memoirs of Sir Rowland Winn, one of the last great purveyors of old Yorkshire hospitality. In his capacity as a country magistrate his name became a byword for justice, his house was thrown open to farmers and cottagers alike at Christmas, and he was a leading patron of the local Ackworth Foundling Hospital.[77] Such a man seemed a standing

---

[73] J. Barrell, *The Dark Side of the Landscape: The Rural Poor in English Painting, 1730–1840* (Cambridge, 1980), ch. 1.

[74] *Memoirs of a Coxcomb* (London, 1751), p. 346.

[75] *Political Disquisitions* (3 vols., London, 1774–5), iii. 45. Burgh was quoting the Tory MP Humphry Sydenham.

[76] p. 12.

[77] *Memoirs of The Life of the Late Mrs Catherine Cappe*, pp. 80–5.

indictment of the polite and uncaring luxury which created an immense gulf between upper and lower classes in the countryside, bridged only by still more snobbish gentlemen farmers and cynical, monopolistic merchants.

HARVESTS AND SHORTAGES

The decay of the old paternalism could be portrayed as the price of improvement. But there were also developments in the 1760s which could not be blamed on any human agency. The period following the Seven Years War produced some freak climatic conditions. Winter temperatures in a number of years were exceptionally low, in 1763, 1766, and 1767 causing particularly serious problems. In February 1766 the newspapers published stories reminiscent of the winter of 1739–40: a peacock frozen to a branch at Birdlip in Gloucestershire, a Sheffield grinder who died in the snow on his way home from work a few hundred yards away, and the destruction in one night of the Duke of Bedford's new tree plantation at Woburn. Succeeding winters added terrible storms to extreme cold. In 1767, 1770, and 1774 there were severe gales and floods: Broadstairs was said to be 'undone' thanks to a storm which wrecked the pier and blocked the harbour in 1767, and Westminster itself was under water at one point in March 1774. 1776 was yet another hard winter: the Thames froze at Mortlake for the first time in many years. Nor did the summers of this period, cold and wet as most of them were, bring relief. Grain production suffered in notable contrast with earlier trends. In the first half of the century there had been major crop deficiencies only in four years, 1709, 1727, 1728, and 1740. The mid-1750s had brought two sharp harbingers of the coming misery, in 1756 and 1757, when high prices provoked food riots. There were at best moderate harvests in 1764 and 1765, and truly bad ones in 1766 and 1767. Then there was a brief respite until 1770, when a cycle of five years of shortage set in.

'We know not in England what belongs to famine,' Defoe had boasted many years earlier.[78] Even in the 1760s and 1770s it was possible to take pride in the fact that absolute want was very uncommon. 'Such a run of wet seasons a century or two ago', reflected the naturalist Gilbert White, 'would, I am persuaded,

[78] P. Earle, *The World of Defoe* (London, 1976), p. 90.

TABLE 6. *Average of wheat per imperial quarter, 1720–1790*
(shillings and pence)

Year	s.	d.	Year	s.	d.	Year	s.	d.	Year	s.	d.
1720	33	10	1739	35	2	1758	45	9	1777	46	11
1721	34	4	1740	46	5	1759	36	4	1778	43	3
1722	33	0	1741	42	8	1760	33	5	1779	34	8
1723	31	9	1742	31	1	1761	27	7	1780	36	9
1724	33	10	1743	22	9	1762	35	9	1781	46	0
1725	44	5	1744	22	9	1763	37	2	1782	49	3
1726	42	1	1745	25	2	1764	42	8	1783	54	3
1727	38	6	1746	35	9	1765	49	6	1784	50	4
1728	49	11	1747	31	10	1766	44	5	1785	43	1
1729	42	10	1748	33	10	1767	59	1	1786	40	0
1730	33	5	1749	33	10	1768	55	1	1787	42	5
1731	30	0	1750	29	8	1769	41	10	1788	46	8
1732	24	4	1751	35	2	1770	44	10	1789	52	9
1733	25	11	1752	38	3	1771	48	7	1790	54	9
1734	35	6	1753	40	10	1772	52	3			
1735	39	4	1754	31	8	1773	52	7			
1736	36	11	1755	31	0	1774	54	3			
1737	34	9	1756	41	4	1775	49	10			
1738	32	5	1757	55	0	1776	39	4			

Source: D. G. Barnes, *A History of the English Corn Laws from 1660–1846* (London, 1930), pp. 297–8.

have occasioned a famine.'[79] The very publicity accorded the discovery of a labourer and his family found dead in their house at Datchworth in 1769 was a reminder of the rarity of actual starvation. But there was no doubting the severity of the crisis, aggravated as it was by winters which put a premium on fuel as well as food. Matters were at their worst in the summer and autumn of 1766 when there was rioting against farmers who were alleged to be holding back supplies, and middlemen who were charged with hoarding grain to drive up prices. Troops were used extensively in the government's efforts to deal with these, perhaps the worst instances of the 'bread riot' in the eighteenth century, and a foretaste of the agonies inflicted on agrarian England in the age of Cobbett. Successive waves of rioting between August and October spread from the south-west to the Thames Valley, the Home Counties, and East Anglia in one direction and the Severn

[79] *The Natural History of Selborne*, ed. R. Mabey (London, 1977), p. 162.

Valley and Midlands in another. The most northerly county
affected was Derbyshire: in the north a somewhat better harvest
and rapid action by magistrates to prevent commercial exploitation
of dearth fended off serious trouble. In London the superior
drawing power of the metropolitan market kept supplies moving
and indeed contributed largely to the resentment of rural rioters,
especially in the hard-hit counties of Berkshire and Wiltshire.

The army was used to protect urban markets and disperse the
mobs which attacked mills and farmhouses. There were deaths in
several places, including eight in a bitter confrontation at Kidderminster, and many arrests—nearly 100 in Gloucestershire.
Special commissions were set up to try offenders, in Berkshire,
Wiltshire, Gloucestershire, and Norfolk, but sentences, in accordance with precedent in cases where the motive for riot was manifest
hardship, were less than draconian. Lord Barrington, the Secretary
of War, who had had the complex task of directing troops to
trouble-spots in most of the counties of southern England, was
dismayed by the leniency which the Crown, judges, and local
magistrates displayed.

Assessments of these events varied widely. Arthur Young was
cynical about the hardship. He claimed that the rioters were the
manufacturing work-force in the west and south, the agricultural
labourers in East Anglia. These were the most favoured elements
in the plebeian community: 'a riot is their best diversion'. If there
had been real deprivation, he thought, it would have affected the
underemployed workers in the decaying textile towns of Suffolk
and Essex, and the depressed farm labourers of the south-west.
Young, ever a defender of the farmer, was all too aware of the
interested use that might be made of such distress. Manufacturers
and tradesmen sought to keep prices of provisions low so that
wages could be held down and the competitive pricing of their
own products maintained. Young called this 'the corner-stone of
a vast fabric in modern politics': it is a remark which looks forward
to the repeal of the Corn Laws many years after his death.[80] This
is not to say that a Parliament of landowners was necessarily
impressed by the bleating of Manchester manufacturers and Trow-
bridge textile-masters. It was always sensitive to rural protest,
partly because of the disturbance which it caused in the county

---

[80] *A Six Weeks Tour through the Southern Counties of England and Wales*, p. 273; *The Farmer's Tour through the East of England*, iv. 319.

community, partly because failure to act at the centre was likely to transfer the financial burden to the poor-rates and the onus of control to disparate and somewhat uncertain authorities in the localities.

It was customary to resort to old arguments against commercial agriculture. The object of the rioting was to compel farmers, millers, and wholesalers to sell their produce at 'fair' prices in the market-place. To the extent that government gave instructions for the enforcing of Tudor legislation against artificially raising prices by 'engrossing, forestalling, and regrating', it encouraged such faith in the subsistence economy and the local market. There was much public pressure in this direction. Newspapers spread stories of profiteering. At the first signs of shortage in the autumn of 1764, it was alleged in Oxford that poor families were starving in parishes which also contained huge stores of wheat destined for other markets. Magistrates were often quick to respond to such concern. The most celebrated Justice of the age, Sir John Fielding, harangued the Grand Jury of Middlesex in October 1764 on the evils of monopoly. Historians agree. Rioters, it has been said, in effect appealed to a 'moral economy' of fair prices and paternalistic government, against a 'market economy' of commercial enterprise and *laissez-faire*.[81] Whether every rioting mob was quite so traditionally minded is open to debate. Many elements were mingled in the rhetoric of the late eighteenth-century rioter, some having to do with long-standing conflicts between employer and employee, some suggesting a levelling, even revolutionary approach to social relations. The relatively favourable conditions of the preceding decades gave the old legislation against middlemen an antiquated and obsolete appearance. Few realists took it very seriously. The fact was that the English corn trade was already arranged on market principles; the supply of London and the industrial centres would have been inconceivable without them. Knowledgeable writers thought that more storage, and more centralization, not less, were needed to feed a growing population without creating major regional blockages.

A more relevant debate concerned the international market, which since the late seventeenth century at least had been treated on the same mercantilist principles as trade in manufactured goods.

[81] See E. P. Thompson, 'The Moral Economy of the English Crowd in the Eighteenth Century', *Past and Present*, I (1971), 76–136.

The bounty on grain exports was becoming controversial by the 1750s as a result of the sheer size of the subsidy and the consequent diversion of national resources to landowners and farmers. Restrictions on food imports caused less difficulty because for most of the period supplies to the home market were plentiful and prices were low. Conditions in the 1760s changed all that. Acute shortages at home raised a great volume of protest against laws which favoured the land at the expense not merely of the labouring classes, but also of the manufacturing and trading interest. In 1764 a series of petitions to Parliament from urban centres concentrated on this point.

Parliament had three methods of dealing with this problem: a ban on exports, suspension of import duties, and prohibition of home distilling. All three were tried on a temporary basis, first in the crisis of 1756–7, then from the mid-1760s to 1773, always for a year at a time to preserve the pretence that this was merely a brief hiatus in policy, not a new departure. None the less, great reliance was placed on such measures, particularly when, in September 1766, Chatham's ministry found itself in the midst of a crisis, with Parliament's most recent legislation having lapsed. The Cabinet's decision to reactivate the legislation by means of the royal prerogative caused constitutional controversy, but also aroused patriotic fervour.[82] Chatham received an impassioned appeal to stop the grain ships sailing by the labourer-poet Simon Hedges, petitions poured in demanding an embargo on exports, and George III was portrayed in the prints granting relief to a grateful people. How much difference such action made, it is difficult to know. At the margin it must have had some effect, but in the longer run it was obvious that more permanent measures were needed.

The result was Thomas Pownall's Corn Law, the most important piece of legislation on the subject between the introduction of the corn bounty in 1689 and the later statutes of 1791–1846. Only a squabble between the two houses of Parliament prevented Pownall's bill reaching the statute-book in 1772; it finally did so a year later. Essentially it revised the existing scales to keep more grain in Britain when prices were high. The bounty was now made payable when corn at home cost less than 44s., not 48s. as before. All exports were banned at 44s., so that the effect was to stop the export market altogether at the point when home prices grew

[82] See above, pp. 371–2.

worrying; virtually unimpeded imports were permitted at a slightly higher level, 48s. The change can be dressed up as a major concession by the landed interest, but since recent history had repeatedly witnessed the granting of similar concessions for short periods, it confirmed an existing trend rather than introducing a new one. Its main and least desirable effect was to promote a whole series of frauds. Among other things the Act encouraged warehousing of corn at points of import and export: the great corn merchants became adept at manipulating supplies to take maximum advantage of the fluctuations of the market and the loopholes in the regulations. The sufferer in this was principally the taxpayer, who footed the bill for higher bounties and lower customs receipts.

Probably the new law made little difference to the supply of food. The truth was that the international and domestic grain trades were increasingly organized by specialized concerns, which made their money by juggling stocks of grain to meet the growing needs of the cities of western Europe. If the poor labourers of Wiltshire were victims of anything, it was of this rather than hard-hearted West Country farmers and millers. The less inhibited champions of the market made no bones about it. Young argued that the impression that high food prices were something 'that can be remedied by the government, must have an extreme bad effect on the minds of people'.[83] In the House of Commons Edmund Burke defended the benevolence of the market as the most effective long-term means of matching supply to the demand of the poorest sections of society. This was in 1772, when Pownall's Act was under discussion. Four years later Adam Smith, in his *Wealth of Nations*, launched his withering attack on monopolist practices in the grain trade. He did little to shake the complacency of the landed interest or even to reshape the law; but he gave intellectual edge to a process of reassessing agrarian policy already initiated by the poor harvests and population growth of the post-war decade.

PRICE INFLATION

Parliament, like the public, placed the staff of life in a special category, but concern about prices had wider scope. Butcher's meat and dairy products were as susceptible as bread to increased costs. The former caused particular alarm, for Englishmen prided

[83] *London Magazine*, 1772, p. 164.

themselves on their meat-eating propensity compared with foreigners. The figures cited by contemporaries need cautious treatment.

Short-term fluctuations could be very sharp and give a distorted picture of overall movement. None the less the essential fact of a significant increase in costs is uncontested. It was reckoned in 1785 that the price of butter in London had risen from 7*d*. or 8*d*. thirty years before to 9*d*. or 10*d*.; of a chicken from 1*s*. 3*d*. or 1*s*. 6*d*. to 2*s*. or 2*s*. 3*d*. Beef and lamb, subject to spectacular increases in the 1760s, had probably risen still more. A variety of causes was suggested, mostly connected with the supposed vices of commercialism and luxury. Nobody kept statistics of the horse population, but equally nobody doubted that the middle of the eighteenth century had seen a great increase in numbers. The result, it was said, was to divert cereals from consumption by cattle, with inevitable consequences for the price of beef and mutton. The new agriculture was also accused of eliminating cottagers as a class, and forcing the rural population, like its urban counterpart, to rely on market meat rather than the cottage economy of vegetable garden, pig and poultry, and common rights to fish and fowl.[84] The demand for butter, milk, and cheese seemed inexhaustible: each new turnpike opened up an area of country to specialized dairying, facilitating the dispatch of cheese and butter to new urban markets. Meat was another matter: improved communications did not help droving very much, and the conjunction of increased demand in the towns, with limited supply in the countryside, pushed up prices with alarming rapidity. Parliament was urged to take action. It was claimed that in London at least the 'carcase butchers' or wholesalers enjoyed an unhealthy monopoly against the 'cutting butchers' and also against the public interest. In 1766, eminent men, some of them involved in more political activities, founded an association in London to reduce meat prices, the aim being to co-operate with counterparts in Bristol and Gloucester. The results were not noticeable.

It was soon realized that the price rise was general. Everything seemed to be going up. House rentals rose, as sharply as agricultural rents, regardless of the fact that housing was barely affected by enclosure and despite the increased house-building in the cities.

[84] *A Political Enquiry into the Consequences Of Enclosing Waste Lands, and the Cause of the Present High Price of Butcher's Meat* (London, 1785).

London rents had actually fallen in the 1740s; their dramatic rise in the 1760s was all the more startling. Fuel went up too—by 3*d*. a bushel in London in the early 1760s. So did many less essential commodities. The rising cost of university education shocked less wealthy customers, notably country clergy anxious to see their sons follow in their footsteps. Precious collections of coins and manuscripts auctioned at the famous London house of Abraham Langford also commanded unexpectedly high prices: even numismatists were startled when a Black Prince coin fetched £25. 14*s*. 6*d*. in March 1766. No generation for one and a half centuries had lived with price inflation such as marked the third quarter of the eighteenth century. It is not surprising that voices were raised in protest.

It was not generally appreciated that population growth might be one reason for the price rise, if only because there was little recognition in the 1760s that the population was now rising rapidly. Some blamed extravagant fashions like tea-drinking, or avaricious producers and middlemen. A few more astute observers grasped that the price rise had to do with an increase in the money supply as well as a shortage of goods. As early as 1758 Soame Jenyns calculated that prices had increased by a third in the eighteenth century, and that one half of that had occurred between 1748 and 1757. He noted that this trend, allowing for a short time-lag, fitted the growth of the National Debt. It followed that anxiety about the malevolent middlemen was entirely misplaced; wealth, and especially paper money, were the real culprits.[85] In one sense, indeed, it was hardly a question of 'culprits'. Robert Wallace, in his *Characteristics of the Present Political State of Great Britain* of 1758 argued that the National Debt was a healthy product of a thriving economy: inflation was a tolerable price to pay. Such explanations were too sophisticated for most contemporaries. There was a persistent desire to believe that impoverishment, not riches, lay behind the price rise. 'Which of you', one journalist asked, 'can now produce undiminished the rent roll of three hundred years back?'[86]

It was a myth that inflation hurt everybody, though one believed by many in the 1760s. In fact the price rise affected some sections of society much more severely than others. Entrepreneurs of all

[85] *The Works of Soame Jenyns*, ii. 172.
[86] *London Magazine*, 1772, p. 218.

kinds, merchants, small traders, manufacturers (at least of domestically consumed goods and probably of exports too), landowners, and farmers, were in a position to defend themselves against its worst effects, even to benefit. There was a huge investment in agricultural improvements, and in public subscriptions to what would, in a modern State, be called the economic infrastructure, especially transport. There was also the less easily quantified investment in industrial enterprises. Such speculative activity was clear evidence of surplus income in the pockets of the propertied classes. It doubtless derived from mild inflation, light taxation, and expanding consumption. Middle-class Englishmen rarely lost by the combination. It was pointed out that merchants raised their prices faster than taxes increased or the value of money fell—creating a state of 'public poverty and private opulence'.[87] Farmers, too, tended to stay one step ahead of their landlords: hence the common belief that a leasehold farm was worth more in some circumstances than freehold land. As for the small businessmen and shopkeepers who represented the backbone of many trading communities, few would have disagreed with the scepticism voiced by Charles James Fox when complaints of a great depression in the capital were put to him in 1771. 'Survey the *unfortunate* citizens of London, sir, and you will find every shopkeeper of any consideration, with his elegant villa, and his variety of equipage.'[88]

Who then suffered? There were a few landowners who, out of idleness, incompetence, or benevolence, watched their tenants grow wealthy while their own incomes stagnated. Some tradesmen overcommitted themselves in specialized markets resistant to price rises and were exposed to the humiliation of bankruptcy. Above all, there were the families of those on fixed incomes, or, in contemporary parlance, 'settled stipends'. Such were schoolmasters and curates whose salaries were fixed by contract. Such too were many of the State's own employees. Government was slow to concede the need to adjust wages to inflation. At the end of the seventeenth century the ordinary excise officer's stipend of £50 made him the equal of many professional lawyers, doctors, and clergy. A hundred years later his successor was likely to be on the same salary and more on a level with small farmers or even skilled labourers.

[87] *The Works of Soame Jenyns*, ii. 184.   [88] *London Magazine*, 1771, p. 289.

Worse still was the plight of those who pledged their lives for the safety of the State. The able seaman's basic pay of 24s. per month was not raised between 1653 and 1797. The low prices and relative stability of the 1730s and 1740s perhaps made this bearable. But in the 1760s and 1770s the grievances of the forces became well nigh intolerable, especially if the graft and extortion which seemed to be normal in both services are taken into account. The common soldier was frequently defrauded by commanding officers who depended for their own living on profitable management of their troops. From time to time the authorities attempted to curb self-interested conduct, particularly on the part of colonels who saw their regiments as a form of commercial enterprise, but only structural reform would have had much effect. In the navy the ordinary seaman had additional hazards to encounter: a Navy Board which gave low priority to payment of wages, and civilian vultures, both in the Admiralty and the dockyard, who made a handsome living from the business of discounting pay tickets and remitting funds to families on shore.

Officers were also under pressure. In the army the cost of a commission rose even faster than prices generally. Genteel families were increasingly anxious to get their sons a place on the ladder; their salaries, however, did not go up. These were compared unfavourably at the onset of the American War in 1775 with day rates of 1s. 6d. earned by common labourers in London and 2s. 6d. earned by mechanics, journeymen, and craftsmen.[89] In the navy rigidly unchanging scales were made worse by peacetime conditions which removed the enticing prospect of prize money and put many officers on half pay. Much concern was expressed about the plight of the half-pay captains. Their petition to Parliament in 1773 was supported by a press campaign. North, for the Treasury, argued that ameliorating the lot of one group must create a precedent for every other, with disastrous consequences for the taxpayer. None the less, the Commons was sufficiently struck by the sufferings of the officers to insist on further enquiry, to North's embarrassment. But little was done. As he had prophesied, other serving officers were quick to press their own claims. So were the advocates of widows and families of officers who had retired from active service or had died in action. In many country towns there were

[89] Thomas Erskine, *Observations on the Prevailing Abuses in the British Army* (London, 1775), p. 22.

impoverished widows with children to support and no prospect
of sustaining the burden of gentility on an income which could
be exceeded by a hard-working labourer.

Significantly, goverment showed itself responsive to pleas for
better rates of pay and conditions only when the labour market
left it no option. In the naval dockyards, for example, there were
all the enemies of the efficient management championed by the
Earl of Sandwich, First Lord of the Admiralty from 1770 to 1780.
These included a skilled, entrenched work-force, a tradition of
'perks' and petty corruption, and a high degree of more or less
formal trade union (in modern terms) activity. Disputes were
not new, but Sandwich's determination to improve productivity,
principally by introducing the use of piece-work, was bound to
be controversial. 'In complying with the Task', he was told by
employees, 'we are committing progressive suicide on our
Bodies.'[90] The resulting conflicts were serious. In the summer of
1775, when the navy's yards were at full stretch to prepare for the
war against America, strikes occurred at Chatham, Woolwich,
Portsmouth, and Plymouth. In the end, Sandwich got his way,
but only by making the 'task work' voluntary and by conceding
the day-workers' claim of 2s. 6d. per day, in compensation for
giving up their 'chips' or customary rights to waste timber. The
non-civilian servants of the State would have been glad of such
consideration.

RESISTING THE PRICE RISE

It was not only lower-class workers who sought to combat inflation.
One group which caused much disquiet by its attempts to keep
abreast of rising prices was the clergy. Clerical incomes depended
heavily on tithes. In principle, tithes were proof against inflation
since they were a fixed proportion, in theory a tenth, of all produce.
They were much hated by those who paid them. Moreover, because
they were levied on gross production, not on net profits, they were
seen as an obstacle to agricultural improvement. Dislike of tithes
was one of the principal causes of anticlericalism in rural communities. But not all incumbents could plausibly be viewed as
leeches on their parishes. The stable conditions of the seventeenth

---

[90] J. M. Haas, 'The Introduction of Task Work into the Royal Dockyards, 1775', *Journal
of British Studies*, 8 (1968–9), 58.

century had often led the clergy to accept local agreements which provided a fixed composition or *modus* in place of tithes. The convenience of collecting a cash sum without disagreeable haggling or time-consuming collection in kind, the pressures brought to bear on priests by their secular patrons and parishioners, the sheer apathy which turned temporary agreements into immemorial tradition, all gave such agreements greater permanence than originally intended.

Conditions changed dramatically in the mid-eighteenth century. Large increases in rent were made possible by improvement, especially by enclosure. Parliamentary enclosure rarely worked to the disadvantage of the clergy, since it was generally approved on the basis that clergy were granted lands in lieu of tithes. Even if lay landowners in the House of Commons were not solicitous of the interests of the parish clergy, there were bishops in the Lords ready to use the legislative powers of the upper house to block bills which did not sufficiently protect the interest of their parish clergy. The allocation of land for rectorial tithes was usually reckoned at one seventh, sufficient evidence in itself that the clergy's tenth of produce was equivalent to far more than that in terms of actual profit. Clergy who had to live with ancient compositions in place of these were more vulnerable. Fixed payments not only left them without a share in improvement, but ensured that their incomes bought less and less in real terms. Ecclesiastical courts, with no power to enforce temporal rights, were unable to provide protection. But to the surprise of many, the secular courts proved more than ready to help. Generations of Whig lawyers consistently treated ecclesiastical law on a strictly secular basis, and dealt with Church lands as property like any other. Many lay gentry, after all, owned tithes and sought their preservation. But the courts also proved unexpectedly generous in construing the rights of clergy.

John Rayner, the contemporary chronicler of 'the parson, struggling with becoming spirit, against wealth, power, and interest', detected strong support for clerical pretensions in the middle of the century.[91] There were some epic battles won by the clergy, creating precedents for the future. In the case of *Bree* v. *Chaplin* (1775) the incumbent of the parish of Racton in Lincolnshire disputed the customary dues of £15 per annum. The principal landowner had found it worth while to invest £12,000 in improvement,

[91] *Cases at Large concerning Tithes* (3 vols., London, 1783), p. vii.

with consequently high profits: the Rector of Racton sought a
share of the proceeds and insisted on his right to collect tithes in
kind, valued at £200 per annum. The courts declared for him.
Laymen often argued that new crops, like new techniques, were
not liable to tithes. In the much followed case of *Adams* v. *Hewitt*
(1781), the Vicar of Kensington claimed tithes of exotic hothouse
fruit grown for the wealthy householders of Westminster, and won
his case. Some strange and disquieting stories were reported.
Bosworth v. *Lambrick* (1779) revealed that in the Gloucestershire
dairy country, at Totworth, tithing day was known as 'devil's Day'.
When the incumbent insisted on collecting in kind rather than put
up with an outmoded composition, human urine and pig's dung
were added to his milk. The roads which he used to collect the
churns were blocked, and the churns themselves were hidden in
impenetrable hedges, or put out on the wrong day. The courts
vigorously denounced such practices. It was calculated in 1782
that of 700 tithes cases recorded in Westminster Hall, 660 had
been determined in favour of the clergy.[92] In the long run this may
have strengthened anticlerical feeling (though it is not clear that
such feeling would not have grown anyway); but it also substantially enhanced the wealth and local standing of the parish
clergy and must have contributed not a little to the revived confidence of the Church in the late eighteenth century. Not least, it
widened the gap between the clergy with tithes and their curates
dependent on discretionary stipends. The growing anxiety of
senior Churchmen to raise the living standards of curates was
plainly connected with this development.

The clergy were well placed to demand a share of the profits of
improvement. More violent commotions occurred lower down the
social scale, at a level not readily granted access to the lawcourts.
Protest of this kind was most effective where it could be concentrated, in London. There it was reckoned that many sections of
the labour force shared in the new prosperity. The trades which
provided consumer goods for middle-class Londoners were relatively well paid, as demand for commodities such as bricks and
other building materials, furniture, wallpaper and carpets, clothes
and jewels, continued to expand. London servants, London
porters, London cabmen, and most involved in the provision of

[92] *Observations on a General Commutation of Tithes for Land or a Corn-Rent* (London,
1782), p. 7.

services, were also thought to benefit. Other groups were less able to protect their position, particularly in face of the recession which marked the period immediately following the Seven Years War. Demobilization in this period, as after earlier wars, contributed to unemployment and helped stimulate a crime wave. Conditions were made worse by a sudden slump in foreign and colonial trade at this time. Overseas demand fell as the conquests of war were returned and glutted colonial markets temporarily contracted. At home a sudden end to the flow of taxpayer's money into the making of war, put a brake on profits, investment, and employment.

Pessimists glimpsed a permanent trend in these developments; but they were answered by the assertion that the depression of the 1760s was only a partial reduction of an unprecedented wartime boom, and in some measure a natural reaction to it. Still, the effects, combined with food and fuel shortages, and sharply rising prices, were severe in some large industries. The Spitalfields weavers suffered particularly; when peace with France brought a reopening of English markets to French silks, they were quick to blame the politicians for their plight. The result was some of the worst rioting of the century in London, culminating in May 1765 in a great siege of the Duke of Bedford's Bloomsbury Square house. Bedford, as negotiator of the peace terms and an avowed supporter of more open trade, was the obvious scapegoat. Troops put the riots down, but Parliament quickly reimposed the silk import tariffs. The weavers were too powerful and potentially dangerous a force in the capital to be ignored altogether. In 1773 they even obtained the passage of a statute providing for minimum wages regulation by the Middlesex JPs. This was a considerable tribute to their strength in an age when neither Parliament nor propertied opinion had much enthusiasm for intervening in relations between employer and employee for the benefit of the latter. Other groups could be equally disruptive. Labour disputes in London in the mid-1760s were as bad as they were anywhere at any time in the eighteenth century.

Much the worst excesses, as contemporaries saw it, were committed by the coal-heavers. Their trade, important and well paid even by comparison with other metropolitan labour, was peculiarly unstable. There was a large Irish element among the coal-heavers, which made them the target of abuse, and supposedly rendered them liable to infiltration by subversive immigrants, including

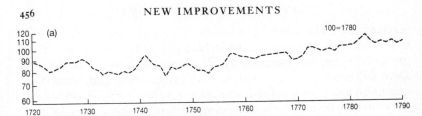

FIG. 8 (*a*). The price trend, 1720–1790

Source: P. Deane and W. A. Cole, *British Economic Growth, 1698–1959: Trends and Structure* (2nd edn., Cambridge, 1967), end paper

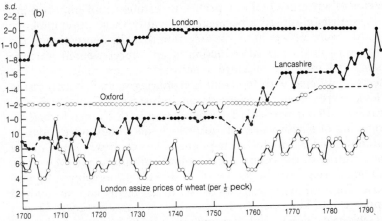

FIG. 8 (*b*). Median daily wage rates of labour in the North, the West, and London

Source: E. W. Gilboy, *Wages in Eighteenth Century England* (Cambridge, 1934), p. 220

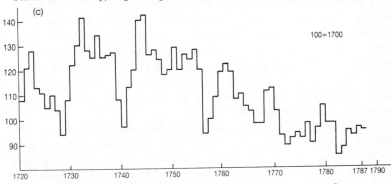

FIG. 8 (*c*). Real wages of London labourers, 1720–1787

Source: B. R. Mitchell and P. Deane, *Abstract of British Historical Statistics*, pp. 346–7

some of the notorious Whiteboys, who terrorized rural society in Ireland in the 1760s. They were also vulnerable to exploitation by their employers the 'undertakers', who in most cases were tavern-keepers and took every opportunity to mulct their workers. Parliament had already, in 1758, authorized the establishment of an official registry, in an attempt to provide a less corrupt alternative to the undertakers. In practice little was done and when the resentment of the work-force against the middlemen was heightened by price rises and shortages, it quickly boiled over. 1768 saw a prolonged strike and major outbreaks of violence in Wapping and Shadwell. Strike-breaking seamen from the colliers were viciously assaulted. (Ironically seamen were themselves on strike in 1768, against the alleged depredations of shipowners and masters, and the use of underqualified marine apprentices.) Unpopular undertakers were mobbed: the siege, in April, of John Green's Roundabout Tavern, was only the most spectacular of these affrays. It was followed by the execution of seven of the besiegers. The immediate grievance was an attempt by the undertakers to reduce rates of pay. In theory, it was resolved, and after the virtual occupation of the dockside parishes by the Guards, the coal-heavers returned to work. In 1770 a new Act of Parliament was passed, in an attempt to restrain the malpractices of the undertakers. But by the middle of the 1770s, its enforcement had been largely abandoned. Like many others the London dock workers were doomed to dependence on the capitalist employers; only occasionally and temporarily did the eighteenth-century State recall its paternalist antecedents.

Many of the industrial disputes of this period had local and temporary causes. Hostile observers were quick to blame the volatile reaction of the better-organized groups of workers; they were also prone to assume, particularly when Wilkesites were active, that manipulation by political agents or merely by demagogic hotheads was to blame. One more searching analysis offered in 1770 was sceptical: 'It has been fashionable of late to join in loud outcries against the working people of this kingdom, on account of pretended extortionate demands of wages, and likewise for idleness and vice.' Three 'partial and self-interested' sources were picked out as being behind these 'insidious reproaches'. These were landlords, farmers, and master workmen, all of whom benefited by the age of improvement. The truth, it was pointed out, was that labour rates had simply not kept pace with taxes and the price of necessities. It was manifest injustice to blame men whose own economic position was worsening while that of their employers strengthened.[93] Such understanding was rare.

How much did the poor earn? There were no adequate statistics to deal with such questions. Modern attempts to reconstruct the trend of real wages are also fraught with difficulty. They suggest an improvement in the manufacturing districts of the north, but stagnation or decline in the third quarter of the century in the south. If the overall pace of change was slow, the contemporary perception was that significant numbers were falling behind in the prosperity stakes. It was calculated in 1777 that a lowly manual labourer and his wife were likely to be earning 8s. 3d. a week, compared with 7s. 3d. forty years before. But ordinary living costs for such a family had risen in the same period from 6s. 5d. a week to 9s. 10d.[94] Slightly higher up the social scale it was thought that the ordinary artisan in London had to bear a fall in real wages of perhaps ten per cent between 1749 and 1787, almost all of it occurring in the 1770s and 1780s. This is not to say that conditions for even these people had not improved sharply in recent decades, or even that in some respects they did not profit by the changes of the late eighteenth century. There is much contemporary testimony that basic conditions of housing and hygiene were better under George III than under his predecessors. English travellers contrasted peasant degradation abroad with 'tight little cottages, inhabited by clean, decent-appearing men, women, and children'.[95] Gilbert White was no hard-hearted middle-class moralist, but he thought that the conditions of the rural labourer had vastly improved in his lifetime. Particularly was this the case with regard to diet.

As to the produce of a garden, every middle-aged person of observation may perceive, within his own memory, both in town and country, how vastly the consumption of vegetables is increased. Green-stalls in cities now support multitudes in a comfortable state, whose gardeners get fortunes. Every decent labourer also has his garden, which is half his support, as well as his delight; and common farmers provide plenty of beans, peas, and greens for their hinds to eat with their bacon; and those few that do not are despised for their sordid parsimony, and looked upon

---

[93] *London Magazine*, 1770, pp. 556–9.
[94] *Reasons for the late Increase of the Poor-Rates* (London, 1777), pp. 12–17.
[95] Philip Thicknesse, *Useful Hints to those who make the Tour of France*, p. 191.

as regardless of the welfare of their dependents. Potatoes have prevailed in this little district, by means of premiums, within these twenty years only; and are much esteemed here now by the poor, who would scarce have ventured to taste them in the last reign.[96]

No doubt the virtual disappearance of that great scourge, land scurvy, owed much to this revolution in eating habits. But even as White wrote, real wages for the lowest of the class he was describing were in decline. Across the border from White, in Berkshire, another clergyman David Davies began his meticulous enquiry into the budgets of rural families in the 1780s.[97] For posterity he provided unimpugnable evidence that the agricultural labourer was at this point entering the long, dark tunnel which Eden and Cobbett were to explore and illuminate. Without population growth to keep the pool of labour always somewhat larger than the demands of the employer, it might have been another story; it might also, of course, have been a less dynamic economy and a distinctly more hesitant progress towards industrialism. In any event the new improvers reaped the profits. The price was paid by others.

[96] *The Natural History of Selborne*, pp. 201–2.
[97] *The Case of Labourers in Husbandry Stated and Considered* (London, 1795).

CHAPTER 10

The Birth of Sensibility

IN the 1760s and 1770s there was a revolution in the making, called by some a sentimental revolution. In part its function was to express the middle-class need for a code of manners which challenged aristocratic ideals and fashions. It also had a bearing on one of the most influential developments of the late eighteenth century, the search for the 'sublime' in religion, literature, architecture, and scenery. There was some concern about the threat which sentiment posed to conventional morality, but in an English context it ultimately served to stem the tide of deism and reinforce the religious conservatism of the day. Its most beneficial consequence was thought to be a heightened sensitivity to the social and moral problems brought by economic change. A new age of philanthropy was born, and a new generation of philanthropists, armed with novel statistical techniques, sought a range of reforms. They were led by men such as Hanway and Howard, eccentric but earnest campaigners in the cause of self-conscious public improvement. Parliament found itself at the centre of an increasingly open debate about the proper direction of social policy. However, progress with institutional change was slow. Criminal law and the Poor Law, both subject to intense criticism, proved particularly resistant to the new climate of opinion. Yet there was a surge of interest in charitable activity, much of it devoted to the discipline as well as the relief of the labouring poor. 'Sensibility' found diverse and suitable objects of appeal in children, animals, and non-European peoples. Many of the attitudes which were to characterize the evangelical revival of the age of Wilberforce were already to be glimpsed in that creation of the third quarter of the eighteenth century, the 'man of feeling'.

THE SENTIMENTAL REVOLUTION

THE third quarter of the eighteenth century witnessed a revolution in manners which had a profound effect on the way that contemporaries conducted and saw themselves. This sentimental revolution was the source of much confusion. Samuel Jackson Pratt described sentiment as a term 'of late invention, to express old emotions in a new way—a term which many use, more affect, few understand, and still fewer, feel'.[1] Its very popularity depended on the diverse interpretations of which it was capable. To ordinary literate (and some illiterate) Englishmen, it meant little more than the capacity to feel strongly, or as one newspaper put it 'a lively and delicate feeling, a quick sense of the right and wrong, in all human actions, and other objects considered in every view of morality and taste'.[2] More than anything else the writings of two men, Jean Jacques Rousseau and Laurence Sterne, gave it currency. English readers were already familiar with Rousseau's early ventures into print but it was the translation of *Julie, ou La Nouvelle Héloise* in 1761 which made his work the centre of attention. Julie came only a generation later than Pamela, but her tale of illicit love seemed an unlikely refinement of the emotional vein which Richardson's novels had uncovered. In fact she shared only the directness and intimacy of her revelations with her famous predecessor. Certainly the lesson which readers drew from Rousseau was the reverse of Richardson's. In Rousseau conventional morality was found wanting against the power of human feelings. Emotional extravagance became a requirement of fashionable worshippers at this new shrine. 'Oh, the dear book!' Pratt had one of his heroines declaim in a Buxton bookshop, 'there are *three* letters in the first volume of that book, worth all the world'.[3]

Sterne's arrival in the literary world had been made in 1759, with the publication of the first two parts of *Tristram Shandy*. Sterne, unlike Rousseau, offered sentiment with vulgarity, but like him he made virtue at best a matter of personal judgement rather than moral prescription. *Tristram Shandy* was packed with low comedy, whimsical characters, and humorous tricks. It attracted an immense readership and attained the status of a cult for a time.

---

[1] *Emma Corbett: or, the Miseries of Civil War* (Dublin, 1780), p. 69.
[2] *London Chronicle*, 6 July 1775.
[3] *The Pupil of Pleasure* (2nd edn., London, 1777), p. 33.

Compared with Rousseau and Sterne, the great triumvirate of mid-Georgian prose, Richardson, Fielding, and Smollett, suddenly looked dated and dull. Picaresque plots with happy endings seemed less real than the dilemmas of Rousseau's modern woman and the ruminations of Sterne's quixotic narcissist. Even Richardson's almost morbid psychological explorations appeared to lack the freshness and originality demanded in the 1760s. For many entering on adolescence or adulthood at this time the primacy of the individual's feelings offered a startlingly new vision of the world. When this generation reached positions of power or influence in the following decades, there were to be far-reaching ramifications. In the mean time even their elders and betters were entranced by Rousseau's rhapsodies and captivated by Sterne's whimsies.

Sentiment, in the broad sense in which it finally predominated, had a special appeal to middle-class England at a time of economic growth and rising standards of living. Gentility was the most prized possession of all in a society obsessed with the pursuit of property and wealth. It could be purchased, but only if the code of genteel conduct was sufficiently flexible to fit the diverse social and educational circumstances of the purchasers. The emphasis on feeling provided this flexibility and removed the sense of repressive social exclusiveness which marked a more aristocratic view of the world. This is not to say that the landed élite was incapable of erecting more subtle barriers against the advance of bourgeois man. Even so the lines of communication were kept open, and the conventions of a common gentility preserved. In this the morality of the new sentiment played an important part. Its function was clearly displayed in the attack on outmoded concepts of gentlemanly honour. Robert Dodsley, who profited both as poet and publisher by the new taste, stressed the socially discriminatory aspect of honour. 'Honour!—What's honour? A vain phantom rais'd, To fright the weak from tasting those delights, Which nature's voice, that law supreme, allows.'[4] 'Nature' also dictated an informal approach to everyday social relations which made the formality of court life seem thoroughly outdated. A few years ago, one commentator remarked, there were endless introductions, bowing, and scraping. Now 'ease is politeness; one bow brings a man into company and he goes off without any'.[5] Then, it was impossible

---

[4] R. Straus, *Robert Dodsley: Poet, Publisher and Playwright* (London, 1910), p. 249.
[5] 'The Contrast', xxviii, *London Magazine*, 1765, p. 347.

to dine without an elaborate parade of passing plates and serving portions. Now, the most anxious host could be sure that his guests would eat without constant attention from himself or concern about precedence. If only the endless toasts and bumpers beloved of drunken Englishmen could be abolished, social intercourse would truly resemble the effortless harmony of nature. (This last proved over-ambitious.) The agony columns and romantic fiction with which the magazines of the day abounded dwelt much on the delights and dilemmas of this newly liberated age.

Intellectuals did their best to appropriate sentiment, and, by restricting its use, to prevent its inflation as the currency of elevated thought and intercourse. But as with every other fashionable pursuit, attempts to monopolize what could be bought with money were bound to fail. The satirist William Combe was severely censured when he had the temerity to tell the citizens of Bristol, the empire's second city, that they were not worthy of the new taste. Combe was 'socially mobile', but in a downward direction. Born to a substantial fortune, educated at Eton and Oxford, he spent his money on high living and descended to a life of literary penury and debt, from which even his most famous work, the *Travels of Dr Syntax*, was not to rescue him. No doubt there was social as well as intellectual snobbery in his treatment of Bristol businessmen. 'Love of gain' he loftily told them in his *Philosopher in Bristol* in 1775, 'entirely envelopes all traits of feeling and delicacy of sentiment, ... I bless heaven that I am not a man of merchandize.' In the resulting controversy Combe was compelled to publish a modified version of his views. Commerce, he reassured his readers, tarnished only those unwilling to cultivate the finer feelings: many of its practitioners were in fact men of refinement and sensitivity.[6] Most contemporary writers were careful to make it clear that sentiment and hard business sense were not only not in conflict but readily went together. For the essayist Edmund Rack it seemed natural to talk of 'men of refined taste and sentiment, who are engaged in the bustle of commercial life'.[7]

The triumph of sentiment was overwhelming. Only in the theatre was its victory contested. Some dramatists resisted demands for a serious, improving stage. George Colman's early successes,

[6] H. W. Hamilton, *Doctor Syntax: A Silhouette of William Combe, Esq. (1742–1823)* (London, 1969), pp. 39, 42–3.
[7] *Essays, Letters, and Poems, by Edmund Rack* (Bath, 1781), p. 401.

such as *The Jealous Wife* in 1761, were essentially robust satires in a strong English tradition of low comedy. But Colman succumbed to the needs of polite audiences even while he pretended otherwise. Of his *English Merchant* in 1767 the *Critical Review* wrote effusively: 'perhaps no comedy was ever produced upon the stage with a more moral tendency, or less offensive to decency ... We enter with concern into the fate of virtuous characters, and we can perceive that the author's feelings always arise in the right place.'[8] This was very much the prevailing note in fashionable dramatic criticism. Goldsmith explored the nature of the resulting conflict between sentimental and low comedy in a celebrated incursion into critical theory. He went on to write *She Stoops to Conquer*, a 'true' comedy in an age of growing mawkishness. Despite its later celebrity, it met with a mixed reception, admired by some critics for its bravery in attacking current trends, condemned by others for its vulgarity. But even Goldsmith seemed refined by comparison with Restoration playwrights.

The social implications of the new drama were clear. It was an established maxim of dramatic theory that comedy belonged with low life, tragedy with high. Only the elevated emotions of the great could provide a proper degree of solemnity for the enactment of serious themes; conversely, only the petty concerns of the ordinary citizen provided matter for mirth. Much ink was spilled for and against this assumption in the 1760s and 1770s. But it could not survive the growing serious-mindedness of middle-class cultural interests. Domestic tragedy shared with sentimental comedy a commitment to sensibility which possessed great appeal for late eighteenth-century audiences. Nor should its intellectual cutting edge be denied. Sentiment could offer an effective challenge to traditional values as well as sending a theatre-goer home with a benevolent tear in his eye. Sophia Lee's *Chapter of Accidents*, a great success in 1780, portrayed as heroine a 'ruined' woman who could formerly have been the subject only of pathos. 'Will you never be above so narrow a prejudice?' asked her lover. 'Are we not the whole world to each other?'[9] If the ghost of Pamela had stirred at the appearance of Rousseau's Julie, it must have shuddered at the arrival of Miss Lee's Cecilia. But heroines were altogether novel in this age of unchained feeling. Twenty years

---

[8] E. R. Page, *George Colman the Elder* (New York, 1935), p. 133.
[9] E. Bernbaum, *The Drama of Sensibility* (Boston, 1915), p. 263.

earlier, in the play which had established Covent Garden's reputation for serious theatre, Dodsley had initiated the new era of
domestic tragedies with *Cleone*, a powerful yet homely melodrama
in which the heroine was falsely suspected of infidelity to her
husband and her son murdered. Bourgeois families were more
familiar with the plight of Cecilia than with Cleone's, but each
embodied something of the contemporary revolution in taste and
susceptibility.[10]

SENTIMENT AND RELIGIOUS REACTION

When sentiment was treated with a becoming moral earnestness,
it also had a certain spiritual significance. In France the sentimental
tradition quickly became associated with the secularism of the
French Enlightenment. But English secularism was a weaker force
by far, and the English contribution to the use of sentiment was
to turn it into a tool of piety rather than paganism. Rousseau's
early fame changed to notoriety. An increasingly prurient interest
in his personal morals was succeeded by reappraisal of the ethical
foundations of his work. His reputation was further weakened
when he visited England with David Hume in 1765. There was a
large element of farce in this visit. He quarrelled publicly with
Hume and ended by displaying obvious signs of persecution mania,
when he fled what he said was Hume's attempt to control him. By
then there was a growing belief, expressed by the Blue Stockings
and their influential friends Edmund Burke and Dr Johnson, that
Rousseau, far from rebelling against the downright atheism of
French intellectual life had merely carried it to new extremes.
'Surely the poor man cannot be a Christian', Mrs Carter mildly
remarked; 'and then all is easily accounted for.'[11] *La Nouvelle
Héloise*, a work of genius, became a work of wickedness; *Émile*,
influential though it was in terms of educational theory, came to
be condemned as dangerous. Sterne also had his critics, when
something of his mode of life became known. Stories of his
raffishness converted his standing as a Yorkshire clergyman from
an asset into a liability. William Warburton, the literary lion of the
day, had initially approved *Shandy*; but he grew increasingly

---

[10] R. Straus, *Robert Dodsley*, ch. 10.

[11] M. Pennington, ed., *Letters from Mrs Elizabeth Carter, to Mrs Montagu, Between the
Years 1755 and 1800* (3 vols., London, 1817), i. 72.

alarmed at Sterne's innuendoes and the tide of popular ribaldry and obscenity which they launched in the popular press. 'Laugh', he warned Sterne 'in good company, where priests and virgins may be present.'[12] Politeness was not appeased by Sterne's other writings, his *Sermons* and his *Sentimental Journey*.

Concern about the moral threat implicit in some aspects of sentiment had more behind it than hostility to the personal morality of its high priests. There was a growing sense in the 1750s and 1760s that the tide of deism had been turned. It is difficult to quantify a belief of this kind. Moreover, it seems strange, given the influence enjoyed by some contemporary deists. But dislike and suspicion of Hume and Gibbon were at least as marked as the popularity which their works enjoyed. Hume himself sarcastically observed that the English were 'relapsing into the deepest Stupidity, Christianity and ignorance'. By the time he died in 1776 his name was a byword for the worst kind of amorality. His friend Adam Smith, who published Hume's candid account of his own life, subsequently claimed that by doing so he had incurred 'ten times more abuse than the very violent attack I had made upon the whole commercial system of Great Britain'.[13] While Hume was dying, Gibbon was publishing the first volume of his majestic *Decline and Fall*. It was a sensationally successful work, acclaimed for scholarship beyond even Robertson, wit which outshone Smollett, and historical judgement more impressive than Hume's. It also had a theme which peculiarly fitted the agonized imperialism of the first year of war against America. But in due course it aroused intense controversy. The fifteenth and sixteenth chapters revealed the full extent of Gibbon's scepticism. Christianity was treated as one of the fundamental causes of the fall of Rome, the herald of medieval barbarism and superstition. The resulting criticism mostly missed its mark, for Gibbon's learning was not easily impugned. But the sneering tone of his jibes against Christians remained as an enduring impression.

Lesser men expressed the evolving concerns of the age more accurately. John Leland had published his *View of the Principal Deistical Writers* between 1754 and 1756. In four volumes it reviewed the champions of deism from the middle of the sev-

---

[12] M. New, 'Sterne, Warburton, and the Burden of Exuberant Wit', *Eighteenth Century Studies*, 15 (1981–2), 252.
[13] E. C. Mossner, *The Life of David Hume*, p. 605.

enteenth century, concluding with a critique of Bolingbroke's voluminous speculations, posthumously published in 1754. Leland lacked elegance and originality but there was a thoroughness about his point-by-point dismissal of the most eminent sceptics which was strongly approved by his readers. Possibly the same climate of opinion which made Methodism so appealing to a popular audience also operated with middle-class opinion. Possibly, too, the direction taken by ecclesiastical politics, under a king devoted to the Church, gave a great boost to the Establishment after forty years of deep division. Oxford, so long proscribed by the Hanoverian regime, was now its ally in the great theological controversies of the day, particularly in the defence of the Thirty-Nine Articles and liturgical conservatism.[14] Anticlericalism was not vanquished, but it concentrated increasingly on aspects of the Church which were almost universally disapproved, particularly pluralism and non-residence, and which did not necessarily weaken its spiritual defences. Admittedly, fratricidal strife continued to cause problems for good Churchmen. One of the most bitter controversies of the 1760s was that between Warburton, now Bishop of Gloucester, and Robert Lowth, an Oxford cleric, also on his way to a distinguished episcopal career. The vehemence of these redoubtable polemicists distressed many of their readers. As the dramatist Richard Cumberland, himself the son of an archdeacon, put it, 'they mouthed and mumbled each other till their very bands blushed and their lawn-sleeves were bloody'.[15] But the issue in question, the historical authenticity and provenance of the Book of Job, seemed less than fundamental. Compared with the dangerous disputes of earlier generations these unedifying squabbles offered little to disturb the foundations of Christian belief. Those who could recall the agitations aroused by a Hoadly or a Middleton were unlikely to be more than irritated by Warburton and Lowth.

There was an appreciation that a broad band of respectable opinion was rallying to the Church. In 1771 the playwright George Colman remarked on 'these, our moral and religious days'.[16] Shortly before, James Beattie had published his *Essay on the Nature and Immutability of Truth*. Beattie was no intellectual giant, though

[14] See pp. 530–1.
[15] *Memoirs of Richard Cumberland*, p. 228.
[16] E. R. Page, *George Colman the Elder*, p. 205.

his writings are said to have had some influence on Kant, mainly (it is to be feared) in transmitting a faulty view of the achievement of British philosophy. But his ambitious assault on the philosophical basis of deism was widely welcomed. Oxford University presented him with an honorary degree, George III awarded him a pension, and Sir Joshua Reynolds painted a controversial scene of Beattie vanquishing Hume, in the 'Triumph of Truth'. Beattie's celebrity was symptomatic of the times, though not every defender of the faith met with such universal approbation.

The old Cambridge-based scepticism which had set out to strengthen Christian belief by limiting the area of controversy that it had to defend was also at work in the 1770s. Soame Jenyns's entry into these matters with his *View of the Internal Evidence of the Christian Religion* in 1776 attracted much interest: 'at the fashionable clubs it is gold to silver, since the appearance of Mr Jenyns's book, that the Christian religion is true.'[17] But Jenyns also got into trouble, like many before him, for conceding too many of the devil's arguments before dispatching their author. His doctrine of evil stirred old embers when he asserted that God, not the abuse of free will by men, created earthly wickedness, a view that was denounced by parties as diverse as the Methodists and the Rational Dissenters. A similar case was that of William Paley, forty years younger than Jenyns, but a representative of the same tradition and a powerful influence on the mainstream of utilitarian thought. His theological writings, culminating in *The View of the Evidence of Christianity* in 1794, aroused suspicion of their unitarian tendencies as well as admiration for their lucid and compelling rationality. The experience of Jenyns and Paley was clear evidence of the lower threshold of tolerance in regard to religious heterodoxy.

Sentiment was intimately connected with the reviving confidence of the believers. In its implied anti-intellectualism or at least its intellectual naïvety it offered a way out of the agonies of earlier debate. 'Revelation agrees with that part of nature which we best understand, our own: the dictate of unsophisticated reason, and the genuine feelings of the human heart.'[18] This was the view of the Blue Stocking Elizabeth Carter, one of the more important influences on the evolution and transmission of the sentimental

[17] *Letters from Mrs Elizabeth Carter, to Mrs Montagu*, iii. 6.
[18] M. Pennington, *Memoirs of the Life of Mrs Elizabeth Carter* (London, 1807), p. 626.

tradition in England. Some of her friends dispensed with the word 'reason' altogether. Mrs Barbauld, daughter of one of Warrington Academy's most distinguished teachers, and herself an author of devotional works for children, described the triumph of religion in distinctly Rousseauistic terms. 'Its seat is in the imagination and the passions, and it has its source in that relish for the sublime, the vast and the beautiful, by which we taste the charms of poetry and other compositions.'[19]

Sublime was a crucial word in this context for it supplied the link between fashionable sentiment and sound religion. Burke had explored its aesthetic implications in his celebrated tract on the *Sublime and Beautiful* in 1756. Sublimity featured too in the Miltonic poems of Christopher Smart, who established his reputation by winning the Seatonian Prize in successive years at Cambridge for his praise of the Supreme Being. Smart was one of the most tortured of eighteenth-century poets: much of his life was spent in madhouses and debtors' prisons. None the less his verse expressed the contemporary yearning for faith in a peculiarly direct manner. John Ogilvie, a saner if less talented poet, also caught something of it in his work. He enjoyed considerable celebrity in the 1760s before his countryman James Beattie delivered a more conclusive message in prose. Sentiment with imagination was the formula for these renewed testimonials to the power of the Almighty, and a generation of preparation, poetic and theological, had gone into it. The search for the sublime, spiritual and secular, perhaps, but rarely secular alone, was on.

ROMANTIC SCENERY, THE GOTHIC REVIVAL, AND CELTIC LEGEND

This search produced unexpected results, including enhanced appreciation of the landscape. Upland Britain came into its own as a paradise of spectacular scenery, guaranteed to satisfy the sentimental visitor's sense of the sublime. Young men and women, like Anna Seward of Lichfield, confessed their 'passion for winding rivers, curtained rocks, devious vallies, and sheltering mountains'.[20] Turnpike roads and the middle-class taste for travel brought hordes of polite tourists to the remoter parts of England and Wales in

[19] B. Rodgers, *Georgian Chronicle: Mrs Barbauld and her Family* (London, 1958), p. 65.
[20] *Letters of Anna Seward* (6 vols., Edinburgh, 1811), i. 301.

search of sights which their predecessors had considered inaccessible and unprepossessing. The Peak District, thanks to its central position, its restricted size, its relatively comfortable towns within a short distance, had enjoyed an earlier vogue than most moorland regions. But such interest had centred on its geological curiosities. In the late eighteenth century it came into its own as mountain scenery. In the case of the Lake District and the northern Pennines the new interest was still more striking. The novelist Thomas Amory was one of the first to exploit its possibilities with his accounts of John Buncle's eccentric rambles through Richmondshire and the Lakes.[21]

The charm of sentimental scenery was difficult to resist. Even the prosaic Arthur Young appreciated the romantic glories described by Amory in the Tees valley: 'you, literally speaking, do not move an hundred yards without being struck with continual waterfalls'.[22] The Welsh marches, Snowdonia, the Wye Valley, all followed. The Wye was especially prized long before William Gilpin made it obligatory for romantic tourists in 1782. At Persfield, a few miles from Tintern, it possessed a magnetic attraction which combined the landscape gardening triumphs of the previous generation with the newly perceived beauties of vale and forest. Already in the 1760s it was being pronounced exquisite, 'in point of striking picturesque views, in the romantic style'.[23]

Tintern was to become the most famous of romantic ruins. The ruin as a source of poetic inspiration had been exploited to the full by the 'graveyard school' of the mid-century. Grand Tourists had a short-lived but important advantage here. John Dyer's *Fall of Rome* in 1741 had suggested exciting new possibilities for the young men who had flocked to Rome to immerse themselves in the classical spirit, and who were now taught to cherish it for its melancholy historical lessons and its haunting architectural decadence. Gibbon's famous account in his *Autobiography* of the effect produced on a susceptible mind by such surroundings put into words what many must have felt, even if few of them conceived a project as grand as the *Decline and Fall* in consequence. Armchair travellers played an important part in reinforcing such images,

---

[21] T. Amory, *The Life and Opinions of John Buncle Esquire*, ed. E. A. Baker (London, 1904), p. xi.
[22] *A Six Months Tour through the North of England*, ii. 202.
[23] *A Six Weeks Tour through the Southern Counties of England and Wales*, p. 140.

with gratifying results for writers and artists. Richard Wilson's sets of classical scenes displaying famous incidents of ancient history and legend exploited the market to its maximum. Dying Niobes and broken statuary became positively hackneyed. But views and the ubiquitous engravings which carried them into ordinary homes were only a substitute for the real thing, and something very like the real thing was available closer to home.

England had virtually no visible classical ruins, but it was not short of medieval buildings, and in the 1760s the mouldering relics of a forgotten past came into their own. The early years of the Gothic Revival will forever be associated with the mannered eccentricities of Horace Walpole and his circle. But Strawberry Hill represents the self-indulgence of the new fashion rather than its scholarly substance. Serious study of medieval architecture was an authentic feature of the period, not just among gentlemen amateurs, but also among surveyors, architects, and builders, who brought earnestness to the preservation of medieval churches, and ingenuity to domestic Gothic imitation. Men like James Essex of Cambridge deserve a historical niche alongside Walpole. Essex devoted much of his life to reviving interest in Cambridge's Gothic buildings and made himself more widely available in connection with cathedral restoration. His treatise on Lincoln Cathedral, published in 1776, reveals historical imagination as well as technical understanding. It displays a determination to place a previously despised style in context, with its judgement that the taste of the Middle Ages was well adapted to the 'religion and genius of the times'. But with or without serious architectural debate, the rage for Gothic would have played its part in the rediscovery of the English heritage.

In the quest for a sublime mixture of sentimental emotion and religious awe, the Blue Stockings were to the fore. 'I always consider', wrote Mrs Carter, 'the sublime as the characteristic of Gothic architecture, and every attempt at elegance and beauty mere foppery, as unsuitable as childish ornaments on a gigantic bulk.'[24] Mrs Carter's letters are indeed an unfailing guide to the obsessions of the middle-class sentimental traveller. They make plain that it was not even necessary to travel as far afield as Tintern. There were evocative reminders of a superstitious past much closer to hand. At Netley Abbey, near Southampton, the proximity of

[24] *Letters from Mrs Elizabeth Carter, to Mrs Montagu*, i. 302.

excellent roads and well-attended resorts created a major tourist attraction. George Keate celebrated it in an extended poem which incidentally provided the visitor with an imaginative historical guide. Significantly Keate had made his name with a long piece on *Ancient and Modern Rome* ('And do I walk the Forum?').[25] Mrs Carter confessed that Gothic living did not go well with London but she found much to her antique taste within easy reach of it. At Windsor she could dream of chivalrous knights and ladies, and deplore the placing of a statue of William III ('not a Gothic hero'). Also in Berkshire, she told her friend the famous Mrs Montagu, 'I longed for you extremely the other night at Reading, to ramble by moonlight amongst the ruins of an old abbey.' On a rare foray abroad she lamented the inferiority of Flemish churches which 'totally shock all my ideas of the sublime' by their bastardized Gothic with its spacious and airy interiors. In fact like many others she was nothing if not nationalistic, even insular, in her cultural preferences. 'I must have visited every remarkable spot on British ground before I feel any curiosity to see the Tarpeian Rock or the Tusculan Villa.' What she expected of Englishmen was veneration for their heritage. To the Duke of Northumberland she awarded high marks for preserving his family's seat at Alnwick Castle, though at Syon on the Thames, Northumberland had also created, with the help of Robert Adam, one of the most lavish essays in the new classicism, a contradiction which Mrs Carter did not remark on. Renovation in general she deplored. 'Those who enjoy the estates of their ancestors should at least show that respect to the place of their abode, and to let it sink with dignity into a venerable ruin.'[26]

The historian John Brand remarked that 'The English Antique has become a general and fashionable Study.'[27] The ramifications went far beyond the viewing of ancient sights. Not least, it fired the contemporary interest in what were taken to be medieval literary conventions and also transformed the way that the more backward parts of Britain were viewed. The poetic heritage of the Middle Ages was explored and analysed for a popular as well as

---

[25] *The Poetical Works of George Keate*, i. 30.
[26] *A Series of Letters between Mrs Elizabeth Carter and Miss Catherine Talbot, from the year 1741 to 1770* (3rd edn., 3 vols., London, 1819), iii. 230, 347; *Letters from Mrs Elizabeth Carter, to Mrs Montagu*, i. 27; *Memoirs of the Life of Mrs Elizabeth Carter*, p. 203; *Letters from Mrs Elizabeth Carter, to Mrs Montagu*, i. 165, 318; *A Series of Letters*, iv. 314.
[27] *Observations on Popular Antiquities*, p. vi.

academic audience by Thomas Percy, whose *Reliques of Ancient English Poetry* was published in 1765, and Richard Hurd, whose critical study of medieval literature *Letters on Chivalry and Romance* had appeared three years earlier. Percy and Hurd were both self-made men and both rose to become bishops; they provided the new interest in the Middle Ages with a solid historical base. But in all this enthusiasm for a distant, romanticized past there was room for more than the scholarly reconstruction of ancient texts. The Gothic novel, announced by Horace Walpole's *Castle of Otranto* in 1765, gave a bizarre but popular twist to the new fashion.

There was also room for impostors, who throve on the naïvety displayed by intelligent and even learned men. Thomas Chatterton's ingenious composition of the poems of a fictitious Bristol priest of the fifteenth century, Thomas Rowley, fooled many. Still more remarkable was the imposture of James Macpherson, whose 'translations' of the early Celtic poet Ossian met with a rapturous reception. *Fingal*, the first of these productions, appeared in 1761, its successor *Temora* a year later. Before very long they were arousing widespread doubt. Authorities on Celtic culture continued to be baffled by them for some forty years and a certain aura of mystery still envelops them today. Ossian had exactly that blend of high drama, raw nature, and primitive emotions on which the sentimentalist throve. Part of Macpherson's skill was to establish this as a kind of cultural missing link, neatly fitting contemporary anthropological speculation. In his introduction to *Fingal* he explained how the warlords of the fifth century enjoyed 'a primeval dignity of sentiment' which later developments in the history of property and government had eroded and corrupted. Such hints to the academics were shrewdly placed. John Millar duly considered Ossian as evidence that in 'the manners of a people acquainted with pasturage, there is often a degree of tenderness and delicacy of sentiment which can hardly be equalled in the most refined productions of a civilised age'.[28] At least one English scholar thought that the most striking proof of Ossian's authenticity was the fact that it contained not 'a single image but what is taken from the views of nature, and scarcely the least allusion to any art or science whatever; an omission scarcely possible in an imposture of

---

[28] *Observations concerning the Distinction of Ranks in Society* (London, 1771), p. 43.

modern invention'.[29] Macpherson stoutly denied that he was guilty of forgery; he went on to become an MP, and a well-paid pamphleteer for Lord North.

There was no Welsh Macpherson, but the same concerns applied in a country where polite tourism was still easier. By the time Thomas Pennant wrote his guides to Wales in the 1770s, it was possible to traverse the most mountainous parts on relatively good roads, and to marvel at the difficulties which former travellers would have encountered on what had been dangerous as well as uncomfortable journeys. In the 1760s and 1770s the monthly magazines carried many enticing advertisements for Welsh tours. Llangollen, for instance, was described as a 'Romantic Country' with 'the most ravishing prospects possible to be conceived by man'.[30] The guidebooks were supplemented by Welsh views. Oddly, Richard Wilson, himself a Welshman, largely missed the artistic opportunities. It was left to Paul Sandby, a friend of the Welsh magnate Sir Watkin Williams Wynn to popularize Welsh scenery. Wynn was one of many Welsh gentry who rediscovered their Celtic origins and willingly subscribed to genealogies which would prove their claim to princely blood. The novelist Mrs Bennett gently satirized this type with her Lady Cecilia Edwin, a fanatical genealogist, who would 'rather have chose to marry her children to the peasant of her own wild hills, than to nobles of any other country'.[31] For the English Wales provided a wealth of pageantry in fantasy. Mary Morgan, author of the *Tour to Milford Haven*, observed that every village had its castle, bringing to mind 'haughty barons and feudal tyranny, the croisades, the age of chivalry, bloody battles, paynim knights, distressed damsels, gallant lovers, haunted towers, ghosts, fairies, and inchantments'. She also noted that the road from Hay on Wye to Carmarthen had more gentlemen's carriages than the roads of the Home Counties.[32] There were snags of course. One Welsh clergyman complained that 'the English mountain hunters had made his country so dear that he could not live in it'.[33]

---

[29] *Letters from Mrs Elizabeth Carter, to Mrs Montagu*, ii. 292.

[30] *London Magazine*, 1766, pp. 446–7.

[31] A. M. Bennett, *Anna; or Memoirs of a Welch Heiress*, i. 234.

[32] (London, 1795), pp. 146, 150.

[33] Mrs C. H. Beale, *Reminiscences of a Gentlewoman of the Last Century*, p. 123.

THE SENTIMENTAL CHALLENGE: MORAL STANDARDS AND SUBVERSION

The cost of living in North Wales was by no means the only casualty of the sentimental revolution, though many of the fears which it generated were exaggerated. The passion for naturalism which infected polite society was a case in point. For a brief period it was fashionable for men to wear their hair without benefit of peruke-maker or powderer. But neither profession was in much danger. The wig made a strong come-back. In the 1770s, it was short enough to date provincial squires wearing the full wigs of an earlier age, but it could hardly be termed 'natural'. Some wondered whether there was a place for anything as artificial as an architect. The young Joseph Banks, on the threshold of a long career as amateur explorer and scientist, rhapsodized about Fingal's Cave, a favourite sight for tourists who could afford to travel to the Western Isles. 'Where is now the boast of the architect! Regularity, the only part in which he fancied to exceed his mistress, Nature, is here found in her possession.'[34] There was little prospect that the profession of architect would founder, however. The late eighteenth century witnessed a building boom of unprecedented proportions. The architect's importance was positively accentuated by the sheer variety of faddish options open to middle-class customers—neo-classical, rococo, English Gothic, Chinese, and so on.

In all this it was obvious that naturalism was a cover for ever more contrived artifice. The leading obstetrician William Hunter liked to observe that labour in childbirth was 'nature's work' and recommended natural techniques.[35] This did not prevent him from making a handsome living out of the gynaecological intervention of the doctor. Actors, too, were ready to satisfy the contemporary taste for so-called naturalism. In his poetic guide to the actor's profession, Robert Lloyd argued that it 'Lies not in trick, or attitude, or start, Nature's true knowledge is the only art.'[36] Critics dwelt on this aspect of acting technique, but most of them must have been well aware how much depended on the sheer professionalism of the contemporary stage.

Concern about the sexual implications of the new mentality was

[34] *London Magazine*, 1774, p. 272.
[35] Ibid. 1772, p. 227.
[36] W. Kenrick, ed. *The Poetical Works of Robert Lloyd*, i. 11.

less easily quieted. The morals of the *Sentimental Journey* were explicitly condemned by Vicesimus Knox. 'Many a connexion, begun with fine sentimentality which Sterne has recommended and increased, has terminated in disease, infancy, madness, suicide and a gibbet.'[37] There was particular anxiety about the tendencies discernible in female education, and in the novels which kept young women of leisure supplied with reading. Hannah More stressed the way in which such books purveyed impossible fantasies. Rank, elegance, beauty, sentimental feelings, sensibility, all displayed at the highest pitch of refinement and ecstasy, made men naïvely disappointed or brutally cynical in their pursuit of women; they also provided women with models of conduct which at best lay beyond any individual's talents, and at worst were a serious distraction from more devout, and more domestic accomplishments.[38] It seems unlikely that Hannah More can have read many of the novels which she condemned. They generally featured vapid, platitudinous good will, which went well with the often equally anodyne devotional literature provided for women. As Knox remarked, 'Most of them tend to recommend benevolence and liberality; for it is the fashion of the age to affect those qualities.'[39]

Faith in the power of feeling produced some eccentric behaviour, the despair of fathers and mothers, brothers and sisters, friends and colleagues. Thomas Day, who was to write one of the classics of children's literature *Sandford and Merton*, became a figure of fun by his strange attempts to adopt what he took to be manners untarnished by civilized society. When he married, his main worry was that his wife had a large fortune, for it laid him open to the charge of a marriage of convenience. Rousseau's *Émile* he thought the most important book after the Bible. His contemporary Anna Laetitia Aikin, who, under her married name of Mrs Barbauld, also became an influential writer for children, was lured into a disastrous marriage with an unstable Frenchman, who entranced her with 'crazy demonstrations of amorous rapture, set off with theatrical French manners'.[40] Her brother John Aikin blamed *La Nouvelle Héloise* for his sister's gullibility. There were not wanting theologians and moralists to condemn the rage for 'Feelings! a

---

[37] *The Works of Vicesimus Knox*, i. 131.

[38] 'The History of Mr Bragwell; or, the Two Wealthy Farmers', *The Works of Hannah More* (8 vols., London, 1801), iv. 82.

[39] *The Works of Vicesimus Knox*, ii. 407.

[40] B. Rodgers, *Georgian Chronicle*, p. 63.

fashionable word, substituted for mental operations, and savouring much of materialism.'[41]

It was believed that suicide was on the increase at this time, and that it owed its popularity to the cult of feeling. The evidence of the London Bills of Mortality suggests on the contrary that the suicide rate peaked in the 1750s and fell thereafter. But the newspapers reported a spate of notable suicides in the 1770s. In 1770 alone there were three such: Charles Yorke, soon after accepting the Lord Chancellorship, Peter Delmé, heir to a huge mercantile fortune, and Thomas Chatterton, whose attempt to establish himself as a man of letters ended in humiliation and poverty in London. But none of these had any direct connection with the literature of sentiment unless it be Chatterton's. More important was the self-generated tendency of the age to intellectual and theological conservatism. Hume's daring *Essay on suicide*, suppressed during his life, was published in 1777 after his own death. It aroused the most bitter hostility, beyond anything that even he had achieved with his sceptical observations on matters of religion.

These anxieties reached a climax at the end of the decade. Goethe's *Werther* was translated into English in 1779. It had an immense effect. Authors in England cashed in with meretricious imitations, mainly 'letters of Charlotte'. One of these writers had the temerity to dedicate his contribution to Queen Charlotte. He also remarked, 'I am confident that a collection of nonsense, under the same title would at least sell an edition.'[42] There were prints and engravings, porcelain figurines and mementoes. Charlotte was endlessly portrayed at Vauxhall and on the stage. In the most appealing scene (though it did not actually appear in Goethe's work), Charlotte at Werther's grave, she was exhibited at Mrs Salmon's Historical Waxworks. Even Richard Graves, a sharp satirist of contemporary morals and manners, was trapped into a half-admiring admission that Charlotte's love for Werther, though illicit on earth, would surely permit them to enjoy a permanent union in heaven. As a clergyman he came to regret this judgement and published a denunciation of suicide by way of retraction.[43] Others were more critical from the beginning. Goethe seemed

---

[41] *The Works of Vicesimus Knox*, vi. 75.

[42] S. P. Atkins, *The Testament of Werther In Poetry and Drama* (Cambridge, Mass., 1949), pp. 22–3.

[43] R. Graves, *Lucubrations* (London, 1786), pp. 199–205.

positively to justify suicide by depicting it as the natural, logical end for a man of powerful feelings foiled by conventional morality. There was evidence at hand to reinforce such alarm. One well-reported case in May 1779 concerned a young man in East India Company service who pursued the object of his passion with Rousseau-like intensity from Calcutta to London and later from Salisbury, via Bristol and Bath, to London. He would pass her time and again on the road in a post-chaise, and pursued her in the streets, 'making motions and faces like a lover turned monkey'. It took a legal prosecution by the lady's father, and seven years' surety, to end this state of affairs.[44] The interest devoted to this case was triggered by a more tragic episode which had taken place a few weeks before, the murder of the Earl of Sandwich's mistress, Martha Ray. Sandwich was a notorious libertine but his manifest distress at her death gave the newspapers a field-day. It transpired that Miss Ray's assailant was a young man who for years had wooed her in vain and finally determined on killing her rather than forfeit his prize. It also emerged that she was a devotee of literary fashion, and had taken a close interest in Chatterton's poetic career. Here was most promising material for the moralist.

These intimations of romanticism perplexed contemporaries. There was, it seemed, a spirit abroad, powerful, beneficent perhaps, yet also sinister, not least in the way it separated generations. Sentiment was not often employed for a frontal attack on traditional morality, nor was its potential as a form of rebellion exploited. Conventions were questioned rather than confronted. Occasionally, however, as in the case of the Ray tragedy, there was an awareness of aspirations which belonged to an alien world. Another bizarre episode which conveyed such a sense was the history of John the Painter, a young man who, in the winter of 1776–7, alarmed the authorities and astonished respectable opinion by a series of arson attacks on dockyards. One of these, at Bristol, caused serious damage and created a short-lived panic redolent of the Gunpowder Plot mentality. When he was arrested and tried, the story which emerged, mainly from the evidence of a spy who had been placed in custody with him, was certainly curious. As an apprentice painter he had been literate enough to make himself a great reader, with the accent on antimonarchical works and (not quite consistently) Voltaire's writings. Above all he had 'the desire

---

[44] *London Magazine*, 1779, p. 237.

of accomplishing some great attainment himself'. He had been on both sides of the Atlantic, and was apparently present at the Boston Tea Party in 1773. In England he enlisted and deserted three successive times, and stole, raped, and burned his way to notoriety. When eventually caught after attempting to set fire to the dockyards at Portsmouth and Plymouth as well as Bristol, he had in his possession only a small bundle in which were copies of Ovid's *Metamorphoses* and *The Art of War and Making Fire Works*. Justice dealt with him conventionally. He was hanged from a gibbet made of a naval mast, after being paraded by cart around Portsmouth docks, and his corpse was hung at the harbour mouth as a lesson to others. His case puzzled many commentators. Some believed he was an American spy. Others thought him mad. Half a century earlier he might have been a Jacobite, before that perhaps a millenarian. Later he might have been a romantic, later still an anarchist. In the 1770s he was baffling.[45]

SENTIMENT AND THE NEW PHILANTHROPY

How could sentiment be rendered useful rather than dangerous? Principally by reducing the scope which it gave to self and self-interest through its emphasis on the individual and his own feelings. In its place would be substituted Sensibility, child, as one journalist put it, of Humanity and Sympathy, and progenitor of Benevolence.[46] Henry Mackenzie's *Man of Feeling*, published in 1770, was a deliberate attempt to display the sentimentalist as a benevolent man: it enjoyed immediate success. Unlike Rousseau and Sterne, Mackenzie offered nothing that would upset the pious or the prudish. His was the melancholy tale of a man whose life was a succession of sentimental encounters with the harsh realities of the world and who devoted it to mitigating them. Viewed in this light, as the motor of essentially social virtues, sentiment came fully into its own in England. It was widely believed that in this 'age of benevolence', or 'age of charity' or 'age of almsgiving' as it was variously called at the time, Englishmen had reached new pinnacles of achievement.

There is no means of quantifying such claims. More intriguing are the novel features of late eighteenth-century benevolence.

[45] *The Life of James Aitken* (2nd edn., Winchester, 1777).
[46] *London Magazine*, 1776, p. 195.

Traditional patterns of charitable activity were associated with individual munificence. The early eighteenth century had witnessed some famous examples of the benefactor as hero, mostly men who had made a fortune and had no heir to pass it on to. Edward Colston, for example, had spent his profits in the Spanish trade on projects which commemorated both his piety and philanthropy. The majestic monument which the architect James Gibbs and the sculptor Michael Rysbrack executed in All Saints Church, Bristol, proudly displayed Colston's numerous benefactions in Bristol, London, Surrey, Devon, and Lancashire, not to mention his gifts to eighteen charity schools and sixty poor livings in various parts of the country. Of Colston's contemporaries, only Thomas Guy and John Radcliffe matched his munificence.

Increasingly the public interest shifted to a different type of benefactor. Pope's Man of Ross, John Kyrle, and the Man of Bath, Ralph Allen, were celebrated for the supposedly unostentatious nature of their benevolence. Paradoxically, in an age of intense individualism, individual philanthropists were expected to suppress their egotism in this respect. Thomas Day praised charitable anonymity, 'that placid unambitious benevolence, which gliding on like a gentle stream, uncelebrated and unknown, delights to scatter blessings upon mankind in obscurity'.[47] Connected with this was doubtless an appreciation of the need to tap the broad base of middle-class wealth as well as the more spectacular accumulations of a few plutocrats with fortunes but no families on which to bestow them. Significantly, the eccentric philanthropist William Hanbury, whose charitable scheme of 1767 envisaged the establishment of a collegiate church, a school, a library, and a hospital in his Leicestershire village, proposed to finance his project from public subscriptions. Hanbury seemed to resemble Colston, Guy, and Radcliffe but his methods were not theirs.

There was much awareness of the deficiencies of the old paternalism. The terms of ancient benefactions were easily ignored or abused, and trustees in perpetuity had a way of giving in to unbusinesslike habits, political manipulation, even downright corruption. It was believed that large sums of money had either been misused or forgotten: in 1786 Parliament initiated a great inquiry

[47] *Select Miscellaneous Productions, of Mrs Day, and Thomas Day Esq. in Verse and Prose* (London, 1805), pp. 89–90.

into parochial endowments in an attempt to arrest such neglect. Charity by subscription was not in principle vulnerable to the same dangers, or if it was, it proved a simple matter to cancel subscriptions. Hospitals were built, schools maintained, poor-houses constructed, all on a model providing scope for middle-class giving and governing. Institutional, 'chartered' charity was evidently a thing of the past. So was the traditional manner of donating. Chancery briefs, generally issued by the Crown to stimulate parish collections on behalf of those affected by sudden disaster, whether at home or abroad, were costly to administer and increasingly shunned even by church-goers. In their place sprang up a new world of committees and causes. 'There is scarcely a newspaper but records some meeting of men of fortune for the most salutary purposes', wrote Hannah More.[48]

A novel kind of philanthropist was required: not great bene-factors, but opinion-makers, men who sought out distress or injust-ice, analysed its causes, campaigned for its alleviation, co-ordinated its eradication. Such was Jonas Hanway, merchant and traveller, advocate of umbrellas and naval free schools, enemy of tea-drinking and tips, friend of chimney sweeps, and opponent of Jews. In one of his many publications, *Virtue in Humble Life*, he described what he called '*my* voyage round the *moral* world'.[49] Hanway made enough to retire from his life as a trader in eastern Europe and the Middle East, but not enough to found a family or even to give very much to the objects of his compassion. However, as an organizer of men and women with more money to spare he was relentless. He and his collaborators defy generalization except in their quixoticism and their preference for publicizing and persuading rather than giving. There was Granville Sharp, grand-son of an archbishop, public servant, conscientious objector to the American War, indefatigable campaigner for the abolition of slavery, and enthusiast for the archaic but democratic machinery of what he took to be the Anglo-Saxon constitution. There was John Howard, country gentleman and Dissenter, who at the age of fifty-three married his landlady after she had nursed him through serious illness. His son, whom he was accused of bringing up with almost savage discipline, grew into insanity. But Howard made the

---

[48] 'An Estimate of the Religion of the Fashionable World', *The Works of Hannah More*, vi. 120.

[49] (2 vols., London, 1774), i. v.

cause of prison reform peculiarly his own, with his remorseless inquisition of prison officers, and his inexhaustible touring of gaols, workhouses, and lazarettos at home and abroad.

There was also William Jones, friend of so many of the political causes of the 1770s and ardent parliamentary reformer, not to say eminent orientalist and legal theorist. One of his more bizarre exercises in useful speculation was the composition of an 'Andrometer' which prescribed a proper career for the new benevolent man: thirty years acquiring knowledge, twenty years of public or professional vocation, ten years literary and social activity, the remaining years preparing for eternity. Clergymen were not wanting to join in the campaign for universal improvement. Martin Madan was a lawyer turned Methodist; as chaplain to the Lock Hospital, he became a tireless champion of charity for the victims of commercialized sex. His career was shattered in 1780 when he published his *Thelyphthora*, advocating polygamy. It was also his declared aim to improve the nation's vital statistics by marrying fallen women to old bachelors and widowers. His colleague Colin Milne, divine and botanist extraordinary, was preacher to the City of London Lying-in Charity: he played a prominent part in the dispensary movement and in the foundation of the Royal Humane Society. Also instrumental in the latter was the physician William Hawes, who in 1773 had offered a reward for the recovery of bodies from the Thames in time to effect a resuscitation. His project reflected the concern of the 1770s with suicides (many of whom ended up in the Thames), but also exploited the intense interest of the times in all aspects of life-saving. In due course it gave rise to the Royal Humane Society, to enthusiastic research into the medical uses of electricity, and to a number of provincial rescue services. Like Milne, Hawes was particularly interested in the dispensary movement, prescribing medicine free or at subsidized rates to the poor.

The list could go on, through Thomas Gilbert, reformer of the Poor Law, Robert Raikes, the 'founder' of the Sunday school movement, to Robert Young, whose Philanthropic Society looked forward to the abolition of poverty and who also found time to promote a Social Union, intended to 'disseminate through all orders a knowledge of the social science'.[50] Young aimed at the achievement of liberty, knowledge, and happiness, with the aid

[50] *Transactions of the Social Union* (London, 1790).

of fourteen committees devoted to subjects which ranged from elocution to public justice. What such men had in common was their enthusiasm for moral as well as material improvement, their skill as publicists, and their tenacity. They were truly entrepreneurs of charity, marketing philanthropy much as Wedgwood marketed porcelain, Arkwright textiles, or Lackington books. Their market included women as well as men and families of small property as well as substantial bourgeois citizens. In the minds of some, including a number of those they sought to help, patronize, and 'improve', they aroused suspicion and occasional hostility. Some of their local imitators met with disappointments, as did Mrs Catherine Cappe, who recorded in her diary the opposition which she encountered as 'a general reformer' when she sought to establish a Sunday school in Bedale.[51] But of their impact on the social policy of late Georgian England there can be no doubt.

The importance of public opinion was widely recognized, especially if it was the opinion of a society galvanized by the new sensibility. 'By this means', wrote Jeremy Bentham, 'we arrive at the seat of the error. Sentiment excites to reflection, and reflection detects the impropriety of the law.'[52] But breaking down the prejudices which stood in the way of reform was a major undertaking. This was particularly the case where legislative action was required to rectify an abuse or improve a procedure. Traditionally, Parliament responded to petitions for redress with some form of inquiry (usually a parliamentary committee authorized to take evidence), and a bill which, after extensive debate and negotiation between interests affected, might pass into law. The procedure worked well for localized problems and produced a huge quantity of *ad hoc* legislation in the late eighteenth century. But the concerns of the new reformers were more sweeping: they sought national solutions to national problems, on a scale which could only be achieved by mobilizing extra-parliamentary as well as parliamentary opinion. Such a process could not even be commenced without careful preparation. Reformers were aware of the importance of the initial groundwork but they suffered the disadvantage of an almost total absence of centrally collated statistics. Government saw it as no part of its duty to collect or record information

[51] *Memoirs of The Life of the Late Mrs Catherine Cappe*, p. 123.
[52] Quoted by L. Radzinowicz, *A History of English Criminal Law and its Administration from 1750*, vol. i: *The Movement for Reform* (London, 1948), p. 388.

which it did not need either for its own (mainly financial and military) purposes or which was not specifically required by Parliament. Parliament itself had the power to order investigations which would have been beyond the resources of other bodies. But it required convincing evidence of some manifest abuse or continuing need before doing so. Poor relief was one matter which it was prepared to take seriously, on the initiative of Thomas Gilbert.

Gilbert was a self-made man who acquired a considerable fortune as steward and financial adviser to a great magnate family, the Leveson-Gowers. He also owed his seat in the Commons to them. But he was by no means a time-server. During thirty-one years as an MP he built up a reputation as a vigorous and enlightened reformer. It was at his urging that the Commons conducted two inquiries into the cost of poor relief, in 1776 and 1786, and the further investigation of charitable endowments in 1786. The resulting reports looked forward to the massive statistical inquiries of the early nineteenth century.

Still more impressive was the legislation promoted by Jonas Hanway, if only because Hanway did not have the advantage of a seat in Parliament himself. His interest in statistics was characteristic of the period, not least in its naïvety. On one occasion, visiting Stonehenge—the St Paul's Catheral of 2,250 years before, he mused—he calculated that heaven and hell between them must contain some 52,941,000,000 souls. But there was nothing amateurish about his investigations of conditions for the children of the poor in London. Using the Bills of Mortality, he showed beyond question the effect of social geography on mortality rates. In the twenty-two 'out-parishes' of Middlesex and Surrey, inhabited by the lowest of London's lower classes, he found an appalling death-rate of 58 per cent compared with only 17 per cent in Westminster. He identified a black list of parishes, such as Bethnal Green, Shadwell, Whitechapel, and Shoreditch, where the need for action to preserve the infant poor was particularly obvious. In St Giles' in the Fields and St George's, Bloomsbury, he found 'The greatest *sink* of mortality in *these kingdoms*, if not on the face of the *whole earth*'. He also identified institutions which he described as slaughterhouses under the name of charity houses, and focused his spotlight on named individuals—for instance, Mrs Poole of St Clement Danes, who as a parish wet-nurse contrived to kill off 18 of the 23 children who were entrusted to her care in 1765. In this early endeavour at serious social investigation he earned the co-operation of a group of kindred spirits in Parliament. The result was an Act of 1762 which compelled the systematic registration of poor children in the capital. By some this measure was called 'An Act for keeping children alive', such was the effect of publicity on the conduct of parish officers.[53]

Even these activities, however, paled by comparison with the more celebrated labours of John Howard. Howard's attention was drawn to the state of prisons when he found himself Sheriff of Bedfordshire in 1773. He died in Russia less than twenty years later, exhausted by his labours and travels, and weakened by his addiction to that most famous of all eighteenth-century patent medicines, Dr James's Powder. In the intervening period he made 'a voyage of discovery, a circumnavigation of charity', as Burke put it, recording conditions with impressive precision in countless gaols, bridewells, and workhouses, and eventually extending his inquiries through Europe to the Near East and to Russia.[54] Not since 1729 had the legislature taken a marked interest in the condition of prisons. Then, it had been shocked by stories of mistreatment and even torture of prisoners. In the 1770s its concern was less ephemeral. Howard was congratulated on his work by the House of Commons and in his subsequent publications almost eliminated the need for official investigations. His book *The State of the Prisons,* published in 1777 and updated in 1780 and 1784 with extensive revisions and additions to assess the extent to which local authorities were responding to pressures for improvement, remains a landmark in the history of social welfare.

POPULATION, FINANCE, AND CREDIT

Compilations like Hanway's and Howard's provided evidence of the need for reform. Its appeal, however, is a more complicated

---

[53] *A Journal of Eight Days Journey from Portsmouth to Kingston upon Thames* (London, 1756), p. 106; *Serious Considerations on The Salutary Design of the Act of Parliament For a regular, uniform Register of the Parish-Poor In all the Parishes within the Bills of Mortality* (London, 1762); *An Earnest Appeal for Mercy To the Children of the Poor* (London, 1766), p. 45; I. Pinchbeck and M. Hewitt, *Children in English Society* (2 vols., London, 1969), i, ch. 7.

[54] 'Speech at the Guildhall, in Bristol, 1780', in *The Works of the Right Honourable Edmund Burke* (8 vols., London, 1854), ii. 142.

matter, involving a wide range of motivations, which are almost impossible to rank, and difficult even to disentangle. Contemporaries understood that most of them had to do with middle-class aspirations and attitudes. Vicesimus Knox commented on the distinctive sincerity of the middle classes compared with their superiors and inferiors: 'They are in earnest in their words and deeds.'[55] Lord Shelburne also made a notable distinction between the character of 'liberality' in France and England. In France it was characteristic of the official classes and depended on their political influence to give it effect; in Britain it was the monopoly of the middle classes and had no direct connection with government.[56] This perhaps restricted its progress in terms of ministerial thinking, yet made it a potent force in the formation of public opinion. But reform was not merely a matter of liberalism and humanitarianism. It was also grounded, at its narrowest, on class interest and crude financial advantage, and even at its widest, on the perceived requirements of an efficient, modern State.

Finance loomed large in discussions of poor relief. It was generally believed that the burden of providing for the poor had increased substantially in the course of the eighteenth century, but there were no reliable statistics. Late seventeenth-century estimates suggested a figure of less than half a million pounds per annum. Annual fluctuations caused by seasonal shortages could be considerable. That there was an upward trend in the middle of the century is not in doubt, though some contemporary guesses, running as high as £3.5 million per annum, were plainly excessive.[57] When Arthur Young was on his travels in the late 1760s he found widespread evidence that poor-rates had doubled during the previous twenty years.[58] The inquiry of 1776 produced a total figure of over £1.5 million, that of 1786 an average for the years 1783–5 of about £2 million. Whether this rate of increase was outstripping price inflation is another matter. In any case it was the anomalous nature of the parochial relief system, producing high rates in decaying urban centres and low rates in growing industrial districts or in closely controlled rural parishes, which

[55] *The Works of Vicesimus Knox*, v. 248.
[56] 'The Price Letters', *Proceedings of Massachusetts Historical Society*, 2nd ser., 17 (1963), 359.
[57] J. Hanway, *A Journal of Eight Days Journey from Portsmouth to Kingston upon Thames*, p. 164.
[58] *The Farmer's Tour through the East of England*, i. 232; iv. 338.

was more striking. But the poor-rate bore heavily on middle-class householders in both town and country, since it effectively took the form of a rate on occupiers. It was accordingly easy to whip up anger about its incidence. In fact every form of humanitarian activity which involved better provision for the indigent, the sick, and the vagrant, gave rise to some supposed financial saving in so far as it reduced the potential burden on taxpayers. Self-help was not a phrase in use in the late eighteenth century but it typified propertied attitudes as much as in Samuel Smiles's day. Growing interest in actuarial principles produced various schemes for State-sponsored life insurance, by which the labouring classes might contribute to their own maintenance in sickness and unemployment. In 1772 William Dowdeswell proposed a bill on these lines: it passed the House of Commons only to be defeated in the Lords. The optimistic reformers of this, the first great age of middle-class reform, had much faith in the notion that it was possible to re-educate the lower orders and by transforming the habits of an entire class completely remove the burden on their betters. Charity which ultimately relieved the rich of its responsibilities had understandable appeal.

Arguments which stressed national advantage were more important, however, for they made it possible to justify greater immediate expenditure as well as promising long-term financial savings. Patriotic fervour and humanitarian endeavour went together. Hanway's Marine Society began in 1756 with the object of finding warm clothing for boy recruits in the navy. By October 1759 it had raised nearly £25,000 through voluntary subscription from individuals, clubs, taverns, colleges, schools, congregations, and casual donors, among them Disraeli's father, at this time a boisterous young currency broker, who gave £4. 4s. 'being so much received as a Composition for an Injury received in a Fray at the Playhouse'.[59] The same techniques were employed by the Society for Encouragement of the British Troops in Germany and North America, which in a short time in 1760 raised £7,261 to purchase comforts for soldiers and consolation for widows and orphans.

It was a small step from ventures of this kind to the more

---

[59] J. Hanway, *An Account of the Marine Society* (6th edn., London, 1759), p. 53; and *An Account of the Society for the Encouragement of the British Troops In Germany and North America* (London, 1760).

generalized campaigns on behalf of the distressed and needy in peacetime. These too had ample justification, so it was said, in terms of return on money invested. Many of the great causes of the period had to do with saving lives by one means or another. These included the projects for reviving victims of drowning accidents and suicide attempts, imitating a similar venture in Amsterdam; the dispensary movement to provide subsidized medicines for the poor, as well as the extension of the hospital system itself; the campaign to improve precautions against fires in the crowded tenements of London and large cities. A similar concern marked Hanway's schemes to improve the lot of children. The devastating mortality in London not only destroyed the labour supply of the next generation, but also swept out of existence vast numbers of future mothers and fathers, thereby casting a long shadow over posterity.

This preoccupation was mixed with others in the demands for legal and judicial reform in the 1770s. It is tempting to suppose that the great strides forward in contemporary legal and penal theory had some impact. Certainly Beccaria was translated fairly quickly, in 1767. But Howard's painstaking investigations probably gave more food for thought than any amount of theory, imported or home-grown. Simple compassion played a large part, not least in the form of sympathy for those who fell foul of laws which had to do with commercial transactions. The severity of the English law of debt was a constant cause of complaint. The power which it gave a creditor over a debtor's liberty and property seemed impossible to defend, yet there was no habeas corpus for debtors. Hardly less objectionable was the administration of the prisons, which exposed poor debtors to degradation, sickness, and death, while it permitted the well-placed debtor with hidden means of wealth a comfortable life.

British commerce depended on a flexible system of credit. It was assumed that without the deterrent of imprisonment that system would collapse. In many areas, where the indebtdness of small tradesmen and wage-earners was rife, small debt courts were set up by local Acts of Parliament in an attempt to ensure more expeditious legal proceedings. But middle-class commissioners in these tribunals were not necessarily more sympathetic than the ordinary lawcourts and their gaolers. Parliament also announced an amnesty from time to time, to reduce the prison population:

seven such Insolvency Acts were passed under George II and a further eight between 1760 and 1781. There were also initiatives outside Parliament. The reforms proposed by the Society for Discharge and Relief of Persons Imprisoned for Small Debts in 1772 included reduction of prison fees, in some cases themselves the cause of continued imprisonment for debt, a more rapid and less obscure legal process, abolition of arrest for debt in a man's own dwelling, and greater powers for a clear majority of creditors against those who might have their own reasons for wanting to see debtors imprisoned (purchase of debts as a form of blackmail was said to be all too common). In practice, the Thatched House Society, as it became known, was only successful in raising funds to purchase the release of some of the more affecting victims of the courts.

The chaplain to the Thatched House Society (and earlier to the Magdalen House) was William Dodd, an adroit and ambitious divine who founded his career on the fashion for sentimental sermonizing. His performances in the pulpit were highly regarded, not least by philanthropic ladies disposed to pity the plight of fallen women and distressed debtors. He was also a swindler. A damaging attempt in 1774 to bribe the Lord Chancellor into appointing him to the lucrative living of St George's, Hanover Square resulted in his dismissal as one of the King's chaplains. A further miscalculation was more serious. He forged the signature of his former pupil the Earl of Chesterfield on a bond for £2,400. The trial which followed detection was reported in detail in the press. Chesterfield was condemned for his remorselessness in prosecuting his old tutor. A public campaign, supported by Dr Johnson and by the societies which Dodd had served, was mounted for his reprieve. Dodd seems confidently to have expected mercy. In prison he composed powerful invocations of the sentimental muse. His *Prison Thoughts*, published posthumously, dwelt heavily on the melancholy plight of the man of feeling as prisoner. 'My friends are gone! Harsh on its sullen hinge Grates the dread door.' It also included explicit appeals for reform. 'Hail, generous Hanway.'[60] When the pleas failed and Dodd was executed the spectacle of a philanthropic parson at the gallows sent a distinct shudder through the propertied community.

Forgery and fraud were sensitive subjects in a commercial

[60] W. Dodd, *Thoughts in Prison* (London, 1777), p. 1.

society. They also gave rise to legal anomalies. Counterfeiting copper coins, in a country starved of small currency, was viewed with relative leniency, and even treated in some circumstances as a natural response to the requirements of circulation. Coining of gold and silver was more serious, though juries were not always ready to support a system which seemed to pay little attention to the needs of businessmen. Thomas Lightouller, the most notorious of coiners, led a charmed life before the courts in the 1750s, thanks to the compassion or complacency of jurymen. But in the manufacturing districts of the West Riding a serious outbreak of coining, counterfeiting, and clipping in the 1760s brought a more systematic campaign of repression, culminating in the murder of a local supervisor of excise by the coiners, and the execution of their leader 'King' David Hartley.[61]

Paper fraud gave rise to still more ambiguous responses. In many cases it was uncertain whether an individual had intended an illegal act. The line between presumptuous use of a friend or acquaintance's credit, and intent to defraud, could be narrow indeed. In the countless paper transactions required in a growing but somewhat unstable economy many businessmen steered close to the wind. Dodd's was not the only case which touched the sensitivity of the public on this point. The execution in 1776 of the Perreau brothers, two businessmen of attested probity supposedly trapped into forgery by a *femme fatale* who escaped scot-free, also after a much-publicized trial and widespread doubts about the fairness of the proceedings, aroused similar concern. The cases of Dodd and the Perreaus also sharpened contemporary interest in the debate about capital punishment.

There was a growing belief, owing much to Howard, that properly regulated imprisonment might provide a more real deterrent than pillory, gallows, or transportation. It was also thought that prison could be used to good effect commercially, as a form of public enterprise, and with a view to training the criminal type in industrious habits. Certainly the prisons as surveyed by Howard seemed woefully lacking in both respects, and indeed in many others. In his first appearance before the House of Commons in 1774 Howard identified their failings. They were badly maintained,

---

[61] J. Styles, ' "Our traitorous money makers": The Yorkshire coiners and the law, 1760–83', in J. Brewer and J. Styles, eds., *An Ungovernable People: The English and their Law in the Seventeenth and Eighteenth Centuries* (London, 1980).

9 (*a*) An Exact Representation

9 (*b*). A Trip to Cocks Heath

Not every one was impressed by the martial ardour displayed at the height of the American War. Manchester volunteers of 1778 are shown above, the supposed attractions of the militia camp at Coxheath below.

10 (a). Pantheon Macaroni

10 (b). S. H. Grimm, *The Macaroni*

The grotesque nature of macaroni fashion was a popular subject for caricature: left, a 'Pantheon Macaroni';
right, a satire by S. H. Grimm.

11 (a). Miss Wicket and
Miss Trigger

11 (b). The Female Bruisers

Female participation in sport was much satirized in the 1770s: above, Miss
Wicket and Miss Trigger; below, Female Bruisers.

12. (*a*). Miss Chudleigh

12. (*b*). The Couch of Adultery

Upper-class morals were endlessly fascinating and frequently censured. On the left, Miss Chudleigh makes her semi-nude appearance in public life at a ball in 1749; she left it in equally spectacular fashion when convicted of bigamous marriage to the Duke of Kingston in 1776. On the right, the cartoonist shows the Duke of Cumberland's ludicrous affair with Lady Grosvenor in 1770; it became widely known from the newspaper reports of her trial and the publication of her royal lover's letters.

13. Magdalen charity ticket

Charitable fund-raising became an important part of the social season in London. This is an invitation to the annual sermon and feast to support the Magdalen Hospital for repentent prostitutes.

A SENTIMENTAL HISTORY
of
Chimney Sweepers,
in LONDON & WESTMINSTER.

SHEWING

The Necessity of putting them under
Regulations, to prevent the grossest
Inhumanity, to the Climbing Boys.

WITH

A Letter to a London Clergyman

ON SUNDAY SCHOOLS,

calculated for the preservation
of the Children of the Poor.

By Jonas Hanway, Esq.

Sold by Dodsley in Pall Mall, &
Sewell in Cornhill.
1785.

Angland sculp.

The abject child of Mis'ry forlorn
Still looks on one below

14. Title page of *A Sentimental History of Chimney Sweepers* (London, 1785)
Campaigns for social reform drew heavily on sentimental taste,
shrewdly exploited by men like Jonas Hanway.

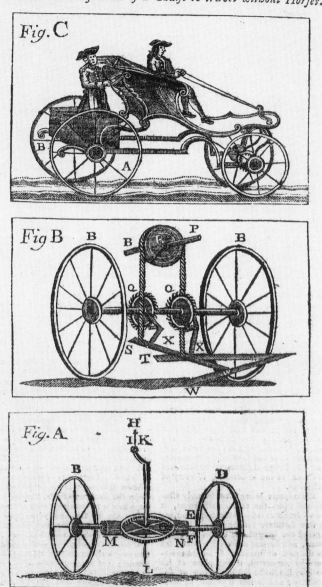

15. Mechanical Projections of a Chaise

Public interest in science and technology was intense, and comprehended both serious academic enquiry and amateur invention. Here the *London Magazine* shows a design of 1769 for a horseless chaise, propelled by a pedalling footman.

16 (a). Can You forebear Laughing

16 (b). Steel Buttons

Even fashion depended on technological advance, as cartoonists enjoyed showing it in the 1770s. Left, the grotesque hairstyle permitted by the elaborate engineering of the hairdressers; right, the devastating radiance of steel buttons from Birmingham.

inadequately cleaned, and disgracefully supervised. They were breeding grounds for fatal fevers: casualties among assize judges provided convincing, and to a Parliament which included many lawyers, compelling evidence to this effect. They mingled prisoners of different ages, sexes, and characters in a demoralizing and dangerous way, and they were managed by officials whose interest it was to extort excessive fees and grant privileges in return for money. The list was supplemented in *The State of the Prisons* by a great quantity of detailed criticism about the physical condition of prisons, the eccentric local customs which affected their administration, and not least the utter lack of interest in their state on the part of otherwise responsible magistrates.

LEGISLATIVE REFORM AND ITS LIMITATIONS

In retrospect the agitation for penal reform seems to establish the 1770s as the seminal period for that reform movement which was to remould so many institutions in the early nineteenth century. But its immediate success was limited. Two Acts of 1774, named after the Somerset MP and Chairman of Quarter Sessions who had taken up Howard's cause with particular enthusiasm, Alexander Popham, were designed to regulate the fees payable by acquitted prisoners, and to reduce the incidence of gaol fever. These were precisely the points which had a special appeal in the light of prevailing sensibilities. The general improvement in conditions of hygiene made gaol fever anomalous as well as outrageous. The confinement of prisoners without the means of bail, at their own cost, also seemed indefensible. Another Somerset man John Langhorne, clergyman, poet, and JP, pleaded their cause in his passionate appeal for a more paternalistic magistracy, *The Country Justice*. 'When found alike in Chains and Night enclos'd, the Thief detected, and the Thief suppos'd.'[62] Whether his fellow countryman's reforms made a great deal of difference is doubtful. Howard recorded with painful accuracy the failure of magistrates and gaolers to implement the new rules. Even in London, where the physician William Smith also carried out a survey, it was found that the 1774 Acts had been largely ignored. The newly rebuilt prison at Newgate was said to be as defective in this respect as more notoriously obsolete gaols.

[62] *The Country Justice: Part the Third* (London, 1777), p. 14.

Reform of the criminal law also made slow progress. In 1772 an attempt was made by leading members of the parliamentary opposition, Sir William Meredith and Edmund Burke, to repeal several statutes inflicting capital punishment. The emphasis was on laws which were plainly redundant, having to do with gypsies, deserted soldiers, and political assassination. They also raised sensitive moral questions: under an Act of James I girls who concealed the birth of a dead bastard child might be convicted of murder. This had frequently been cited as an extreme example of the inhumanity of the English criminal code, not least because it conflicted with a central principle of natural justice, the presumption of innocence. Similar exception was taken to an Elizabethan statute which was directed against the abduction, rape, and forced marriage of young women, but did not extend its protection to those who were not heiresses to substantial property. Even this tentative programme of reform proved controversial. Part of it was defeated in the Commons, the remainder was lost in the Lords.

Parliamentary interest in stemming the advance of capital punishment had been stimulated by a revival of public debate, culminating in the publication of William Eden's precocious *Principles of Penal Punishment* in 1771. Eden's argument was that if the death penalty were genuinely to operate as a deterrent it must be employed only for the most serious offences. The English system, which employed it indiscriminately as a threat but enforced it only as an occasional punishment, seemed designed positively to deprive it of its deterrent effect. Combined with growing hostility to the taking of human life this view did much to sustain interest in reform during the following years. Samuel Romilly's first essay on the subject, his *Observations ... on Executive Justice* in 1786, employed it to some effect. But the argument, supported though it was by increasingly accurate information about the actual incidence of the death penalty, did not win an easy victory. Romilly's tract was written in opposition to Martin Madan's *Thoughts on Executive Justice* of 1785. Madan had argued adroitly but brutally that it was the uncertain enforcement of the death penalty, not its widespread availability, which rendered it useless as a deterrent: it was the prerogative of mercy that needed curbing. Somewhat less draconian but more influential were the views of the utilitarian William Paley, also published in 1785. His comforting assertion that the discretionary use of execution was a rational deterrent, peculiarly appropriate to a country which enjoyed extensive political liberty, provided invaluable ammunition for defenders of the status quo. Romilly's campaign was to be long and arduous.

Parliament was none the less compelled to consider the alternatives to capital punishment. In the 1770s judges seem to have entertained increasing doubts about the advantages of transportation.[63] Moreover the American War effectively removed the principal destination of transportees. The result was an Act directing suitable convicts to be housed on naval hulks in the Thames. Two important objectives of contemporary reformers were thereby brought within reach. The hulks could be supervised with less difficulty and certainly with less contact between prisoners and their friends or family than in conventional gaols. They also provided for useful hard labour, initially dredging the river. High hopes were entertained of the reforming effect of physical work. As William Smith put it, 'Where labour ends vice certainly begins'.[64]

The public was fascinated by the installation of the hulk *Justitia* at Woolwich. William Dodd, awaiting his execution, did not miss the chance to exploit the pathos: 'see the chain'd Britons, fetter'd Man by Man'.[65] Judges were at pains to stress that the law would apply equally to criminals of rank. The first to suffer attracted much interest. David Brown Dignam was convicted of fraudulently offering to procure a place in the Custom House at Dublin. Appalled by his sentence, he tried to bribe the guards, and eventually committed suicide. His fellow convict George Barrington was a genteel pickpocket, and something of a celebrity. Barrington pleaded in vain with the judge to exempt him from the hulks, on account of the 'delicacy of his frame and constitution', and also because the 'ignominious, slavish punishment of working on the Thames' was unacceptable for gentlemen.[66] Crowds of spectators appeared at Woolwich to see him in convict clothes with wheelbarrow and spade. The hulks did not, however, turn out an unqualified success. They were crowded, insanitary, and prone to infestation. Their new supervisors also proved less superior to the old-style gaolers than reformers had anticipated. Not surprisingly

[63] J. M. Beattie, *Crime and the Courts in England, 1660–1800* (Oxford, 1986), p. 560.
[64] *State of the Gaols in London, Westminster, and Borough of Southwark* (London, 1776), p. 67.
[65] W. Dodd, *Thoughts in Prison*, p. 90.
[66] *London Magazine*, 1777, p. 227.

the experts began once again to think in terms of transportation, to the West Indies, to Africa, and eventually to a new gem in the imperial crown, Australia. Barrington shared in this experiment too. Released from Woolwich he took up his old ways, was convicted, and deported to New South Wales. There he became a reformed character and rose to the dignity of High Constable of Paramatta.

Reformers looking for a new initiative in penal policy were much encouraged by a statute of 1779, which authorized the creation of two penitentiaries on the latest principles. Unfortunately, three commissioners were appointed to execute the Act, Howard himself, the physician John Fothergill, and the treasurer of the Foundling Hospital, George Whatly. It proved a highly impracticable combination. Howard, indefatigable as critic and analyst, was not a natural conciliator. The commissioners were unable even to agree on a site for the first prison. There were also major questions of policy as yet unresolved. Much ink was spilled on the problem of confinement. Some argued that the ultimate deterrent to criminal activity was total isolation; others had doubts about the psychological consequences. Jeremy Bentham, the most innovative, but not the most practical of theorists, changed his mind on this matter, after starting as an enthusiast for solitary confinement.

The most notable changes occurred in a local context, where the subtleties of penal theory could be ignored and the obstructions overridden. It was in Gloucestershire, under the leadership of Sir George Onesiphorus Paul, that steps were taken towards a more coherent policy. Paul was a magistrate who had read his Howard, but also knew his quarter sessions politics and was able to bring weight to bear in the county community. Although Gloucestershire's authorizing statute was not obtained until 1785, its principles were thrashed out in 1783 and quickly communicated to other counties. Paul envisaged four county bridewells operating on clear maxims of deterrence for minor offences, and a central gaol for lengthy incarceration. The prisons were to be administered by staff who were, in theory at least, deprived of an interest in corrupt management. There was also much emphasis on a new regime of hard work, close supervision, and sexual segregation. The path of reform did not prove smooth but the Gloucestershire magistrates were widely applauded for setting out on it.

Reformers were frequently made aware of the difficulty of overcoming powerful vested interests. Certainly this was the case with Edmund Burke's bill of 1776, which was designed to deter coastal communities from the ransacking of wrecked vessels, by requiring the hundred to provide compensation for damage and theft. The facts were undeniable: the complicity of entire villages in robbery and even murder was obvious, and there were well-known instances of the killing of crews who might testify to the activities of wreckers. Yet the opposition of MPs who represented maritime constituencies brought Burke's efforts to nought. Similar lessons could be learned from attempts to reform the Poor Law. After nearly two decades of agitation the only result of importance was Gilbert's Act of 1782.

The Act envisaged the gradual elimination of the anomalies of parochial relief by encouraging parishes to unite for Poor Law purposes. It also looked to the establishment of workhouses which might meet the demand for a social and industrial discipline, without giving rise to the inhumanity and corruption associated with schemes for 'farming out' the poor. It had that mixture of utilitarian rigour and high-minded benevolence which was to inspire the austere reforms of the 1830s. But unlike those reforms, and more characteristically of eighteenth-century attitudes, it was permissive legislation, which operated only where local communities could agree on the need for change. In this respect it was merely extending a procedure which had been adopted in Suffolk and Norfolk since the late 1750s. There a series of local acts had granted permission for parishes to collaborate (at hundred level) in borrowing, consolidating rates, and building workhouses. These schemes were meant to provide better care for the genuinely poor, to deter the 'sturdy beggars', and, given a suitable spirit of enterprise, to reimburse the ratepayer with the profits of workhouse industry. The result was some striking, even handsome new buildings, grander, as it was pointed out, than many East Anglian mansions. In the short term the new establishments helped keep poor-rates down (their major objective for most ratepayers) but the initial investment was costly, and by the 1790s, when Frederick Eden made his famous survey of poor relief, it was clear that they had neither reduced the long-term expense nor rendered the relief itself more effective. No doubt it was for this reason that few areas took advantage of Gilbert's Act.

In such local obstructionism lay the single most powerful

restraint on reform. Even Jonas Hanway found that parliamentary statutes could do little on their own. The climax of his campaign to improve the treatment of the infant poor in London was an Act of 1767, which set up parochial boards of supervisors in and about London, charged with ensuring that children at risk were sent into the country. The Act provided for financial support, and gave wet-nurses an incentive to ensure the survival of their charges rather than their extinction. It was said to have had a marked effect, but even Hanway admitted that it was not invariably enforced. Infant mortality in the capital during the early decades of the Industrial Revolution remained a fearful problem.

CHILDREN, ANIMALS, AND POPULAR RECREATIONS

The most successful reforms were those which depended on voluntary activity and needed neither encouragement nor endorsement by legislators. Especially was this the case if they challenged no vested interest and seemed to offer improved social conditions at small financial cost, preferably in a way which reinforced political conformity. A feature of the reforming ideals of this era, and one which remained to characterize the evangelical revival, was their intense conservatism, all the more striking at a time when natural rights theory was making progress in some quarters. Hannah More's famous tracts, one of the most coherent attempts to drum respect for authority into the lower classes, belong to a slightly later period, when the menace of revolution abroad heightened social anxieties at home. But it needed no Robespierre or St Just to turn the philanthropists of the age into arch-conservatives. Jonas Hanway stressed that the intention of his reforms was to reinforce law and government, not to undermine them. His *Soldier's Faithful Friend*, published in 1766, instructed not only soldiers but many other classes of manual labourer on their duty to their betters. Like the later evangelicals, he made religious consolation the centre-piece of his conservatism. There were some who glimpsed the sheer humbug of middle-class reforming attitudes in this respect, long before it reached the pinnacle of hypocrisy which their successors claimed to see in early nineteenth-century evangelicals. The satirist Richard Owen Cambridge complained of the condescending attitude of many patrons of the populace, not least in denying its cultural aspirations. 'Shall you be struck with Titian's tints, And may'nt I stop to stare at prints?'[67] But Cambridge was essentially of gentry stock, and worldly at that: he understood nothing of the new puritanism of earnest men like Hanway and Howard.

Much attention was bestowed on the need to discipline the poor, partly by eliminating all practices which seemed to threaten political order and religious conformity, partly by enforcing the kind of regimentation appropriate to the labour requirements of a rapidly industrializing society. 'Reformation of Manners' was in the air again in the 1760s and 1770s, though formal institutions comparable to the societies of the early eighteenth century did not reappear for some time. The London Methodists undertook prosecutions of immorality during the Seven Years War but found themselves defeated by a judicial counter-attack which ended with heavy financial costs awarded against them. Thereafter it was not until the celebrated royal Proclamation of 1787 against Vice and Immorality, itself the result of a co-ordinated campaign by Churchmen and politicians, that organized efforts at moral improvement took place. In the mean time, however, informal pressure mounted steadily. A stream of sermons and tracts urged an end to drinking, swearing, gambling, and all activities which made the poor labourer a less dependable employee, as well as a vile sinner. Hanway and his friends were great Sabbatarians: one of their standard arguments was that good conduct on the day of rest was an essential part of a disciplined approach to six days of work. In 1781 Beilby Porteus, the Bishop of Chester, piloted through Parliament a measure reinforcing the laws against sabbath-breaking.

There was much lofty criticism of those popular recreations which were rooted in the traditions of communal life. They often involved 'wasted' time not merely on Sundays but on the many patronal festivals or holidays which supposedly interfered with the labouring calendar. Englishmen were for ever contratulating themselves on the wickedness of Roman Catholic practice in this respect, contrasting the numerous holidays enjoyed in southern Europe with more frugal attitudes in England and northern Europe, but they would gladly have reduced the holiday period further. It was not merely idleness that was feared. Sexual licence,

[67] 'A Dialogue between a Member of Parliament and his Servant (1752)', in G. O. Cambridge, *The Works of Richard Owen Cambridge*, p. 259.

drunken brawling, cruelty to animals, even the threat of violence and political unrest, all were associated with specifically popular entertainment and relaxations. Paradoxically, it was at this very time that antiquarian interest in folklore was growing. Foremost in this field was the Newcastle clergyman John Brand, who revised and reissued the work published by a predecessor at Newcastle, Henry Bourne, in 1720. The result, Brand's *Observations on Popular Antiquities* of 1777 is an intriguing guide to the social tensions implicit in such scholarship. Brand himself plainly shared a sense of the moral dangers of undisciplined lower-class revelries. At the same time, he was too honest not to admit their long history, their wholesome good humour, and their gratuitous victimization by the champions of commercial society. Misgivings of this kind were rare, however. At the time when Brand was writing, there were also appearing many tracts and chapbooks specifically intended to reform the lives of illiterate Englishmen and women. Typical of the values involved was *The School Mistress for the Poor*, an anonymous work published in 1778 and reprinted well into the nineteenth century. Its obsession with the virtues of obedience, labour, and godliness makes understandable its long-lived appeal to Victorians. The clear implication of its title was that in matters of morality and politics the poor were to be treated as children. It also dealt much with children themselves. Children were favourite objects of the reformers, and in no position to resist the benevolent despotism of the new puritans.

The significance of these attitudes was made clear by the Sunday school movement, the most successful of all philanthropic campaigns in this period. The Sunday schools were not strictly the invention of the printer Robert Raikes and his collaborator, the Gloucester clergyman Thomas Stock. There were a number of precursors, including a school run by the most famous of the Unitarian converts of the 1770s Theophilus Lindsey, when he was Rector of Catterick. But it was Raikes who gave the idea the publicity to turn it into a national sensation. His objective was typical of the hard-headed realism of philanthropists of the evangelical school. As he pointed out, there was much to be said for a form of schooling which took children off the streets and kept them from breaking windows. Opposition to the schools was based on the assumption that it was absurd to invest money in a scheme which would fill children's heads with dangerous ideas and aspirations. But as the defenders never tired of reiterating, education could be used to quell the spirit of free enquiry, not to stimulate it, to enforce discipline and conformity, not to challenge them, and to teach duties, not inculcate rights. The argument helped inspire thousands of middle-class citizens to make a modest contribution to the cause. By 1785, when the Sunday School Society was instituted, it was clear that Raikes's formula would be applied on a nation-wide scale.

Children were appropriate beneficiaries of the philanthropic sensibility of the age. Rousseau's *Émile* had given a stimulus to interest in education, and initiated an era of crackpot theories and eccentric experiments. It cannot be said that much progress was made in terms of solid analysis. Locke's psychology remained the basis of educational theory, and the vast superstructure of moralizing erected on it in the 1760s and 1770s added little of substance. Many parents subscribed to the fashionable faith in a relatively relaxed upbringing. The Derbyshire poet and physician Erasmus Darwin carried this approach to extremes (and also to the irritation of his friends) by his utter refusal to discipline his children. Yet even devotees of Rousseau could be ruthless disciplinarians. Darwin's friend Thomas Day, who, in a spirit of experiment, took charge of two young orphan girls whom he intended to bring up as his own daughters on enlightened educational principles, practised physical discipline and mental control to a horrifying degree. Not surprisingly they failed to live up to his ideals of feminine development. One was discharged at an early stage; the other, designed for marriage to Day, demonstrated insufficient self-discipline for her high destiny and had to be married off to a friend.

Such conduct is more remarkable as evidence of interest in children than for anything it achieved with them. This interest reflected the improved survival rates for children of upper and middle-class families, as well as the wealth and leisure available to them. It was exploited by painters who specialized in family groups, with children displayed increasingly as objects of central importance, rather than mere appendages. It also brought profit to authors of improving children's literature and handbooks on the upbringing of children. The early classics, Day's *Sandford and Merton* and Sarah Trimmer's *Sacred History*, were marked by uncompromising moral didacticism, if not downright priggery.

Even when they genuinely expanded the intellectual horizons of the reading child, for example where geography and history were concerned, their prime object was to model children with a view to piety and conformity. It was such qualities which Mrs Trimmer had in mind when she remarked that her Sunday school children at Brentford, 'who were in a very rude state are now wonderfully civilised'.[68] But it would be quite unfair to charge the reformers with neglect of material in favour of moral welfare. Hanway devoted much attention to the fate of children brutally exploited by those who should have been their protectors. His view was not based on a sentimental horror of hard labour for children. In fact he was shocked to find 'parents importune for charity, whose children were arrived to 8 years old, up to 13 or 14, and not gaining a penny a day'.[69] He was still more shocked, however, by the way so many employers, particularly of the smaller kind, abused their younger employees.

The most harrowing case was that of the London chimney-sweeps. As new lines of terraced houses advanced across the Middlesex landscape, most of them built with chimneys too narrow to admit any but the tiniest of bodies, infant sweeps became a familiar sight. Parish authorities, desperate to rid themselves of the burden of care, 'sold' them as apprentices to indigent masters; they began their work, often at the age of four or five, walking a mile or two to work in all weathers, with little on their backs (clothes got in the way of chimneys), and without benefit of shoes or stockings. Injuries of every kind abounded and the normal condition of the child chimney-sweep was characterized by abrasions, wounds, and contorted bones. Contact with soot, external and internal, caused a high incidence of urinary complaints and cancer of the scrotum. In summer, with little work available, they were hired out to other tradesmen or left to roam without food or money. If they lived to reach the age of twelve or fourteen, they were too big for their trade and broken in health. In 1773 a self-appointed committee attempted to secure better conditions by putting pressure on employers, but the voluntary nature of the indentures which it sought to introduce made effective improvement unlikely. Even the first statute regulating the conditions of

---

[68] B. Rodgers, *Cloak of Charity: Studies in Eighteenth-Century Philanthropy* (London, 1949), p. 123.
[69] *Proposal for County Naval Free-Schools, to be built on Waste Lands* [1783], p. 5.

work for sweeps, in 1788, was by no means universally enforced. In this as in so many other cases, the vested interest of employers, often men eking out a bare subsistence themselves, made change impossible. The chimney-sweeps numbered about 600 in 1785, but they were only the most affecting cases in what seemed a boundless landscape of urban despair. The laws of apprenticeship, obsolescent though they were, positively facilitated exploitation of child labour, and came in for growing criticism. Perhaps the most serious instance to prick the public conscience was that of Elizabeth Brownrigg, a poor-house midwife who brutally mistreated a succession of serving girls, one of them to the point of death. Convicted of murder, she repented on the scaffold and urged 'that all overseers, etc. would look now-and-then after the poor young persons of both sexes, to see that their masters and mistresses used them well'.[70] This was a pious hope indeed, but the speech and the plea (sincerely meant or not) were peculiarly characteristic of the changing climate of opinion in the 1760s and 1770s.

The appeal of children lay in their helplessness, their utter dependence on parental benevolence and enlightenment. It was matched, if not exceeded, by the plight of animals. The optimistic secularism of much eighteenth-century thought bred a growing belief in the essential innocence of the animal world. Scientists who found it difficult to distinguish clearly between the physical characteristics of men and those of brutes reinforced this tendency. In a controversial tract Thomas Percival, author of *A Father's Instructions*, claimed that conscious sensation extended throughout the vegetable world. Not many of his readers swallowed this, but there was sufficient romance in the new botany to make an appealing subject for sentimental poets, as Erasmus Darwin's great success, the *Botanic Garden*, testifies. Animal rights created awkward problems for theologians. Richard Dean, curate of Middleton, accepted the challenge in full with his *Essay on the future life of Brute Creation*. His argument that animals were more than biological mechanisms and might well share in mankind's privilege of eternal life provoked threats of prosecution in the courts. But even less daring theologians stressed man's duty towards the creation which the Deity had placed in his charge. The evangelicals turned this theme to advantage, drawing on chapbook folklore. Sarah Trimmer's *Fabulous Histories designed for the Instruction of*

[70] *London Magazine*, 1767, p. 484.

children respecting their treatment of Animals, published in 1786, found support for benevolence in popular tales like the *History of the Robins*.

The fashionable poets of the age also made great play with so promising a theme, relishing the paradoxes which it suggested, in that human progress so often required harsh treatment of animals. Mrs Barbauld, in the *Mouse's Petition*, lamented the loneliness of Joseph Priestley's mice, confined for his experiments on the composition of air: she also extended her sympathy to the lowest of God's creation. 'Beware, lest in the worm you crush, A brother soul you find; And tremble lest thy luckless hand Dislodge a kindred mind.'[71] The mawkishness of enthusiasts for animal welfare met with some mockery. Goldsmith derided sighing sentimentalists who ate the flesh of six different animals in one fricassee.[72] Reviewing William Jackson's *The Beauties of Nature Displayed, in a Sentimental Ramble through her Luxuriant Fields* in 1770, the Dissenter Jabez Hirons caustically observed that in practice God's benevolent design for animal life resembled nothing more than a great slaughterhouse.[73] Satirical commentators portrayed the agonies of young men who accidentally trod on earthworms while rescuing flies from spiders, or young women who feared to breathe for fear of killing the 'animalcula which naturalists say are thereby murthered'. One such could hardly walk for fear of 'exterminating an ant who was laden with food, which I could not but fancy was designed to a sick friend in the neighbouring hillock'.[74] Soame Jenyns helpfully suggested that the torments of animals were best explained by the theory of transmigration of souls. The poor fox had once been a corrupt minister, the bull a brutal tyrant, the bird in its cage a merciless creditor; even the lobster boiled alive must once have been a cruel Spaniard in Mexico or a Dutch murderer at the Massacre of Amboina. There were evidently limits to sentimental credulity.[75]

The practical effect of the new sensibility was limited where animals were concerned. Some ostentatious vegetarians paraded their preferences. The antiquarian Joseph Ritson was one of those

[71] L. Aikin, *The Works of Anna Laetitia Barbauld* (London, 1825), i. 37.
[72] 'The Citizen of the World', xv, in *The Collected Works of Oliver Goldsmith*, ii. 66.
[73] *Monthly Review*, 42 (1770), 169.
[74] S. J. Pratt, *Shenstone-Green; or, the New Paradise Lost* (3 vols., 2nd edn., London, 1780), i. 7–8.
[75] 'The World', clxiii, in *The Works of Soame Jenyns*, ii. 130–1.

who did so, though his habit was widely attributed to insanity. The barbarities of Smithfield, in theory at least, were scrutinized more closely by the City authorities.[76] Hygiene as well as humanity dictated more control of the slaughterers' activities, as indeed did the growing unpopularity of the butchers and drovers themselves at a time when meat prices were rising faster than almost any other commodity. More vulnerable, but also more resistant to middle-class criticism, was hunting. It is possible that the growing emphasis on formality and ritual which characterized the history of the fox-hunt in this period represented an attempt to present it in a more defensible, less casually cruel, form. On the whole, however, the field sports of the rich were hardly affected. It was quite different with the poor. Cock-shying, a popular custom in many towns, had long been the subject of polite distaste, not least because of the general disorder which it was said to provoke. Cock-fighting was a trickier problem. Middle and upper-class interest in it was considerable, if somewhat in decline. Old-fashioned country gentlemen certainly saw no harm in it. Sir John Astley of Shropshire even built an elaborate monument to his most famous cock, which had won 100 guineas in one fight.[77] Nevertheless, the criticism may have had some effect. It was commonly said that Englishmen had made cock-fighting a particularly barbarous sport, partly by the frequent use of steel spurs, partly by resort to exhausting contests, like the battle royal, in which the birds fought until only one was left, or the notorious Welsh main which started with sixteen pairs, and ended with a victor who had won five fights. Some rural sports were identified with lower-class enthusiasm and were accordingly condemned outright: in the case of badger and hedgehog-baiting, for instance, double standards were plainly being applied.

TRAVEL AND EXPLORATION

Sensitivity to the plight of animals derived partly from growing knowledge of the world of flora and fauna, knowledge often somewhat distantly related to the serious-minded scientific investigations of botanists and biologists, but none the less dependent on them. All the more was this the case with the rapid assimilation

[76] S. J. Pratt, *Gleanings in England* (2nd edn., 3 vols., London, 1801), iii. 273 ff.
[77] *London Magazine*, 1775, p. 480.

of new historical, geographical, and anthropological information concerning man himself. There were vastly increased opportunities for travel. 'There is scarcely', wrote the poet George Keate, 'any considerable object, between Shooter's Hill and Mount Aetna, which hath not been described, well or ill, by some author or other.'[78] Travel literature, as distinct from travel itself, which at least beyond English shores was still primarily for people of wealth, was one of the great publishing triumphs of the late eighteenth century, riding high on vicarious pleasure in a multitude of sights and impressions. Rare indeed, said Hannah More, were 'travellers of that rare tribe, Who've *seen* the countries they describe'.[79] The main interest of these accounts was not topographical, though appropriate scenic descriptions were *de rigueur*. Nor, for the most part, were their readers antiquarians, though antiquities ranked high among the ostensible objects of tourism. Their focus seems rather to have been on social customs and peculiarities, especially in matters, for instance sexual relations, of special sensitivity in contemporary England. Philip Thicknesse, driven abroad by debt, cashed in on this need. He dwelt heavily on the vulgarity and coarseness of French women, a source of contamination for English women not firmly supervised by their husbands. Gambling was rife in Paris and would ruin young Englishmen foolish enough to become involved.[80] These warnings were not necessarily intended for actual use. Rather they reinforced English prejudices, and met the need for a sense of contrasting customs. In his wickedly innocent *Sentimental Journey* Laurence Sterne carried the conventions of this genre to their limit, and most travel writers stepped back from a precipice which could only be negotiated with talent as well as enterprise. But the same interest in mores and manners and their impact on the sensitivities of middle-class Englishmen is unmistakable. Even scholarly writers like Francis Carter, whose *Journey from Gibraltar to Malaga* of 1777 was concerned with the survival of Roman antiquities, were aware of the need to supply this commodity of sentimental social comment.

It was also vital to reinforce native patriotism. Comparisons of continental Catholicism with English Protestantism were almost invariably unfavourable to the former. Travellers who violated this

---

[78] *Sketches from Nature*, ii. 14.
[79] 'The Bas Bleu', in *The Works of Hannah More*, i. 23.
[80] *A Year's Journey through France and Part of Spain* (2 vols., Bath, 1777), ii. 230, 239.

rule and mistook middle-class liberalism for middle-class tolerance did so at their peril. Mrs Kindersley, who published an account of her voyage in the South Atlantic, made the fatal mistake of offering some mildly sympathetic remarks about the Catholic Church in Brazil and received a lambasting from clerical opinion.[81] It is significant in this respect that the country which featured most of all in travel literature, Italy, was precisely that which enjoyed the most satisfying mixture of elements: a cultural heritage important to Englishmen conscious of their own debt to Rome and the Renaissance, a priest-ridden society which gave rise to comforting reflections about the intellectual torpor and economic decline attending popery, and sexual conventions which offered opportunities for censure and titillation alike. At a time when the status of women in general was much debated, it was unsurprising that the one essential topic for writers on Italy was the peculiar position of Italian women, involving, so it seemed, a strange combination of subjection and sexual liberty. The Italian *cicisbeo* exerted an overwhelming fascination on the English. When the writers were themselves women, as in the case of Anna Miller's *Letters from Italy* in 1777, the appeal seemed greater still. A foreigner with a good command of English and a shrewd appreciation of the market might also profit by his special knowledge. Giuseppe Baretti's *Account of the Manners and Customs of Italy* of 1768 was acknowledged as the most authoritative of all such productions. It included an agreeably controversial attack on the inventions and exaggerations of less knowledgeable reporters, notably the unfortunate Samuel Sharp, whose ignorance of the Italian language was said to have led him into particularly gross errors.[82] Lacking the guidance of cosmopolitan authors like Baretti, there was always the possibility of translation. A large international market flourished for travel literature, one in which the English participated eagerly. The translated accounts of journeys in the less well-known parts of eastern Europe were guaranteed a readership.

Naïve interest in ethnic diversity was reinforced by the historical and anthropological preoccupations of many scholars and writers. Eighteenth-century man had a profound curiosity about where he had come from and a corresponding interest in the light which other

---

[81] *Letters from The Island of Teneriffe, Brazil, The Cape of Good Hope, and the East Indies* (London, 1777); H. Hodgson, *Letters to Mrs Kindersley* (London, 1778).
[82] S. Sharp, *Letters from Italy* (London, 1766).

societies might throw on the origins of the modern, commercial age. For many, of course, all such information fitted into pre-existing conceptions. The most celebrated instance was probably Jacob Bryant's *A New System or An Analysis of Ancient Mythology*, which sought to reconcile a vast mass of history and myth with the literal interpretation of the Old Testament. But this line of argument, although bringing comfort to the conventional Christian, had limited appeal. Most were ready to admit that the Bible was at best unhelpful on many matters of special contemporary concern. Extended contact with primitive peoples, or, indeed, sophisticated peoples whose societies seemed alien to the European tradition, required intellectual and psychological adjustment. In all this there was particular fascination with the way in which individual cultures grew and died, and an understandable curiosity about the prospects for society in the West, as it was coming to be labelled.

Even at home there was room for empirical research on this theme. Highland society, described so profitably by Thomas Pennant in his *Tour in Scotland* of 1774 and by Boswell and Johnson in the published accounts of their Hebridean tour, seemed to offer just this sense of a civilization, or at least a culture, which was visibly changing under the impact of novel economic forces. Pennant's solution was a romantic appeal to the paternalism of the landlord in Scotland, Johnson's a more realistic assessment of the economic and political pressures which had doomed feudal society, particularly since the Forty-Five. In either case English readers were able to experience a compound of stimulating sensations, triumph, sadness, guilt, on behalf of a superior but all too successful commercialism.

Still more influential were overseas explorations. After the Seven Years War Britain and France authorized ventures to the Southern Hemisphere which captured the public imagination in both countries, and in time transformed the European view of primitive society. The motives for these expeditions were mixed. Cook's initial voyage in 1768 was commissioned to observe the Transit of Venus from a good vantage-point in the South Pacific. The results were expected to be of the first importance for navigators as well as for astronomers. This voyage also yielded a wealth of new information about natural history, especially botany. The second voyage in 1772 proved equally productive in scientific terms. A persistent conundrum, the difficulty of devising a reliable means of ascertaining longitude at sea, was resolved by vigorous testing of a new generation of chronometers. Strategy and commerce offered less certain but still more glittering prizes. High hopes were entertained of territories in the South Atlantic and South Pacific, and contributed to the Falkland Islands dispute in 1770. There were two ancient speculations to dispose of, each as enticing as the alchemist's gold, or the philosopher's stone. In the south there beckoned the Terra Australis, a future Peru which might yield who knew what minerals, raw materials, and markets. There was also the question of a north-west passage. Christopher Middleton, on his expedition of 1741, had forecast the futility of further searching in the Arctic, but an enthusiastic armchair explorer, Arthur Dobbs, kept interest alive long enough to lead Parliament to offer a reward for its discovery in 1745. Even the proof offered in 1771 by one of the servants of Hudson's Bay Company, Samuel Hearne, that if a such a passage existed it did not lead out of Hudson Bay, failed to deter the Admiralty and Royal Society from offering Cook hopeful instructions on the point for his third and final voyage in 1776.

Cook died in an absurdly inconsequential brawl in the Hawaiian Islands, least favourite of island paradises among his generation of discoverers. None the less his deputy Charles Clerke was able to report the end of any hope of a north-west passage. But Cook's reputation had been made in the Southern Hemisphere. His first two voyages, despite the competition of Bougainville and the previous efforts of Byron and Wallis, put the geography and navigation of the South Pacific on a new basis and made Cook a legendary figure in his own lifetime. In particular, on his second voyage, when the *Resolution* made two great sweeps of the islands of the South Pacific, and when he penetrated as far as the ice-packs of Antarctica, he disposed of the myth of Terra Australis. As he noted himself, proudly: 'final end put to the searching after a Southern Continent, which has at times engrossed the attention of some of the Maritime Powers for near two centuries past and the Geographers of all ages'.[83]

Cook had started from humble beginnings on the Yorkshire coast. In his own record of the second voyage published in 1777,

[83] J. C. Beaglehole, *The Life of Captain James Cook* (London, 1974), p. 433, and subsequent quotations, pp. 471, 292, 252, 218, 359.

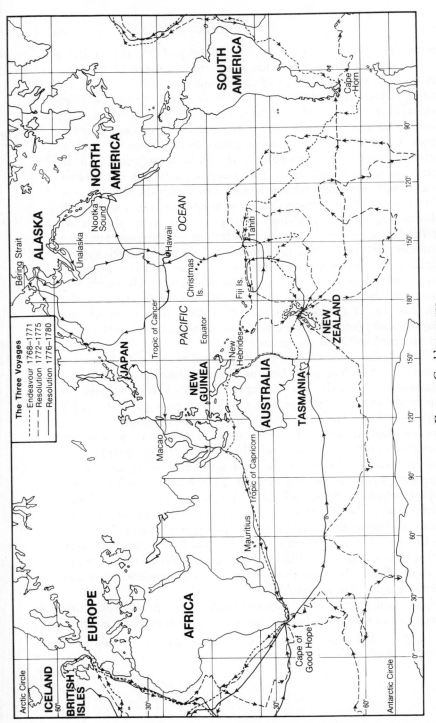

Fig. 9. Cook's voyages

Source: J. C. Beaglehole, *The Life of Captain James Cook* (London 1974), p. 704

he self-deprecatingly but piously admitted his limited education and his progress 'from a prentice boy in the Coal trade to a Commander in the Navy'. His triumph was one of practical seamanship, humane, sensible leadership, and painstaking surveying, learned in Canadian waters during the campaigns of the Seven Years War. He suffered a good deal at the hands of officers, academics, and amateur scientists. Alexander Dalrymple, an overblown adventurer, was originally designed for the expedition of 1768 and Cook was spared him only because, without any credentials as a sailor, he attempted to bully the Admiralty into giving him command. He had the misfortune to publish in embarassing detail his belief that South Georgia, off the Falklands, was the northerly point of a great southern continent; this was in 1775, the year of Cook's return from the myth-dispelling second voyage. Hardly less of a prima donna was Joseph Banks, gentleman scientist and explorer, who accompanied Cook in 1768 and initially outshone him in fame. Banks had very grand plans for the second voyage, which included taking along celebrities such as the naval physician James Lind, and the artist Johann Zoffany. Cook was saved having to cope with this trio by Banks's impossible demands, which would have turned his ships into lavishly furnished laboratories, at the expense of their seaworthiness. Banks went off on a less than successful Icelandic voyage with his Swedish botanist Dr Solander. It is a measure of Cook's diplomacy that their relationship was only temporarily affected by Banks's arrogance, and Cook's subsequent triumphs.

In his early journals, Cook occasionally revealed a naïve ambition. 'O how Glorious would it be to set my heel upon the Pole! and turn myself round 360 degrees in a second.' Soon after naming Botany Bay he rhapsodized about the Australian Aborigines. 'They live in Tranquillity which is not disturb'd by the Inequality of Conditions.' Such romanticism may have helped him persevere, particularly during his first voyage. Both Byron and Wallis, only a few years before him, had found the endless succession of sea, sky, and scurvy far from home a disincentive to adventurous navigation. Even on Cook's *Endeavour* there was a 'no-continent party' who hoped that New Zealand would turn out very quickly to be an island and longed to return to roast beef and home. But Cook was also capable of a more sober realism, which increasingly predominated in his encounters with primitive peoples. Tahiti already had an extraordinary reputation as a land of enchantment. Cook retained a certain caution and had a conscience about the effect of European contact on a society so long isolated. This stood him in good stead in less attractive parts, in Melanesia, the antithesis of the Friendly Isles, and in New Zealand where other less cautious visitors were shocked out of innocent wonder at the unrestrained joy of South Pacific life by the horror of cannibalism. Cook offered a judicious assessment. New Zealanders, he was forced to concede, 'are certainly in a state of civilisation'. They were by no means mere primitives; cannibalism accordingly must be an ancient practice sanctioned by religious authority and tradition. It was a warning of the dangers of custom, perhaps, but not a sign of the degenerate nature of some inhabitants of the hoped-for Arcadia.

Readers in England were soon called upon to make judgements of similar sophistication. The market for tales of the South Seas was huge, and the profits to be made from recounting the exploits of the explorers far greater than those of making the explorations. French accounts, particularly of the pioneering Bougainville, were quickly translated into English. The official version of the early voyages of Byron, Wallis, and Cook was given by a literary man with no previous knowledge of the subject, John Hawkesworth. The Admiralty handed over the official materials for these voyages and left Hawkesworth to negotiate his own terms, which amounted to £6,000, one of the most remunerative publishing ventures of the eighteenth century. Hawkesworth's work was disastrously inept. Cook first saw it when he was returning from his second voyage at the Cape. He confessed himself 'mortified' by the ignorant bowdlerization which Hawkesworth presented as a scientific summary of the early expeditions. Hawkesworth himself died within a few months of publication, his death apparently hastened by the avalanche of recrimination which descended on him.

There was a considerable scramble for a share in this literary eldorado. Even the gunner's mate of the *Resolution*, John Marra, an Irishman whose alcoholic and sexual lapses had caused Cook many problems, managed to sell his account to the chapbook publisher Francis Newbery of St Paul's Churchyard. Cook himself published his somewhat crude, but competent account, in 1778; his literary adviser for that edition, Canon John Douglas, wrote a matching report of the final voyage in 1784. There was an embarassing brush with Johann Reinhold Forster, the botanist who had accompanied Cook on the second voyage in place of Banks. Forster's scientific credentials were undoubted. His personal industry and perseverance were also remarkable: he had endured much hardship in finding his way to England and the attention of the Admiralty. But he expected to be in charge of the presentation of the second voyage and its findings, and took well-meaning attempts to improve his English, including the proffered advice of the poet and essayist Richard Owen Cambridge, very badly. In the end he was to publish on his own, to considerable effect as it turned out, especially when his son George Forster wrote up a popular version of his work which he published in advance of Cook himself.

ENLIGHTENED OPINION AND NON-EUROPEAN PEOPLES

What did the public make of this flood of information? There was some scepticism about the importance of the discoveries. One anonymous 'Rhapsody' extolled the more sensational benefits of the new settlements.[84] The gigantic human beings allegedly seen by Byron and his crew in Patagonia would make excellent night watchmen in London, 'bunches of riotous young fellows hanging at their belts'. The Polynesian ignorance of gold and silver would reform the materialism of Englishmen; moreover, their want of horses would eliminate horse-racing and reduce the price of oats. The exposure of illegitimate children would solve the problem of London's poor infants, and cannibalism offered a promising new source of food as well as a means of reducing poor-rates. But such cynicism was rare. The more sensational aspects of the discoveries soon outran the sober judgements which Cook offered. The sexual licence of Tahiti aroused intense interest and censure. Cook very reasonably enquired whether the morals of Englishwomen would normally be decided on the basis of encounters by sailors with street-walkers in London's dockland, but his plea fell on deaf ears. Cannibalism proved equally fascinating to vicarious voyagers.

Closer contact did not necessarily make for a more intelligent response. Bougainville had brought back from Tahiti a native who had delighted Parisian society. Cook was not enthusiastic about such imports, but his fellow commander on the second voyage,

[84] *London Magazine*, 1775, pp. 74–7.

Tobias Furneaux, returned with Omai, a young Tahitian who was quickly promoted to the rank of prince by some of his hosts, and whose doings were followed with rapturous attention. Omai was introduced to the most distinguished men of his day, fêted at court and in clubs, subjected to the constant glare of public attention and private curiosity. He was not very clever or very industrious. Granville Sharp's efforts to instruct him in the humanities proved tedious, and his English remained poor. When he returned home with Cook on the third voyage he distressed some commentators by taking, in place of 'useful' acquisitions, a barrel-organ, a suit of armour, and some experimental electrical machinery. Omai's principal function was to heighten public awareness of the South Sea Islanders. There were paintings by Reynolds, and engravings by Bartolozzi. Tahitian beads and shells achieved instant popularity, and Omai caused a minor sensation by censuring the Duchess of Devonshire's déshabillé dress and natural hair-style.

More serious matters were at issue however. Theologians who worried about that aspect of the divine dispensation which left pagans and savages uninformed of Christ's saving message worried still more when presented with the disagreeable rituals of remote religious practices. Hawkesworth's scepticism led him straight into this trap, and aroused controversy. But there is not much evidence of a significant South Sea dent in conventional belief. High priests of the religion of man drew little comfort from the cannibalism of New Zealand, and many an evangelical was more impressed by the need to convert the heathen than by the deficiencies of previous divine plans. The first overseas missionary effort had to wait a while, until the 1790s, but in retrospect it is not difficult to discern its distant outline in the debates of the 1770s. At the very least the new discoveries made for greater understanding of the diversity of human society, and stimulated speculative if not scientific invest-igation. The dilemma which they posed seemed to occur wherever European man looked beyond his own continent. Red Indians, much celebrated in contemporary art, were brave, generous, self-sacrificing. They were also deceitful, ruthless, and infinitely cruel. The South Sea Islanders presented still more perplexing con-tradictions. On balance, optimism generally won through, partly because the rampant commercialism of western society threw the joys of more primitive life into higher relief, partly because con-temporary social and anthropological analysis stressed the unity of human experience, notwithstanding the diverse climates and environments in which it operated. There was little suggestion of specifically racial differentiation. Biblical scholars cheerfully fitted new colours and creeds into the pattern of Genesis. One of the most systematic attempts to remove the romance from Red Indians was James Adair's *History* which offered twenty-three arguments for regarding them as the descendants of one of the tribes of Israel. Their colour, he assured his readers, was merely the result of a sunny climate and excessive use of oil.[85]

This growing appreciation, simultaneously, of the unity of man and the diversity of mankind, had a profound effect on attitudes towards non-European peoples who took the brunt of European commercialism. Even Cook and his colleagues had been lectured by the Earl of Morton, the President of the Royal Society, on their duty to treat native people respectfully, justly, generously, as, in the strictest sense, the legal proprietors of their lands. In this respect at least Cook's often sympathetic and unvengeful view was typical of the times, as well as the man. His deputy Clerke, after the horrific events at Kealakekua Bay, went ashore under intense pressure to take a swift and bloody revenge, but came away only with Cook's remains to be buried at sea: the bodies of four marines who had died with him were scattered among the petty princes of Hawaii. Examples of brutal treatment of primitive men were guaranteed to arouse middle-class indignation at home. The sudden transformation of British attitudes towards the sufferings of Asians under the rule of the East India Company plainly owed much to a readiness to believe that Europeans on the make were a blot on the reputation of their mother countries. Anna Seward, the Swan of Lichfield, in her *Elegy on Captain Cook* of 1780, rhetorically asked, 'What Pow'r inpir'd his dauntless breast to brave, The scorch'd Equator, and th' Antartic wave?'[86] The answer was not, it transpired, what Cook had once frankly spoken of, his desire to 'go as far as man could possibly go', but rather that 'Nymph divine! Humanity'. Educationists seized on this point. Geography as a school subject had a special function: it taught us to 'look upon the savage Indian, as our fellow creature, who has a mind as capable of every exalted satisfaction, as ours'.[87]

---

[85] James Adair, *The History of the American Indians* (London, 1775), pp. 1–4.
[86] pp. 4–5.
[87] M. Pennington, ed., *The Works of the late Miss Catherine Talbot* (London, 1809), p. 147.

Even legislators were carried on the crest of this wave of moral outrage at the injustice of racial discrimination, at least outside England. In the prolonged debate over the fate of St Vincent, where British speculators in a newly acquired colony were brutally exterminating the native Caribs, with a view to establishing a conventional sugar colony, there was much concern at the ruthlessness with which white men treated brown. When one witness, examined by the House of Commons as to these matters, observed of the Caribs that they had an excessive love of women and wine, the MP Isaac Barré raised a sympathetic laugh by pointing out that such a disposition merely made them indistinguishable from Englishmen. On the same subject Hans Stanley, a friend of Lord North and firm opponent of the American colonists, declared that 'he should not think of either the stature or complexion of any man, whether he was a Pygmy or a Patagonian, or whether he was white, yellow or black.'[88]

Enlightened views of this kind could not exist long without encountering the malodorous subject of slavery, one of the central institutions of the British empire, one of the staple trades of Englishmen, and, so it was reasoned, one of the most impious and malign forms of oppression invented by man. Some historians of slavery have argued that abolitionism was a natural counterpart of industrialization and free-market economics. If so, this was a perception which entirely escaped contemporaries, conscious as they were of the profits which continued to flow from the African and American trade, and the importance which the sugar plantations retained in the imperial system. Moreover, viewed against the sentimental background in which it belongs, abolition takes its place among the manifold expressions of the new sensibility, most of which can only be tangentially related to economic analysis. This is not to say that political economists did not point out the advantage of doing away with slavery as an institution. Adam Smith and John Millar both argued that liberty was the essential stimulus to industry; without the capacity to acquire property (almost a definition of slavery in a propertied age) no man would work harder than brutality and desperation dictated.

Arguments from natural equality and the sheer injustice of slavery were much commoner. Many of them preceded the abolitionist era. A wide range of mid-eighteenth-century authorities

[88] *Parliamentary History*, xvii. 727, 732.

placed on record their dislike of slavery. Some of these, like the poets Shenstone and Dodd, the lawyer Blackstone, the philosopher Ferguson, were by no means known for their liberal politics. The trickle of enlightened opinion which such men represented grew to a torrent in the 1770s, just in time to embarrass and confuse many earnest reformers. Those who supported America in her fight with the mother country, while denouncing slavery at home and throughout the empire, were often all too aware that slavery as a practice and an institution was growing most rapidly in the southern colonies of America. This was more a coincidence of chronology than a profound paradox. In much of America north of Maryland the same mixture of conditions which made abolition popular in England made it so there. In fact it was the Quakers of Pennsylvania, operating through their close correspondence with Dissenters in London, who did most to propel anti-slavery sentiment into something like organized activity. One of them, Anthony Benezet, had published his *Caution and Warning to Great Britain* as early as 1767. During the following decade some of the most famous appeals were made public, from Wesley's *Thoughts on Slavery* in 1774 (a tract which for all the political conservatism of its author unmistakably yoked the growing influence of Methodists to the abolitionists' cause), to the poems of Thomas Day, who most clearly represented the secular, even utilitarian assault on slavery.

Progress was slow, given the immense weight of vested interest that opposed change. The most notable victory of the early years was the verdict in 1772 in the case of James Somersett, a negro on whose behalf a group of London reformers sought legal redress. Mansfield was a cautious judge in such matters and was reluctant to offer a definitive verdict in a test case of this kind. None the less he eventually ruled that slavery was 'so odious that nothing can be suffered to support it but positive law. Whatever inconveniences, therefore may follow from the decision, I cannot say this case is allowed or approved by the law of England; and therefore the black must be discharged.'[89] Though he hedged his judgement about with qualifications, it was widely taken to signify that slavery was illegal in England itself. This victory had a major psychological effect. It was in large measure the work of Granville Sharp, in many

[89] W. C. Costin and J. Steven Watson, *The Law and Working of the Constitution: Documents, 1660–1914* (2nd edn., 2 vols., London, 1961), i. 315.

ways a representative figure of the 1770s. Like other reformers of
the period, Sharp had eccentric views, including somewhat bizarre
plans to recreate the political communities of Anglo-Saxon
England. Whether, like Wilberforce, he could have created the
mass campaign of the 1780s, with its appeal to polite society and
to a broad spread of religious beliefs, must be doubtful. At any rate
the American War intervened, taking the edge off the intellectual
consistency of the pro-American abolitionists, and distracting
attention from the iniquity of slavery. As with so much else
attempted in the 1770s the new sensibility was not sufficient to
bring about change. It needed the somewhat harder core of moral
earnestness provided by the evangelicals to turn it into a weapon
of real weight and effectiveness.

CHAPTER 11

Britannia's Distress, 1770–1783

LORD NORTH'S ministry began propitiously. *Much of its success derived from North's gifts as a parliamentarian, much too from the confidence which he inspired among the back-bench country gentlemen. It was clear, however, that the ferments of the 1760s had had permanent consequences, not least in the searching scrutiny to which the traditional assumptions of the eighteenth-century constitution were subjected by critics of the regime. These included Dissenters in matters of Church as well as State. North's handling of imperial affairs, in India, in Canada, and in America, suggested resourcefulness and firmness. His decision to use force against the American colonies was widely supported and positively strengthened his political position. But when the war began to go badly in 1777, a crisis of unprecedented dimensions unfolded. Recognition of American independence came to be seen as unavoidable. Something of the same sort threatened in Ireland with the appearance of the Volunteer movement. In England a campaign in favour of 'economical reform', and to a lesser extent parliamentary reform, made itself felt. The Gordon Riots of 1780 heightened the sense of impending catastrophe. North's survival until the surrender at Yorktown nearly two years later only postponed a resolution of these conflicts. The Peace was unpopular, though less humiliating than had been feared. A succession of short-lived ministries reflected the instability of parliamentary politics after the fall of North. The desperate struggle between George III and his Whig opponents, culminating in the dismissal of the Fox–North Coalition, suggested the possibility of sweeping constitutional change. In the end the King triumphed, and the reformers were defeated. Britannia's revival was to depend not on the popular appeal of Fox, but on the personal pre-eminence of the younger Pitt.*

NORTH'S MINISTRY

NORTH'S initiation as Prime Minister suggested none of
the trials and tribulations with which his name was later
to be associated, and compares well with that of other
great Georgian statesmen. Walpole had scrambled through the
squalor of the South Sea Bubble and the confusion of the Atterbury
Plot. Pelham had struggled to an equally hard-earned supremacy
at a divided Court and in the midst of a dynastic crisis. The younger
Pitt staked his political career on a desperate and unpredictable
constitutional conflict. North, seemingly the least assertive of the
four, moved smoothly, rapidly, and conclusively to a position of
commanding power. On his first important Commons division, yet
another motion relating to Wilkes's incapacitation, he achieved a
majority of forty. This was little more than Grafton had been able
to register on the eve of his resignation, but as the King pointed
out, 'a Majority of 40 at this particular crisis considering it is upon
the old ground that has been at least ten times before the House
is a very favourable auspice on Your taking the lead in Administration. Believe me a little spirit will soon restore a degree of
order in my Service.'[1]

This confidence was justified. Grafton's ministry, notwithstanding appearances, had crumbled from within. North did
not depend, like his predecessor, on a wavering band of Chathamites, ready to desert at a signal from their leader. Moreover, the
very extremism of some of the ministry's opponents served to
rally moderate support. In March William Beckford, as Lord
Mayor of London, presented the King with a formal Remonstrance
of the Livery, by implication comparing his conduct with that of
James II. The Wilkesites had attracted widespread support when
the issue was the Middlesex election; but increasingly they seemed
to be adopting a republican, even a revolutionary stance. Harsh
words were said in Parliament and the King himself was restive
under the public rebukes of the City. But North urged caution,
and the Remonstrators were left to stew in their own juice. Before
very long the administration's majority rose to almost a hundred:
its future seemed suddenly secure.

North was a House of Commons man through and through,
with most, if not all the attributes of a first-rate minister. Men of

[1] *Correspondence of George III*, ii. 128.

business and back-benchers alike had high regard for his command of fiscal policy. In this respect his apprenticeship, both as a Lord of the Treasury under Newcastle and Bute, and as Chancellor of the Exchequer since 1767, proved invaluable. His shrewd but diplomatic (if somewhat dilatory) management of patronage made him fewer enemies than most of his predecessors. His debating powers were of a high order in what posterity has considered a golden age of parliamentary rhetoric. He made no attempt at the grand manner, but preserved a reputation for solid groundwork, honest argument, and unfailing good humour. His fund of wit, never malicious, and often directed at himself, made him an engaging opponent.

Temperament was much of North's strength; it was also something of his weakness. A man who remained so long in office cannot have been as unambitious as he claimed, but he was as George III put it, 'easily disturbed',[2] and his propensity to panic was to become a liability during the final stages of the American War. In Cabinet he was prone to defer to others, though it later suited him to exaggerate the extent to which he was merely a departmental minister in his own ministry. Particularly after 1775, when his cousin Lord Dartmouth made way as Secretary for America to the powerful mind and dominant will of Lord George Germain, he gave the appearance of being somewhat isolated among his colleagues. He depended much on the advice of three men who held no ministerial portfolio. John Robinson, Secretary to the Treasury, grew adept at making decisions for his master. Lord Mansfield, who was widely seen as the *éminence grise* of the Cabinet, and the true successor of Bute, played a large if unofficial part in ministerial deliberations. Above all there was the King himself, who was strongly attached to his minister, even lending him money to ease his financial embarrassments. These derived equally from the burdens of a large family and a parsimonious father, the Earl of Guilford. It has been observed that George III governed Lord North as Newcastle had never governed George II.[3] Yet it was a genuine partnership. At times George III seemed rather to resemble North's secretary than his sovereign—as when he promised to keep him informed of State affairs while on holiday. Scandal relied on Frederick Prince of Wales's interest in Lady Guilford

[2] *Correspondence of George III*, ii. 68.
[3] R. Pares, *King George III and the Politicians* (Oxford, 1967), p. 183.

and a certain facial similarity between North and the King, to attribute their close relationship to consanguinity. It seems to have depended more on two minds which on most matters thought alike, and two natures which were remarkably complementary.

The ministry was more unified than its predecessors. With the King's Friends North was on excellent terms: Bute no longer had influence at court, and his last remaining link with it was severed with the death of the King's mother, the Princess Dowager of Wales, in 1771. More important, George Grenville died in 1770, and his followers quickly came to terms. Two of them, Alexander Wedderburn in the Commons, and the Earl of Suffolk in the Lords, were to prove major acquisitions for government. By now all the natural Court Whigs of the 1750s were once again in office. The Bedfords had returned in 1768, the Grenvilles in 1770. Most of Newcastle's supporters had either declined to leave office in 1762, or returned to it permanently in 1765. George III's so-called Tory government included many famous names of Hanoverian Whiggism: Onslow, Townshend, Fitzroy, Manners, Pelham.

In opposition there remained the dwindling, divided remnant of the Old Whigs. The followers of Rockingham and Chatham were rarely able to co-operate in Parliament. Typical were the divisions which they displayed when Dowdeswell proposed his Jury Bill in 1771. Mansfield had ruled, in a prosecution arising from the letters of Junius, that in libel cases juries might only determine the fact of authorship and publication, leaving the substantive verdict to the judge. He had much precedent on his side, but some lawyers, including his long-standing rival Camden, against him. Dowdeswell's bill would have given juries the exclusive right to determine guilt. It was designed, however, as an 'enacting' measure, governing the future without touching on the past. Rockingham had no desire to become involved in the legal arguments nor did he entertain any animus against Mansfield, his uncle by marriage. But Chatham detested Mansfield, and regarded the legal principles as crucial; he insisted on a 'declaratory' measure directly stating not only what the law must be in future but what it had been in the past. The result was a farcical scene in the Commons, with Dowdeswell's bill defeated by 218 votes to 72, and the friends of Chatham appearing as its principal opponents. The episode was clear evidence that the so-called Revolution Whigs were unable to agree even on the contents of their case let alone to collaborate in pressing it against the court of George III.

A distinctive feature of North's regime was its reliance on back-bench support. Estimates of the size of the Court and Treasury party vary according to the criterion by which membership is decided. Under Newcastle, at the end of George II's reign, MPs with places or pensions numbered as many as 250. Thereafter, the ministerial instability of the 1760s somewhat reduced this figure, and under North it hovered around 200. This was partly offset by the parliamentary absenteeism of the late eighteenth century. In Walpole's time important issues had occasionally commanded the attendance of more than 500 MPs; in North's, divisions involving more than 400 were rare, and the role of the inner core of reliable government supporters all the greater. None the less, the ministry derived equally valuable, and certainly more valued support from independent country gentlemen, men who in an earlier age might have been Tories, and who in some cases continued to consider themselves true representatives of the old Tory tradition. It was their Church and King mentality, their latent royalism and authoritarianism, which did much to create a coherent court politics during these years. They were a source of immense strength to North, himself married to the daughter of a Somerset squire and by temperament more a country gentleman than an aristocrat. On major issues of the day he had a better claim to represent the broad body of landed opinion than any other minister of the century.

There was, however, one snag. The independents were not unthinking supporters of the court: men such as Sir Roger New-digate, MP for Oxford University and a Tory veteran of George II's reign, and Sir William Bagot, cousin of North himself, and representative of the enduring strain of Staffordshire Toryism, were perfectly capable of voting against government. When they did so their object was not to bring it down, but rather to register their conscientious objections to a particular measure. North was made fully aware of the mixed nature of their blessing in his first session when they supported a proposal of George Grenville, in what proved to be his last session. Grenville's bill, passed for a trial period in 1770 and made perpetual in 1774, transferred jurisdiction in election disputes from the house as a whole to committees of MPs chosen by lot. The Tory country gentlemen had suffered much from the practice of 'weeding the House' in previous reigns: their readiness to deny it even to a King and a minister whom they admired demonstrated that their support was by no means unconditional.

Grenville's Act represented one of North's few parliamentary rebuffs. In 1770 he carried out Grafton's promise of the previous year, with the ready concurrence of the Commons. The Townshend duties, he pointed out, were contrary even to Britain's own interests, levied as they were on domestic exports. Only the tea duty was retained, in the same spirit that the Declaratory Act had been passed in 1766, signifying Parliament's refusal to concede the constitutional demands of America. British exports to the colonies had fallen by nearly half during 1769 as a result of American non-importation but in America there was little interest in prolonging the dispute outside Boston, and not much even there. The non-importation campaign collapsed and a boom in Anglo-American trade followed.

More problematic than the North Atlantic was the South Atlantic. There the Governor of Buenos Aires had ejected a British party which had established itself in the Falkland Islands following a naval expedition dispatched in 1766. Sceptics could point out the worthlessness of the Falklands: Dr Johnson did so in a devastating contribution to the pamphlet debate.[4] But a Spanish insult to the navy demanded a firm riposte. North, no more enthusiastically than Walpole in 1739, prepared for war. In the event he was saved by Louis XV, who proved unready to support his Spanish ally. A convention was negotiated with Spain: Madrid renounced the action of its officials, and North secretly undertook to evacuate the islands in due course. When Parliament debated the matter in January 1771 the opposition did its best to identify the settlement with the notorious Convention of the Pardo in 1739. But the minister's contention that British honour had been preserved proved sufficient to convince the country gentlemen. The King even contemplated a veritable diplomatic revolution, an alliance with France which would end the long history of Anglo-French conflict. But the international scene proved too troubled for such daring initiatives. In Sweden, in 1772, a monarchical revolution supported from Versailles compelled North's ministry to rattle its sabre again. The partition of Poland and the Russo-Turkish war

[4] *Thoughts on the Late Transactions Respecting Falkland's Islands* (London, 1771).

kept both Britain and France in a state of unease and uncertainty about the relative balance of forces in Europe. As a result an escape from diplomatic isolation seemed no more practical than it had for the previous decade.

The North ministry's greatest embarrassment during its first years was self-inflicted. In March 1771 a junior minister Colonel George Onslow urged the Commons to take note of the reports of parliamentary debates with which the newspapers of the day were filled. Technically they constituted a breach of privilege. During the 1750s a combination of parliamentary prohibition and political torpor had indeed largely banished them from the columns of the press. But the Wilkesite crisis naturally stimulated their reappearance. The action taken by the Commons on Onslow's initiative proved counter-productive. The House became entangled in a ludicrous tussle with the City of London, which predictably supported the printers and publishers involved. Two of the magistrates concerned were MPs, Richard Oliver and Brass Crosby: they were dispatched to the Tower. A third, John Wilkes, was wisely ignored. Proceedings dragged on until the session closed. The Commons did not withdraw its claim to forbid reporting, and North's supporters regularly used procedural motions closing the galleries to strangers, in order to exclude the reporters. But Onslow's turned out to be the last significant attempt to prevent the publication of debates. 'Memory' Woodfall and his harassed colleagues of the press were to make the 1770s the decisive decade in the establishment of parliamentary reporting on a professional basis.

NORTH'S OPPONENTS: WHIGS, REFORMERS, AND DISSENTERS

The parliamentary disarray of North's opponents strengthened the ministry, but the minister did not underestimate the resilience of the Whig opposition. Chatham's party, indeed, was based on little but its leader's past achievements and continuing megalomania: it was to prove no more permanent than those of Bute, Bedford, and Grenville. Rockingham's had a more lasting base, if only in the unappeasable arrogance of the aristocrats who laid claim to the Whig tradition. Partly because long years of opposition forced it to adopt a popular stance, partly because Rockingham's Yorkshire connections provided a robust, independent element which it would have been difficult to derive from Newcastle, the party was restored to something of its ancient 'Country' appeal. Many of Rockingham's friends and followers were admittedly personal dependants of the Whig magnates. But others were independent country gentlemen: such were Sir George Savile, a pillar of northern Whiggism, and William Dowdeswell, leader of a group of West Country Tories who had cast their lot with Rockingham in the novel conditions of George III's reign. What unified aristocratic interest and country sentiment was hostility to the King. This remained a potent cause.

In Edmund Burke the Rockingham party had a thinker capable of reworking so hackneyed a theme, adapting it to contemporary circumstances, while exploiting its atavistic appeal. His *Thoughts on the Cause of the Present Discontents* was published in May 1770, too late to take full advantage of the crisis which had followed the Middlesex election. None the less it made a considerable impact. Aside from Burke's characteristic rhetorical force, which lent power even to commonplace sentiments, it was a precise and compelling piece of political analysis which opponents found it difficult to combat. Burke made a point of avoiding the personalities which had marred recent debate, but the 'strange distemper' which he traced to its origin at the accession of George III was unmistakably the political strategy adopted by the King and Bute. His evidence was drawn from a highly coloured account of the Rockingham administration of 1765–6. To preserve and extend the influence of the Crown, so he alleged, the King's Friends had evolved a system of 'double cabinets', undermining the authority of ministers who were formally responsible to Parliament, but who in reality were kept without any executive power. The King's Friends were not his only target. He treated Chatham's cry of 'measures not men' as the cant it was. He also contemptuously dismissed the 'Bill of Rights' people for the absurdity of their faith in triennial parliaments. The true solution, naturally, was to give the Rockingham Whigs a monopoly of power. Later, Burke's defence of party, and his emphasis on the need for a Cabinet united by collective responsibility, were to seem far-sighted. At the time there was understandable cynicism about Burke's motives. Many who were impressed by the tightness of his reasoning and the power of his analysis, were also convinced that the *Thoughts* (the 'political Creed of our Party', as Burke described it)[5] was merely a sublime and beautiful form of sour grapes.

The most telling criticism came not from the court, which was content, in Burke's words, to treat his tract as a 'piece of Gentlemanlike hostility',[6] but from another quarter. Catherine Macaulay counter-attacked on behalf of her republican friends; her brother John Sawbridge was one of the founders of the Bill of Rights Society and a prominent figure in City politics. She treated the Rockinghams as a selfish aristocratic clique which depended as much as the Crown itself on influence and bribery. More importantly, she sought the origins of the present discontents long before the accession of George III. The extended rule of Walpole and the Pelhams became in her perspective a disastrous period of corruption, during which the ideals of Whiggism were betrayed by its supposed champions. Her arguments were not altogether new; they resembled those of generations of Commonwealth Whigs and Country Tories who had resisted the oligarchical tendencies of early Hanoverian government. This link between old style 'patriot' ideology, even old Toryism, and the new 'patriotism' of the 1760s and 1770s was important. It was to provide the reformers of the late eighteenth century with a fund of arguments and a sense of continuity. It also departed from the conventional Whig defence of Walpole and Newcastle and looked forward to the historic division of the Whig party under the stress of the French Revolution a quarter of a century later.

Significantly, the Revolution of 1688 was dragged into the controversy. In the volume of her celebrated *History of England* which dealt with the events of 1688-9 Mrs Macaulay displayed little reverence for the sacred memory of the Glorious Revolution. Rather she treated it as a lost opportunity, wasted by the Court Whigs who saw in it only a chance to establish themselves in power, employing the very means employed previously by the Stuarts. She also drew on contemporary politics. George III's ministries were mixtures of former Whigs and Tories, not easily identified as supporters of divine right and absolutism. Certainly their rallying point was not so much the supremacy of the Crown, as the supremacy of Parliament; it was that supremacy, which, in Middlesex and in America, was put to the test. But Mrs Macaulay

---

[5] *Correspondence of Edmund Burke*, ii. 136.
[6] Ibid. ii. 139.

argued precisely that the King and his friends had transformed Parliament from the representative of the people into the pawn of the Crown. If that were so all the the old arguments against divine right monarchy could be levelled against the supremacy of King in Parliament. Moreover, some of the old Tories made extravagant assertions of loyalty to their new King, claims which seemed to hark back to the seventeenth century. There was a confident regality about the court of George III which made it vulnerable to such charges. The neo-classical splendour and Van Dyck costumes which featured in Zoffany's royal portraits capture something of this sense of reviving royalty. The close alliance of Church and King, based equally on the gathering confidence of the former and the undoubted piety of the latter, gave a tinge of Laudianism to the new court.

Against this background trivial disputes took on undue significance. One such arose from the sermon which an Oxford cleric, Thomas Nowell, preached before the House of Commons in memory of Charles I on 30 January 1772. Nowell was Principal of St Mary Hall, and successor in that office to the celebrated Jacobite William King. His sermon included some challenging comparisons of the opponents of George III with the enemies of Charles I. He thereby provoked an attempt to repeal the statute requiring annual commemoration of the execution of Charles I, and a correspondingly furious defence of the royal martyr by the Tory country gentlemen. Another nine days' wonder was Sir John Dalrymple's claim, published in his historical *Memoirs* in 1771, to have found documentary evidence that the celebrated Algernon Sidney, venerated by republicans as Charles I was by royalists, had been a pensioner of Louis XIV.

Such controversies perhaps helped offset the decline of the Wilkesite movement. Wilkes's official career in the City itself continued to prosper. But the Bill of Rights Society had disintegrated and it proved difficult to maintain the popular interest of 1769 in the Middlesex election. In the general election of 1774 a handful of urban constituencies were induced to instruct their MPs in favour of specific reforms, including triennial parliaments. But this hardly suggested that great bodies of electors were eager to be convinced of the justice of the reformer's cause. Perhaps this was partly because Parliament was thought capable of reforming itself. One effect of Grenville's Election Act was to bring public interest as well as parliamentary impartiality to bear on electoral malpractice. The reports of the Commons committees entrusted with the determination of disputed elections stimulated discussion of representative theory and practice. James Burgh's *Political Disquisitions*, published in 1774-5, was the first attempt in many years to offer a systematic analysis of the deficiencies of the parliamentary constitution. It was a rambling work, with a somewhat eccentric and antiquarian flavour. But it provided more realistic champions of reform, men like Alderman Sawbridge in the House of Commons, and Major Cartwright out of it, with the chapter and verse for their allegations.

Even Parliament was roused to action. The independent supporters of George III were as outraged by evidence of deep-rooted corruption as were his City opponents. The borough of New Shoreham, where it was found that a body of electors calling themselves the Christian Club had in effect put up the borough for sale to the highest bidder, was disfranchised in 1771 and its seats awarded to the freeholders in the surrounding Rape of Bramber. Hindon in Wiltshire was threatened with a similar fate. Here was the first evidence that Parliament might proceed to carry out piecemeal what the reformers demanded on principle. It did not appease the Wilkesites; it did suggest to men of moderation that the assembly which had defied the freeholders of Middlesex might none the less prove capable of its own redemption.

Perhaps more important in sustaining the challenge of reform than the debate about the rights of electors was the debate about the rights of religious minorities. Dissent in politics and in religion had always been in some measure linked; the connection was particularly clear in the case of 'Rational Dissent', the essentially Unitarian reliance on a faith which required a minimum of liturgical baggage, and treated the divinity of Christ as a superstitious divergence from defensible theological doctrine. Within the Church this had its roots in Cambridge and its intellectual antecedents in the deism of some Whig Churchmen in the 1730s and 1740s. The tone under George III was set by Francis Blackburne, Archdeacon of Cleveland; his *Confessional*, published in 1766, commenced an intense debate about the validity of the Thirty-Nine Articles, particularly in so far as they embodied trinitarianism. Blackburne's followers included men such as John Jebb, John Disney, and Theophilus Lindsey, who eventually left the Church to preserve their Unitarianism. They had close links with kindred spirits who derived similar principles from a Nonconformist, especially a Presbyterian, background. When clergy of liberal persuasion met at the Feathers Tavern in 1772 and petitioned Parliament for a relaxation of subscription to the articles, they naturally aroused interest among Dissenters. Their petition provoked an avalanche of protest from the universities and from the bishops. If the petition had not been crushed in the Commons it would certainly have been buried in the Lords. But the issue itself did not disappear.

By the Toleration Act of 1689 Dissenting schoolmasters and ministers were required to subscribe to those of the Thirty-Nine Articles which concerned doctrine, as opposed to discipline. To many it seemed difficult to defend this imposition by the State Church on the pastors of legally tolerated sects. On the other hand, its defenders argued that most of those who sought relief were in effect atheists, whose insidious influence, especially in schooling, was fatally threatening to a Christian society. (It did not go unnoticed that they were also opponents of government; one active offshoot of the Wilkesite movement, the Honest Whig Club, was dominated by Rational Dissenters.) With a general election in prospect the Commons was brought to support amending legislation both in 1772 and 1773, though there was much dispute over the form of declaration required of Dissenters in place of subscription to the articles. In the upper house the bills were heavily defeated; only one bishop, John Green of Lincoln, formerly a tool of Newcastle, a Cambridge Head of House, and representative of a now despised ecclesiastical tradition, voted for them. Eventually, in 1779, the bill was permitted to pass. In the mean time this flurry of sectarian agitation, like that of the mid-1730s, had important repercussions. If any point marked the historic termination of the long-standing alliance between Dissent and Low Church Whiggism, it was this. Rational Dissenters did not have numerous congregations but they commanded both property and power in some of the larger cities. At least in the 1770s they possessed influence in polite society far beyond that of their evangelical brethren; Lindsey's own chapel in Essex Street could vie with the fashionable congregations of the West End in its appeal to sections of the social and political élite in London. But growing resentment of an outdated system of discriminations and proscriptions made enemies as well as friends, and not merely among inflexible defenders of the traditional order in Church and State. Burke supported the Dissenters in the subscription controversy, but it would not be long before he came to see the political aggression and intellectual heterodoxy of Rational Dissent as characteristics of a sinister new force which would help to launch a revolution in France and threaten one in Britain.

INDIA: THE REGULATING ACT

Lord North, as Chancellor of Oxford University, was in honour bound to defend the Church and its privileges, but his awareness of the electoral influence of Dissenters made him a reluctant meddler in such matters. He also had other distractions. The early 1770s were marked by rapid economic recovery after the spasmodic recessions of the 1760s. But even commercial expansion was marked by strains, especially when renewed confidence intensified financial speculation. The result, in 1772, was a credit crisis, which threatened to engulf the East India Company. The Company was the victim of the excessively high expectations which investors continued to entertain of India. These expectations could not be met by trading prospects, and were made even less realistic by a devastating famine which occurred in Bengal. As in 1766, the threat of bankruptcy compelled the government to help with a loan; in return the Company was required to demonstrate its financial self-discipline by reducing dividends. North, no reformer, might have left the matter there, but in Parliament he came under intense pressure to impose additional conditions. The consequence was the Regulating Act of 1773, subjecting the Company to a stiff dose of reform, which its proprietors found singularly unpalatable. The directors, previously elected annually, were given a tenure of four years at a time, in order to lend more stability to their affairs; the proprietors were permitted voting rights only for stock amounting to £1000, held for at least a year. In India the two outlying presidencies of Bombay and Madras were placed under the control of Calcutta; in Bengal itself a new Supreme Council, composed in the first instance of nominees of government, was placed under the leadership of one of the Company's most capable servants, Warren Hastings.

In due course it proved easy to criticize the Regulating Act.

Hastings, in his long struggle to maintain British power in the subcontinent, found himself hamstrung by the factiousness and personal animosities to which his Council was prone. At home the supposed elimination of the small proprietor did little to improve the management of Company affairs. Indeed North himself helped to make the Court of Proprietors an arena for the combat of government and opposition second only to Parliament itself. With this in mind one of the most senior East India politicians, Lawrence Sulivan, characterized North as 'the boldest minister this realm has been blest with since the days of Oliver Cromwell'.[7] The truth was that India was simply too important to the State and therefore to statesmen, to be left to the discretion of interested directors and avaricious officials. The Rockingham Whigs bitterly opposed the Regulating Bill as an outrageous invasion of chartered privileges and propertied rights; yet before very long they were to recognize that what was needed was more State intervention, not less. Many of their contemporaries had already reached this conclusion.

Aside from North's scrutiny of Company affairs, the Commons insisted on a separate inquiry, conducted by a Select Committee under the chairmanship of General Burgoyne. North had no intention of permitting the Committee to determine policy, but it was allowed to investigate some of the matters which most concerned MPs, and indeed a wider public. The returned oriental adventurer was already established in many minds as a threat to the integrity of public life. No doubt disappointed candidates for parliamentary seats did their best to encourage the impression that they were ruthless, rapacious, and corrupt. Samuel Foote, always a shrewd satirist of current taste, helped to make the 'Nabob' a stock figure with his play of the same name, first performed in June 1772. The nature and extent of Britain's new Asiatic responsibilities naturally aroused curiosity. It was stimulated as well as partly satisfied by one of the first major books in its field, Alexander Dow's *History of Hindustan*, published between 1768 and 1772. But there was also more pointed concern about the character of English rule. William Bolts's *Considerations on Indian Affairs* led the way with a damning indictment of misgovernment by the Company's agents. Burgoyne, nothing if not an adventurer himself, did not hesitate to fix the resulting obloquy at the highest level. Robert Clive, an MP, an Irish peer, a magnate in his home county of Shropshire,

[7] P. J. Marshall, *Problems of Empire: Britain and India, 1757–1813* (London, 1968) p. 34.

and a powerful if wayward force in Company politics, found himself pilloried before the Commons for the share which he had taken in the plunder of Bengal. He escaped formal prosecution but he had few friends who were prepared to deny the truth of the Burgoyne Committee's scorching verdict on British rule. 'In the east the laws of society, the laws of nature have been enormously violated. Oppression in every shape has ground the faces of the poor defenceless natives; and tyranny in her bloodless form has stalked abroad.'[8] This concern with the fate of the native Indian struck a new and important note. It was left, somewhat unjustly, to Warren Hastings to bear the brunt of public criticism, and to Burke and Pitt to formulate the means by which the Company should be controlled. But in the process which eventually brought about the major changes of the 1780s, 1773 was undoubtedly a landmark.

THE AMERICAN CRISIS

One additional measure which North took to assist the East India Company had important consequences elsewhere. The Tea Act of 1773 reduced the duties on tea re-exported to the colonies, with the object of making British tea cheaper than its smuggled competitors in America. Whether this was done primarily with a view to the expansion of the Company's trade, or whether North deliberately sought to bring about American submission to the remaining duty on tea imports, is not entirely clear. In retrospect the provocation seems imprudent. But the ministry had reason to be irritated with the colonies. In 1772 a naval cutter, the *Gaspée*, in pursuit of smugglers, had been caught and destroyed by a party of Rhode Island men whom it proved impossible to identify and prosecute. Moreover the continued activity of New England agitators, especially in stimulating the establishment of intercolonial committees of correspondence, had not gone unnoticed by the Secretary for America, Lord Dartmouth. No doubt the Tea Act presented itself as a subtle means of bringing America to provide a modest contribution to imperial funds, without either the fanfare or the odium of a new revenue act. If this was the reasoning it misfired. Subtlety had not saved the Townshend duties and it did not save the Tea Act. The Sons of Liberty in Boston saw it as a deliberate attempt to impose an otherwise nominal duty

[8] *London Magazine*, 1773, p. 12.

and to enforce the Declaratory Act of 1766. On 16 December they unceremoniously boarded the first tea ships to arrive in Boston harbour, and dumped their cargo in the harbour. Their action was applauded in the other colonies and would have been widely imitated if the Company had not wisely refrained from landing tea elsewhere.

The response in England to the Boston Tea Party only makes sense when viewed against the lengthening history of Anglo-American conflict. The Tea Party could not be described as a direct affront to the authority of the Crown or Parliament: it was technically an invasion of private property. In this sense it was less outrageous than the burning of the *Gaspée*, or the Stamp Act riots. But from a British standpoint it was the last straw, the final evidence that the colonists, or sufficient of their number to require chastisement, were intent on defying imperial authority. There is no mistaking the wave of indignation which swept through the ranks of propertied opinion in England. Even the supporters of Chatham, men who had consistently presented themselves as the champions of America, joined in demanding punishment for the malefactors. The measures which North duly brought before Parliament in 1774 were carried overwhelmingly in both Houses, and there is no evidence that they were opposed by a substantial body of opinion outside it. But just as the Boston Tea Party had confirmed the analysis of those who viewed every American action as part of a deep-laid conspiracy against imperial authority, so North's Coercive Acts perfectly corresponded with the colonial conviction that the mother country was aiming at despotism. It had previously been argued in London, with encouragement from friends of government in America, that British policy had erred in treating the colonies as a unit. The coercive legislation of 1774 was accordingly directed at what was considered the most troublesome colony, Massachusetts Bay. But this did nothing to allay colonial fears. On the contrary the severity of the new laws made many colonists suspect that Massachusetts was the guinea-pig for harsh medicine which would soon be tried elsewhere. One of these Acts closed the port of Boston until reparation was made to the Company; the penalties laid on Edinburgh after the Porteous affair of 1737 were cited as precedent. A second remodelled the Massachusetts Charter, replacing the elected council with a nominated one, and taking control of juries out of the hands of the electorate. Two further Acts provided for tighter control of the judicial and military organization of the province.

Little more was needed to convince Americans that this was not spontaneous retribution but a preconceived plan for assault on their liberties. That little was obligingly provided by North's Quebec Act of 1774. Its central features were approval of French civil law, and acceptance of the need to govern through conciliar co-operation with the French seigneurs rather than through the traditional British machinery of an elected assembly. There was much to be said for this policy. Without extensive settlement by British immigrants it seemed a prudent as well as liberal recognition of the rights of the French colonists. In this respect it merely continued the approach of successive Governors on the ground and of their superiors in London. However, the judgement of Lord Mansfield in the case of *Campbell* v. *Hall* in 1774 made it clear that a permanent settlement required formal implementation by statute. Hence, no doubt, the decision to proceed with the Quebec Act. The timing, however, was unfortunate. The opposition treated the Act as a violation of the English common law tradition. It also fastened on other controversial clauses. One of these recognized the Roman Catholic establishment in Quebec and permitted it to collect tithes. North further proposed to extend the Quebec frontier to include the region between the Ohio and the Mississipi: his object was cheaper and more effective management of the western lands, but it aroused the ire of those who had an eye to future settlement in the Indian territories.

In England the Quebec Act provided a useful handle for North's opponents; the Wilkesites in the City, unable to gain support for Boston's action against the Tea Act, found it easier to denounce the popish, arbitrary menace of the Quebec Act. In America it provided apparently conclusive evidence that the nightmare of the Sons of Liberty, a tyrannical regime, based on popery, prerogative rule, and parliamentary taxation, was at last coming true. The transatlantic response to the legislative programme of 1774 was one of outrage. By November news arrived in Whitehall that a new Congress, imitating that of 1765, intended imposing a commercial embargo to bring about the repeal of the Coercive Acts. The dilemma of 1766, and of 1769, was repeating itself, in a still more intractable form.

During the parliamentary session of 1774 North impressed

observers with his display of calm authority. By instinct he was a 'consensus politician': he strove to obtain the approval of the country gentlemen and throve on it when it was bestowed. In September he called a general election six months earlier than the Septennial Act demanded, with the object of exploiting the favourable climate of opinion. There were ninety-five electoral contests, few with much sense of ideological conflict about them. Opposition drew comfort from the fact that the prestigious city of Bristol returned two enemies of the court. One was a radical merchant from New York, Henry Cruger, the other Edmund Burke, selected unexpectedly, and by special invitation from Bristol, at the moment of his nomination for a close borough provided by his patron Rockingham. But America as an issue hardly figured in the election, nor was North's majority in the Commons remotely threatened by it. Even so, facing a highly supportive, indeed belligerent Parliament, North was far from complacent.

The reports from America were discouraging. There were signs that New England would not be brought to heel without substantial reinforcements of troops. North's colleagues in the Cabinet, with the exception of his cousin Dartmouth, favoured firm action, as did the King himself. Legislation was accordingly introduced to restrain the trade and fisheries of the New England colonies until they submitted; in due course the remaining colonies were subjected to similar restrictions. The commander in Boston, General Gage, was encouraged to show his teeth. Attempts by the opposition to promote milder measures were easily overridden. Burke proposed repeal of the statutes which had offended America, and, more vaguely, a new spirit of co-operation and trust in the management of imperial affairs. His *Speech on Conciliation*, like his earlier *Thoughts on the Cause of the Present Discontents*, had a profound influence on nineteenth-century students of government, but none at all on the conduct of policy at the time. Nor did Chatham's suggestion of a permanent American legislature which would exercise the powers of taxation claimed by Parliament. It was not clear that either of these projects would have appealed to the colonists themselves.

North had an olive branch of his own to offer, to the irritation of some of his supporters. His conciliatory plan exempted from parliamentary taxation those colonies which voluntarily provided funds for imperial support. To many this seemed a distinction without a difference. But the constitutional conflict was rich in such distinctions. Possibly North was concerned to satisfy independent opinion of his desire to achieve a peaceful settlement. Possibly he was appeasing his own and Dartmouth's conscience. He was certainly aware of the wisdom of dividing the colonies. New York and Pennsylvania, in particular, were notoriously reluctant to engage in armed struggle with the mother country. In the event only tiny Nova Scotia accepted North's offer. Just when news of North's gesture reached America, in April 1775, reports were spreading of the historic battles at Lexington and Concord. Gage had taken advantage of his orders to attempt the seizure of an arms depot. The result did not confirm the boasted superiority of British troops over colonial militia. In a European setting these would have been skirmishes of no consequence. Their psychological significance in America was immense. For the first time American blood had been deliberately shed by English hands. Nothing was better designed to rally colonial moderates to the rebel cause.

War was now a fact. The American Declaration of Independence was delayed until 4 July 1776, when, after much manœuvring, the colonies were brought to agree on a formal renunciation of their allegiance. Such is the importance of the Declaration in national history and myth that it is easy to forget that Britain had moved first. The Proclamation of Rebellion was issued on 23 August 1775. In a sense it was less painful for Englishmen than the Declaration was for Americans. Partly this was a matter of the respective stakes. For Americans independence was truly awesome. If it failed, it made its advocates traitors, whose lives and properties counted for nothing; even if it succeeded, the old certainties of political life were gone. By contrast, no class of Englishmen faced unavoidable risk to person or property. Moreover North's ministry continued to enjoy widespread support. The summer of 1775 saw a considerable campaign of petitions against the war, and addresses in favour of it. Broadly speaking, the forces involved reflected the relative strengths of government and opposition. Up to a point, too, they indicated the divergent political interests of Church and Dissent, for this was a war in which the influence of the Church was unhesitatingly placed alongside the authority of Crown and Parliament. The old Tory language of passive obedience enjoyed something of a revival in tract, sermon, and address; the Americans were 'Sons of Anarchy', 'mad Enthusiasts and desperate Republicans'.[9] Government did all it could to maximize and publicize its following, but the petitions, too, were numerous. They were ineffective in two respects, however. In the first place, the petitioners found it difficult to support America on grounds of constitutional principle. At issue, after all, was the authority of Parliament itself. No self-respecting Whig could lightly disregard the legislative supremacy of Westminster. Secondly, the support of the commercial interests, whose involvement was essential to shake the resolution of government and Parliament, was simply not available.

This was less surprising than it may seem. For merchants, not least those in colonial trade, there was a real fear that America would end by throwing off parliamentary regulation of trade along with parliamentary taxation. It was widely assumed that the Navigation Acts were the basis of British prosperity. A few hardy souls challenged this orthodoxy. Josiah Tucker, Dean of Gloucester and an experienced controversialist, argued that Britain would be better off without her colonies. Adam Smith's *Wealth of Nations*, published in 1776, demolished the intellectual case for monopoly and regulation. But these arguments had little influence with hard-headed businessmen who could count the advantage of protected markets, and regarded the benefits of abandoning them as speculative. Moreover the early years of the war were a prosperous time. American non-exportation followed later than non-importation; in the gap between the two, great quantities of grain and tobacco poured in to reduce America's debts. The loss of colonial markets was made up by growing European consumption of British goods and by a variety of devices for evading the embargoes of Congress and Parliament alike. Above all, government spending on the war provided a stimulus to manufacturing production. Armies had to be clothed, fed, and transported, and the taxpayer's investment paid rich dividends to armament makers in the Midlands and textile manufacturers in Yorkshire, Lancashire, and the West Country. War lined the pockets of countless shopkeepers and small tradesmen who provided consumer goods and services for a market galvanized by full employment. It was also reasoned that the conflict would be a short one. The greatest empire in the

[9] *London Gazette*, 17 Oct., 4 Nov. 1775.

memory of mankind was not to be shaken by the puny pretensions of a provincial congress.

THE AMERICAN WAR

Steady progress towards the subjugation of America was essential, if only to maintain morale at home, and to discourage foreign intervention. From early in the war the French court offered sympathy and informal support for the American rebels. But there was little danger of more active or official backing until America had clearly demonstrated its capacity to resist. In this respect the diplomatic isolation which successive British ministries had reluctantly accepted since the end of the Seven Years War was not necessarily a handicap, however imprudent it was to seem in retrospect. British policy was based on the premiss that while a European alliance would have been desirable, it was not worth the price which potential allies were demanding. A strong navy capable of securing the British Isles against invasion and controlling all the waters on which the empire and its trade depended, was worth far more in strategic terms. Under Sandwich as First Lord of the Admiralty the navy had been brought to as flourishing a state as could be expected on a peacetime budget. Directly and indirectly, the military, diplomatic, and political situation hinged on events in America.

There was evidence during the first years of war that success would not be long delayed. Admittedly, Gage's initial activities in New England in 1775–6 produced little. The Battle of Bunker Hill was a bloody, inconclusive affair which suggested that the occupation of Boston was not worth the effort which it cost. The British had their first hero of the war, Lord Percy, whose feats of valour at Bunker Hill filled the newspapers at home, but also a realization that the conquest of America would not be the work of one campaign. It could be argued, however, that this was before serious war preparations had been set on foot. Lord George Germain, brought in as Secretary of State for America in 1775, proved an efficient, resourceful minister. As naval and military estimates soared and troops and supplies poured across the Atlantic, the war news improved. The campaign of 1776 saw Canada preserved from American occupation: it also brought General Howe's promising victory at the Battle of Long Island, followed by the occupation of New York and the prospect of the capture of Philadelphia, the seat of Congress.

Before the war North had hoped to keep New York and Pennsylvania loyal to the empire, dividing the colonies and ensuring a British stranglehold on colonial lines of trade and communication. The war seemed about to accomplish what his political strategy had failed to achieve. 1777 was intended to complete this process, with a small army under General Burgoyne advancing from Quebec to join with Howe on the Hudson, thereby cutting off New England. Burgoyne's march turned out to be a mistake. Howe took Philadelphia in September 1777 but he was not able to pin down his enemy and finish his campaign in Pennsylvania in time to provide support for Burgoyne. The result was the humiliation of the latter's surrender at Saratoga. Germain and the generals blamed each other for the breakdown in communications which seemed the most plausible explanation of Burgoyne's isolation. It was hardly a disastrous defeat: Burgoyne's forces numbered only 5,000 and the overall strength of Britain's military position was little affected. Yet it proved a watershed in the history of the war. In February 1778 France negotiated a full-scale alliance with the United States; a year later Spain also entered the war. In America British forces, under a new commander, Sir Henry Clinton, withdrew to their base at New York, and turned their attention to the south, in the hope that the loyalists there would permit more effective occupation than in the north. Not least, North, whose enthusiasm for the war had never matched that of his Cabinet colleagues, produced a peace plan, which involved sending a commission led by the Earl of Carlisle to America. Carlisle was a lightweight, and his instructions were unclear. Moreover, in the wake of Saratoga and the Franco-American alliance there was no prospect of Congress accepting anything less than full independence. The real significance of the commission lay at home. As one of North's back-bench supporters, the Lincolnshire country gentleman Robert Vyner, put it, 'his favourite object of taxation could not now be had'.[10] Thus the cause for which so much ink and blood had been spilled since 1763 was abandoned with hardly a word said in its defence.

The domestic implications of Saratoga were grave. North's opponents had been overwhelmed by parliamentary and public

[10] *Parliamentary History*, xix. 770.

support for the war in 1775 and 1776. Saratoga hardly proved the Whigs right, for they too had expected British arms to succeed in America, however much they deplored the likely consequences. But it did offer the distinct possibility that North would either lose the war, or win it at a cost which would be politically fatal. In the House of Commons independent support for the government wavered, and North's normal majority sank from over 150 to under 100. But politics became more polarized than ever. Saratoga promoted a definite rallying of patriotic opinion, creating problems for opposition: the friends of America could not afford to appear the friends of France and Spain. Chatham, in his last, highly theatrical speech before the Lords, appealed for a revival of national unity to preserve the empire which he had so signally served. The image of the great commoner, vainly devoting his final words (he died six weeks later) to the redemption of his country, was firmly imprinted on the public mind, and eventually, through the medium of J. S. Copley's engraving, found its way into countless homes. Theatre audiences themselves were treated to an appropriate new tragedy, *The Battle of Hastings*. On the first night, Earl Edwin's 'heroic exclamation—"all private feuds shall cease when England's glory is at stake"' was 'so sensibly felt by the audience that a repetition was called for, but judiciously refused—as out of character in a tragedy'.[11]

Loyal sentiment was exploited when the friends of government started collecting subscriptions to support the war. New regiments of volunteers were raised, with particular support, as critics pointed out, from the old Jacobite heartlands, in Scotland, at Liverpool, and at Manchester. The war of the Hessian mercenary was becoming the war of the true blue Englishman. But not all Englishmen were true blue. Since the beginning of hostilities the radical fringe, isolated by bellicose public sentiment and, as it seemed, by the pusillanimity of the parliamentary Whigs, had kept up a thin but strident chorus of protest. This included Richard Price's *Observations on Civil Liberty*, an influential plea on behalf of 'natural rights' in England and America, and Lord Abingdon's furious assault on Burke for his insistence, in the *Letter to the Sheriffs of Bristol*, that MPs were not subject to the direction of their constituents. Abingdon, Geneva-educated and a republican representative of an old Tory family, also challenged the right of

[11] *London Magazine*, 1778, p. 37.

private citizens to raise subscriptions for the war, alleging that they were analogous to the forced loans and benevolences of Tudor and Stuart monarchs. Success in the Seven Years War had bred a mood of national unity; it was obvious by 1778 that further reverses in the American War would breed division and acrimony.

The escalation of the war had other consequences. Until 1778 the war at sea had been one of legalized piracy, with the honours more or less even between British and American privateers. Now imperial trade came under intense pressure. Fending off privateers was not easy, as the activities of John Paul Jones in British waters demonstrated. Neutralizing the Bourbon invasion threat and maintaining control of the Atlantic at the same time also stretched the navy to its limit. It was in no position to protect commerce as it had in the Seven Years War. The merchants who had looked on the American war with equanimity could not look on a French and Spanish war with anything but alarm. Nor indeed could the British taxpayer. Stamp duties, custom duties, and excise duties were multiplied. Carriages, auctions, and male servants were taxed in the cause of throwing the cost of war 'as much as possible on the opulent', as North put it.[12] This laudable intention could not be maintained indefinitely. Alcohol, sugar, salt, and soap, heavily burdened already, to the disadvantage of the poor, were selected for further taxation in the last years of the war. North's war loans, garnished with premiums and lotteries, were also costly. In December 1774 three per cent consols had stood at a commanding 92; in December 1776, they dropped to 82, and in December 1777 to 76. Saratoga brought the realization that the war must be a prolonged one and its financial burden heavy. By February 1778 three per cents had fallen to 60. Inevitably North's borrowing policy was affected. In 1780 he was driven to offer substantial bonuses of stock to induce further loans to government. The policy was not new: it had been employed at the end of the Seven Years War. But it was to prove highly controversial in the context of a losing war and a falling ministry.

Equally unpopular was North's method of conducting business. His loans were negotiated with small groups of financiers who could answer for the large sums involved. His wartime contracts, for the supply of food, fuel, clothing, and specie, also involved informal dealings with favoured businessmen. Again there was

[12] P. D. G. Thomas, *Lord North* (London, 1976), p. 103.

nothing new in this. Newcastle, like North, had dealt with the great City capitalists; the belief of both that the results benefited the taxpayer has been endorsed by historians. But the intermingling of personal and professional relationships gave rise to accusations of corruption. Contracting companies saw the advantages of having a representative in Parliament. Again, a war that was going badly made it all the easier to denounce jobbery. War profiteers were obvious targets. When an opposition supporter, Philip Jennings Clerke, urged the Commons to prohibit government contractors from sitting in the Commons, his bill was only narrowly defeated. Snobbery and high-mindedness joined forces on this occasion. Anthony Bacon, attacked in scathing terms by Clerke as a coal-merchant and cobbler, begged not 'to be treated in so unbecoming, nay, contemptuous manner—as if they were monsters, and not fit for human society!'[13] Bacon, ironically, had started his career as a storekeeper in Maryland. He became a highly successful indus-trialist (one of the first great iron and coal-masters of South Wales), a government contractor, merchant, and MP for one of the most corrupt of all constituencies, Aylesbury. His superiors suffered with him. The wild Lord George Gordon openly described North's dealings as 'villainous'.[14] North hardly deserved the charge. As a Treasury minister he enjoyed a reputation with expert judges for economical, even innovative administration. The Commission of Public Accounts, which undertook a searching scrutiny of public administration and paved the way for reform, was actually estab-lished by North in 1780. But in the increasingly heated atmosphere which came to prevail after Saratoga, the management of the war was bound to prove contentious. There was a perceptible sense, by 1779, that unless the war situation improved rapidly the great dam of North's political security would break under the pressure of public anxiety and political animus.

VOLUNTEERS AND ASSOCIATORS

The dam seemed likely to give way first not in England, but in Ireland. The Irish crisis, even, as some would have it, the Irish Revolution, was only in part a result of the war. As in England, George III's good intentions had had unexpected consequences.

---

[13] *Parliamentary Register*, ix. 157.
[14] Ibid. 158–9.

In the 1760s his ministers made it their aim to reshape Irish politics, creating a strong Dublin executive based on a resident viceroy in constant touch with the Cabinet in London, and depriving the parliamentary 'undertakers' of their control of patronage and policy. This was not necessarily to the disadvantage of the Irish patriot movement. Lord Townshend, who as Lord-Lieutenant between 1768 and 1772 did most to implement the new design, had begun his viceroyalty by conceding an Octennial Act, providing for regular elections to Parliament on the English pattern. This hint of an alliance between popular forces and the 'Castle' against parliamentary managers and borough-mongers was somewhat misleading but it offered patriot politicians new openings, as fissures opened up in the oligarchical structure of Hanoverian Ireland. In 1773 the authorities in both Dublin and London even encouraged demands for an Irish absentee tax. Fiscal convenience and patriotic indignation joined in this attack on Anglo-Irish landlords who spent their rents as well as their lives in England. The intended victims, led by the leader of the Whig opposition Lord Rockingham, protested violently. There were also doubts in Ireland itself about the wisdom of introducing any kind of property tax. A duty on absentees could easily be converted into a general land tax such as applied in England. The plan was accordingly dropped against the better judgement of the Lord-Lieutenant of the day, Lord Harcourt. Such paradoxes made Irish politics perplexing, but they did not remove the objections to British domination of Irish politics. A resident viceroy, for instance, was an all too obvious reminder of the dependence which represented the reality of Irish relations with England.

The dispute with America stimulated matching controversy in Ireland. But more important was the economic effect of the war, which proved particularly damaging to Irish exports of provisions. The Irish recession preceded that in England and Scotland by at least three years (for all their dependence on the American tobacco trade, Glasgow merchants and their suppliers proved remarkably flexible in adapting to wartime conditions). Patriotism and penury came together in predictable fashion, producing a clamour for the dismantling of the protectionist system with which Britain had so long constrained its Irish competitors. In this the Dublin Parliament was positively abetted by the Earl of Buckinghamshire, Lord-Lieutenant from 1777. At Westminster a bill to open

Ireland's trade with British colonies found North trapped between his Lord-Lieutenant and the Irish Parliament on the one hand, and enraged home manufacturers on the other. The only result, one of doubtful value to its supposed beneficiaries, was an Act which authorized the export of Irish goods to the colonies, but without the legalized imports which would have made direct trade viable. It took a full-scale boycott of British goods in Ireland, recalling the non-importation campaigns of America, to persuade opinion in England of the wisdom of concession. The 1780 session duly produced the granting of colonial free trade, and the removal of those restraints on the free export of Irish goods, notably woollens, which had marked Britain's commercial stranglehold on Irish manufacturers since the previous century.

By this time the Irish situation had deteriorated further. Just as in America commercial grievances proved difficult to disentangle from constitutional complaints, so in Ireland there were demands for political change. Poynings law, which had subjected Irish legislation to the scrutiny of the Privy Council in London for nearly three centuries, and the Irish Declaratory Act of 1720, which proclaimed the legislative supremacy of Westminster over Dublin, came under intense criticism. Henry Grattan, the most effective opposition orator, proposed a historical view of the constitution which recalled earlier manifestos of Irish rights, such as Swift's *Drapier Letters* and Molyneux's *The Case of Ireland's being bound by Acts of Parliament in England*. On this view the Irish Crown, though perpetually united with that of England, was a distinct entity; so far as legislation was concerned Ireland already enjoyed complete independence. This resembled the constitutional doctrine which had come to prevail in America shortly before the Declaration of Independence. It had considerably more historical and legal plausibility in Ireland than it ever had in the thirteen colonies. More importantly it had behind it the active support of Protestant opinion. The Volunteer movement, established in theory to supply the want of an organized militia and to defend Ireland against invasion, was in reality a form of extra-constitutional agitation. It was beyond the influence of government, it worked closely in hand with the patriot opposition in the Irish Parliament, and it seemed to threaten something almost incredible to English eyes: an Irish rebellion, not of papists, but Protestants.

In England, too, events seemed to be conspiring against North. Naval victory in the war against France and Spain was the pre-condition of strategic security at home as well as in the colonies; but off Ushant in July 1778 Admiral Keppel's fleet proved unable to achieve it. At the resulting court martial in February 1779 Keppel succeeded in clearing himself and laying the blame for his failure at the door of a brother officer and ministerial supporter, Palliser. In Parliament the Whig opposition made effective use of this controversy. Their tactics were shrewdly devised to isolate the ministers most directly concerned with the conduct of the war, Sandwich at the Admiralty, and Germain at the American Office. North's fragile morale came close to collapse in the summer of 1779: only the support of the King himself and North's principal subordinates, Charles Jenkinson, William Eden, and John Robinson, kept him in office. As George III gently reminded him, the opposition's target was not the Prime Minister but his master. Relations between alienated aristocrats and the Crown were notice-ably acrimonious. There were widely reported duels arising from political disagreements, between the Earl of Shelburne and a Scottish MP William Fullarton, and between the Duke of Grafton and a court supporter, the Earl of Pomfret. When a former Prime Minister resorted to the duelling sword to settle his differences, his inferiors could hardly be expected to show restraint. Some of the opposition leaders positively encouraged a resort to violence. In the House of Lords the Duke of Richmond openly accused the ministry of submitting to the vicious influence of Bute; his col-league the Duke of Manchester publicly referred to the execution of Charles I and deposition of James II 'for offences against the constitution, of infinitely less magnitude than those which marked the administration of the present reign'.[15]

The parliamentary session of 1780 was the worst that North suffered, yet his discomfiture was extra-parliamentary in its origin. In December 1779 a great public meeting had been held at York, with the emphasis on the vices of government in general rather than on the failings of ministers as such. The resulting Yorkshire petition concentrated on the waste, inefficiency, and corruption of government. It was followed by the setting up of a committee to devise a 'plan of association'. Rockingham, in his home county, was nervous about some of these proceedings, but Christopher

[15] *Parliamentary History*, xx. 1173.

Wyvill, the leading light of the Yorkshire movement, proved a vigorous agitator as well as an effective organizer. The petitioning caught on quickly: in the end there were nearly forty committees or Associations, with their echoes of the extra-legal associations adopted at times of dynastic crisis in 1696 and 1745. Not all were lasting, but the intensity of the initial protest was undoubted, and it was given additional edge by the enthusiasm of radical groups in the metropolis. The Quintuple Alliance, representing London, Westminster, Southwark, Middlesex, and Surrey, was to be much the most active element in the Association movement, apart from Yorkshire. With a general election at most two years away it was to be expected that even a House of Commons complaisant to Lord North would respond to such pressure.

Prudently, opposition MPs concentrated on those objectives of the extra-parliamentary agitation which commanded moderate support. Essentially this involved 'economical reform', the reduction of useless expenditure at court, the purification of Parliament by the exclusion of certain categories of placemen and contractors, and some modest electoral reform. These proposals had a very familiar look: they were in the same country tradition which had produced so many demands for place bills from the age of Danby onwards. But in the context of nearly a century of relatively stable parliamentary government, and with the active support of men who treated these measures as the first instalment of a more ambitious programme, they represented a greater threat to the constitution of the unreformed Parliament than might appear in retrospect. At first there was considerable independent support. On 6 April John Dunning made his historic motion, unsupported by evidence but sustained by emotion, that the 'influence of the crown has increased, is increasing and ought to be diminished': it was carried by 233 votes to 218. Charles James Fox pronounced 'that if he died that night, he should think he had lived to a good purpose in having contributed to bring about this second revolution'.[16] Both apprehension and assumption proved premature. The country gentlemen, having registered their discontent, retreated. Burke's Economical Reform Bill, abolishing Crown sinecures, was unravelled clause by clause. Another bill, prohibiting revenue officers from voting in parliamentary elections, was thrown out by 29 votes. Dunning's motion opposing the dissolution of

---

[16] *London Magazine*, 1780, p. 271.

Parliament, with its echoes of 1641, was rejected by 254 votes to 203. Fox's 'second revolution' was indeed short-lived.

THE GORDON RIOTS

Many contemporaries attributed this failure to the Gordon Riots. Certainly they provided an appropriately violent climax to the drama of 1780. They also revealed some ambiguities of late eighteenth-century life. Educated Englishmen were prone to congratulate themselves on their treatment of the Roman Catholic minority in their midst, and visiting foreigners readily concurred. Papists continued to suffer a degree of penal taxation, principally in the form of double assessments to the land tax; they were also excluded from all public offices, except perhaps those which, at parochial level, were most burdensome. But even at times of tension, for example during the Jacobite Rebellions of 1715 and 1745, local communities and their leaders tended to protect Catholic families with whom they lived on amicable, if slightly distant, terms. When the Jacobite threat passed, the last pretence for prosecution passed with it. Roman Catholic gentry continued to be educated abroad, married mostly within their own faith, and, when they sought an official or military career, found it in other countries. But in lifestyle and mentality they were increasingly assimilated to the propertied classes of their own country. The novelist Henry Brooke, whose transformed attitude was typical of the generation to which he belonged, had penned a bitter denunciation of Catholicism at the time of the Forty-Five. In old age he felt encouraged to revise his view by popish conformity to the values of ordinary Protestant Englishmen and Irishmen. 'Even the vulgar and ignorant among the Roman laity, would grumble at departing from an inch of their property, though the priest should advise, and the pope himself should enjoin it.'[17]

Admittedly, there were parish constables and professional informers ready to work on public prejudice against papists, often with the connivance of alarmist writers in the press. But in the 1760s attempts at prosecution were discouraged by the judges as well as by respectable opinion. It was easy for educated men to deride the scaremongers. Archibald Bower, 'the Ecclesiastical Mountebank of this time', as the diarist William Cole called him,

[17] *Brookiana* (2 vols., London, 1804), i. 199.

had made a considerable impact when, as a renegade Jesuit, he wrote a *History of the Popes* retailing in gruesome detail the horrors of the Inquisition.[18] His credibility was punctured, however, when John Douglas, later Bishop of Salisbury, revealed that Bower had returned to his mother Church after initially forsaking it, had a well-deserved reputation for sexual immorality, and had cobbled together his history by a combination of plagiarism and translation from earlier authors. Bower's literary career, which only ended with his death in 1766, revealed a considerable gap, between the entrenched anti-popery which marked popular attitudes, and the tolerant complacency of polite society.

Ferocious laws remained on the statute-book, and it was on these that liberal concern increasingly focused. Party politics were not involved. It was Lord North whose Quebec Bill had granted extensive concessions to the Catholics of Canada. At home, the Roman Catholic Relief Bill passed in 1778 was proposed by a leading opposition Whig, Sir George Savile, and strongly supported by Cabinet ministers. It removed three mainstays of the laws against papists, none of which had been enforced in recent years, but which constituted an embarrassment to enlightened opinion and a standing encouragement to hostile informers. One made popish priests guilty of felony; another rendered Roman Catholics educated abroad liable to be deprived of their property, 'debarring', as the Attorney-General put it, 'the parent from exercising the noblest and best of all affections, the educating his child in the manner that he thought best for the happiness of his beloved offspring'; a third prevented Catholics from acquiring real property by purchase—it had 'only to be mentioned', John Dunning observed, 'to excite the indignation of the House'.[19] Eighteenth-century hard-headedness and sentiment thus combined in this assault on ancient bigotry.

The extra-parliamentary response to Savile's Act was delayed, but violent. It was triggered by the anti-popish agitation which followed the proposal of a related measure for Scotland in 1779. In England itself, Lord George Gordon's Protestant Association proved diabolically active. Commentators who had grown accustomed to smile at the mild excesses of an English mob soon had

---

[18] F. G. Stokes, ed., *A Journal of my Journey to Paris in the Year 1765, By the Rev. William Cole* (London, 1931), p. 183.
[19] *Parliamentary History*, xix. 1140.

cause to wipe the smile from their faces. Gordon's march to petition Parliament on Friday 7 June proved only the beginning. Attacks on prominent papists and their chapels quickly turned into undiscriminating orgies of brutality, fuelled by plundering breweries. The most eminent victim was Lord Mansfield, whose discountenance of legal persecution combined with his public image as a Scottish perpetuator of Butean principles made him doubly vulnerable. His house in Bloomsbury was pillaged and his celebrated library destroyed. The authorities proved almost powerless to arrest this wave of destruction, which went on for nearly a week. Gaols were burned and their inmates released. The Bank of England was briefly besieged. Ministers were reluctant to order in troops, magistrates were still more terrified to call on them to fire; the militia and law officers of the capital proved utterly incapable of effective countermeasures. It was eventually firm action by the King which restored London to a charred and battered tranquillity. The Proclamation against the rioters was issued on Wednesday 7 June. Thereafter the army quickly brought the disturbances to an end.

The reverberations of the riots were prolonged. The execution of a number of rioters initiated a difficult debate about the legitimacy of the attitudes which they had represented and the use of the law against them. Some critics of the King's action apprehended the creation of an arbitrary state, and anxiously began discussing the merits of diverse schemes for a metropolitan militia or constitutional force, or as some of them called it, 'a police'. Parliament was almost prompted to revoke its concession concerning Catholic education.

The strength of popular feeling, as well as its violence, was difficult for contemporaries to explain, let alone excuse. There was no hard evidence of an increased Catholic presence. The Catholic Joseph Berington argued that his faith had steadily lost ground in the course of the eighteenth century. He was probably exaggerating the plight of his co-religionists but two surveys conducted by the bishops in 1767 and 1780 revealed at most a modest upward trend which did no more than keep abreast of the general population increase. They also displayed the regional distribution of English Catholicism before the age of Irish immigration. Lancashire, with nearly 23,000 papists in 1767, had fully a third of what remained a relatively small national total, London a further 11,000. For the rest, Catholicism was essentially a faith maintained by the gentry, with its most enduring pockets in places where landowners remained true to it, in the North-East, in the Thames Valley, in Hampshire and Sussex, in the West Midlands. In some places where it had once been strong, for instance in Monmouthshire, it was in notable decay. The eighteenth century had indeed seen a fairly steady trickle of defections, some of them from famous families. In the 1770s the heir to the Dukedom of Norfolk itself, the Earl of Surrey, conformed to the established Church. Berington was contemptuous of the personal and political rewards of conformity: 'I pity an Earl of Surrey, who can sink down to a paltry service of a party-declaimer in the Lower House of parliament.'[20] At lower levels of society, however, it is possible that the reverse process was operating. Bishops were understandably jittery about their slender hold on popular religious feeling. Bishop Newton, an arch-conservative in politics, connected the strength of Methodism, of which he had local experience in his diocese of Bristol, with the influence of Jesuit priests and the non-enforcement of the law by magistrates in a common threat to the Church of England.[21] He may have had clearer insight into popular anxieties than Lord Mansfield, on the one hand, or indeed John Wilkes, on the other. Wilkes, whose scepticism hardly permitted him to take religious bigotry seriously, played a courageous part in putting down the riots, and was howled down by the mob: 'off, off, no popish chamberlain'.

Reformers blamed the rioters for their own declining fortunes. Looking back on this period the Whig Vicesimus Knox found in it the roots of that crippling conservatism which characterized the ruling class in the age of the French Revolution. 'Almost immediately a damp was cast on the generous ardour ... Toryism saw the change with delight.'[22] This was an over-simplification. The Association movement itself was deeply divided. Wyvill worked earnestly with the metropolitan reformers but found it difficult to harness the energies of the diverse groups involved. There was suspicion in the provinces that the movement had fallen into the hands of extremists. At some of the public meetings early

[20] *The State and Behaviour of English Catholics from The Reformation to the year 1780* (London, 1780), p. 131.
[21] *Works of Thomas Newton*, ii. 669–79.
[22] *The Works of Vicesimus Knox*, v. 192.

in 1780, dangerous doctrines had been voiced. Manhood suffrage was advocated, along with annual elections and strict constituency control of MPs. The aristocratic and monarchical elements in the famed mixed constitution came in for some severe republican strictures, in language which recalled a more robust but also more violent age. When delegates from the county committees were summoned to meet at London the belief that they were openly challenging Parliament's own representative credentials caused a manifest falling away of support. The fear that reform might be carried by a self-appointed Convention in effect declaring war on Parliament was a real one. James Burgh had written of the need for a Grand National Association to restore the Constitution.[23] John Jebb, a leading light in the metropolitan reform movement, asked 'Would not an act of delegates, freely chosen by the people, assented to by the king and hereditary nobility, be sufficient for this purpose?'[24] Even at local level the Associations carried an implicit threat to the traditional institutions of county government. Rockingham had been disturbed by this possibility in his own country. The Scottish philosopher Adam Ferguson took a serious view of events in Yorkshire. 'That county seems to be turning itself into a Republic.'[25]

Such fears could only work to the advantage of the government. There was also good news from America in 1780 as British troops advanced through the South and finally captured its greatest city, Charleston. At home the invasion threat passed for the moment. North resisted the intrigue within his own Cabinet as he had beaten off opposition outside it. In the autumn of 1779 Lord Gower, son of the Tory 'traitor' of 1745, led a series of desertions from the ministry by the old Bedford faction. It was widely assumed that when the Bedfords left a ship, it was indeed sinking. But with the support of one of their number, Lord Chancellor Thurlow, North held steady. Soon after the Gordon Riots he tentatively offered Rockingham a coalition, but the Whig terms, including the recognition of American independence, the enactment of economical reform, and the dismissal of Germain and Sandwich, proved too much for the King.

[23] *Political Disquisitions*, iii. 428–9.
[24] *The Works Theological, Medical, Political, and Miscellaneous, of John Jebb, M.D.F.R.S. with Memoirs of the Life of the Author, by John Disney* (3 vols., London, 1787), ii. 507.
[25] D. Kettler, *The Social and Political Thought of Adam Ferguson* (Ohio, 1965), p. 86.

In September North called a snap election. Both Rockingham and the reformers were unable to capitalize on the mood of the previous spring. There was a strange contrast here. In 1779 a by-election in Hampshire had caused intense excitement and suggested the possibility of a national conflict polarized on party lines. In 1780 this failed to materialize. Edmund Burke's defeat in the popular constituency of Bristol owed something to local considerations, especially his preference of Irish free trade to the commercial interest of his constituents. But it was also a fair sign of the apathy, even hostility, encountered by the opposition. North's majority in the new House of Commons remained above forty even on the difficult question of economical reform. Had there been a substantial shift of opinion in the summer of 1780? Or had the great upheaval of the previous winter and spring been but a short-lived response to a tempory crisis? On either reading there was little immediate prospect of change. As ever, all hinged on the war in America.

THE FALL OF NORTH AND THE PEACE

Cornwallis's surrender at Yorktown in October 1781, following a period of reassuring reports from the war theatre, came as a considerable shock. It was partly the result of an over-confident march through Virginia, partly an indication of the strain on naval resources in the North Atlantic. When the news arrived, North considered it conclusive so far as the war was concerned: 'Oh God, it is all over.' This was not his master's view. It remained George III's belief that the war could and should go on. As a result the parliamentary battles of the next three months were only nominally between North and his opponents; in reality they were between the King and an increasingly high proportion of the House of Commons, with North caught in the middle, the reluctant defender of a war in which he no longer believed. In the Commons his majority dropped quickly to around twenty. On Henry Conway's motion in favour of ending the war, on 27 February, it vanished altogether; the motion was carried by 234 votes to 215. A further four weeks were needed to bring down the government. News of the loss of Minorca was not as politically devastating as it had been in 1756, but it intensified the prevailing sense of gloom. On 18 March a group of North's independent supporters, staunch country gentlemen who had loyally supported him for a decade and more, warned him that they could no longer do so.

Before opposition could relish the pleasure of humiliating him on a vote of no confidence, North announced his resignation. His discreet but firm lecture to the King on his constitutional duty to accept the verdict of Parliament made little impact. George III never forgave North for abandoning him. Yet perhaps it was his own obstinacy which had made it impossible for North to continue. In 1742 the men who brought about Walpole's fall had lost faith in the minister as well as his measures. It is not clear that this was the case in 1782. Already, in January, North had prudently sacrificed Germain to the demands of his colleagues. Germain, not for the first time in his career, proved a satisfying sacrificial victim; certainly his dismissal took much pressure off the Cabinet. North was by nature a survivor; he was also a skilled if not masterful manager of the House of Commons. Given the opportunity to cut loose from the American War and a clear direction from the King to strengthen his political position at whatever cost, it is not impossible that he might have battled through the spring of 1782 to be the minister who negotiated peace with America after waging war on it.

The ministries which succeeded North's were by no means appealing to the great mass of independent back-benchers. Rockingham's, which lasted only three months until terminated by his death at the end of June 1782, was a coalition of the principal elements formerly in opposition, the Rockingham Whigs, and Chatham's followers, now marshalled under Shelburne. The animosity between Charles James Fox and Shelburne himself, as the Secretaries of State principally responsible for the government's policy, made it highly unstable. Its successor, led by Shelburne, whom George III found more to his taste than Fox, was even weaker, for it rested on an unlikely alliance of Chathamite Whigs and Court and Treasury placemen. Fox and Rockingham's followers, deprived of their leader, refused to support Shelburne. In the House of Commons William Pitt, the youthful Chancellor of the Exchequer and son of Chatham, was expected to cope with the rhetorical skills and debating power of North, Fox, Burke, and Sheridan. But Parliament was in recess in the summer of 1782 and Shelburne's attention was chiefly directed to the negotiations with enemy powers which were being conducted in Paris.

There was much, after all, to be negotiated. Some even thought it was worth fighting on. They were probably over-optimistic. Financial exhaustion, economic crisis, and military failure had sapped the public will to continue the war. There was no denying, however that the prospects were improving. Gibraltar was preserved against a final Spanish assault in September 1782. In India the Company's beleaguered forces, reinforced from home, proved successful in resisting both the native powers on the subcontinent and the threat of the French navy in the Bay of Bengal. Above all, in the West Indies, in the spring of 1782, Rodney won a decisive naval victory, the Battle of the Saints. He wrote home: 'You may now despise all your enemies.'[26] Britain's enemies were hardly despicable but they were divided and somewhat distracted. The American negotiators were acutely aware of the slender thread of interest which linked them with the court of Louis XVI; they also knew that in the United States itself the British military position was by no means hopeless. There were 30,000 British troops in North America after Yorktown. New York, Halifax, Charleston, Savannah, and St Augustus, not to say Quebec, were all still in imperial hands. Neither Spain nor France had made the territorial gains for which it had hoped. They were financially in the same straits as the British government, and they feared an Anglo-American *rapprochement* at their expense. The Dutch, dragged into war in 1780 as a result of insisting on their right to trade freely with combatant countries, were incapable of defending a scattered empire: partition by either their British enemy or their French ally seemed its likely fate. The League of Armed Neutrality, with Russia at its head, was formed to resist Britain's attempts at commercial and naval blockade of its enemies. In London it was considered more of a diplomatic embarrassment than a strategic threat.

The Rockingham and Shelburne ministries did not make the best use of this hand. Under Rockingham, Fox was precipitate in his anxiety to grant America what she asked, Shelburne unduly sanguine in his belief that an enduring form of transatlantic empire might be saved. Vergennes and Franklin had the measure of their envoys in Paris. When Shelburne acquired exclusive control of the negotiations in June 1782 he made substantial concessions. The lands between the Ohio and the Mississippi, incorporated in

[26] P. Mackesy, *The War for America, 1775-1783* (London, 1964), p. 459.

Quebec in 1774, were now ceded to the United States, effectively depriving Canada of its natural hinterland, one of huge potential value for the future. The provision made for the protection of loyalists who had risked everything for their King was manifestly inadequate, as was that for the repayment of pre-war debts owed to British merchants. Shelburne's generosity was not without purpose; indeed there was something visionary in his plan. He looked forward to an era of renewed Anglo-American co-operation based on commercial collaboration, leading perhaps to a recreation of that empire which he and his master Chatham had been so reluctant to dismember, notwithstanding their reputation as friends of America.

This was hardly a realistic prescription: certainly it proved too advanced for Parliament. Plans for a free trade treaty with the new United States were killed in the Commons. Arguments drawn from fashionable *laissez-faire* doctrine made little headway against the conviction that it was illogical as well as imprudent to reward America for her resistance, by continuing the commercial privileges which she had enjoyed as a full member of the empire. The American treaty itself remained profoundly unpopular. Parliament had willed the peace but it did not like it. In this respect Shelburne was perhaps unfortunate as the minister who had to take responsibility for a necessary but unpalatable degree of national humiliation. Even so, the terms which he had negotiated made it easier for his predecessor North and his rival Fox to combine and defeat them in the Commons. In the end, however, the settlement which he had offered was largely adhered to. In retrospect the gains made by Britain's European enemies were not excessive, bearing in mind the desperate situation of only two years earlier. The restoration of Florida and Minorca to Spain, and the return of Tobago and Senegal to France, with minor concessions in the Newfoundland fishery and in India, could plausibly be portrayed as relatively insignificant.

However debatable its terms, the Peace of 1783 was the work of ministers who had been placed in power to negotiate it against the expressed will of the Crown. This was a considerable novelty. Indeed the Rockingham Ministry, short-lived though it proved, represented a landmark in constitutional history. The ministerial changes of 1782 involved a more extensive upheaval among office-holders than any since 1714, virtually replacing one administration with another drawn from opposition. Rockingham also came to power with what would have to be described in modern parlance as a legislative programme. The economical reform measures of 1780 were finally passed. Burke was granted his opportunity to set about abolishing redundant offices. It has become customary to dismiss the significance of his labours in this respect. Yet the extensive reduction in the royal household and the elimination of supposedly useless offices of state, including the entire Board of Trade, was bitterly opposed by the King and would indeed have been unthinkable even a decade earlier. Burke also established the principle of parliamentary accountability for civil list expenditure. In addition, Clerke's Act, named after Philip Jennings Clerke, removed the contractors from the Commons. Crewe's Act, named after another opponent of Lord North, John Crewe, disabled revenue officers from voting in parliamentary elections.

In Ireland, where the Volunteers had virtually issued an ulti-matum demanding Irish legislative independence, concessions which would have amazed earlier generations were made. In a tactical sense they were probably unnecessary. With the American War practically over, the Irish crisis was no longer the strategic concern it might have been. Moreover, for all the attempts of the patriots to forge an enduring bond between Protestant and Catholic nationalism, it is difficult to regard the implied threat to secede from the empire as anything other than a gigantic bluff, albeit one in which Protestants half-believed. But Rockingham and some of his friends were great Irish landlords. They were also friends and natural allies of Irish Whigs like Grattan and Lord Charlemont. In 1782 they repealed the Declaratory Act of 1720, leaving the Irish Parliament to demolish the remains of Privy Council supervision of Irish legislation. A further Renunciation Act in 1783 removed the lingering suspicion of some Irish patriots that British law had not specifically been deprived of its status in Dublin. These conces-sions, second in importance only to American independence itself, placed Ireland somewhat in the situation of Scotland before the Union, with alarming implications for the future of Anglo-Irish relations. In the months which followed March 1782 it was becom-ing clear just how momentous the fall of North's ministry had been, as the changes which it wrought in America, in Ireland, and in England itself, took effect. Many an independent who had voted to force North out of office had cause to regret his conduct.

CONSTITUTIONAL CRISIS

The independents were an important element in a shifting pattern of politics. They wanted peace, retrenchment, and good house-keeping, a return to stability after the storms of recent years. They wanted the King respected but not necessarily deferred to. As to men, they would have supported almost any coalition of the principal politicians—perhaps in 1783 one of North and Shelburne, in 1784 one of Fox and Pitt. The King was also a force in his own right, and his views were clearer, as well as stronger. North he had come to despise, almost to detest. The bitterness with which he now regarded his former friend and servant was displayed when he attempted to make North responsible for the election expenses which he had incurred on the government's behalf in 1780. Fox he hated as much as any man who ever crossed him. In his youth Fox had been offered every opportunity of a conventional court career; he had preferred to throw himself into a reckless opposition. By opposing the Royal Marriage Act in 1772 he had marked himself out for special animosity. Nor did his notorious profligacy help him with a puritanical monarch. Above all, he had carried Rockingham's aristocratic dislike of kingly power to new heights. In the second Rockingham Ministry Fox's doctrine that the party in power should in effect choose its own leader and direct both measures and men without reference to the wishes of the Crown infuriated the King.

George III's own preference was for Shelburne as the least of current evils, and perhaps, with an eye to the future, for the young William Pitt, elected to the Commons only in 1781. At any other time Pitt's elevation would have seemed grossly premature. But the times were not ordinary and Pitt made the best of his opportunity in 1782–3. He had his father's prestige, and also his father's priggish high-mindedness to impress those who did not have to deal daily with him. He acquired an early reputation as an orator, one for which he had prepared himself at Cambridge. Already in July 1782 North remarked that no ministry would be able to withstand him.[27] As Chancellor of the Exchequer in Shelburne's Cabinet he identified himself with progressive causes but without displaying the anti-aristocratic virulence of many reformers. The Whig poet

[27] *Letters from Mrs Elizabeth Carter, to Mrs Montagu, Between the Years 1755 and 1800,* iii. 170.

William Mason, as early as June 1782, caught something of his peculiar inheritance and promise: 'Be thou the People's Friend.'[28]

The King had a measure of personal influence but he could not save Shelburne against the determined opposition of Fox and North and the opprobrium of an unpopular Peace. Two divisions in February 1783 saw the ministry defeated by 224 votes to 208, and 207 to 190. The King wanted to fight on, but Shelburne took the same view as North, in March 1782, a view which represented, after all, the development of the doctrine of parliamentary accountability in the century separating the impeachment of Danby from the fall of North. With the politicians divided between three different parties, North's, Fox's, and Shelburne's, it was plain that an alliance would have to be negotiated. The obvious one, between Shelburne and North, was ruled out by Pitt, whose personal vindictiveness in his relations with North expressed the malignancy so often displayed by his family. Fox and Shelburne had quarrelled definitively in 1782. Only a coalition between Fox and North remained to be tried. It was made in a spirit of compromise on both sides. The American War lay in the past. North was left free to oppose parliamentary reform as Fox was to support it. The alliance was not more hypocritical than Pitt's with some of the men who had figured at the court of George III during the North years, Henry Dundas, Edward Thurlow, Charles Jenkinson. Many parliamentarians saw it as a sensible and healing measure. By the King it was seen in a different light. But there was no escape.

The Fox–North Coalition was formed on 12 March 1783 under the nominal leadership of the Duke of Portland, with North as Home Secretary and Fox as Foreign Secretary. There was no doubt of a handsome majority in Parliament. The King persisted in his hostility, to the extent of refusing to create peerages at the recommendation of the new Cabinet. In Pitt he saw a potential first minister, albeit one untried at the highest levels. There were constant calculations with John Robinson, who had declined to follow North into coalition with Fox, as to the prospects of securing a majority by calling an early general election. But Pitt himself had no intention of staking his political career on a desperate throw. The ministry provocatively supported the Prince of Wales, who delighted in an opportunity to offend his father, in his demand for a separate allowance. Enraged, the King renewed his

<hr>

[28] *Ode to the Honourable William Pitt* (London, 1782), p. 11.

pleas to Pitt. The latter, knowing the history of his country and his family, sensibly decided that 'King versus Prince' was not a promising issue to put before the electorate. He did not have to wait long for a more appealing cause.

In retrospect it seems the highest folly in Fox to have provided the King with an issue which exactly suited his purpose, permitting him to appeal to extra-parliamentary opinion on grounds of high principle as much as personal interest. Fox's East India Bill perhaps seemed innocuous to its authors. In the last years of North's ministry only the distractions of the American War had prevented North himself from devising a settlement which would improve the administration of India, control the factiousness of the East India Company, and repair the deficiencies of his earlier Regulating Act. In 1781 he had pushed through a modest reform of judicial machinery in Bengal, and Robinson had long been planning more extensive legislation. Most authorities agreed that the proprietors of the Company should be further restrained from manipulating its affairs, and that the servants of the Company should be more rigorously disciplined. Most, too, saw that State intervention in Indian affairs must increase, and the directors be induced to concentrate on commerce rather than politics and patronage. But Fox and his friends contributed two distinctive items to their East India reform, both of which proved political gifts to the King.

One was the supervision of the Company's affairs by a Commission composed of Fox's friends, removable only on an address from Parliament. Such an arrangement departed from the tradition of vesting all executive appointments in the Crown, albeit subject to parliamentary accountability. Only the judges had been rendered more or less independent of the Crown by making their tenure dependent on a parliamentary vote; to elevate Fox's political nominees to this status seemed to be adding insult to injury. Secondly, the ministers contrived to unify the East India interest against them, and not merely by their proposals for a new commission. Since 1780 Burke had immersed himself in East India affairs. He played a prominent part in the parliamentary committees of investigation into Indian administration, and penned the famous *Ninth Report* which highlighted the most glaring defects of British rule in India. He also acquired more knowledge of India than anyone who had not actually been there and more authority on the subject than many who had. But thanks partly to his enquiries, partly to the network of interests with which he and his party were involved, he had committed himself to the view that much of the responsibility for maladministration in India was to be laid at the door of the Governor-General, Warren Hastings. Circumstances and the exigencies of survival during the war had identified Hastings with a motley collection of interests and factions, both in London and in Asia. In time Burke's obsession with the prosecution of Hastings became a liability to his party. In the short run it served to alienate his friends from some of the richest, most powerful, and also most corrupt elements in the Company, among them the 'Arcot gang', led by Paul Benfield. Contemporaries greatly exaggerated the influence and patronage at the command of such interests. But the Foxites were the victims both of the myth and the reality. To outsiders they seemed intent on appropriating an immense reservoir of corruption. Yet the men who wielded real influence were provoked by them into employing it on behalf of the King.

George III could not stop the bill passing the Commons. Instead he killed it in the Lords by making it clear that no peer who voted for it would be considered his friend. Whether this was a legitimate ploy has long remained a nice point of constitutional controversy. Judged by his own criterion of parliamentary independence, expressed to the Rockingham Whigs in connection with the repeal of the Stamp Act in 1766, it would appear dubious; no doubt the extremity of the crisis and the strength of his own feelings in 1783 placed his relationship with the legislature in a new light. He went on to dismiss the Coalition and put Pitt in office. This was widely expected to be a 'mince pie' ministry which would last over Christmas before succumbing to the majority of Fox and North. In January 1784 Fox appeared to have a majority of about a hundred when he attempted to insist on the right of Parliament to determine the composition of the ministry. But his position was weaker than it seemed. He could not take strong measures against Pitt, such as withholding supply or blocking the annual Mutiny Act, without recalling the spirit of 1641 and raising the spectre of civil war. Some of his back-bench supporters were shaken by the crisis into which the King's action had plunged them, but they did not necessarily hold the King entirely to blame. In the Commons Pitt stood the test, and Fox's majority began to wither. The columns of the *London Gazette* were flooded with addresses to the Crown applauding the King's actions. He responded by calling a general election in the spring of 1784, three years before one was required by the Septennial Act. Few seriously questioned his right to do so, though there was no Hanoverian precedent for so premature a use of the royal prerogative of dissolution. The propaganda war was won handsomely by the Crown. Independent electors, in the open constituencies, were persuaded to see the issue in terms of a corrupt aristocratic conspiracy versus a principled, embattled monarch. Both Fox and North lost many of their Commons supporters, some of them former placemen who were ousted by Pitt's nominees in close boroughs, but many others victims of a clear electoral verdict against them. Robinson actually underestimated the swing against Fox in open constituencies, but his overall prediction of a majority well in excess of 100 was borne out.

The constitutional crisis of 1783–4 was thus resolved firmly in favour of the Crown. Yet it was not an inevitable victory. The King's strength was that he was able to identify the cause of his government with integrity in public life, and that of his opponents with oligarchy and corruption. This was positively revolutionary in terms of traditional eighteenth-century politics; the Whigs themselves were staggered by the way their rhetoric was turned against them. Circumstances and political misjudgement in the last months of 1783 largely accounted for their discomfiture. The Whig doctrine of collective responsibility and the Whig party's hopes of power perished together. Fox's friends were relegated to years of opposition in what looked a very familiar mould, with the Prince of Wales supporting them against a pragmatic Prime Minister whose position seemed as unassailable as that of Pelham or Walpole.

Another casualty seemed to be any realistic hope of reform. The rivalry of Pitt and Fox hastened the distintegration of the Association movement and when he moved for parliamentary reform from the Treasury Bench in 1785 Pitt was decisively defeated. Whether this really had much to do with the political crisis of the previous year is, however, debatable. Pitt had tried two similar motions earlier, in 1782 and 1783, with the same result. Primarily this was because the cause no longer had deep-rooted or extensive support. By 1783 Wyvill and the Associators represented only themselves; briefly, in 1779–80, they had appeared to represent the nation as a whole. It required no revolutionary threat from abroad to render the reformers powerless. The fact that one of them was now Prime Minister may have seemed a paradox; it was not, however, a contradiction.

CHAPTER 12

Macaroni Manners

THE economic growth of the 1760s and 1770s had important consequences for public and private finance. A wave of speculation and gaming, some of it associated with the State lottery, caused intense anxiety in the early seventies. The financial crash of 1772 revived memories of the South Sea Bubble and aroused exaggerated fears of impending national bankruptcy. Such concern also reflected the growing belief that the age was peculiarly afflicted by the vices of luxury, extravagance, and immorality. This was the heyday of the macaronis, outrageous offenders against the canons of bourgeois respectability, not least in the effeminate dress and manners which they adopted. Marital fidelity and family life were widely thought to be threatened. The moral standards of the new King and Queen visibly clashed with the supposed degeneracy of upper-class life. Scandals associated with other, less disciplined members of the royal family, enhanced this impression of a crisis in the highest reaches of polite society. Aristocratic power and values generally came under increasing criticism. 'Chesterfieldism' seemed to embody all that was most cynical and depraved in an outmoded concept of gentility. The sexual freedom of educated women, and the prominence accorded female writers and artists, gave rise to an increasingly tense debate, as scholarly

*argument combined with sensational journalism to
investigate the changing roles of the sexes. Other
features of the age, for instance the sense of cultural*
malaise *created by meretricious theatrical fashions,
were similarly subjected to searching examination. In
all these concerns the mentality of a powerful and
serious-minded middle-class was discernible: its object
to control and discipline the very forces which were
spreading prosperity and 'politeness' throughout the
ranks of propertied society.*

SPECULATION AND BANKRUPTCY

THERE was a certain flavour about the 1760s and 1770s, which contemporaries found puzzling and even distasteful. Charles Dickens later caught something of it when he chose the early 1770s for the opening scenes of *A Tale of Two Cities*. 'It was the best of times, it was the worst of times.' Much of this sense of paradox derived from a peculiar combination of heightened sensibility with vulgar materialism. Many who subscribed to the former were dismayed by the latter. Jonas Hanway, a great philanthropic busybody, denounced what he called the 'age of Pleasure'; others used still more disapproving epithets, Vanity, Extravagance, Luxury, and so on, to characterize it. The Bishop of Bristol, Thomas Newton, offered a complete series of coupled condemnations; it was, he said, an age of novelty and singularity, of pride and vanity, of luxury and pleasure, of venality and corruption, of licentiousness and wickedness.[1]

Moralists are often ready to believe that they live in sinful times, and certainly the rapid economic growth of the period made for abundant temptations. In this respect there were obvious parallels with that other age of excess and extravagance, the early 1720s. Even the South Sea Bubble seemed to have a successor in the financial crash of 1772–3. In 1753, and again in 1763, the City had suffered sudden crises of confidence. But on each of those occasions the rot began in Amsterdam, and had more to do with Dutch difficulties than fiscal instability in London. Indeed in both instances it was the buoyancy of the British stock-market, and the desire of Continental investors to take their profits, which made it temporarily vulnerable to strains in the money-markets abroad. But in June 1772, as the Dutch newspaper *De Koopman* pointed out, the cycle of speculation, panic, and bankruptcy started in London and then spread to the Continent.[2] This crisis, which continued well into 1773, was a good deal worse than any of the preceding half-century, provoking dark comparisons with the Bubble itself.

Yet most of the anxiety proved unfounded. There were, indeed, features of the fiscal recession of 1772 which made it far less

[1] *The Defects of Police the Cause of Immorality* (London, 1775), p. 265.
[2] C. Wilson, *Anglo-Dutch Commerce and Finance in the Eighteenth Century* (Cambridge, 1941), p. 174.

threatening than its predecessor of fifty years before. Nobody seriously suggested that corruption in high places might be involved, and the financial standing of government was virtually unaffected. Public stock had looked vulnerable during the Falkland Islands crisis, but remained unshaken by the storms of 1772 and 1773. The poet-merchant Richard Glover, who gave influential testimony before the House of Commons as to the cause of the crisis, blamed Scotland, 'that land of projects', where it was possible to find 'erudition and science, jurisprudence, theology, history, oratory—in short, Sir, every sense, but that common sort, upon which all worldly welfare, both public and private, depends'. He claimed that if the speculation in paper securities had continued much longer the resulting slump would have ruined public credit.[3] To others the resilience of the financial institutions seemed at least as striking as their fragility.

In part, this confidence derived from enhanced public awareness of the economic utility of credit. In the early eighteenth century those, like Daniel Defoe, who sang the praises of the god Circulation, had to contend with widespread scepticism. But in the early 1770s there was no retreat into bullion or land. Typical of the prevailing optimism was the reassurance offered by one financial journalist: 'simply to create wealth in a nation, is not in modern politics the only end; but it must be circulating wealth, or it will not be effective.'[4] Until the heavy taxation and military disasters of the later stages of the American War there was certainly no halt to circulation, as the growth of provincial banking demonstrated. It was remarked that England was more of a 'Paperwealth' than ever.[5] Admittedly, there was legislation, in 1765 for Scotland, in 1775 and 1777 for England, restraining the use of small denomination notes. But the object of these acts was to provide a measure of protection for the poorer classes against exploitation by their betters. In Yorkshire employers were paying wages in notes for very small sums. These notes might be made payable only at a future date and were subject to frauds undetectable by the illiterate.

So far as the great mass of property and business transactions was concerned, paper credit continued to flourish with the encouragement of the courts and without interference from government.

---

[3] *Parliamentary History*, xvii. 1113.
[4] *London Magazine*, 1777, p. 523.
[5] Ibid., p. 469.

North's recoinage of 1773–6, the first major exercise of its kind since 1696, was a limited operation and was designed to underpin, not undercut, confidence in paper. In this it proved successful. Silver was left to decay into the token currency which it clearly became by the early nineteenth century. The standard set in 1696 had left it distinctly overvalued and in the 1760s it was reckoned that every ounce of silver intended to pass as current coin at 5s. 2d. would cost nearly 5s. 7d. to purchase in bullion, a disparity which made large-scale minting impracticable. In fact there had been no substantial issue of silver since the minting of Lima silver in 1745–6, and throughout the late eighteenth century the silver currency diminished rapidly in quantity and quality. Half-crowns were said to be very rare, and even sixpences and shillings were notoriously worn or 'light'. Gold, by contrast, commanded wide acceptance and confidence; a favourable balance of trade with Portuguese Brazil, one of the great gold exporters, made it less likely than silver to be drained away in overseas or foreign trade. Even so it suffered from deficiencies. Sheer wear and tear reduced the value of older coins; moreover, clipping and counterfeiting caused concern about the viability of the gold standard. North's recoinage, which involved calling in over £16 million worth of gold coins, restored its prestige. The new guinea on which George III appeared after fourteen years' rule, with double chin and patriarchal authority, was highly esteemed. Travellers found that French innkeepers now took pleasure in receiving gold coins from Englishmen landing at Calais, and on their return dispensed bagfuls of questionable 'Birmingham shillings' rather than give them up again.[6]

Currency was not the only evidence of the new fiscal confidence. It was also convincingly displayed in the sympathy bestowed on bankers who might have been held responsible for the misfortunes of 1772. Public attention was focused on the house of Neale, James, Fordyce, and Down. It was not the biggest concern to founder: probably the firm of Glyn and Halifax qualified for this doubtful honour. It was, however, the first, and in Alexander Fordyce it certainly had the most colourful victim of the recession. Alexander came from a modestly prosperous, intensely ambitious Aberdeen background. He was the risk-taker of the family, though his

[6] Philip Thicknesse, *A Year's Journey through France and Part of Spain* (2 vols., Bath, 1777), i. 9–10.

brothers William and James, respectively physician and priest,
exploited the opportunities offered by fashionable society in
London just as shrewdly as he. His fortune was made by speculating in two great 'booms': the Peace Preliminaries of 1762, and
the rise in India stock after Clive's return to Calcutta. Thereafter
he lived the life of a merchant prince. He married the daughter of
a Scottish earl, erected a handsome seat at Roehampton, and spent
heavily if fruitlessly on parliamentary elections. His fortunes were
affected by the Falklands Crisis, but the cause of his fall in 1772
was his involvement in the affairs of the Ayr Bank, a recently
founded Scottish company which had engaged in some imprudent
lending. Initially Fordyce tried to bluff his way out of trouble,
producing a flurry of banknotes with which to reassure his creditors. But his downfall was only delayed.

There is an intriguing family account, published long after
Fordyce's death, of his strange conduct on the eve of his disgrace
in June 1772, when he returned home to Roehampton for dinner
(like many other City businessmen in the 1770s, he was an early
'commuter'). 'I always told the wary ones,' he raved, 'and the wise
ones, with heads of a chicken and claws of a corbie, that I would
be a man or a mouse; and this night, this very night, the die is
cast, and I am . . . am . . . A man! Bring champaign; and, Butler,
Burgundy below! Let tonight live for ever! Champaign above,
Burgundy below! The gods shall celebrate this night, for Alexander is a man.'[7] Not until the next day did his family learn
what was about to befall them. In the subsequent bankruptcy
proceedings there were surprisingly few ready to condemn him,
let alone his hapless partners. Fordyce absconded but when he
returned to face the music he stressed that he had taken no money
with him, having lost in all a fortune of £150,000. 'And here nature
burst forth, and a few tears eased the anguish of an aching heart.'
The reporter of his partners' hearing was even more sympathetic.
One of them, James, begged to retain his wife's dowry for the
benefit of his children, a plea which visibly impressed the presiding
commissioner of bankruptcy, who praised his humility and resignation, and read out the request like a 'man of feeling'. The
creditors, who had to be content with a dividend of 4s., may have
felt less sentimental, but the atmosphere of relative calm and

---

[7] *Memoirs of the late Mrs Henrietta Fordyce, Relict of James Fordyce* (London, 1823),
pp. 53–4.

compassion is remote indeed from the bitterness of the 1720s.[8] It was conveyed to posterity in Samuel Foote's notably mild satire *The Bankrupt*. Foote was a merciless exposer of contemporary hypocrisy, but he evidently felt there was nothing to be gained by pillorying Fordyce.

GAMING AND THE STATE

Compassion was not the same as complacency. The more disreputable forms of speculation aroused much irritation. A great deal that came under this heading was actually described as insurance, though the distinction between some forms of insurance and outright gambling was far from clear. 'I remember', an eminent banker, Benjamin Hopkins, told the Commons in 1773, 'when the business of underwriting was respectable.'[9] Some of the ventures which attracted unfavourable comment were in fact well-intentioned but imprudent schemes for retirement pensions, based on faulty actuarial assumptions at a time when reliable statistical information was hard to come by. Others hardly pretended to be more than gaming.

A notorious case of this kind arose from the activities of the bizarre Chevalier D'Eon. D'Eon was a French diplomat who had come to England at the end of the Seven Years War and got himself into all kinds of scrapes in the course of a short but tempestuous career. Constant bickering with his colleagues and a taste for appearing in women's dress made him the object of public interest as well as a source of embarrassment to his compatriots. There were many wagers, masquerading as 'insurances', on the vexed question of his sex. One of these came before the Court of King's Bench, in the case of *Hayes* v. *Jacques*, in 1777, when it was reported that reputable medical authority in France had settled the matter in favour of womanhood. Hayes had ventured fifteen guineas to fifteen hundred that such proof would be forthcoming, but Jacques declined to accept the report as sufficient evidence. D'Eon, denying complicity in this and any other bet, wisely returned to his native land to await the outcome. Lord Mansfield expressed his anger that the majesty of the law should be engaged in such a frivolous matter but was forced to rule the wager legal.

[8] *London Magazine*, 1772, pp. 432, 397–8.
[9] *Parliamentary History*, xvii. 795.

The jury found for Hayes though his 'insurance' was eventually disqualified on a technicality. The difficulty in the case was a serious one and came not infrequently before the courts in different contexts. How was it possible to draw a line which would outlaw morally dubious forms of insurance without penalizing respectable companies and threatening the legitimate interests of trade and property? Parliament not only declined to draw the line itself, but seemed indirectly at least to encourage its transgression by the public at large, with its endorsement of national lotteries, 'the ruin of trade, the parent of poverty, and the destruction of morality', as one critic put it.[10]

State lotteries had flourished since 1694. But certain features of their use in the 1770s were new. In the first place, several private lottery schemes were authorized by Parliament at this time. The sale of Cox's Museum, a celebrated collection of gems, automata, and timepieces, was managed by means of a lottery, as was the disposal of the Adam brothers' ambitious building speculation on the Strand, the Adelphi. It was argued that the capital value of such assets put them beyond all but a handful of individual purchasers, and that a lottery provided a legitimate means of compensation for enterprising ventures in the public interest. But there were those who regarded such lotteries as a form of public corruption akin to Elizabethan monopolies. Moreover, even less objectionable lotteries, like the State lottery itself, were accused of fostering the English vice of gaming, especially among the lower classes.

The national lottery was certainly popular. Minimum tickets had been reduced from £20 to £10, bringing them well within the purchasing power of the middle sort. Tickets were sold in small shares at prices easily afforded by all but the indigent. The sudden celebrity which went with a big win always aroused great interest. In 1767, for example, when a small tavern-keeper in Abingdon won the first prize, and scattered largess among his neighbours, he enjoyed a brief blaze of glory. Some important changes were made at about this time. Until 1768 prizes took the form of government stock. Thereafter they were paid in cash, enhancing their appeal to the man in the street. Still more influential was the decision to raise the first prize from £10,000 to £20,000 and to cancel the value of tickets which drew a blank, thereby converting the lottery

[10] *London Magazine*, 1780, p. 15.

into a simple game of chance in which the stake might be lost altogether. As many critics pointed out, it was difficult to detect the moral distinction between such gambling and that involved in less approved but more traditional forms, such as card-games or cock-fights.

Defenders of the lottery replied that much of the gaming associated with the lottery was unauthorized and illegal. Lottery tickets were paid for by instalments and there was great trafficking in them, with City brokers characteristically inventing their own vocabulary to describe them: 'light horse' were tickets on which only the first instalment had been paid, 'heavy horse' were fully subscribed tickets. The draw itself took up to forty-two days and speculating in tickets increased as it progressed. It was held in some state at the Guildhall and the number and prizes drawn each day were widely reported. In the last days of the draw, with a diminishing number of tickets still known to be in play, excitement would reach fever pitch.

In this excitement the ticket-holders were by no means the only interested parties. For the office-keepers whose business was trading in lotteries it offered an interesting range of 'insurances'. Where a ticket-holder paid a premium to cover himself against the failure of his ticket it was conceivably proper to describe the procedure as insurance; but in many cases such premiums were merely further wagers on a given number coming up, regardless of whether the office-keeper or the investor had the ticket in question. Nominal sales of goods such as handkerchiefs, trinkets, and even beef dinners, were made with these premiums to legitimize or enhance their attractions. Fraudulent practices were commonplace and there were many brokers whose object was literally to stay a step ahead of their winners. One of the master criminals of the age, Charles 'Patch' Price, was a practitioner of lottery frauds. He escaped conviction for many years before being condemned for a felony in 1786, when he committed suicide rather than submit to the noose. Parliament periodically tried to eliminate the worst practices but with little success. Most of those employed to sell this form of gaming were merely the agents of wealthy, faceless capitalists: the metropolis and Home Counties swarmed with these 'morocco men' (so named from the wallets which they carried). When the net was cast it generally caught only these smaller fry, whose imprisonment was in any case rendered painless by their paymasters. In all this it is easy to understand the success of the lottery. The sports on which so many Englishmen customarily bet, horse-racing, cock-fighting, boxing, and cricket, were local events. Only the legislature could make betting a truly national sport. It was small wonder that the moralists blamed rulers, as well as ruled, for the corruption of the times.

FASHIONABLE DIVERSIONS

Upper-class gaming was a favourite subject of censorious pens. Brooks's, White's, and other clubs in which rich young men proverbially lost their patrimony were nothing new, though the generation of Charles James Fox seems to have set records in this respect, with reports in 1770 of up to £15,000 lost in an evening. When John Damer, son of the immensely wealthy Lord Milton committed suicide in 1776 because his father refused to pay gambling debts of £70,000, there was a spate of moralizing about the temptations of aristocratic life. It was noticed that sports which depended on upper-class betting throve in the 1770s. Cricket owed much to the support of noblemen, some of whom played the game as well as wagered on it. Horse-racing, which acquired three of its classics at this time, the St Leger in 1776, the Oaks in 1779, and the Derby in 1780, similarly benefited by the rage for gambling.

Not only the well-born were at risk. The memoirs of William Hickey testify to the perils which beset young men of comfortable, middle-class background in the London of the 1760s and 1770s, though Hickey himself claimed to be immune to the gaming infection, except for a few shillings which he readily lost to the sharks who frequented billiard-rooms, in order to learn from their skill with a cue.[11] There were complaints about the spread of card-playing as a fashionable pastime in homes which, it was supposed, would have shunned it in earlier times. Sunday, increasingly a day of diversion rather than rest for business families, was thought to be vulnerable to this threat. It was easy to point to the bad example set by prominent public figures. If there was a presiding genius in the polite vices of the 1770s it was probably Mrs Theresa Cornelys, an Italian immigrant whose mixture of operatic and sexual conquests prepared her for a leading role in London's social life. She established herself at Carlisle House in Soho about 1760 and in

[11] A. Spencer, ed., *Memoirs of William Hickey* (9th edn., 4 vols., London, 1948), i. 64–5.

due course turned it into what Horace Walpole called a 'fairy palace, for balls, concerts, and masquerades'.[12] There were dark rumours about life at Carlisle House, but Mrs Cornelys's balls attracted royalty as well as riff-raff. Her Harmonic Meetings became so fashionable that they were eventually prosecuted as illegal theatrical performances at the instance of the managers of the Opera House in the Haymarket. This, and mounting indebtedness, brought her career to a temporary halt in 1772, though she subsequently reappeared to manage, with much criticized parsimony, the great regatta held on the Thames in 1775. In 1776, she even attempted to reopen Carlisle House. But by then she seemed to have lost her touch.

In this Mrs Cornelys may have been a victim of the famous Pantheon, built at a cost of £60,000 in Oxford Street, and opened in 1772. Its mighty, neo-classical dome, illuminated by thousands of candles, captivated fashionable taste and handsomely repaid its proprietors. Critics were appalled by its extravagance and pointlessness. Most people, it was observed, simply went to the Pantheon to see and be seen. Soame Jenyns had it in mind when he observed that 'Thousands are collected from the idle and extravagant for seeing dogs, horses, men and monkies perform feats of activity, and, in some places, for the privilege only of seeing one another.'[13] But here as at Ranelagh and Vauxhall, the most important activity going on was the marriage market. At Carlisle House this had sometimes been conducted in a way which seemed a little too gross. 'There, I beheld full many a youthful Maid, like colts for sale to public view display'd', wrote the satirist William Combe.[14] At the Pantheon it seemed that the vulgarity was dimmed and only the politeness illuminated.

The 1770s were marked by an apparently limitless desire for new sensations. The ideal social event, both from the commercial standpoint, and for those who attended, was one which carried an air of exclusiveness while exhibiting to the public at large an extravagant spectacle. The Thames regatta, patronized by princes of the blood, met this criterion. So did elaborate public gardens and firework displays, though some of the latter caused much annoyance in the new suburban surroundings in which they were

[12] *Horace Walpole's Correspondence*, xxiii. 271.
[13] *The Works of Soame Jenyns*, ii. 291–2.
[14] H. W. Hamilton, *Doctor Syntax*, p. 81.

located. One of the more influential innovations of the period was the *fête-champêtre*, the most celebrated of which was held on the marriage of Lord Stanley at his Surrey house, The Oaks, in June 1774. The invitation list was impressive, and there were complaints that the business of Parliament had been suspended so that Lord North and his friends could attend. Stanley took full advantage of the rage for rural fantasy. There were shepherds and peasants, druids and dryads, fairy lights, rustic sports and games. The occasion cried out for a Hogarth to display its ironies. Stanley was a notorious rake and wastrel, remembered in retrospect as the founder of the Derby and the Oaks, rather than as the statesman he aspired to be. His bride was daughter of one of the great beauties of the age, the Duchess of Hamilton (née Elizabeth Gunning); she had been practically dragged to the altar to sustain her mother's social ambitions. The marriage ended disastrously, with Lady Stanley, or Derby, as she became, detected in a lurid affair with the Duke of Dorset, a great cricketer and a great philanderer. Her story, which concluded with the social death of a formal separation and ostracism at court, seemed thoroughly symbolic of the aristocratic life-style of the 1770s. In the mean time the idyll of the Oaks was much imitated, not always with very satisfactory results. In the summer of 1776 Mrs Chapone reported a *fête* in which wind ruined the alfresco breakfast, rain compelled Arcadian haymakers to don English cloaks, and the hired operatic singers failed to arrive.[15] None the less, if the newspapers are to be believed, lowly variants of the *fête-champêtre* were practised by ordinary London families and their servants, if only in the form of glorified picnics on the banks of the Thames.

Display was the most consistent and most disapproved element in the recreations of an age of an extravagance. At its worst it was alleged to produce horrifying foppery and effeminacy. This was the heyday of one of the more bizarre figures in the history of fashion. The macaronis took their origin from a society of enthusiasts for Italian culture who were determined to display their contempt for the values represented by the Beefsteak Club. Their intention, and it was one which many young men of education and rebellious instincts found engaging, was precisely to offend the sober, stuffy insularity which seemed to be the essence of their fathers' patriotism. George Colman satirized the type in his suc-

---

[15] *The Works of Mrs Chapone*, ii. 174–5.

cessful play *Man and Wife* in 1770, stressing absurd affectation in dress, as well as the deliberate flouting of traditional virtues in preference for foreign vices. Thereafter the term came to describe almost any form of folly or excess. There were macaroni lords, macaroni lawyers, macaroni parsons. There were even macaroni soldiers and sailors. An extreme example of the latter was exhibited by Edward Thompson in his adaptation of *The Fair Quaker: or The Humours of the Navy*. His Captain Mizen was one of many 'only fit to seduce their brother officers' wives'. In his cabin he boasted girandole glasses, a fortepiano, a fine Turkey carpet, and a blue damask sofa, all of which had to be protected against the tobacco-spitting of his colleagues. He had two visiting days a week, one for sea lieutenants, one for marine officers, his great object being to reform the service so that every sailor would 'be more polite than our country members of parliament'. His downfall took the form of marriage to a 'Strand bird', or 'Drury nymph', a union into which he was tricked in the belief that she was a Quaker heiress.[16]

Some of Thompson's success with the character arose from his implied warning that the new foppery had infected the very source of martial valour and national honour. But the much feared effeminacy of macaronis was largely a matter of daringly delicate head-dress and artificial nosegays. In practice there was nothing to prevent such affectations going with boisterous and boorish masculinity. Young men with too much money and too few inhibitions prospered in the permissive climate of the years between two great wars. When they ran amok in the university towns or in London they seemed even more undisciplined than generations of their predecessors. They were certainly no less offensive to bourgeois respectability. A London shopkeeper who was awarded £200 damages against an educated ruffian in 1764 won great applause in the press. However, it was daughters who were most at risk, as the anonymous author of the 'Description of the animal called a Buck' pointed out. Bucks were particularly mischievous in the rutting season, which 'unfortunately lasts all the year round'.[17] In the relative social freedom of the late eighteenth century it was precisely this familiarity which was both feared and desired. 'Perdita' Robinson, who, after a polite education, achieved notoriety

[16] (London, 1773), pp. 5, 8, 9, 58.
[17] *London Magazine*, 1764, p. 334.

as the Prince of Wales's first acknowledged mistress, thought
she had been corrupted by the Pantheon itself, that 'circle of
enchantment' where young women underwent 'the gaze of impertinent high breeding'.[18]

The marriage market throve on a delicate balance of sexual
tension and social discipline; not surprisingly those who upset
convention attracted much notoriety. The most sensational episode
of this kind, the Vauxhall Affray, occurred, in an appropriately
inconsequential way, in the eighteenth-century equivalent of the
'silly season', July 1773. It began with insulting looks cast at a
woman escorted by a group of young men in Vauxhall gardens,
and quickly got out of hand. A duel was averted partly because
the principal defender of the lady's honour was a clergyman, Henry
Bate. But Bate was not a conventional cleric. He was a journalist,
and a man about town with literary pretensions. He also shared
the enthusiasm of many of his generation for boxing. His antagonist, the Honourable George Fitzgerald, was a practised duellist
but confessed that 'Nature, Sir, has not cast me in an athletic
mould, nor has the science of bruising had any share in my
gymnastic education.' However, Fitzgerald got his friend Captain
Myles to box against Bate. Not only did Bate resoundingly win
the contest, but it transpired that Myles was actually Fitzgerald's
footman. The newspapers revelled in this bizarre triumph of a
clerical pugilist over a 'little effeminate macaroni', after a Vauxhall
evening of a kind generally found only in novels. And for the
censors of youthful fashion it abounded in promising material for
general application to the folly of the times.[19]

ROYALTY AND MORALITY

Even members of the royal family presented an inviting target to
critics of modish moral laxity. Of George III's brothers and
sisters only Princess Augusta, uncontroversially if not very happily
married to Prince Ferdinand of Brunswick, enjoyed a blameless
reputation. The Duke of York led a raffish social life, marked by
puerile escapades and pranks. The most notorious of his practical
jokes, involving a supposedly docile colt, cost the actor and playwright Samuel Foote a leg. York also irritated the King by his

[18] *Memoirs of the Late Mrs Robinson* (London, 1930), p. 52.
[19] *The Vauxhall Affray; or, the Macaronis Defeated* (London, 1773), p. 31.

political intrigues with the Bedford party. He died prematurely, in September 1767, confessing his past neglect of duty. By then the tragedy of his youngest sister was far advanced. Princess Caroline Matilda had made a disastrous marriage to the young King of Denmark, Christian VII. Her husband suffered from a form of progressive dementia which led him into obscene and bestial exploits. The Queen of Denmark was foolish enough to share her own bed with the chief minister of the Danish court, Struensee. She also shared in his fall when the inevitable palace revolution occurred in January 1772. Only the firm conduct of George III's envoy in Copenhagen, and the mobilization of a naval squadron, secured the Queen's release to safe but tedious exile at Celle in the Hanoverian dominions. Her fate provoked comparison with that of her great-grandmother Sophia Dorothea, whose indiscretion as consort of George I had caused her immurement at Ahlden nearby. The inevitable plotting for a return to Copenhagen inspired interest among romantically inclined adventurers, but the Queen's brother in London, a realistic judge of her part in the calamity of 1772, would have nothing to do with them.

Closer to home, her other brothers, the Dukes of Gloucester and Cumberland, were equally troublesome. Gloucester, the King's favourite, had clandestinely married a celebrated beauty, the widowed Lady Waldegrave, in 1766. The secret was kept well enough to pass muster with the King until 1772, when Lady Waldegrave became pregnant. In the mean time Cumberland was involved in one scrape after another. The worst was his trial in July 1770 for adultery with Lady Grosvenor. It emerged that Cumberland, disguised as a young Welsh squire, had pursued his affair at a number of public houses on the road between London and the Grosvenor family seat in Cheshire. To the delight of the newspapers, witnesses present at the White Hart Inn, St Albans, were called to testify to the lovers' antics. Hardly less salacious and still more risible were Cumberland's love-letters, which duly found their way into the papers. They revealed a wealth of bad spelling and incorrect grammar, not to say embarrassingly fatuous sentiment. Lord Grosvenor's counsel demanded the staggering sum of £100,000 in damages, bearing in mind the 'bad example to the subordinate classes of society'.[20] The court declined to award punitive damages but compensation was set at the exceptionally

[20] *London Magazine*, 1770, pp. 341–56.

high figure of £10,000. The King was mortified, not least because he had to lend his brother the money to pay this bill. Matters did not improve. In November 1771, on an unexpected visit to the King at Richmond Lodge, Cumberland announced his marriage to Mrs Anne Horton, the widowed daughter of a notorious libertine, Lord Irnham. Shortly after this interview and a few days before the *Public Advertiser* got wind of the marriage and reported it, he fled with his bride to France.

Cumberland's marriage and, when it was confirmed, Gloucester's, angered the King as much as anything in his long reign. Some political capital was made of the fact that Mrs Horton was the sister of Henry Lawes Luttrell, Wilkes's supplanter in Middlesex. 'It is now', the *Public Advertiser* observed, 'happily for this country, within the limits of possibility, that a Luttrell may be king of Great Britain'.[21] But George III was less worried by Wilkesite propaganda than by the threat to the purity of his blood. He talked, somewhat wildly, of the dynastic disaster of the Wars of the Roses, conveniently forgetting Tudor and Stuart intermarriage with commoners. Perhaps he had a painful recollection of his dutiful sacrifice of 'the most charming of her sex' Lady Sarah Lennox, for an alliance with the house of Mecklenburg-Strelitz. In any event he made plain his displeasure by demanding legislation to prevent future royal marriages without the consent of the reigning monarch. This caused much disquiet in Parliament. Burke spoke loftily of marriage as a divinely ordained institution, subject only to the laws of nature. At a lower level many otherwise loyal courtiers defended the legitimate aspirations of British parents, and resented the implication that their daughters might do as mistresses but not as wives. Though the Crown's powers under the Royal Marriage Act were confined to members of the royal family below the age of twenty-five, the scope of the statute was extensive, embracing as it did all the descendants of George II. The populist Surrey politician Sir Joseph Mawbey caught the prevailing mood when he suggested it be entitled 'an act for enlarging and extending the prerogative of the crown, and for the encouragement of adultery and fornication'.[22] In the end it

[21] *Junius: including Letters by the Same Writer, under other Signatures (Now First Collected)* (London, 1890), p. 494. J. Cannon, ed., *The Letters of Junius* (Oxford, 1978), pp. 527–8, discusses the possibility that this was the work of Junius.

[22] *London Magazine*, 1772, p. 156.

was carried through both Houses, though at one point the majority in the Commons fell to a mere eighteen.

The indiscretions of the royal princes were humiliating for the King, but they did have the incidentally beneficial effect of accentuating his own domestic virtues. The popular view of his marriage pictured a model of propriety and homeliness, highly suitable for the bringing up of a large family. (Fifteen children were born between 1762 and 1783, all but two of whom lived beyond infancy.) After 1777 when the King and Queen began to spend much time at Windsor, dabbled in farming, and generally adopted a style of life somewhat resembling that of a country squire's family, cartoonists enjoyed depicting them as Farmer George and his wife. In fact a more accurate analogy might have been drawn with the countless middle-class households who saw in the royal couple the living embodiment of respectable family life. Like all monarchs George III lived among aristocrats; but he made no attempt to adopt the grand manner. St James's Palace, in the dust of London, was used only for ceremonial purposes and was allowed gently to decay. The royal residence in the metropolis was far from impressive: the Queen's House (later Buckingham Palace) was bought on account of its open situation among green fields for £28,000 in 1762. In an unconsciously symbolic act, the palaces of the Revolution monarchs, Hampton Court and Kensington, were abandoned, in preference for a somewhat motley collection of buildings at Kew and later for Windsor.

The unpretentiousness of life in the royal household is confirmed by the most authoritative source for the early years, the diary of Lady Mary Coke. Both the King and Queen led abstemious and well-regulated lives. Nothing worse than a little card-playing was ever alleged against either of them, and Queen Charlotte was positively strait-laced. At an early stage in her marriage, with the aid of her old nurse, Madame Schwellenberg, she established a firm ascendancy over the court ladies. According to some of them this came close to tyranny. Lapses from the highest standards of sexual propriety and marital fidelity were strongly disapproved, and the gulf between aristocratic mores in the West End and the conventions observed at court grew immense. It was not only for the ambitious widows who had trapped Cumberland and Gloucester that the royal enmity proved implacable.

The Queen also battled hard, if somewhat unavailingly, against

French frippery, bestowing her patronage puritanically as well as patriotically on sober English goods. When fashion absolutely required submission to the *mode*, as in the rage for polonaises with daringly low-cut waistcoats in 1775, the impact was reduced, and no doubt the aesthetic effect somewhat endangered, by the Queen's insistence on wearing hers with high stiff stays to preserve royal modesty. She was lauded as a true First Lady and a model of womanhood by the moralizers and sermonizers. The King's unfailing fidelity and piety seemed even more remarkable. 'Not Alfred's self could ever be, More *dully* regular than He!'[23] Bourgeois respectability and prudery were rising stocks in the 1760s and 1770s and they did not suffer by the subscription of such eminent persons.

ARISTOCRATIC VICE

Contemporaries thought they had an objective yardstick of the deterioration of moral standards in the growing demand for divorce. It is not easy to share their confidence. Divorce was a cumbersome procedure involving both a hearing before an ecclesiastical court and a private Act of Parliament. It was available only to the rich and its incidence was very rare. Applications for divorce bills certainly increased in the early 1770s, giving rise to concern among the bishops. However, when the Lords debated the problem in 1771, it was the speech of Lord Pomfret, a backwoods peer who was not known for mincing matters, which attracted most attention. He complained bitterly that 'they got no business done that session, on account of these damn'd divorces. Every wife (sayd he) that can creep into a back room or a corner is a whore. They are always fresh from this business—morning and evening—noon and night. They go to it with the keenness of the wren, and with the quickness of the sparrow.'[24] Shute Barrington, a well-connected courtier and Bishop of Llandaff, sought to turn this kind of anxiety into legislative action. Twice, in 1771 and 1779, a bill was carried through the upper house only to fail in the lower. The main provision would have made it illegal for the 'guilty' parties in a divorce case subsequently to marry. Critics thought this distinctly hard on women, who were likely to be the main sufferers by such

---

[23] *Satire for the King's Birth-Day* (London, 1779), p. 11.
[24] *London Magazine*, 1772, p. 403.

a prohibition. Charles James Fox observed that it seemed 'very unjust to serve the ladies as we had done the Americans, punish them without representation'.[25] It was also far from certain that the proposed legislation would have much effect. Lord Effingham, who earned some cheap popularity when he refused to go with his regiment to fight in America and was not unknown for his exploits in the bedchamber, sarcastically suggested that potential adulterers would be more deterred if they were compelled to marry, rather than prohibited from marrying. In any event divorce applications diminished again in the 1780s, as inexplicably as they had increased.

More impressive than the divorce rate was the widespread conviction, of which Pomfret's outburst was merely an example, that responsibility for falling standards lay very largely with women. The author of *The Female Congress* in 1779 linked 'the frequent violations of the marriage bed, and the rising licentiousness of female manners, which in our days have dishonoured *Britain*'.[26] However, identifying the culprits was not the same as isolating the cause, and on this opinions varied. One explanation concerned the changing relationship of women with their doctors. No doubt much of the hostility to the growing use of male gynaecologists arose from the vested interest of midwives. But the resulting bickering gave the moralists a field-day. Medical students, it was pointed out, only knew the female body from anatomical specimens. Confronted with the living reality, nature would prove too much for them. 'When a man is in free possession of the citadel, and all the out-works surrendered at discretion, it is then too late to attempt guarding the town from plunder.' A few doctors might be able to resist temptation. In particular, exception was made for the eminent gynaecologist William Hunter, 'by the help of his cold constitution and dint of very long practice'. Even in such a case, however, women patients tended to lose all sense of modesty and in their enthusiasm for '*dear* Doctor Hunter', '*angelick* Doctor ...', '*enchanting* Doctor ...' quickly fell victim to less scrupulous men.[27]

These anxieties were symptomatic of a wider fear concerning the uses to which fashionable women might put their increasingly extensive liberties. In a notable reversal of the usual logic, it was

---

[25] Ibid. 1779, p. 267.
[26] p. viii.
[27] *London Magazine*, 1772, pp. 225–8.

thought that they might be corrupted by the example of their inferiors. Politely brought up women might join in a 'jovial sisterhood, unable to endure with patience the restraint the imaginary laws of honour laid them under, while they saw the amorous shoeboy and the happy cinder-wench roll down the hill at *Greenwich* Park together; resolved on the same scene of happiness'.[28] Whatever the inducements there was considerable agreement about the consequences. Particularly in London, where the paternalism and purity of the countryside were unavailable to curb female sexuality, feminine virtue seemed to be a thing of the past, as Edward Thompson, whose art was a curious mixture of the censorious and sentimental, pointed out. His poems *The Meretriciad* and *The Demi-Rep* were immensely popular when they first appeared in the 1760s and were much reprinted thereafter. Thompson knew the Town well and exploited his knowledge to great effect. He spoke of a capital city infested with over-sexed 'Dames', of footmen employed for their sexual prowess, of hypocritical maids who each year spent a time in 'those convenient places of the town, where Maiden Ladies lay their bantlings down'. He also held out chaste models of womanhood, readers of Langhorne's pure and limpid verse, and attenders at fashionable charity sermons, who were seduced from the duties of wife and mother by the corrupt atmosphere of the city in which they lived. He even hinted at sodomy and incest.[29]

The vulnerability of women to the temptations and pressures of an age of vanity seemed infinite. But if they were blue-blooded women there was all the more interest in their fate. The monthly magazines never tired of printing portraits of court ladies and society beauties with accounts of their lives and conquests which ranged from the indelicate to the downright defamatory. The same could be said of their husbands and lovers. In the late 1770s, there was published a number of more or less 'complete peerages', with identities thinly disguised and exploits described at length. This seems to have started in earnest with the poet William Combe, himself something of a macaroni in an earlier, more prosperous phase of his career. Combe's *Diaboliad* of 1777 was a poetic fantasy concerning the election in Hell of an heir apparent to Satan. The

---

[28] *London Magazine*, 1780, p. 253.
[29] *The Demi-Rep* (2nd edn., London [1766]), pp. 9, 11, 13–14, 21; *The Meretriciad* (4th edn., London, 1763).

main candidates included personal enemies of Combe's but also some notorious rakes, led by that Lord Irnham whose daughter had married the Duke of Cumberland. This vein of low literature was worked for some years and yielded considerable rewards to Combe and his many imitators in the art of mass libel. Its success derived in part from the factual support which the great scandals of the period seemed to provide.

Those looking for evidence of aristocratic delinquency were delighted by the trial of the Duchess of Kingston for bigamy in 1776. The Duchess was found guilty of contracting an illegal union with the Duke in 1769 but claimed that she had reason to believe her earlier marriage with Augustus Hervey (later Earl of Bristol) had been dissolved. She was found guilty but pleaded her privilege as a peeress to evade punishment, and fled abroad to escape abuse. It was tempting to make comparisons with the trial earlier, in 1768, of Lord Baltimore for rape. Baltimore's case had a special interest in that it promised a real life enactment of the plot of *Pamela*. He was charged with abducting a milliner named Miss Woolnoth, whom he carried off to his country residence at Epsom and after many attempts at seduction, raped. As the victim unfolded her story in court public interest became intense: she was a Dissenter and the newspapers took evident pleasure in her picturesque biblical language. Baltimore's London home was attacked and severely damaged by a mob, and all seemed set for a most satisfying indictment of aristocratic vice. Regrettably, nature refused to imitate art. Evidence was presented which suggested the complicity of Miss Woolnoth and her family, and Baltimore was exonerated. Even so, like the Duchess of Kingston, he found the prominence afforded by popular prurience more than he could stand. He left shortly afterwards for Italy and died there in 1771.

A no less convincing aristocratic villain was the notorious Lord Lyttelton, who earned high marks from Combe as a potential prince of evil. Lyttelton was arguably no more remarkable than many other rakehells of the 1770s but his offence was heightened by the contrast with his father George, Lord Lyttelton, who had been considered the embodiment of refinement, culture, and piety in the higher reaches of society. On the Grand Tour the young Lyttelton acquired an awesome reputation for excess and debauchery, even by the standards of rich Englishmen abroad. Later he sought a degree of respectability, with a view to a political career, but his earlier misdeeds were not forgotten when he died prematurely, at the age of thirty-five, in 1779. Shortly before his death he had told his friends of an apparition which had warned him that he had not long to live. The press was naturally intrigued. Medical authorities were not wanting to point out the physical strain imposed by a dissolute youth and there was clear evidence of prolonged ill health in Lyttelton's last months. But not all were convinced by such rationality. There were hints of a Faustian compact in so strange a story. At the very least Lyttelton's death provided confirmation of the dire fate which attended dark deeds.

Not many opponents of aristocratic vice can have expected their enemies to offer a barefaced defence of dissolute habits. But this was what seemed to have happened when the Earl of Chesterfield's letters to his natural son Philip Stanhope were published in 1774. There were 430 letters, written over a period of thirty years and providing a complete system of education for the man of fashion. Dr Johnson was provoked to make one of his most celebrated and crushing judgements, describing it as teaching 'the morals of a whore, and the manners of a dancing master'.[30] Defenders pointed out that the letters contained much that was good sense and morally unexceptionable. But what made most impact at the time was the controversial advice as to sexual relationships. Chesterfield's opinion was that deceitful affairs in high society were infinitely to be preferred to 'low company, and their low vices'. The pleasures of 'high life, and in good company (though possibly in themselves not more moral), are more delicate, more refined, less dangerous, and less disgraceful; and, in the common course of things, not reckoned disgraceful at all'.[31] These views did not appeal to a public enraptured by Mackenzie's *Man of Feeling*, published only three years before. Chesterfield's snobbery controverted the notion of gentility by nature. His emphasis on calculation challenged the primacy of unaffected feeling. Above all, his recommendation of dissimulation simply outraged the moral earnestness of the sentimentalists. Distressingly, the son had practised only the deceitfulness, for when he died in 1768 it emerged that he had clandestinely married a low-born Irishwoman. It was she, Eugenia

---

[30] *Boswell's Life of Johnson*, i. 266.

[31] B. Dobrée, ed., *The Letters of Philip Dormer Stanhope, 4th Earl of Chesterfield* (6 vols., London, 1932), iv. 1536.

Stanhope, who, after Chesterfield's own death, sold the letters to the publisher Dodsley, to the chagrin of the Earl's executors.

Of the many attacks on Chesterfield's principles the most instructive in retrospect is Samuel Jackson Pratt's *The Pupil of Pleasure*, a satire appropriate for what Pratt called an 'age of voluptuousness'. His story was set in the newly fashionable spa of Buxton, 'a place of politeness', and described the seduction of an honest curate's wife by a cynical young practitioner of Chesterfieldian maxims. The emphasis was on the dangers of ethical self-deception: 'Where then the ruin?' asked the villain Philip Sedley, when he reflected that the curate would know nothing of his wife's infidelity. But the author also asserted the morally blinding effect of upper-class refinement and artificiality. The wife Harriet Homespun was brought by Sedley to despise her husband's gauche manner, his inability to handle a knife and fork gracefully, his habit of eating bread and butter from the side not the end, his drinking tea from the saucer rather than the cup, his insistence on ignoring the *ton* by turning up his cup rather than laying a spoon across it when he had finished. Even after the fateful seduction she could only lament 'having thrown away my charms upon a country curate, that does not know how to behave in company—who is unable to carve a chicken, or lead his wife into a ball-room, without hanging down his head and biting his nails'. The conclusion of this tale was tragic, though morally satisfying. She came to a sad end, eventually realizing her shame and dying of it; her seducer to a bad end, killed in a duel by the husband of another of his victims.[32]

DUELLING

Death in this manner was appropriate, for duelling was also a favourite target of contemporary moralists, and similarly associated with high society. Many of the arguments adduced were familiar. 'Appeals to heaven' were a form of blasphemy, since a benevolent deity could never have intended such barbarism. Justice could only be served incidentally, for the duel was at best equivalent to throwing dice and at worst a test of skill at murder. And how could it be honourable to kill the husband of the woman one had seduced when, as custom required, he issued a challenge in defence of his

[32] (2nd edn., London, 1777), pp. vii, 103, 130, 134.

own honour? Such reasoning had a long and unavailing history. But some new twists were given to the argument. Antiquarians confidently traced duelling and the 'phantom honour' on which it depended to a primitive society bereft of strong legal institutions and dominated by feudal magnates. Modern legal theory left little room for such outmoded practices. No theory of punishment could make death appropriate for the trivial offences which often gave rise to affairs of honour, nor did a duel reform the offender (assuming he lived) or compensate the sufferer (assuming he lived). Above all, how could public law, the law of the community, be respected, if highly placed individuals invented laws for themselves?[33]

In an age of benevolence these arguments were unanswerable. Indeed in public virtually no one attempted to answer them. But the incidence of duelling was not noticeably reduced. In fact there were many well-publicized fights in the 1760s and 1770s, some involving distinguished peers such as the Duke of Grafton, Lord George Germain, the Earl of Shelburne, and Viscount Townshend. On one occasion Lord Stormont, British ambassador to the French court, became embroiled in a quarrel with a French prince of the blood royal. He was extracted from the embarrassment of an international duel only after delicate diplomatic negotiation. The example of such men exacerbated the problem but they were hardly the cause of it. Political duels were relatively uncommon. Both Houses of Parliament did their best to prevent them, and contemporaries sometimes expressed surprise that political quarrels did not more frequently lead to bloodshed. In local politics duelling would have made for carnage at election time but there was never much likelihood of this happening. In a rare case in 1763, the Court of King's Bench stamped heavily on a duellist in Monmouthshire foolhardy enough to challenge a knight of the shire.[34]

It was among young men with military training or connections, that the practice proved virtually impossible to control. Critics pointed out that the nineteenth article of war specifically forbade duelling.[35] But this was a dead letter: senior officers connived at duels to settle debts of honour. Military notions of justice did not

[33] *Sentimental Magazine*, 1773, pp. 204–5.
[34] *London Magazine*, 1763, p. 277.
[35] Lewis Lochée, *An Essay on Military Education* (2nd edn., London, 1776), p. 34.

correspond with civilian theory. In the army the vindication of personal honour was considered crucial to the maintenance of officer morale and enterprise. The court martial itself was as much a means of defending reputations as of punishing indiscipline—it would have occurred to few civilians to seek trial in a court of justice in the way that many officers demanded a court martial to clear their name. Against such customs it was perhaps futile to reason. Certainly the most offensive cases, precisely those which fuelled opposition to the practice, had a marked military complexion.

The two most notorious duellists of the period were both army officers: 'Tyger' Roche, and 'Fighting' Fitzgerald. Captain Roche was a young desperado who had a connection with Wilkes and had stood as candidate at the famous Middlesex contest between Wilkes and Luttrell, when he achieved the distinction of registering no votes at all. His own hour came in 1773 when he got into a series of quarrels with fellow officers aboard a vessel on its way to India. According to his version of what happened, the honour of both his own wife and Wilkes's daughter had been called in question by a 'faction of Scotchmen'. There were many who regarded picking quarrels with Scotsmen as a patriotic duty in the early years of George III's reign. While ashore at the Cape Roche contrived to kill one of his antagonists in what looked suspiciously like a premeditated act of butchery. He was eventually brought back to London for trial in 1775, and found not guilty by a complaisant jury.[36]

Roche's contemporary George Fitzgerald was even more notorious. Though humiliated by the clerical pugilist in the Vauxhall Affray, Fitzgerald was a skilled user of more deadly weapons. He had fought eleven duels by the age of twenty-four (it was said that brain damage caused by one of these accounted for his later recklessness) and many extraordinary stories were recounted of him, including the claim that when put up for Brooks's he was blackballed by every member, but that none would tell him for fear of having to fight. For many years he led a charmed life, until, eventually, he went home to Ireland. Following a series of wild escapades arising from a violent feud with his father and brother, he was executed for murder.[37]

[36] *A Plain and Circumstantial Account of the Transactions between Captain Roche and Lieutenant Ferguson* (London, 1775); *London Magazine*, 1775, p. 375.
[37] J. Ashton, *Eighteenth-Century Waifs* (London, 1887), pp. 141–9.

Hardened duellists like Roche and Fitzgerald flourished for so long not merely because they were nurtured and protected by a military code, but also because the ordinary law found it difficult to reach them. Possibly the not so respectable elements to be seen on common juries conspired with military tradition. Unless there was evidence that a duellist had offended against his own rules of honour he was unlikely to be convicted. Typical was the case reported at Kingston Assizes in 1780. Mr Justice Gould clearly told the jury 'there could be no honour in so savage a custom'. Yet the accused, who had killed his opponent, and argued subsequently that the deceased had been interfering in another man's quarrel, was convicted of manslaughter and escaped with a derisory £10 fine.[38]

ARISTOCRATIC POWER

It is tempting to see in criticism of blue-blooded delinquents the beginnings of a systematic campaign against aristocracy and the values which it represented. 'Chesterfieldism' was particularly provoking in this respect. As the essayist Vicesimus Knox put it, 'nothing has of late militated more powerfully against nobility than the publication of Lord Chesterfield's letters ... Lord Chesterfield has let us all behind the scenes: he invites us to see the peer dress for public exhibition.'[39] The glimpse thus afforded was certainly unedifying and there were not wanting critics to cast doubt on the validity of hereditary honours. The *Patricians* in 1773 argued, that '*birth* alone has no pretence, To truth, or honour, dignity, or sense.'[40] Another review of the life style adopted by peers, *Ways and Means* of 1782, floated the idea of a wholesale auction of peers, and having examined their failings in unpleasant detail, concluded that the nation would get little return on its investment in a hereditary aristocracy. In politics there was always an undercurrent of republican distaste for the House of Lords, which surfaced at times of turbulence. Catherine Macaulay, in her onslaught on the Rockingham Whigs in 1770, treated the vested interest of great noblemen as an affront to Harringtonian values at least as great as

---

[38] *London Magazine*, 1780, p. 187.
[39] *The Works of Vicesimus Knox*, v. 116–17.
[40] *The Patricians: or, A Candid Examination into the Merits of the Principal Speakers of the House of Lords* (London, 1773), p. 4.

that represented by the corruption at the command of the Crown. A decade later, the orientalist William Jones, writing on behalf of the Society of Constitutional Information, warned, 'lest by reducing the regal power to its just level, we raise the aristocratical to a dangerous height'.[41] Such anxieties were widely entertained. Many of the county Associators involved in the reform agitation of the early 1780s proved extremely wary of magnates, even of those who promised support.

The feeling that aristocratic influence was getting stronger during this period was probably mistaken. If peers controlled more constituencies at the end of the eighteenth century, when reformers first began conducting systematic surveys, it was as much a result of the deliberate expansion of the peerage in the 1780s and 1790s as of a tendency to electoral oligarchy. In parliamentary boroughs the inroads of 'nabobs', contractors, and other carpet-baggers were frequently made at the expense of local families. In the corrupt constituency of Shaftesbury, for instance, the rocketing cost of elections forced both the Earl of Ilchester and the Earl of Shaftesbury to withdraw from a town which they had long dominated and fought over. The fact was that the price of a parliamentary seat was rising faster than the income even of improving landlords. In the counties, always a sensitive barometer to the standing of the magnates, there was little sign of heightened aristocratic dominance. Despite the large number of county election contests in the 1760s and 1770s, only in three counties was there real conflict between a noble family seeking to increase its electoral influence and the community of gentry and freeholders. In Wiltshire in 1772 the Earl of Pembroke permitted his cousin to hoist the Wilton banner for the first time in many years. Two years later in Northumberland, the Duke of that name, a parvenu who owed his elevation to a fortunate marriage with the heiress of the Percies, sought to fill both county seats. Less ambitiously but no less controversially, a Duke of Rutland in 1775 ventured to interfere in Leicestershire for the first time since the election of 1741. Significantly, in all three cases aristocratic intrusion was indignantly repelled. Using the name Herbert, Percy, or Manners, it seemed, was more likely to harm than help a candidate.

---

[41] Lord Teignmouth, *Memoirs of the Life, Writings, and Correspondence, of Sir William Jones* (London, 1804), p. 209.

Elsewhere the great families rested on their laurels and often observed an ostentatious neutrality. In Derbyshire the house of Cavendish remained content with its claim to one of the county seats, first successfully asserted in 1734, and in the contest of 1768 declined to become involved. Similarly in Sussex the Duke of Richmond refused to join in the contested election of 1774. Such instances belie much of the rhetoric of the period. Objections were raised to the influence of members of the House of Lords in elections to the House of Commons. In 1780 the Duke of Chandos found himself denounced in the lower house for his part in the Hampshire contest of the preceding year. His friends countered with similar accusations against his rival the Duke of Bolton. This currency was old and long since debased. The truth was that magnates continued to enjoy their traditional influence in the county community, often providing leadership and a rallying point for great coalitions of electoral interests. But in most counties power lay with the country gentlemen or indeed with the small freeholders who required much wooing, especially in the towns. The popularity of the watchword 'independence' in the late eighteenth century can easily suggest a reaction against excessive aristocratic activity in county society and politics. But independence was a meaningless slogan. Nobody would oppose independence any more than advocate sin. As a rhetorical device its object was to distance politicians from the very corruption which most of them employed but which was so offensive to the public morality of the age. As a pointer to anti-aristocratic feeling, it is worthless.

The sanctity attaching to property in the eighteenth century made it highly unlikely that there would be much interest in punitive taxation or the redistribution of wealth. None the less arguments were dredged up from time to time, mainly from republican sources, in opposition to the immense concentrations of wealth represented by the great landowning families. John Brown, author of the celebrated *Estimate*, pointed out that commercial development actually facilitated the accumulation of wealth in landed hands.[42] A *loi agraire* to govern the distribution of property had attractions for radical critics of the status quo. Thomas Spence of Newcastle even designed a utopian scheme for

---

[42] *An Estimate of the Manners and Principles of the Times* (London, 1757), p. 156.

common ownership of land in 1775.[43] Projects of this kind attracted little interest and virtually no support.

Whether the great families were actually increasing their share of the nation's wealth was and is far from certain. Local studies suggest that aristocratic aggrandizement, at least in terms of the growth of the great estate as the dominant feature of the English agriculture, is a historical mirage which disappears when subjected to close inspection.[44] In Buckinghamshire, for example, the great landowners seemed particularly active in the early eighteenth century. Yet in 1784 the top thirty propertied families in the county paid almost exactly the same proportion of the land tax as the top thirty had in 1650.[45] Major landowners were naturally well placed to exploit the opportunities offered by agricultural improvement, but the part which they played can seem more important than it actually was. The propagandists for the new agriculture had an obvious interest in exaggerating it. Moreover, the consolidation of estates gave a thoroughly misleading impression. Intensive estate management worked best on compact holdings within a convenient distance for supervision. Remote properties, often acquired by marriage or by dynastic accident, were expensive to oversee and difficult to control. There were also political considerations. A few votes in a distant county brought only embarrassing requests for the exertion of pressure on tenants whom it might be particularly difficult to manipulate. Consolidation maximized influence in local affairs, enhanced the standing of the landowner, and in elections or in patronage negotiations, brought the highest possible return, especially from men at Whitehall and Westminster primarily impressed by the size and weight of local influence. Families like the Cokes of Norfolk and the Temples of Stowe consciously sought to sacrifice distant holdings in return for acquisitions nearer to home, with important consequences for politics in Norfolk and Buckinghamshire respectively.[46] The result

[43] P. M. Ashraf, *The Life and Times of Thomas Spence* (Newcastle, 1983), pp. 120–3.

[44] The thesis of substantial growth of great estates was first developed in a celebrated article: H. J. Habakkuk, 'English Landownership, 1690–1740', *Ec. Hist. Rev.*, 10 (1939–40), 2–17. It has been subjected to circumspect but weighty criticism: see Bibliography, p. 752.

[45] Buckinghamshire Record Office, Land-Tax Assessments for 1784 and list of property-owners in Richard Grenville's notebook, c.1650.

[46] R. A. C. Parker, *Coke of Norfolk: A Financial and Agricultural Study, 1707–1842* (Oxford, 1975), pp. 27, 37–8.

was certainly to enhance the family's local importance, but it did not necessarily imply a real increase either in acres or disposable wealth.

Landowners were notable investors in the mining mania stimulated by the fuel needs of a growing population and expanding industry. But mining was naturally associated with the ownership of land, and there is no evidence that men of broad acres played a disproportionately large part in other sectors of speculative or commercial enterprise. On the contrary, where statistics are available, as in the case of canal investment, they merely confirm the important but far from dominating role played by large property-owners in the areas affected.[47] Turnpike trusts, drainage schemes, enclosure projects, all attracted the landowner's attention but not beyond what might be expected given his evident interest in investment so intimately connected with the rural economy. Urban growth, admittedly, brought windfall profits, but only to the few who owned property in the right places. Families like the Grosvenors and Russells were not displaying exceptional commercial aggression and enterprise in seeking to exploit the very obvious advantages of land-holdings on the edge of a rapidly expanding London. In fact the Dukes of Bedford were slow to exploit the potential of their estate. Great Russell Street remained part of the northern frontier of London for practically a century before the fourth Duke's wife authorized the development of Bedford Square in 1775. By then the Bloomsbury estate was already bringing in over £9,000, nearly a third of the family's rental income from all sources. Forty-four years later its London profits were to exceed all its very considerable country receipts.[48] Such enterprise was matched by many others, including less likely powerhouses of capitalist expansion, such as municipal and ecclesiastical corporations. In the last quarter of the century the development of the Finsbury estate in north London, in which both the City and the Prebendary of Finsbury had interests, is as striking an example of urban property speculation as the better-known activities of the Russells.

---

[47] J. R. Ward, *The Finance of Canal Building in Eighteenth-Century England*, ch. vi.

[48] D. J. Olsen, *Town Planning in London: The Eighteenth and Nineteenth Centuries* (New Haven, 1964), ch. 4, appendix 1.

ARISTOCRATIC INFLUENCE

More sensitive than the question of wealth was that of patronage. It is hardly surprising that a peerage was closely associated with access to a vast range of offices and openings.[49] In the royal household, even in government itself, peers had always been highly favoured and were to continue so until well into the nineteenth century. Resentment may have owed more to intensified competition generally than to a higher real incidence of aristocratic jobbery. Complaints about career prospects in the army inevitably dwelt on the superior advantages of wealthy young noblemen, particularly those who appeared so prominently in fashionable Guards and cavalry regiments. But the competitive pressure which helped give rise to such complaints also stemmed from mounting investments of bourgeois wealth in a genteel military career. Rather more specific allegations concerned the Church. Here there is little reason to doubt that advowsons owned by peers, as by gentry generally, were increasingly bestowed on their own families rather than on their inferiors and dependants. At parish level as well as in the higher ecclesiastical echelons, particularly the cathedral chapters, the title 'Honourable and Reverend' became distinctly more common. In the 1760s and 1770s there was a crop of blue-blooded bishops in the House of Lords. Well known noble names, Lyttelton, Keppel, Yorke, North, and Cornwallis, graced the bench. Yet its complexion remained socially mixed.[50] George III was a conscientious promoter of merit rather than a tool of his courtiers, and he stipulated genteel origins only in a high-placed household post such as the Deanery of Windsor. Of the four bishops chosen in the 'bumper year' 1769 only one, Shute Barrington, brother of the Secretary of War and son of an Irish peer, could plausibly be described as being of high birth. The three others, Edmund Law, John Hinchcliffe, and Jonathan Shipley were sons, respectively, of a poor schoolmaster, a Westminster livery stable keeper, and a London stationer.

It was plainly possible to resist aristocratic demands, but the demands themseves were mounting. The eldest sons of peers rarely sought an official career: their principal duty before succeeding to the title was to make a good marriage, and perhaps to lay the

[49] J. Cannon, *Aristocratic Century: The Peerage of Eighteenth-Century England* (Cambridge, 1984), esp. ch. 4.
[50] See pp. 262–3.

basis of a political 'interest'. Younger sons were another matter, representing as they did a great potential drain on the resources of landed families. There is no evidence that the eighteenth-century obsession with primogeniture led to greater ruthlessness on the part of harassed fathers. On the contrary, financial provision for younger children of both sexes was one of the constant pre-occupations of aristocratic parents and rising standards of living if anything made more generous treatment necessary. But for sons access to patronage provided an invaluable source of support and it needed only a small increase in the number of such well-born young men to intensify competition for jobs. Demographic change added to the social tensions created by the shortage of patronage. Mortality in aristocratic families was forbiddingly high in the early eighteenth century, and comparable to that affecting the population at large. But improvements in medical techniques, in hygiene, and in living conditions, particularly benefited the opulent. Aristocratic life expectancy increased markedly in the middle of the century.[51] The patronage system was inevitably affected.

The resulting pressures are easily demonstrated. In 1734 there were twenty sons of earls in the army, navy, or Church: fifteen of these were the children of only four peers, the Earls of Plymouth, Bristol, Harborough, and Albemarle. Albemarle represented a newly ennobled Dutch family which traced back to the reign of William III a tradition of diplomatic and military service. Plymouth, Bristol, and Harborough were all impoverished peers with large families. Fifty years later there were thirty-five sons of earls in official service. They were widely distributed among families and reflected the higher survival rate of aristocratic children. The total numbers involved were relatively small, but the earls were only one rank of the peerage and a seventy-five per cent increase in their sons' demand for a lucrative career indicated a considerable stiffening of competition for the patronage provided by the State.[52] It is noteworthy that in the same period the sons of earls did not appear more prominently in Parliament, despite long-standing concern about aristocratic infiltration of the lower

---

[51] T. H. Hollingsworth, 'The Demography of the British peerage', Population Studies, 18 (1964), suppl.

[52] The earls are cited because they included at any one time a very small proportion of the newly ennobled, whose 'aristocratic' credentials are open to question. Statistics for the peerage as a whole necessarily include those recruited to the baronage from the ranks of commoners.

house. Seats in the Commons were subject to market economics. Commissions in the army and livings in the Church, while in principle open to allcomers with money, offered the aristocracy more opportunity for the exploitation of favour and patronage.

Paradoxically, contemporary suspicions of a tendency to oligarchy were strengthened by the more or less fixed size of the peerage as a class. Despite growing wealth and a marked rise in living standards in the middle of the century, admission to this class remained a carefully guarded privilege, open only to real plutocrats, or to those whose services in public life, especially in law or in politics, gave them strong claims on ministers and monarchs. In the thirty years before 1750 the peerage of Great Britain (that is, excluding Scottish and Irish peers) had increased by only three to a total of 181. Between 1750 and 1783 there were ninety-eight further creations. But of these, thirty-two were elevations from one rank to another, and the rest were largely counterbalanced by peerages which became extinct. The result was a net increase of only four during the period 1750–83. George III was as miserly as his grandfather in this respect. He complained bitterly about the way he was pestered for peerages, and did his best to resist the importunities of ministers and courtiers. Lord North's political needs during the American War brought the first signs of an expansion which was to be a notable feature of the years after 1784. The relative stability in the House of Lords, which lasted throughout the early Hanoverian period, contrasts very strikingly with other periods. In the seventeenth century the peerage had more than doubled. In the nineteenth century it was to expand enormously. Yet the exclusiveness of the aristocracy in the mid-eighteenth century seems not to have been associated with an obvious hardening of its social arteries. The extent to which peers married outside their own class is a subject of historical controversy. What is not in doubt is that they were notably less prone to do so in the seventeenth than the eighteenth century.[53] Increasingly, the hunt for good dowries and wealthy fathers-in-law took precedence over snobbish prejudices or the quest for a perfect pedigree.

The tensions created by an aristocracy, even an aristocracy that shared fully in contemporary prosperity and was not afraid to utilize its status, remained, by one means and another, well under

[53] See J. Cannon, *Aristocratic Century*, ch. 3.

control in Georgian England. The absence of anything resembling
a caste was one of the most vaunted features of English society,
endlessly extolled by foreign visitors. Why did peers have no tax
exemptions, they enquired? Why did they pay turnpike tolls like
anyone else? Why were their property rights indistinguishable
from those of other Englishmen? Why were their exclusive legal
privileges so restricted? Even aristocrats themselves sometimes
seemed reluctant to employ all their rights. Lord Chesterfield
aroused much interest in 1776 when, at the trial of Dr Dodd, he
waived his right to give his word on honour rather than on oath,
sooner than draw unpopularity upon himself. The fact was that
even the peers perceived the advantages which they derived from
their immersion in a society where wealth rather than landownership or hereditary rank determined status. The influence
which they possessed was shared with a much larger class—one
which, for all its power, was difficult to define at the edges. There
were a few impecunious peers, like the last Viscount Say and Sele,
who claimed that he could not afford to live in London to attend
the House of Lords, and there were a number who, like the fourth
Earl of Cholmondeley, enjoyed 'but a small fortune for an earl',
as Horace Walpole put it. With an annual income of £2,500
Cholmondeley reckoned that he could not afford to maintain his
country seat.[54] Many country gentlemen could outpoint peers in
riches, political influence, and lavish life-style; so could some of
the merchant princes of London and the great cities.

The aristocracy was so divided politically that it was in little
danger of acquiring a 'dyed in the wool' appearance, whatever the
prevailing tone of its politics. In this respect the consistent tendency of the Lords to support the Crown and its ministers was
somewhat misleading. The twenty-six bishops and sixteen elected
Scottish peers played a large part in maintaining government
majorities in the upper house. Without them, the built-in loyalty
of the Lords would have been questionable. There was always a
substantial body of peers in opposition, some of them, in the case
of the Rockingham Whigs, amongst the greatest magnates in the
realm. Others were far from being the disappointed courtiers
denounced by Catherine Macaulay. In the 1770s and 1780s there
were several aristocratic firebrands who gave strong support to
the demands of reformers, including the Dukes of Richmond and

[54] *Horace Walpole's Correspondence*, xxiii. 217.

Manchester and Lord Mahon, later Earl Stanhope. The young Earl of Abingdon yielded nothing to the metropolitan reformers in zeal, and proved a powerful adversary of moderate Whigs like Edmund Burke. The political pluralism of such a class made it difficult to develop a consistent grudge. To oppose a duke who spent his days at court was one thing; to outface one at a freeholders' meeting, or in a reforming society, was quite another.

If, then, there was sometimes an anti-aristocratic tone to contemporary social criticism its object was reform rather than revolution. In an acquisitive society there was still need for the men of blue blood and broad acres, provided (a crucial provision) they shared the values of that society. Inherited wealth was no obstacle and indeed attracted greater respect when increased further. The Duke of Bridgewater was described in his obituary as 'the benefactor of his country. By his active spirit and his unshaken perseverance, he amassed immense wealth. But the public grew rich with him; and his labours were not more profitable to himself, than they were to his country'.[55] Arthur Young praised improving aristocratic landlords to the skies, while boasting that in doing so he deliberately placed them alongside ingenious farmers and mechanically minded tradesmen. The Marquess of Rockingham's farming experiments at Wentworth Woodhouse were valued far above his political activities; and in Young's favourite county of Norfolk the third Earl of Orford was awarded marks for his interest in matters of utility: 'leave the lieutenancy of a county, the rangership of a park, and the honours of the bedchamber, to those in whose eyes such baubles are respectable. I would rather dwell on the merit of the first importer of South down sheep into Norfolk.'[56] Noblemen who sought the role of leader on such terms were eminently acceptable. In subscription lists for learned books, appealing charities, moral causes, they were welcomed, less for the money they contributed than the example they set. Every charity, county infirmary, agricultural or learned society, looked better with a peer at its head or a good stock of peers on its council.

There remained room for the old patriarchalism, particularly in the context of agrarian society, when election contests or an heir's coming of age stimulated great rallies of rural tenantry and their labourers. But the new pageantry of urban, bourgeois England was developing fast, subtly transforming the role of noblemen as principal gentlemen, without their fully realizing it. Ostentatious display was still permissible, but display which suggested commitment to an open, equal society rather than one which savoured of lordly superiority. The point was strongly made by James 'Athenian' Stuart, one of the many writers who criticized the nobility's contribution to the architectural heritage of London. Tucked away behind gloomy walls and enclosed courtyards, the palaces of the great offered nothing to less exalted inhabitants of the capital. 'It may procure respect in Algiers or Tunis; but here it can only excite disgust.' The ideal was a house, grand indeed, but one which 'shall still present something that intimates a relation to the society in which you live'.[57] That relation, of course, was meant to suggest harmony. There were some who enjoyed wide public esteem, even adoration. The chorus of public and poetic lamentation which followed the tragic death of the young Marquess of Tavistock in a riding accident in 1766 displayed something of the sentimental potential in the appeal of aristocratic virtue. When aristocrats like Lyttelton and Chesterfield diverged from the patterns of conformity required by the society around them, they were punished and their example held up for its deterrent effect. Knox remarked that 'the rich and the great may be considered as beacons on a promontory.'[58] Only if they burned brightly and truly would the multitudes who steered by them keep a true course.

FEMALE ACCOMPLISHMENTS

Manners rather than men were the main target. There was widespread recognition that the social mobility which seemed such a feature of eighteenth-century England had to do with a consuming desire to imitate one's betters. 'Vanity', as a critical commentator put it, 'has possessed itself of all ranks of people; their schemes of life are not to be really happy, free from want, poverty and oppression; but how to mingle every man with the class that is superior to him, and how to support a gay and splendid appearance, utterly inconsistent with their station and circumstances.'[59] The

[57] *Critical Observations on the Buildings and Improvements of London*, pp. 26, 24.
[58] *The Works of Vicesimus Knox*, ii. 271.
[59] *London Magazine*, 1780, p. 61.

emphasis here may have been on men, but the vanity identified as the cause of this restless quest for higher social standards was more commonly attributed to women. The *ton* or *bon Ton*, that is to say the fashionable taste which was paraded and emulated at every conceivable venue from Ranelagh and the Pantheon to the humblest country assembly, was particularly associated with female snobbery. Naturally, the favourite targets were those which seemed most incongruous, especially among London's socially self-conscious business classes. Soame Jenyns found 'hair has curled as genteely on one side of Temple-Bar, as on the other, as hoops have grown as prodigious a magnitude in the foggy air of Cheapside, as in the purer regions of Grosvenor-square and Hill-street'.[60] Garrick also had fun with City women in his *Bon Ton; or, High Life above Stairs.* His Madam Fussock was 'warm from Spital-fields', and 'Sunday riding in a one-horse chaise, to Bagnigge Wells'. His Miss Tittup revelled in balls, masques, plays, French stays, fruit out of season, and paint.[61]

Criticism was not directed only at such parvenues. In fact in the same spirit of exemplary exposure which gave rise to censure of aristocratic bucks, it was particularly upper-class women who were held up for public condemnation. 'Harlequin' in 1775 recounted the wasted day of the fashionable woman, prone to

rise at ten, throw herself into a hurry, dress before she goes out, fly away to the exhibitions of painting, and models and wax, and a thousand other things: take a peep at a play to encourage a poor player on his benefit night—fly to the pantheon to hear Agujari sing—whisk from thence to Ranelagh, to meet dear Lord William, and adjourn with the dear creature to Vauxhall to finish the evening with a glass of burnt Champagne: then yawning on her return, assure her dreaming lord, that she cannot support it; it is too much; the human spirit will not endure it, sink dead as a flat into her bed, and rise next morning in pursuit of similar follies.[62]

There were always individual women to provide case-studies. The young Duchess of Devonshire was the toast of the 1770s and a source of endless delight to gossips. Her affectations and indiscretions laid her open to earnest criticism as well as ribald satire. She was pursued through a number of poetic satires, and warned

---

[60] 'The World', cxxv, in *The Works of Soame Jenyns*, ii. 98.
[61] (London, 1775), Prologue, written by George Colman.
[62] *London Magazine*, 1775, pp. 271–3.

that even hairdressers, milliners, and mantua-makers treated her as a subject of folly. 'Popular opinion possesses a judicial power, and will condemn the error, even though it crown a character as dignified as Your Grace.'[63] The public may have condemned the Duchess of Devonshire but it did not cease to emulate her manner and her dress.

Women's fashions aroused more enduring interest than the brief notoriety enjoyed by male macaronis. The mid-1770s, especially, saw some alarming extremes: bizarre, top-heavy head-dresses, provocatively plunging necklines, and pronounced backsides, sustained by the cork rump. The result was a sudden outburst of hostility to feminine extravagance which led even the cartoonists to concentrate on women's clothes, for the first time since the rage for hoops in the 1740s. Part of the hostility had to do with the way in which women seemed to be aping men. There was a theatrical tradition, which gathered force in the 1770s, of dressing females in men's clothes: the so-called 'breeches parts', manifestly designed to titillate. 'Perdita' Robinson, one of many young actresses of slender talent but ample physical charms, proved popular in these roles and boasted of having slain her princely lover, the heir to the throne, with such a part in *The Winter's Tale*.[64] By the time George IV actually succeeded, one critic claimed, women would 'throw away the cap, the top knot, and the tippet, and clip the petticoat close to the knee', displaying stockinged calves like men.[65] The truth was that there was a growing tendency for women to travel, to participate in outdoor leisure activities, and generally to exploit the opportunities offered by contemporary enthusiasm for family life in a social setting. They required garments more sturdy and costumes more versatile than those available to their mothers and grandmothers. One result was the widespread adoption of the male's riding-habit, including the frock-coat, which itself had seemed so revolutionary when introduced to England in the second quarter of the century. But sensitivity to the implications of sartorial masculinity was pronounced. Colours were not in question: in this respect there seems to have been little sexual differentiation. But there was a vigorous debate about textures and also about

---

[63] William Combe, *A Second Letter to her Grace the Duchess of Devonshire* (London, 1777), pp. 2, 5.

[64] *Memoirs of the Late Mrs Robinson*, pp. 122–8.

[65] *London Magazine*, 1772, p. 404.

buttons and buckles. Broad cloth and buttoned coats, it was suggested, were inherently masculine; except perhaps on horseback they must not be permitted to supersede appropriately feminine draperies and less abrasive textiles.

The controversy concerning female fashions is a pointer to the sometimes stormy sexual politics of the 1770s. The supposedly feministic tendencies glimpsed with such alarm thirty years before seemed to have developed into a full-blown revolution. Female poets, playwrights, and novelists abounded. Their works were still preceded by prefaces or prologues apologising for the sex of the writer, but such archness deceived nobody. The most talented of these women, much celebrated in the periodicals of the day, were said to have given the England of George III the first place in the long annals of womanhood. There was much celebration of the 'Nine Living Muses', a diverse group which illustrates the cultural prominence accorded some of these women. They included Catherine Macaulay, whose *History of England* and republican views attracted controversy as well as admiration. Her popularity was affected in the late 1770s by her much publicized addiction to cosmetics, and by her startling second marriage at the age of fifty-seven to a man thirty-six years her junior. A less wayward muse was the Blue Stocking Elizabeth Carter: her poems were praised by Johnson, Burke, and their circle, and by her translation of Epictetus she earned a considerable reputation as a classical scholar.

Mrs Barbauld, formerly Anna Aikin, was also a poet; her published collection of 1773 laid a reputation on which she subsequently built with her famous 'Hymns for Children'. There were also Hannah More, in the 1770s best known for her poems and tragedies, and Charlotte Lennox, perhaps the most successful female novelist prior to Fanny Burney. All three of these women owed much to early recognition and recommendation by Samuel Johnson. Patronage, in the shape of David Garrick, was also important in the career of the playwright Elizabeth Griffith, the sixth muse. It played a smaller part in the career of the seventh, Elizabeth Linley, whose angelic voice was widely admired in sacred as well as profane surroundings before she married Richard Brinsley Sheridan. It was perhaps rather cheeky to claim Angelica Kauffmann, who had only come to England in 1766, as another English muse. It could, however, be argued that the enthusiasm of polite society in London, including the King, was needed to bring out her genius as a decorative artist. The last of the muses, and leading light of all literary ladies, Mrs Montagu, owed nothing to patronage, foreign or domestic, and was herself a celebrated patroness. In fact it would be wrong to impute disproportionate significance to male patronage in the history of these women. In the case of Angelica Kauffmann, for instance, the leading patron was indeed herself a woman, the wife of the British Ambassador in Venice, Lady Wentworth. Moreover, in England itself Mrs Montagu had many imitators in the art of bestowing social respectability and genteel encouragement, most notably, perhaps, Lady Miller. At her seat of Batheaston, unkindly called by Horace Walpole the 'puppet-show-Parnassus', she organized poetic Olympiads in which prizes were awarded and the successful entries published.[66] It was on public awareness of female accomplishment in this period that the confidence of the next generation of literary women, beginning with Anna Seward and Fanny Burney, would rest.

Interest in the doings of women was not restricted to the favoured and the great. In the novels of the day women were frequently allocated an active part far exceeding the passive piety of Pamela. Duty and domesticity reigned supreme in the final pages of such works, but before that, feats of courage, even heroism, were evidently much to the taste of readers. Women who imitated such fictional heroines in real life received much publicity. Female soldiers and sailors had always attracted attention, and the figure of the virago was a familiar literacy device from the chapbook upwards. But positive, even masculine, qualities in the new woman of the 1760s and 1770s were treated seriously. Particular interest was displayed in women who maintained their femininity while outdoing the men around them, and in this case nature did occasionally imitate art. The story of Lady Harriet Acland, wife of an officer in Burgoyne's army, who advanced into battle with a corps of grenadiers, and penetrated enemy lines to console her wounded husband, could easily have appeared in a novel.[67]

Fascination with the place of women in contemporary society was reinforced by growing interest in the history and sociology of their sex. In the middle of the century the public had been

---

[66] *Horace Walpole's Correspondence*, xxxii. 221.
[67] See p. 626.

offered catalogues of female worthies through the ages. Later, more systematic and disciplined analysis became available, typically presenting women as the beneficiaries of commercial society. John Millar's *Observations concerning the Distinction of Ranks in Society*, published in 1771, described their progress from an ancient state of slavery, mitigated only by the influence which in primitive societies they derived from their child-bearing, to the domesticity and refinement brought about by the successive developments of agrarian and commercial civilization. He gave special prominence to relations between the sexes, and to the requirement in sophisticated societies for ever more repressive yet more romantic modes of courtship. Like William Alexander, whose *History of Women* of 1779, was perhaps the first systematic study of its subject in English, he was engrossed by the phenomenon of chivalry, in an age when 'passion had been wrought up to the highest pitch'.[68] Significantly, both men saw the chivalric ideal as a kind of false dawn for women, combining affected romanticism with political impotence. In the commercial Europe which had emerged since the Middle Ages, women enjoyed more real, if less exaggerated, respect from their menfolk. 'We cannot hesitate a moment to declare', Alexander pronounced, 'that the present condition of the fair sex, every thing impartially considered, is greatly preferable to what it was while they were approached as demigoddesses and in the scale of political society treated as cyphers.'[69]

This is not to argue that the new concern with the historical progress of women implied concessions to feminists. In retrospect the design seems to have been to fit women to take the place required of them in the family life of a newly affluent and mobile society, while repressing those tendencies which suggested any challenge to male authority. Alexander's work, a rambling survey of the treatment of females in non-European societies, was admittedly ambivalent in this respect, questioning whether 'there were not a public employment between that of superintending a kingdom, and the affairs of her own kitchen, which would be managed by the genius and capacity of women'.[70] But in general his tone was complacent. Women were intended, not indeed as slaves, but as companions. Their role was to complement, not to challenge their fathers and husbands. He described without wincing the lengthy list of legal disqualifications which women

[68] p. 56.   [69] i. 168.   [70] ii. 336.

suffered, particularly in the management of property, and insisted that they were fully compensated for their disabilities by the informal privileges which they enjoyed. In this he was merely endorsing the predominant view.

Underlying delight in the accomplishments of eighteenth-century woman was a pronounced fear that liberty might turn to licence, and indeed that women might demand of right what they were granted by way of liberties. *Female Government* in 1779 blamed the ills of contemporary society on the excessive social mixing of the sexes. 'A Woman is the downy pillow on which a Man should repose from the severer and more exalted duties of life; from his studies, his labour, and his cares.' The author recommended that men should only see women at night and that the male child should be removed from his mother's presence as soon as he was taken from her breast 'and by no means suffered to see that dangerous parent, until by a masculine and proper education he may be judged to be superior to the contagion of effeminate manners'.[71] The torrent of sermons and addresses which descended on wives and daughters in the 1760s and 1770s was meant to extinguish any flickers of feminism. First and foremost among these were James Fordyce's *Sermons to Young Women*, in 1765. Fordyce, a successful Nonconformist minister, and brother of the banker Alexander Fordyce, was an appropriate mouthpiece of the comfortable puritanism of the period. He was also a great entrepreneur, for he made large sums from his improving writings, and shrewdly exploited the market for such literature among anxious mothers and fathers. He stressed the usual bugbears: the dangers of boarding-school education, the folly of extravagant dress, the damage done by novel-reading and play-going. Primacy was accorded to domestic economics, scriptural support being cited for the moral value of needlework. Especially important matters, like Modest Apparel, Artful Behaviour, Dangerous Connexions, and Good Manners, were dignified with capitals, and the general effect set the tone for such writing well into the nineteenth century.[72]

Intellectually the sermons were feeble, and earned their author the magisterial Knox's dismissal as a 'frothy declaimer'.[73] Nothing

---

[71] pp. 7, 11.
[72] (3rd edn., 2 vols., 1766).
[73] *The Works of Vicesimus Knox*, ii. 216.

in them was likely to make conscientious parents think too hard, let alone think anything that might prove uncomfortable. The formula was for anodyne prescriptions, compatible with a decently undisturbing middle-class form of virtue. But most important was Fordyce's determination to block off any escape routes for well-educated young women of a mutinous nature. Women were not made for war, politics, commerce, arduous exercise, or even for abstract thought in philosophy and science. What they did possess was 'a degree of complacence, yieldingness, and sweetness, beyond what we look for in "men"'. Queen Charlotte was cited as an outstanding example: 'Royalty itself derives Lustre from Meekness.' 'There is an empire', Fordyce told his female readers, 'which belongs to you ... I mean what has the heart for its object, and is secured by meekness and modesty, by soft attraction and virtuous love.'[74] It is difficult to believe that many daughters wanted to hear Fordyce's message, though in the pulpit he was said to have an actor's diction and manners, and was much admired as a clerical Cicero by female congregations. No doubt to parents he was balm itself. And there were many imitators, some of them women. Hannah More's *Essays Addressed to Young Ladies* of 1777 taught that the freedom enjoyed by women in England imposed a greater obligation to be 'exemplary in their general conduct'. Even intellectual challenge to male authority was discouraged. 'Girls should be taught to give up their opinions betimes, and not pertinaciously to carry on a dispute, even if they would know themselves to be in the right.'[75] Hestor Chapone's *Letters on the Improvement of the Mind* was perhaps the least flaccid of such advice, but no less concerned to endorse the conventional desiderata in a woman of 'gentleness, meekness, and patience'.[76]

CULTURAL CRISIS

The sermons of the 1770s suggest something of the connection between social change, sexual tension, and repressive morality. The same themes predominated in the contemporary debate concerning what was seen as an alarming cultural crisis. Macaroni

---

[74] ii. 222–3, 247; i. 272.
[75] 'Essays Principally designed for Young ladies', 1777, in *The Works of Hannah More* (6 vols., London, 1833–4), vi. 326.
[76] *The Works of Mrs Chapone*, iii. 113.

manners were meretricious as well as morally threatening. The trashy novels and verse which accompanied the growth of literacy and the triumph of sentiment were used by moralists as examples of a decline in aesthetic taste, closely matching the decay of moral principles. Respectable novelists like Fanny Burney and Clara Reeve were conscious of the need to rescue the moral standing of their art. Mrs Reeve observed that 'the business of Romance is, first, to excite the attention; and, secondly, to direct it to some useful, or, at least innocent, end.'[77] But it was perhaps in the theatre that the battle of vanity with virtue seemed to be joined in its most critical phase. For contemporaries, the issue was somewhat obscured by accidents of time and talent. Several of the great figures of the stage departed in the mid-1770s. Foote, the darling of the comic theatre, was already having a grim time of it before his death in 1777. 1776 had brought public charges of homosexuality and an end to his charmed life with the critics. 'Laughter is all the public require of Mr Foote, and laughter he gives them', it had been said in 1772.[78] But in his last years he was accused of mere buffoonery, below the notice of fashionable taste.

Charles Macklin did not altogether give up acting until he reached the age of 92 in 1789, but he was rarely seen in London after the riotous campaign which was mounted to prevent him acting Macbeth in 1772. Macklin was considered a comic, not a tragedian. Moreover he had the temerity to portray Macbeth in Scottish costume, something not done for many years and highly unpopular with a London audience. Though he successfully defended his right in court, it was a pyrrhic victory. The spectacle of one of the century's greatest actors driven from the stage at the peak of his career was poignant. Thomas Weston, generally expected to succeed and even surpass Foote as premier comedian, died in debt and drink before him in 1776. Above all the reign of Garrick the Great was drawing to a close, not altogether happily. In May and June 1776, in a final season, he performed eight of his most celebrated characters to packed theatres. His famous role of Richard III was acted three times, but the magic that had captivated Chesterfield, Lyttelton, and Fielding, was gone. The King

[77] The Old English Baron: A Gothic Story (London, 1778), p. v.
[78] 'The British Theatre', in London Magazine, 1772, p. 310.

commissioned one special, last performance, but it proved disappointing.

The passing of some famous names in dramatic history cast a temporary shadow over the future prospects of the theatre. But there were claims that it was degenerating, even before these final exits. It was easy to view the vulgarity and exhibitionism which were displayed on stage as representative of public taste generally. The apparently inexhaustible demand for exhibitions in the 1770s seemed to prostitute art and scholarship. 'It is incredible', observed Horace Walpole, 'what sums are raised by mere exhibitions of anything; a new fashion, and to enter at which you pay a shilling or half a crown.'[79] In retrospect the contemporary enthusiasm for Cox's Museum of Automata, and for the Lever collection of natural history, displayed in Leicester Square as the Holophusikon, seems innocent enough. Certainly they performed a service which the British Museum refused to match, declining to make charges, while restricting the flow of numbers and information, to the irritation of a genuinely enthusiastic public. Nor was it necessarily reprehensible for artists to exploit the interest suggested by attendance at the Royal Academy exhibitions. Much of the criticism of J. S. Copley for holding 'raree-shows' of his works prior to having them engraved for the mass market, savours of sour grapes.[80] On the other hand, concern about the commercialism of contemporary art seemed to have support in the cheap sensationalism of Boddly's magic lantern. There was also the ingenious theatricality of Philippe De Loutherbourg, who offered mechanically operated vistas to a ticket-paying audience at his Eidophusikon and of Patience Wright, who used her modelling talents in wax to draw a mass following.

The essence of many of these ventures was a combination of technical ingenuity (involving clockwork, hydraulics, and mirrors) with artistic effect. Greek etymology provided suitably striking names to express the resulting visual novelty: not only the Holophusikon, the Eidophusikon, and the Eidoranion were products of these years, but also, with a longer lasting place in the English language, the Panorama. Such activities seemed to match what was happening on the stage. It could be argued that Garrick had begun the descent with his use of the Stratford Jubilee to stimulate public

[79] *Horace Walpole's Correspondence*, xxiii. 211.
[80] J. D. Brown, *John Singleton Copley* (2 vols., Cambridge, Mass., 1966), ii. 284.

interest in pageantry and display. Short pieces were alleged to be
the enemy of dramatic standards in the early 1770s, with jubilees,
processions, Christmas tales, pantomimes, mimicry, and mere
'singsong' predominating. Two-act operas invaded the 'once classic
stage of Drury Lane'.[81] The rewards must have been considerable
to justify the capital invested in some of these productions. Garrick
was said to have spent £1,500 on the scenery for *The Maid of
Oaks*, exploiting interest in Lord Stanley's famous *fête-champêtre*
of 1774. 'The landscapes of Claud', it was reported 'are scarcely
equal to some of the views exhibited.'[82] In this case at least it
could be argued that theatrical scenery was attaining higher artistic
standards. It was the Royal Academician De Loutherbourg, criticized for prostituting his talent in the Eidophusikon, who played
the largest part in this development. But critics were not reassured.
Even when, with Sheridan's *School for Scandal* in 1777, 'a mar-
vellous resurrection of the stage' presented itself, it was tempting
to dismiss it as the exception that proved the rule.[83] Its success
depended on satirizing the very values which seemed to make the
age so tawdry, and many of those who applauded Sheridan's
comedy could even be loftily criticized for not appreciating the
subtlety of his irony.

The future of the theatre as an artistic medium was more
secure than many contemporaries supposed. To some extent the
showmanship of the 1770s was itself evidence of the extensive
market opened up by rising standards of living. Theatrical managers were tapping a new audience, one which in time would
provide a broader and more dependable base for the drama. But
the contemporary anxiety about what was happening on the stage
is a significant pointer to trends in contemporary opinion, particularly in public morality. Middle-class audiences had changing
expectations of the theatre. Partly this was a question of ensuring
that sexual morals were not endangered. In this matter, however,
politeness and sentiment were already achieving what was desired.
Thus the *Sentimental Magazine* put it in 1773: 'As we have
increased in Politeness, we have likewise increased the Chastity of
our literary Productions: ... Our Ancestors placed their Amuse-

[81] 'The British Theatre', in *London Magazine*, 1776, p. 565.
[82] Ibid. 1774, p. 518.
[83] *Horace Walpole's Correspondence*, xli. 363.

ment in Laughter, we place our's on Chastity of Sentiment.'[84] Authors went out of their way to ensure that potentially racy themes, like that of Tom Jones in the opera of that name, were purged of all indelicacy, and no revision of Congreve or Vanbrugh was neglected which might leave room for polite censure.

Whether the results were improving in a wider sense is another matter. The extension of regular theatre in purpose-built houses produced much anxiety on the part of respectable middle-class opinion concerned by the threat to the morals and industry of the labouring population in commercial and manufacturing cities. In Parliament, bishops ritually appeared to cast doubt on the wisdom of licensing new theatres, but Bishop Lowth of London, at least, was not above observing that only custom prevented him from attending the theatre himself.[85] Permanent theatres were technically a breach of the law and therefore required statutory authority. A succession of local bills, most of them eventually successful, kept the issue before Parliament. At Birmingham and Manchester there were particularly punishing controversies on this score in the mid-1770s.

Travelling companies were notoriously suspect. They depended entirely on the readiness of local magistrates to tolerate them. In practice this consent was usually forthcoming. The universities alone put up determined resistance, and then only at the cost of diverting entertainers and their student audiences to nearby towns: Abingdon was long a profitable venue for playing companies, thanks to Oxford's opposition to them. The moral consequences were much debated. The novelist James Thistlethwaite urged managers to transform what could be seen as a 'seminary of vice', into 'a moral mirror'.[86] This laudable objective could not be achieved without a heroic campaign to clean up the stage and make it suitable for the most unimpeachably respectable audiences. 'Were the theatre under certain regulations, a man might go to it as he goes to church, to learn his duty; and it might justly be honoured with the appellation which it has often assumed, and will be called the School of Virtue.' Knox, who made this plea, urged, as many others did, that this process depended on eliminating the cheap comedy and light opera which dominated the stage, both in the

---

[84] *Sentimental Magazine*, 1773, p. 3.
[85] William Combe, *The Fast-Day: A Lambeth Eclogue* (London, 1780), p. x.
[86] *The Child of Misfortune; or The History of Mrs Gilbert* (2 vols., Dublin, 1777), i. 129.

provinces and in London. He thought 'no method more effectual in softening the ferocity, and improving the minds of the lower classes of a great capital, than the frequent exhibition of tragical pieces, in which the distress is carried to the highest extreme, and the moral at once self-evident, impressive and instructive.' Predictably, Knox looked to works such as Lillo's *George Barnwell*,[87] the classic tale of doom which afflicted a Londoner destroyed by greed and sexual passion, to achieve this end, and thought the *Beggar's Opera* the very embodiment of the evils which it was designed to counteract.[88] He had ample support from others, especially those prepared to bowdlerize Shakespeare and those waiting in the wings with new tragedies on classical or historical themes.

Some famous names throve on the desire to bring improving tragedy into the theatre in the 1770s, including Hannah More, whose *Earl Percy* was one of the more successful of such ventures. It is significant of the contemporary belief that the stage was redeemable that she was among its would-be reformers at this time. Twenty years later, when she was preparing a complete edition of her works, she thought the enterprise had altogether failed and the school of virtue degenerated into corruption and irreligion. In her preface she admitted to a 'revolution in the sentiments of the author', and reprinted her own productions only to escape the charge of hypocrisy.[89] Such defeated reformers thought they had succumbed to the innate viciousness of an institution ultimately beyond redemption. But it was also their own snobbery which made the theatre so suspect. The stage was one of the few entertainments shared by all ranks. The prominence in the auditorium of the servant class, that most effective mediator between polite and plebeian values, was an irritation to some of those who sat with them, and also to managers such as Garrick, who unwisely attempted to impose an admission charge on the footmen of his fashionable customers. The low-brow productions in the 1770s reflected in part the wishes of lower-class audiences.

According to the proprietors of the Haymarket Theatre there was a distinct drop in the social status of theatre attenders at this time, a development which they put down to the shortage of seats

---

[87] See pp. 126–7.
[88] *The Works of Vicesimus Knox*, ii. 19.
[89] *The Works of Hannah More*, iii. 2.

in theatres artificially restricted by royal monopolies.[90] But it is equally likely that the preference of upper and middle-class society for genteel recreation which would not be tainted by mass attendance was having an effect. This may account for interest in public readings of plays, proceedings unlikely to attract the less respectable elements present in the theatres. It may also explain the vogue for country house dramas, like those of the Earl of Essex, attended by the Prime Minister Lord North, or the annual productions organized at Wynnstay by Sir Watkin Williams Wynn, on one occasion supervised by Garrick himself. Such affairs were, of course, secluded from the profane gaze of plebeian theatre-goers. In this the theatre was typical of the 'improving' character of the age. If there were signs of puritanism at work, they rarely conflicted with the exploitation of leisure and luxury by those with the money to enjoy it. For all the moralizing, it was vanity which gained the upper hand, and virtue which, to fulfil a role in a polite plutocracy, did the accommodating.

[90] *Correspondence of George III*, ii. 196–7.

CHAPTER 13

Opulence and Glory

THE success of the Seven Years War bred a certain complacency about Britain's place in the world. It was temporarily shattered by the American War and replaced by a cautious optimism about a future which was not meant to include imperial ambitions. War in general was an inescapable experience for Englishmen born after 1720, but for most of them it was acquired at second hand or viewed more as theatre than reality. There was some sentimental dismay at the horrors of armed conflict, rarely developing into authentic pacifism. War had important economic consequences, though it is difficult in retrospect accurately to assess them. At the time there was concern about the underlying economic trends. In the absence of reliable statistics, it was possible to believe that the population was diminishing. The need to increase the nation's stock of manpower was a characteristic preoccupation of the age. There was matching concern about the size of the National Debt, and the consequent strains imposed on fiscal policy. Pessimism on these scores was offset, especially after 1760, by growing faith in the commercial vitality of British society. Technological advance aroused great enthusiasm. Voluntary organizations and associations expressed the contemporary interest in practical enlightenment. Particularly among businessmen, the emphasis was on marketing *as much as mechanics. Industrial advance provoked some opposition, including violent resistance to the introduction of labour-saving machinery. But features of industrialization which were later to arouse controversy, for example the employment of women and children, attracted praise rather than criticism. Its aesthetic dangers were rarely stressed. Above all, there was awareness, by the 1780s, that regional change was shifting wealth and population towards the North and the Midlands.*

BRITISH ARMS: SUCCESS AND FAILURE

ENGLISHMEN had always had a high opinion of their inherent virtues as a nation, particularly in those matters, their legal and political traditions, for example, which had to do primarily with domestic affairs. During the Seven Years War they also acquired a matching pride in their achievements *vis-à-vis* other nations. An extraordinary succession of victories brought an unprecedented accession of power and prestige. An empire which exceeded even that of the Romans sprang into being. It was sustained by a commerce which bestrode the world and threatened to overwhelm every competitor. All this had been accomplished in a startlingly short time. The contrast with the preceding age seemed striking indeed. From Malplaquet to Minorca British army had enjoyed few successes and no undisputed triumphs. Important though they were at the time, the brief success of Puerto Bello and the slaughter of the Highlanders at Culloden provided little lasting cause for complacency. Criticism of the feebleness of British statesmanship when exerted on the international stage had been strident throughout the reigns of George I and George II. Few of the economic analyses of the same period offered more than guarded optimism and most were distinctly pessimistic. The consequent gloom may have been misleading, but for the generation which emerged into the sunlight of the 1760s and the 1770s there was no doubt of the significance of the transformation. As an Oxford don John Dupré, put it in one of the many platitudinous sermons preached on this theme, 'From a state of mediocrity we have made a rapid advance to opulence and glory.'[1]

Dupré's statement was made in 1781, and was meant to offer reassurance at a time when clouds were once more darkening the horizon. Many of his brethren were less sanguine. Nemesis seemed to have followed hard on hubris. The campaign for moral reformation throve on the resulting sense of guilt. 'How fat we were when the war terminated in the year 1763,' exclaimed the evangelical John Newton, 'and how we have kicked and forsaken the rock of our salvation of late years.'[2] There was an understandable tendency to draw into one depressing diagnosis the diverse social and cultural ills which had beset the British during their apparently

[1] *A Sermon, Preached at the Parish Church of Tring, Hertfordshire, On Wednesday, Feb. 21, 1781* (Oxford, 1781), p. 9.
[2] *The Works of the Rev. John Newton* (6 vols., London, 1808), ii. 249.

short-lived age of extravagance. *Anticipation*, published in 1781, and envisaging the voyage of an American to England in the year 1899, described the British Museum housing skittles and boxing, St Paul's occupied by a pantomime company, the Royal Society transformed into a fish-market, Chelsea Hospital inhabited by French servants, Swiss painters, and Italian rope-dancers, and a roofless Westminster Abbey filled with Scottish trinket-sellers. There was a strongly felt need for scapegoats, conveniently met from the stock of villains identified by opponents of government. It was all too easy to assume that the war had been the work of a corrupt oligarchy tyrannizing over the national will. Long after the event Thomas Somerville recalled that no war in the annals of Britain had been more popular at its commencement. 'Persons of my own age, who were wont, as I well remember, to express themselves with a passionate zeal on this subject, and who considered all those who held a different opinion the tools of faction and abettors of rebellion, have not only changed their own sentiments, but seem to have forgotten them as much as they had lost all sense of personal identity.'[3] But the actual agony of expiation was short-lived, its principal victims being the ministers who had presided over 'Britannia's ruin', and Lord Shelburne who had had to negotiate an unpopular peace.

It quickly became clear that the lasting damage inflicted by the American War was slight. The military record in the last year of warfare in the West Indies and India was reassuring, and the terms of the Peace Treaty proved less demoralizing than had once seemed likely. The pamphleteer Baptist Noel Turner had the temerity to describe it as 'a war, more truly glorious than any thing Lewis XIV could boast of'.[4] Even the forfeiture of the American colonies quickly came to seem less catastrophic than had been feared. The speedy recovery of overseas trade belied the pre-war assumption that a captive colonial America was essential to British interests. Nor did the loss of three million turbulent subjects seem a very grave one. For some, of course, America was the scene of an inspiring experiment in the politics of virtue. 'Next to the introduction of Christianity among mankind,' Richard Price confidently asserted, 'the American revolution may prove the most important

[3] *My Own Life and Times, 1741–1814*, p. 185.
[4] *The True Alarm* (London, 1783), p. 4.

step in the progressive cause of human improvement.'[5] His expectation was not shared by many of his countrymen. Reports of
the discord and corruption which marked the early years of the
American republic fed the consoling English conviction that American independence would prove short-lived or at least insecure,
and that even if it worked, the British Empire was well rid of its
authors. The idea that the 1780s witnessed a decisive shift to
a new concept of empire, commercial rather than territorial in
character, and oriental rather than occidental in direction, is somewhat speculative. But there is little doubt that the fate of the
western empire left Englishmen as ready to believe that they had
been foolish to want to keep it as regretful that they had lost it.
The concern in the 1780s to find a means by which Canada might
become in effect self-financing and self-governing showed that a
few years of war could do far more to revise long-standing concepts
of empire than any amount of challenging analysis and argument
by experts.

The brief meridian of the first empire lessened the agony of its
passing. Its prosperity had been so short-lived that there was hardly
time for national attitudes to be enduringly affected. Eighteenth-
century Englishmen had no real belief in themselves as imperialists,
no notion that they had a special mission to conquer and rule,
notwithstanding some signs of an incipient sense of imperial
responsibility among administrators in the 1760s. Traditional
wisdom had it that the English genius was for liberty and self-
government. Skill in ruling subject nations was not prized by those
brought up in this tradition. It was associated with more degenerate societies and more despotic constitutions. The sheer un-
Englishness of what was taking place in Bengal in the age of Clive
and Hastings contributed largely to the mood of revulsion which
affected East Indian politics. It was difficult even to envisage the
problem of governing other people in any but an English context.
Burke, no narrow-minded patriot, supported his contention that
Hastings had subverted the laws of the country, by describing the
native zemindars with whom he dealt almost as if they were English
squires equipped with freehold estates and the protection of the
common law. From a quite different perspective Granville Sharp
refused to accept that native subjects should not enjoy their

[5] *Observations on the Importance of the American Revolution, and the Means of making it a
Benefit to the World* (London, 1785), p. 6.

'*Natural right to a share in the government* of those countries which they inhabit'. He advocated a representative assembly open to low-caste Indians so that they 'may have confidence to reject and confine that detestable lie of the Brahmins, by which they are holden in slavery, and rendered the prey of Tartarian, as well as European, wolves and tigers'.[6]

Englishmen had never completely believed in the grandeur which they enjoyed in the 1760s. One commentator in 1767 attributed the dazzling successes of the Seven Years War to four 'P's: Pitt, Pompadour, Prussia, Providence.[7] None of these assets could be taken for granted in future. There was a brittle quality about British power after 1763 which Whigs attributed to a foolish and pusillanimous peace treaty, but which had more to do with nervousness about the permanence of the verdict gained between 1759 and 1761. Much printer's ink was spilt on comparisons of the underlying strength of Britain and France. One of the most important dialogues of the 1760s was the pamphlet exchange on the 'State of the Nation', which took place in 1768-9 between William Knox and Edmund Burke, the former arguing for the continuing superiority of Bourbon resources, the latter for the essential resilience of post-war Britain. Doubt in such matters extended to the future viability of the British empire. Was it wise, some wondered, for a small and essentially insular nation to imitate the great imperial powers of the past? Would not the sheer size of the empire, and the commercial system required to sustain it, threaten the fundamental integrity of English society? History suggested that large empires were inherently unstable and that even in their prosperity they sapped the vigour and subverted the virtue of their masters. Gibbon's thesis that Rome had suffered from 'immoderate greatness' was the most distinguished statement of a commonplace historical view; published during the American War, it naturally brought to mind disheartening parallels. It may seem ironic that Gibbon was a loyal supporter of Lord North in the House of Commons and a minister at the Board of Trade, but his scepticism was shared by others responsible for the supervision of the empire. Soame Jenyns, who had sat at the Board of Trade many years longer than Gibbon, 'always considered the

---

[6] *A Defence of the Ancient, Legal, and Constitutional, Right of the People, To elect Representatives for every Session of Parliament* (4th edn., London, 1780), pp. 5–6.

[7] *London Magazine*, 1767, p. 59.

British empire as enlarged beyond the bounds dictated by sound policy'.[8]

ATTITUDES TO WAR

Britons born between about 1730 and 1800 could hardly escape having their adult lives affected by war, whatever its strategic and economic consequences. By contrast, those born during the last years of Anne's reign or in that of George I were brought up against the background of the prolonged if not entirely placid peace of 1713 to 1739. They saw war in middle and old age, if they lived long enough to see it at all, in an era when average life expectancy rarely rose as high as thirty-five years and sometimes fell below thirty. This was the generation of Johnson and Gray, Wesley and Warburton, Chatham and Mansfield. Their privilege, a childhood and adolescence unmarked by memories of war, made them unique among the generations born between the beginning of Charles I's reign and the end of George III's. Laurence Sterne, born in 1713, the year that the Treaty of Utrecht was signed, later conveyed a sense of this remoteness in his portrait of Uncle Toby, teller of interminable tales of trench warfare in King William's War. The fact that *Tristram Shandy* was published in 1760, in the midst of another great European war, of very different character, merely sharpened the perception of changing experiences in this respect.

The sheer inexperience of those who went to war in the 1740s remains striking. Of the naval leaders of the war, Vernon, Mathews, Lestock, Anson, Warren, only Mathews had fought in a senior capacity in the War of the Spanish Succession. Among the generals there were some, including Stair and the King himself, who had witnessed the carnage of Marlborough's campaigns. But the forces which they commanded were necessarily untried. Part of the pride of Dettingen lay in an awareness of the English soldier's unfamiliarity with warfare compared with his French and German counterparts. 'The far greater part of our *British* soldiers labour'd under the disadvantage, of having never yet had an opportunity to see an enemy in the field.'[9] Soldiers and sailors old enough to have fought against the might of Louis XIV were invalids. To his

[8] *The Works of Soame Jenyns*, i. xii–xiii.
[9] Joseph Stennett, *A Sermon Preach'd In Little-Wild-Street, The 17th of July 1743* (2nd edn., London, 1743), p. 27.

dismay Anson was compelled to take as his marine complement for the voyage to the South Seas the superannuated pensioners of the Chelsea Hospital. The vast majority of them never returned. For most, war was a matter of applying theory rather than repeating practice. This did not remain true for long. Between 1739 and 1783, twenty-four years were spent at war, twenty at peace. During peacetime itself war seemed all too close. The early 1750s were dominated by diplomatic manœuvres and military skirmishes which plainly looked forward to the resumption of hostilities with France. Even the more enduring peace which followed the Seven Years War was interrupted by repeated emergencies, one of which, the Falkland Islands crisis of 1770, put the country on a war footing.

Despite the fragility of peace, the pity of war was not much regarded. Quakers continued to object to its contaminating associations. But they found it difficult to draw a clear line between what was permissible and what was not. One of their number, William Cookworthy, famous for his ingenuity in the perfecting of porcelain manufacture, was shocked in 1745 to be told that it was 'grown a settled maxim, that Friends may deal in Prize-Goods'.[10] Some Quakers even found it compatible with their principles to supply goods to the armed forces. The Birmingham manufacturer Samuel Galton roundly declared that 'Men are not responsible for the abuse of what they manufacture.'[11] Galton was formally disowned for making armaments, as were others who shared his attitude. But it was a repeated complaint of strict Friends that their more modish brethren had destroyed the reputation of their sect for uncompromising pacifism.

By and large the established Church did its patriotic duty. In every war the Crown proclaimed general fasts which gave an opportunity for solemn reflection on the nation's moral fitness to receive the divine favour in battle. Such occasions frequently degenerated into State occasions for patriotic preachers to display their loyalty. It helped to fight alongside Protestants (though claiming the deist Frederick II as such in the Seven Years War involved a very loose definition of Protestantism) and it helped to fight against Papists (every war of the period was sooner or later a war against France and Spain). But these were not necessary

[10] *Memoirs of William Cookworthy* (London, 1854), p. 22.
[11] H. Pearson, *Doctor Darwin*, p. 100.

conditions for enlisting religion in the cause of war. The Queen of Hungary was enthusiastically supported in 1741, as were the Portuguese in 1762, for all their Catholicism; the old Protestant allies of the Grand Alliance, the Dutch, were readily identified as enemies in 1781. Every war was treated as a just one, though the American War stretched even elastic consciences uncomfortably far in this respect. As Sir John Dalrymple put it, 'the present war is a singular War; it is a War of English Subjects against English Subjects.'[12] It was also a war against fellow Protestants. This difficulty was somewhat eased by the association of American Protestantism with fanatical Puritanism. Some of the bishops, notably William Markham, Archbishop of York, and John Butler, Bishop of Oxford, were bellicose supporters of Lord North's ministry. Only two or three, John Hinchcliffe, Bishop of Peterborough, Frederick Keppel, Bishop of Exeter, and Jonathan Shipley, Bishop of St Asaph, opposed the war, and that on political rather than moral grounds. The bench came in for some bitter invective when it declined to condemn the use of Red Indian auxiliaries and their scalping knives against the colonists in 1777. But even among other Churchmen, refusal to rejoice in the triumphs of war, in terms such as those expressed by William Warburton in the Seven Years War, was unusual: 'I look upon war with horror: I regard it as one of the blackest sufflations of Hell, which blasts all the flourishing works of God.'[13]

There was some concern that progress in military and naval technology was rendering warfare increasingly terrible. 'In the modern methods of destruction,' pleaded one preacher before the University of Oxford in 1779, 'let men, if they can bear the dreadful picture, imagine to themselves the ruin of springing a mine, or of a sea-fight.'[14] The influence of the sentimental school perhaps did something to temper the inherent belligerence of contemporary patriotism. The artists and engravers of the second half of the century, emboldened by the vogue for contemporary history-painting, doubtless contributed to the glorification of war. But some of their most successful efforts were those which portrayed its poignancy. Edward Penny's famous representation of

[12] *Considerations upon the Different Modes of finding Recruits for the Army* (London, 1775), p. 13.

[13] A. W. Evans, *Warburton and the Warburtonians*, p. 274.

[14] George Bellas, *A Sermon Preached before the University of Oxford, On Sunday the Seventh of November, 1779* (Oxford, 1779), p. 14.

the Seven Years War hero Lord Granby depicted him relieving a
sick soldier and his family. The runner-up to Penny's painting in
terms of the quantity of engraved prints sold was West's hardly
less celebrated picture of Wolfe, not at the head of his troops in
the famous advance across the Heights of Abraham, but on the
point of death, surrounded by his appalled officers. Some aspects
of war became increasingly repugnant. Killing out of patriotism
remained defensible, even laudable. But much killing went on for
profit. Prize law made naval warfare a kind of gigantic wartime
lottery. Though the profits were distributed with gross inequity in
favour of the officers, it was reckoned that nothing did so much
for recruiting as the prospect of a Spanish war, with its promise
of Peruvian plunder.

Given a choice, seamen preferred another form of mercenary
warfare. Privateering was big business, offering some compensation
for the commercial losses suffered in wartime. In 1779 it was
calculated that 120 privateers, crewed by nearly nine thousand
men, were based at Liverpool alone.[15] Privateering was in theory
controlled by the Admiralty, and owners themselves were not
necessarily rapacious and inhumane. But the officers and men who
served on privateers were not known for their squeamishness. The
most successful of them were little better than pirates. Such was the
famous Fortunatus Wright, whose exploits in the Mediterranean
during the War of the Austrian Succession and the Seven Years
War, until he disappeared with his ship in 1757, made him a
popular hero. He combined unusual daring with extreme dis-
respect for the property of neutrals, and in one case at least for the
property of his own countrymen in the Levant Company. Neutral
rights were a major diplomatic issue in successive naval wars, and
though British governments had an obvious interest in minimizing
them, their task in defending the right of search was not rendered
easier by the cynicism of the privateers. From a national standpoint,
too, it was not clear that the balance sheet of privateering produced
a net profit. In the American War, at least, losses and gains
cancelled each other out. Enemy privateers tended to be more
successful than enemy naval commanders. The most feared privat-
eer of the Seven Years War was a Frenchman, François Thurot.
He inflicted considerable damage on shipping in the Atlantic

---

[15] G. Williams, *History of the Liverpool Privateers and Letters of Marque with an Account
of the Liverpool Slave Trade* (London, 1897), p. 183.

approaches before, having accepted a commission in the French navy, he was brought to battle and killed off the Isle of Man in 1760. In the American War John Paul Jones achieved similar fame. His audacious raids on coastal targets, including his descent on Lord Selkirk's house, brought privateering uncomfortably close to home, even if in this instance Lady Selkirk was able to testify to his chivalry. By this time attitudes were certainly beginning to change. The young Gilbert Wakefield, high-principled or priggish depending on viewpoint, made himself unpopular in Liverpool by condemning both its privateering and its slaving. He also declined to pray for success against the American colonies, to the fury of his churchwardens.[16]

Wakefield was a somewhat extreme case of the influence of a new school of enlightened thought and benevolent sentiment. The humanitarianism which he represented had many beneficiaries. Prisoners of war, often unsupported either by their own or their captors' government, were relieved by subscriptions to provide them with food and clothes during both the Seven Years War and the American War. Officers were particularly well treated, especially when they were released on parole. The first historian of Leicester, John Throsby, noted of the thirty prisoners held there in 1756–7, 'for their genteel behaviour they were much esteemed by the inhabitants of Leicester, and they mingled in all polite assemblies, with, as it were, a native agreeableness.'[17] The calculation that they spent some £9,000 during their detention at Leicester doubtless added to their popularity. In the following war this happy history of civilized conduct in the midst of hostilities continued, though with one unfortunate interruption, when a French officer killed an Englishman in a brawl. As a known duellist, his plea that he had discharged his pistol by accident seemed implausible. His request for a jury made up of Frenchmen and Englishmen in equal numbers was rejected, and he was duly convicted of murder. But the King pardoned him, and both the trial and the outcome were treated as a suitably impressive demonstration of the principle that nationality was no bar to justice in an English court.[18]

[16] *Memoirs of the Life of Gilbert Wakefield*, i. 190–3, 197–8.
[17] J. Throsby, *The Memoirs of the Town and County of Leicester* (6 vols., Leicester, 1777), v. 90.
[18] J. Thompson, *The History of Leicester in the Eighteenth Century*, pp. 165–8.

The cult of feeling was particularly vulnerable to the strains of the American War, if only because it was so readily portrayed as fratricidal. The brotherhood of man had much appeal, but the brotherhood of English subjects had more. The fact that rigid opponents of the colonists described them not as brothers but as rebellious sons in need of paternal correction accentuated this domestic dimension to the Anglo-American conflict. It was exploited by critics of the war to some effect, for example by Samual Jackson Pratt in his novel *Emma Corbett* in 1780. The tale was of a heroine torn between her brother, fighting to defend his uncle's property in America, and her lover, an officer in the army of George III. The uncertainties of war permitted Pratt to maximize her suffering by having both brother and lover die twice, the second time for good in each case. Emma herself died only once, giving birth to her child. She might have suffered a still worse fate, but General Washington had released her when she was captured, assuring her: 'I am not at war with the *affections*.'[19] Reviewers expressed the hope that the novel would have an effect comparable to Mauduit's *Considerations on the German War* in 1761; what close analysis and sceptical argument had achieved in one generation was evidently to be accomplished by sympathy and sentiment in the next.

Men were readier to address this theme than women, but they had in mind a female as well as male readership. Thomas Day, an eccentric worshipper of Rousseau, penned passionate outbursts against the war, including *The Desolation of America*. It particularly invoked the horrors of war for women and children.

> The cries of wretched mothers, that in vain
> Lament their fate, and mourn their children slain;
> The virgin's shriek, who trembling in the dust,
> Weeps the pollution of a ruffian's lust;
> The mangled infant's wail, that as he dies,
> Looks up in vain for pity to the skies.[20]

Yet Day was no pacifist. Like many other self-consciously radical reformers of the day he had an appreciation of the military basis of patriotism which made war in a noble cause thoroughly defensible. The time had not yet come to abandon that rich ideological

---

[19] p. 236.
[20] (London, 1777), p. 19.

tradition which connected 'patriotism' with the defence of hearth and home, and which made the landed men who could beat their ploughshares into swords the very embodiment of civic virtue. On this view it was the Americans, pitting a volunteer militia against the mercenary Hessians and Hanoverians of a despotic king, who were the true patriots, even if men like Thomas Day and Richard Price were embarrassed by some of their practices, for example their sanction of slavery. Ironically, when America proved so successful that France was brought into the war, traditional, 'anti-Gallican' patriotism was revived in its full force, swamping the tentative pacifism of the early years of the war. The almost hysterical atmosphere which obtained in 1778 and 1779 left no room for negotiation. As the Moravian James Hutton told Benjamin Franklin, 'There is such a spirit and temper now in the nation, that I cannot think Independency could be successfully proposed.'[21] The novelty of a sustained anti-war movement was postponed until the Revolutionary War of the 1790s.

THE EXPERIENCE OF WAR

Though Englishmen were used to the idea of war, most of them experienced it at second hand. Only during the Forty-Five were they subjected to the presence of enemy troops on English soil. In that instance their experiences were hardly comparable to those of other nations. The terrors inflicted by barbarous Highlanders could not plausibly be bracketed, for instance, with the sufferings of Frederick II's subjects in the Seven Years War. The gulf between the experience of English warriors and English civilians in this respect was enormous. One of the few in a position to bridge it, recording his impressions for posterity, was the young Samuel Kelly, a seaman who had visited Charleston before the American War and found himself among the crew of a vessel which called there in 1782. It was not simply the human suffering and sorrow which struck him, but the sheer scale and impact of destruction which war could bring. Houses were destroyed, mansions ruined, the tea-garden in which he had once lingered devastated, the church steeple painted a sinister black to prevent it serving as a landmark for those at sea. Even the famous statue of Lord Chatham had been symbolically defaced by the siege-guns.[22]

[21] D. Benham, *Memoirs of James Hutton*, pp. 511–12.
[22] C. Garstin, *Samuel Kelly: An Eighteenth-Century Seaman* (London, 1925), p. 51.

War resembled a remote form of theatre in which spectators and actors were forever separated. There was also a somewhat theatrical quality about those manifestations of war which did make themselves obvious to ordinary citizens. The reform of the militia in 1757 brought large numbers of men into temporary military service, and made their marches, exercises, and encampments a presence more obtrusive than the peacetime activities of a small standing army. In the American War two great camps were formed for the protection of London against potential invasion, at Coxheath in Kent, and Warley in Essex. They became the objects of intense interest to Londoners. A primitive coach service was organized, and various forms of commercial exploitation took place, including side-shows, prostitution, and gaming.[23] The militia themselves operated in a rather unreal atmosphere, training in the midst of civilian society for a war which might never come close, but which, if it did, would become one of deadly seriousness.

Champions of the militia thought they had 'proved there was scarce any degree of perfection at which a Militia Battalion could not arrive.'[24] But militiamen were not the doughty yeomen envisaged by patriot theorists. Most of them were too poor either to buy themselves exemption from service or to resist the temptation of the bounty payable if they volunteered. In fact it was admitted that they differed very little from those who served in the army, where discipline and training were at least likely to be more rigorous. Possibly they did something to boost civilian morale. Their accomplishments were not exclusively, perhaps not primarily, military. The young Lord Althorp, at Warley with the Northants militia in 1779, noted the lively competition for the title of crack regiment between the North Gloucesters and the Dorsets, but saw nothing incongruous in the observation that much of the latter's superiority derived from their band. The Colonel of the Dorsets was said to have refused an offer of £300 from his first clarinetist to buy himself out, such was his pride in the musical prowess of his command.[25] Perhaps it was not surprising that professional entertainers saw the potential of the camp. On the London stage there was a successful production of a musical

[23] T. L. S. Sprigge, ed., *The Correspondence of Jeremy Bentham*, vol. ii: 1777–80 (London, 1968), p. 154.

[24] *A Plan of Internal Defence in the Present Crisis* (London, 1778), p. 9.

[25] British Library, Althorp Papers.

comedy entitled *Warley Camp*, with words by Sheridan and music by Dibdin.

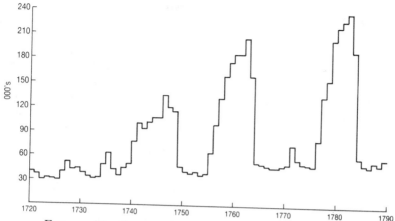

FIG. 10. Numbers serving in the armed forces, 1720–1790
Source: Parliamentary Papers. 1868–9, xxxv. Part II, 693ff.

Authentic experience of war was, of course, the fate of many men, more than might be supposed, given Britannia's boasted success in paying other people to fight for her, and the relatively small size of the peacetime army. At the height of the American War the total number serving in the army and navy approached a quarter of a million. Death or injury on the battlefield was not necessarily the main fear for serving soldiers and sailors. The men who went to war with the Liverpool Blues, raised at a time of intense patriotic ardour in 1778, had more serious matters to contend with than the Dorset Regiment at Warley. At their destination in Jamaica they found oppressive heat, rampant disease, the constant threat of French invasion, and countrymen who appalled them by their barbarity. Major Stanley, son of Lord Strange and grandson of the Earl of Derby, died not as he and his family would have wished, sword in hand, but in bed, rotting of putrid fever, and cursing 'the Ministry in the bitterest terms, for sacrificing him to the inclemencies of an infernal Clime'.[26] It was not necessary to go to the tropics to expire ingloriously on behalf of King and country. In the Forty-Five the volunteer regiments

[26] O. F. Christie, ed., *The Diary of the Revd William Jones, 1777–1821* (London, 1929), p. 64.

raised against the Pretender suffered terribly from the infectious diseases which they encountered. According to the memoirs of the dramatist Richard Cumberland, whose father had helped raise troops in Northamptonshire, smallpox at Carlisle made 'cruel havock' among the 'young peasantry'.[27] In the navy, confinement for long periods on a poor diet in unhygienic conditions ensured an equally grim record. A few weeks on blockade duty in the western Channel was quite as devastating in this respect as service in the Caribbean or Africa. In 1763 it was calculated that whereas only about 1,500 sailors had died in action against the enemy, some 133,708 had been lost by disease and desertion.[28] These figures are hardly credible but they suggest something of the contemporary concern with the problem.

Some of the most distinguished physicians of the day enlisted in the cause of maintaining the nation's seapower. The navy acquired its own infirmary, the Haslar Hospital at Portsmouth, founded in 1746. Hygiene and diet attracted by far the most interest. The connection between crowded conditions and disease was well known. It was to be the subject of a matching campaign to improve the health of gaols, slums, and not least hospitals themselves. In the navy it began earlier, when the wars of the mid-century brought home to the authorities the gravity of the situation. Ventilators were designed to improve the supply of clean air in naval vessels. There was a lively competition between their designers, Stephen Hales and Samuel Sutton, to secure the patronage of the Admiralty.[29] Scurvy was the principal cause for concern. Its peculiarly enervating symptoms made it the nightmare of naval commanders and administrators. The good effects of a diet of fresh vegetables and fruit were widely understood, but proving the precise connection and identifying the magic component proved extraordinarily difficult. James Lind in effect solved the problem with his discovery of the efficacy of citrus fruits at the end of the War of 1739–48, but the impracticality of organizing strict scientific tests under laboratory conditions meant that his prescription was not generally adopted for many years. This delay was not the result of blind prejudice and ignorance on the part of the naval authorities.

---

[27] *Memoirs of Richard Cumberland*, p. 57.

[28] G. J. Marcus, *Heart of Oak: A Survey of British Sea Power in the Georgian Era* (London, 1975), p. 130.

[29] A. Zuckerman, 'Scurvy and the Ventilation of Ships in the Royal Navy: Samuel Sutton's Contribution', *Eighteenth Century Studies*, 10 (1976–7), 222–34.

Senior officers recognized that medicine had a vital part to play in the work of creating an efficient navy. Rodney, for instance, took the resourceful Gilbert Blane as his private doctor to the West Indies in 1779 and subsequently made him Physician to the Fleet, in order to give him more scope. Blane was to play an important part in promoting antiscorbutics. Britain was always short of cannon-fodder, and the saving of lives was a contribution to national security as much as it was evidence of growing humanitarianism.

THE ECONOMIC EFFECTS OF WAR

Successful warfare was expected to bring notable economic benefits in a world accustomed to the notion that trade followed the flag. New markets might be acquired, new sources of raw materials might be exploited, and, occasionally, completely new trades might be developed. In the debate about the peace terms which ended the Seven Years War economic arguments were as prominent as strategic considerations. Given that it was not practicable to retain both French Canada and the French West Indies, much attention was devoted to the relative advantages of Canada for fish, fur, and an expanding Indian trade, and of Guadeloupe and Martinique for a dominant position in world sugar production. Behind these arguments could be discerned some powerful vested interests. There was a suspicion that one of the considerations which tilted the balance in favour of Quebec was the anxiety of the sugar merchants and planters to protect British West Indian sugar from further competition within the empire.

The American War ended with a still more difficult debate, which challenged the premises of mercantilist strategy as a whole. Should the newly independent United States of America be treated as privileged trading partners, in effect enjoying the advantages of membership of the empire without its political responsibilities? Should the traditional protectionism maintained against the commercial rivalry of most of the Continental powers be abandoned in favour of the uncertain but exciting possibilities of freer trade? Should that most sacred principle of the Navigation System, the merchant marine's monopoly of the British and colonial carrying trade, be breached by permitting American and even European vessels to compete on equal terms? With the notable exception of the reciprocal lowering of duties on Anglo-French trade in 1787, the answers eventually given to these questions were generally negative and invariably cautious. But the very attention devoted to them is a reminder that war could change perspectives on economic policy.

The actual impact of war on the economy is difficult to determine, partly because conclusive statistical evidence either way is not available, partly because the question itself is a somewhat unreal one. Claims that war had on balance a disadvantageous effect depend on the assumption that the alternative to war was peace on the existing terms. But most wars were fought more to prevent change than to bring it about. In 1756 the advocates of war believed that continued peace would permit the French to expand their empire and trade both in the Americas and Asia, with disastrous consequences for Britain. A fair assessment of the commercial consequences of the Seven Years War does not mean comparing the realities of 1763 with those of 1756; rather it requires a comparison of the realities of 1763 with the hypothetical effects of a further seven years' peace. Any model employed to make the first comparison is irrelevant. Any devised to cope with the second is highly speculative.

What is not in doubt is that war brought dramatic changes, sometimes temporary, sometimes permanent. The damage which the War of Jenkins' Ear did to the long-standing trade with mainland Spain was one of the first consequences of a war waged to facilitate commercial penetration of the Spanish empire. It was not readily repaired thereafter. The severe blows inflicted on colonial trade by the conflict with America resulted from a war designed to secure the economic benefits of that trade on an enduring basis. Though the war failed, the trade itself rapidly recovered. The most spectacular advantages brought by war were likely to be short-lived. Territorial expansion and naval mastery in the Seven Years War generated an extraordinary boom in overseas trade and domestic production, which made the post-war recession seem all the more disastrous. It is a commonplace observation that before the era of total war peacetime activities of all kinds often proceeded as if they were little affected by the fortunes of war. But the impression is somewhat misleading. Every kind of enterprise could be affected by wars and the taxation required to finance them. Agriculture, for instance, was by no means immune. At the very least, wartime borrowing by the State tended to reduce the price of government stock while increasing its yield, thereby rendering land an unattractive investment. High land taxes as well as multiplying excises in wartime ensured that landowners suffered along with ordinary consumers. A bad harvest or more general strains in commerce and credit could complete a dangerous cycle of crisis for the land. In the disastrous year of 1779 it was widely believed that the landed interest suffered even more than others. Certainly the 'economical reform' campaign with which it ended testifies to the anxiety engendered by the war in the county communities.

It did not help at such times that those who profited most by war often had a shady reputation. Privateering was not the only morally dubious beneficiary of warfare. Many men made fortunes out of supplying the armed forces, and it was easy to assume that they were enabled to do so by corrupt means. The hostility to government contractors during the American War was the most extreme example of a recurrent preoccupation. But this was not the full extent of the illegal profiteering promoted by war. Smugglers had a doubly unpatriotic interest in war, which flourished in proportion as British arms faltered. During the Seven Years War they found it difficult to compete with prices kept relatively low by their country's temporary dominance in world trade, and difficult also, to conduct their operations once the navy completely controlled the seas around the British Isles. But during the War of the Austrian Succession and the War of American Independence, neither of these restraints applied. Naval forces were severely stretched until the last stages of each of these wars, and in no position to reinforce the laws against smuggling. In each war, too, supplies of foreign goods were disrupted, and a vast market in illegal imports sprang up.

Smuggling is not, by its nature, susceptible to statistical analysis, but there is ample evidence that it reached new heights in each of these periods, the 1740s and the 1770s. The report which the Excise Board submitted at the end of the American War reveals its significance in colourful detail. It reckoned that duties on spirits and tea, the principal commodities involved, would be doubled if smuggling could be stopped. There were some hundred vessels of anything from ten to three hundred and fifty tons engaged in it, most of them armed with heavy guns. In Cornwall a fortified cove, in theory meant as a form of voluntary coastal defence against the enemy, was used for the landing of goods in perfect security. In Sussex a typical operation involved delivering 3,000 horse-loads, from three large vessels protected by gangs of between thirty and sixty men. There were well-established inland smuggling bases: in London, for instance, Stockwell was notorious as a distribution centre. Transport was painstakingly organized. Marlborough in Wiltshire was cited as a major staging post on a thoroughfare which ran from the Dorset and Hampshire coast to lucrative markets in Oxfordshire, Warwickshire, and Worcestershire.[30] The sheer scale of the organization involved in smuggling not only made it, as contemporary parlance often recognized, a 'trade' in its own right, but one which was well adapted to benefit by the disruption of war.

Eighteenth-century government did not normally involve itself in commercial and manufacturing activities directly. But the requirements of war sometimes compelled it to do so. In these matters its view was dictated by practicalities rather than economic principles, the usual result being some form of collaboration between the State and private enterprise. The Royal Brass Foundry, for instance, had been established in 1716 after a disastrous explosion in the privately managed ordnance works at Moorfields. Under George III its history revealed how government could participate in rapid techological development and indeed stimulate it in others. The Verbruggen family, seduced from Dutch service and brought to Woolwich in 1770, introduced new founding and boring techniques, and set standards of construction which forced others to display equal initiative. It was their devastating report about the inferior naval cannon manufactured by the famous Carron works, which gave Anthony Bacon, later a no less famous ironmaster, his chance to contract for the supply of the latest, solid-bored guns.[31] Similar inventiveness characterized naval construction. Anson and Sandwich, between them responsible for the Admiralty for the greater part of three decades, made strenuous efforts to erase the navy's reputation for inferior naval architecture and shipbuilding. They both had to gear up a decaying peacetime fleet to the requirements of world

[30] PRO, CUST. 48. 21.
[31] M. H. Jackson and C. de Beer, *Eighteenth Century Gunfounding* (Newton Abbot, 1973), Part II.

war, and both relied heavily on stimulating private shipbuilders to compete with the royal dockyards. They were quick to recognize the advantages of new techniques and skills. Copper-sheathing of hulls, perhaps the single most important innovation of the period, was introduced under Anson and extended to become a matter of routine by Sandwich. The most intractable problem faced by both was the shortage of good quality timber. It is not easy to see what either could have done to solve it in the space of a few years.

The economic effects of government spending on warfare in a wider sense are difficult to quantify but equally difficult to deny. Some industries owed much to munition requirements. The rapid expansion of iron manufacturing from the 1750s onwards is partly to be explained in these terms. It is not surprising that some of its most prominent figures, Samuel Garbett, Matthew Boulton, John Roebuck, the Wilkinsons, were experts in the art of lobbying ministers and Parliament. Brass and copper developed as rapidly, not least to meet the requirements of the armed forces. In wartime this was also true of industries less commonly associated with such a market. Textiles were required in volume when armies and navies had to be fitted out. At the beginning of the American War, the losses incurred in the West Riding woollen manufacture by embargoes on Anglo-American trade were in large measure made up by orders for the supply of clothing to British troops.

Some of the expenditure of war was of marginal or no economic advantage. Subsidies of foreign allies, for example, though often praised as protecting the domestic labour force from the manpower needs of war, were virtually a dead loss, though sometimes they came back in the form of orders for British goods. But most wartime expenditure went to the financing of goods and services which had a stimulating commercial and industrial effect. In this sense war was a means of compelling the taxpayer to make an investment in home production. There was a price: the National Debt rocketed upwards, and borrowing was financed by raising new taxes which in time added to the costs of production. Moreover, war diverted capital from what Adam Smith considered its natural channel. On the other hand, artificial injections of demand have had their advocates in modern economies, and there is no doubt that the industries directly affected developed more speedily than was likely in normal conditions. In peacetime investment in agriculture and communications rose rapidly. During wartime many of the funds used for these purposes were diverted to government, either through taxation or lending. The result was an alternating series of investment patterns, which may well, in the result, have produced an unintended balance.

POPULATION AND PROCREATION

Contemporaries not only found it difficult to assess the impact of the war on the economy, they were also uncertain of some of the most basic features of economic development. Demographic growth itself was doubted. Three papers published in the transactions of the Royal Society between 1751 and 1756 by William Brakenridge offered a gloomy interpretation of the limited information available, notably the London Bills of Mortality. His critics, George Burrington and Richard Forster, did not deny the depressing logic of the Bills, but asserted that it was compatible with healthy growth in provincial towns and in the countryside.[32] Even in the immediate environs of London, they found grounds for consolation. To set against the evidence of declining house-building and occupancy in the City, it was possible to point to the continuing expansion of Paddington, St Pancras, and Marylebone, all of them outside the Bills of Mortality, but very much within the expanding metropolitan areas.

When Brakenridge was writing, the upturn in population was only just beginning. He reckoned the total for England and Wales at 5,340,000, when it was probably nearly a million more. In the next generation similar arguments were put with less justification but more force by the relentless controversialist Richard Price. When Price published his *Essay on the Population of England, From the Revolution to the present Time* in 1780, the population was more than seven million, and growing at an unprecedentedly fast rate, Yet Price put it at less than five million, not much more (as he pointed out) than the kingdom of Naples, and less than one-fifth of the French total. He met with some redoubtable opponents: William Eden, who was to enjoy a distinguished political and diplomatic career, William Wales, mathematician, astronomer, and scientific adviser on Cook's second and third voyages, and John

---

[32] D. V. Glass, *Numbering the People: The Eighteenth-Century Population Controversy and the Development of Census and Vital Statistics in Britain* (Farnborough, Hampshire, 1973), p. 51.

Howlett, a clergyman who became known for the thoroughness of his statistical enquiries. Howlett argued, correctly, that the population had been growing for a period of some twenty years, and that by 1780 it was at least a third more than it had been in 1688, Price's base year. Howlett's own estimates, variously between eight and nine million, were too high, but he delivered some telling blows. Price had relied on three bodies of evidence, the house and window tax returns, excise revenues, and the Bills of Mortality. All three were misleading. Many houses and cottages were exempt from duty, and Howlett found it easy to demonstrate that the returns were seriously defective. The excise statistics were similarly rendered worthless by major uncertainties about the accounts recorded in the 1690s, which made comparisons with the late eighteenth century futile. The Bills of Mortality were not representative of other parts of the country.

Though Price was wrong, he was not easily discredited. Only a census would have settled the matter definitively. Such a solution had been proposed in Parliament in 1753 but dropped because of its unpopularity. It was feared that it would be used to exact oppressive taxes and invade civil liberties. The numerous amateur censuses conducted in the 1770s and 1780s were taken mainly in great and growing cities. Though they certainly revealed rapid growth, this did not answer the broader question. Even Price had not denied that the population was increasing in large manufacturing towns. Indeed, the proposition that urban growth occurred at the expense of the national stock in general, and that towns sucked in healthy lives only to destroy them, was an old one. It fitted well with conventional anxieties about the corrosive effect of commerce on the body politic. It also seemed to be supported by complaints of rural depopulation in an age of enclosure and engrossment.

The obsession with manpower was at times overwhelming. Many preoccupations which otherwise make little sense were closely associated with it. Not the least was the connection discerned between sexual morals and vital statistics. Historians of public morality have sometimes found themselves at a loss to explain the eighteenth century's curious mixture of attitudes, its comparatively relaxed view of sexual excesses in some respects, combined with continuing austerity in others. The relative tolerance which extended to libertines and rakes may be exaggerated, but there is no doubt that it contrasted with a marked intolerance of practices identified as aberrant. Homosexuality, for instance, could neither be avowed nor approved. Even in the theatrical world, where lower standards were taken for granted, it could prove disastrous. In the 1770s, Samuel Foote had the last years of his life ruined by a revelation of his sexual preferences, and the playwright Isaac Bickerstaffe sacrificed a promising career for the same reason. In Bickerstaffe's case the reverberations were so serious that two of the most celebrated performers of the day, David Garrick and Charles Dibdin, had to resort to legal action to dissociate themselves from the resulting scandals.

There seems to have been a flourishing market for books which brought the combined weight of morality and medicine to bear. Even if some of those who read *Onania*, in one of the nineteen editions produced between 1707 and 1759, were investing in pornography rather than puritanism, the unanimity of the condemnation remains striking. Fanciful explanations have been ventured, ranging from the need to defend paternal authority to the supposed connection of puritanism with capitalism.[33] A simpler and more plausible suggestion has to do with the conviction that the political and economic well-being of the country depended above all on procreation. Population growth was assumed to be synonymous not merely with national power but with civilized progress. Lord Kames, whose *Sketches of the History of Man* brought him a mixture of mockery and praise in 1774, argued that American Indians remained at their primitive stage of social development in large part because their males 'are feeble in their organs of generation, [and] have no ardour for the female sex'.[34] Failure to procreate was a source of much guilt, not least among men who turned to philanthrophy by way of expiation. Hanway was one of a number of childless benefactors of children; he told his public that 'since he could not be married to his mind, he had endeavoured to make ample satisfaction to his country.'[35] There were frequent proposals to encourage marriage by taxing bachelors and spinsters. They probably foundered more on recognition that marriage for propertied people was a far from easy matter, than

---

[33] P.-G. Boucé, 'Aspects of Sexual Tolerance and Intolerance in Eighteenth-Century England', *British Journal for Eighteenth-Century Studies*, 3 (1980), 173–91.
[34] R. L. Meek, *Social Science and the Ignoble Savage* (Cambridge, 1976), p. 159.
[35] *Virtue in Humble Life* (2 vols., London, 1774), i. 251.

on doubts about their equity. On these topics the double standard was not invariably adopted. Masculine privilege and patriarchal authority did not extend to those who would not or could not carry out the first responsibility of their sex. Women encumbered with such a husband were morally relieved of their duty to obey before they were legally freed of it, as the commentaries on published divorce cases, a popular literary category in its own right, testify.

The medical profession had a special part to play in these matters. Doctors had a stronger incentive to marry than their peers in other professions. It was a recognized axiom that a doctor who sought the custom of respectable and fashionable women must first take a wife. The famous James Currie, who made himself Liverpool's most popular physician, commenced his successful career after some years of indigence, by marrying. (It helped, in his case, that he found a bride in one of Liverpool's most opulent mercantile families.) Doctors were enthusiastic advocates of conventional sexual morality. This was true even of the bizarre James Graham, whose Temple of Health and Hymen, established in 1780 to restore fertility and bliss to married couples, attracted notoriety. After three years he was compelled to transfer his interest to the stimulating effects of mud-baths. Yet he subscribed to the received wisdom in sexual matters: the desirability of marriage, the viciousness of prostitution, the wastefulness of masturbation.[36] Inventiveness could be displayed in less spectacular ways than Graham's. It was easy enough to describe and deplore the medical consequences of promiscuity. The bad effects of masturbation required more imagination, and got it, with elaborate discussions of the physical and eventually mental debilitation which it caused. In this as in many other respects doctors were considered good citizens as well as good counsellors. They saw themselves, no doubt, as relieving suffering in a manner which could be supported by Christian piety and enlightened reason alike. But they also saw themselves as true patriots, even when they were not, like Lind and Hales, improving the health of the armed forces as such.

The campaign to popularize the use of inoculation against smallpox will always be associated with the name of Lady Mary Wortley Montagu who initiated it in 1721, after learning the technique on

<hr />

[36] R. Porter, 'The Sexual Politics of James Graham', *British Journal for Eighteenth-Century Studies*, 5 (1982), 199–206.

her travels in Turkey. But it was much later, in the mid-1760s, that Robert Sutton and his son Daniel devised a system of mass treatment. They emphasized its utility to a nation recurrently at war. Extensive claims were made for its efficacy. Thomas Dimsdale, one of its most successful promoters, boasted of having cleared the town of Hertford of the disease between 1766 and 1774. Howlett reckoned that a decisive improvement in Maidstone had occurred with the introduction of inoculation in 1767. It is difficult to assess the propriety of such boasts.[37] Medical authority is not wanting to endorse the propaganda of Dimsdale and Howlett. On the other hand, modern demographers stress increasing fertility rates more than declining mortality rates. The prospects of employment and the possibility of establishing an independent family may well have improved sufficiently to explain a small but notable lowering of the average marriage age of women from somewhat under twenty-six years in the second quarter of the century to twenty-four in the last quarter.[38] High real wages did not last very long, but help explain the shift on to a new plane of population growth, one which survived subsequent changes in economic conditions. Whatever the truth, there is no doubting the social earnestness and patriotic concern of the men who interested themselves in the production and preservation of people.

FINANCE AND TAXATION

Statistical analysis and patriotic concern were brought to bear on financial resources as well as human stock. Recurrent warfare after 1739 threatened to make the National Debt as grave a worry as it had been in the early years of the century, before the era of Walpolian peace and fiscal prudence. 'Modern wars,' it was noted in 1778, 'especially between England and France, have been in great measure competitions of expence.'[39] The strain of the War of the Austrian Succession was absorbed with relative ease, as Pelham's triumphant reduction of interest rates in 1749 showed. But the Debt climbed to dizzy heights during the Seven Years War and the American War, from less than 80 million in 1757 to

[37] P. Razell, *The Conquest of Smallpox: The Impact of Inoculation on Smallpox Mortality in Eighteenth-Century Britain* (Firle, 1977).

[38] E. A. Wrigley and R. A. Schofield, *The Population History of England, 1541–1871*, p. 423.

[39] *A Plan of Internal Defence in the Present Crisis.*

more than 240 million in 1783. In the same period the sum required annually to service the Debt rose from £2,735,925 to £9,406,406. In wartime it was all too easy to rely on public borrowing as the main means of meeting extraordinary expenditure. Any attempt to pay for war by taxation would have required a total recasting of the land tax, the introduction of a direct levy on personal and business incomes, and the establishment of a centralized bureaucracy capable of assessing and collecting the new revenues. Such radical solutions were politically unacceptable except in the most dire emergency: not until 1798, when the State was threatened by bankruptcy and revolution, were they adopted.

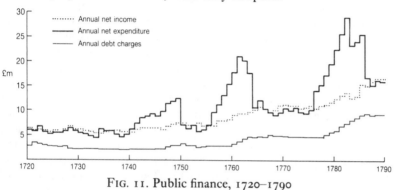

FIG. 11. Public finance, 1720–1790

Source: B. R. Mitchell and P. Deane, *Abstract of British Historical Statistics*, pp. 386–8, 389–91

In the mean time ministers preferred to borrow, mortgaging the future rather than rendering the present unduly uncomfortable. Both Newcastle and North did so on terms which favoured the investor at the expense of the public. North, especially, could only raise funds in the last years of the American War by offering bonuses and inducements which gratuitously burdened the capital account. The sum actually borrowed in the American War was £91.8 million, but the capital debt funded rose by £115.3 million. It was a matter of judgement as to whether such desperate generosity was necessary. Investors who could afford to put their money in government stock under these circumstances certainly profited handsomely. It was not just that the terms of war loans were attractive in themselves. Peacetime conditions inevitably raised the capital value of stock, just as war lowered it. An investor who waited for peace to have its effect could make a handsome capital gain. As one London Welshman put it, writing home to his family in 1759, 'Stock being so low every one is for buying that has money to spare, on a prospect of getting above 20 per cent on the peace, and about 4 per cent interest in the mean time.'[40] It was not necessary to be patriotic to take a share in British warfare. Foreign investors did so on a large scale. It was reckoned in 1776 that three-sevenths of the debt was owned by the Dutch. This was a considerable exaggeration, but there was a widespread belief that a Debt owned in part by foreigners must in effect make government their pawn. From a foreign standpoint the relationship looked rather different. The Debt could be seen as a means by which Englishmen mortgaged their political system and made foreigners sustain them in prosperity. 'The English State sinks away under its debt, but the substance of that debt is spread among the nation, which becomes rich and prospers, although the State is poor.'[41]

The political ramifications of the Debt were extensive. In the early eighteenth century the principal creditors of the State had been the great financial corporations, the Bank of England, the East India Company, and the South Sea Company. Nominally all three remained important. But the reality was different. The South Sea Company, since its disaster in 1720, enjoyed an independent financial existence only on paper. The East India Company, as a territorial power, was required after 1767 to make a contribution to the Exchequer, but its share in the National Debt was relatively insignificant. Even the Bank became a managerial agency for the Treasury, rather than a funding institution. The critical stage in this respect was the War of the Austrian Succession, when the government in effect engaged in borrowing from the public at large. The novelty of this proceeding was masked partly by the gradual nature of the change, partly by the fact that the initial floating of a loan was negotiated with City financiers. They were usually well represented on the great corporations themselves and in a sense they constituted a powerful informal corporation in their own right, one essential to the everyday running of the country. But the money for the supply of which they contracted ultimately came from a numerous class of investors drawn from all sections

[40] J. H. Davies, ed., *The Letters of Lewis, Richard, William and John Morris, of Anglesey (Morrisiaid Mon) 1728–1765* (2 vols., Aberystwyth, 1907–9), ii. 109.

[41] C. Wilson, *Anglo-Dutch Commerce and Finance in the Eighteenth Century*, p. 188.

of propertied society and extending well down the social scale. The annuities offered by government, the most important of them, after Pelham's Debt Conversion in 1749, the famous Reduced Three Per Cents and Consols, became the principal stocks. The substantial share of the national wealth tied up in government debt, the proportion of economic growth which went to sustain it, and the erratic, speculative nature of the contemporary market in industrial capital made for a highly distinctive system of public finance, quite unlike that of Victorian times. The consequences for the politics have never been precisely calculated, and perhaps remain incalculable. But at the very least they strengthened the community of interest which bound together the propertied nation in its widest sense and the political élite.

In the early nineteenth century this nexus of financial interests could be seen for what it was, an important element in the system which subjected government to the will of the propertied classes. At the time criticism focused more on the sheer risk and instability of such a system. During the American War, the old fear, long dormant, that the National Debt might become insupportable was once again commonplace. The reformer James Burgh thought that the ultimate catastrophe of constitutional collapse would commence with a run on the stocks. He advocated associations of the kind which had been seen in 1745, to support public credit in the event of such a crisis.[42] A variety of schemes was proposed to stave off bankruptcy, usually involving new taxation. The most influential came appropriately from the self-appointed censor of the age Richard Price, whose early tracts on the subject were published in 1771 and 1772. The fiscal horrors of the American War bestowed a prophetic plausibility on his warnings, and induced politicians, led by Price's friend Lord Shelburne, to take them seriously. Price's praise of the beauty of compound interest and his insistence on the need for a new sinking fund eventually bore fruit in Pitt's legislation of 1786. As with most of Price's projects, theory and practice turned out to be very different things. Even in peacetime it would have required higher interest rates and additional taxes to give the sinking fund a prospect of success. As it was the Revolutionary and Napoleonic Wars engulfed it in a torrent of new borrowing.

What made speculations like Price's peculiarly interesting to a

[42] *Political Disquisitions*, iii. 434.

wider public was not so much the size of the Debt in the future as the burden of paying interest on it at present. Traditionally, ordinary peacetime expenditure was met largely from direct taxation, principally in the form of the land tax. There was a certain simplicity about budgeting under George II, well summarized by an entry in George Bubb Dodington's diary for 1751: 'Voted 3s. per £ on the land, which with the malt, and £40,000 out of the Sinking Fund, makes the Supply.'[43] Indirect taxation, in the form of customs and excise duties, went partly to support the Crown's civil list, partly to sustain the interest payments on the National Debt. In essentials, this system remained unaltered from the days of Walpole to those of the younger Pitt. But the burden imposed by wartime borrowing imperceptibly changed its character. As the proportion of the annual budget allocated to the payment of interest rose, so the part played by the indirect taxes which sustained it became more prominent. In the 1730s, out of an annual budget of about five million, two million represented interest payments, most of it funded from excise duties established during the wars of William and Anne. By the 1780s some nine million of a budget of about thirteen million went to pay for the Debt. Indirect taxation as a proportion of the whole naturally rose. Even in wartime, when the land tax was levied at its highest rate, direct taxes played a limited part in the calculations of Treasury ministers. In 1720 they produced 38 per cent of the total tax yield, in 1760 26 per cent, and in 1780 20 per cent.

This trend toward indirect taxation caused concern, not least because it was obvious that taxes on consumption bore disproportionately hard on the poor consumer. In fact Walpole's successors at the Treasury were conscious of the social hardship inflicted by excises, and sought at least to divert them from the basic necessities of life. The four taxes regarded as objectionable in this respect, those on salt, soap, candles, and leather, contributed a much smaller part of North's budgets than they had of Walpole's.[44] But this caution hardly removed the cause for concern.

[43] J. Carswell and L. A. Dralle, eds., *The political Journal of George Bubb Dodington* (Oxford, 1965), p. 99.
[44] The comparison is based on the accounts summarized in the *Calendar of Treasury Books* for the earlier period, and in *Parliamentary Papers* for the later. The four taxes yielded only 6% of revenue in 1785, about a third of the proportion which they had provided in 1718.

In the second half of the century the rising price of most foodstuffs made even light taxation onerous. There were also items, notably tea and ale, which for practical purposes were necessities rather than luxuries, and which were undeniably taxed at a high and increasing rate. Tea, admittedly, could be treated as an enervating drug and a symptom of oriental effeminacy, well deserving of the taxman's attention. Jonas Hanway waged furious war on it, characteristically appealing to patriotic opinion for support. 'Were they the sons of tea-sippers, who won the fields of Cressy and Agincourt, or dyed the Danube's stream with Gallic blood?'[45] Arthur Young advocated a heavier tea excise, aimed specifically at the poor.[46] The reverse happened. In 1785 Pitt drastically reduced the tea duties in order to take the profit out of smuggling. By 1787 when David Davies was undertaking his careful investigation of lower-class budgets, tea had ceased to seem either so noxious or so luxurious. He criticized it only as 'the occasion of much idle gosiping among the women'.[47] There was no difference of opinion about beer. The most atavistic critics of popular taste could not approve duties which raised the price of the ordinary Englishman's ale. Government taxed it heavily, while publicly regretting the necessity.

High-minded anxiety about the effect of taxation on the poor was reinforced by anger at its impact on the standard of living of the modestly well off. The list of excisable commodities was considerably longer at the end of the American War than it had been at the commencement of the War of the Austrian Succession. Glass, silver plate, carriages and post-horses, auction sales, male servants, hair powder, advertisements, receipts, wagons and stage-coaches, offices, all were newly taxed between 1740 and 1783. This was in addition to increases in the rates of existing duties. The whole range of alcoholic beverages, together with the hops and malt which went into their manufacture, everything subject to import duties, the house and window taxes, stamp duties on paper, newspaper, dice, and cards, and a variety of business and legal transactions, all were loaded with additional taxation as a consequence of the wars. Some of these impositions were designed as a form of concealed income tax. But the fact that most of them fell

---

[45] *A Journal of Eight Days Journey from Portsmouth to Kingston upon Thames*, p. 245.
[46] *The Farmer's Letters to the People of England*, p. 534.
[47] *The Case of Labourers in Husbandry Stated and Considered*, p. 39.

on middle-class consumers who could well afford to pay did not lessen dislike of them. Nor did it meet the argument that in extending taxation the State was augmenting its power. Much of the new taxation, especially the stamp duties, the licences required of a wide range of professions, and the inland duties, were assessed and collected by the excise department, and thereby predictably unpopular.

It is no coincidence that one of the reforms adopted at the end of the American War was the Act of 1782 which disfranchised excise and customs officers in parliamentary elections. Public criticism of the means used to enforce the collection of the excise, notably the powers of search vested in officers and the summary jurisdiction employed in excise trials, was as marked in the 1780s as it had been earlier in the century. Some voices were admittedly heard in defence. The elder Pitt eventually confessed himself ashamed of his part in the outcry against the excise scheme of 1733, and Adam Smith denounced the popular and political clamour which had attended it.[48] The Excise Board was not unreasonably proud of its professionalism and efficiency, at least by comparison with other branches of government. Though constantly under pressure from the Treasury to use its patronage for electoral and political purposes, it resisted many ministerial demands, including those which involved anticipating reversions and selling offices in the manner which had become common in other departments. The Board was also conscious of its unpopularity and reluctant to increase it. In 1775 it virtually refused to employ its legal powers to collect the plate duty on the grounds that it 'would bring such an Odium upon the Law of Excise, as would prove extremely inconvenient to the Management of the Revenue'.[49] The following year, faced with a parliamentary suggestion that the carriage and duty be reinforced by means of a licence to be displayed on every carriage and renewed annually, it killed the proposal by pointing out the extreme difficulty which would attend relations between carriage owners and the officers empowered to license them.[50] Such caution needs setting against the hostility which the excise encountered throughout the period, but

---

[48] R. H. Campbell and A. S. Skinner, eds., *An Inquiry into the Nature and Causes of the Wealth of Nations* (2 vols., Oxford, 1976), ii. 886.

[49] PRO, CUST. 18. 19, 19 Jan. 1775.

[50] Ibid.

which rose to alarming heights when the exigencies of war forced government to extend it.

COMMERCIAL OPTIMISM AND EARLY INDUSTRIALIZATION

Not every response to the changes taking place in the second half of the century was pessimistic. One powerful riposte to the Jeremiahs was Robert Wallace's *Characteristics of the Present Political State of Great Britain*. It is remarkable not least because it was published in 1758, at a time when the omens seemed unpromising. Wallace dismissed as unjustified the national mood of self-doubt captured by John Brown's *Estimate of the Manners*, of the preceding year. Periodic clamour about luxury he treated as so much pious nonsense. There was a sense in which everything was a luxury. 'Few things are more popular, than severity against national vices.'[51] He also parried some of the most telling blows of the sceptics. Against Hume he argued that paper credit had a stimulating, not a debilitating, economic effect. The National Debt he considered a modest burden, which could be paid off with the proceeds of one year's rental of Britain and Ireland. Industry, not silver and gold, was true riches, and every indication suggested that since the early seventeenth century Britain's wealth had multiplied threefold. In 1758 it was perhaps not easy to be convinced by Wallace's robustness, however much one admired it. But after the success of the Seven Years War, and the accompanying economic growth, there were more ample grounds for confidence. Sir James Steuart's *Inquiry into the Principles of Political Economy*, published in 1767, was characterized by Arthur Young as 'two large quarto volumes, seemingly in defence of all modern politics (in them, *whatever is, is right*).' Yet Young himself found on his travels 'the strongest marks of a rich, a happy, and a flourishing people'.[52] Most expansive and most ebullient of all, on the eve of the American War, was John Campbell's prolix *Political Survey of Britain* of 1774. The subtitle of Campbell's book explained that it was 'intended to Shew That we have not as yet approached near the Summit of Improvement, but that it will afford Employment

[51] p. 193.
[52] *The Farmer's Letters to the People of England*, p. 343; *A Six Months Tour Through the North of England*, iv. 549.

to many Generations before they push to their utmost Extent the natural Advantages of Great Britain'.

None of these works matched Adam Smith's *Wealth of Nations* in 1776 for intellectual distinction and subsequent influence. Smith's offered a simple but pioneering analysis of the fundamental division of income into rents, wages, and the profits of stock, and identified their respective owners, the landlord, the wage-earner, and the capitalist, as the 'three great, original and constituent orders of every civilised society'.[53] This understanding of the essentially unified character of capital, however and by whomever invested, created a new platform of economic theory on which the heroic stage of liberal economics (and later its Marxist derivative) could be constructed. Much of its argument was a merciless battering of the 'mercantile system' and the obstructions which it offered to the creation of wealth. Moreover, Smith was notably ambivalent about the long-term prospects of commercial society, even one liberated from the dead hand of monopoly.

Anxieties about the economic limitations of commercial development, not to say its moral and political consequences, were long-standing. They form one of the central and most inescapable themes of eighteenth-century thought. But turning the clock back was an option seriously considered only by a few hare-brained enthusiasts who had read their Rousseau without thought. Most of the social theory of the age accepted commercialism as a historical necessity for human improvement. The celebrated four-stage theory of human evolution treated hunting, pasturage, agriculture, and commerce as the successive modes of subsistence which determined the progress of civilization. Its claim to be 'conjectural history' is perhaps unduly modest. The men who expounded it, Adam Smith himself, Lord Kames, and Sir John Dalrymple, and those who developed it into a tool of sophisticated social analysis, notably John Millar and Adam Ferguson, supported their conjectures with a remarkable range of evidence, biblical, archaeological, literary, linguistic, and anthropological. But scholarly confirmation of the importance of commerce was hardly needed. Dr Johnson's complacent comments on the superiority of a fully developed manufacturing economy were representative of much received wisdom in the 1770s. 'Where flocks and corn are the only wealth, there are always more hands than work, and of that work

[53] i. 265.

there is little in which skill and dexterity can be much distinguished.'[54] Patriotic self-congratulation relied much on this argument, and foreigners were aware of its value in the context of international competition. It was often noted that Britain's economic strength and military potential ultimately derived from the vitality and variety of its manufacturing industry. As one French analyst put it, the British had 'grown richer by consuming'.[55]

The first half of George III's reign is often given a special place in the process of industrialization. Victorians invested the age with extraordinary significance, and made its leading entrepreneurs, Josiah Wedgwood, Matthew Boulton, James Watt, heroic figures worthy of a role in a historical epic. Modern economic analysis is less comfortable with the notion of a great Industrial Revolution, sweeping Britain into a completely new era.[56] This is a question of perspective. Compared with later industrial growth in other countries, the progress made in the eighteenth century can be made to look hestitant and unspectacular, though nobody has yet denied that Britain was the first society to tread the path of industrialization. Rather it is claimed that it did so at a gentle pace with measured steps. On this argument, growth took place at a faster rate during the early eighteenth century and a slower rate during the late eighteenth century, than enthusiasts for the concept of rapid industrialization have admitted. Beyond the confines of the cotton industry, the idea of 'industrial take-off' has come to seem implausible.

Unfortunately the evidence on which these contentions are based is highly unsatisfactory. Much of it consists of contemporary speculation refined but not necessarily reinforced by modern techniques of statistical analysis. On matters as crucial as the distribution of wealth, and spending on services, it is impossible to have confidence in what is essentially conjecture rather than computation. Moreover, the problems which most stand in need of a solution, concerning the chronology of growth, are those which most demand scepticism. Individual years have to be treated as

---

[54] R. W. Chapman, ed., *Johnson's Journey to the Western Islands of Scotland and Boswell's Journal of A Tour to the Hebrides with Samuel Johnson*, p. 92.

[55] F. Crouzet, 'The sources of England's Wealth: Some French Views in the Eighteenth Century', in P. L. Cottrell and D. H. Aldcroft, eds., *Shipping, Trade and Commerce: Essays in memory of Ralph Davis*, p. 69.

[56] See, for example, N. F. R. Crafts, *British Economic Growth during the Industrial Revolution* (Oxford, 1985).

base years for statistical purposes but they rarely lend themselves to short-term comparisons. 1760 and 1780, for example, create special difficulties, though the period which they encapsulate is a critical one for the debate about industrialization. The first belonged at the zenith of a successful war, in which a large proportion of world trade was sucked into a rapidly expanding domestic economy. The second coincided with the nadir of an unsuccessful war, marked by recession in many sectors of the economy. Only a reliable statistical series permitting annual or at least quinquennial comparisons could resolve such problems; it is unlikely that the available evidence will ever permit such precision.

This is not to say that a concern with the continuities of economic development rather than its sudden shifts is not revealing about the process of industrialization. The emphasis on the decades before 1760 is particularly rewarding. Growth in many sectors during the first half of the century was impressive. This is true not merely of industries in which early progress has long been recognized, for instance coal production, but also in some of those traditionally associated with a later period. The establishment of the Staffordshire potteries is difficult to disentangle from the career of Josiah Wedgwood. Yet their historian professes to find, as early as 1735, most of the characteristics of the mature industry: the supersession of essentially domestic manufacturing by relatively large-scale production, the introduction of specialized processing, dependent on division of labour, the concentration on a national and overseas market, the rapid urbanization of small manufacturing villages increasingly independent of their agrarian surroundings.[57]

The challenge to long-standing ideas about the process of industrialization extends beyond the question of chronology. The traditional model postulates linear progression from domestic manufacture towards a factory system, financed on a capitalist basis, reliant on a specialized system of production, and restructuring family organization, daily rhythms, and popular culture as it proceeds. This is highly inapplicable to the eighteenth century. If the essential criterion for factory organization is the concentration of a number of processes under one roof, there were few such by 1783, and virtually all of them in the cotton and silk industry. But the teleological assumptions involved in adopting

---

[57] L. Weatherill, *The Pottery Trade and North Staffordshire, 1660–1760* (Manchester, 1971).

such criteria are themselves somewhat dubious and perhaps have more to do with the requirements of nineteenth-century political economy than the realities of eighteenth-century economic growth. Technological change did not automatically produce factories. It affected different trades and different areas diversely, sometimes the same trade and the same area diversely according to local context. The Yorkshire woollen manufacture was famous for its dependence on small artisans and craftsmen, and its integration in the agricultural life of the West Riding; the Yorkshire worsted manufacture had early developed a high degree of centralization, based on the clothier's exploitation of the 'putting out' system in the manner of the West Country cloth industry. Both grew rapidly in the course of the eighteenth century, both expanded spectacularly at its end. But neither succumbed at once to the factory system as Lancashire cotton did.

Birmingham, home of the famous toy trade, was to become a byword for the survival of workshop industry in the nineteenth century. At a time, in 1770, when Matthew Boulton's celebrated establishment was employing a work-force nearing one thousand, there were hundreds of small foundries and metal-working shops. Perhaps no industrial centre benefited so consistently from the new features of the eighteenth century: an environment of enterprise unmarred by corporate restrictions, production of goods peculiarly adapted to the requirements of colonial and overseas markets, exploitation of a newly developed transport and mining structure which transformed the character of the West Midlands, and identification with some of the most innovative techniques of manufacturing. Yet it preserved small capitals, a skilled workforce of whom technology made greater, not lesser demands, and, not least, a diverse culture, tortured by political and religious contentions.

Generalizations about the character of early industrialization are difficult. Technological change often depended on, and was designed to improve, hand skills rather than mechanical adaptations. Family life was affected by growing reliance on women and children for the operation of easily manipulated machinery, but some machines, including the famous spinning mules, required the muscle power of men. Apprenticeship often gave way before the changing requirements of mass manufacturing but employers also proved capable of adapting it, both by varying the terms of apprenticeship and diversifying the training which they offered.

Domestic manufacturing sometimes caved in before the competition of highly centralized and capitalized concerns, but in some places, for example in the south and east, in the lace, straw, and glove manufactures, the effect of economic growth was to create new putting-out industries. Conversely, much 'industrialization' was short-lived, even ephemeral. Shropshire was almost synonymous with the early growth of the iron industry yet in retrospect it can be viewed as an example of abortive development.

CLASS AND INTEREST

One of the advantages of an economic history more cautious about the onset of industrialism and more conscious of its diversity is that it helps explain what once seemed like blindness to a transformation of enormous significance. Adam Smith's famous account of the effects of the division of labour on pin-making, and his speculations about the stultifying effect of drudgery on the minds of manufacturing workers, foreshadow some of the preoccupations of later commentators, but it would obviously be anachronistic to expect him to be familiar with an industrial landscape of factories and chimney-stacks. Even so, it is possible to trace some of the perspectives of an industrializing society in the outlook of his age. The language of class, for instance, owes its origin to the mid-eighteenth century. In part, resort to such language doubtless had to do with the advances made in scientific typology. The Linnaean classification of species is perhaps the best known example of this central concern. Its terminology offered advantages over the traditional vocabulary of social commentary. 'Order' and 'rank' were associated with relatively fine gradations, exemplified by the division of the peerage into ranks which meant a great deal to their possessors, but which obscured the broader similarities and unities obvious to those who were not peers. Status was increasingly seen as a complicated mixture of wealth, education, occupation, and manners, not readily defined with precision. It was best treated in broad terms which rendered the position of individuals problematical but captured the unifying tendencies of modern life. It was particularly useful to have a means of referring to the great mass of the population who did not belong with their propertied betters. The phrase 'lower class' was

already in use in the early part of George II's reign.[58] It appeared
quite frequently in the 1740s and 1750s and thereafter became
commonplace, though remaining interchangeable with other
expressions, the 'lower orders', the 'lower sort', and so on.[59]

References to the 'upper class' and 'higher class' were similarly
common by the 1770s.[60] Intriguingly, it was somewhat less usual
to talk of the 'middle class'. As late as 1784, when the Cambridge
don William Keate spoke simply of 'the middle class', he was
employing a comparatively novel expression.[61] It is not difficult
to see why it took longer to come into common currency. The
language of class was used by polite, educated, propertied society
principally as a means of identifying all those who were possessed
of little or no politeness, education, or property. Differences of
income and status which were crucial to a lower class teetering
perpetually on the brink of poverty but striving constantly to
avoid falling over it, appeared of little consequence to their social
superiors. Using comparable language to differentiate between
those with some property and those with more was a perilous
business. It also conflicted with the middle class's own vision
of itself. It was united in nothing more than in its members'
determination to make themselves gentlemen and ladies, thereby
identifying themselves with the upper class. Though Englishmen
prided themselves on the social mobility which they enjoyed, there
was a certain element of hypocrisy in such claims and a continuing
awareness that for the very great majority, such mobility was out
of the question. In a very real sense class was meant to indicate a
permanent, unchanging status: something which set its members
aside, so completely that for all purposes they could be treated as
a separate category. There was no embarrassment about describing
the lower class in such terms. But for middle-class men and
women to classify themselves thus would have been decidedly
uncomfortable.

The implications of this vocabulary should be taken seriously

---

[58] e.g. *Grub-Street Journal*, 27 Feb. 1735.

[59] W. Gordon, *A Sermon Preach'd in the New Church of St Matthew's, Bethnal Green, On the 20th of July, 1746* (London, 1746), p. 12; J. Rutty, *The Liberty of the Spirit and the Flesh Distinguished* (Dublin, 1756), p. 31.

[60] e.g. *The Lottery Magazine*, July 1776, p. 26; E. Bentham, *Charity Schools Sermon, 30 April 1772* (London, 1772), p. 15.

[61] *A Sermon, Preached upon the Occasion of the General Thanksgiving, for the late Peace, July 29th, 1784* (Bath, 1784), p. 24.

but not too seriously. The eighteenth century invented the modern terminology of class. It did not entertain the notion of class conflict, at any rate in its modern sense. On the contrary, the attraction of class as a concept borrowed from scientists was that it described distinctions which belonged, or were seen to belong, to an essentially balanced and harmonious world of nature. The concept of social conflict was commonplace enough; so was the belief of propertied people that they were vulnerable to the envy and resentment of the non-propertied. But there was a deep need, perhaps reinforced by the very instability of commercial society, to stress the divine requirement and political desirability of social subordination. Whether or not the world was the best of all possible worlds, most propertied people could agree that the lower classes occupied an unchangeable place within it. Class conflict was inconceivable as part of the divine plan, as part of the natural world, and as part of a well-organized society.

It was not easy to view individuals in other than an individualist framework, as the view even of many so-called 'radicals' testifies. Conflict between groups was commonly described using a terminology, that of interest, which could equally well account for the views of their individual members. The very idea that collective identity could transcend the individual was uncongenial and belonged rather in the philosopher's study than the practical world of politics. Part of the advantage of class was precisely that it made it easier to treat conflicts of interest as relatively minor matters which could be contained within the broader harmonies of social existence. The most threatening enmities of all were rendered as innocuous as it was possible to make them. In the early eighteenth century the antagonism of the landed interest and the moneyed interest had been sufficiently intense to arouse deep concern about its destabilizing effect. Thereafter it came to seem less important. When matters such as agricultural protection and the taxation of property were under discussion, or when financial crises brought bankers and brokers into uncomfortable public prominence, the old slogans were dusted off and put to use. But it suited almost everyone with property to play down such distinctions. Most landowners in some measure depended on the world of money and merchandise; most of the men who dominated the latter either owned land or desired to do so. Above all, the polite code of manners depended on treating the possession of wealth rather than land as the essential determinant of social standing. In the late eighteenth century the play of interests was at the centre of politics, and there was a sense in which parliamentary politics consisted of little else. But the interests were so numerous and complex that they did not need to be made the basis of any broader philosophy of conflict. Individuals had various interests, personal, professional, propertied. These required constant balancing, negotiating, and compromising. Emphasis on the unifying character of class made it easier to cope with their sometimes unsettling turbulence, but only religious differences, and the political conflicts which they engendered, truly threatened the propertied consensus. The 1790s were to prove a turning-point in this respect; until then they remained manageable.

INVENTION

If contemporary commentators were not always prophetic about the consequences of industrialization, they were well aware of the importance of technological change. The British had long prided themselves on their skill as manufacturers. But their special gift was a matter of dispute. Defoe had argued that the English were not great inventors, but rather great improvers of other people's inventions.[62] This view could not be sustained by the 1770s. Interest in technical improvement and innovation was intense in the first decades of George III's reign. 776 patents were registered between 1760 and 1785, 79 more than the total for the period 1617–1760. Controversy about the patent system was itself a symptom of the interest which was aroused by the rage for invention. Patents amounted to a form of monopoly, effectively placing a tax on the introduction of new techniques. The defeat in 1774 of the booksellers' attempt to secure a perpetual copyright in literary works had obvious implications for scientific creativity.[63] Both the legislature and the judiciary were wary about extending the rights even of the most ingenious inventors. There were some gigantic battles over patents in the 1770s. In one, in 1775, the Bristol porcelain manufacturer Richard Champion eventually obtained parliamentary sanction for the renewal of the patent which he had bought from William Cookworthy. In another, in 1781, Richard

[62] P. Earle, *The World of Defoe*, p. 125.
[63] See pp. 93–4.

Arkwright was defeated when he sought to prolong the patent of his successful carding and spinning machines. He was opposed by a committee set up in Manchester specifically to resist the legal protection of inventions. Yet it was obvious that without the guarantee of profit which a patent provided there was little incentive for the ingenious to employ their talents. Samuel Crompton, whose mule represented a breakthrough in the mechanization of the cotton industry, was unable to afford even the expense of obtaining a patent and opted for a local subscription to make his invention available in 1780. He obtained only £70 and spent most of his life in poverty.

The critic and poet William Kenrick argued in 1774 that it was precisely the function of patent law to provide incentives and that the system needed strengthening to increase its effectiveness.[64] Most commentators preferred the alternative of rewarding inventiveness without restricting the availability of its fruits. The example frequently used was the statutory reward offered in 1713 to the inventor of a reliable method of determining the longitude at sea. John Harrison's chronometers, developed and perfected over a long period between 1735 and 1773, were the result. But it was voluntary association rather than parliamentary policy which provided the most notable stimulus. The Society of Arts, founded in 1754, made practical invention its prime concern. In 1783 it boasted that the improvements of the preceding twenty years had been stimulated by its premiums and prizes for inventions of proven or potential worth.

It is difficult to adjudicate such claims. There is a sense in which technological promotion was in itself a form of entrepreneurial activity, distinct from any benefits which it actually brought. William Shipley, in effect the founder of the Society of Arts, conceived of his brain-child as a means of furthering his private drawing school, as well as an experiment in public spirit. Edmund Rack also had a personal interest in the famous society which he founded in 1777 at Bath, forerunner of the Bath and West. He drew a salary as its secretary and charged it a rent for giving it rooms in his own house.[65] Nor is there any simple means of

---

[64] W. Bowden, *Industrial Society in England towards the End of the Eighteenth Century* (New York, 1925), p. 25.

[65] D. G. C. Allan, *William Shipley: Founder of the Royal Society of Arts* (London, 1968), pp. 76 ff.; T. F. Plowman, *Edmund Rack: The Society He Founded and the Company He Kept* (Bath, 1914), p. 22.

elucidating the relationship between invention and industrial advance. One of the most famous examples of an engineering breakthrough, the improvement in furnace technology which made possible the use of coal rather than charcoal in iron-smelting, clearly reveals this difficulty. In essence the process had been initiated by Abraham Darby at Coalbrookdale in 1709. Failure to apply it on a wide scale has been attributed to technical deficiencies which were not overcome until the 1750s. But it is equally possible, and more plausible, to account for it in terms of the rising price of wood and the falling price of coal in the middle of the century. When the gap became big enough to make an alternative to traditional charcoal-smelting urgent, the technology of coke-smelting was to hand and quickly employed.[66] Even where completely new technology was involved, market requirements probably provided the crucial stimulus. Altogether it is difficult to believe that the premiums offered by the Society of Arts were a more effective incentive to ingenuity than the profit motive of individual manufacturers.

Machinery had an understandable fascination, one which emerges strongly from the attention devoted to it in contemporary literature. The popular monthly magazines regularly carried feature articles with appropriate illustrative matter. The *London Magazine*, for instance, offered a series of such articles by a mining engineer, Edward Barrass, between 1764 and 1766, with engraved prints of coal wagons and wagon ways, a coal-pit nearby, and a coal staith. Later, in 1777 and 1778, it returned to the subject with detailed accounts and drawings of a coal-pit, section by section, and a boring machine.[67] Though this kind of interest expanded in the early part of George III's reign, it built on a well-established tradition. The silk engine erected at Derby by Sir Thomas Lombe, nearly half a century earlier, became positively hackneyed as a subject for popular amazement. Malachy Postlethwayt included an account of it in his celebrated *Dictionary*. Like many others, he concentrated on the impressive statistics of the machine. There were 26,586 wheels and 97,746 movements; 318,504,960 yards of silk thread could be twisted on it in twenty-four hours. 'By the aid

---

[66] C. K. Hyde, 'The Adoption of Coke-Smelting by the British Iron Industry, 1709–1790', *Explorations in Economic History*, 10 (1972–3), 397–418.
[67] *London Magazine*, 1764, pp. 144–5; 1765, pp. 40–1; 1776, pp. 40–1; 1767, pp. 464–7; 1778, pp. 136–7.

of mechanics, this little being, not above five or six feet high, with two arms only, will dispatch as much work as a giant, whom one would imagine to have a thousand.'[68] Few doubted the contribution made by such machines to Britain's prosperity.

Both Parliament and government devoted much attention to the protection of the skills on which technical progress depended. The emigration of workmen and engineers was a subject of continuing anxiety; so was the activity of foreign spies who made the discovery of manufacturing secrets their special concern. When free trade was under discussion at the end of the American War one of the standard objections was that it would render the arts of innovation vulnerable to foreign imitation. Richard Watson, who prided himself on his enlightened views, and whose varied academic and clerical career included a time as Professor of Chemistry at Cambridge, opposed the reduction of tariffs on Anglo-French trade in the 1780s on the ground that it made available to French rivals the 'machines, presses, dies, and tools' on which Britain depended for its technical superiority. Burgundy would be enabled to compete with English ironmasters, and Moulins would match Sheffield in cutlery making.[69] Such concern reflected the belief that skills and techniques were precisely what made British manufactures competitive in world markets. Wages at home were believed to be higher than in other countries, and natural resources fewer. It was all the more necessary to protect scientific knowledge and mechanical know-how.

Admiration for technical inventiveness was not just a matter of hard-headed business sense, but belonged with faith in rational progress and recognition of the beneficence of scientific empiricism. Historians recorded its triumphs with the same enthusiasm which they devoted to archaeological discoveries. One of several county histories published in the 1770s, the *History and Antiquities of Westmorland and Cumberland*, written by Joseph Nicolson and Richard Burn, included an account of the coal industry in the area, and praised recent innovations on the grounds of their humanity. In the Whitehaven collieries, the authors reported, Spedding's friction lighting system offered a safe alternative to dangerous candles or lamps. Moreover, the latest fire-engines were the equi-

---

[68] *The Universal Dictionary of Trade and Commerce, sub* 'Derbyshire'.
[69] R. Watson, *Anecdotes of the Life of Richard Watson, Bishop of Llandaff* (London, 1817), pp. 173–4.

valent of 2,520 men with buckets. Others were adept at seeing a
benevolent purpose where it was not initially obvious. When
Matthew Boulton applied Watt's steam-engine to the mechanization of coin pressing in 1788, his friend Erasmus Darwin
observed that the results were so superior that they were virtually
impossible to counterfeit, and 'in consequence, save many lives
from the hand of the executioner; a circumstance worthy the
attention of a great Minister. If a civick crown was given in Rome
for preserving the life of one citizen, Mr Boulton should be covered
with garlands of oak.'[70]

One of the lauded features of industrialization was the opportunity it offered to child labour. Machinery which could be operated by women and children, or increased the need for sweated
labour in the preparation or finishing of materials, seemed progressive to an age which fretted at the perpetual surplus of orphan
children and which considered female labour as a valuable means
of supplementing the income of poor families. In a rope-twisting
establishment at Bridport, a visitor was moved to record ''tis
charming to see how industrious their poor are—every child of
five years being able to earn threepence or a groat a day.'[71] Similar
enthusiasm was displayed by the writer Richard Joseph Sullivan,
who described a new silk manufactory near Basingstoke in which
some 140 children were employed, with a further 50 maintained
until they were of an age to work. He noted that its foundation
was the result of 'a benevolent desire of employing so many
unprotected beings, and of saving them perhaps from infamy and
want'. The mistress who was placed in charge of the children
assured him, 'they are poor, it is true, but still they are lovely little
innocents. God protects them; and sure I am, he will reward their
generous benefactor with peace and happiness hereafter!'[72]

Fears of exploitation were not much in evidence and those that
were expressed could be quelled by the paternalism of the early
factory masters. In the rural areas where many of the early factories
were built, communities were literally being constructed from
the ground up. Their builders stressed the provision of healthy

[70] R. Ruding, *Annals of the Coinage of Britain and its Dependencies* (4 vols., London, 1817),
iii. 121.

[71] E. J. Climenson, *Passage from the Diaries of Mrs. Philip Lybbe Powys of Hardwick House,
Oxfordshire, from 1756 to 1808*, p. 65.

[72] *Observations made during a Tour through parts of England, Scotland, and Wales* (London,
1780), pp. 87–8.

housing, fresh produce, educational facilities, humane working practices, and wholesome discipline. Such was Samuel Greg's factory at Styal, nine miles south of Manchester, built in 1784 at a cost of £16,000.[73] Such too was Arkwright's famous establishment at Cromford in Derbyshire, under construction from 1771. William Bray recorded his admiration for it in his *Sketch of a Tour into Derbyshire and Yorkshire* in 1778: 'Every thing wears the face of industry and chearfulness ... How different this from the description given some years ago, when this place was described as "the habitation of a few grovers who dug for lead-ore, and whose huts were not bigger than hogsties!"'[74] There were certainly some philanthropists. The community created at Leadhills by the mathematician James Stirling looked forward to utopian Owenism in some respects. Leadhills had limited hours, minimum wages, solid stone houses with gardens, a school, elementary health insurance, a library, and the professional services of doctors and clergymen. This was not however, very typical. In the early years there was doubtless a strong temptation to take an optimistic view of these developments. It did not survive subsequent experience, more particularly in an urban setting where this kind of paternalism was rarely attempted, and where the sheer physical overcrowding and squalor of the manufacturing areas created problems of health and welfare beyond the conception of earlier generations.

INNOVATION AND ENTERPRISE

Invention had to do with more than technical ingenuity, more even than innovation widely construed. Historians have debated in what sense men like Matthew Boulton and Richard Arkwright were inventors and innovators. Some of the uncertainty arises from the fact that they were first and foremost businessmen. Distinctions of this kind tend to obscure two of the most significant features of late eighteenth-century enterprise, the way in which it exploited an almost indiscriminate mixing of talents, ranks, and interests, and the extent to which it depended on skills as much in marketing as manufacturing.

The most famous of all eighteenth-century scientific societies,

---

[73] F. Collier, *The Family Economy of the Working Classes in the Cotton Industry, 1784–1833* (Manchester, 1964), ch. v.
[74] (London, 1778), p. 74.

the Lunar Society, which first met formally at Birmingham in 1775, had no sense of the need to establish the rigid lines of demarcation which were later to characterize the development of science as an academic discipline. Its most distinguished chemist was James Keir. Starting as a doctor, Keir spent some years in the army, took up glass manufacturing, managed Boulton's Soho works, wrote treatises on a number of chemical and geological subjects, and in 1780 set up a factory for the production of alkali, employing his own discoveries. His friend James Watt had no formal academic training, though he owed much to his time as an instrument-maker at Glasgow University. He was there when Joseph Black, whose lectures were to earn him the title of father of modern chemistry, was a young professor. There too he met the mathematician John Robison. 'I saw a workman, and expected no more; but was surprised to find a philosopher,' Robison later recalled.[75] Watt was encouraged by Robison, and by John Roebuck, one of the partners in the Carron ironworks, to improve on existing versions of the steam-engine. His invention of a separate condenser for the conservation of steam power, the foundation of his success, took place in 1765 and was patented four years later. Watt remained sensitive about his humble origins, yet when he joined Boulton in the enterprise which was to make the steam-engine viable in the mining industry, and eventually in manufacturing, there was never any doubt about his acceptance as an equal. Boulton himself came from a manufacturing background, and in effect had two careers, the first as founder of the 'toy' works at Soho in 1760, the second, after 1772, as Watt's partner. He had a flair for publicity and adroitly manipulated patrons and politicians. It was his skill as a lobbyist which obtained a statutory extension of Watt's patent. Without that extension the long, and at times rough, road to a profitable steam-engine would not have been open to Watt and his partner.

Boulton and Watt had been introduced by a Scottish physician practising in Birmingham, William Small. Small's circle of friendships was remarkable, and included transatlantic connections, not least Benjamin Franklin and Thomas Jefferson, whom Small had taught during a period of residence in Virginia. Small appealed to Watt because, as an experimenter with clocks and barometers, he added the practical craftmanship of the engineer to the more

[75] Quoted in J. G. Crowther, *Scientists of the Industrial Revolution* (London, 1962), p. 113.

predictable arts of a man of letters. He died prematurely in 1775, but his medical colleague in the Lunar Society, Erasmus Darwin, contributed a similar mixture of interests. Darwin was one of many eighteenth-century physicians who made alcoholic abstinence a pre-condition of physical as well as spiritual health. It was said that he had sobered the county of Derbyshire. He dabbled in mechanics, having invented his own 'fiery chariot', and dominated a literary circle which made Lichfield a prominent centre in the production of sentimental poetry. He and Small were particular friends of Richard Edgeworth and Thomas Day, whom they brought into the Lunar Society. Edgeworth and Day were both Oxonians, both had a legal training which they subsequently ignored, and both were ardent advocates of Rousseau's educational and political theories. Edgeworth engaged in numerous mechanical experiments, including a friendly rivalry with Darwin's projects for self-propelling carriages. Day was the only member of the Society who was manifestly incapable of competing as an empirical scientist. But his educational doctrines and poetic effusions made him a worthy member of a group in which eccentric speculation and practical wisdom were more or less equally mixed.

It would be rash to claim that the Lunar Society was typical of provincial association, even at the level of serious intellectual activity. The early Literary and Philosophical Societies had some similar features, but none of them was so involved in the practical concerns of manufacturing industry and most had a more obviously dissident political tone than the Lunar Society. The first societies devoted to encouraging innovation in an institutional sense, including Rack's society at Bath, had practical experimentation at heart, but lacked the free-ranging informality of the Lunar Society. There were many literary and debating societies which provided local counterparts in the dissemination of 'enlightened' knowledge, but wanted both its distinction and its peculiar mixture of talents. Most obviously there were a great number of 'gentleman's societies' which laid claim to similar cultural or scientific seriousness, but which rapidly degenerated into genteel drinking or election clubs. None the less the Lunar Society has its own significance as the epitome of some of the most striking features of provincial culture.

In London scientists looked to the Royal Society. It has suffered in retrospect for two failings, its reluctance to distinguish real science from pointless research and pedantic antiquarianism, and its excessive deference to the patronage of the great. The Society was certainly given to inquiries which to the natural and physical scientists of the nineteenth century were to seem at best irrelevant, at worst meretricious. From 1727, the year of Newton's death, until 1753, it had only two Presidents, Sir Hans Sloane and Martin Folkes. In this period it sometimes seemed difficult to distinguish from the Society of Antiquaries. It also paid the compliment of membership to men who combined blue blood with dilettante leanings, but who were deficient in evident originality or authentic scholarship. 'It is', wrote William Wales in 1784, 'in a great measure become lately a *genteel* Society, rather than a *learned* one.'[76] Two peers in succession, the Earl of Macclesfield and the Earl of Morton, followed Folkes, and only a brief interlude under the physician Sir John Pringle intervened before the long, genteel presidency of Sir Joseph Banks. Yet Macclesfield, Morton, and Banks were by no means aristocratic ciphers. Moreover, in the 1770s and 1780s, the Royal Society retained a unique distinction, its accolade coveted as much by genuine researchers such as Priestley and Keir as by social climbers. To a visiting scientist like Faujas de Saint Fond in 1784, a society at which it was possible to meet Banks himself, the chemist Henry Cavendish, the astronomers Nevil Maskelyne and Alexander Aubert, and the Linnaean Sir Henry Englefield, on what was essentially an honorary occasion, the admission of the Elector Palatine, needed no defending. Still more was he impressed by the close relations which such men enjoyed with ingenious instrument-makers and engineers.[77]

There is a Whig history of science, as there is of politics, which makes it difficult to judge the eighteenth century on its own terms. But one of the most important points about the learning of the day is that it did not readily fit modern conceptions of material and scientific progress. The English had their own Enlightenment, challenging, uncompromising, and even unconventional. It was not necessarily progressive, it was far from invariably right, and in retrospect it seems bizarrely blinkered. It shared with Continental counterparts its essentially secular concerns and its wide-ranging speculations. But in England it was remarkably unfettered and potentially profitable, as much in terms of the interest it aroused

[76] D. V. Glass, *Numbering the People*, p. 44.
[77] B. Faujas de Saint Fond, *A Journey through England and Scotland to the Hebrides in 1784*, i. 49–53.

as the technological progress which it made possible. This, no
doubt, was why Continental scientists came to England to achieve
recognition, in exactly the way that many artists did, seeking a
land of opportunity, not a realm of superior genius. Herschel and
Forster are to be seen against the same background as Zoffany and
Kauffmann, prudent investors in the enterprise of a vigorous
society.

With most investors the ultimate consideration is the market.
Whether or not the late eighteenth century was an age of mechanical genius, it was certainly an age of marketing flair. In part this
was a consequence of the revolution in communications which had
occurred in the preceding decades, generating a national market
serviced by a sophisticated transport system and powerful, widely
accessible media. The close connection between what Macaulay
was to call the 'age of intelligence' and commercial fashion was
exemplified in the pharmaceutical industry. Booksellers and publishers played a crucial part in the sale of medical nostrums. The
traditional idea of the quack was of a mountebank who sold his
prescriptions by his rhetorical and conjuring skill, displayed before
the populace in the showbooth and at the fair. It took a long time
to disappear but it was supplemented by a more powerful image,
that of the quack by correspondence, whose cures were proclaimed
in the press, expressed in pseudo-scientific language, supported
by published testimonials from satisfied customers, and sold
through the booksellers who often advertised them.

The most famous of all eighteenth-century medicines, Dr
James's Powder, made a fortune for its inventor and for the
publishing firm Newbery, which owned a half-share in it. Doubts
about the wisdom of ingesting antimony, the crucial ingredient in
James's patent, were strengthened in 1774 by the publicity which
attended Goldsmith's death, allegedly hastened by doses of the
powder. But James was only one of many medical men who
profited by an alliance with the press. In the nineteenth century
professionalism came to be incompatible with commercialism of
this crude kind. In the eighteenth century professional men (whatever his failings, James was a trained medical man and a licentiate
of the Royal College of Physicians) were uninhibited in their
exploitation of its possibilities. Incipient signs of hypocrisy in such
matters provoked some lively debate. When the solicitor John
Rayner was censured because he had advertised for custom in

bankruptcy cases, he defended himself on the grounds that the famous Dr John Hunter had in effect advertised himself by his writings, most of which were plainly designed for more than a strictly medical readership. He also pointed out that the legal luminary Sir William Blackstone, Vinerian Professor at Oxford, had advanced his career and his earnings by his books.[78] Rayner, dismissed as a Commissioner of Bankruptcy by the Lord Chancellor for improperly transferring a case to himself, was evidently accustomed to sail close to the wind, but his argument was not without force. He might have added the Church to his examples. The market for published sermons was big, but many sermons had their origin in the preacher's anxiety to bring his name to the attention of a wider public, perhaps attracting a potential patron. Hack writing was notoriously the resort of impecunious clergymen, well qualified by education to employ the pen when they had no pulpit from which to preach. One such, Dr John Trusler, went further than most when in 1773 he advertised the sale of ready-made sermons at 1s. each, engraved on copperplate to resemble manuscript and disarm the suspicions of congregations. William Cowper, evangelical as well as poet, gently chided him in *The Task*. 'Are there who purchase of the doctor's ware? Oh, name it not in Gath!—it cannot be, That grave and learned clerks should need such aid.'[79]

Business marketing was not open to the same objections as the commercialization of professional services. But it required similar organization. Stories of serendipity were commonplace, but misleading. It was claimed of John Taylor, Birmingham's first manufacturing magnate, that the japanning technique which made his fortune was discovered by accident when his wife dropped a candle on a pile of caddies.[80] In practice great pains went into design and marketing. The most adroit entrepreneurs were those who exploited the connection between polite patronage and a mass market. This was the *métier* of Josiah Wedgwood. The popularity of his creamware in the late 1760s was secured by the custom of Queen Charlotte at home and the Tsarina Catherine II in Russia. In the following decade the market which he achieved both for his

[78] *Readings on Statutes ... Passed in the Reign of his late Majesty, King George the Second*, p. v.

[79] H. S. Milford, ed., *Cowper: Poetical Works* (4th edn., London 1967), p. 154.

[80] W. H. Ryland, ed., *Reminiscences of Thomas Henry Ryland* (Birmingham, 1904), p. 46.

black basalt ware and his celebrated 'jasper', had a good deal to do with his success in exploiting the snob value of 'antique forms', while adapting them to the requirements of middle-class taste. He catered not merely for china services, but for a vast range of knick-knacks, snuff-boxes, buckles, earrings, rings, brooches, and so on, many of which competed with the productions of his friend Boulton at Soho.

Wedgwood and Boulton were similar types, not least in the combination of talents which they brought to bear on behalf of their businesses. Wedgwood's remark that he scarcely knew 'whether I am a landed gentleman, an engineer, or a potter, for indeed I am all three, and many other characters by turns' could equally have been made by Boulton. To later generations it was their inventive techniques which seemed most important about them. But their astute exploitation of contemporary taste was at least as impressive. So, perhaps, was their talent for pulling strings and currying favours at the highest levels of society. Both were friends of Joseph Priestley, and Wedgwood, especially, had many connections with Dissenters; but as businessmen they were cautious in their politics, no doubt prudently, given the need to collaborate with a range of interests and propertied families in a region known for its old-fashioned Toryism. If it was stimulating to be intimate with irreverent spirits like Priestley, Darwin, and Day, it was positively profitable to be on friendly terms with Earl Gower and the Earl of Dartmouth.[81]

THE IMPACT OF INDUSTRIALIZATION

Slow though the pace of industrialization may appear in the light of later developments, contemporaries had little doubt of the importance of what was taking place. The correspondence of the Shropshire ironmaster Richard Reynolds reveals his sense of the 'prodigious advancement of the iron trade' and the no less spectacular expansion of the coal industry.[82] Samuel Oldknow's letters provide similar insight into the remarkable developments taking place in cotton manufacturing. Oldknow, in collaboration with Arkwright, started manufacturing at Stockport in 1782, turned his

[81] N. McKendrick, J. Brewer, and J. H. Plumb, *The Birth of a Consumer Society: The Commercialization of Eighteenth-Century England* (new edn., London, 1983), pp. 71–4.
[82] H. M. Rathbone, *Letters of Richard Reynolds* (London, 1852), pp. 280–1.

attention to the London market in 1783, and by 1786 made himself the country's first muslin-maker. Nowhere is the hectic excitement of the mid-1780s better captured than in the letters which he received from his London middleman, Samuel Salte. Salte was an engrossed observer of the expansion of the cotton industry. In three years, he boasted in 1785, what had been widely regarded as a 'Chimerical Scheme', that of rivalling Indian production of calicoes and muslins, had exceeded the most sanguine hopes of those who undertook it. Salte's enthusiasm starts out of his letters. 'You must give a look to Invention, Industry you have in abundance,' he urged Oldknow in April 1786: 'as the Sun Shines let us make Hay.' A little later: 'You may defy united all competitors and all usurpers, but remember you must not Slacken your ardent Zeal in this race. You must both have the perseverance of Saints, and the resolution of Martyrs.'[83]

Changes in manufacturing industry struck those not directly responsible for it in various ways. In the 1780s there was understandable interest, half-admiring, half-envious, in the fortunes being made by manufacturers. Spectacular agglomerations of wealth in this way were not completely unprecedented. The textile industry in the West Country and in East Anglia had a history of producing clothiers who could take their place in landed society, though traditionally they rather resembled merchant capitalists than the factory masters associated with later industrialization. In the mid-eighteenth century it was common to cite Taylor of Birmingham as an outstanding example of the way in which it was possible to progress from modest circumstances to opulence in the space of a few years. In the following decades such cases became commonplace in manufacturing regions, particularly in Lancashire. There it was observed in 1780 that in ten years 'a poor man not worth £5, now keeps his carriage and servants, is become Lord of a Manor, and has purchased an estate of £20,000'.[84]

Awareness that there was a large element of risk in such rewards made the riches thus accumulated seem all the more remarkable. Manufacturing was not considered a safe investment and the first generations of industrial capitalists relied on a variety of fiscal

[83] G. Unwin, *Samuel Oldknow and the Arkwrights* (2nd edn., Manchester, 1968), pp. 64, 79.

[84] Quoted A. P. Wadsworth and J. De L. Mann, *The Cotton Trade and Industrial Lancashire, 1600–1780* (Manchester, 1931), p. 500.

expedients. Friends and relations contributed, and profits were ploughed back into the business. Investors in the modern sense, working either through large institutions or by the professional channel of brokers and bankers, were virtually unknown. The rate of capital accumulation was relatively low (how low remains a matter of dispute) and while there is little evidence of capital starvation, individual entrepreneurs often led a somewhat desperate life in their struggle to build up profits before bankruptcy intervened. Men who were to become famous for their success, Arkwright and Boulton, for example, were no exceptions to this rule. 'All the great manufacturers that I have ever known', remarked Boulton, 'have begun the world with very little capital.'[85]

Not surprisingly, manufacturers themselves were drawn disproportionately from the middle ranks. Typically they were men with a background in trade or manufacturing, access to a minimum of funds required for independent enterprise, and, not least, ambition to take advantage of promising but not guaranteed prospects. In their own society their origins did not set them apart. Nor, it should be stressed, were those who hit the jackpot viewed with contempt or excessive jealousy. Manufacturing had highly favourable connotations in the public mind. The manufacturer provided employment for the poor, and helped make his country independent of its competitors. This could not be said of financiers, nabobs, contractors, and other representatives of the class who had got rich quickly. In the minds of some it could not even be safely said of landowners and merchants. It is significant in this context that the landed interest rarely saw itself as being in conflict with manufacturing. Landowners were quick to exploit the potential value of their lands for mining purposes, and some, like the Dudley family in the West Midlands, made a substantial contribution to the industrialization of their region.[86] Above all, a strong sense of the essential integration of the local economy made the landowner at worst a neutral observer, and at best a committed partner in developments which served industrial development.

There was one important, though partial, exception to the favour with which contemporary propertied society looked on

[85] H. Hamilton, *The English Brass and Copper Industries*, p. 271.

[86] T. J. Raybould, *The Economic Emergence of the Black Country: A Study of the Dudley Estate* (Newton Abbot, 1973); 'Aristocratic Landowners and the Industrial Revolution: The Black Country Experience, c.1760–1840', *Midland History*, 9 (1984), 59–86.

the manufacturer. In some places at least the proposition that improvement was synonymous with greater employment was open to question. Most notably was this the case in Lancashire. There mechanization proceeded more rapidly than anywhere else. In other places it was easy to demonstrate that machines were compatible with expanded employment opportunities. In Cornwall, for example, Watt's steam pumps created additional mining jobs; in the metallurgical industries of the Midlands, skilled labour was more rather than less necessary as the pace of technological change speeded up. But in the manufacture of textiles, especially the light textiles of Lancashire and the East Midlands, it was another story. The spectacular advances made by the spinning-jennies in the era of Hargreaves and Arkwright seemed to present a real threat to spinners. When their introduction coincided with temporary recession, it was natural to blame them for shortage of work. Economic historians are confident that mechanization in this period usually created more opportunities for work. This was also argued at the time. The *Leicester Journal* asserted in 1773 that 'The pretence that fewer workmen would be employed is vain; unless the English already possessed the trade of the whole world; nor even then unless new fashions in the mode of work could be no longer invented.'[87] But this was not invariably the contemporary perception. Even those who advocated machinery did not always claim it.

Confronted with widespread resistance to the use of jennies in Bolton during the American War, the local magistrate Dorning Rasbotham urged the sheer inevitability of technological innovation. He recalled how Lewis Paul's flying shuttle of some thirty years earlier had aroused opposition so intense as to compel its inventor to flee to France; yet the shuttle was now in general use. He also appealed to the sectional interest of the weavers, 'urging the former insolence of spinners, and the happiness of such as had already relieved themselves, and procured employment for their children'.[88] The work-force was not readily convinced. Lancashire experienced recurrent riots, some of the worst of them in the autumn of 1779. The Yorkshire militia had to be used to disperse a crowd of 2,000 demonstrating against one of Arkwright's machines at Chorley, and a body of 300 'respectable housekeepers'

[87] J. Thompson, *The History of Leicester in the Eighteenth Century*, p. 148.
[88] W. E. A. Axon, *Manchester A Hundred years Ago* (Manchester, 1887), p. 89.

joined with the Twenty-Fifth Regiment for the protection of Preston against machine breakers.[89] There was comparable violence in the hosiery industry, not always as a result of temporary recession. At Leicester the use of machines met with bitter resistance before and after the American War, as well as during it. Leicester's traditional politics lent a particularly acrimonious note to these conflicts. The spinning machines which provoked the most serious riots there, in 1785, were financed by two men who were acknowledged Whigs and Dissenters. 'No presbyterians, no machines' was the resulting cry.[90] Disturbances also occurred in the West Country. Outbreaks of this kind were not on the scale of the later Luddism, but there were sufficient to alarm Parliament. What laid the fears temporarily to rest in most places, especially Lancashire, was the sheer pace of expansion after the American War. The optimistic view that the lower prices promoted by mechanization would expand the market faster than labour savings could reduce employment, seemed, at least for the moment, to have been proved correct.

The possibility of unemployment aside, there was little sense of the damage which industrialization might do. Contemporary comment was overwhelmingly favourable, as contemporary interest in the character of new enterprises was immense. The novelty of large machines in motion fascinated visitors to the first ventures in heavy industry. The same Sullivan who delighted in child labour near Basingstoke was amazed by the Carron works. 'How far the powers of mechanism can go in the great style, is here tremendously displayed: hell itself seems open to your view, nor do the bellows afford a less horrid noise than the yelling of all the infernal deities put together.'[91] The contrast which manufacturing sites presented with rural settings heightened appreciation of their visual impact. The majestic Severn valley scenery in which Coalbrookdale was situated was guaranteed to stimulate such appreciation. Anna Seward, the 'Swan of Lichfield', was conventionally astonished on her visit in 1787 to find 'a town, noisy and smouldering, and almost as populous as Birmingham, amidst sylvan hills, lofty rocks, and meandering waters'.[92] The Victorian authoress Mrs Schim-

[89] London Magazine, 1779, p. 478.
[90] C. H. Beale, Catherine Hutton and Her Friends, p. 90.
[91] Observations made during a Tour through parts of England, Scotland, and Wales, p. 229.
[92] Letters of Anna Seward: written between the years 1784 and 1807, i. 339.

melpenninck later recalled childhood visits to the Shropshire ironworks, and particularly the impression made on her by the extraordinary lighting effects which they had incidentally created. 'The roaring of the blast furnaces, the long beds of glowing coke, the jets of flame and showers of sparks, and the stalwart forms of the various forge-men, mingled with the woods, the rocks, and caverns, or reflected in the broad waters of the Severn, gave it a peculiarity of appearance which I have never seen elsewhere.'[93] Those who lived in the midst of these spectacles were equally enthusiastic about them. Hannah Darby, brought up at Coalbrookdale, recorded in her diary in 1753 an ideal walk in fields and woods, terminating at the works and viewing the 'stupendious Bellows' and 'mighty Cylinders'.[94] This amalgam of complacency and wonder was characteristic of the early response to industrial works.

Similar scenic contrasts made Merthyr Tydfil exciting, when John Guest and Anthony Bacon began exploiting its potential as an iron manufacturing centre in the 1770s. The language used by visitors—the fifth Duke of Rutland called it 'grand and sublime beyond all description'—carries no suggestion of revulsion, only an acceptance of industrial art as setting off the more familiar delights of nature.[95] Where there were reservations they concerned urbanization rather than industrialization. Great cities like Birmingham, Manchester, and Glasgow had frequently been praised for their neatness, modernity, and order. But by the 1780s their size, and the squalor which it eventually brought, began to sow doubts. Moreover, though the picturesque vogue could cope with spectacular irruptions of art in the midst of nature, it could not readily accommodate the ordered mediocrity of urban building on an unprecedented scale. William Gilpin's disapproval of Birmingham and its frivolous arts did not commend itself to all, but it plainly pointed the way to a less confident assertion of the aesthetic credentials of urban modernity.[96] When completely new industrial sites were found objectionable it was generally on the grounds that they threatened to become small cities, blotting out their surroundings. 'Every rural sound', John Byng noted at Cromford,

[93] Life of Mary Anne Schimmelpenninck, i. 231.
[94] E. Greg, Reynolds-Rathbone Diaries and Letters, 1753–1839 (London, 1905), p. 63.
[95] Journal of a Tour through North and South Wales (London, 1805), p. 63.
[96] B. Faujas de Saint Fond, A Journey through England and Scotland to the Hebrides in 1784, ii. 347.

'is sunk in the clamours of cotton works; and the simple peasant (for to be simple we must be sequester'd) is changed into the impudent mechanic.'[97] Impudence was not the only characteristic of workmen. It was sometimes difficult for polite tourists to ignore the Caliban-like creatures who laboured in physically demanding industries. Joseph Heely described 'half-burnt cadaverous looking animals' to be found at the Stourbridge glass works in 1777.[98] Occasionally, too, a realization that the forces released by economic growth might threaten traditional values, broke through complacency about the benefits of expansion. When it was proposed to extend the Midland canal network to Oxford, reservations were voiced. 'That Oxford should be made a place of commerce, is contrary to the genius of the place, the necessary retirement and employment of the students. The making the seat of the Muses the center of traffic, or even the principal road of communication, ought by all means to be avoided.'[99]

Comparable in importance to a sense of the change which industrialization brought to the familiar landscape was an awareness of its effect on provincial identity and regional balance. The redistribution of wealth and population in favour of the Midlands and North was to be one of the most obvious consequences of industrial growth. It was, in fact, well advanced by the middle of the eighteenth century. Though growth was by no means restricted to the North, the drift away from East Anglia and the South-West, historically the great centres of manufacturing, was obvious. But for the continuing importance of London as political, administrative, and social capital, and to some extent as commercial entrepôt, the trend would be still more marked. As it was there is little doubt where the most impressive development was occurring. Eight counties embracing the most vigorous areas of the manufacturing North and Midlands were growing rapidly in population terms. Individual counties display striking contrasts in this respect. Some counties in the rural east (despite modern doubts about the depopulating effects of enclosure, areas of high parliamentary enclosure), for instance, Huntingdonshire, Cambridgeshire, Lincolnshire, suffered a net loss of population at a time when Lancashire was doubling in size. Estimates of the national housing

[97] C. B. Andrews, ed., *The Torrington Diaries* (4 vols., repr. New York, 1970), ii. 195.
[98] *A Description of Envil* (London, 1777), p. 13.
[99] *London Magazine*, 1772, p. 473.

TABLE 7. *Regional distribution of population*
(percentages)

	1701	1720	1751	1758	1781	1801
South-West	15.60	14.46	14.83	13.13	13.14	12.46
South-East	23.91	28.82	23.83	24.94	23.93	24.87
East	16.06	16.75	14.43	15.24	13.92	12.59
Midlands	20.18	20.19	20.78	22.69	21.73	21.29
North	17.67	17.02	19.25	20.07	20.66	22.63
Wales	6.64	5.07	6.84	5.69	6.55	6.10
Eight counties (Lancs., Notts., Yorks., Derby., Leics., Staffs., Ches., War.)	21.74	22.50	23.34	26.58	26.61	29.34

Sources: Population for 1701, 1751, 1781 and 1801 is derived from P. Deane and W. A. Cole, *British Economic Growth, 1688–1959* (Cambridge, 1969); population for 1720 from Cox's *Magna Britannia* and *A Collection of Voyages and Travels*, vol. i (London, 1745), 'Don Gonazales Voyage'; houses for 1758 from PRO, T. 35. 19. The regions represent counties as follows: SW: Corn., Devon, Dorset, Som., Wilts.; SE: Middx., Kent, Sussex, Surrey, Hants., Essex, Herts., Berks.; E: Norfolk, Suffolk, Hunts., Cambs., Beds., Northants, Lincs., Bucks.; Midlands: War., Worcs., Leics., Rutland, Notts., Staffs., Shropshire, Oxon., Ches., Derby., Glos., Herefords., Monmouths.; N: Westmorland, Cumberland, Northumb., Dur., Lancs., Yorks.

stock suggest a twelve per cent fall overall during George II's reign, a period of sluggish population growth at best. Yet they attribute to Lancashire growth of more than fifteen per cent in that period.

Lancashire, indeed, is the outstanding case of a region of unceasing expansion in the eighteenth century. Its population grew from somewhat over 200,000 at the start of George II's reign to nearly 320,000 by 1758, and more than 420,000 by 1781. Its unusual features provide some food for thought about the social and political conditions which could accompany the most dynamic regional economy of eighteenth-century England. Lancashire had the fastest growing seaport of the period in Liverpool, the fastest growing city in Manchester, and the fastest growing industrial hinterland in south-east Lancashire. It also had a history of internal conflict. There were more Roman Catholics than in any other region outside London and a marked incidence of Protestant Dissent of all kinds, all in proximity to a notably High Church tradition. Local politics had long been divisive and included a notorious propensity to Jacobitism. Labour was imported on a massive scale. Liverpool was already known as a centre of Scottish and Irish immigration and there is no doubt that cotton manufacturing attracted large numbers from neighbouring regions. The county benefited from a very low land tax, a notable lack of central direction (its palatine status still gave it an unusual degree of independence), and a relatively dispersed structure of landowning which offered little scope to aristocratic oligarchy of a kind common in the eastern counties.

Awareness of the changing pattern of regional wealth was not wanting, even before it became obvious to the most blinkered observers in the early nineteenth century. In the early years of George III's reign observers were struck by the vigour of manufacturing in Yorkshire and Lancashire.[1] It was not customary to think of the North as a land of smoke, grime, and opulence, but in the 1780s this perception was beginning to become commonplace. It appears strongly in Charles Dibdin's *Musical Tour*, in which music was by no means the only subject. This book was published in Sheffield, the 'regions of smoke', as Dibdin called it, and had a good deal to say about life beyond the environs of London.

Manufactories that begin about the center of the kingdom, push on to the north; till—having taken up their residence in Yorkshire—they expand to the east and west; but particularly the west, in a most astonishing way. Thus, from Leeds to Liverpool—through Bradford, Halifax, Rochdale, Manchester, Warrington, and Preston—the population is wonderful. The workmen are like to many ants employed about their heaps; but they are so different from those in London, that while the arts of the north labour for the *general benefit*, the other pismires work hard for the general confusion.

Dibdin found the middle class of the North by no means unappreciative of what he had to offer by way of musical sophistication. 'Their manners', he noted at Wakefield, 'appear to be simple and unaffected; their conversation is polished, and in their musical pursuits they go my way to work, and praise every thing that pleases upon reflection.'[2] Dibdin had had his share of metropolitan

---

[1] J. Long, *The Golden Fleece: or, some Thoughts on the Cloathing Trade* (Dublin, 1763), pp. 9, 11.
[2] *The Musical Tour of Mr Dibdin* (Sheffield, 1788), pp. 15, 83, 194.

disappointments and expected to make a profit by publishing his appreciation of provincial manners. Even so his observations reveal something of the vigour and distinctiveness of what was already an industrial culture.

CHAPTER 14

This Happy Constitution

THE changes which marked eighteenth-century life were sometimes difficult to absorb, not least in political matters, where tradition and the 'ancient constitution' were much prized. Different interpretations of the Revolution of 1688 rested on the assumption that its function had been to restore old laws and liberties rather than introduce new ones. The contemporary achievement was often thought of as one of preservation, especially the maintenance of balanced government against the encroachments of the Crown and the nobility. But there was also clear evidence that the State was undergoing a transformation, as the requirements of war, the growth of deficit financing, and the expansion of government took effect. It was not, by Continental standards, an authoritarian State; it was, however, an extremely flexible and resilient one. Public administration was relatively decentralized, and a marked degree of particularism and provincialism suggested almost a federal structure. But at its core was the consolidated power of Parliament and the doctrine of parliamentary supremacy. The very prominence of Parliament laid it open to criticism in the late eighteenth century. Yet in terms of its primary function, the representation of a diverse and increasingly prosperous society, it proved both efficient and adaptable. The result was not olig-

archy in any meaningful sense, but neither did it
have any tendency to democracy. Parliament and the
State which it sustained were responsive to the expressed
requirements of the propertied public. They secured
the interests and embodied the ideas of an essentially
middle-class political culture. In this respect the
regime of the younger Pitt, in the 1780s, was a notable
advance on that of Walpole, in the 1730s, for all
the apparent resemblances.

CHANGE AND THE CONSTITUTION

THE transformation, social, cultural, religious, economic, which occurred in Britain between the 1720s and the 1780s was nothing if not spectacular. Some even believed that it had wrought a fundamental alteration in the English people. This was the conclusion of the historian of manners John Andrews, looking back on the developments of the mid-eighteenth century, from the standpoint of 1782. 'The whole mass of the people of England was infected to such a degree, that they might be said to have changed, in some very material respects, the character and the temper of Englishmen.'[1] Change was in principle not at all congenial according to the values which the age inherited from its predecessors. The English genius was associated with the preservation of ancient virtues, not the introduction of novelties. As a result, the acceptance of change was a painful process. Many people responded by emphasizing what had not changed, thus maintaining a comforting faith in their surroundings. Some of the most popular figures were those who represented resistance to change. Part of the fascination which attended Dr Johnson even among people who had never met him, was his standing as a representative of the traditional English virtues. In reality Johnson throve on modernity and derived his living from it. His career was one long exemplification of the impact of commercialism on the profession of letters. But a familiar image, indicating old-fashioned Toryism, Churchmanship, and manners, was not less marketable than the talent which he brought to his *Dictionary*, his essays, and his *Lives of the Poets*. Another tactic of the age was to pretend that the change which did take place was for the better, and more in the nature of developing existing traditions than inventing new ones. 'Improvement not innovation' was the watchword of the late eighteenth century. This, too, was largely hypocrisy. Most improvements were in the strictest sense innovations, and not a few of them hurt the interests of some party or individual. But the preferred terminology is significant of the potential strain between the inherited mentality of the age and its material progress.

It was in politics that the resulting tensions showed most clearly. Even if the era of Walpole and Pelham was treated as one of relative

---

[1] *An Inquiry into the Manners, Taste, and Amusements, of the Two last Centuries, in England* (London, 1782), p. 6.

stability, itself a highly questionable proposition, few contemporaries would have denied that the early years of George III's
reign were tempestuous. The turmoil of the American War and
the uncertainty which succeeded it heightened this sense of dis-
continuity. The author of *A Brief and Impartial Review of the State
of Great Britain* in 1783 saw his country embarking on a difficult
and unpredictable enterprise for which its history hardly fitted it.
'It is not the least of her misfortunes, that Britain should be obliged
to quit her ancient maxims, and be compelled, in her old age, to
enter upon a new study of experimental policy, where knowledge
is to be gradually gleaned from laborious discovery, independent
of any known established theory.'[2] The virtues of the English
constitution were pre-eminently historical virtues. In politics it
could be argued that there was not even room for improvement,
let alone innovation. How could so perfect a design as the Englishmen's liberty be improved? It could only be preserved and
handed on to posterity as the priceless inheritance it was. On the
other hand, much that Englishmen valued was of less than venerable origin. It was customary to refer to the events of 1688 as
the 'recent revolution' for long into the eighteenth century. The
Hanoverian monarchy was manifestly a novelty, at least in the
sense that George I and George II would not have been Kings of
England if the traditional rules of succession had been observed.
Englishmen were proud of their 'ancient constitution' but preferred for the most part to talk of their 'excellent' or 'happy
constitution', a formulation which side-stepped the question of its
historical legitimacy. Arguments about change none the less tended
to dominate political debate. Opponents of government contended
that it was carrying its subjects away from the time-honoured
liberties and safeguards of the constitution. Government denied
that it was doing so and claimed, on the contrary, that its opponents
wished to introduce innovation in the guise of former practice.
Walpole and the *Craftsman* school, George III, Bute, North, and
their Whig enemies, all operated within this framework. Every
statesmen, it seemed, must prove himself a true 'Revolution'
statesman.

The Revolution was generally seen, not as a break with the past,
but as a reassertion of historic liberties. Whether it could be
repeated was a hotly disputed point. No government, even an

[2] (London, 1783), p. 6.

unimpeachably Whig government, wished to encourage further Revolutions. Whig Churchmen played a notable part in rendering the Revolution a unique necessity, a freak in the history of freedom, dictated by the aberration of a popish, absolutist king. Oppositions preferred to maintain the status of the Revolution as living history, a perpetual warning to posterity and a precedent for similar action in future. As a result the debate about the legitimacy of successive Hanoverian governments was also a debate about the meaning and implications of 1688. But by the 1770s and 1780s this was changing. Increasingly, governments were content to treat of the constitution as it had actually developed in the course of the eighteenth century, in effect itself the sole source of legitimacy. The old battlefield became irrelevant from their standpoint. The most intellectually distinguished defenders of the status quo in the first half of George III's reign, David Hume, Samuel Johnson, Josiah Tucker, either ignored it or pronounced it not worth winning. Instead they justified the sovereignty exercised by George III in Parliament on utilitarian grounds and appealed for historical justification merely to its prescriptive acceptance by successive generations of Britons.

When the centenary of the Revolution occurred in 1788 the court of George III made no attempt to claim it for political purposes. Rather it was left to Richard Price and the radical opponents of government to make it their own. In the ensuing years the Revolution controversy became part of a private war between different claimants to the Whig tradition, not the central preoccupation of court and country, government and opposition. The 'ancient constitution' also fell increasingly into the exclusive possession of the radicals. Their enemies hardly needed it, though they were not afraid to use arguments drawn from tradition to support Church and King as embodied in the government of George III and the younger Pitt. There was no contradiction here. The radicals attached legitimacy to rights, liberties, and contracts which they found in history, not to the prescriptive charms of a system that had stood the test of two or three generations. Ultimately, they were compelled to resort to authentic novelty in their arguments for reform, particularly once the French Revolution had opened up a fascinating new world of novelties. For their part the defenders of the status quo had the best of both worlds. They thought in terms of a constitution sanctioned by the passage of time, yet incorporating all that was valuable in the progressive developments of the eighteenth century. In this sense the 'happy constitution' was indeed 'improvement without innovation', a characteristic piece of self-deception by a propertied society which changed what suited it while denying that it ever offended against the traditional virtues of English life.

What had actually changed in politics? Fifty-six years separated the accession of George II from his grandson's humiliating surrender of a large portion of the British empire. This was roughly the adult lifetime of the generation born in the second decade of the century, in the last years of Queen Anne, or the early years of George I, either side of the Jacobite Rebellion of 1715. The passage of time was considerable and it spanned very different epochs. At the death of George I, the father of the House of Commons was Francis Gwyn, MP for Wells and a landowner in Glamorgan and Dorset.[3] Gwyn had been born a year before the execution of Charles I, and first sat in Parliament in 1673. He had lived through seven reigns and an era of acute dynastic instability. Rump, Restoration, and Revolution had all taken place by the time he was forty; by his eightieth birthday, he had also seen the bitter party conflict of the post-Revolution era, including the Church in Danger crisis of Queen Anne's reign, the Jacobite rebellion in 1715, the South Sea Bubble, and a series of famous enactments, the Act of Settlement, the Riot Act, the Septennial Act. Monck and Marlborough, Sheldon and Sacheverell, Lady Castlemaine and the Duchess of Kendal might jostle in his memory.

Half a century later Thomas William Coke, Coke of Norfolk, entered Parliament. Coke was the youngest Member of Parliament in 1776 and the father of the House of Commons when he retired in 1832, at the time of the great Reform Act. He witnessed events scarcely less dramatic than those which had occurred before Gwyn's eyes. The French Revolution, the defeat of Napoleon, the political tumults which accompanied early industrialization, the struggles over Catholic Emancipation and parliamentary reform, all belonged to his lifetime. When he entered Parliament the bounty on corn exports was still a matter of extreme financial interest to his Norfolk farmers; when he died in 1842 they were engaged in

---

[3] Sir Nicholas Pelham had technically sat in the Commons even earlier than Gwyn, in 1671. But he had long since retired, only to be brought back briefly in 1726–7 as a stopgap for the Duke of Newcastle in the borough of Lewes. It is unlikely that he attended Parliament.

their historic struggle to preserve even the home market for English grain. He sat in Parliament with the elder Pitt at the end of his career, and with Sir Robert Peel when he was about to assume the leadership of the Tory party.

Between Gwyn's withdrawal and Coke's arrival there lay something like the maximum parliamentary career of any man. One whose tenure of a seat in the Commons approximately coincided with this intervening period was William Aislabie, son of Walpole's predecessor as Chancellor of the Exchequer at the time of the South Sea Bubble. MP for Ripon from 1721 until his death in 1781, he sat in the Commons with Gwyn in his youth and with Coke in his old age. Sadly, he did not record the impressions of a lifetime as a parliamentarian. As the owner of Studley Royal and restorer of Fountains Abbey he had interests which went beyond politics. None the less his career as a legislator spanned a period of considerable change. How might he have summarized it?

BALANCED GOVERNMENT

If Aislabie had been able to anticipate the verdict of posterity the answer would be one word: stability. Not only is it frequently associated with the eighteenth century, it is often considered its peculiar achievement, permitting the political convulsions of a post-industrial age, in the nineteenth and twentieth centuries, to be absorbed without revolution or catastrophe. This stability is commonly identified with the evolution of a system of parliamentary politics which laid the basis for an enduring tradition of party government. If the British constitutional achievement is the development of parliamentary democracy as a means of conducting affairs in a complex, industrial society, then it might be said that the eighteenth century made it parliamentary and the nineteenth century made it democratic. This essentially Whig perspective has not altogether lost its attractions among modern historians. It remains commonplace to view the early eighteenth century as a critical stage in the establishment of political stability, and the late eighteenth century as the decisive test of its solidity amidst the storms of revolution.[4] In between, the structure had been allowed to settle on its foundations, brought to a high degree

[4] J. H. Plumb, *The Growth of Political Stability in England, 1675–1725* (London, 1967); I. R. Christie, *Stress and Stability in late Eighteenth-Century Britain* (Oxford, 1984).

of external order and internal convenience, and generally made a suitable home for a nation which was to dazzle the world with its lasting parliamentary tradition as well as its more transitory imperial achievements.

This thesis has serious weaknesses. If stability means either tranquillity or unchanging government it will not do to describe the experience of the eighteenth century, let alone the period which separated the 1720s from the 1780s. Nobody who had heard his father talk of the excise crisis and the Forty-Five, and lived through the Middlesex election and the Gordon Riots could suppose that Englishmen were essentially subdued or submissive in their response to political controversy. Nor could anybody who had witnessed the chronic instability which accompanied the fall of Sir Robert Walpole, the succession of ministerial coups and convulsions which marked the 1760s, or the desperate crisis which accompanied the conflict of George III and his Whig opponents between 1782 and 1784, suppose that Britons had found a means of choosing governments without undue strife. These points are too important to be buried in the complacent conservatism which the era of the French Revolution brought to many who looked back on the preceding era, and which inevitably colours later perceptions of the eighteenth century. In the 1780s contemporaries emphatically did not think of the preceding half-century as one of calm and orderly progress in the direction of decorous politics. Nor did they see their countrymen as models of political maturity and discipline. On the contrary, the general assumption was that Englishmen were well nigh ungovernable in their political wilfulness, and English politics itself incessantly subject to the unpredictable influence of popular opinion. They also thought, for the most part, that the system of government was on balance much the best yet tried by mankind, that Englishmen were freer than any other nation in the civilized world, and that their destiny was one uniquely favoured by Providence. But these arrogant assumptions expressed their faith in English liberty, the product of centuries of libertarianism, not in English stability.

Aislabie, as the restorer of the Gothic glories of Fountains, would surely have been more interested in liberty than stability. If safeguarding it was a somewhat negative achievement, it was none the less supremely important and closely connected with another boasted triumph of the age, also somewhat negative. Preserving the balance of the constitution was an almost universally accepted priority, at a time when it was still normal to analyse the working of the constitution in mechanistic terms. In this respect much of the debate conducted in the 1780s would have been comprehensible to the men of the 1680s or even earlier, however startled they might have been by some of the developments of the intervening period. Mixed government was something which the British had long prided themselves on, and by the late eighteenth century its merits were well known and widely appreciated abroad. Traditional theories of the State identified a balanced polity, with the Crown representing the principle of monarchy, the Lords that of aristocracy, the Commons that of democracy. Contemporaries never tired of repeating this rather tedious but by no means contemptible platitude.

History suggested that complacency would be most unwise. It was supported by the impression gained from current affairs. States which lacked strong monarchical government did not prosper in the second half of the eighteenth century. The Dutch veered between a feeble Stadtholdership and republican dependence on France. The Poles succumbed to partition in 1772, the Swedes to a royalist *coup d'état* in the same year. Moreover a long tradition of political theory emphasized the difficulty of maintaining a liberal political constitution. Utopianism was emphatically not to the fore of eighteenth-century thought. The great majority of those who thought about such things were aware of the dangers which threatened even so excellent a constitution as that enjoyed by Britons. One of the most obvious was the possibility that the balance of government would tilt too far towards the Crown. It was not necessary to be a republican critic of government to hold this view. David Hume, condemned for his favourable opinion of the Stuarts in his *History of England*, considered the erection of an absolute monarchy the outcome of contemporary politics.[5]

Contemporaries were proud of having kept despotism at bay, though nervous about their chances of continuing to do so. But they did not necessarily expect an immediate catastrophe. The Whig preoccupation with the supposed menace of George III helps obscure the contemporary faith in the continuance of mixed government. Acknowledging its force requires a sense of proportion, beyond that displayed by Whig historians. George III

[5] *Essays Moral, Political and Literary* (Oxford, 1963), pp. 48–53.

was a controversial King, and in terms of his personal and political will a difficult one to control. But he never envisaged, let alone threatened to bring about, an absolute system of government comparable to that at the command of his Continental cousins. His insistence on a say in the appointment of his own ministers was hardly tantamount to a declaration of war on his subjects. In many respects the first twenty-four years of his reign witnessed major concessions. By 1783 he had given up all power to remove judges and lost control of his own civil list; he had been forced to yield up his household offices, and humiliatingly compelled to dismember his empire. His tyranny in America, if such it was, was a parliamentary, not a royal tyranny. His political victories were small ones in the long history of constitutional monarchy: his success in ousting George Grenville in 1765, at the cost of a continuing cycle of ministerial instability; his conquest, in the midst of a desperate crisis, and only with great difficulty, of a coalition fortuitously placed in power by the disastrous outcome of the war in America. Compared with his grandfather, his control of foreign policy was at best limited, his command of patronage restricted, his independence of the legislature minimal.

George III was no mean politician, and in the circumstances of his reign, a tolerably successful one. But to compare him with a Frederick II, or even a Louis XV, would be absurd. In the last analysis it is doubtful if even his opponents did so. Lord Rockingham and Charles James Fox, as leaders of the Whig opposition, were sincerely convinced of the danger which the King and his ministers represented. But there was a large element of rhetoric and theatre about their positions. Lord Rockingham, after all, when dismissed in 1766, did not ride back to Yorkshire to raise the standard of revolt; nor did Fox, when foiled in 1784, urge the Westminster Associators to arm themselves and seize the Tower. Despotism was always one step further on in Whig rhetoric, and when the French Revolution revealed whence it might come, not a few Whigs, including most of those who represented the tradition handed down by Rockingham, were to revise their view of the danger presented by a Hanoverian monarch. Long before then, most of their contemporaries had concluded that they were merely crying wolf. The supreme test of 1783–4 made it clear that most Britons saw George III as the victim and the Whigs as the despots. Fox and his friends thought it a wildly unfair verdict. They hardly troubled to dispute, however, that it was the verdict, and a popular one at that.

In theory the ministers of the Crown were responsible to the King himself. In practice this accountability was shared with the House of Commons. The extent of its powers was demonstrated by the establishment of the doctrine of ministerial responsibility. Impeachment remained, technically, a means of enforcing parliamentary accountability. Walpole was threatened with it; so was Bute, and among the papers of Edmund Burke there is a draft of a proposed impeachment of Lord North.[6] But such threats were not executed, because ministers accepted that when they lost the support of the Commons they had no choice but to resign the offices they held under the Crown. The retirement of Walpole in 1742 and North in 1782 was conclusive proof of this. George III, indeed, resisted the doctrine in 1782 and received from his minister a courageously firm lecture on the subject: 'Your Majesty is well apprized that, in this country, the Prince on the Throne, cannot, with prudence, oppose the deliberate resolution of the House of Commons.'[7] Two years later the King's battle with the Fox–North Coalition, though conducted in terms of King versus Commons, Prince versus People, in no sense cancelled this judgement. George III's dissolution of Parliament in 1784 clearly showed that he recognized the need to change the Commons itself, by appealing to the electorate, in order to alter his ministry. The alternative, which he seriously contemplated, was to abdicate his crown, not to defy the legislature.

Depotism, in the sense in which it was understood at the time, was related to the political implications of the standing army. Under George II fear of the army was genuine, widespread, and at times intense. Militarism was the nightmare of 'patriot' politicians. It was associated with the worst excesses of Continental absolutism, not to say popery. There was a strong belief that in order to compete with the great European land powers Britain was risking subjection to a mercenary force at the command of an alien King. Much of the hostility to the Hanoverian regime was founded on this apprehension, as not a little lingering faith in the Stuarts was based on the idea that they would make it possible to cut loose from all Continental entanglements. By most standards the English

[6] Sheffield City Library, Wentworth Woodhouse MSS, Burke Papers.
[7] *Correspondence of George III*, v. 395.

army was absurdly small during peacetime. Walpole considered a force of 18,000 the bare minimum with which government could be defended against insurrection and the coasts guarded against invasion. Yet his opponents thought even this might enable the King to dispense with Parliament. The standing army was viewed as a pistol perpetually pointed at the Englishman's liberty. Under George III this preoccupation virtually vanished. The firm action eventually taken against the Gordon Rioters in 1780 reawakened worries about the dangers of militarism, but chiefly in the minds of radical opponents of government. Interest in new 'policing' arrangements, a term which began to acquire its modern usage in the 1780s, owed something to the nightmare of those June days of 1780, but did not signify widespread doubts about the political dangers presented by the army. In fact as an issue of major political importance the standing army was dead. What future it had was in terms of class dictatorship rather than central absolutism.

What accounts for this change? In part it reflected the sense that the English legal system had coped better with the threat of an armed force than had been anticipated. The civil liability of soldiers for actions committed against civilians remained unchallenged. Under George II party strife and the threat of Jacobitism had made it possible to justify vigorous use of the military and easy to suspect its abuse. After the accession of George III, the Jacobite danger was removed and the army kept out of electoral politics. The use of troops against the Wilkesites indeed raised the spectre which had haunted opponents of the early Hanoverians. But the St George's Fields Massacre and the prosecutions which succeeded it could hardly be considered a triumph for a militaristically minded government. Accounts of the Massacre like that of the young William Hickey, who was present throughout, make it seem rather a series of bungles than a systematic attack on civil liberty.[8] There was a widely held view that the net effect of these developments had been to weaken the army as an agent in the maintenance of law and order, possibly to the point of anarchy. Dr Johnson thought this an indication of the feebleness of government in the 1770s. 'Our great fear is from want of power in government. Such a storm of vulgar force has broke in.'[9] When the Gordon Riots

[8] *Memoirs of William Hickey*, 1. 92–4.
[9] R. W. Chapman, ed., *Johnson's Journey to the Western Islands of Scotland and Boswell's Journal of A Tour to the Hebrides with Samuel Johnson*, p. 195.

provided alarming evidence that he might be right, even republican opponents did not deny the need for an armed force to keep order. Their concern was rather to create a civilian, volunteer force which might render the army redundant in this respect.

By this time there was a civilian, though hardly volunteer, force in existence. The militia, revived and reformed in 1757, could be considered a standing counterbalance to the menace of the army. It was officered and manned on a county basis, and became a familiar part of local life. Still more important was the fact that the standing army itself had in a sense proved a dependably patriotic force. 'There is nothing reasonably to be feared from a standing army of double the numbers of the present,' it was asserted in 1775.[10] The sterling achievements of the British infantry in the Seven Years War created intense pride within and without the ranks of the army. Moreover, army officers were difficult to distinguish from ordinary gentlemen. Because they purchased their commissions, serving officers were independent of their political masters. Though mercenary in the sense that they were paid by the Crown, or rather by Parliament, through annual army estimates, they were essentially young men of property, inherited or acquired. They chose to invest in a military life in the same way that they might have invested in government stock, a living in the Church, or a share in a commercial business. It was a question whether this state of affairs served the military interests of their country. Successive monarchs and ministers sought to limit the effects of commission by purchase in the cause of greater efficiency.[11] It was believed that a higher degree of professionalism required an officer class selected on the basis of individual merit and directed by no interest but its loyalty to its commanders. However, the political cost of such an army would have been very high.

Absolutism was one threat to the balanced constitution; oligarchy was another. From time to time worries were expressed on this score. Since 'oligarchs' were among the leading opponents of monarchical power, and thereby the principal patrons of 'patriotism', the theme was muted compared with the tyrannical pretensions of kings. Moreover it was difficult to identify the precise

[10] T. Erskine, *Observations on the Prevailing Abuses in the British Army*, p. 6.
[11] J. A. Houlding, *Fit for Service: The Training of the British Army 1715–1795* (Oxford, 1981), pp. 100 ff.

source of an aristocratic threat, when the main characteristic of magnate power, the ownership of great estates, was shared with gentry families who made it a point of honour to oppose their over-mighty colleagues who were also peers. The best hope was to fix the resulting obloquy on the upper house of Parliament. The Lords had threatened to 'overbalance' the precious scales of the constitution with the attempt to restrict the creation of new peer-ages in 1719. Again, in the 1750s, when the Lords promoted the Marriage Act and defeated the Habeas Corpus Bill, it was believed that aristocracy was showing an unhealthy tendency to self-aggrandizement. Conflicts occurred between the two houses of Parliament, sometimes over the great issues of the day like the Habeas Corpus Bill itself, and Fox's East India Bill, more fre-quently over the old questions of money bills and parliamentary privileges. But there was much to support the belief that serious disagreement was largely precluded by the influence of the peers in the elections of MPs. In this sense a lower house with a distinctly aristocratic tinge rendered an aristocratic upper house almost unnecessary. Nor could it be argued that peers did not have a fair share of place and power. The evidence of the Hanoverian period suggests that it was essential for the Prime Minister to sit in the Commons, where he could directly answer critics and personally supervise the dispensing of patronage. But most Cabinets were dominated by peers, from the time of Walpole, who was the only commoner in that of 1727, to the time of the younger Pitt, who was similarly isolated in his Cabinet of 1783.

Peers had influence, but not power, let alone hegemony. It has been argued, none the less, that Georgian England was an essen-tially aristocratic society. This view mistakes appearance for reality, and consequence for cause. Blue blood and rank, without property, counted for very little in late eighteenth-century England, and rendered their possessors objects of pity rather than envy. It was wealth which brought power and prestige. Inherited wealth was a large proportion of the whole in a society which resisted direct taxation and social reconstruction by the State. The great land-owner, with or without a title, was guaranteed his share of power and prestige. But the base of propertied society was broadening and diversifying in the late eighteenth century. If the result was aristocratic it was so only in the novel sense that Burke defined it when he provided the ruling establishment in Britain with its most systematic vindication in the 1790s. His *Letter to a Noble Lord* fully exposes the ironies involved.[12] The young Duke of Bedford he attacked as the very type of irresponsible aristocracy. Against him he pleaded for a concept of social responsibility and widely diffused benevolence which characterized a large propertied class, not a narrow oligarchy.

Many of Burke's contemporaries offered advice to aristocrats who wished to share in the power permitted in a propertied but pluralistic society.[13] To the extent that this conceded the role of leader, it did so on terms which subordinated mere self-interest and oligarchy to the requirements of middle-class mores. The anti-slavery and reformation of manners movements of the 1780s, headed by Churchmen, bourgeois philanthropists, peers, and landed gentry is a better pointer to the mixed character of leadership in late eighteenth-century England than the statistics of borough ownership or the make-up of party caucuses. The emphasis on what Vicesimus Knox called personal nobility was similarly indicative of the preoccupation of the age with aristocracy as an accessible and above all strictly accountable ruling class.[14] There is a long, mainly Tory tradition which would make this the rule of the few, in the strict sense an oligarchy. It lies behind Disraeli's celebrated observation that 'there were ten families in this country, who, if they could only agree, could always share the government.'[15] It is as preposterous a view as the simplistic Whig attribution of tyrannical designs to George III. But Disraeli had not read Knox, any more than Macaulay had read the letters of George III.

Impartial contemporaries would have found it difficult to grasp a view of their age which made it one of aristocratic power. For the most part they thought the challenge of aristocracy had been faced and defeated in the crisis which accompanied the end of the American War. The attempt by the Rockingham Whigs, and then the Fox–North Coalition, to dictate men and measures to George III was widely seen as a desperate attempt to entrench aristocratic rule. It seemed ironic, no doubt, that the House of Lords, the Crown, and the parliamentary electorate should combine to defeat it. But the House of Lords was itself a decidedly mixed body, the

[12] (London, 1796).
[13] See p. 599.
[14] *The Works of Vicesimus Knox*, v.
[15] *Sybil*, ed. S. M. Smith (Oxford, 1981), p. 259.

Crown, as directed by King George and Queen Charlotte, could lay claim to a large fund of middle-class goodwill, and the parliamentary electorate at its widest was by no means unrepresentative of the broad mass of propertied opinion. In a real sense, Fox, the man of the people, was also the leader of a quintessentially ducal party, though one which combined populism with aristocratic arrogance. What it lacked was the moral values and political weight associated with the propertied class as a whole, especially its massive middle-class core. George III and William Pitt exploited them to the full.

THE STATE

Supposing the balance beloved of the theorists to have been maintained, what resulted? In short a State which was well adapted to war, yet throve in peace; in structural terms flexible and resilient rather than aggressive or authoritarian; durable but lacking rigidity; above all the product of a decentralized, pluralistic, voluntary-minded society. The most successful State of eighteenth-century Europe was an eccentric, even anomalous construction, by no means the mighty machine advocated by enthusiasts for enlightened, unitary government. Yet in some respects its coherence and capability far outdid its competitors among the absolute monarchies of the Continental world.

In the mid-eighteenth century Britain became the supreme example in the western world of a State organized for effective war-making. This is not to say that it was a military State. Had it been required to support vast armies in peacetime it would probably have subsided into the bankruptcy which was the fate of the French monarchy in the 1780s, or the bureaucratic inertia which befell Prussia. No other country proved so successful at shifting from the demands of peacetime commercial expansion to wartime concentration on military objectives and then back again. It did so primarily by evolving a system of deficit finance which took the strain of massive expenditure on a relatively narrow economic base. But this was possible only bcause the parliamentary politics which characterized the eighteenth century had the public confidence to underpin what many considered a dangerously overcommitted system of credit. To this extent it was politics as much as commerce which determined the growth of British power. A society which made war by borrowing money and buying men on the open market rather than by taxing and conscripting its citizens by its coercive force could only function if it carried the broad support of its propertied classes. When the Hanoverian regime was at its most unpopular and Jacobitism at its strongest, under Walpole, this might have proved difficult: it was probably as well that he did not have to fight a war until 1739, a priority second to none in his own calculations. Thereafter, as the benefits of Revolution politics to propertied society became obvious and rival claims on the individual's dynastic loyalty subsided, the system worked to astonishing effect.

When it made war the British State seemed remarkably efficient, even centralized, in its capacity to find funds, and raise forces. But appearances were somewhat misleading. It was precisely when fighting wars, especially the relatively limited wars of the period, none of which produced an actual invasion by a foreign army, that the State showed its capacity for flexible response. In peacetime, and for many purposes in wartime, it remained a highly decentralized system. This is true even if the diverse traditions, conventions, and laws of Scotland, Ireland, and the colonies are ignored. English government was still overwhelmingly federal in character, so much so that Tom Paine considered it 'republican' in its extreme lack of central direction.[16] Almost all government was, in fact, local government. But the term 'local government' was not employed. It was invented by a later age which gave it subordinate status in a centralized democracy. In the eighteenth century what went on in the locality was at least as important as what occurred at Westminster. Significantly it was at this level, too, that the mid-eighteenth century was at its most creative. This was exactly because it treated such matters as all-important. The result was a great deal of change, but change so uneven that in some respects later generations were able to consider it an age of peculiar stability.

Municipal government, strictly defined, remained virtually unaltered. No new charters were granted in the eighteenth century, though a number of boroughs which already possessed charters were granted new versions of them to clarify or modify their provisions. Veneration for chartered rights and a vivid memory of

[16] *Rights of Man*, ed. H. Collins (London, 1969), pp. 148, 216, 234, 258.

the Stuart infringement of local liberties made systematic revision of the structure of urban administration unthinkable. On the other hand, municipal corporations were increasingly despised by those not directly involved in them, and it was only with reluctance that Parliament could be induced to give them additional authority, however defective their existing powers. In the great unincorporated cities of Manchester and Birmingham there was some discussion of the desirability of applying for chartered government: the view that prevailed was that its vices would far outweigh its virtues. Urban growth created acute problems in many places, ranging from sewage disposal and street lighting to poor relief and lower-class indebtedness. But it was widely assumed that the corporations could not be trusted in such matters. They were for the most part self-perpetuating and beyond public accountability. In their management of municipal property they were frequently charged with self-serving and corruption. Sometimes they were identified with religious and political interests which were at odds with the communities they represented. Consequently, when new powers were given they were granted for specific purposes to named or elected commissioners. Victorian reformers thought these bodies as oligarchical, irrational, and even corrupt as the municipal corporations whose work they supplemented. In the eighteenth century they seemed a sensible response to the deficiencies of urban government, one which respected political sensitivities without compounding the vices of the existing system.

In the countryside the social standing of the magistracy and its enthusiasm for taking on more and more executive functions obviated the need for specific institutions, with the exception of the turnpike trusts. None the less, statutory powers enhanced the importance of JPs as a class. The County Rates Act of 1739 in effect gave them extensive powers of taxation. In the late eighteenth century the county came to have an administrative life in a novel sense, as the county rate multiplied and public works—highways, bridges, prisons—became increasingly the conscious concern of quarter sessions. The preoccupations were not necessarily new, but the readiness of the magistrates to initiate, direct, and plan, rather than respond to parochial neglect or local complaint, was strikingly so. By the 1790s Parliament was treating the county benches as so many superior sources of information for legislation as well as agents for its implementation.

Innovation of this kind did not provoke much protest in point of principle, though in a local context it could be the occasion of intense debate and division. Matching expansion of the scope and personnel of central government was less palatable. Its operations tended to be regarded as at best a regrettable necessity, whereas those of local administrators were assumed to be genuinely concerned with the solution of social problems. The difference was seen very clearly in attitudes to public borrowing. The National Debt was thought a disgrace and a scandal, but lending to help construct a poorhouse or a hospital was a contribution to the public good. There was also the constant dread of generating new funds of patronage for the use of ministers and politicians. Even if eighteenth-century governments had been sufficiently inspired by the example of their Continental counterparts to engage in reconstruction and reform they would soon have come to grief on this rock. None the less, warfare ensured that public spending grew apace. During the Walpole era the annual budget hovered around five or six million. Thereafter it increased rapidly, breaking the psychologically important barriers of ten million in 1747 and twenty million in 1762. These were war years; the peacetime budgets of the 1760s ducked briefly below ten million before the American War sent them spiralling upwards. Annual expenditure reached nearly thirty million in 1782 and even in peacetime it never again dropped below fifteen.

Because such a high proportion of wartime expenditure was met by borrowing, in a form which permanently added to the National Debt, the burden of taxation did not contract even in years of low expenditure and good housekeeping—it merely stabilized for a while, before resuming its upward trend. Moreover the land tax, the main form of direct taxation, remained unaltered until 1798. The rate at which it was levied varied according to the exigencies of war, but not in proportion to the actual burden of wartime expenditure. After 1750 price inflation rendered the maximum rate of four shillings in the pound increasingly insignificant. It was indirect taxation which met the greater part of the nation's bills: stamp duties multiplied dramatically during the wars of the second half of the century as did customs duties, and excises. This affected a wide range of luxuries and a narrow but dangerously burdensome range of common necessities. In this sense one of the recurrent nightmares of early eighteenth-century

Englishmen, a vision of almost endless excises, was realized. There were important bureaucratic consequences. Local taxes, together with the land tax and the house and window duty, were assessed and collected by amateurs. The rest required a growing army of revenue officers. By 1782 there were some fourteen thousand of them, probably exceeding, for example, the total number of clergymen in England and Wales. It is not surprising that they figured so prominently in the contemporary mind, nor that they gave rise to despairing prognostications about the health of the body politic. The building of a handsome new headquarters for the excise department on the site of Gresham's defunct college in Broad Street in 1767 provoked some gloomy reflections on the symbolic significance of subjugating learning to tax-collecting.

It was the pressures of high taxation which brought a radical rethinking of administrative matters at the close of the American War. The fifteen reports of the Commissioners of Public Accounts, issued between 1780 and 1786, set out the maxims which were to transform the structure and character of British administration in the following century. Their respect for prescription did not lessen their determination to enforce new criteria of good government. 'The principles which secure the rights of private property are sacred, and to be preserved inviolate; they are landmarks to be considered as immovable. But the public have their rights also, rights equally sacred, and as freely to be exercised.'[17] The public's rights required direct performance of duties without recourse to deputies or delegates, fixed salaries which obviated the need for fees and the accompanying bribery, and above all rules to eliminate the laxity and abuse which seemed to characterize so much of the administrative fabric of the Tudor and Stuart State. The clarity and forcefulness with which these principles were advanced seems startling, yet their novelty can be exaggerated. The Commission itself was reasserting a tradition of administrative reform which belonged securely with earlier commissions, under Charles II, and in the years which followed the Revolution of 1688. Moreover the practice of some departments of State had long accorded with the new recommendations. The hated revenue services, headed though they were by boards of political appointees, consistently sought to enforce similar principles in the nomination and supervision of customs and excise officers. Yet many con-

[17] *Commons Journals*, xxix. 779–80.

temporaries thought of these services as alien impositions, threatening the liberty and property of Englishmen. This mixture of tradition and innovation in the business of government was altogether typical of the age. So was the fact that it was brought about by the pressures of war. An important administrative change in the arrangements of central government, the decision in 1782 to divide the responsibilities of the Secretaries of State, not in terms of the geographical location of the foreign courts with which they dealt, but in terms of a basic distinction between foreign and domestic affairs, for the first time gave the Crown a front-rank minister concerned with home affairs distinct from financial administration or enforcement of the laws.

How strong was the eighteenth-century State? It is tempting to argue, especially in the light of its record in warfare, that it was institutionally stronger than many of its rivals.[18] The temptation should be resisted. The State was efficient as a war-making machine because in its warlike activities it implemented the wishes of the propertied forces which dominated society, while attracting the patriotic support of the classes who provided the cannon-fodder. Every war began with commercial interests convinced that they would benefit by war, with a sufficient number of landed gentlemen prepared to support the assertion of the nation's dignity, and with a rabidly jingoistic press reminding everyone else of the justice, necessity, and feasibility of the war. This was invariably followed by a cycle of immense government spending, increased manufacturing activity, high employment, windfall profits, price inflation, and threatening recession. By the end of every war only a small minority of interests saw much profit in continuing the process, and many were protesting vociferously that it had been allowed to continue so long. But the strains, except on unfortunate individuals and the unconsulted 'industrious poor' were short-lived once peace resumed. The key, of course, was borrowing, which stimulated the economy, promoted mild, profitable inflation, devalued the Debt, and constantly shifted its burden on to posterity. Warfare on the English model was a triumph for an enterprising and acquisitive society, not an authoritarian State.

If the test of a strong State is its capacity to enforce its will on recalcitrant citizens, the evidence is weak. During the first half of the period, when dynastic tensions and the unpopularity of the

---

[18] L. J. Hume, *Bentham and Bureaucracy* (Cambridge, 1981), pp. 21–2.

Hanoverian monarchy made for a deeply divided society, only one war was fought. It was not an entirely happy experience. Even when, from the 1750s, the State was able to call on a relatively united ruling class, it was not always successful. Enforcing the Militia Act of 1757, an elementary and comparatively painless form of military service recommended by both Whigs and Tories and supported overwhelmingly by propertied people, proved an extraordinarily difficult task. Compared with Continental States, Britain may have been successful in imposing and collecting taxes. Even so its record was not impressive. It was notoriously the case that the Excise Board, a professional, bureaucratic body of renown, found it difficult to levy taxes beyond London and the counties around it. In peacetime it was well nigh impossible to impose a new tax which would not provoke serious opposition and which would yield something like its expected product. Both the Seven Years War and the American War were followed by a succession of taxes tried and repealed in desperate attempts to make the books balance after an expensive war. Wartime taxes were hardly popular, but generally stuck. Peacetime levies were another matter altogether.

Beyond taxation the record of the State was still worse. The British reputation for passing laws which nobody bothered to observe was so marked that it was considered an important element in the libertarian tradition.[19] Only laws which some individual or group had an obvious interest in enforcing were likely to be fully put into practice, not by the State, but by virtue of local action. In this respect it is difficult to detect any substantial change in the course of the mid-eighteenth century. Theorists were looking, for all sorts of reasons, to a new kind of State. But there is not much evidence that Lord North and the younger Pitt called on an apparatus which was notably more impressive than that at the command of Sir Robert Walpole. Changes in the interim stemmed from changes in the political community, not the increased power of government. If anything, it seems likely that the early Hanoverian State was more intimidating than the late. The threat to the succession made the notorious general warrants virtually unchallengeable before 1760; after 1760 the argument of State necessity was swept aside.

What the State lacked in forcefulness, it made up in durability.

[19] See p. 296.

In this respect its growing unity was particularly important, for it made possible an increasingly firm response when the moral support of its citizens was forthcoming. This unity was a novel development, and by no means without limitations. Since it was compatible with a high degree of political and administrative decentralization, it needs defining with care. In 1727 the British monarchy was an extraordinary conglomeration of diverse identities and units, resembling rather the Habsburg dominions in their colourful particularism than the unified government beloved of Enlightenment theorists. In England, Scotland, Ireland, and Hanover, it had four distinct systems of government, the three latter regarded in London as essentially alien and suspect. Hanover never was assimilated, or even more than nominally attached. Ireland was united with the British Crown but had its own rebellious legislature; for reasons of religion it was considered perpetually at risk, a liability as much as an asset. The Union with Scotland was only twenty years old. It left a degree of autonomy north of the border, and, until Jacobitism died, Scotland was regarded as barely more dependable than Ireland. In addition there was a diverse, disunited set of colonies in America and the West Indies, which were permitted a large measure of self-government, and in some cases had only the common ties of commerce to bind them to the mother country.

In some respects little of this had changed by the early 1780s. Scotland's autonomy remained in its full extent. The changes made in the Highlands after the Forty-Five had the consent of the Whig rulers of Scotland: they were changes within Scotland, not changes between England and Scotland. In other matters, respect for the settlement negotiated in 1707 was reinforced rather than weakened under George III. Ireland positively strengthened its position. In 1782–3 it was granted complete legislative independence, reversing the tendency to incorporation which had marked the early part of the century. Colonial government, after the agonizing attempt to enforce British supremacy in America, was increasingly left to its own devices in the 1780s. The object of imperial administrators was to get settler colonies to pay for themselves, but without enforcing total submission.

Even in England the process of decentralization seemed to be speeding up. This is somewhat paradoxical. Some of the basic trends of the age were breaking down the barriers between regions and especially those between town and country. But the same gentry who lived much of their lives in London or Bath, married their sons and daughters into families from distant provinces, spoke with the same accents and pursued the same fashions as their counterparts in other places, and promoted the development of what was essentially a national market, were fiercely resistant to any attempt to encroach on their control of county government.

Yet it is possible to discern a greater sense of an overriding loyalty to one, British State in the later eighteenth century. It can be substantiated not in institutional terms, but in the way ordinary citizens regarded their government. In the everyday literature of current affairs, newspapers, magazines, cartoons, and broadsheets, Britain had superseded England for many purposes. In the 1730s most Englishmen still thought of the State in severely insular fashion, as an English realm with outlying members, most of them dependencies, some of them positive encumbrances. Such was the pressure of this conformity that in political matters even Welshmen called themselves Englishmen, lest they be suspected of falling into the category of despised Celtic dependants, like the Scots and Irish. For the cartoonist Britannia was an English symbol in the early years of George II, often beset by Scotsmen in kilts. Contemporaries seem not to have grasped the irony of this appropriation of the emblem of Britain to one part of the island. Fifty years later Englishmen remained aggressively xenophobic and in their attitudes to other inhabitants of the British Isles at best patronizing. Even in this respect, however, the worst was over. The feverish anti-Scottish sentiment of the Bute era gradually diminished. The prominence of Scots in the armies sent to America may have confirmed the paranoid suspicions of Jacobite influence among the colonists and their English friends. It also made clear to other Englishmen that Scots were not merely freebooters in a union of expediency and enterprise, but loyal fellow citizens prepared to contribute more than their share in defending it. In this respect, as in others, the court played an important role, once the embarrassment of George III's personal connection with Lord Bute had been left behind. The King's boast in 1760 that he was truly a Briton was amply fulfilled in a long reign which revealed no national prejudices or discrimination on his part.

The trauma of the War of American Independence is particularly significant as a pointer to changing attitudes towards the State.

Some Englishmen and most Americans believed that the war did not reflect the wishes of the British as a nation. This convenient fiction, which made the British and American peoples friends, and only their governments enemies, was repeated by Whiggish historians in the nineteenth century. It placed the blame for the breakdown of Anglo-American relations clearly with the King and his ministers. Another fiction, widely entertained in America, though not altogether consistent with the first, was the claim that the colonies were in effect a nation in the making, and about to throw off their dependent status as émigré Englishmen. This served the cause of nineteenth-century American nationalism, and incidentally permitted Victorian Englishmen to consider the American Revolution a natural outcome of the Anglo-Saxon tradition, albeit one hastened by the unfortunate policies of English governments.

Modern scholarship has rendered both fictions thin indeed. The policies which offended America, and the war to enforce them, were approved by a majority of the political nation, perhaps by an overwhelming majority. Equally the evidence is clear that of real nationalism there was almost nothing in America. Americans were Englishmen and Virginians or New Englishmen first, Americans second if at all. In this their perspectives were very like those of their fellow citizens in the British Isles. It took the threat of British encroachment to unite them. American nationalism may have followed the American Revolution: it did not precede it.

British policy in the colonies reflected the confidence of a State swollen by the triumphs of the Seven Years War and the economic growth which accompanied it. George III was no Joseph II, but his governments made a real attempt to weld the diverse societies which he ruled into a unit with common objectives, or at least common principles of commercial and administrative life. Although the weapon, parliamentary supremacy, was distinctive, its resemblance to enlightened despotism was not superficial. This great venture, a vision shared by many who at one time or another opposed George III, faltered at Bunker Hill, crumbled at Saratoga, and collapsed at Yorktown. But it had enduring effects. Englishmen in the 1780s were the leading citizens of an empire which for all its internal liberties, particularisms, and anomalies, had a perceived unity. The implications need careful weighing. They do not signify, at any rate after the American War, an uncompromising authoritarianism in dealing with colonies. In the 1780s there was a tendency to avoid further adventures in centralization, and in many ways, growing sympathy for the subjects of the Crown in distant parts. But this was itself the product of a developing view of the functions and duties of the State. The sympathy and humanity for which Americans looked in vain were much more likely to be granted once they had left the empire. The new kind of State was reflected in the attitudes which guided propertied opinion rather than the authority of central government.

Nationalistic distinctions did not disappear overnight. Individual Englishmen remained as contemptuous of their fellow citizens of the empire as before, as many Irishmen, Scots, and Welshmen testified. If Indians, Canadians, and West Indians had emigrated to England in numbers they would doubtless have met with a similar or worse reception. But the crucial fact was that these tensions were kept well within bounds, at least for the purposes of economic development and political harmony. The State in its eighteenth-century form, a State based on the power of parliamentary supremacy, the vigour of commercial growth, and the moral force of a predominantly middle-class culture was well placed to face the revolutionary turmoil which lay ahead.

PARLIAMENTARY SUPREMACY

At the level of ordinary individuals, the very expression 'State' was an awkward one, whatever the reality which it represented. Yet its competitors were still more objectionable. 'Commonwealth' was already outmoded. It also had dangerous, mid-seventeenth-century connotations. The Commonwealthmen of the early eighteenth century went to great lengths to explain that they were not king-killers, but nobody with a tincture of monarchism could be happy with the term, still less with the more explicit 'Republic'. The beauty of 'State' was precisely that it had no specific implications as to the proper composition of government. It could be used neutrally to indicate government in general, and it was the property of no particular group or sect. But the extension of its usage took time. It was sometimes employed to distinguish secular concerns from those of the Church, sometimes as a synonym for 'country' or 'kingdom' in the context of international relations. By the late eighteenth century it was being employed increasingly to express the sense of a society organized for political or legal purposes. Men like Priestley and Bentham gave it its modern meaning, usually because they wanted it to adopt policies or programmes in what is now a recognizably modern way. But not many ordinary men and women thought like Bentham and Priestley, and when they did grapple with concepts of government they were most likely to reach first for Parliament as the institutional expression of the nation as a collective body.

In a sense Parliament was a surprising candidate for this position. It had no executive authority of its own. When arresting Alexander Murray in 1750, or the offending printers in 1771, it could barely enforce its will. For roughly half of every year it did not sit at all, and to summon it out of season was highly controversial. When famine threatened in the autumn of 1766, the Chatham ministry used the prerogative of the Crown rather than convene the 'grand inquest of the nation'. It consisted of nearly eight hundred men, 558 MPs, 26 bishops, 16 elected representatives of the Scottish peerage, and roughly 180 hereditary British peers. Few had deliberately prepared themselves for the exercise of sovereignty, and most were subject to the influence of patrons or electors. Those who were not answerable to anybody were likely to be relatively uninterested in what went on in Parliament. Particularly in the second half of the century, attendance by more than half the members of either House was uncommon. When they did attend, the effect was not always very impressive, at least where the more important of the two chambers, the House of Commons, was concerned. St Stephen's Chapel was a cramped, unhealthy room in which MPs jostled with each other and members of the public. It was a standing embarrassment to architectural experts who looked for a magnificent baroque or Palladian home for the world's most powerful deliberative assembly. Lord Tyrawley, who carried aristocratic disdain to unusual lengths, professed not to know where the House of Commons was.[20] Neither House recorded its debates, made a practice of printing all its bills, codified its procedures and standing orders, or concerned itself much about the image which it presented to the public. This was the great legislative Leviathan of Georgian England, the setting for the elder Pitt's philippics and Burke's Ciceronian orations, the terror of absolute monarchs and unrepresented colonists alike.

[20] Horace Walpole, *Memoirs of King George II*, iii. 15.

It would be difficult to exaggerate the overwhelming importance of Parliament in eighteenth-century England, hackneyed though it is as a historical theme. The doctrine of parliamentary supremacy expressed by Blackstone in his famous *Commentaries* of 1765–9 was uncompromising. It admitted of no check on the legislative authority of the Crown in Parliament.[21] By coincidence Blackstone's statement was made at a time when Parliament itself was asserting its authority in the American colonies, with disastrous results. The doctrine reflected a number of developments, many of them originating in the late seventeenth century. The decisive defeat of absolute monarchy in 1688 and the establishment of annual parliamentary sessions helped install Westminster at the centre of political life. But its permanence remained open to question at least until the 1740s. Although Jacobites talked of their ambition of summoning a free Parliament, a dynastic revolution could have eliminated it altogether. Nor was Hanoverian rule synonymous with parliamentary supremacy. George II considered the House of Commons at best a tedious necessity, its main function to 'do the King's business', that is finance his foreign policy and pension list.

There were real fears under Walpole that an ingenious minister and a malevolent monarch would find means of putting Parliament back where it had belonged in the seventeenth century, an occasional, almost ephemeral feature of political life. A long peace and prudent fiscal policy placed Walpole on the brink of making parliamentary taxation unnecessary in the 1730s, and without parliamentary taxation there was no guarantee of regular, let alone frequent Parliaments. It took the renewed warfare of the mid-eighteenth century and the vast increase in taxation associated with it to confirm the verdict of the Revolution of 1688. In this, as in many other ways, Walpole's fall was a great watershed, not less important than the stirring events of fifty years before. Thereafter it became impossible to conceive of a constitution without Parliament. By the 1760s, when local and private legislation was multiplying, it would have been unthinkable to turn back. Not even the worst enemies of George III seriously accused him of seeking the abolition of Parliament, however much they accused him of seeking to mould it to his will. But this had often been alleged against Walpole and George II.

[21] i. 156.

Parliament's significance in political discourse grew steadily. An important change which occurred during the early years of George III was the growing attention focused on its debates. Admittedly, parliamentary debates had long been of interest to the public at large. For much of the reign of George II there were brief reports of parliamentary proceedings, usually in the monthly magazines. They were generally printed some months or even a year after delivery, at a time when Parliament was not sitting, and lightly, ludicrously camouflaged as the proceedings of a gentleman's club or the senate of Lilliput. But they were at best short summaries, and many of them bore only the most remote resemblance to what was actually said. From time to time both Houses reinforced their rules against the publication of debates, but rarely troubled to execute them. In the 1750s, such was the relative tranquillity of parliamentary politics that the journals virtually gave up covering such proceedings. John Wilkes brought this state of affairs to an end. After 1771 there emerged a small but highly skilled corps of parliamentary journalists, adept at evading the Commons and Lords prohibition on actual stenography and at summarizing speeches without sacrificing their sense. By the late 1770s major parliamentary debates were appearing in virtually every newspaper.

The ubiquity of these reports is very striking. In the 1720s and 1730s the main matter in a newspaper, metropolitan or provincial, was likely to be an extract from one of the papers devoted to essays on controversial topics, and items of foreign news. Both continued to feature in late eighteenth-century papers. But pride of place was given to a parliamentary report. This put Parliament and its doings at the very centre of current affairs and familiarized the most distant communities not merely with the subjects debated, but also with the personalities, the quirks, and the conventions of each House. Lord North, Charles James Fox, and William Pitt were present in every coffee-house and in not a few homes in a way which would have seemed extraordinary to Sir Robert Walpole, William Pulteney, and William Shippen. The change influenced the way the public thought of Parliament, and helped promote criticism of its representative credentials. It must also have had some effect on contemporary polemic. Debating clubs and disputing societies were a feature of the age. The famous Robin Hood Club, open to all classes from mechanics to magnates, was only the best-known of what was a widespread and to some rather alarming institution. It did not hesitate to imitate the procedures and employ the language of Parliament. There was a belief in the 1770s and 1780s that popular irreverence for government was stimulated by these self-appointed State deliberators.

Parliament itself was affected. The first great parliamentarian who consciously addressed the House of Commons in the knowledge that his words would be relayed to a mass audience in something more than slogans or bowdlerisms was Edmund Burke. He assisted the process by publishing his own version of some of his orations. His *Speech on American Taxation* in 1774 and his *Speech on Conciliation* in 1775 came to be regarded as classics both of imperial thought and parliamentary rhetoric. Even five years earlier they would have been unthinkable as the actual record of what a member of the House of Commons had told his fellow legislators. Burke, of course, was exceptional as thinker, speaker, and writer. But it is the case that from the 1770s every MP and peer who chose to address his parliamentary colleagues was engaging in an act of public information and education, or, as it might be seen, public propaganda and manipulation. Parliament as an arcane mystery vanished overnight. MPs, once prized as 'knowing Parliament men', were now public orators.

Government was becoming in a real sense a function of the legislature. Terminology understandably lagged behind reality in this respect. Foreign ministers were still accredited to the court of St James, government was still the King's, and even humble land-tax assessors frequently described the impost which they levied as the 'King's tax'. But these appearances were misleading. Foreign affairs were, under George III especially, conducted according to the will of Parliament, however much the day-to-day management of diplomatic relations had to be carried out by the Secretaries of State and their subordinates. Every tax was approved and regulated by Parliament, primarily by the House of Commons. The royal prerogative was guarded as far as possible by Whig Ministers as much as by Hanoverian monarchs. In colonial and Irish affairs, Crown, Cabinet, and Privy Council to some extent excluded Parliament. But Cabinet ministers were invariably Members of Parliament. Walpole, in a justly celebrated and typically artful speech of 1739, boasted to the Commons that for all his power, he was their creature. Under any of his successors the boast would have seemed redundant and faintly absurd, if not offensive in its implication that an alternative state of affairs was imaginable.[22]

The weakness of the Cabinet as an institution accentuated the importance of Parliament. Much historical ingenuity has been deployed to locate the origins and trace the development of Cabinet government. So far as the eighteenth century is concerned it has mostly been wasted. The formal Cabinet Council was largely neglected for practical purposes. Walpole characteristically remarked on the accession of George II that he was 'against having the Cabinet; no good ever came from them'.[23] His view was shared by all his successors. It is easy to see why. The Cabinet Council was a relatively large body which included office-holders best kept out of the secrets of government: the Archbishop of Canterbury and major household officials, for example. Administrative action which proceeded from the royal prerogative still required its endorsement, and when the King was abroad, as George II frequently was, the presence of the principal ministers as Lords Regent breathed a temporary vitality into its activities. But for purposes of practical politics it was a mere shell. In its place there evolved the inner Cabinet, a small body of ministers, entrusted with the confidential management of the King's affairs. The Prime Minister and Secretaries of State invariably sat in it. Beyond that its membership was a matter for negotiation. Almost everything about it depended on the personalities of those involved and on the circumstances of the day. Some Cabinets kept minutes, some did not; some Prime Ministers dominated their colleagues, others were no more than first among equals. There plainly had to be regular meetings of important ministers, and some agreement on the adoption of common policies, but even these minimal requirements were not always met: the Cabinet remained a startlingly unbusinesslike and casual body for much of the period. Nor did it promote that solidarity which was to be the hallmark of its later history. Cabinet accountability was very slow to develop. Facing an irate Commons or Lords ministers could not shelter behind Prime Ministerial or collective decision-making. Under the stress of the American War North and his colleagues insisted on their joint responsibility, but the opposition's campaign against

---

[22] *Parliamentary History*, x. 946.
[23] *The Life and Letters of John Locke, with extracts from his Correspondence, Journals, and Common-Place Books. By Lord King*, ii. 52.

individual ministers, and the disintegration of the ministry in the last two years of the war revealed this as a fiction.

Cabinets technically advised the Crown. But nothing that implied spending money could be proposed to the King without an assurance of parliamentary support: this effectively meant any important measure of public policy. Privy Counsellors were themselves for practical purposes the leading ministers of the day and therefore parliamentarians themselves. The tendency was for even Council matters to come increasingly before the legislature. The Privy Council's responsibility for the maintenance of order, the regulation of employment, and the supervision of laws maintaining the supply of food, was gradually superseded by Parliament acting through the magistracy. By the 1760s Parliament was poised to intervene directly in the affairs of the American colonies and the East India Company. Having raised the funds to protect and extend the empire its determination to make imperial policy could hardly be resisted. George III, usually portrayed as an ardent defender of the royal prerogative, was positively prodigal in his surrender of his rights to Parliament. This could never have been said of his predecessor, who kept a tight guard on his kingly powers, however much he left the management of Parliament to his ministers.

Even judges, by instinct conservative guardians of their inheritance, responded to the pull of Parliament. The most influential of them, Lord Hardwicke and Lord Mansfield, enjoyed immense standing not merely in Westminster Hall and the royal closet, but also in Parliament. Important judges had always been members of the House of Lords, but in an age of annual parliamentary sessions and constant legislation, a seat in the Lords and the respect which attended the leading Crown lawyers' opinion gave them additional importance. At its height this power could rival that of Prime Ministers. Hardwicke as Newcastle's Lord Chancellor enjoyed vast political influence; so did Mansfield as Lord North's leading legal adviser, though not Lord Chancellor, a position which he considered judicially uninteresting. Even lesser men could wield power beyond their personal pretensions. Lord Northington was a thorn in the side of the ministries which included him as Lord Chancellor in the 1760s, as Lord Thurlow was in the 1780s. The younger Pitt eventually had Thurlow dismissed in 1792 but similar problems were to occur under his successors, notably with Lord Eldon. It was a problem which had its origin in the mid-eighteenth century and its expression in some of the most important legislative enactments of the age—Hardwicke's Marriage Act, Mansfield's Quebec Act, as well as in some highly controversial political activities, including Hardwicke's campaign against Henry Fox in the 1750s and Mansfield's crucial support for the King's American measures in the 1770s.

Parliament's growing prominence in government was not more important than the place it came to occupy in the lives of ordinary citizens. The positive explosion of legislative activity which marked the mid-eighteenth century had profound consequences. In the 1720s Parliament added barely fifty statutes a year to the statute-book: half of these were private bills, revising estate settlements, naturalizing foreigners, and so on. By the 1780s the annual total was approaching 200, the great majority of them public in the sense that they applied to the public at large, albeit in a restricted locality. Most parliamentary activity in the second half of the eighteenth century was concerned not with implementing or reviewing government policy, but with endorsing and enforcing the initiatives of commercial interest or particular localities. The promoters of such legislation might be no more than a handful of individuals, the enclosers of a small rural parish, the manufacturers of an insignificant commodity which needed protecting against its rivals, the advocates of a new church in a growing suburb. Or they might represent great numbers, a large city seeking powers to pave its streets, a body of subscribers to a canal project, or the merchants and manufacturers in an entire industry. In either case what they were doing was to employ the new legislative force of Parliament to bring about change.

Parliament responded readily to such demands. Lobbying by commercial interests was a highly organized business. Commercial groups raised funds, set up committees, dispatched their own delegates to Westminster. In the 1780s the celebrated Chamber of Manufactures, which sought to co-ordinate the activities of the lobbyists under the direction of some of the leading industrial entrepreneurs of the day, Josiah Wedgwood, Matthew Boulton, Samuel Garbett, though over-ambitious in its plans for one voice on behalf of very diverse trades, was merely extending a commonplace activity. When manufacturers and merchants chose to influence national policy, for example in their support for the

repeal of the American Stamp Act in 1766, or in their opposition
to free trade with Ireland in the late 1770s and 1780s, they put on
an impressive display of commercial power. But even on a regional
or national basis they were accustomed to mount sophisticated,
expensive campaigns. So were many cities, towns, and parishes,
in search of specific policy changes. Very often, of course, one
demand clashed with another. When they conflicted there was a
tendency to compromise or to apply the desired law within as
confined a scope as possible. The process of legislation was expensive in terms of parliamentary fees and the cost of preparing a bill:
most petitioners preferred accommodation to losing their bill and
their money. When compromise was impossible, however, the
conflict could be devastating. Whenever the interests of the linen
and woollen industries conflicted, as they did frequently, the
result was a bitter confrontation in Parliament; this rivalry was
exacerbated by the regional and national loyalties which reflected
the linen trade's base in Scotland and Ireland and the woollen
manufacture's traditional importance in the West Country, in East
Anglia, and in Yorkshire. The most divisive issue in Parliament in
1749 was not a matter of national policy, but the attempt by the
Grenville family to secure a bill asserting Buckingham's right to
act as host to the summer assizes for the county against the claims
of its rival Aylesbury. Competition of this kind was the very essence
of eighteenth-century politics.

PARLIAMENTARY REPRESENTATION

The efficiency displayed by Parliament in coping with the growing
volume of legislation points to the continuing acceptability of
the political structure of which it was a part. A major consideration was the readiness of MPs to serve the propertied interests
of the communities with which they were associated. A famous
twentieth-century scholar made his reputation by demonstrating
that eighteenth-century MPs were rather servants of their own
families, connections, and interests, than of that public opinion
which Whigs identified as the magical basis of parliamentary representation. Sir Lewis Namier's essay 'Why men went into Parliament?' remains a classic of historical sociology.[24] It is also
misleading. Men went into Parliament for all kinds of reasons, but

[24] *The Structure of Politics at the Accession of George III* (London, 1961).

what they did when they got there almost always had a bearing on their staying there. This was not, however, a matter of party politics. Edmund Burke lost his Bristol seat to a supporter of Lord North in 1780 not because he was one of the leaders of the Whig opposition in the Commons, but because he declined to submit to the direction of his constituents in the commercial questions which most concerned them. Country gentlemen who sat as the natural representatives of their counties, borough-owners who commanded the votes of their electors, placemen and businessmen who looked to Parliament for advancement, all were expected to engage in the complex and tiresome business of legislation, even when they were not required to take a particular line in national politics. There were few constituencies so closed that an MP could afford to ignore the requests of his constituents for assistance with legislation; those that were, were frequently represented by local property-owners who had an interest of their own in promoting local bills. This was a dimension of parliamentary life which Namier largely ignored, as his Whig predecessors had before him.

Not only parliamentary constituencies were represented in Parliament. Much legislation was promoted by places which lacked seats in the House of Commons. Birmingham, Manchester, the suburbs of London, all notoriously unrepresented, were frequent applicants for legislation. They were served by the diverse propertied interests of MPs and peers who gained valuable local credit by their help, and in any case thought twice about resisting the pressure of their tenants, their neighbours, or their friends. To a marked extent eighteenth-century legislators were as much representatives of the localities where they resided or held property as those for which they sat in Parliament. Many of those elected technically by the rotten boroughs of the south-west were in effect the servants of other regions where parliamentary boroughs were less generously allocated. Contemporaries were well aware that landlord representation was a valuable parliamentary weapon. The *London Magazine* in 1768 claimed that it was one of the peculiar virtues of the English constitution compared with the French that every neighbourhood had 'the happiness to have some gentleman in the neighbourhood who has the honour of a seat in our supreme legislature, and consequently a power to command the attention of our ministers of state'.[25]

[25] p. 388.

Certain developments of the mid-eighteenth century made this form of 'virtual representation' particularly effective. One was the gradual elimination of party as a cause of dissension in most legislation. The party strife of George II's reign was such that it proved difficult to protect relatively uncontentious legislation from its effects. Battles between interests or localities offered all too clear an opportunity for the Whigs or Tories incidentally affected to appeal to their party colleagues for support. Divisions on some seemingly minor matters, such as turnpike bills, were astonishingly high: they not infrequently found more than 250 MPs voting. This changed in the 1750s. The decline of party identities in the traditional sense made such tactics unavailable to individual MPs. As a result debates and divisions in Parliament tended increasingly to reflect the relative balance of property and interests concerned rather than the artificial involvement in court and country, Whig and Tory. The late eighteenth-century legislature, inundated by demands for statutory intervention, could not afford the bitter party rivalries of the early eighteenth century.

Nor could it afford an unduly restrictive view of the doctrine of parliamentary representation. Strict constituency control of MPs would have produced a dangerously unbalanced system, one reflecting the bizarre distribution of parliamentary boroughs. Middlesex had 8 MPs and a million residents compared with Cornwall's 42 MPs and a population of barely a hundred thousand. But in practice Middlesex commanded the services of as many as 57 MPs with permanent residences in the county. It also attracted the interest of almost the whole body of MPs and peers who were resident in London for the purpose of attending parliamentary sessions. By the late eighteenth century an MP who lacked a house which he rented, leased, or owned in the capital was decidedly unusual. Such considerations put a rather different complexion on otherwise indefensible anomalies of electoral geography. There was even a complaint in 1783 that London had too much representation for the public good.[26]

Legislators were encouraged to interpret their representative duties broadly. One of the advantages of the doctrine that an MP represented the country as a whole, rather than his particular electors, was precisely its appeal in these terms. When Edmund Burke defended it in the face of his Bristol electors in 1774 he

[26] Baptist Noel Turner, *The True Alarm*, p. 3.

aroused much controversy.[27] But Burke's opponents were Wilkesites who advocated electoral control of MPs in the form of 'instructions' specifying the conduct which they were expected to pursue in Parliament. Instructions had an honourable history. They were used against Walpole's excise scheme and foreign policy to some effect. MPs found them increasingly repugnant. It is easy to see why. It would have been impossible for Parliament to answer to the needs of a propertied society in its broadest and most flexible form if ordinary MPs had been controlled by their immediate constituents. Liberation from such dictatorship was a pre-condition of effective representation of the manifold interests of the day.

This argument did not impress the champions of electoral reform. But there was almost no meeting point between them and their opponents. At issue was a conflict of values which could be described but not compromised. In essence, the parliamentary reformers demanded that the representation of the individual be made the supreme criterion of a rational political system. By the 1780s arguments to this effect were being put which looked forward decades. Participatory democracy had its advocates long before the fully fledged class conflict which placed it on the agenda of practical politicians. Against them there was asserted a scale of values which made little allowance for the ordinary citizen's wishes. But the defeat of parliamentary reform was not the victory of reactionaries against radicals. Rather it was the pragmatic verdict of the interests and individuals resorting to Parliament. It did not need the horrors of the revolutionary era to demonstrate the functional effectiveness of the legislature. When Parliament was subjected to a series of petitions for parliamentary reform in 1782 and 1783 it was noticeable that most of them came not from unrepresented communities but from excluded majorities in existing parliamentary boroughs. In essence, their complaint was that the privilege of electing a Member of Parliament had been unfairly entrusted to an oligarchical minority of their fellow citizens. The Society for Constitutional Information hoped for much wider support, especially among urban populations entirely without parliamentary representation. But Birmingham did not petition, nor did Manchester, Leeds, Sheffield, or any other great city which lacked MPs of its own. In such places propertied men entertained a certain scepticism

[27] *Speech at the Conclusion of the Poll, 3 Nov. 1774* [Bristol, 1774].

FIG. 12. Electoral geography and parliamentary reform proposals

Note: The distribution of parliamentary boroughs is shown, together with the total number of seats in each county. The figure in parentheses gives the seats allocated to each county under a scheme proposed in Sir John Sinclair's *Lucubrations during a short recess* (London, 1782). Sinclair's proposals were less radical than those of most parliamentary reformers but more likely to accord with realistic expectations.

about the advantages of reform. The parliamentary franchise was expected to bring corruption and tumult at election time, continual intrigue and faction between elections. The defence for the status quo was that it provided access to the legislature without the inconvenience and irritation of elections.

The commonest worry about Parliament's functioning was not its deficiency where the public at large was concerned, but rather its vulnerability to the pressures exerted by the executive. The *power* of the Crown was not viewed as the main enemy of the authority and virtue of Parliament. Its *influence* certainly was. Montesquieu's celebrated assertion that the Englishman's liberty, invented 'first in the woods of Germany', consisted primarily in a parliamentary independence which would perish 'when the legislative power shall be more corrupt than the executive', was considered a truism.[28] There was no perennial hardier than place and pension bills to minimize the Crown's influence in the Commons. (It was not suggested that members of the House of Lords should not hold office or receive a pension.) In this way the old bogey of influence came to seem more relevant than ever, as the principal, perhaps the only, threat to legislative independence. The 'economical reform' campaign of 1780 was the most determined of all attempts to defeat it. How much effect it had is another matter. It is customary to deride the impact of such movements. The place legislation of Queen Anne's reign had left a vast amount of potential influence at the command of government, and the further Acts of 1742 and 1782 made only limited inroads into it. This does not necessarily reveal the faint-heartedness of the legislators, however. Realism, as opposed to rhetoric, suggested that while influence could be forced to flow through new channels it could rarely be removed altogether. The customs and excise officers, for instance, had been barred from seats in the Commons under William III; they lost their right to vote in parliamentary elections much later in 1782. But they did not cease to be an important source of political influence. Brothers, sons, cousins, and friends of MPs and voters continued to be revenue officials. The words of John Robinson, one of the most experienced of all eighteenth-century electioneers, when surveying the effects of the 1782 Act at Hastings, might be applied to many valiant attempts of Georgian reformers to restore the purity of the constitution. 'The disfranchising bill

[28] *The Spirit of the Laws* (New York, 1949), p. 162.

has made great alterations in this and other boroughs, yet it is hoped that this borough with great attention may as formerly be got to return two friends, but this cannot be known until the time comes for conversation.'[29] Conversation proved him right.

The scrutiny of influence was part of a much wider debate about the problem of corruption. But it was easier to denounce the Crown than ordinary propertied citizens. Corruption was the single most important political issue of the eighteenth century. It never lost its importance, yet there was never much danger of a root and branch approach to eliminating it. Everybody denounced it; most politicians dealt in it. A 'pure' patriot like the elder Pitt could not avoid engaging in bribery and patronage any more than a frankly cynical one like his rival Henry Fox. The very anxiety which the age experienced in this respect has made it all the easier for posterity to condemn it. If it had been more hypocritical in its acceptance of corruption it would probably have escaped censure to a greater degree.

Corruption was at its most obvious and damaging where the Commons itself was concerned. Roughly half of all seats in the lower house were occupied by members whose electors were so few that there was a likelihood that the result was procured by bribery. It was a general rule that the smaller the constituency, the stronger the temptation for voters to collaborate with a view to selling their votes. There were exceptions. Some large and important cities had small electorates which discharged their duty without reference to their personal interests. Bath was a well-known example. Its franchise was vested in the corporation, and its electors opted freely for some well-known public figures, including the elder Pitt. But small boroughs were subject to immense temptations. Moreover, as the value of a parliamentary seat rose with inflation and the growing importance of a voice in the Commons, there was a tendency for marginally vulnerable boroughs to fall victim to the logic which had long since corrupted the smallest and rottenest.

Short of statutory reform, what could a House of Commons genuinely concerned about this state of affairs do? The lower house had control of the determination of controverted elections. A system which made the borough franchise depend on uncertain and

---

[29] W. T. Laprade, ed., *Parliamentary Papers of John Robinson, 1774–1784* (Camden Society, 3rd ser., vol. 33), 80.

variable local charters or conventions left much room for disputes of this kind, and the consequent hearings were a major parliamentary distraction, particularly in the session following a general election when a host of petitions protesting against the declared outcome were likely to be put forward. Government had an obvious interest in using its influence to sway the resulting decisions. At least before Grenville's Act of 1770, it did so to some effect.[30] It has been argued that the Commons itself was biased when it considered election petitions, usually preferring small, oligarchical electorates to large, open ones.[31] This contention has a bearing on the consequences of an important statute designed to limit electoral malpractice, the Bribery Act of 1729. A clause in this Act required the Commons perpetually to abide by its previous or 'last' determination of a particular franchise dispute. It thereby offered some relief to an assembly plagued with requests to reopen previous decisions as to a local convention, custom, or charter. Its effect was to close constituencies where the last or only decision on record was in favour of a small electorate, to open those where it had favoured a larger body. If, as has been suggested, the Commons generally opted for a narrow rather than a broad franchise, the effect was to preserve and entrench electoral oligarchy.

This conclusion is misleading. Very few electoral petitions offered the Commons a chance to choose between a large electorate, based on a franchise vested in the freemen or ratepayers of a borough, and a small body of burgage owners or corporation members. Many disputes involved fine distinctions and pedantic points of legal interpretation. The Commons was often influenced by personal or political bias. But it also sought to establish the historical evidence on which most borough disputes turned. For the rest two critical considerations seem to have guided its deliberations. One was a horror of permitting voting by men who depended on public charity. It was assumed that such voters could not be expected to exercise an independent judgement, uninfluenced by the magistrates, overseers, and ratepayers who supervised the distribution of relief. The other was a dislike of the means by which borough interests bought the support of elements with no real standing in the borough. Particularly in 'freemen boroughs', where voting was the privilege of those who enjoyed

[30] See pp. 524–5.
[31] J. Cannon, *Parliamentary Reform, 1640–1832* (Cambridge, 1973), p. 34.

the freedom of the municipality, there was a party advantage to be gained by the sale of the freedom to outsiders, or by the mass creation of non-resident 'honorary' freeman. This was one of the admitted scandals of the age. When it could, the Commons curbed it by restricting the vote to resident townsmen. (It also passed the Durham Act in 1763, to make it more difficult for honorary freemen to vote immediately after election.)[32] The statistical effect was to reduce the size of the electorate, thereby creating a 'narrower' electoral body. But the object was to ensure that oligarchical interests could not artificially manufacture votes.

A similar intention dictated Parliament's treatment of the county constituencies. The franchise was vested by statute in the forty-shilling freeholder, a landowner whose property was rated at £2 per annum. This was a low qualification and constantly made lower by inflation. There was concern about the vulnerability of the smaller freeholders to bribery, and some talk of raising the quali-fication. But the status of freeholder was much prized and Par-liament confined itself to ensuring that it was reserved for bona fide landowners. Following the Oxfordshire election of 1754, copyholders were prohibited from assuming the rights of forty-shilling freeholders. Acts of 1745 and 1780 required voters to be assessed to the land tax, a form of electoral registration which probably excluded considerable numbers of small freeholders from voting. On the accession of George III Parliament required the registration of annuity grants, a means by which landowners created blocks of freehold votes without conveying land to those involved. The technique of manufacturing votes by splitting prop-erty was one of the scandals of the age, whether the manufacturers were county magnates or East India Company proprietors. Par-liament did its best to inhibit them at the cost of reducing the potential electorate. Again, the object was not to promote oligarchy but to confine it, by ensuring that voters were authentically men of property and thereby relatively resistant to undue influence.

Beyond such measures Parliament did not, and could not, go, given prevailing assumptions. Harrington's maxim that power followed property was one of the unchallenged nostrums of mid-eighteenth-century thought. Corruption was merely one ex-pression of the power of property. Men with property, that is to say wealth, would inevitably use it to bend others to their will. In

[32] See p. 344.

a highly mobile, enterprising society, where property took many forms, and constantly changed its nature, the simplest expression of its force was the sovereign power of cash. There was much hypocrisy about this. Landed gentlemen protested bitterly when their own form of corruption, essentially the use of influence over their tenants, was overcome by other forms, imported by moneyed men. The former was 'natural interest', the latter was bribery. This distinction was nonsense, though it often appealed to a House of Commons in which landlords, many of them ironically descended from moneyed men, were well represented. It also revealed why corruption could not be eliminated, only replaced with some other form of corruption. A total revision of political values, denying the power of property, was required: one which accepted the equal validity of every man's will, regardless of his wealth, and registered it by some means such as a secret ballot and office-holding by competition. These would have been quite unacceptable in the eighteenth century. In the last analysis it was thought better to put up with corruption in its numberless forms than admit its egalitarian alternative.

A POLITICAL CULTURE

Politics was not merely a question of the machinery by which propertied men settled their differences and enforced their will. It was a reflection of society as a whole, in short a product of a political culture. This was well understood. Contemporaries thought of the public interest as something more than politics narrowly defined. Democratic egalitarians, of whom there were not a few in the first half of George III's reign, even sought to integrate political life and the public domain by making every man and even every woman rightful participants in the business of politics. But they remained a minority. An older view associated rights with law and duties with politics: it unashamedly prescribed a hierarchy of ranks, distributing both privileges and responsibilities without regard to the natural equality of man. Those who took this view were not necessarily naïve in their expectations of statesmen. Cynicism about 'politicians' was as marked as in any other age: in fact the final devaluation of the term, to signify merely one who engaged in political activity rather than one who had an expertise in the art and craft of politics, belongs with the eighteenth century. But cynicism about the way political life was conducted was perfectly compatible with a healthy interest in the wider world of which politics was merely a part, and a strong sense of the public responsibility of those who transacted public affairs.

There is no doubt that England's was an essentially popular political culture. But it was not supposed that the British constitution was democratic: on the contrary, to describe it in such terms was considered offensive. A balanced system of government must no more tilt towards the people than to monarch or magnates. On the other hand, the advocates of balance did not deny either that for practical purposes politics was a mass activity. Foreigners commented on the political sophistication or at least political precocity of the ordinary Englishmen whom they encountered, regardless of rank. In this respect at least there was no widening of the political nation, for it was already, in the early eighteenth century, at its widest possible extent. It was common to talk of the English as a 'nation of politicians' or even a 'nation of Prime Ministers' at the beginning of George II's reign, a time when the very term 'Prime Minister' was a novelty. It was and remained a platitude that Englishmen were politicized beyond any of their Continental counterparts.

It is arguable, if anything, that the mid-eighteenth century witnessed a certain narrowing of the political nation, not in terms of an aristocratic or oligarchical reaction but in the sense that the strengthening of the bourgeois presence in politics tended to squeeze out the lowest elements. Political discourse in a public context, increasingly the essence of politics as such, was conducted largely in the columns of the newspaper press. The illiterate had their own means of access to this discourse, but only at an inferior level. In an age of information, or, as was said at the time, of 'intelligence', the ill-informed were truly second-class citizens. Paradoxically the parliamentary reformers of the 1770s and 1780s had little understanding of the need to mobilize the politically uneducated, however much they exploited the popular discontent aroused, for instance, by the Middlesex election. Their weapons were the pamphlet and the treatise, their ammunition facts and statistics, their battleground the debating clubs and literary societies. Polemical literature was an immensely potent force but Burgh, Price, and Priestley had no notion of how to bring home its ultimate object to the poor. Wesley's example might have taught them much, and perhaps was to teach their radical successors in the next generation a good deal about infiltrating the most unpromising regions of popular culture.

Most middle-class politics were innately anti-plebeian. The politics of aristocratic oligarchy and also those of landed gentry allowed for a certain robust populism, albeit within a paternalistic framework. In the electoral battles of the early eighteenth century, and still more in the war of riot to which party strife not infrequently descended, the need for cannon-fodder was met by the so-called mob. There was a tradition of cautious tolerance of popular protest and even a readiness to legitimize it. The salutary violence of a mob bent on chastising extortionate bawdy-house owners, or enforcing the laws against monopoly, could be excused as a rough but ready form of achieving what laws and governments did not always accomplish very efficiently. So could the riot as an expression of fundamental political liberty. But the political climate of the mid-eighteenth century was less favourable to popular exertions of power, and that of the late eighteenth century decidedly hostile. The Wilkesite disturbances were perhaps the last in which riot was considered legitimate by very large numbers of propertied people. Newspaper readers of the day were reminded of the old Duke of Newcastle's boast that at the time of the Hanoverian Accession he had put himself at the head of a mob. This would have been an unthinkable boast for Lord North and the younger Pitt. Electoral violence remained characteristic of populous cities, but aroused growing irritation and alarm. What had been acceptable half a century before was increasingly reprobated in the 1770s and 1780s. The last vestige of propertied enthusiasm for popular justice as mediated by a mob was dissipated by the Gordon Riots.

This is not to say that extra-parliamentary politics ceased to be necessary. Rather they were made to serve the needs of propertied society. The arts of information-gathering, propaganda, campaigning, petitioning, and lobbying were increasingly organized and concentrated. The Parliament which met in 1784 was to be subjected to a stream of such efforts: Manchester's successful campaign to repeal the fustian tax, a widespread protest against Pitt's proposals for Irish free trade, vigorous lobbying to influence a commercial treaty with France, and, not least, the great assault on the slave trade. The ultimate victory of politeness was its success in creating a highly disciplined form of political protest, one which left the impolite, especially that labouring poor whose activities were being increasingly disciplined, regulated, and controlled in other ways in the late eighteenth century, out of contention.

What was the vision offered by the politics of the late eighteenth century? Not, certainly, that which had been held out at its beginning. Then a choice was presented to the public at large. It was the choice between two different kinds of society. One offered persecution of religious minorities, a retreat from deficit finance, expanding government and crude commercialism, a minimal part in European affairs, and a reversion to traditional, paternalistic values. The other offered oligarchical rule, protection for Protestant sects, acceptance of a prominent place in the Continental State system, and an unrestricted financial and commercial market. In their extreme form these essentially party prescriptions were tried only briefly, during the decade 1710–20, when Tories and Whigs successively sought to entrench themselves permanently in power. The Tory effort was wrecked by the divisions of the party of Oxford and Bolingbroke, and the impossibility of bringing back a popish pretender. The Whig attempt was ruined by the Whig split of 1717 and the disaster of the South Sea Bubble. Walpole's regime was very different. His measures were a mixture in party terms and provoked a matching coalition of parties in opposition. One consequence of the Walpole years was intense disillusion with the programme earlier offered by the parties, and eventually with the Utopian prospect held out by the *Craftsman* school.

The politics which emerged thereafter were the politics of interest, not the interests of the old kind, land versus money, threatening an intolerable division of the nation and an unacceptable choice of commercial alternatives, but every conceivable kind of interest, ranging from those of small groups of individuals to large classes, competing and combining within a political consensus of impressive proportions. In essence, that consensus weathered the political storms which accompanied the accession of George III. It also survived the final overthrow of the Whig magnates, the last survivors of the party which had grasped at permanent hegemony under Stanhope, shared in the less exclusive coalition mustered by Walpole, and increasingly accepted accommodation with all kinds of enemies in the days of the Pelhams. Parties did not vanish but they were kept within the bounds acceptable to a society in

which the requirements of 'improvement' took precedence over
sectarian and partisan strife. There were protestors, of course,
including a majority of colonial Americans, and a minority of
mutinous Englishmen, especially among Dissenters. But the net
effect was a pluralistic State. Its resources were deployed to devastating effect in the Seven Years War, and only narrowly failed
to achieve similar feats against colonial rebellion and a hostile
world in the War of American Independence.

Montesquieu, whose wisdom appealed to very diverse spirits
in contemporary Britain, observed that whereas other societies
subjected the requirements of commerce to those of government,
the English had succeeded in subordinating their political system
to their commerce.[33] Certainly this was what seemed to have been
achieved in the course of the mid-eighteenth century. It was not,
however, a narrowly material triumph. Its ideological and moral
implications were extensive. The accumulation of wealth and the
political system which endorsed it had to cope with relative, if not
absolute, immiseration on a massive scale. The control, relief, and
direction of the lower orders, was in the broadest sense a political
challenge, though not one which can be analysed in mechanistic
or psephological terms. Very few people lacked a view about the
proper arrangements of the State and the use of politics to transform morals and manners. As the philanthropist Jonas Hanway
put it, 'We are all politicians.'[34] Even Methodism, a seeming revolt
against the materialism of the age was in part a political statement,
with implications extending to party politics, as Wesley's controversial ventures into polemic demonstrated. But above all there
was a moral dimension to late eighteenth-century politics which
reveals the ideals as well as material interests and ambitions of the
classes who most benefited by them.

Perhaps no development of the mid-eighteenth century was
more important than the growing success of government in tapping
this moral force. Under Walpole, opposition, in its 'country',
'patriot', form, had virtually a monopoly of moral indignation.
Walpole stood for many things, fiscal economy, political prudence
in the defence of the Protestant Succession, pragmatic wisdom in
handling religious controversies, robust but unadventurous self-
interest in dealing with foreign powers. Men of the world and

[33] *The Spirit of the Laws*, p. 321.
[34] *Virtue in Humble Life*, ii. 349.

political experience admired him. Sir Matthew Decker, banker, economic theorist, and shrewd businessman, thought Walpole a genius.[35] What neither he nor anyone else claimed for Walpole was inspirational quality or deep moral appeal. Worse was to follow in the squalid manœuvring which succeeded Walpole's fall. Pitt did something to revive the cause of political morality, but most of his popularity was a consequence of the jingoism unleashed by the Seven Years War. It was George III and Lord Bute who grasped it for government, though in the short run they were unable to realize its full value. This was in part their own fault, a result of their inexperience, perhaps, too, of their personal animus and arrogance. None the less the underlying trend was clear. North was more successful in mobilizing the idealism of the age than his opponents liked to admit. Still more was the younger Pitt, in collaboration with a monarch increasingly respected for his personal integrity, his unwavering assertion of patriotic English values, his staunch traditionalism. A patriarchal King and a priggish Prime Minister were well placed to appeal to a bourgeoisie rediscovering its puritan heritage in an evangelical setting. The contrast with the Prince of Wales and Fox, representatives, so it seemed, of aristocratic irresponsibility and vice, was striking.

Students of history were well aware that no nation could rely on hereditary monarchy to produce the ruler it needed. There was a growing belief by the 1780s that Britain was, for the moment at least, blessed in this respect as it had not been more than briefly since the reign of Elizabeth. George III was truly regarded by many as 'The Father of his People', as the antiquarian John Nichols expressed it in a dedication.[36] Prime Ministers were more particularly the product of a political culture. In this the transition from Walpole to Pitt is not a bad indication of the changing priorities of Georgian society. In some ways Walpole and Pitt had much in common. Both were naturally cautious statesmen and authentic administrative reformers, both shrewd manipulators of the House of Commons and the court, both past masters at exploiting the disarray or divisions of their opponents. But they were also very different. Walpole was the last great minister to found a fortune and a dynasty on service to a court. He belongs with the most skilful royal ministers of the past, Wolsey and Burghley, for

[35] Wilton House, Pembroke MSS, Decker's tours.
[36] *The History and Antiquities of the County of Leicester*, dedication.

example. Though his friends were often men of business and commerce, his natural milieu was that of the country gentleman. He was prouder of nothing than his pretentious Palladian palace, his broad acres, and his paternalistic care for his Norfolk tenants. In public affairs, to settle the Protestant Succession was no mean ambition but it was his only overriding one, and it carried with it no sense of the enormous changes which were coming over contemporary society. His highest priority in terms of social policy was to preserve a beleaguered landed interest against further fiscal encroachment by the State. His opponents thought him meretriciously modern, but in fact his values were those of his youth, and not so very different from their own, though the proclaimed means of achieving them seemed very different.

Pitt, Prime Minister within forty-two years of Walpole, had been born eighty-three years after him, and represented the values of another epoch. He was no aspiring magnate, but the hero of the improving middle class. A villa in Putney, the friendship of earnest evangelicals and methodically minded administrators, these were highly appropriate for a young man who had a lively interest in the economic changes which were transforming his country, and a mission to ameliorate their less desirable consequences. In their different ways both accepted the challenge of their times. Walpole carried the Hanoverian regime through testing dynastic crises in the face of an often hostile nation. Pitt was to guide a propertied political establishment through the storms of Revolution abroad and disorder at home. It was altogether characteristic of eighteenth-century Britain that the stability which they both seem to represent in the eyes of posterity should mask such striking changes. The polite and commercial people of the 1730s was still polite and commercial in the 1780s: it did not, in any fundamental sense, inhabit the same society.

Chronology

THE object is to display the sequence of major events discussed in the text. Their location there may be found in the index. In the 'legislation' column date is determined by royal assent according to the year on which the parliamentary session in question ended; regnal year and designation are given in brackets.

Date	Politics	Legislation
1727	Accession of George II General Election	Civil List Act (1 George II, Sess. 1, c. 1)
1728		
1729	Agitation against Spanish depredations	Act regulating Attorneys (2 George II, c. 23)
	Treaty of Seville	Bribery Act (2 George II, c. 24)
1730	Townshend's resignation as Secretary of State	Repeal of Salt Duty (3 George II, c. 20)
		Special Juries Act (3 George II, c. 25)
1731	Treaty of Vienna	English in Law Proceedings Act (4 George II, c. 26)
1732	Charitable Corporation scandal	Revival of Salt Duty (5 George II, c. 6)
		Qualification of JPs Act (5 George II, c. 18)
1733	Excise crisis War of the Polish Succession	Molasses Act (6 George II, c. 13)
1734	General Election	Repeal of Septennial Act defeated
1735		Engraving Copyright Act (8 George II, c. 13)
1736	Porteous Riots	Repeal of Test and Corporation Acts defeated
		Quaker Tithe Bill defeated
		Witchcraft Act (9 George II, c. 5)
		Gin Act (9 George II, c. 23)
		Smuggling Act (9 George II, c. 35)
		Mortmain Act (9 George II, c. 36)
1737	Hardwicke Lord Chancellor Prince Frederick expelled from court	Stage Licensing Act (10 George II, c. 28)
	Death of Queen Caroline	Financial settlement on Prince Frederick (10 George II, c. 29)
		Porteous Act (10 George II, c. 35)
1738		
1739	Convention of the Pardo War of Jenkins' Ear Victory at Puerto Bello	County Rates Act (12 George II, c. 29)

People and Projects	Publications	Date
Death of Sir Isaac Newton		
Moravians arrived in London	John Gay, *The Beggar's Opera* Alexander Pope, *Dunciad*	1728
First 'Methodist' meetings at Oxford		1729
Trial of Francis Charteris Colley Cibber made Poet Laureate	Stephen Duck, *The Thresher's Labour*	1730
	Gentleman's Magazine, first issue George Lillo, *The London Merchant, or the History of George Barnwell* first performed	1731
Georgia founded Society of Dilettanti founded Vauxhall Gardens opened	William Hogarth, *A Harlot's Progress* *London Magazine*, first issue	1732
	William Hogarth, *A Rake's Progress* Benjamin Martin, *Philosophic Grammar* Alexander Pope, *Essay on Man*	1733
Prosecution of Philip Doddridge Bristol Hospital founded		1734
	Henry Brooke, *Universal Beauty*	1735
Gin riots	Joseph Butler, *The Analogy of Religion* William Warburton, *Alliance between Church and State*	1736
John Potter succeeds William Wake as Archbishop of Canterbury		1737
Last report by London Society for Reformation of Manners Wesley's 'conversion'		1738
Charter of Foundling Hospital Field preaching by Whitefield and Wesley Turpin executed	Richard Glover, *Hosier's Ghost* *Journals* of John Wesley and George Whitefield	1739

Date	Politics	Legislation
1740	War of the Austrian Succession	Seaman's Act (13 George II, c. 3)
		Gaming Act (13 George II, c. 19)
		Vagrancy Act (13 George II, c. 24)
1741	'The Motion' to remove Walpole defeated	
	General Election	
	Failure of attack on Cartagena	
1742	Walpole's resignation: Carteret ministry	Place Act (15 George II, c. 22)
1743	Battle of Dettingen	Gin Act (16 George II, c. 8)
	Treaty of Worms	
1744	Granville (Carteret) dismissed: Broad-Bottom ministry	Suspension of Habeas Corpus (17 George II, c. 6)
	War declared on France	
	Anson's expedition	
1745	Battle of Fontenoy	County Election Act (18 George II, c. 18)
	Capture of Louisburg	
	Landing of Young Pretender: battle of Prestonpans	
1746	Final defeat of Granville: Pelham ministry	Repeal of City Elections Act (19 George II, c. 8)
	Battle of Culloden	Disarming of Highlands Act (19 George II, c. 39)
	Loss of Madras	
1747	Battle of Laffeld	Heritable Jurisdictions Act (20 George II, c. 43)
	Naval victories of Finisterre and Belle-Île	
	General Election	
1748	Treaty of Aix-la-Chapelle	Disarming of Highlands Act (21 George II, c. 34)
1749	Westminster Election	
1750		Interest rate reduction (23 George II, c. 1 etc.)
1751	Death of Prince Frederick	Calendar Act (24 George II, c. 23)
1752		Murder Act (25 George II, c. 37)

People and Projects	Publications	
		Date
	John Dyer, *The Ruins of Rome*	1740
	Samuel Richardson, *Pamela*	
	James Thomson, *Rule Britannia*	
	David Hume, *Essays, Moral and Philosophical*	1741
Convocation permitted to sit for last time		1742
	Henry Fielding, *Jonathan Wild*	1743
Levant Trade opened	John Armstrong, *The Art of Preserving Health*	1744
	Edward Moore, *Fables for the Female Sex*	
	William Hogarth, *Marriage-à-la-Mode*	1745
	Edward Young, *Night Thoughts*	
Lock Hospital founded	Tobias Smollett, *The Tears of Scotland*	1746
Thomas Herring succeeds as Archbishop of Canterbury	Thomas Carte, *History of England*, vol. i	1747
	William Hogarth, *Industry and Idleness*	
Henry Fielding appointed as Westminster magistrate		1748
Lady Huntingdon's house opened for preaching		
Bosavern Penlez riots	Henry Fielding, *The History of Tom Jones*	1749
British Lying-in Hospital (first of its kind)	Sarah Fielding, *The Governess*	
	Conyers Middleton, *A Free Inquiry into the Miraculous Powers*	
	Monthly Review, first issue	
London earthquake	Henry Fielding, *An Enquiry into . . . the late Increase of Robbers*	1750
St Luke's Hospital for insane founded	Brakenridge on population in *Philosophical Transactions*	1751
Lloyd Committee on crime and poverty	Malachy Postlethwayt, *Universal Dictionary of Trade and Commerce*	
	Charlotte Lennox, *The Female Quixote*	1752

Date	Politics	Legislation
1753		British Museum Act (26 George II, c. 22)
		Jewish Naturalization Act (26 George II, c. 26)
		Marriage Act (26 George II, c. 33)
1754	Death of Pelham: Newcastle ministry General Election	Repeal of Jewish Naturalization Act (27 George II, c. 1)
1755	Boscawen's expedition	
1756	Convention of Westminster Fall of Minorca Resignation of Newcastle: Pitt–Devonshire ministry	
1757	Pitt–Newcastle ministry Battle of Plassey	Militia Act (30 George II, c. 25)
1758	2nd Treaty of Westminster Capture of Louisburg	Habeas Corpus Bill defeated
1759	Capture of Guadeloupe Battle of Minden Capture of Quebec Battle of Lagos and Quiberon	
1760	Accession of George III	MPs Qualification Act (33 George II, c. 20)
1761	General Election Resignation of Pitt	Civil List Act (1 George III, c. 1) Judges Tenure Act (1 George III, c. 23)
1762	War with Spain Capture of Martinique Resignation of Newcastle: Bute ministry Breach with Prussia Capture of Havana and Manila	Hanway's Act for Registering Infant Poor (2 George III, c. 22)

People and Projects	Publications	Date
British Museum founded		1753
Elizabeth Channing controversy		
Census proposed		
Society of Arts founded	Thomas Chippendale, *The Gentleman and Cabinet-Maker's Director*	1754
	David Hume, *History of England*, vol. i	
	Lord Bolingbroke, *Works*	1755
	Samuel Johnson, *Dictionary*	
	Edmund Burke, *Essay on the Sublime and Beautiful*	1756
First appearance of John Baskerville's new typography	John Brown, *Estimate of the Manners and Principles of the Times*	1757
Militia riots	John Dyer, *The Fleece*	
Thomas Secker succeeds as Archbishop of Canterbury		
William Whitehead made Poet Laureate		
Magdalen Hospital founded	*Annual Register*, vol. i	1758
Trial of Eugene Aram	David Garrick, *Heart of Oak*	1759
Bridgewater's Canal commenced	Laurence Sterne, *Tristram Shandy*, vol. i	
Execution of Lord Ferrers	Samuel Foote, *The Minor*	1760
Public exhibition of paintings at Society of Arts	Robert Lloyd, *The Actor*	
Rolvenden prosecution of Methodists	Israel Mauduit, *Considerations on the present German War*	
	Ossian (James Macpherson), *Fingal*	1761
	George Colman, sen., *The Jealous Wife*	
Mystery of Cock Lane ghost	James Stuart and Nicholas Revett, *The Antiquities of Athens*, vol. 1	1762
Westminster Paving Commission established		

Date	Politics	Legislation
1763	Peace of Paris	Cider excise (3 George III, c. 12)
	Proclamation for government of American conquests	Durham Electoral Qualification Act (3 George III, c. 15)
	Resignation of Bute: Grenville ministry	
1764	Grant of *diwanni* to East India Company	Sugar Act (4 George III, c. 15)
	Expulsion of Wilkes from House of Commons	
1765	Dismissal of Grenville: Rockingham ministry	Stamp Act (5 George III, c. 12)
		Regency Act (5 George III, c. 27)
		American Mutiny Act (5 George III, c. 33)
1766	Dismissal of Rockingham: Chatham ministry	Repeal of Stamp Act (6 George III, c. 11)
		American Declaratory Act (6 George III, c. 12)
		Repeal of cider excise (6 George III, c. 14)
		Free Ports Act (6 George III, c. 49)
		Revenue Act (6 George III, c. 52)
1767	Bedford party joined ministry	East India regulations (7 George III, cc. 49, 57)
		Townshend duties (7 George III, c. 46)
		Act suspending New York Assembly (7 George III, c. 59)
1768	General Election: Middlesex Election	
	St George's Fields Massacre	
	French annexation of Corsica	
	American non-importation movement	
	Chatham's resignation	
1769	Wilkesite petitioning movement	Crown Lands Act (9 George III, c. 16)
1770	Grafton's resignation: North ministry	Repeal of Townshend duties (10 George III, c. 17)
	Boston massacre	Grenville's Elections Act (10 George III, c. 41)
	Falkland Islands crisis	

People and Projects	Publications	Date
	Catherine Macaulay, *History of England*, vol. i	1763
	Robert Adam, *Ruins of the Palace of the Emperor Diocletian, at Spalatro*	1764
	Horace Walpole, *Castle of Otranto*	
General warrants ruled illegal by Pratt	William Blackstone, *Commentaries on the Laws of England* commenced	1765
	Samuel Foote, *The Commissary*	
	James Fordyce, *Sermons to Young Women*	
	Thomas Percy, *Reliques of Ancient Poetry*	
Death of James III	Christopher Anstey, *The New Bath Guide*	1766
Grand Trunk canal projected		
Food riots	Francis Blackburne, *Confessional*	
	Oliver Goldsmith, *The Vicar of Wakefield*	
	Evan Lloyd, *The Methodist*	
Elizabeth Brownrigg executed		1767
Lord Baltimore's trial	Arthur Young's *Tours* commenced	1768
Cook's first voyage		
Frederick Cornwallis succeeds as Archbishop of Canterbury		
Royal Academy founded		
Shakespeare Jubilee	Sir Joshua Reynolds, first *Discourse*	1769
Hargreaves' spinning-jenny patented	Edmund Burke, *Thoughts on the Cause of the Present Discontents*	1770
Suicide of Thomas Chatterton		
	James Beattie, *Essay on Truth*	
	Oliver Goldsmith, *The Deserted Village*	
	Tobias Smollett, *Humphry Clinker*	

Date	Politics	Legislation
1771	Printers' controversy	New Shoreham Disfranchisement Act (11 George III, c. 55)
1772	Feathers' Tavern Petition Gaspée burned	Royal Marriage Act (12 George III, c. 11)
1773	Recoinage Boston Tea Party	Dowdeswell's Insurance Bill defeated Pownall's Corn Law (13 George III, c. 43) Tea Act (13 George III, c. 44) East India Regulating Act (13 George III, c. 63)
1774	American non-importation General Election	Popham's Prison Acts (14 George III, cc. 20, 59) Boston Port Act (14 George III, c. 19) Justice Act (14 George III, c. 39) Massachusetts Government Act (14 George III, c. 45) Quartering Act (14 George III, c. 54) Madhouse Act (14 George III, c. 49) Quebec Act (14 George III, c. 83)
1775	Battles of Lexington and Concord Proclamation of Rebellion	North's conciliatory resolution
1776	American Declaration of Independence Battle of Long Island	American Prohibitory Act (16 George III, c. 5) Poor Relief Survey Act (16 George III, c. 40) Hulks Act (16 George III, c. 43)
1777	Battle of Saratoga	

People and Projects	Publications	Date
Arkwright's manufacture at Cromford commenced	Henry Mackenzie, *The Man of Feeling*	1771
Warren Hastings appointed Governor of Bengal	John Millar, *Observations concerning the Distinction of Ranks*	
Wesley's controversy with Calvinistic Methodists		
Cook's second voyage	Samuel Foote, *The Nabob*	1772
Financial crash		
Lord Mansfield's slavery judgment in case of Somersett		
Pantheon opened		
Partnership of Boulton and Watt		
Society for Relief of Small Debtors		
Adelphi Lottery	*Encyclopaedia Britannica*	1773
	Oliver Goldsmith, *She Stoops to Conquer*	
Theophilus Lindsey's Unitarian Chapel founded	Jacob Bryant, *A New System or Analysis of Ancient Mythology*, vol. i	1774
Failure of proposed examination reform at Cambridge University	James Burgh, *Political Disquisitions*, vol. i	
Copyright law settled by Lords	John Campbell, *Political Survey*	
Humane Society formed	Lord Chesterfield, *Letters to His Son*	
Joseph Priestley's discovery of 'dephlogisticated air'	Samuel Johnson, *Taxation No Tyranny*	
	John Langhorne, *The Country Justice*, pt. I	
Lunar Society's first formal meeting	Edmund Burke, *Speech on Conciliation with America*	1775
	Samuel Johnson, *Journey to the Western Islands of Scotland*	
Cook's third voyage	Jeremy Bentham, *Fragment on Government*	1776
National report on poor relief expenditure	Edward Gibbon, *Decline and Fall of the Roman Empire*, vol. i	
Retirement of David Garrick	Thomas Paine, *Common Sense*	
Duchess of Kingston's trial	Richard Price, *Observations on Civil Liberty*	
	Adam Smith, *Wealth of Nations*	
Bath Society founded	Richard Brinsley Sheridan, *The School for Scandal*	1777
Execution of William Dodd	John Howard, *State of the Prisons*	
Execution of John the Painter		

Date	Politics	Legislation
1778	War with France Carlisle peace commission	Catholic Relief Act (18 George III, c. 60)
1779	War with Spain	Dissenters Relief Act (19 George III, c. 44)
1780	Association movement: Dunning's motion Gordon Riots Capture of Charleston General Election	Irish Trade Act (20 George III, c. 18)
1781	Surrender at Yorktown	Audit of Public Accounts Act (21 George III, c. 45)
1782	Battle of the Saints Resignation of North: Rockingham ministry Death of Rockingham: Shelburne ministry	Crewe's Place Act (22 George III, c. 41) Clerke's Contractors' Act (22 George III, c. 45) Repeal of Irish Declaratory Act (22 George III, c. 53) Burke's Establishment Act (22 George III, c. 82) Gilbert's Poor Law Act (22 George III, c. 83)
1783	Peace of Versailles Fox–North Coalition Pitt ministry	Fox's East India Bill

People and Projects	Publications	Date
	Arminian Magazine, first issue	1778
	Frances Burney, *Evelina*	
Machine riots	William Alexander, *History of Women*	1779
	Samuel Johnson, *Lives of the Poets* commenced	
	William Mason, *The English Garden*	
		1780
Arkwright's patent overturned		1781
		1782
Public executions moved from Tyburn to Newgate		1783

Bibliography

THIS list of about five hundred titles is designed to provide balanced coverage of the subjects discussed in the text. The emphasis is on recent books, but articles which are of exceptional importance or which have not yet been absorbed into the literature are also listed, as are a few older works, for similar reasons. Some edited collections of documents are cited at the appropriate points, and one section consists of diaries, memoirs, and letters available in modern editions. For the rest, primary materials, now available in immense quantity and in diverse published forms, including microfilm and microfiche, are not included. They have been liberally employed in support of the text and many are to be found in the footnote references. Fuller bibliographical information is available in the following: S. Pargellis and P. J. Medley, *Bibliography of British History: The Eighteenth Century, 1714–1789* (Oxford, 1951), though not updated, an indispensable guide to earlier works, including primary sources; G. R. Elton, *Modern Historians on British History, 1485–1945: A Critical Bibliography, 1945–1969* (London, 1970); R. Schlatter, ed., *Recent Views on British History: Essays on Historical Writing since 1966* (New Brunswick, New Jersey, 1984), particularly valuable for its comments and assessments; W. H. Chaloner and R. C. Richardson, eds., *Bibliography of British Economic and Social History* (Manchester, 1984), and R. A. Smith, *Late Georgian and Regency England, 1760–1837* (Cambridge, 1984), both essentially listings.

GENERAL

J. B. Owen, *The Eighteenth Century, 1714–1815* (London, 1974), D. Marshall, *Eighteenth Century England* (London, 1962), W. A. Speck, *Stability and Strife: England, 1714–1760* (London, 1977), I. R. Christie, *Wars and Revolutions: Britain, 1760–1815* (London, 1982), all emphasize, though in varying degree, political narrative. The following are primarily economic histories: T. S. Ashton, *An Economic History of England: The Eighteenth Century* (London, 1955); R. Floud and D. McCloskey, eds., *The Economic History of Britain since 1700*, vol. i: *1700–1860* (2 vols., Cambridge, 1981), a collection of essays by specialists; B. A. Holderness, *Pre-Industrial England: Economy and Society, 1500–1750* (London, 1976); P. Mathias, *The First Industrial Nation* (2nd edn., London, 1983);

E. Pawson, *The Early Industrial Revolution* (London, 1979). Social history at its most ambitious has the virtue that it treats almost nothing as wholly foreign to its purpose. On the other hand, it lacks the clear sense of a distinctive technique and a definable subject which sustains political and economic historians. R. Porter, *English Society in the Eighteenth Century* (London, 1982) makes up in vigour and colour for what it sometimes lacks in discipline. J. C. D. Clark's *English Society: Ideology, Social Structure and Political Practice during the Ancien Regime* (Cambridge, 1985) has been derided by scholars but is not without insight.

There are some valuable collections of essays on diverse aspects of the period: S. B. Baxter, ed., *England's Rise to Greatness* (Los Angeles, 1983); P. Mathias, *The Transformation of England: Essays in the Economic and Social History of England in the Eighteenth Century* (London, 1979); J. Cannon, ed., *The Whig Ascendancy: Colloquies on Hanoverian England* (London, 1981); D. C. Coleman and A. H. John, eds, *Trade, Government and Economy in pre-Industrial England* (London, 1976). Essays by two distinguished scholars are collected in L. Namier, *Crossrⱦds of Power* (London, 1962), and A. Newman, ed., *L. Sutherland: Politics and Finance in the Eighteenth Century* (London, 1984).

DIARIES, MEMOIRS, LETTERS

The most celebrated of all eighteenth-century memorists, Horace Walpole, has received regal editorial treatment in recent years. W. S. Lewis prints a highly readable selection of letters from the immense Yale edition of the correspondence which he founded, in *Selected Letters of Horace Walpole* (New Haven, 1973). The earlier memoirs have also been given scholarly treatment by J. Brooke, *Memoirs of the Reign of King George II* (3 vols., New Haven, 1985). R. Sedgwick, the modern editor of Lord Hervey's memoirs, presents an abridged version in *Lord Hervey's Memoirs* (London, 1952). Court memoirs of a later period are found in *The Letters and Journals of Lady Mary Coke* (fascimile edn., 4 vols., Bath, 1970).

Political participants as well as observers are represented in published editions: T. J. McCann, ed., *The Correspondence of the Dukes of Richmond and Newcastle, 1724–1750* (Sussex Record Soc., lxxiii, 1982–3); A. N. Newman, ed., *Leicester House Politics, 1750–60, from the Papers of John, Second Earl of Egmont* (Camden Miscellany, xxiii, 4th ser., vol. 7); P. D. Brown and K. W. Schweizer, eds., *The Devonshire Diary* (Camden, 4th ser., vol. 27); T. W. Copeland and others, eds., *The Correspondence of Edmund Burke* (10 vols., Cambridge, 1958–78); Sir J. Fortescue, ed., *The Correspondence of King George the Third from 1760 to December 1783* (new impression, 6 vols., London, 1973); J. Carswell and L. A. Dralle, eds., *The Political Journal of George Bubb Dodington*

(Oxford, 1965). The most effective polemic of the age is found in J. Cannon, ed., *The Letters of Junius* (Oxford, 1978); D. J. Greene, ed., *The Yale Edition of the Works of Samuel Johnson*, vol. x: *Political Writings* (New Haven, 1977); P. Langford and others, eds., *The Writings and Speeches of Edmund Burke* (Oxford, 1981–).

Editions of letters which illuminate a broad swathe of eighteenth-century life include C. F. Burgess, ed., *The Letters of John Gay* (Oxford, 1966), G. Cannon, ed., *The Letters of Sir William Jones* (2 vols., Oxford, 1970), D. M. Little and G. M. Kahrl, eds., *The Letters of David Garrick* (3 vols., London, 1963). Three classics, Boswell's *Life of Johnson*, Gibbon's *Autobiography*, Gilbert White's *Natural History of Selborne* are available in a variety of modern editions. R. Lonsdale's selection *The New Oxford Book of Eighteenth-Century Verse* (Oxford, 1984) displays a remarkable range of social and political concerns as well as poetic talents. D. Vaisey, ed., *The Diary of Thomas Turner, 1754–1765* (Oxford, 1984) provides a fascinating glimpse of life at a relatively humble level in a Sussex village, B. Mitchell and H. Penrose, eds., *Letters from Bath 1766–1767 by the Rev. John Penrose* (Gloucester, 1983), an equally absorbing sketch of manners at a fashionable resort. S. Markham, ed., *John Loveday of Caversham, 1711–1789: The Life and Tours of an Eighteenth-Century Onlooker* (Salisbury, 1984) charmingly portrays the mind of an antiquarian with wide-ranging interests, L. G. Mitchell, *The Purefoy Letters* (London, 1973), the concerns of a Buckinghamshire country squire.

IDEAS AND THEIR TRANSMISSION

On political ideas, H. T. Dickinson, *Liberty and Property: Political Ideology in Eighteenth-Century Britain* (London, 1977), marshalls a multiplicity of arguments. J. A. W. Gunn, *Beyond Liberty and Property: The Process of Self-Recognition in Eighteenth-Century Political Thought* (Kingston, 1983) is an absorbing and refreshingly unpretentious study. C. Robbins, *The Eighteenth-Century Commonwealthman* (Cambridge, Mass., 1959) remedied a considerable deficiency when it was published and continues to provide a mine of information about republican thinkers. Their opponents are examined by R. Browning, *Political and Constitutional Ideas of the Court Whigs* (London, 1982). D. Forbes, *Hume's Philosophical Politics* (Cambridge, 1975), reveals the political thought of one of the most powerful minds of the age. The principal features of anti-Walpolian thought are described by I. Kramnick, *Bolingbroke and his Circle: The Politics of Nostalgia in the Age of Walpole* (Cambridge, Mass., 1968), and the difficulties caused by Walpole's defeat by M. M. Goldsmith, 'Faction Detected: Ideological Consequences of Robert Walpole's Decline and Fall', *History*, 64 (1979), 1–19. The literary opposition to the Robinocracy is discussed by B. Goldgar, *Walpole and the Wits, the Relation of Politics and Literature, 1722–1742* (Lincoln, Nebraska, 1976).

Important trends in the thought of the period are explored in the following: C. Vereker, *Eighteenth-Century Optimism* (Liverpool, 1967); J. G. A. Pocock, *Virtue, Commerce, and History* (Cambridge, 1976); K. V. Thomas, *Man and the Natural World: Changing Attitudes in England, 1500–1800* (London, 1983); I. Hont and M. Ignatieff, *Wealth and Virtue: The Shaping of Political Economy in the Scottish Enlightenment* (Cambridge, 1983); K. Tribe, *Land, Labour and Economic Discourse* (London, 1978); R. Porter, 'The Enlightenment in England', in R. Porter and M. Teich, eds., *The Enlightenment in National Context* (Cambridge, 1981); P. J. Korshin, *Typologies in England, 1650–1820* (Princeton, 1982); R. J. Smith, *The Gothic Bequest: Medieval Institutions in British Thought, 1688–1863* (Cambridge, 1987); L. Whitney, *Primitivism and the Idea of Progress in English Popular Literature of the Eighteenth Century* (Baltimore, 1934). G. Newman, *The Rise of English Nationalism: A Cultural History 1740–1830* (London, 1987), offers a challenging, if ultimately unconvincing thesis.

A number of cultural institutions have found historians: E. Miller, *That Noble Cabinet: A History of the British Museum* (London, 1973); S. C. Hutchison, *The History of the Royal Academy* (London, 1968); D. Hudson and K. W. Luckhurst, *The Royal Society of Arts, 1754–1954* (London, 1954) and D. G. C. Allan, *William Shipley: Founder of the Royal Society of Arts* (London, 1968); R. E. Schofield, *The Lunar Society of Birmingham* (Oxford, 1963). Provincial culture offers a promising field: R. S. Porter, 'Science, Provincial Culture and Public Opinion in Enlightenment England', *British Journal of Eighteenth-Century Studies*, 3 (1986), 20–46; T. Fawcett, 'Eighteenth-Century Debating Societies', *British Journal of Eighteenth-Century Studies*, 3 (1986), 216–29; P. Kaufman, *Libraries and their Users* (London, 1969); G. A. Feather, *The Provincial Book Trade in Eighteenth-Century England* (Cambridge, 1985).

The newspaper's development is reviewed by J. Black, *The English Press in the Eighteenth Century* (Beckenham, 1987). More detailed studies include M. R. Harris, *London Newspapers in the Age of Walpole: A Study of the Origin of the Modern English Press* (London, 1987) and L. Werkmeister, *The London Daily Press, 1772–1792* (Lincoln, Nebraska, 1963). L. Hanson, *The Government and the Press, 1695–1763* (London, 1936) has yet to be superseded. A famous monthly is the subject of C. L. Carlson, *The First Magazine: A History of* The Gentleman's Magazine (Providence, Rhode Island, 1938). R. D. Spector, *English Literary Periodicals and the Climate of Opinion during the Seven Years War* (The Hague, 1966) provides a case-study of the relationship between the magazines and public opinion. Various aspects of the book world are examined in two collections of essays edited by R. Myers and M. Harris, *Sale and Distribution of Books from 1700* (Oxford, 1982), and *Author/Publisher Relations during the Eighteenth and Nineteenth Centuries* (Oxford, 1983).

ARTS IN CONTEXT

Aristocratic leadership is illuminated by J. Lees-Milne, *Earls of Creation: Five Great Patrons of Eighteenth-Century Art* (London, 1962). M. Foss, *The Age of Patronage, 1660–1750* (London, 1971) attacks the artistic effects of commercialization in the eighteenth century. Its implications are more coolly analysed by L. Lippincott, *Selling Art in Georgian London: The Rise of Arthur Pond* (New Haven, 1983). F. T. Herrmann, *The English as Collectors* (London, 1973), prints extracts from contemporary sources. Art historical works of enduring interest include J. Lees-Milne, *The Age of Adam* (London, 1947), J. Steegman, *The Rule of Taste from George I to George IV* (London, 1936), L. Lipking, *The Ordering of the Arts in Eighteenth-Century England* (Princeton, 1970), M. R. Brownell, *Alexander Pope and the Arts of Georgian England* (Oxford, 1978), P. Bicknell, *Beauty, Horror and Immensity: Picturesque Landscape in Britain, 1750–1850* (Cambridge, 1981). The sociology of art is to the fore in J. Barrell, *The Dark Side of the Landscape: The Rural Poor in English Painting, 1730–1840* (Cambridge, 1980).

Perhaps because they are increasingly addressed to a readership which lacks the training and assumptions of traditional art criticism, exhibition catalogues have in recent years displayed a commendable readiness to place artists and their work in historical context. Some of the most rewarding are: N. Penny, ed., *Reynolds* (London, 1986); B. Allen, *Francis Hayman* (New Haven, 1987); D. H. Solkin, *Richard Wilson* (London, 1982); W. L. Pressly, *James Barry: The Artist as Hero* (London, 1983); *Rococo: Art and Design in Hogarth's England* (London, 1984).

D. Cruickshank, *A Guide to the Georgian Buildings of Britain and Ireland* (London, 1985) is a lucid historical exposition as well as a gazetteer, M. Girouard, *Life in the English Country House: A Social and Architectural history* (London, 1978), a widely acclaimed investigation of the social history of the great house, and J. R. Harris, *The Artist and the Country House* (rev. edn., London, 1985), a refreshing approach to its pictorial representation. The most innovative architect of the mid-eighteenth century is the subject of G. Beard, *The Work of Robert Adam* (London, 1978). J. Dixon Hunt, *The Genius of the Place: The English Landscape Garden, 1620–1820* (London, 1975) presents a selection of contemporary views and statements of the art. Recent studies of masters are R. Turner, *Capability Brown and the Eighteenth-Century English Landscape* (London, 1985), M. Wilson, *William Kent: Architect, Designer,*

Painter, Gardener 1685–1748 (London, 1984), and G. Carter, P. Goode, K. Laurie, *Humphry Repton Landscape Gardener, 1752–1818* (Norwich, 1982). The potential of eighteenth-century music studies beyond musicology itself has yet to be exploited, but there is much of value in E. D. Mackerness, *A Social History of English Music* (London, 1964), D. Johnson, *Music and Society in Lowland Scotland in the Eighteenth Century* (London, 1972), and C. Hogwood and R. Luckett, eds., *Music in Eighteenth-Century England* (Cambridge, 1983). Standard histories of particular arts showing sensitivity to the historical implications include J. Burke, *English Art, 1714–1800* (Oxford, 1976), E. Waterhouse, *Painting in Britain, 1530–1790* (4th edn., London, 1978), G. Hughes, *English Glass for the Collector, 1660–1860* (London, 1958), J. Fowler and J. Cornforth, *English Decoration in the 18th Century* (2nd edn., London, 1986), P. Ward-Jackson, *English Furniture Designs of the Eighteenth Century* (London, 1984); A. Buck, *Dress in Eighteenth-Century England* (London, 1979), and A. Ribeiro, *A Visual History of Costume: The Eighteenth Century* (London, 1983).

Satirical art has obvious appeal for the historian. The following are liberally illustrated: D. G. Kunzle, *The Early Comic Strip* (Berkeley, 1973); M. D. George, *English Political Caricature to 1792: A Study of Opinion and Propaganda* (Oxford, 1959); H. M. Atherton, *Political Prints in the Age of Hogarth: A Study of the Ideographic Representation of Politics* (Oxford, 1974); R. Paulson, *Hogarth's Graphic Works* (2 vols., New Haven, 1965). Also by George, there is a lively selection of satires, *Hogarth to Cruikshank: Social Change in Graphic Satire* (London, 1967). Six volumes of caricatures from the British Museum's collection of prints, representing diverse aspects of English politics and society, make up a series edited by M. Duffy, *The English Satirical Print, 1600–1832* (Cambridge, 1986).

LITERATURE IN CONTEXT

The historical context of literature has received growing attention both from historians and literary scholars. One of the former provides a useful introduction for the earlier period, W. A. Speck, *Society and Literature in England, 1700–60* (Dublin, 1983), one of the latter for the later period, M. Butler, *Romantics, Rebels, and Reactionaries: English Literature and its Background, 1760–1830* (Oxford, 1981). The sociology of bibliography has aroused similar interest; see, for example, I. Rivers, ed., *Books and their Readers in Eighteenth-Century England* (Leicester, 1982). Because Augustan letters were so politicized, some essentially literary studies have particular historical interest: examples are M. Mack, *The Garden and the City: Retirement and Politics in the Later Poetry of Pope, 1731–1743*

(Toronto, 1969); P. Fussell, *The Rhetorical World of Augustan Humanism: Ethics and Imagery from Swift to Burke* (Oxford, 1965); P. K. Elkin, *The Augustan Defence of Satire* (Oxford, 1973).

The stage as political propaganda is discussed by J. Loftis, *The Politics of Drama in Augustan England* (Oxford, 1963), and the imposition of censorship by V. T. Corfield, *The Licensing Act of 1737* (Madison, Wisconsin, 1984). The social setting of the theatre is described by L. Hughes, *The Drama's Patrons: A Study of the Eighteenth-Century London Audience* (Austin, 1971), and S. Rosenfeld, *The Theatres of the London Fairs in the Eighteenth Century* (Cambridge, 1960). Provincial theatre has been studied with profit: see, for example, E. Grice, *The Rise and Fall of the Theatre in East Anglia during the Eighteenth and Nineteenth Centuries: Rogues and Vagabonds or the Actors' Road to Respectability* (Lavenham, 1977).

Women were important both as writers and readers in the expanding book world of the eighteenth century. R. P. Utter and G. B. Needham, *Pamela's Daughters* (London, 1937) retains its interest and originality. Early feminist literature is the subject of R. Perry, *The Celebrated Mary Astell: An Early English Feminist* (Chicago, 1986), and K. M. Rogers, *Feminism in Eighteenth-Century England* (Brighton, 1982). It also figures in J. Rendall, *The Origins of Modern Feminism* (Basingstoke, 1985), and J. Todd, *Women's Friendship in Literature* (New York, 1980).

RELIGION

The most recent, but rather disappointing, survey is E. G. Rupp, *Religion in England, 1688–1791* (Oxford, 1986). N. Sykes, *Church and State in England in the Eighteenth Century* (Cambridge, 1934) is the standard work on the Church as an institution, though the same author's *From Sheldon to Secker: Aspects of English Church History, 1660–1760* (Cambridge, 1959), is more stimulating. Two works now in their second century, C. J. Abbey, *The English Church and its Bishops, 1700–1800* (2 vols., London, 1887), and C. J. Abbey and J. Overton, *The English Church in the Eighteenth Century* (2 vols., London, 1878), remain valuable mines of information. G. F. A. Best, *Temporal Pillars: Queen Anne's Bounty, the Ecclesiastical Commissioners and the Church of England* (Cambridge, 1964), has implications far beyond its title. The quality of worship is investigated by F. C. Mather, 'Georgian Churchmanship Reconsidered: Some Variations in Anglican Public Worship, 1714–1830', *Journal of Ecclesiastical History*, 36 (1985), 255–83. Two bishops have full-scale biographies by Sykes: *William Wake, Archbishop of Canterbury, 1657–1737* (2 vols., Cambridge, 1957) and *Edmund Gibson, Bishop of London, 1689–1748* (London, 1926). The critical stage in Gibson's break with his political masters is explained by N. C. Hunt, *Two Early Political Associations:*

The Quakers and the Dissenting Deputies in the Age of Sir Robert Walpole (Oxford, 1961) and further elucidated by S. Taylor, 'Sir Robert Walpole, the Church of England, and the Quaker's Tithe Bill of 1736', *Historical Journal*, 28 (1985), 51–78. On another bishop, A. W. Evans, *Warburton and the Warburtonians: A Study in some Eighteenth-Century Controversies* (London, 1932) is of particular interest because Warburton's interests were so diverse.

Scholarly studies of the Church in its local setting are less numerous than the richness of the archives might suggest, but include G. N. Evans, *Religion and Politics in Mid-Eighteenth Century Anglesey* (Cardiff, 1953), and A. Warne, *Church and Society in Eighteenth-Century Devon* (Newton Abbot, 1969). L. P. Curtis, *Chichester Towers* (New Haven, 1966), presents an unflattering picture of politics in a cathedral close. The economics of the Church feature in C. Clay, ' "The Greed of Whig Bishops"? Church Landlords and their Lessees, 1660–1760', *Past and Present*, 87 (1980), 128–57, and E. J. Evans, *The Contentious Tithe: The Tithe Problem and English Agriculture, 1750–1850* (London, 1976). Evans also helps explain the unpopularity of the clergy in 'Some Reasons for the Growth of English Rural Anti-Clericalism, *c.*1750–*c.*1830', *Past and Present*, 66 (1975), 84–109, and reveals their plight in the North in 'The Anglican Clergy of Northern England', in C. Jones, ed., *Britain in the First Age of Party, 1680–1750: Essays Presented to Geoffrey Holmes* (London, 1987). The deist assault is described by R. N. Stromberg, *Religious Liberalism in Eighteenth-Century England* (Oxford, 1954), and J. Redwood, *Reason, Ridicule and Religion: The Age of Enlightenment in England, 1660–1750* (London, 1976). Rhetoric and theology come together in J. Downey, *The Eighteenth-Century Pulpit: A Study of the Sermons of Butler, Berkeley, Secker, Sterne, Whitefield, and Wesley* (Oxford, 1969).

M. R. Watts, *The Dissenters*, vol. i: *From the Reformation to the French Revolution* (Oxford, 1978), provides a sensible survey. The politics of Dissent are the subject of J. E. Bradley, 'Whigs and Nonconformists: "Slumbering Radicalism" in English Politics, 1739–1789', *Eighteenth-Century Studies*, 9 (1975–6), 1–27, and J. Seed, 'Gentlemen Dissenters: The Social and Political Meaning of Rational Dissent in the 1770s and 1780s', *Historical Journal*, 28 (1983), 299–325. I. Grubb, *Quakerism and Industry before 1800* (London, 1930), is the only substantial work on an important subject.

The literature of evangelical revival is vast but variable in quality. A useful introduction is A. Armstrong, *The Church of England, the Methodists and Society, 1700–1850* (London, 1973). A. D. Gilbert, *Religion and Society in Industrial England, Chapel and Social Change, 1740–1914* (London, 1976) provides a sociological analysis. The standard history of Methodism is R. E. Davies and E. G. Rupp, *A History of the Methodist*

Church in Great Britain, vol. *i* (London, 1965). R. F. Wearmouth, *Methodism and the Common People of the Eighteenth Century* (London, 1957) continues to be useful as a catalogue of popular responses to Methodism. Individuals of particular importance have found capable biographers: G. F. Nuttall, *Howel Harris, 1714–1733: The Last Enthusiast* (Cardiff, 1965); E. Evans, *Howel Harris Evangelist* (Cardiff, 1974); A. S. Wood, *Thomas Hawels, 1734–1820* (London, 1957); G. G. Cragg, *Crimshaw of Haworth* (London, 1947); G. C. B. Davies, *The Early Cornish Evangelicals, 1735–60: A Study of Walker of Truro and Others* (London, 1951). A long-running debate on the political consequences of Methodism is brought up to date by D. Hempton, *Methodism and Politics in British Society, 1750–1850* (London, 1984). Some of the most illuminating writings on evangelicals of all kinds are those of J. D. Walsh, for example, 'Origins of the Evangelical Revival', in G. V. Bennett and J. D. Walsh, *Essays in Modern English Church History* (London, 1966).

J. Bossy, *The English Catholic Community* (London, 1975), is suspect so far as the eighteenth century is concerned. An admirable corrective is E. Duffy, *Peter and Jack: Roman Catholics and Dissent in Eighteenth Century England* (London, 1982). The same author also presents a collection of essays: *Challoner and his Church: A Catholic Bishop in Georgian England* (London, 1981). R. K. Donovan, 'The Military origins of the Roman Catholic Relief Programme of 1778', *Historical Journal*, 28 (1985), 79–107, explains the background to Savile's Act. Some of the best of recusant history may be sampled in the works of H. Aveling, for example his 'Post-Reformation Catholicism in East Yorkshire, 1558–1790' (East Yorks. Local History Society, No. 11, 1960).

MANNERS AND MORALS

M. T. Quinlan, *Victorian Prelude: A History of English Manners, 1700–1830* (New York, 1941), is principally concerned with the later part of the period. The duelling controversy is analysed by D. T. Andrew, 'The Code of Honour and its Critics: The Opposition to Duelling in England, 1700–1850', *Social History*, 5 (1980), 409–34. The early reformation of manners movement is the subject of G. V. Portus, *Caritas Anglicana or, An Historical Inquiry into those Religious and Philanthropical Societies that flourished in England between the Years 1678 and 1740* (London, 1912), and, more recently, T. Isaacs, 'The Anglican hierarchy and the Reformation of Manner, 1688–1738', *Journal of Ecclesiastical History*, 33 (1982), 391–411. Sabbatarianism is examined by W. B. Whitaker, *The Eighteenth-Century English Sunday: A Study of Sunday Observance from 1677 to 1833* (London, 1940).

A transformation in sexual relations is argued by L. Stone, *The Family, Sex and Marriage in England, 1500–1800* (London, 1977); it is pressed within a narrower compass by R. Trumbach, *The Rise of the Egalitarian Family in Eighteenth-Century England: Aristocratic Kinship and Domestic Relations in Eighteenth-Century England* (New York, 1978), and placed in longer perspective by A. Macfarlane, *Marriage and Love in England: Modes of Reproduction, 1300–1840* (Oxford, 1986). A lucid, elegant essay by D. Foxon, *Libertine Literature in England, 1660–1745* (London, 1964), is worth much else of what is written on the tempting but testing subject of pornography. A recent account is P. Wagner, *Eros Revived: Erotica of the Enlightenment in England and America* (London, 1988).

R. W. Malcolmson, *Popular Recreations in English Society, 1700–1850* (Cambridge, 1973), defends, and H. Cunningham, *Leisure in the Industrial Revolution* (London, 1980), challenges, some received wisdom about the assault on popular recreation. On polite flesh-pots there are are L. C. Jones, *The Clubs of the Georgian Rakes* (New York, 1942), R. D. Altick, *The Shows of London* (Cambridge, Mass., 1978), and W. Wroth, *The London Pleasure Gardens of the Eighteenth Century* (London, 1896). R. Longrigg, *The History of Horse Racing* (London, 1972), has chapters on the eighteenth century. For travel and tourism, W. E. Mead, *The Grand Tour in the Eighteenth Century* (Boston, 1914), continues to provide a useful summary. J. Black, *The British and the Grand Tour* (Beckenham, 1985), presents a great deal of information. P. G. Adams, *Travellers and Travel Liars, 1660–1800* (Berkeley, 1962), investigates some bizarre travellers' tales.

EDUCATION AND PHILANTHROPY

Literacy is the subject of L. Stone, 'Literacy and Education in England, 1640–1900', *Past and Present*, 42 (1969), 42–139, and R. S. Schofield, 'Dimensions of Illiteracy, 1750–1850', *Explorations in Economic History*, 2nd ser., 10 (1972–3), 436–54. The world of the hornbook and the chapbook are investigated by V. Neuburg, *Popular Education in Eighteenth Century England* (London, 1971), and *The Penny Histories* (London, 1965). M. G. Jones, *The Charity School Movement: A Study of Eighteenth-Century Puritanism in Action* (Cambridge, 1938), describes religious schooling at the beginning of the period, and T. Laqueur, *Religion and Respectability: Sunday Schools and Working-Class Culture* (New Haven, 1976), does a similar service for its end.

Education cannot be profitably separated from attitudes towards the young more generally, especially at a time when more than a third of the population were minors. J. H. Plumb's 'The New World of Children in Eighteenth-Century Society', *Past and Present*, 67 (1975), 64–95, is an important essay, and R. Bayne Powell, *The English Child in the Eighteenth Century* (London, 1939) contains information not readily available elsewhere. However, the only full-scale study remains the invaluable

I. Pinchbeck and M. Hewitt, *Children in English Society* (London, 1969). H. McLachlan, *English Education under the Test Act* (Manchester, 1931) is a survey of Dissenting Academies. Grammar schools and 'public schools' are examined by R. S. Tompson, *Classics or Charity? The Dilemma of the Eighteenth-Century Grammar School* (Manchester, 1971), and N. Hans, *New Trends in Education in the Eighteenth Century* (London, 1951). Individual school histories are numerous. On higher education there is L. Stone, *The University in Society*, vol. i: *Oxford and Cambridge from the Fourteenth Century to the Early Nineteenth* (Princeton, 1974). Oxford has modern scholarly treatment in L. S. Sutherland and L. G. Mitchell, eds., *The History of the University of Oxford*, vol. v: *The Eighteenth Century* (Oxford, 1986), but for Cambridge, D. A. Winstanley's *Unreformed Cambridge: A Study of Certain Aspects of the University in the Eighteenth Century* (Cambridge, 1935), and *The University of Cambridge in the Eighteenth Century* (Cambridge, 1922), have still to be replaced.

Historical surveys of the charitable impulse are offered by B. K. Gray, *A History of English Philanthropy* (London, 1905), and D. Owen, *English Philanthropy, 1660–1960* (Cambridge, Mass., 1965). B. Rodgers, *Cloak of Charity: Studies in Eighteenth-Century Philanthropy* (London, 1949), portrays some leading philanthropists, while F. K. Brown, *Fathers of the Victorians* (Cambridge, 1961) puts them in evangelical perspective. Hanway's labours are discussed by J. S. Taylor, *Jonas Hanway, Founder of the Marine Society: Charity and Policy in Eighteenth-Century Britain* (London, 1985), Howard's by R. Morgan, 'Divine Philanthropy: John Howard Reconsidered', *History*, 62 (1977), 388–410, Coram's by R. K. McClure, *Coram's Children: The London Foundling Hospital in the Eighteenth Century* (New Haven, 1981). E. H. Pearce, *The Sons of the Clergy, 1655–1904* (London, 1904) tells the story of one of the most successful charities.

A large proportion of eighteenth-century charity had to do with medicine. M. C. Buer, *Health, Wealth and Population in the Early Days of the Industrial Revolution* (re-issued, London, 1968), has yet to be superseded in some respects. Individual hospitals have their historians, for example G. McLoughlin, *A Short History of the First Liverpool Infirmary, 1749–1824* (London, 1978). More generally, there is J. Woodward, *To Do the Sick No Harm: A Study of the British Voluntary Hospital System to 1875* (London, 1974). On institutions for the insane, see W. L. Parry-Jones, *The Trade in Lunacy: A Study of Private Mad-Houses in England in the Eighteenth and Nineteenth Centuries* (London, 1972). S. Razzell, *The Conquest of Smallpox: The Impact of Inoculation on Smallpox Mortality in Eighteenth-Century Britain* (Firle, 1977), urges the importance of inoculation in improving the demographic statistics.

CLASS

Modern analysis of contemporary efforts at statistical analysis is offered by P. H. Lindert and J. G. Williamson, 'Revising England's Social Tables, 1688–1812', *Explorations in Economic History*, 19 (1982), 383–408. In what sense it is legitimate to talk of class in pre-industrial society has much vexed historians. The most effective contribution is the work of E. P. Thompson, which stimulates even when it does not convince: 'Eighteenth-Century English Society: Class Struggle without Class?', *Social History*, 3 (1978), 133–65, and 'Patrician Society, Plebeian Culture', *Journal of Social History*, 8 (1974), 382–405. These writings have been enormously influential. The contemporary terminology is examined by P. J. Corfield, 'Class by Name and Number in Eighteenth-Century Britain', *History*, 72 (1987), 38–61.

The upper classes have received much attention. Interest has long centred on two questions: how wealthy were they, and how exclusive were they? In a famous article, H. J. Habakkuk argued that the landed aristocracy benefited by the trends of the late seventeenth and eighteenth century: 'English Landownership, 1680–1740', *Economic History Review*, 2nd ser., 10 (1940), 2–17. This view was supported by G. E. Mingay, *English Landed Society in the Eighteenth Century* (London, 1963). It has since come in for considerable criticism. The key arguments may be found in L. Bonfield, *Marriage Settlements, 1601–1740* (Cambridge, 1983), C. Clay, 'Marriage, Inheritance and the Rise of Large Estates in England, 1660–1815' *Economic History Review*, 2nd ser., 21 (1968), 503–18, B. A. Holderness, 'The English Land Market in the Eighteenth Century: The Case of Lincolnshire', *Economic History Review*, 2nd ser., 26 (1974), 557–76. Habakkuk himself has modified his stance somewhat in 'The Rise and Fall of English Landed Families, 1660–1800', *Transactions of the Royal Historical Society*, 29–31 (1979–81). The resulting state of play is judiciously summarized by J. V. Beckett, *The Aristocracy in England, 1660–1914* (Oxford, 1986). P. Roebuck, *Yorkshire Baronets, 1640–1760* (London, 1980) is the only full-scale local study which has found its way into print. Exclusiveness is also a complicated matter. The current trend is to doubt the openness of the English ruling class: J. Cannon, *Aristocratic Century: The Peerage of Eighteenth-Century England* (Cambridge, 1984); L. Stone and J. C. F. Stone, *An Open Élite? England, 1540–1880* (Oxford, 1984). It is unlikely that these are the last words on the subject. County studies are not numerous, but P. Jenkins, *The Making of a Ruling Class: The Glamorgan Gentry, 1640–1790* (Cambridge, 1983), shows what can be done within a narrower framework.

Middle-class life has not been adequately explored and studied in its own right. It is difficult to define, its concerns incidentally occur in a vast range of other contexts, and middle-class people themselves went out of their way to identify with the class above them. N. Rogers, 'Money, Land and Lineage: The big bourgeoisie of Hanoverian London', *Social History*, 4 (1979) 437–54, brings welcome precision to the study of London's merchant oligarchy, and R. G. Wilson, *Gentlemen and Merchants: The Merchant Community in Leeds, 1700–1830* (Manchester, 1971), does a similar service for a great provincial city. The social background of early industrialists is analysed by S. D. Chapman, *The Early Factory Masters* (Newton Abbot, 1969), F. Crouzet, *The First Industrialists: The Problem of Origins* (Cambridge, 1985), K. Honeyman, *Origins of Enterprise: Business Leadership in the Industrial Revolution* (Manchester, 1982).

Superficially, lower-class life has benefited by the vogue for popular history, but much practised under this heading is actually the history of social policy, economic improvement, and cultural assault, all conducted on behalf of other classes, and drawn from the materials which they accumulated. R. W. Malcolmson, *Life and Labour in England, 1700–1780* (London, 1981), surveys this scene. The standard of living debate turns largely on what happened after 1780, but L. D. Schwarz, 'The Standard of Living in the Long Run: London, 1700–1860', *Economic History Review*, 2nd ser., 38 (1985), 24–41, attempts a longer view. J. J. Hecht, *The Domestic Servant Class in Eighteenth-Century England* (London, 1956) is thoroughly researched.

There is an extensive literature concerning poor relief in the era of Spheenhamland and the Poor Law Amendment Act, which should be treated with caution for what it assumes about the eighteenth century in general. G. W. Oxley, *Poor Relief in England and Wales, 1601–1834* (Newton Abbot, 1974) is a reliable short history. D. Marshall, *The English Poor in the Eighteenth Century: A Study of Social and Administrative History* (London, 1926) includes an essential account of the contemporary debate about poverty, further illuminated in A. W. Coats, 'The Relief of Poverty: Attitudes to Labour, and Economic Change in England, 1660–1782', *International Review of Social History*, 21 (1976), 98–115.

E. P. Thompson, 'The Moral Economy of the English Crowd in the Eighteenth Century', *Past and Present*, 50 (1971), 76–136, has set the tone for much writing about popular protest. A rare challenge is offered by D. E. Williams, 'Morals, Markets and the English Crowd in 1766', *Past and Present*, 104 (1982), 56–73. The long view is taken by J. Stevenson, *Popular Disturbances in England, 1700–1870* (London, 1979), and a still longer if rather narrow view by K. D. M. Snell, *Annals of the Labouring Poor: Social Change and Agrarian England, 1660–1900* (Cambridge, 1985). W. J. Shelton, *English Hunger and Industrial Disorder: A Study of Social Conflict during the First Decade of George III's Reign* (Toronto, 1975) examines the testing crisis of the mid-1760s. Geographical exactitude is provided in A. Charlesworth, ed., *An Atlas of Rural Protest in*

Britain, 1548–1900 (London, 1982). Early trade unionism is discussed by J. Rule, *The Experience of Labour in Eighteenth-Century Industry* (London, 1981), and C. R. Dobson, *Masters and Journeymen: A Prehistory of Industrial Relations, 1717–1800* (London, 1980), crowd control by T. Hayter, *The Army and the Crowd in Mid-Georgian England* (London, 1978).

LAW

W. S. Holdsworth, *A History of English Law* (3rd edn., 16 vols., London, 1922–66) is a quarry of legal arguments and judgments. In a smaller compass, P. S. Atiyah, *The Rise and Fall of Contract* (Oxford, 1969), also has much to say of interest to historians. L. Radzinowicz, *A History of English Criminal Law and its Administration from 1750* (4 vols., London, 1948–68), did for the subject what the Webbs did for local government and brought a similar perspective to bear, that of the 'progressive' in search of early signs of 'reform'. For the rest, legal historians having largely ignored the eighteenth century, social historians have colonized it. The results naturally reflect their interests. Criminality is central, and social crime favoured. A pioneering series of studies was published by D. Hay, P. Linebaugh, and E. P. Thompson as *Albion's Fatal Tree* (London, 1975). One of the authors, D. Hay, took a crucial argument further in 'War, Dearth and Theft in the Eighteenth Century: The Record of the English Courts', *Past and Present*, 95 (1982), 117–60. Doubts about some of this research have been expressed, for example by P. King, 'Decision-Makers and Decision-Making in the English Criminal Law, 1750–1800', *Historical Journal*, 27 (1986), 25–58, and J. H. Langbein, 'Albion's Fatal Flaws', *Past and Present*, 98 (1983), 96–120. P. B. Munsche, *Gentlemen and Poachers: The English Game Laws, 1671–1830* (Cambridge, 1981), also diverges from the 'Albion' school. But the most systematic independent study, with broad implications, is J. M. Beattie, *Crime and the Courts in England, 1660–1800* (Oxford, 1986). A critical bibliography is provided by J. M. Innes and J. Styles, 'The Crime Wave in Recent Writing on Crime and Criminal Law', *Journal of British Studies*, 25 (1986), 380–435. J. Brewer and J. Styles, eds., *An Ungovernable People: The English and their Law in the Seventeenth and Eighteenth Centuries* (London, 1980) is a stimulating and wide-ranging collection of essays on diverse aspects of the law, less coherent than *Albion* but more creative.

Punishment follows crime. R. A. Cooper, 'Ideas and their Execution: English Prison Reform', *Eighteenth-Century Studies*, 10 (1976–7), 73–93, explains the context of Howard's proposals. M. Ignatieff, *A Just Measure of Pain: The Penitentiary in the Industrial Revolution* (London, 1979) puts 'prison reform' in perspective, and M. De Lacy, *Prison Reform in Lancashire, 1700–1850: A Study in Local Administration* (Manchester,

1986) suggests that the old prison system was less benighted than is sometimes supposed. Since Radzinowicz, crime and punishment have aroused more interest than policing and prevention, but a refreshing view of the Fieldings is presented by J. Styles, 'Sir John Fielding and the Problem of Criminal Investigation in Eighteenth-Century England', *Transactions of the Royal Historical Society*, 5th ser., 33 (1983), 127–49.

The legal profession is examined by R. Robson, *The Attorney in Eighteenth-Century England* (Cambridge, 1959), P. Lucas, 'A Collective Biography of Students and Barristers of Lincoln's Inn, 1680–1804: A Study in the "Aristocratic Resurgence" of the Eighteenth Century', *Journal of Modern History*, 46 (1974), 227–61, and D. Duman, *The Judicial Bench in England, 1727–1875* (London, 1982). C. H. S. Fifoot, *Lord Mansfield* (Oxford, 1936), describes the legal principles of the most influential lawyer of the age.

KINGS AND MINISTERS

There is no adequate biography of George II, but J. B. Owen, 'George II Reconsidered', in A. Whiteman, J. Bromley, and P. G. M. Dickson, eds., *Statesmen, Scholars, and Merchants* (Oxford, 1973) is an essential corrective to traditional prejudices about him. J. H. Plumb, *Sir Robert Walpole: The King's Minister* (London, 1960), covers the years up to 1734. H. T. Dickinson, *Walpole and the Whig Supremacy* (London, 1973) is an admirably incisive analysis of Walpole's rule, which is also examined from a variety of perspectives in J. Black, ed., *Britain in the Age of Walpole* (London, 1984). P. Langford, *The Excise Crisis: Society and Politics in the Age of Walpole* (Oxford, 1975), analyses Walpole's most testing ordeal, but his decline and fall await a scholarly history. J. B. Owen, *The Rise of the Pelhams* (London, 1957) is Namierite history at its most convincing. A detailed study of the mid-1750s is provided by J. C. D. Clark, *The Dynamics of Change: The Crisis of the 1750s and English Party Systems* (Cambridge, 1982). There are biographies of the Pelham brothers: J. Wilkes, *A Whig in Power, the Political Career of Henry Pelham* (Evanston, 1964) and R. Browning, *The Duke of Newcastle* (New Haven, 1975). Jacobitism has ceased to be the exclusive preserve of cranks. Scholarly studies include P. S. Fritz, *The English Ministers and Jacobitism between the Rebellions of 1715 and 1745* (Toronto, 1975), B. P. Lenman, *The Jacobite Risings in Britain, 1689–1741* (London, 1980), E. Cruickshanks, *Political Untouchables: The Tories and the '45* (London, 1979), W. A. Speck, *The Butcher: The Duke of Cumberland and the Suppression of the 45* (Oxford, 1982). Pitt's bubble remains unpricked, though it has shrunk somewhat, under the meticulous inspection of M. Peters, *Pitt and Popularity: The Patriot Minister and London Opinion during the Seven Years War* (Oxford, 1980). A. F. B. Williams, *The Life of William Pitt,*

Earl of Chatham (2 vols., London, 1913), is still the most thorough biography, S. Ayling, *The Elder Pitt, Earl of Chatham* (London, 1976), the most balanced treatment of recent years.

The ancient debate about the intentions and practice of George III has lost its urgency. J. Brooke, *King George III* (London, 1972) registers the Namierite victory and is also the best biography, but R. Pares, *George III and the Politicians* (Oxford, 1953) remains valuable for the outstandingly balanced judgement which it provides. T. C. W. Blanning, '"That Horrid Electorate" or "Ma Patrie Germanique"? George III, Hanover, and the Furstenbund of 1785', *Historical Journal*, 20 (1977), 311–44, reassesses royal attitudes towards Hanover, while L. Colley, 'The Apotheosis of George III: Loyalty, Royalty and the British Nation, 1760–1820', *Past and Present*, 102 (1984), 94–129, considers his function as totem-pole. Stimulating perceptions are also offered by J. Brewer, *Party Ideology and Popular Politics at the Accession of George III* (Cambridge, 1976), and by I. R. Christie, *Myth and Reality in Late Eighteenth-Century British Politics* (London, 1970). Though its substantive conclusions have long since been assimilated, Sir L. Namier, *The Structure of Politics at the Accession of George III* (rev. edn., London, 1957) has lost none of its freshness and sense of originality.

Monographs on the years following 1760 are numerous: Namier's own *England in the Age of the American Revolution* (2nd edn., London, 1963); P. Langford, *The First Rockingham Administration, 1765–6* (Oxford, 1973); J. Brooke, *The Chatham Administration, 1766–8* (London, 1956); B. Donoughue, *British Politics and the American Revolution: The Path to War, 1773–75* (London, 1964); I. R. Christie, *The End of North's Ministry* (London, 1958); J. A. Cannon, *The Fox–North Coalition: Crisis of the Constitution, 1782–4* (Cambridge, 1969). Bute is the subject of a collection of studies: K. R. Schweizer, ed., *Lord Bute: Essays in Re-interpretation* (Leicester, 1988) and there are a number of biographies, e.g.: P. Lawson, *George Grenville: A Political Life* (Oxford, 1984); P. D. G. Thomas, *Lord North* (1976); J. W. Derry, *Charles James Fox* (London, 1972).

PARLIAMENT AND POPULAR POLITICS

Constitutional histories with valuable insights into the politics of this period are E. N. Williams, ed., *The Eighteenth-Century Constitution: Documents and Commentary* (Cambridge, 1960), M. A. Thomson, *A Constitutional History of England, 1640–1801* (London, 1938), and B. Kemp, *King and Commons, 1660–1832* (London, 1957). A. S. Foord, *His Majesty's Opposition, 1714–1839* (Oxford, 1964) is a useful narrative. B. W. Hill, *The Growth of Parliamentary Parties, 1689–1742* (London, 1976), and *British Parliamentary Parties, 1742–1832* (London, 1985), tells a story which begins with conviction but loses some of it by the 1760s.

Two parties with more in common than they supposed have found their historian: L. Colley, *In Defiance of Oligarchy: The Tory Party, 1714–60* (Cambridge, 1982), and F. O'Gorman, *The Rise of Party in England: The Rockingham Whigs, 1760–82* (London, 1975). O'Gorman has also written a short introduction to the late eighteenth-century history of party *The Emergence of the British Two-party System, 1760–1832* (London, 1982). P. D. Brown, *The Chathamites* (London, 1967) is a series of biographical essays.

R. Sedgwick, *The History of Parliament: The House of Commons, 1715– 1754* (2 vols., London, 1970) and Sir L. Namier and J. Brooke, *The History of Parliament: The House of Commons, 1754–1790* (3 vols., London, 1964) contain a wealth of introductory material as well as constituency histories, and short biographies of every MP who sat during the period. Parliamentary debates still have to be read in contemporary compilations apart from those relating to America, which were published by F. Stock, *Proceedings and Debates of the British Parliaments respecting North America* (5 vols., Washington, 1924–41), now continued by R. C. Simmons and P. D. G. Thomas (New York, 1982–).

Legislative procedure is examined in S. Lambert, *Bills and Acts* (Cambridge, 1971), and the workings of the lower house in P. D. G. Thomas, *The House of Commons in the Eighteenth Century* (Oxford, 1971). For the House of Lords, it is necessary to rely largely on an estimable but outmoded study by A. S. Turberville, *The House of Lords in the Eighteenth Century* (Oxford, 1927). However, there are relevant essays in C. Jones and D. L. Jones, *Peers, Politics and Power: The House of Lords, 1603–1911* (London, 1986) and also by C. Jones, 'The House of Lords and the Growth of Political Stability, 1701–1742', in C. Jones, ed., *Britain in the First Age of Party, 1680–1750: Essays Presented to Geoffrey Holmes* (London, 1987).

The electoral structure of the unreformed Parliament is described in E. Porritt, *The Unreformed House of Commons* (2 vols., Cambridge, 1903, repr. New York, 1963). Recent scholars have been at pains to prove that electoral participation was less constrained by influence and corruption than has been thought: J. A. Phillips, *Electoral Behaviour in Unreformed England: Plumpers, Splitter and Straights* (Princeton, 1982); F. O'Gorman, 'The Unreformed Electorate of Hanoverian England: The Mid-Eighteenth Century to the Reform Act of 1832', *Social History*, 11 (1986), 33–52. There are many election studies, including one of a county over a prolonged period, E. G. Forrester, *Northamptonshire Elections and Electioneering, 1695–1832* (Oxford, 1941), and one of a famous contest, R. J. Robson, *The Oxfordshire Election of 1754* (Oxford, 1949). There is much of value in H. Wellenreuther, *Repräsentation und Grossgrundbesitz in England, 1730–1770* (Stuttgart, 1979).

The story of the reform movement is told in J. Cannon, *Parliamentary Reform, 1640–1832* (Cambridge, 1973), and its extra-parliamentary structure analysed in E. C. Black, *The Association: British Extra-Parliamentary Organisation, 1769–1793* (Cambridge, Mass., 1963). The Wilkesites have attracted some high-quality writing: J. Brewer, 'English Radicalism in the Age of George III', in J. G. A. Pocock, ed., *Three British Revolutions, 1641, 1688, 1776* (Princeton, 1980); G. Rudé, *Wilkes and Liberty* (Oxford, 1962). Rudé's *Paris and London in the Eighteenth Century: Studies in Popular Protest* (London, 1970) touches a variety of tumults.

THE STATE

P. G. M. Dickson, *The Financial Revolution in England: A Study in the Development of Public Credit, 1688–1756* (London, 1967), is the definitive treatment of public finance in the first half of the period. J. D. Binney, *British Public Finance and Administration, 1774–92* (Oxford, 1958), considers the later part from a slightly different perspective. W. R. Ward, *The English Land Tax in the Eighteenth Century* (Oxford, 1953) is an administrative history, M. Turner and D. Mills, *Land and Property: The English Land Tax, 1692–1832* (Gloucester, 1986) an exploration of the uses to which land-tax records in the localities can be put. There is much in E. Hughes, *Studies in Administration and Finance, 1558–1825* (Manchester, 1934) which cannot be found elsewhere. A comparative dimension is lent by P. Matthias and P. O'Brien, 'Taxation in Britain and France, 1715–1810: A Comparison of the Social and Economic Incidence of Taxes collected for the Central Government', *European Economic History*, 5 (1976), 610–50. On the civil list, see E. R. Reitan, 'The Civil List in Eighteenth Century British Politics', *Historical Journal*, 9 (1966), 318–37, and 'From Revenue to Civil List, 1689–1782', *Historical Journal*, 13 (1970), 571–88. J. Norris, *Shelburne and Reform* (London, 1963) helps establish Pittite credentials for economical reform, but J. R. Breihan questions them in 'William Pitt and the Commission on Fees, 1785–1801', *Historical Journal*, 27 (1984), 59–81. On the Treasury, there are H. Rosaveare, *The Treasury, 1660–1870: The Foundations of Control* (London, 1973), and N. Baker, *Government and Contractors: The British Treasury and War Supplies, 1775–1783* (London, 1971). K. Ellis, *The Post Office in the Eighteenth Century* (London, 1958) is concerned with central administration, B. Austen, *English Provincial Posts, 1633–1840: A Study based on Kent Examples* (London, 1978), with local practice. The principles of public service are considered by G. E. Aylmer, 'From Office-Holding to Civil Service: The Genesis of Modern Bureaucracy', *Transactions of the Royal Historical Society*, 5th ser., 30 (1980), 91–108, and J. Torrance, 'Social Class and Bureaucratic Innovation: The Commission for Examining the Public Accounts, 1780–1787', *Past and*

Present, 1 (1978), 56–81. The series by J. C. Sainty and J. M. Collinge, *Office-holders in Modern Britain* (London, 1972–), provides valuable essays in administrative history as well as biographical information. S. and B. Webb, *English Local Government* (9 vols., London, 1906–29), towers over the local scene. Their researches were exhaustive but the questions they asked were not those which always interest modern scholars. B. Keith-Lucas, *The Unreformed Local Government System* (London, 1980) is a lucid general survey. N. Landau, *Justices of the Peace, 1679–1760* (Berkeley, 1984) is in large measure a local study, as is that of E. Moir, *Local Government in Gloucestershire, 1775–1800* (Bristol and Gloucestershire Archaeological Society, 1969). L. Glassey questions the autonomy of local authorities in C. Jones, ed., *Britain in the First Age of Party, 1680–1750: Essays Presented to Geoffrey Holmes* (London, 1987).

Sir J. Fortescue, *A History of the British Army* (13 vols., London, 1899–1930), a remarkable achievement in its time, is outmoded, and there is no successor. There are, however, some valuable monographs and essays on different aspects of the army: J. A. Houlding, *Fit for Service: The Training of the British Army, 1715–1795* (Oxford, 1982); A. Bruce, *The Purchase system in the British Army, 1660–1871* (London, 1980); A. N. Gilbert, 'Law and Honour among Eighteenth-Century British Army officers', *Historical Journal*, 19 (1976), 75–87. Regimental histories are numerous but of variable quality: those by C. T. Atkinson are not the most recent but they are among the most thorough, e.g. *The South Wales Borderers, 24th Foot, 1689–1837* (Cambridge, 1937). J. R. Western, *The English militia in the Eighteenth Century* (London, 1965) is authoritative, as is O. F. G. Hogg, *The Royal Arsenal: Its Background, Origin and Subsequent History* (London, 1963). H. C. B. Rogers, *The British Army of the Eighteenth Century* (New York, 1977) provides a short survey.

D. Baugh, *Naval Administration, 1715–1750* (London, 1977), B. Pool, *Navy Board Contracts, 1660–1832: Contract Administration under the Navy Board* (London, 1966), S. F. Gradish, *The Manning of the British Navy during the Seven Years War* (London, 1980), D. Syrett, *Shipping and the American War, 1775–83: A Study of British Transport Organisation* (London, 1970), all offer cautious but convincing reassessments of naval management. A more daring revisionist is N. A. M. Rodger, whose *The Wooden World: An Anatomy of the Georgian Navy* (London, 1986), makes life below deck seem almost attractive.

WAR AND FOREIGN RELATIONS

Helpful background is to be found in D. McKay and H. M. Scott, *The Rise of the Great Powers, 1648–1815* (London, 1983). Surveys of foreign policy in the period as a whole are provided by D. B. Horn's *Great Britain and Europe in the Eighteenth Century* (Oxford, 1967), and J. R. Jones,

Britain and the World, 1649–1815 (London, 1980). Horn has also assessed *The British Diplomatic Service, 1689–1789* (Oxford, 1961). A characteristically unpretentious but illuminating essay on attitudes towards the Continent is J. S. Bromley, 'Britain and Europe in the Eighteenth Century', *History*, 66 (1981), 394–412. D. Jarrett, *The Begetters of Revolution: England's Involvement with France, 1759–1789* (London, 1973) explores Anglo-French relations of an unofficial kind.

On Walpole's foreign policy, see J. Black, *British Foreign Policy in the Age of Walpole* (Edinburgh, 1985) and *The Collapse of the Anglo-French Alliance, 1727–1731* (Gloucester, 1987). France is treated in relation to the Forty-Five by F. McLynn, *France and the Jacobite Rising of 1745* (Edinburgh, 1981), and more generally by J. Black, *Natural and Necessary Enemies: Anglo-French Relations in the Eighteenth Century* (London, 1986). G. Niedhart, *Handel und Krieg in der Britischen Weltpolitik, 1738–1763* (Munich, 1979), puts war in its mercantilist context, and R. Middleton, *The Bells of Victory: The Pitt–Newcastle Ministry and the Conduct of the Seven Years War* (Cambridge, 1985) takes some of the gilt off Pitt's reputation as a war minister.

M. Roberts, in *Splendid Isolation, 1763–1780* (Reading, 1967), picks out the crucial features of foreign policy after George III's accession, and analyses relations with one court in depth in *British Diplomacy and Swedish Politics, 1758–73* (London, 1980). P. Mackesy, *The War for America, 1775–1783* (London, 1964) has yet to be bettered as an account from the British side. The diplomacy is well approached via I. de Madariaga, *Britain, Russia and the Armed Neutrality of 1780* (London, 1962), with S. F. Bemis, *The Diplomacy of the American Revolution* (Bloomington, 1967), providing coverage from the American standpoint. The story of the peace negotations is told by R. B. Morris, *The Peacemakers: The Great Powers and American Independence* (New York, 1965).

THE BRITISH ISLES

There are many Irish studies which have a bearing on English history, partly because Irish relations with England in the eighteenth century were in process of rapid change. General histories are T. W. Moody and W. E. Vaughan, *The New History of Ireland*, vol. iv: *1692–1800* (Oxford, 1986), E. M. Johnston, *Ireland in the Eighteenth Century* (Dublin, 1974), and J. C. Beckett, *The Making of Modern Ireland, 1603–1923* (new edn., London, 1981). The Irish economy is examined by L. M. Cullen, *Anglo-Irish Trade, 1660–1800* (Manchester, 1968), and F. G. James, *Ireland in the Empire, 1688–1770* (Cambridge, Mass., 1973). T. Bartlett and D. W. Hayton, *Penal Era and Golden Age: Essays in Irish History, 1690–1800* (Belfast, 1979) is an important collection of essays on diverse subjects. The growing turmoil of the late eighteenth century is the subject of E. M.

Johnston, *Great Britain and Ireland, 1760–1800: A Study in Political Administration* (Edinburgh, 1963), M. R. O'Connell, *Irish Politics and Social Conflict in the Age of the American Revolution* (Philadelphia, 1965), and R. B. McDowell, *Ireland in the Age of Imperialism and Revolution, 1760–1801* (Oxford, 1977).

Scotland has an excellent survey in T. C. Smout, *A History of the Scottish People, 1650–1830* (2nd edn., London, 1970), and a short economic history by B. P.Lenman, *An Economic History of Modern Scotland, 1660–1976* (London, 1977). There is a wealth of writing on the Scottish Enlightenment as a product of specifically Scottish culture. General accounts include A. C. Chitnis, *The Scotch Enlightenment: A Social History* (London, 1976) and J. Rendall, *The Origins of the Scottish Enlightenment* (London, 1978). R. H. Campbell and A. S. Skinner, *The Origins and Nature of the Scottish Enlightenment* (Edinburgh, 1982), discuss some of the major questions which interest Scottish historians but in a broad historical context. There are two absorbing studies of politics: J. S. Shaw, *The Management of Scottish Society, 1707–1764: Power, Nobles, Lawyers, Edinburgh Agent and English Influence* (Edinburgh, 1983) and A. Murdoch, *'The People Above': Politics and Administration in Mid-Eighteenth Century Scotland* (Edinburgh, 1980). H. Hamilton, *The Industrial Revolution in Scotland* (Oxford, 1932) has yet to be fully superseded.

Wales is the subject of a useful survey with the emphasis on culture, P. Morgan, *A New History of Wales: The Eighteenth Century Renaissance* (Llandybie, 1982), and a narrative history by G. H. Jenkins, *History of Wales*, vol. iv: *The Foundations of Modern Wales: Wales, 1642–1780* (Oxford, 1987).

OVERSEAS

British treatment of the American colonies before the Seven Years War is examined by J. A. Henretta, *'Salutary Neglect': Colonial Administration under the Duke of Newcastle* (Princeton, 1972), A. G. Olson, *Anglo-American Politics, 1660–1775: The Relationship between Parties in England and Colonial America* (Oxford, 1973), P. Marshall and G. Williams, eds., *The British Atlantic Empire before the American Revolution* (London, 1980). J. Shy, *Towards Lexington* (Princeton, 1965), explains the military background to British policy.

I. R. Christie provides a short summary of the American Revolution in *Crisis of Empire* (London, 1976), and with B. W. Labaree, a fuller narrative, *Empire or Independence, 1760–1776* (Oxford, 1976). A stimulating, remorselessly polemical analysis, emphasizing the dilemma of British ministers, is R. W. Tucker and D. C. Hendrickson, *The Fall of the First British Empire: Origins of the War of American Independence*

(Baltimore, 1982). Two authoritative monographs on British policy have been written by P. D. G. Thomas, *British Politics and the Stamp Act Crisis, 1863–1767* (Oxford, 1975), *The Townshend Duties Crisis: The Second Phase of the American Revolution, 1767–1773* (Oxford, 1987). Thomas also establishes George III's credentials as a moderate, well-intentioned sovereign of America: 'George III and the American Revolution', *History*, 70 (1985), 16–31.

British support for the American stance is discussed by A. H. Lincoln, *Some Political and Social Ideas of English Dissent, 1763–1800* (Cambridge, 1938), C. Bonwick, *English Radicals and the American Revolution* (Chapel Hill, 1977), and J. E. Bradley, *Popular Politics and the American Revolution in England: Petitions, the Crown, and Public Opinion* (Macon, Georgia, 1986). Works primarily concerned with American attitudes, but illuminating for the British response, are B. Bailyn, *The Ideological Origins of the American Revolution* (Cambridge, Mass., 1967) and P. Maier, *From Resistance to Revolution: Colonial Radicals and the Development of American Opposition to Britain, 1765–1776* (London, 1973).

F. Madden and D. Fieldhouse, eds., *The Classical Period of the First British Empire, 1689–1783: The Foundations of a Colonial System of Government* (London, 1985), present a wide-ranging selection of documents. V. T. Harlow, *The Founding of the Second British Empire, 1763–1793* (2 vols., London, 1952, 1964), offers a distinctive interpretation of imperial policy after the Seven Years War, and incidentally includes thorough coverage of a wide range of imperial problems. Attitudes to overseas peoples are surveyed by P. J. Marshall and G. Williams, *The Great Map of Mankind: British Perceptions of the World in the Age of Enlightenment* (London, 1982). As introductions to the importance of the Pacific discoveries, J. C. Beaglehole, *The Life of Captain James Cook* (London, 1974) and B. Smith, *European Vision and the South Pacific, 1768–1850: A Study in the History of Art and Ideas* (Oxford, 1965) are invaluable.

R. Anstey, *The Atlantic Slave Trade and British Abolition, 1760–1810* (London, 1975) is much the most balanced and thorough account of the subject. F. Shylloh, *Black People in Britain, 1555–1883* (London, 1977) examines racial attitudes in a domestic setting. On India, L. S. Sutherland, *The East India Company in Eighteenth Century Politics* (Oxford, 1952) is indispensable, as is P. J. Marshall, *East India Fortunes: The British in Bengal in the Eighteenth Century* (Oxford, 1976). The same author's *Problems of Empire: Britain and India, 1757–1813* (London, 1968) introduces a series of critical documents charting the progress of British rule over India. His *'A Free though Conquering People': Britain and Asia in the Eighteenth Century* (London, 1981) asks fundamental questions about British involvement in India.

ECONOMIC TRENDS

Economic historians used to argue about the causes of the Industrial Revolution; they now debate whether it occurred at all. P. Deane, *The First Industrial Revolution* (2nd edn., Cambridge, 1979) provides an admirably clear-cut analysis. R. M. Hartwell's writings may be sampled in *The Industrial Revolution and Economic Growth* (London, 1971). T. S. Ashton, *Economic Fluctuations in England, 1700–1800* (Oxford, 1959), stays close to the historical evidence. P. Deane and W. A. Cole, *British Economic Growth, 1688–1959* (2nd edn., Cambridge, 1967), presents a great array of statistics in intelligible form. N. F. R. Crafts, *British Economic Growth during the Industrial Revolution* (Oxford, 1985), relies on sophisticated analysis of such statistics and exemplifies the scepticism now fashionable about the extent of growth. A. J. Little, *Deceleration in the Eighteenth-Century British Economy* (London, 1976) and J. V. Beckett, 'Regional Variation and the Age of Agricultural Depression, 1730–50', *Economic History Review*, 35 (1982), 35–51, consider the problem of recession under George II. A crucial subject was opened up many years ago by A. H. John, 'War and the English Economy, 1700–63', *Economic History Review*, 2nd ser., 7 (1954–5), 329–44, and has yet to be fully developed.

The definitive calculations of population, with a mass of allied and supporting material, are to be found in E. A. Wrigley and R. S. Schofield, *The Population History of England, 1541–1871* (London, 1981). A stimulating discussion of modern demographic trends as they emerged in the eighteenth century is N. L. Tranter, *Population and Society, 1750–1940* (London, 1985). D. V. Glass describes the contemporary debate in *Numbering the People: The Eighteenth-Century Population Controversy and the Development of Census and Vital Statistics in Britain* (Farnborough, 1973).

FINANCE AND COMMERCE

A. C. Carter, *Getting, Spending and Investing in Early Modern Times: Essays on Dutch, English and Huguenot Economic History* (Assen, 1975) helps place British finance, both public and private, in its Continental setting. H. P. R. Hoare, *Hoare's Bank: A Record, 1672–1955* (rev. edn., London, 1955) is a good example of a class of individual bank histories. L. S. Pressnell, *Country Banking in the Industrial Revolution* (Oxford, 1956), deals with the provincial banking scene. J. Hoppit, *Risk and Failure in English Business, 1700–1800* (Cambridge, 1987), investigates the bankruptcy records with profit. The role of capital in industrialization is debated in F. Crouzet, *Capital Formation in the Industrial Revolution* (London, 1972) and its place in transport improvement by J. R. Ward,

The Finance of Canal Building in Eighteenth-Century England (Oxford, 1974).

The theme of commercialization is explored by N. McKendrick, J. Brewer, and J. H. Plumb, *The Birth of a Consumer Society: The Commercialization of Eighteenth-Century England* (new edn., London, 1983), and D. Alexander, *Retailing in England during the Industrial Revolution* (London, 1970). T. S. Willan, *An Eighteenth-Century Shopkeeper: Abraham Dent of Kirkby Stephen* (Manchester, 1970) is a useful case-study. Studies of overseas commerce include W. E. Minchinton, ed., *The Growth of English Overseas Trade in the Seventeenth and Eighteenth Centuries* (London, 1969), J. B. Williams, *British Commercial Policy and Trade Expansion, 1750–1850* (Oxford, 1972), H. E. S. Fisher, *The Portugal Trade* (London, 1971), H. S. K. Kent, *War and Trade in Northern Seas: Anglo-Scandinavian Economic Relations in the Mid-Eighteenth Century* (Cambridge, 1973), R. Davis, *Aleppo and Devonshire Square: English Traders in the Levant in the Eighteenth Century* (London, 1967), P. L. Cottrell and D. H. Aldcroft, eds., *Shipping, Trade and Commerce: Essays in Memory of Ralph Davis* (Leicester, 1981), R. Davis, *The Rise of the English Shipping Industry in the Seventeenth and Eighteenth Centuries* (London, 1962).

TRANSPORT AND INDUSTRY

Many manufactures have their own history, e.g. S. D. Chapman, *The Cotton Industry in the Industrial Revolution* (London, 1972), J. de L. Mann, *The Cloth Industry in the West of England from 1640 to 1880* (Oxford, 1971), P. Mathias, *The Brewing Industry in England, 1700–1830* (Cambridge, 1959), M. W. Flinn, *The History of the British Coal Industry: vol. 2: 1700–1830* (Oxford, 1984), H. Hamilton, *The English Brass and Copper Industries to 1800* (London, 1926), L. Weatherill, *The Pottery Trade and North Staffordshire, 1660–1760* (Manchester, 1971), M. H. Jackson and C. de Beer, *Eighteenth Century Gunfounding* (Newton Abbot, 1973), C. K. Hyde, *Technological Change and the British Iron Industry, 1700–1780* (Princeton, 1977).

M. Berg, *The Age of Manufactures, 1700–1820* (London, 1985) overturns some widely entertained assumptions about the character of early industrialization, A. E. Musson and E. Robinson, *Science and Technology in the Industrial Revolution* (Manchester, 1969), and D. S. Lowndes, *The Unbound Prometheus: Technological Change and Industrial Development in Western Europe from 1750 to the Present* (Cambridge, 1969), assess its technological sophistication.

D. Aldcroft and M. Freeman, eds., *Transport and the Industrial Revolution* (London, 1983) is a wide-ranging collection of essays. P. J. G. Ransom, *The Archaeology of the Transport Revolution, 1750–1850* (Tadworth, 1984) has excellent illustrations. The turnpike movement is analysed in E. Pawson, *Transport and Economy: The Turnpike Roads of Eighteenth-Century Britain* (London, 1977), and W. Albert, *The Turnpike Road System in England, 1663–1840* (Cambridge, 1972), the canal movement in E. R. C. Hadfield, *British Canals: An Illustrated History* (6th edn., Newton Abbot, 1979).

AGRICULTURE

E. Kerridge, *The Agricultural Revolution* (London, 1967), argues for a revolutionary process which occurred before the eighteenth century, while J. D. Chambers and G. E. Mingay, *The Agricultural Revolution, 1750–1880* (London, 1966), take a more conventional view of its timing. E. L. Jones, ed., *Agriculture and the Industrial Revolution* (Oxford, 1974) and *Agriculture and Economic Growth in England, 1650–1815* (London, 1967) contain some pointed expositions of the relationship between agriculture and industry. The debate was reviewed by P. O'Brien, 'Agriculture and the Industrial Revolution', *Economic History Review*, 2nd ser., 30 (1977), 166–81. The literature of improvement is assessed by P. Horn, 'The Contribution of the Propagandist to Eighteenth-Century Agricultural Improvement', *Historical Journal*, 25 (1982), 313–29.

On the Corn Laws there are A. H. John, 'English Agricultural Improvement and Grain Exports, 1660–1765', in D. C. Coleman and A. H. John, eds., *Trade, Government and Economy in Pre-Industrial England, Essays presented to F. O. Fisher* (London, 1976), R. V. Jackson, 'Growth and Deceleration in English Agriculture, 1660–1790', *Economic History Review*, 2nd ser., 38 (1985), 333–51, and D. G. Barnes, *A History of the English Corn Laws from 1660 to 1846* (London, 1930). Enclosure has a considerable literature, but the current state of the art is summarized conveniently by M. Turner, *English Parliamentary Enclosure: Its Historical Geography and Economic History* (Folkestone, 1980). Detailed local study has not made generalization about the social consequences of enclosure easier.

There are several important estate studies: R. A. C. Parker, *Coke of Norfolk: A Financial and Agricultural Study, 1707–1842* (Oxford, 1975); J. R. Wordie, *Estate Management in Eighteenth-Century England: The Building of the Leveson-Gower Fortune* (London, 1982); T. J. Raybould, *The Economic Emergence of the Black Country: A Study of the Dudley Estate* (Newton Abbot, 1973).

URBAN LIFE

P. J. Corfield, *The Impact of English Towns* (Oxford, 1982), provides an outline history for the eighteenth century. There is also much bearing on the period in J. De Vries, *European Urbanisation, 1500–1800* (London,

1984) and P. Clark, ed., *The Transformation of English Provincial Towns* (London, 1984). C. W. Chalklin, *The Provincial Towns of Georgian England: A Study of the Building Process, 1740–1820* (London, 1974) is of wider consequence than its title might suggest. P. Borsay, 'The English Urban Renaissance: The development of provincial culture, *c.*1680– *c.*1760', *Social History*, 5 (1976–7), 581–603, focuses on an earlier period, and D. Cannadine, *Lords and Landlords: The Aristocracy and the Towns, 1774–1976* (Leicester, 1980), on a later period, but both are of unusual interest.

Studies of individual towns include R. Newton, *Eighteenth-Century Exeter* (Exeter, 1984), Sir F. Hill, *Georgian Lincoln* (Cambridge, 1966), A. T. Patterson, *A History of Southampton, 1700–1914*, vol. i: *An Oligarchy in Decline, 1700–1835* (Southampton, 1966), P. M. Horsley, *Eighteenth-Century Newcastle* (Newcastle, 1971), and G. Jackson, *Hull in the Eighteenth Century: A Study in Economic and Social History* (London, 1972). J. Money, *Experience and Identity: Birmingham and the West Midlands, 1760–1800* (Manchester, 1977), provides rich but rather dense documentation of urban development in a regional setting. As yet there is no major work devoted to urban politics in a broad context, but useful pointers to what might be achieved with the wealth of sources available are N. Rogers, 'The Urban Opposition to Whig Oligarchy', in M. and J. Jacob, *The Origins of Anglo-American Radicalism* (London, 1984) and P. Jenkins, 'Tory Industrialism and Town Politics: Swansea in the Eighteenth Century', *Historical Journal*, 28 (1985), 107–23.

London has inspired two historical classics, of social and architectural history respectively: M. D. George, *London Life in the Eighteenth Century* (London, 1966) and J. Summerson, *Georgian London* (rev. edn., London, 1962). Equally authoritative in its field is D. J. Olson, *Town Planning in London: The Eighteenth and Nineteenth Centuries* (New Haven, 1964). G. Rudé, *Hanoverian London* (London, 1971) provides broad-brush treatment of the capital's history, and M. Byrd, *London Transformed: Images of the City in the Eighteenth Century* (New Haven, 1978), a useful reminder of its evocative literary image. London's immediate environs have yet to receive the detailed attention they deserve in what was a period of rapid suburban expansion, but there are two books which show the way: F. H. W. Sheppard, *Local Government in St. Marylebone, 1688–1835* (London, 1958); F. M. L. Thompson, *Hampstead: Building a Borough, 1650–1984* (London, 1974). J. Stevenson, ed., *London in the Age of Reform* (Oxford, 1977) includes essays on the City's opposition to mid-eighteenth-century government.

Index